The Lives Of Saints

Anonymous

Nabu Public Domain Reprints:

You are holding a reproduction of an original work published before 1923 that is in the public domain in the United States of America, and possibly other countries. You may freely copy and distribute this work as no entity (individual or corporate) has a copyright on the body of the work. This book may contain prior copyright references, and library stamps (as most of these works were scanned from library copies). These have been scanned and retained as part of the historical artifact.

This book may have occasional imperfections such as missing or blurred pages, poor pictures, errant marks, etc. that were either part of the original artifact, or were introduced by the scanning process. We believe this work is culturally important, and despite the imperfections, have elected to bring it back into print as part of our continuing commitment to the preservation of printed works worldwide. We appreciate your understanding of the imperfections in the preservation process, and hope you enjoy this valuable book.

THE
LIVES
OF
SAINTS

COLLECTED FROM

Authentick Records

OF

CHURCH HISTORY.

With a full ACCOUNT of the other

FESTIVALS throughout the YEAR.

The whole Interspersed with

Suitable REFLECTIONS.

VOLUME IV.

LONDON:
Printed for THOMAS MEIGHAN, in *Drury-Lane*.

MDCCXXIX

An ACCOUNT

Of the AUTHORITIES made Use of in this

WORK.

VOLUME the Fourth.

OCTOBER.

I. THE Life of St. *Remigius*, which we have follow'd, is the Work of *Hincmar*, who sate on the See of *Rheims* in the Middle of the IX Century; to which we have added the advantageous Testimonies of *Sidonius Appolinaris* Ep. 14. b. 8. and St. *Gregory* of *Tours*, Hist. b. 2. c. 31. and *Of the Glory of Confessors* c. 79.

II. Our Account of St. *Thomas*, Bishop of *Hereford*, is taken from his Life written by an anonymous Author, of good Credit, whose Performance may be seen in *Surius*, with some Alterations of the Stile.

III. The Life of St. *Cyprian* Bishop of *Toulon*, composed by one, who has not left us his Name, is by some thought antient, while others are not willing to allow it an earlier Date than the XI Century. We had some Assistance in writing this Saint's Life from that of St. *Cesarius*, Bishop of *Arles*.

IV. the History of St. *Francis* is written by St. *Bonaventure*, the eighth General of his Order. We learn several curious Particulars from *Father Wadding*'s *Library of the Minor Friars*, and his *Annals* of the same Order.

V. Our Account of St. *Placidus* and his Companions in Martyrdom is extracted from their Acts as they appear in *Surius*; in which *Baronius* owns are some Things that want Correction; what we have reported agrees with what St. *Gregory the Great* says of the Martyrs, *Dial.* b. 2. c. 3, 7.

All we know of St. *Galla* may be seen in the Writings of the Author last named, *Dial.* b. 4. c. 13.

VI. The chief Materials for compiling St. *Bruno*'s Life are found in his own Writings, and particularly his Letters. The rest is sufficiently supplied by *Guibert*, Abbot of *Nogent*, and *Guigues* the fifth General of the *Carthusians*; the former in the History of his Life, the latter in that of *Hugh* Bishop of *Grenoble*.

Our Account of St. *Faith* and St. *Caprasius* is taken from the Acts of their Martyrdom as they stand in *Surius*'s Collection.

VII. What we have said of St. *Mark*, Pope, wants the Support of no other Authority, but what is there specified.

The History of St. *Sergius* and St. *Bacchus* is taken from the Acts of their Martyrdom; that of the Veneration paid their Relicks is found in *Procopius*'s Treatise of *Justinian*'s Buildings b. 2. c. 9. b. 5. c. 9. and *Anastasius* c. 91.

VIII. St. *Bridget*'s Life is taken chiefly from the Bull published for her Canonization eighteen Years after her Decease, which is reckon'd much more exact than the Account published by *Surius* from an anonymous Author.

The Life of St. *Thaïs* is among the Lives of the Fathers of the Desart written by an ancient *Greek* Author.

IX. For what regards St. *Dionysius* the *Areopagite*, and the Apostle of *France*, see the *Acts* of the *Apostles* c. 17. St. *Chrysostom of the Priesthood* b. 4. c. 7. *Eusebius* b. 3. c. 4. St. *Gregory of Tours Hist. Fran.* b. 1. c. 30, 31. *Baronius*'s Notes on the Martyrologe, *Monsieur de Tillemont* and other modern Writers of *France*, who have had Occasion to touch on that Subject.

X. St. *Francis Borgia*'s Life was written originally by *Ribadeneira* a *Spanish Jesuit*, who was personally acquainted with the Saint, and well furnish'd with what was necessary for executing such a Task. Since his Canonization the same was perform'd by *Father Verjus* of the same Society in *French*, who beside the Assistance he met with in *Ribadeneiras*'s Composition, had the Advantage of a *Spanish* Manuscript written by a Jesuit of that Country, who had the Direction of the Saint's Conscience nine Years, and spent a considerable Part of his Time in his Company.

The History of St. *Paulinus*, Bishop of *York*, is scatter'd in several Chapters of *Bede*'s second Book.

XI. We have the original Acts of the three holy Martyrs of this Day, viz. *Tarachus, Probus,* and *Andronicus,* which consist of two Parts; the former is a Transcript of their Trial; the latter an exact Relation of what happen'd from their Condemation to their Burial. This valuable Piece was publish'd by *Baronius* in his Annals, but imperfect. The *Greek* Text appear'd first by the Care of Monsieur *Bigot* at *Paris* in 1680. but was not complete and entire 'till *Dom. Ruinart* revised it with a good Manuscript and obliged the World with it in his Collection, which was very useful to us through the whole Course of this Work.

XII. St. *Wilfrid*'s Life is the Work of *Heddius Stephanus*, Chanter of the Church of *Canterbury*, and inseperable Companion of his Labours. This Piece may be seen in Dom. *Mabillon*'s fourth *Benedictin Age*: to this add Venerable *Bede,* b. 3. c. 25, 26, b. 5. c. 20.

XIII. The Life of St. *Edward the Confessor* was penn'd by *Elred*, Abbot of *Revesby*, who died in 1166. The best Edition of it is that published at *London* by Ro. *Twysden* 1652.

XIV. *Baronius*

XIV. *Baronius* mentioning the Acts of St. *Callistus* speaks of them as an incorrect Piece, and refers to his *Annals* for the more certain Parts of his History, *Anno* 226.

XV. Our Account of St. *Teresa* is taken from her own Works; what is wanting there is supplied from *Ribera* a *Spanish Jesuite* some Time her Confessor, and from *Yepez* Bishop of *Tarragona*.

XVI. The Life of St. *Gallus* was first written by *Walafrid*, who spent great Part of his Time at the Monastery which bears the Saint's Name, and died Abbot of another House in 849; the Main of his History is acknowledged to be compiled from good Materials; the last who published that Piece is *Dom. Mabillon* in his second *Benedictine Age*.

XVII. The Author of St. *Hedwigis*'s Life is not known by his Name, but is esteem'd a grave and creditable Writer. See likewise *Chromer's History of Poland*.

XVIII. Our Account of S. *Luke* is taken from *the Acts of the Apostles*, and some Passages from St. *Paul's* Epistles, referr'd to in the Margin. St. *Jerom's Quest. on Genesis*. His *Hist. of Illustrious Men*, c. 7. St. *Iren*. b. 3. c. 1. *Epiphan. Her*. 51, c. 11. See also *Baron*. on the *Roman* Martyrologe.

XIX. The Life of St. *Peter* of *Alcantara* was first written by *John of* St. *Mary* in 1619. and by *Martin* of St. *Joseph* in 1644. The same has been since perform'd by two *Franciscans*, one a *Spaniard*, the other a *Frenchman*. To which we have added something from St. *Teresa*, who was well acquainted with the Saint.

XX. Our Acount of St. *Artemius* is drawn from St. *Athanasius*'s Letter about *his own Flight*; that *to the Solitaries*. *Theodoret*, b. 3. c. 18. the Life of St. *Pachomius*, and *Julian* the *Apostates*' tenth Epistle.

XXI. St. *Hilarion* had the Advantage of an able and judicious Historian; we have the Particulars of his wonderful and edifying Life written by St. *Jerom*, and directed to St. *Asella*. That Father died about fifty Years after the Saint of this Day, but had taken Care to procure exact Informations from all Places, which had been favour'd with his Presence.

The Story of St. *Ursula* and her Companions, as usually reported, may be seen in *Surius*. *Baronius* in his Notes on the Martyrologe owns their Acts had suffer'd much from Persons of great Credulity, and a fruitful Imagination.

XXII. The Acts of St. *Philip* Bishop of *Heraclea*, written in *Greek* were published for the first Time by *Dom. Mabillon* in his fourth Volume of *Analecta* with a *Latin* Translation. By the Help of a good Manuscript *Dom. Ruinart* has given us that valuable Piece more correct, with some useful Observations of his own.

XXIII. The Life of the Patriarch *Ignatius* is faithfully written in *Greek* by *Nicetas David*, a Native of *Constantinople* and Bishop of *Paphlagonia*, cotemporary with that holy Man.

XXIV. St. *Magloire*'s Life compofed by an anonymous Writer is inferted among *Mabillon*'s *Acts of Bened. Saints*. See alfo the Life of St. *Samfon*, fpoken of *July* the twenty eighth.

XXV. The Acts of St. *Chryfanthus* and St. *Daria* are fufpected by *Baronius*, *Annal. an.* 284.

What we have quoted from St. *Gregory of Tours* concerning thefe Martyrs occurs in his Treatife *of the Glory of Martyrs* c. 38.

The Hiftory of *Gaudentius* is taken from his own Sermons, publifhed in the *Library of the Fathers*, and *Baron.* Annals anno. 405.

XXVI. What we have faid of St. *Evariftus* is found in *Eufeb.* b. 3, c. 34, and St. *Ignatius*'s Ep. to the *Romans*.

The Acts of St. *Lucian*, and St. *Marcian*, publifh'd correctly by *Ruinart*, are divided into two Parts; whereof the former contains what Informations the Compiler could get on the Spot concerning the Converfion and penitential Life of the holy Martyrs: the latter feems an exact Copy of that Trial taken from the publick Records.

XXVII. Our Account of St. *Frumentius* is collected from *Rufinus* Hift. b. 1. c. 19. *Theodoret* b. 1. c. 22. *Socrates*, b. 1. c. 19. *Sozomen*. b. 2. c. 24. and St. *Athan.* firft *Apology*.

XXVIII. The Gofpel, *Acts of the Apoftles*, and fome few Paffages from the Fathers were our only Guides in fpeaking of St. *Simon* and St. *Jude*. See the Commentators and Criticks on the *Epiftle* which bears St. *Jude*'s Name, and *Eufeb*. b. 3. c. 2.

XXIX. The Life of St. *Narciffus* is taken from *Eufeb*. b. 5. c. 12, 23, 24. b. 6. c. 9, 10, 11, 12. and St. *Jerom Of illuftrious Men* c. 62.

Our Accounts of St. *Mary the Penitent* makes Part of the Life of her holy Uncle compofed by St. *Ephrem*, who fpent great Part of his Life with them in the Defart.

XXX. The Original Acts of St. *Marcellus* had been publifh'd by *Surius* and *Baronius* before *Dom. Ruinart* undertook his Collection; but that learned *Benedictin* has revifed them with two other Manufcripts and inferted them in his *Acts of the firft Martyrs*.

XXXI. St. *Quintin*'s Acts, as they ftand in *Surius*, are efteem'd correct, and antient. St. *Wolfgang*'s Life is the Work of one well acquainted with that Saint, and may be feen in its original Purity in *Mabillon*'s 5. *Bened.* Age.

NOVEMBER.

I. THE Hiftory of the *Pantheon*, it's Dedication &c. is taken from *Dio.* b. 53; the *Theodofian Code* l. *ult. de Paganis*, and b. 15. with the fame Title and *Gregory the Great* Ep. 71. b. 9. Our Account of the Feaft of *All Saints* is collected from *Anaftafius*'s Life of *Gregory* III; *Mabillon*'s *Diplomata*, p. 537.

The

The Life of St. *Marcellus*, which furnished us with Materials bears the Name of *Fortunatus*, whom some with great Probability think to be the famous Bishop of *Poitiers* in the VI Century.

II. Our Account of *All Souls Day* wants no References in this Place.

III. The Life of St. *Malachi*, to be seen among St. *Bernard*'s Works, was composed from good Materials sent him from *Ireland*, and what he could relate on his own Knowledge.

IV. The Life of St. *Charles* was first written by *Charles Bascapé*, General of the *Barnabites*, afterwards Bishop of *Novara*, who had been educated in the holy Prelate's House, and employ'd under him in some of the most important Affairs of his Church. We have a second Piece of the same Name composed by *Augustin Valerio*, Bishop of *Verona*, who was intimate with the Saint. These two are in *Latin*. *John Baptist Guiffano*, who spent some Time under St. *Charles*'s Roof, perform'd the same in *Italian*; and our Account is collected from these three original Writers, whose Credit is beyond Dispute.

The Martyrdom of St. *Vitalis* and St. *Agricola* is recorded by St. *Ambrose*, c. 1, and 2. of his *Exhortation to Virginity*.

V. The Authorities alledged concerning St. *Zacharias*'s violent Death are *Origen*, on *Matt.* 25. St. *Basil*, Hom. of *Christ's humble Generation*. St. *Gregory Nyssen*, *Orat.* on *Christ's Nativity*. St. *Peter* of *Alexandria*, can. 13. and St. *Cyril*, Bishop of the same See, in his Treatise *against the Anthromorphites*. St. *Jerom*'s Sentiments of the Matter may be seen in his Commentary on the twenty third of St. *Matthew*.

VI. St. *Winock*'s Life, by an anonymous Writer, at some Distance from the Saint's Time, is published corectly by *Dom. Mabillon*, *Bened. Age* 3. part 1.

VII. Our Account of St. *Willibrord* is taken from his Life, written by *Alcuin* about fifty Years after his Death; *Venerable Bede*, b. 5. c. 12; and St. *Boniface*'s ninety seventh *Epistle*, directed to Pope *Stephen* II.

VIII. *Baronius*, in his Notes on the *Roman* Martyrologe says that the Acts of the *four crown'd Martyrs*, are thought to be the Work of *Anastasius*, the *Library Keeper*; but does not give us his own Opinion of the Matter.

St. *Willebad*'s Life, from which our Account is taken, was written by *Anscarius* his third Successor in the See of *Bremen*.

IX. The whole History of St. *John Lateran*'s Church may be seen in *Baronius*'s Notes on the Martyrologe.

Our Account of St. *Theodore* is transcribed from St. *Gregory Nyssen*'s Panegyrick on that *great Martyr*, as he stiles him.

X. The Acts of St. *Trypho* and St. *Respicius*, which we have follow'd, were first published by *Octavio Gaëtan*, a *Jesuit* in his *History of the Sicilian Saints*; and appear'd since in *Ruinart*'s second Edition, which he had prepared for the Press, but died before it was printed. See *Bibliotheque des Auteurs de la Congregation de St. Maur.* p. 436.

XI. Our

XI. Our Account of St. *Martin* of *Tours* is taken from his Life, as written by St. *Sulpicius Severus*, who writes nothing on that Subject but what he saw, or heard from the Saint's other Disciples; and St. *Gregory* of *Tours's*, *Hist.* b. 1, 10; and his four Books of the Vertues and Miracles of St. *Martin*.

The Life of St. *John the Almoner* was written by *Leontius*, a *Cyprian* Bishop of the VII Century, and composed of such Materials as he received from, a Priest, and Treasurer of the Church of *Alexandria*. This Piece was originally penn'd in *Greek*, and translated into *Latin* by *Anastasius* the *Library Keeper*.

XII. The Life of St. *Martin* Pope and Martyr, published by *Surius*, seems to be the Work of a cotemporary Writer, well acquainted with that Saint's Actions. To which may be added the Epistles of that holy Pope, the Acts of the Councils of his Time, and a Collection of Pieces, which regard the *Monothelites*, thrown together by *Anastasius* the *Library Keeper*, and published by *Father Sirmond*.

The History of St. *Theodore the Studite* may be found in his Life, as written by *Michael* his Disciple, translated into *Latin* by *Father Sirmond*; the Saint's own Letters; his Account of St. *Plato*; and the Life of St. *Nicholas* the *Studite*, his Disciple, written by an anonymous Author.

XIII. Our Account of St. *Didacus* is taken from his Life, as composed in *Latin* by *Peter Galesini*, an *Italian* about one hundred and twenty Years after his Death.

The Life of St. *Stanislaüs Kostka* has been written by several of the Society of *Jesus*; the chief are those composed by *Francis Sacchini*, in *Latin* and *Italian*; by *Eusebius de Niremberg* in *Spanish*; *Daniel Bartoli* in *Italian*; and *Father Orleans* in *French*.

XIV. St. *Laurence*'s Life, written about forty five Years after his Decease, is the Work of a Regular Canon of *Eu*, who had seen him at *Canterbury*, and was well furnished with Materials from *England* and *Ireland*, and the Monastery where he died.

XV. Our Acount of St. *Malo* is taken from his Life, penn'd by an anonymous Author of the VIII or IX Century; which may be seen in *Mabillon*'s first *Benedictin* Age.

XVI. What we have related of St. *Eucherius* is collected from St. *Hilary of Arles*'s Life of St. *Honoratus: Cassian's Preface to his Conferences: Salvian* of *Marseilles*, Ep. 8. *Sidonius Apollinaris* Ep. 3, b. 4.

The Life of St. *Edmond*, from which we have copied our Account of that holy Prelate, is the Work of an anonymous Author inserted in *Surius*'s Collection. See *Matthew Paris* an. 1234; and *Godwin of the Bishops of England*.

XVII. Our Account of St. *Gregory Thaumaturgus* is collected from his elegrnt Panegyrick on *Origen* upon his leaving that learned Master, St. *Gregory Nyssen*'s Discourse on the Saint: St. *Basil*'s Treatise *Of the holy Spirit*: and St. *Jerom Of illustrious Men* c. 65.

The

The History of St. *Dionysius* of *Alexandria*, taken chiefly from his own Works, is very exactly written by *Eusebius Hist.*: b. 6, c. 29, 40, 44, 45, 46. b. 7, c. 11, 17, 20. See also St. *Jerom Of illustrious Men* c. 69.

The Life of St. *Hugh* Bishop of *Lincoln*, published by *Surius*, is an Extract from a larger Piece written by an anonymous Author, well acquainted with the Saint.

XVIII. The History of St. *Peter*'s and St. *Paul*'s Churches at *Rome* may be read at large in *Baronius*'s *Notes on the Martyrologe*, and other modern Writers on that Subject.

What we know with Certainty of St. *Romanus* occurs in *Eusebius*'s second Book of the *Resurrection* of *Jesus Christ*, and the *History of the Martyrs in Palestine* c. 2.

XIX. almost sixty Years after St. *Elizabeth*'s Death her Life was composed by *Thierry* a *Dominican* of *Thuringia*: that Piece was imperfect till *Lambeius* supplied what was wanting in the second Volume of his *Library of the Emperor's*. A Letter to *Gregory* IX from *Conrad* a Priest of *Marpurg* mention'd in our Account gives us some Particulars, either omitted or but slightly touched by other Writers.

Our Account of St. *Pontianus* is taken from the *Roman* Martyrologe, and *Pagi*'s Remarks on *Baronius an.* 235.

XX. The Life St. *Felix* of *Valois* is related with that of St. *John* of *Matha*; see our Account *Feb.* 8.

What we have said of St. *Edmund* King and Martyr is taken from his Life penn'd by *Abo* a Monk of St. *Benet*'s an the *Loire* one hundred Years after his Death; see *Matthew Paris an* 855, and other *English* Historians.

XXI. The Authorities on which we proceed in speaking of the *Presentation of the Blessed Virgin* are there sufficiently mention'd.

The Life of St. *Columban*, which appears in *Mabill.* 2 *Ben. Age*, was written by *Jonas*, a Monk of *Bobbio*, who lived soon after the Saint, and could not be at a loss for good Informations from the Disciples of that holy Abbot. *Usher*'s *Antiq*; of the *British Churches* p. 919. *Cave*'s *Ecclesiastical Library* p. 302, 303: and St. *Columban*'s *Epistles*, publish'd at *Louvain* in 1667.

XXII. Our Account of St. *Cecily* is taken from her Acts, which are antient. All we know of St. *Philemon* and his Wife is found in the Epistle of St. *Paul* to that holy Man.

XXIII. Beside what St. *Paul* says of St. *Clement*, we have deliver'd what we could learn of him from his first Epistle: St. *Chrysostom* on *Tim.* 1. Preface; *Eusebius*, b. 3, c. 15, b. 4, c. 23, *Epiphanius Heres.* 27, c. 6. and St. *Jerom Of illustrious Men* c. 15.

XXIV. Our Account of St. *Chrysogonus* is drawn from the Acts of St. *Anastasia*'s Martyrdom; see *Dec.* 25.

The History of St. *Flora* and St. *Mary* is the Work of St. *Eulogius*, Bishop of *Corduba*, Eye-Witness of Part of what he relates, and well inform'd of what pass'd in Regard to those Martyrs, while he was confin'd in another Prison of the same Town.

XXV. The learned *Baronius* says that no Man who is acquainted with the History of the IV Century can suppose St. *Catharine*'s Acts correct.

Our Account of the Sufferings of St. *Moses*, St. *Maximus* &c. is taken from several Epistles that pass'd between them, Pope *Cornelius*, and St. *Cyprian*, which are preserved among their Saint's Works viz. Ep. 25, 26, 46, 47, 50, 51.

XXVI. The History of St. *Peter* of *Alexandria* is collected from *Euseb.* b. 7, c. 32, b. 8, c. 13, b. 9, c. 6. St. *Jerom*'s *Chronicle*: St. *Athan.* 2d *Apology*: *Theodoret* b. 1, c. 8, *Socrat.* b. 1, c. 7, and *Sozomen* b. 1, c. 24.

XXVII. The Life of St. *Maximus*, printed in the *Chronicle* of *Lerins*, was composed by *Dynamius* a *Patrician*, employ'd in *Gaul* by Pope *Gregory the Great*: to which we have added St. *Gregory* of *Tours* of *the Gl. of Conf.* c. 83. St. *Eucherius Of a solitary Life*, and the *History of the Councils*.

The Life of St. *Virgilius*, written about the Middle of the XII Age, by an unknown Author may be seen in *Mabillion*'s third *Bened. Age.*

XXVIII. St. *Stephen*'s Life, written by *Stephen*, a Deacon of *Constantinople*, forty two Years after the Saint's Death, is inserted among the *Greek Analects* of the *Benedictins*, Tom. 1.

XXIX. The Martyrdom of *Saturninus*, as recorded by an anonymous, but good Author, may be seen in *Ruinart*'s Collection, who supposes them written about fifty Years after the Saint's Death.

XXX. In our Account of St. *Andrew*'s Mission we have produced the Opinions of *Origen*, in *Euseb.* b. 3. c. 1. *Sophronius*'s Supplement to St. *Jerom, Of illustrious Men*, c. 2. *Theodoret*, on *ps.* 116. St. *Gregory Naz. Orat.* 25. St. *Jerom*, Ep. 29. *Paulinus*, Poem, 34.

DECEMBER.

I. THE Life of St. *Eligius* is the Work of St. *Owen*, his particular Friend, who composed it twelve or thirteen Years after his Decease. This Piece was publish'd by *Surius* with much Alteration; but has been since given to the Publick by *Dom. d'Achery* in 1661 in a more perfect Manner; 'though, as some learned Men think, not in it's Original Purity.

II. *Baronius* in his Notes on the *Roman* Martyrologe tells us he had seen St. *Bibiana*'s Acts in Manuscript, which he adds, stand in Need of some Correction; for which Reason we have given those Parts only, which admit of least Exception.

The Life of St. *Peter Chrysologus* is collected from some of his own Discourses, where he had Occasion to speak of himself; and *Rubeus*'s *History* of *Ravenna*, b. 2.

III. St. *Francis Xaverius* has been made known to us by several able Pens of the Society of *Jesus*; those whom we had Recourse to on this Occasion were *Horatio Turselin* who published his Piece at *Rome* in 1594. He wrote in *Latin*, and translated the Saint's Letters into the same Language in 1596. *Daniel Bartoli* an *Italian*, who wrote in his mother Tongue; Father *Boubours*, whose *French* Performance was translated into *English* by Mr. *Dryden*; and *Nic. Orlandin's History of the Society*.

The little we were able to say of King *Lucius* is taken from *Ven. Bede's History* b. 1. c. 4.

IV. What we have said of the different Accounts of the Place and Time of St. *Barbara's* Martyrdom is taken from *Baronius* on the Martyrologe.

St. *Clement* of *Alexandria's* History may be gather'd from his *Stromata*, and *Pedagogue*; *Eusebius* b. 6. c. 18. *Epiphanius*, heref. 32. c. 6; and St. *Jerom, Of illustrious Men*, c. 39.

V. The Life of St. *Sabas* is the Work of *Cyril*, a Monk, and his Disciple; and is allow'd to be an exact and faithful Piece; but has suffer'd somewhat from *Metaphrastes*'s Pen.

VI. The Life of St. *Nicholas*, attributed to St. *Methodius* Patriarch of *Constantinople*, and the Account of his Relicks being removed to *Bari*, were published by *Surius*.

St. *Asella's* Life fills St. *Jerom's* fifteenth Epistle, addres'd to St. *Marcella*; to which may be added his ninety ninth Epistle, to *Assella*, and his hundred and fortieth directed to *Principia*, a holy Virgin.

VII. Beside St. *Ambrose's* Epistles, his funeral Orations, and some other Pieces by the same Hand, we had Recourse to his Life as written by *Paulinus*, who had been his Secretary.

VIII. Concerning the Feast of the *Conception of the Blessed Virgin* the curious may read St. *Bernard's Epistle* to the *Canons of Lyons*, which is the 174. *Paris Edit*. 1621. *Baronius* on the *Roman* Martyrologe: and *Dugdales's Monasticon*, 1 Vol. p. 240.

The Life of St. *Romaricus*, by an anonymous Monk, well acquainted with that holy Abbot's Disciples, has been rescued from several Corruptions by *Dom. Mabillon*, who inserted it in his second *Bened. Age*.

IX. St. *Gorgonia's* History is deliver'd in a funeral Oration pronounced at her Grave by her Brother St. *Gregory Nazianzen*.

X. What we have related of St. *Melchiades* was found in *Eusebius* b. 7. c. 14. b. 10. c. 5. St. *Augustin's* Account of the third Days Conference with the *Donatists* at *Carthage*, and *Ep.* 162.

We have presented our Readers with the Account of St. *Eulalia's* Martyrdom, as recorded by *Prudentius*, Hymn 3. of *the Crowns* of Martyrs.

XI. The Life of Pope *Damasus* is compiled from his own Poems; St. *Jerom*, Ep. 50. *Chron.* a. 367, St. *Augustin's Account of the Conference of Carthage*,

thage, d. 3, St. *Athanasius ad Afric.* p. 941. St *Basil*, Ep. 220, 272, 321, St. *Gregory Nazianzen*, Or. 51, 52. and the *Theodosian Code* b. 20. *de Episcopis.* b. 16. *Leg.* 2. *tit.* 1.

XII. The Sufferings of St. *Epimachus*, St. *Alexander* &c. are related by St. *Dionysius* Bishop of *Alexandria*, an Eye-witness; and the Account preserved by *Eusebius*, b. 6. c. 41.

XIII. Our Account of St. *Lucy* is taken from her Acts, as published by *Surius*.

The Martyrdom of St. *Eustratius* and his Companions was written originally in *Greek* by *Eusebius* a Monk of *Sebaste* in *Armenia*, and translated into *Latin* by *John*, who stiles himself a *Servant* of St. *Januarius*, i. e. one belonging to the Church at *Naples* which bore his Name. See *Baronius* on the Martyrologe.

XIV. What we have said of St. *Spyridon* is taken from *Sozomen*, b. 1. c. 11. St. *Jerom Of Illustrious Men.* c. 92. *Rufinus* b. 1. c. 5.

XV. The Life of St. *Eusebius*, Bishop of *Vercelli* is gather'd from St. *Jerom, Of illustrious Men*, c. 106. St. *Ambrose* Ep. 63, *Edit Bened.* Liberius, Ep. 4, 5. in the Acts of the Councils. *Sulpicius Severus*, b. 2. *Athanasius*, *Epistle to the Solitaries. Socrates*, b. 3. c. 56. *Sozomen*, b. 5. c. 12. and *Theodoret* b. 3. c. 4, 5.

XVI. Our Account of St *Ado* is taken from his Life, as compiled by *Dom. Mabillon* in his fourth *Bened. Age*, part second; from an old Breviary of a collegiate Church in *Dauphiny*, and other antient Monuments.

XVII. The History of St. *Lazarus* is recorded by St. *John* the Evangelist, as referr'd to in our Margin.

The Life of St. *Olympias* is collected from *Palladius*, a cotemporary Writer *Hist: Laus.* c. 144. *Dial. of the Life of St. Chrysostom* p. 164, &c. *Sozomen* b. 8. c. 24. and 17 Epistles written by St. *Chrysostom* to the holy Woman of whom we are speaking.

XVIII. What we have said of St. *Paul the Simple* is taken from *Palladius's Hist: Lauf.* c. 28. That Historian assures us the Account was taken from two of the Saint's Disciples.

St. *Winebald's* Life is the Work of a Nun of *Heidenheim*, personally acquainted with the Saint, whom some suppose to be his Sister. It may be seen in *Surius*, and 3. *Bened. Age.* part 2.

XIX. What we have reported of St. *Meuris* and St. *Thea*, &c. is extracted from the Acts of St. *Porphyrius*, Bishop of *Gaza*, written by *Mark* a Deacon, and the Acts of St. *Timothy* and St. *Maurice*, two of the Martyrs of this Day published by *Henschenius*, who continued the Work of *Bollandus* in his first Vol. for the Month of *May*.

XX. St. *Chrysostom's* Panegyrick on St. *Philogonus* Bishop of *Antioch* furnished us with Materials for the History of that Prelate.

XXI. The

XXI. The Gospel of St. *John* is our best Guide in the Life of St. *Thomas*. The Tradition concerning his Apostolical Mission may be seen in *Eusebius* b. 3, c. 1. *Rufinus*, b. 10, c. 9. and St. *Chrysostom* Hom. 61 on St. *John*.

XXII. The Martyrdom of St. *Ischyrion* and St. *Cheremon* is related by St. *Dionysius* Bishop of *Alexandria* in his Letter to *Fabius* of *Antioch*; of which we have a considerable Fragment in *Eusebius*, b. 6, c. 42.

XXIII. All we know of the ten Martyrs of *Crete* is contain'd in their Acts, as published by *Surius*.

Our Account of St. *Servulus* is transcribed from St. *Gregory the Great*, who knew the Saint. *Hom.* 15 *on the Gospel*. *Dial.* b. 4, c. 14.

XXIV. What we have said of St. *Delphinus* was found in St. *Ambrose*, Epistle 70, *Sulpicius Severus*, b. 2, and several Epistles of St. *Paulinus* of *Nola*.

The History of St. *Thrasilla*, and St. *Emiliana* is written by St. *Gregory the Great* in his 28 *Hom.* on the Gospels, and *Dial.* b. 4. c. 16.

XXV. Our Margin will inform the Reader where to look for the Scripture Account of our Lord's Nativity. What regards the Day on which that Blessing is commemorated may be found in St. *Augustin*, on *Psalm* 132; and *Of the Trinity*, b. 4. c. 5.

The Acts of St. *Anastasia*, from which our Account of that holy Martyr is taken are mentioned by *Monsieur de Tillemont, Mem. Eccl.* Tom. 5.

XXVI. St. *Stephen*'s History has the Stamp of Divine Authority.

XXVII. Beside what the holy Scripture relates of St. *John*, we found some Assistance from St. *Jerom* on *Isaiah* b. 5, c. 4. Ep. 16. St. *Chrys.* on Matt. *Hom.* 85. St *Iren.* b. 3, c. 3, 11, *Euseb.* b. 3, c. 23, b. 6, c. 14. St. *Chrysostom* to *Theodore who had fallen* c. 11. *Ephiph. Her.* 51, c. 12, and St. *Jerom, Of illustrious Men.* c. 9.

XXVIII. The History of the holy Innocents has the same Authority as that of St. *Stephen*.

Our Account of St. *Theodore* is taken from the Life of St. *Pachomius*, published in *Greek* and *Latin* by Father *Papebroch* in his Continuation of *Bollandus, May* 14.

XXIX. Beside the Life of St. *Thomas* of *Canterbury* abridged from four Authors, which is well known, we made use of the Saint's Letters collected by his Friend *John of Salisbury*, afterwards Bishop of *Chartres*; and other Historians of our Nation, who wrote since that Time.

XXX. Cardinal *Baronius* had seen the Acts of St. *Sabinus* in Manuscript, which are probably the same that have since appear'd in *Baluze*'s *Miscellanies*

lanies Vol. 2, who thought them faithful and correct; but *Monsieur de Tillemont*, in his Notes on *Dioclesian*'s Prosecution, declares for the contrary Opinion.

XXXI. Our Account of St. *Silvester* is taken from the Acts of the Councils held in his Time, *Eusebius, Life of Constantine* b. 3, c. 7, *Sozomen* b. 1, c. 17, and *Theodoret*, b. 10, c. 8.

ERRATA.

PAGE 2 line 6 for *Arms* read *Arm*. p. 35 l. 26. for *their* read *three*. p. 45 l. 17 after *that* read *be*. p. 66 l. 24 for *former* read *latter*. p. 126 for *very* read *every*. p. 140 l. 23 for *now*, read *no*. p. 156 l. last for *are*, read *as*. p. 161 l. 5 after *declared* read *be*. p. 221 l. 2 after *then* read *in*. p. 223 l. last before *as* read *such*. p. 127 for *Disciple* read *Discipline*. p. 237 l. 13 for *made* read *make*. p. 238 l. 6. for *Disciple* read *Disciples*. p. 241 l. 2 for *consider* read *considerable*. p. 243 l. 5 for *arising* read *among*. p. 303 l. 1 for *contentions* read *contentious* p. 312 l. 1 for *that* read *their*. p. 332 blot out *in what*. p. 349 l. 9 blot out the second *was*. p. 361 l. 1 for *Millions* read *Thousands*. p. 367 l. 28 for *PHILONUS* read *PHILOGONUS*. p. 394 l. 29. blot out *to be*. p. 411 l. 11 for *him* read *the Pope*.

THE
LIVES
OF
SAINTS;

COLLECTED FROM

AUTHENTICK RECORDS,

OF

CHURCH HISTORY.

With a full Account of

THE OTHER

FESTIVALS throughout the YEAR.

The whole Interspersed with

Suitable REFLECTIONS.

Number X. *for* OCTOBER.

LONDON:

Printed for THOMAS MEIGHAN, in *Drury-Lane*, MDCCXXIX.

Advertisement.

THE following Work is collected from such Authorities, as are universally acknowledged to be unexceptionable. And therefore what is omitted, and might by some be expected here, is not judged or declared false and spurious by such Omission; but only not inserted, because doubted of by some.

AN Alphabetical TABLE

OF

The Saints in *October*.

A	Day
ARTEMIUS, *Martyr*.	20
B	
Bridget, *Widow*,	8
Bruno,	6
C	
Callistus, *Pope and Martyr*,	14
Chrysanthus *and* Daria, *Martyrs*,	25
Cyprian, *Bishop of* Toulon,	3
D	
Dionysius *the* Areopagite,	9
E	
Edward *King and Confessor*,	13
Evaristus, *Pope*,	26
F	
Francis, *of* Assisio,	4
Francis, *of* Borgia,	10
Frumentius, *Apostle of* Ethiopia,	27

G	Day
Gallus, *Abbot*,	16
Gaudentius, *Bishop of* Brescia,	25
H	
Hedwigis,	17
Hilarion, *Abott*,	21
I	
Ignatius, *Patriarch of* Constantinople,	23
L	
Lucian, *and* Marcian, *Martyrs*,	26
Luke *Evangelist*,	18
M	
Magloire, *Bishop*.	24
Marcellus, *Martyr*.	30
Mark, Pope,	7
Mary, *Penitent*,	29

Narcissus,

An Alphabetical Table.

	Day
N	
Narcissus, *Bishop of* Jerusalem,	28
P	
Paulinus, *Bishop of* York,	10
Peter *of* Alcantara,	19
Philip *Bishop, and his Companions Martyrs,*	22
Placidus *and his Companions Martyr,*	5
Q	
Quintin *Martyr,*	31
R	
Remigius, *Bishop of* Rheims,	1
S	
Sergius *and* Bacchus, *Martyrs,*	7
Simon *and* Jude, *Apostles,*	28
T	
Tarachus *and his Companions, Martyrs,*	11
Teresa, *Virgin,*	15
Thaïs, *Penitent,*	8
Thomas *Bishop of* Hereford,	2
W	
Wilfrid, *Archbishop of* York,	12
Wolfgang *Bishop of* Ratisbone.	31

OCTOBER the First.

Saint REMIGIUS,
Bishop of RHEIMS.

REMIGIUS, descended of an antient and honourable Family in Gaul, was born in the Middle of the fifth Century. His Parents took all imaginable Care of his Education, as soon as he was capable of receiving Instruction; and their Child's excellent Capacity made that an easy Task. His Progress in Learning was such as obliged *Sidonius* a cotemporary Prelate to acknowledge him one of the most considerable Men of that Age. But as Vertue makes the brightest Part of the Character of a Saint, we are to observe, after the *French* Authors of his Life, that *Remigius* was from his very Infancy so remarkable for Innocence, Gravity, and all that could recommend him to the most important Posts in the Church, that upon the Death of *Bennadius*, Bishop of *Rheims*, he was placed in that See by the unanimous Voice of all concern'd in the Election, tho' then but twenty two Years old; and the Success of his Ministerial Labours were a sufficient Proof that the Choice was directed by Divine Providence.

The Grace, which he receiv'd at his Consecration supplied his want of Experience in Ecclesiastical Affairs so effectually, that from the first Moment he appear'd in the Episcopal Chair, he govern'd his Flock with all the Prudence and Vigilance of an old Pastor. But, while thus intent on the Salvation of those committed to his Care, he was as solicitous as ever to secure his own Soul.

St. Remigius, *Bishop*.

Oct. 1 *Sidonius* is very strong upon the Chastity and Purity of Heart and Mind, with which he and his Brother *Principius* approached the Altar, where they receiv'd fresh Supplies of that divine Flame, the Love of God, which animated all their Actions; the same holy Author tells us they sate loose to all the Interests, and Satisfactions of this World, and knew no Pleasure but in the Execution of their Ministry. St. *Gregory* of *Tours*, who died in the Close of the sixth Age, observes that he was so remarkable for eminent Sanctity that he was look'd on as another St. *Silvester*; by which Expression that holy Bishop means to say that the Church of *Rheims*, while in Possession of our Saint, had no Reason to envy the Happiness the Christians of *Rome* enjoy'd under that good Pope.

Remigius had lived some Years an exact Model of that Vigilance, Humility, and Paternal Tenderness, which compose the Character of a good Prelate, when *Clovis*, destroying the Remains of the Roman Power in *Gaul*, became Master of all that is now known by the Name of *France*, and *Rheims* was one of the Towns that came into the Hands of that victorious Prince. *Clovis* treated the conquer'd People with so much Sweetness and Humanity that they all chose to remain under their new Master, who made no Alteration in the Laws and Customs which he found established among them, and left them all in quiet Possession of their Goods and Estates. But what endear'd him most to his new Subjects was his tolerating the Christian Religion, which they profess'd, 'though He and his *Franks* were Pagans. In 493, six Years after this Conquest, *Clovis* married *Clotilda*, of whom we have spoken at large on the third of *June*. Her Solicitude for her Royal Consort's Conversion, has been already represented, as the Effect of an ardent Zeal for the Glory of God, and the real Good of that Prince. An unexpected Victory over the *Germans* in 496 determin'd *Clovis* to embrace the Faith; upon which *Clotilda* engaged our Saint to come to Court, and improve his good Inclinations into an entire Conversion. *Remigius*, always glad of any Opportunity of propagating the Kingdom of *Jesus Christ*, undertook to instruct him in the Principles, and Obligations of our most holy Religion. *Clovis* received the great Lessons of Christianity with Docility; but, upon the Bishop's proposing the Conversion of his People by his Influence and Authority, he was startled and urged the Difficulty of the Attempt with much Concern; for he had some Reason to apprehend that the *Franks* were so bigotted to their antient Superstitions, and Idolatry, that an Attempt to disturb them in their abominable Religion would put them upon rebelling. The King, however, to shew his Obedience to the holy Prelate's Directions, promised to speak to them on that Subject; and was beginning a Speech to his Army on the Vanity of the Gods they worship'd, when

the

the Grace of God work'd so powerfully in their Hearts, that they declared themselves ready to renounce the Heathen Deities and obey the God which *Remigius* preached to his Majesty. The Saint, transported with this happy Disposition, proceeded with all possible Expedition to baptize *Clovis*, and his Nobility at *Rheims*.

Oct. 1.

While *Remigius*, assisted by St. *Vedast*, of whom see our Account *February* the sixth, and the Clergy of *Rheims* were employ'd in instructing the numerous Body of Catechumens, several Bishops made their Way to the Court and Camp, and contributed their Endeavours toward carrying on that glorious Work. On *Christmas* day, the Time appointed for performing the Ceremony, the King, follow'd by a prodigious Number, went into the great Church, and asked the Favour of being washed from his Sins in the Lifegiving Waters. *Remigius* receiv'd him with all the Dignity of a Christian Pontif, and exacted a formal Renunciation of Idolatry, and express Confession of the Blessed Trinity; after which he was baptized, and receiv'd the sacred Unction; and the same was perform'd in Favour of above three thousand *Franks* the same Day. Thus the Kingdom of *France* owes it's Conversion to our holy Prelate under God, and venerate him as their Apostle.

Some of those, who have undertaken to write our Saint's History, give us an Account of a Council of Bishops, or a celebrated Meeting of Clergy and Laity for discussing the *Arian* Controversy, in which *Remigius* signalized his Zeal and Capacity against the Errors of that Sect. The Eastern, and Southern Parts of *Gaul*, then in the Hands of the *Visigoths* and *Burgundians*, were generally infected with the Heresy in Question, which gave him frequent Occasions of disputing the controverted Points with their Neighbours the *Franks*. This Meeting therefore was order'd with a View of confirming the Catholicks in their Faith, and gaining the Hereticks. The Bishop of *Rheims* who was deservedly esteem'd the most holy and learned Prelate in *Clovis*'s Dominions, was invited; and, 'though then well advanced in Years, obliged to be the Mouth of the Orthodox on that Occasion. His Adversary, fond of his own Abilities, enter'd the Lists with our Champion with a full Persuasion of defeating him; but, at our Saint's opening the Debate, the Heretick was seiz'd with an Awe, which struck him dumb for some Time; upon the first Recovery of his Speech he employ'd it in begging Pardon for his Vanity and Presumption, and owning the Divinity of the Son of God. This Miracle being soon noised abroad went farther in destroying *Arianism* and reducing the Number of it's Votaries, than all the Discourses and Arguments of the most able Divines.

St. Thomas, Bishop.

Oct. 2. Our Saint's Vertue, which had been exposed to severe Trials in the Course of a long and laborious Pontificate, was in the Close of his Life exercised by much Sickness, which brought him to a happy Death in a great Age, after having worthily fill'd the See of *Rheims* seventy four Years. 'Though there is some Dispute concerning the Year in which he died, the thirteenth of *January* is universally allow'd to be the Day of his Death.

The Body of our Saint was first buried in a small Church at *Rheims*, which bore the Name of St. *Christopher*; but the Number of Miracles perform'd by his Intercession soon made the Place famous; and St. *Gregory* Bishop of *Tours* assures us that several were done in his Time. In the Middle of the ninth Century the Church, already mention'd was rebuilt, or much enlarged, and the venerable Relicks placed in a Silver Shrine; this Translation was perform'd on the first of *October*, the Day on which the *Roman* Martyrologe has placed the Saint's Name. In the Year 901 the Body was with great Solemnity removed from the Cathedral, where it had been deposited for some Time to the Abbey then built on the Ruins of St. *Christopher*'s Church. *Leo* IX, who held a Council at *Rheims* in 1049, deposited the Ashes of the holy Bishop of that City in a new Church, which is still known by the Name of our Saint; and fixt his Festival on the first of *October*.

The II Day.

N. B. *The* CHURCH *this Day testifies her Gratitude to the Almighty for the Protection he affords us by the Ministry of* ANGELS; *but, as we have already spoke sufficiently on that Subject on the twenty ninth of September, the Reader is referr'd to what is said there.*

Saint THOMAS Bishop of Hereford.

THOMAS, the Son of *William Cantilupe*, and *Millecent* Countess of *Evreux*, and thus descended from two of the most considerable of those Families which came from *Normandy* with the Conqueror, was born in *England* about the Year 1225, and in his very Infancy gave several Proofs of his being the particular Choice of the Almighty. He seem'd raised above the common Weaknesses of Nature; all his Inclinations tended to Vertue; his Words and Actions were full of a manly Gravity; and he had no Relish for those Diversions which are the usual Employments of Children. With these happy Dispositions, he was blessed with an excellent Capacity for Learning; but understanding

standing the Glory aud Service of God ought to be the ultimate End of all his Studies, he divided his Time so as to devote much the greater Part of it to pious Exercises. He heard Mass every Day with an edifying Devotion, and said the Canonical Hours long before he was engaged in the Ecclesiastical State.

Having receiv'd the first Rudiments of Learning, and strong Impressions of Religion at home, he was sent to *Oxford*, where he went through his Humanity, and then removed to *Paris* for his Improvement in superiour Studies. After he had appear'd with universal Applause in that University, and signalized himself for his Skill in Philosophy he took his Master of Arts Degree, and return'd to *Oxford*. After some Time spent there in the Study of the Canon Law, he proceeded Doctor of that Faculty; and, upon the Death of the Chancellor of that famous University, no Man was judged more proper to succeed him than our Saint. His Behaviour in that exalted Station gave the whole Nation a most advantageous Idea of his Piety, Learning, and Wisdom, and recommended him very strongly to the Notice of *Henry* III then on the *English* Throne. That Prince, desirous of acknowledging our Saint's Merit in the best Manner in his Power, and providing for the Ease and Interest of his Subjects, made him Lord high Chancellor. All the Change this Promotion made in his Manners was for the better; he was now more vigilant, over his own Motions than ever; and discharged all the Obligations of that important Post with a disinterested Fidelity, admirable Prudence, and inviolable Integrity. Neither Favour nor Recommendations from Persons of the first Rank could influence him to the Prejudice of Truth and Justice; and he made no Distinction between those who appear'd at his Tribunal, but what was determin'd by the Merits of their Cause, and the Law of Equity.

'Though no Man was more capable of that Office, he was so sensible of the Weight of it and the Difficulties which attend it, that he frequently desired Leave to resign it; but King *Henry* always press'd his Continuance in that Station- so that as long as He lived, the Saint was obliged to groan under the Load. Upon that Prince's Death, which happen'd in 1272, *Thomas* deliver'd up the Seals to *Edward* his Son and Successor, and desired Leave to return to the Seminary of Learning where he began his Studies. As his whole Thoughts were now bent on the Ecclesiastical State, he enter'd on Divinity, shew'd the same Capacity and Solidity in that, as had appear'd in his Application to other Branches of Learning, and proceeded Doctor with great Applause. Tho' we are not told the precise Time of his taking holy Orders, we are to suppose
it

Oct. 2 it was either before or soon after his Graduation; for the Author of his Life, after large Commendations of his Regularity, Modesty, Charity, Devotion, and Sobriety, all which he possess'd in an eminent Degree from that Period of Time, adds, that it was impossible to see him offer the tremendous Sacrifice without being inspired with a Seraphick Ardour in Prayer, or touched with Remorse for Sin. As his Heart was full of Purity and Sincerity, he could not bear Lying, Detraction, and Dissimulation.

Such was our Saint, when the See of *Hereford* became vacant by the Death of *John de Breton* in 1275. Some Authors tell us he was then Canon of that Cathedral; but all agree that his Merit was so well known there that he was declared Bishop by the unanimous Voices of the Clergy and People. He receiv'd so fruitful a Grace at the Time of his Consecration that every Vertue, which had been observed in him before, shone out with a double Lustre on his appearing in the Episcopal Chair. His Humility was more profound than ever: his Indifference to the things of this Word more perfect: his Vigilance over his own Actions more exact: and his Inclinations to do Good to others increased with his Fortune. Endeavouring to secure his own Soul by labouring for the Salvation of those committed to his Charge, he exerted a truly Pastoral Vigour in reforming the Manners of his Flock, and establishing good Discipline in his Diocese. Nor was he less strenuous in asserting the Rights of his Church, which he thought infringed by the Pretensions of the Archbishop of *Canterbury*. The Dispute ran so high on that Article between our Saint and his Metropolitan that he was obliged to make a Journey to *Rome* in 1285, where he obtain'd all the Redress he could desire, and left that City in 1287. His Design was to return to *England*; but as soon as he reached *Monte Fiasconi* in the Territories of *Florence* he was taken ill, and died after a short Sickness.

His Body was exposed to publick View six days, after which the Flesh was buried in a Church on the Spot, and the Bones carried to *Hereford*, where they were joyfully receiv'd and honour'd by the whole Town. The Saint was canonized by *John* XXII, who was raised to the holy See in 1316, and his Festival fix't to the second of *October*, as it stands at present in the *Roman* Martyrologe.

The

The III Day. Oct. 3.

St. CYPRIAN, Bishop of TOULON.

THE Saint of this Day, a Native of *Marseilles*, enter'd young into the celebrated Monastry of St. *Victor* in that City, where he was well grounded in the Principles and Obligations of the Christian Religion, and made no small Progress in Learning. He was thus qualified, when *Cesarius* Bishop of *Arles* invited him to that City, completed his Education, and made him Deacon of his Church. The *Visigoths*, who reign'd in *Spain*, were then in Possession of *Arles*, and *Marseilles*. *Alarick* the King of that barbarous People 'though a profess'd *Arian*, treated the Catholicks in his Dominions with Equity and Moderation, and allow'd them to meet and take their own Measures for maintaining the Orthodox Faith among the *Gauls*. The Council of *Agatha* or *Agde* in 560 was the Result of this Indulgence. *Cesarius*, who presided in that venerable assembly, was attended there by his Deacon *Cyprian*.

Licinian, a Notary of the Church of *Arles*, having insinuated somewhat to his Disadvantage, that holy Prelate was banished to *Bourdeaux*. *Cyprian*, full of Affliction for the Distress of the Flock thus deprived of it's worthy Pastor, undertook a Journey to Court, and pleaded the Saint's Cause so successfully that he was immediately restor'd to his Bishoprick; but before his return to *Arles*, that Town fell into the Hands of *Theodorick*, King of the *Ostrogoths* in *Italy* by the Death of *Alarick*.

After *Cyprian* had signalized his Zeal and Capacity at *Arles* for some Years, and given sufficient Proofs of a consummate Prudence and great Piety, he was placed at the Head of a Religious Community at *Toulon*; and about the Year 516 consecrated Bishop of that Place by *Cesarius* his Metropolitan. He discharged all the Duties of his Station with great Activity and Vigilance; and proved such as those troublesome Times required. We cannot suppose he wanted Employment when we consider the *Arian* Heresy threatning the Faith of his Flock, and the Disorders introduced by the late Wars corrupting their Morals. Nor was he less attentive to the Necessities of the whole Church than to those of his own particular Charge, always strictly united with his holy Master; he had a Share in all the Resolutions, and Negotiations of that great Prelate; and claim'd a Right to divide his Sufferings for the Truth.

The fourth Council of *Arles* was held in 524; in which *Cesarius* presided, and *Cyprian* assisted. Our Saint was present likewise at the second Council of *Orange* in 529, and consequently one of those excellent Prelates, who defended

Oct. 4. fended the Grace of *Jesus Christ* against the Attempts of the *Semipelagians*. *Cyprian* appear'd in several other Councils; but in none to more Advantage than in that of *Valentia* in *Dauphiny* the same Year. He assisted in that Assembly both as Bishop of *Toulon*, and Representative of his Metropolitan, who was then Sick. Several difficult Questions concerning *Grace and Freewill* were discussed in that Council, which gave our Saint an Opportunity of shewing Skill in that Controversy; for he proved all his Assertions by the Scriptures, and Authority of the holy Fathers. What he said on that Occasion was adopted and confirm'd by *Cesarius*, and approved of by the holy See.

Toulon, and the rest of *Provence* was incorporated with *France* in 536; a Change that gave the orthodox Prelates the cheerful Prospect of Protection, and Encouragement of their Endeavours for extirpating Heresy: in which Work our Saint exerted himself with a becoming Vigour. The Time of *Cyprian*'s Death is not certainly known; *Cesarius* mentions him in his Will in 542; but he was not alive in 549, as appears from the fifth Council of *Orleans* being sign'd by his Successor *Palladius* that Year. He was buried in his own Cathedral, in which a magnificent Chapel was afterwards built in his Honour; where his Relicks are still preserved with due Veneration. The Church of *France* keeps the third of *October* in his Memory, and the City of *Toulon* looks on him as their Patron.

The IV Day.

St. *FRANCIS*, Founder of the Order of *Minor Friars*.

ST. *Francis*, a Native of *Assisio* in *Italy*, was born in the Year 1181. His Parents bore a good Character among their Neighbours; but, being engaged in Trade, were more intent on getting Money than educating their Children. *Francis* was applied to Business as soon as he was capable of it; and, 'though he was not remarkable for any Vice, his whole Time was divided between Interest and Pleasures. He had a natural Tenderness for the Poor, which encreased with Age, and shew'd itself on all Occasions. He made it a Law to himself never to refuse relieving any one that asked for the Love of God; being one Day very busy in his Shop, he chanced to let a poor Man go away without Assistance; but upon reflecting on the Omission, he was so touched with a Sense of what he thought a great Fault that he left his Business, went in Quest of the same miserable Object, gave him a large

Alms,

Alms; and made a Promise to Almighty God never to refuse any that should Oct. 3. ask in his Name, as long as it was in his Power to relieve them; an Obligation, which he observed most punctually the remaining Part of his Life. He had several other excellent Qualities which recommended him to the Affection, and Esteem of all who knew him; his Honesty, Liberality, Politeness, and obliging Behaviour gave the Inhabitants of *Assisio* abundant Reason to hope he would one Day become the Ornament of their Town. But Providence had other Views in his Favour, and design'd to employ those valuable Dispositions in a very different Way.

Francis, full of the Spirit of the World, and entirely taken up with Business, did not for some Time comprehend the Will of God in his Regard, and seem'd to have no Relish nor Concern for any thing but what brought a present Satisfaction. Upon his Recovery from a long and dangerous Fit of Sickness, he was one Day going abroad in a fine Suit of Cloaths, when meeting one, whom he knew to be a Gentleman of a good Family, very shabby, he was so struck with the melancholy Object that he gave him his Coat. The following Night he dreamt he was in a large Room full of Arms, all marked with a Cross; and upon asking for whose Use they were design'd, was told they were for him and, his Soldiers. When he 'waked, he concluded he should be advanced to some considerable Post in the Army, and began to think how to put himself in the Way of military Preferment; in this View he left his Business, undertook a Journey into *Apulia*, in order to offer his Service to a Nobleman there, who had raised a considerable Body of Forces. As he was on the Road, he was favour'd with another Dream which undeceived him, brought him back to *Assisio*, and let him know he was design'd for the Service of God in a particular Manner. This Admonition made so deep an Impression on him that from that Moment he enter'd into himself; and concluded that the Enemies whom he was to engage were such as attack the Soul, and that Instruments of Penance were the Arms, which he was to employ in that holy War.

At his Return to his Father's House, the Change of his Heart was visible in every Circumstance of his Behaviour: he seldom went abroad; broke with all his old Companions; and began to allow Prayer and Meditation some Share of his Time. As he had now serious Thoughts of Eternity, he resolved to leave off his Business, and break from every Engagement that fix'd him to the World. Full of these excellent Dispositions he was one Day on Horseback in the Plains of *Assisio*, where he met a poor Man cover'd with a loathsome Leprosy; Nature recoiled at the shocking Sight; but *Francis*, reflecting on the Obligation of Self Conquest, as an indispensible Condition of the Service

Oct. 3 of *Jesus Christ*, alighted, embraced the miserable Object, gave him a handsome Alms, and then pursued his Journey. He had scarce mounted his Horse, when to his great Surprize, the Person he had relieved disappear'd; but *Francis* was so far from being afrighted at what had happen'd, that he receiv'd fresh Courage and Resolution, and from that Moment proposed to make every Action of his Life a Step to Perfection. In this View he now took all Opportunities of retiring, and seem'd to have no other Pleasure but what he found in Silence and devout Tears.

As he was one Day absorp'd in Prayer, and transported into a Sort of Extasy, he was favour'd with a Vision, which represented our Redeemer expiring on the Cross. That Object made so deep an Impression on the happy Convert that from that Time he never heard the Sufferings of *Jesus Christ* mention'd without testifying his Sense of the Enormity of Sin, and the infinite goodness of God in rescuing us from it's Tyranny, by Tears and Sighs. The Evangelical Maxims of Self-denial, and Carrying the Cross were always in his Mind, and the Life of our divine Master continually before his Eyes. The Humility, Poverty, Patience, and boundless Tenderness of his crucified Saviour were the daily Subjects of his Meditation, and the grand Model on which he endeavour'd to form his own Life.

Soon after *Francis*'s Return to *Assisio*, as he was conversing with the Almighty in St. *Damian*'s Church, near that Town, he heard a Voice like that of a Man, which seem'd to proceed from the Crucifix on the Altar, and order'd him to repair that Building, then in a ruinous Condition. Being convinced that he was alone, he was at first startled at what he had heard; but upon reflecting on the Matter, receiv'd the Command as an authentick Declaration of the Will of God, and resolved to perform what was thus recommended to his Care. Upon going home, he loaded a Horse with Goods, which he disposed of at *Foligno*, and carried the Money to the Priest who had the Care of St. *Damian*'s Church, desiring it might be employ'd in repairing the House of God, and feeding the Poor, and that he might be allow'd to live with that Ecclesiastick for his Improvement in Vertue. The Priest, whose Circumstances were very narrow, agreed to the last Article of his Request; but declined accepting of the Money. *Francis* then assured him he did nothing in this whole Affair without the immediate Direction of the Almighty, and threw his Purse into a Window. He had spent some Days with his new Companion in Fasting, Prayer, and Self-mortification before his Father knew what was become of him; but upon being inform'd of his whole Conduct since he went from home, the old Gentleman accompanied by some Relations hasten'd.

sten'd to St. *Damian*'s in the first Transports of his Passion, and demanded Oct. 3. his Son. *Francis*, not thinking it proper to confront an angry Parent, hid himself in a Cave, where he pass'd several Days in Tears and Penance, begging to be deliver'd from the Hands of those, who attempted to drag him from his religious Retreat; at last, fortified by the Grace of God, he ventured out and resolved to bear the worst that could befal him. Upon his appearing at *Assisio* in a Dress and Manner vastly different from what he wore when among them before, the most favourable Opinion they entertain'd of him was that this Change proceeded from a Disorder in his Mind; and his Discourse, which now turn'd on Subjects not usually admitted by such as live in the World, confirm'd his Neighbours in their Opinion of his Distraction. But our Saint was to begin with the great Lessons of Christian Morality, and be inured to Contempt and ill Usage from the first Moment of his entring into the School of *Jesus Christ*; he was accosted in the Streets with Stones, and Dirt, and treated as an incurable Madman. *Francis*'s coarse Reception at *Assisio* drew the whole Town together; and the Saint's Father being alarm'd at the Noise made on that Occasion, ran out, seiz'd him, carried him home, beat him, bound him, and confined him like one who had really lost his Senses. Upon his Father's going into the Country, the Prisoner was recommended to the Care of his Mother, with Directions to treat him as He had done. She had not been long in Possession of that Commission, when being convinced that *Francis*'s Resolution was proof against the most vigorous Attempts, she gave him his Liberty; and he went back to St. *Damian*'s.

His Father returning to *Assisio*, and missing the Saint, flew to the Place of his Retreat with all the Rage of a disappointed Worldling, who imagined his Son lost, if not employ'd in increasing his Fortune. At his Arrival, *Francis* met him, and with an undaunted Courage assured him he was ready to bear the Weight of more Chains and Blows for the Love of *Jesus Christ*, whose Disciple he was, and resolved to remain. The angry Father, finding he gain'd no Ground, seem'd willing to compound for the Loss of his Son by securing the Money he took at *Foligno*, and grew much calmer as soon as that Darling of his Heart was in his Possession. The old Gentleman then gave him his Choice either to return to his House, or renounce all his Hopes and Expectations in the Family. Upon *Francis* preferring the latter, he was carried before the Bishop of *Assisio*, and required to do it in Form. As soon as they came into the Presence of that Prelate, the Saint perform'd what he had promised by stripping himself, and giving up all his Cloaths; after which expressive Ceremony, turning to his Father, "*hitherto* said he, *I have called You*

Oct. 4. "*my Father; but now I am to make my whole Application to my Father, who is in Heaven.*" The Bishop, strongly affected with *Francis*'s Resolution and Disinterestedness, embraced him, and cover'd him with his own Cloak 'till he could find somewhat more proper for his Use, which was an old Cloak belonging to a Country Fellow, who chanced to be in the Episcopal Palace at that Time. The Saint receiv'd it cheerfully, and made a Cross on it with Chalk, or Mortar, that the Passion of *Jesus Christ* might always be in his Mind.

This Conversion is dated in the twenty fifth Year of our Saint's Life. Upon his leaving the Bishop he quitted the Town, went in Quest of a convenient Solitude, and sanctified every Step by singing the Praises of the Almighty. Submitting his own will to the Direction of the holy Spirit, he travell'd where he thought that Guide led him; and, coming to *Gubbio*, was met by one of his old Acquaintance, who receiv'd him very kindly, made him several Profers which his Indifference to all the Enjoyments of Life made him decline, and with much difficulty prevail'd with him to accept of an old Coat, to wear under his Cloak. Thus accommodated *Francis* made some Stay in that Town, during which Time the Hospital was the most constant Scene of his Actions; where dressing leprous Sores, kissing the most Offensive Ulcers, and other Acts of Charity and Humility were his whole Employment. But the Remembrance of the Order he had receiv'd in St. *Damian*'s Church brought him back to *Assisio*, and made him enter on Means for performing what was then recommended to him. In this View he submitted to beg where he had once lived in Plenty, and his Applications were crown'd with a Success that enabled him to repair the said Building; at which he work'd, 'though much wasted, and disabled by rigorus Fasts. Having thus experienced his own Strength, and the charitable Dispositions of the People, he undertook to repair two other Churches; one of which bore the Name of St. *Peter*, the other was dedicated in Honour of *our Lady of the Angels*. The latter of these lay about three Quarters of a Mile from the Town, was called *Portiuncula* i, e. *a small Part*, and then belong'd to the *Benedictin* Monks. The Situation of this Building was so agreeable to our Saint, that he resolved to make it the Place of his ordinary Residence. Here it was that he laid the Foundation of the flourishing Order, which carries his Name, after two Years spent in Silence and Mortification. Being one Day at Mass that Passage of the Mat. 10 Gospel was read in which our Lord recommends to his Apostles a perfect Dis-
9, 10. engagement from the World and all it's Cares, and forbids their providing themselves with Money, Shoes, or two Coats, when employ'd in the Evangelical

Message;

Message; upon hearing this Advice, he took it as a direct Command to him- Oct. 4 self, immediately conform'd to the Letter of it, and resolved to make it the inviolable Rule of his own Life. Being thus reduced to the Circumstances of the first Founders of Christianity, he preached the Necessity of Penance in so strong, and serious Terms that several Persons were converted; which carried the Reputation of his Virtue, and Apostolical Life to distant Parts of *Italy*. Some of those, whom God had touched by the Ministry of the Saint, press'd to be admitted as Members of one Family under so excellent a Father, that the Model of the Perfection which he taught might be always before their Eyes. *Bernard*, a substantial Tradesman of *Assisio*, was the first of that Number: *Peter* of *Catana* Caron of the Cathedral in the same City, the second: and *Giles* a poor ignorant Peasant of great Simplicity and Virtue, the third. *Bernard* and *Peter*, after some necessary Instructions in our Saint's Design, were dispatched into *Romagna* with Directions to recommend the Poverty and Sufferings of *Jesus Christ* both by Word and Example; while the Saint, attended by Brother *Giles*, was employ'd in the same Manner in the *Marca* of *Ancona*.

As soon as *Francis* found the Number of his Disciples arise to Six, he call'd them together, made them most pathetick Discourses on the Necessity of Self denial and corporal Mortifications, in order to gain the Kingdom of Heaven; and then let them know that he proposed sending them into different Parts of the World to preach the same Doctrine to others. Before he could execute this holy Design, his Family was considerably encreased; upon which the Saint depending on large Additions to their Number, drew up a Set of Rules, containing the several Precepts he had given his Disciples since they had engaged to share the Labours of an Apostolical and Penitential Life with him. The Bishop of *Assisio*, whom he consulted on all Occasions, advised him to admit of Lands and Revenues for the Maintainance of himself and his Companions; but *Francis* would not hear of a Proposal so foreign to his original Design of leaving the World; and, when the Property of the *Portiuncula* was offer'd him, he would only accept of the Use of it, that he and his Disciples might always appear Strangers on Earth.

Having thus established his Order on the Foundation of Evangelical Poverty, his next Care was how to continue and perpetuate the new Establishment; which was not to be done effectually without the Approbation of the holy See. This Affair carried him and his whole Community to *Rome* in the Year 1210; where *Innocent* III, after some Delay, approved of his Plan by Word of Mouth. Being now Master of all he desired in this World, he
conducted

Oct. 3. conducted his spiritual Children to the Valley of *Spoleto*, where he spent some Time in forming them to the Spirit of his Institute, and then conducted them to the *Portiuncula*, sent them about the Country with the Evangelical Commission, and provided a convenient Number of Cells for their Reception at their Return from those charitable Journeys. The holy Founder was indefatigable in the Labours of his Vocation, which were rewarded and encouraged by a Success equal to the Holiness of his Intentions.

We have already told our Readers what Share St. *Francis* had in the Conversion of St. *Clara*, and founding a Monastery of his Order for Women, in our Account of that holy Virgin on the twelfth of *August*; and therefore proceed to acquaint them with the prodigious Increase of that Part of our Saint's Family which was more immediately under his Direction. As a Proof of his own Humility, and to inspire his Disciples with the same Vertue, he gave them the Name of *Minor Friars*. Their Love of Poverty, and Mortification, and Zeal for the Souls of their Neighbours had such Powerful Charms for all who were inclined to give Eternity a serious Thought, that our Saint had the Satisfaction of seeing above five thousand Apostolical Labourers of his Institute at the first general Chapter in 1219. It is scarce possible to describe all the Mortifications practiced by our Saint for his own Sanctification, and the Edification of others, who were thus moved to do Penance for their Sins; his Fasts were long and rigorous: his Food coarse, and disagreeable: his Cloaths mean, and scarce able to defend him from the Injuries of the Weather: the bare Ground his Bed: and a close Union with God in Prayer, and Meditation his chief Pleasure.

Our Saint's Charity, which knew no Bounds, inspired him with a Desire of labouring for the Conversion of remote Countries, particularly those inhabited by Infidels. This was his Disposition when he made a Journey to *Rome* for the Pope's Consent to his carrying the Light of the Gospel among the *Saracens* in *Syria*. His Holiness easily granted his Request, and assisted him in raising a Convent of his Order at *Rome*. Thus authorized he took Shipping; but by the Direction of a wise overruling Providence, was thrown on the Coast of *Sclavonia*, and obliged to return to *Italy*. Soon after this Disappointment he fell dangerously ill, and, before his Recovery was complete, set out for *Spain*, from which Country he design'd to go for *Africa*, where he hoped he might be honour'd with the Crown of Martyrdom. Several great Miracles perform'd by his Ministry on the Road were so many Proofs of the Power of God, and his Approbation of the Saint's Views in this Expedition; but *Francis* was not yet to enjoy the wished for Satisfaction of preaching the Kingdom of *Jesus Christ*

Christ to the *Mahometans*, and a violent Fit of Sickness in *Spain* lead him to conclude the Almighty had reserved that Task for other Hands, and design'd to insinuate by this second Disappointment that the Preservation of his Conquests in *Italy* was his present Business. Full of this Persuasion he return'd to his first Retreat as soon as his Health allow'd him to travel. At his Return to his Convent, he reassumed his Labours for the Propagation of his Order in other Parts of *Europe*; which succeeded so well that in a little Time Communities of his Friars were established in all the chief Towns of *England*, *France*, and *Germany*.

Oct. 3.

Upon the breaking up of the general Council of *Lateran*, held in 1215, *Francis* made a second Journey to *Rome* in Hopes of obtaining a Bull in Confirmation of his Rule. *Innocent* III died during the Saint's Stay in that City; and his Successor *Honorius* III, used him with all the Respect due to his Vertue; but having the Rules of three other Orders before him at that Time, he was obliged to defer the formal Approbation of the *Franciscan* for some Years. In the mean while the pious Founder prevail'd with his Holiness to allow them a Protector, and Cardinal *Hugolin*, Bishop of *Ostia*, was named on that Occasion. That Prelate presided in the first General Chapter of the new Order, which was held in the open Fields near the Convent *of our Lady of the Angels*, being too numerous to be contain'd in any Building in that Neighbourhood, where all his Business was to moderate the excessive Austerities of several, who had form'd their Lives rather by the Example than Precepts of the Saint.

Soon after this Assembly was dissolved, *Francis* made a third Attempt to visit and enlighten the Infidels, which succeeded to his Wish. He took Shipping at *Ancona* in Company with eleven of his Friars, and landed at *Acon*, in *Palestine*, known formerly by the Name of *Ptolomaïs*; from which Port he travell'd to *Damiata* in *Egypt*, the Subject of a long Contest between the Sultan of *Egypt*, and the Christian Army engaged in the holy War. That Prince, incensed at the Boldness of these resolute Strangers, had promised a very considerable Reward to any one who should bring him the Head of one of them. A Danger like this could have no Influence over a Man, who had left his own Country in Quest of Martyrdom; full of the cheerful Hope of dying in the glorious Cause of Religion, the Saint, attended only by one of his Companions, known by the Appellation of *the illuminated Brother*, made his Way to the *Mahometan* Camp, where after much ill Usage they were carried before the Sultan. Upon their Appearing, that Prince asked them what Business had brought them into that Country; to which *Francis* readily answer'd that the only true God had sent them thither to shew Him and his Subjects the Path

of

Oct. 4. of Salvation. The *Sultan*, seeing his Courage, heard him with great Attention for several Days together, and invited him to stay in his Dominions, and near his Person. The Saint let him know his Conversion and that of his People would be the only Means to detain him in *Egypt*; and, to convince him of the superiour Excellency of the Religion which he proposed, offer'd to throw himself into a large Fire in Company with one of the Mahometan Priests, and put the whole Issue of the Dispute upon the Escape or Death of one of the Parties. The *Sultan* was too well acquainted with the Dispositions of his Priests to imagine any of them would stand the Trial; and when the Saint profer'd to undergo it alone, upon Condition this his Delivery from the Power of the Flames should determine the Conversion of the Infidels, the Sultan thought proper to decline the Proposal; but acknowledged *Francis*'s Merit by rich Presents, which the holy Man would by no Means receive. This generous Contempt of what the Generality of Mankind pursue so vigorously, and with so much Anxiety, inhanced the Sultan's Opinion of his Merit; who dismissed him in the civilest Manner possible, recommended himself to his Prayers, and gave him the Liberty of making what Conquests he could in his Dominions. But it appear'd on this Occasion that it is in vain for Man to talk to the Ear, unless God touches the Heart; for *Francis* left *Egypt* without any other Satisfaction than that of a good Intention, and a disinterested Zeal for the Glory of God.

It was our Saint's Custom to divide his Time between God and his Neighbour; the former Part was employ'd in Prayer and Contemplation: the latter in serving all who wanted his Assistance. He had now discharged all the Obligations under which he lay to his Neighbour, procured the Pope's Confirmation of his Order, reduced his Rule to a more regular and methodical Form, and resign'd his Character of Superior General into the Hands of *Peter* of *Catana*; so that his own Sanctification seem'd now the only Employment left. In the Year 1224 he retired to Mount *Alverno*, where he undertook to observe his usual Fast of forty Days from the Assumption of the Blessed Virgin, to the End of *September*, in Honour of St. *Michael*. While he was employ'd in a Close Conversation with the Almighty in that Retreat, he received the Impressions of our Lord's Passion in his Hands, Feet, and Side, after being favoured with the glorious Vision of a *Seraph*. This Circumstance of our Saint's Life, from which he derives the Appellation of *Seraphick*, is related by St. *Bonaventure*, who was well convinced of the Reality of the Wounds in his venerable Body, and tells us he had heard Pope *Alexander* IV declare from the Pulpit that he had seen them.

From

From the Time of his receiving that Favour 'till the Conclusion of his holy Life, which happen'd two Years after, the Saint could only instruct his Disciples by Patience under continual Sickness. Finding his End approach, he hasten'd to his Convent of *Our Lady of the Angels*, desired the whole Community to come into his Cell, employ'd his last Breath in exhorting them to the Love of God, the Practice of Evangelical Poverty, and Steadfastness in the Catholick Faith, and expired in their Arms on the fourth of *October* 1226. The next Day his Body, attended by great Crouds of People, was carried to *Assisio*; and buried in St. *George*'s Church, where he had receiv'd some slight Instructions in his Infancy, and preached several Times since his Conversion. The Number and Lustre of the Miracles perform'd at his Grave seem'd such evident Marks of his Sanctity to *Gregory* IX, then in the holy See, that he undertook to canonize him in Form, as soon as it was possible. It was not necessary to make long and perplex'd Enquiries in this Affair; the sacred College was unanimous on that Article, and his Holiness, while Cardinal Protector of the Order, had been an Eye Witness of the Sanctity of his Life and the many Favours conferr'd on the Sick, and Lame by his Ministry. The Ceremony was perform'd at *Assisio* with great Solemnity on the seventeenth of *July* 1228, and his Festival fix'd on the Day of his Death.

Oct. 5.

The V Day.

St. *PLACIDUS*, and his Companions MARTYRS.

PLACIDUS, Son to *Tertullus* a Senator of *Rome*, was put into St. *Benedict*'s Hands in his Infancy, and placed under his Direction about the Year 522 in the Monastery of *Subiaco*, where he made a happy Progress in Virtue, and became one of that Saint's most considerable Disciples. He was sent in Company with a convenient Number of Monks into *Sicily*, with Commission to build a Monastery in that Island. That Building being finished, our Saint was placed at the Head of the new Community, which by his prudent Management soon encreased. *Eutychius* and *Victorius*, the holy Abbot's Brothers, and *Flavia* his Sister, made him a Visit when in that Station. While they were there, a Company of Pirates landed, probably at *Messina*, plunder'd the Monastery, and put our Saint his Brother and Sister, with thirty Monks to the Sword. As they fell by the Hands of *Barbarians*, the Church honours them as Martyrs on the fifth of *October*.

Oct. 5.

St. GALLA, Widow.

GALLA was Daughter to the illustrious Patrician *Symmachus*, who was put to Death at *Ravenna* in the Year 525 by Order of *Theodorick* King of the *Goths* in *Italy* for endeavouring to support the Dignity of the *Roman* Senate against that Prince's Attempts. History has not preserved the Name of our Saint's Husband; but St. *Gregory* the Great tells us she lost him in less than a Year. Her Youth, the Affluence of her Fortune, and the Pleasures of the World which smiled on her, and courted her Acceptance were so many strong Inducements to engage again in a married State; but *Galla*, blind to all the Charms of created Beings, chose to devote the Remainder of her Days to her Heavenly Spouse. In this View she retired to a small Monastery joining to St. *Peter*'s Church, where she spent several Years in Solitude, Prayer, and Mortification; which Employments were never interrupted but by Acts of Charity that required her to converse with Mankind. The Saint was very punctual and diligent in the Practice of all those Virtues which make Retirement agreeable to the Almighty by sanctifying the Person. Toward the Close of her Life she was afflicted with a Cancer in her Breast, but suffer'd all the Pain of it with most edifying Patience and Submission to the Divine Will, 'till the happy Moment which deliver'd her from Life and all the Evils of it. The Time of her Death is not known; but the *Roman* Martyrologe places her Name on the fifth of *October*.

The VI Day.

St. BRUNO, Founder of the CARTHUSIANS.

BRUNO, descended of an ancient and honourable Family, was born at *Cologn* about the Middle of the XI Century, and in his very Infancy shew'd such Dispositions to Virtue as made it easy to judge that God had prevented him with his holy Grace, and design'd him for a singular Instrument of his Glory. His Parents, whose Virtue was still more considerable than their Birth, made it their first Care to improve the Blessing they enjoy'd in so promising a Child by a religious and liberal Education. As he was happy in an excellent Genius and good Memory, he made a considerable Progress in his Studies at an Age when the Generality are scarce acquainted with the first Rudiments of Learning. The Innocence of his Life, and an uncommon

Ripeness

Ripeness of Understanding recommended him so strongly to the Esteem of St. *Amnon*, then Bishop of *Cologn*, that he was made Canon of St. *Cunibert*'s Church in that City, when very young. Upon the Death of that holy Prelate *Bruno* removed to *Rheims*, where he finished his Studies, was admitted Canon of the Cathedral, and Chancellor of the University; and, according to all Accounts of his Life, he was reckon'd one of the most learned Men of the Age.

Oct. 6.

Bruno, being one Day in Company with *Raoul* Provost of the Church of *Rheims*, and an other Friend, their Discourse turn'd on the Vanity of the Pleasures and Enjoyments of this World, and the Solidity and eternal Duration of those which are promised in the other. They had dwelt some Time on these important Topicks when, finding themselves inflamed with an ardent Desire of eternal Happiness, they made a Vow to leave the World as soon as it was possible, and retire to a Monastery. The Execution of this Design was deferr'd 'till the Return of one of his Friends, who was then going to *Rome*; but, he staying longer than was at first proposed, and the other growing cold in the Affair, *Bruno* persevered in his Resolution, and consider'd of Means to acquit himself of the Obligation under which he lay. The Loss of his two first Companions was more than made up by the Addition of six Persons of great Vertue, and other valuable Qualifications, viz. Dr. *Landuin*, a Native of *Lucca* in *Italy*: *Stephen du Bourg*, and *Stephen de Die* Canons of St. *Rufus*'s near *Avignon*: *Hugh*, the only Priest in the Company; and *Andrew* and *Guerin*, two Laymen. These seven were bent on retiring together, and were considering of a proper Place for their Purpose, when *Bruno* observed to them that finding a Desart for their Reception was much the least Part of their Business, and desired they would endeavour to engage the Direction and Advice of some able and holy Man in that Undertaking. Upon this necessary Hint the two Canons already mentioned told him they knew a Prelate in that Country, who made the Salvation of his Neighbour his first Care, and would be glad to receive and encourage such as were disposed to end their Days in penitential Austerities. The Person of whom they spoke was *Hugh*, the famous Bishop of *Grenoble*, whose real Character exceeded all the Panegyricks that have been bestow'd on his Vertue; and the Mention of that excellent Master and great Patron of a solitary Life determin'd the whole Company to make a Journey to *Grenoble*; where they threw thmselves at the holy Prelate's Feet, begging his Direction, and the Liberty of retiring in some Part of his Diocese, where they might serve God without Interruption, or being burthensome to others. The Sight of the seven Strangers put the Bishop in Mind of a Dream, in which he he saw seven Stars move before him to an uncultivated, mountainous Desart called in the *French* Tongue *La Chartreuse*, where he thought the Almighty raised a Place of Worship. Upon hearing their Petition, he immediately applied his Dream to Them, and concluded these were the Persons represented by so many Stars; full of this Persuasion, and transported at a Proposal so conducive to the Glory of God, and the Salvation of the Men before him, he receiv'd them with all Marks of Affection and Respect, gave them Leave to inhabit the *Chartreuse*, and assured them of all the Protection and Assistance in his Power. That they might not be surprized at their Arrival there, *Hugh* thought it would not be improper to give them an exact Description of the Desart; but, 'though all the Horrors of that Place were drawn in strong Colours, *Bruno* and his Companions were so far from being shock'd at the Representation that they seem'd the more impatient to begin their Penance in a Place so suitable to their Design and Inclinations. The Bishop, observing their Fervour, desired they would consider that it would be impossible for them to practice the same Austerities in a cold Country, which were used by the holy Solitaries of *Egypt*, *Syria*, and *Palestine*, and remember that Prudence obliged them to make considerable Abatements in the Article of Fasting, which was much easier in those hot Climates. The Saint and his Companions assured the Bishop that they went to that Desart with more Pleasure than could be imagined; were too well persuaded of their own Weakness to place their Confidence in any thing but God; and, as they believed Him the sole Author of their Resolution, and proposed the Advancement of his Glory as the only End of all their Undertakings, hoped they might depend on the Divine Assistance, as long as they continued faithful to the Directions of Heaven.

Hugh, charm'd with these excellent Dispositions, kept them in his House 'till toward the Close of *June*, and then conducted them to the Scene of their intended Penance, and put them in Possession of all the Ground that lay between two or three high Mountains, where our Saint and his Companions built a small Chapel, and several low Cells at a convenient Distance one from another, not unlike the antient *Laura*'s of *Palestine*. This was the humble Beginning of the *Carthusian* Hermitage, which has communicated it's Name to the whole Order; the Foundation of which is by some dated in 1084, by others two Years later.

The holy Inhabitants of this Desart lived there in a Manner, which cannot well be described, because they took no small Care to conceal their Austerities from every Eye but his, who has promised a publick Reward for good Actions done privately. *Guibert*, Abbot of *Nogent*, who saw this Family of Penitents

soon

soon after their Establishment in *Dauphiny*, tells us that in his Time they had each a seperate Cell in which they worked, eat and slept, received their Stock of Provisions for the Week every Sunday, which consisted only of Bread and Legumes; the Water, they drank, ran before their Doors; on Sundays and great Festivals they eat Fish and Cheese; took no Money; admitted no superfluous Ornaments in their Place of Worship; observed strict Silence; and thus their whole time was divided between Prayer, Contemplation, and Labour. Their chief Employment was to transcribe pious Books, which brought Money enough to keep them from being burthensome to others.

Bruno was consider'd as the Head and Master of this Body of Hermits, a Station due to his superiour Vertue as well as to his other Qualifications. The Saint had been six Years in that Post when *Urban* II, who had been his Scholar at *Rheims*, sent for him to *Rome* in Order to advise with him about the Affairs of the Church. When his Holiness's Will was signified to our holy Recluse, the Companions of his Penance were inconsolable under the Loss they should sustain by the Absence of their Father; and when the melancholy Hour of his Departure was come, they assured him he should not leave them, for they would follow him wherever he went. The Saint did all in his Power to dissuade them from quitting their dear Solitude, and endeavour'd to make them easy under the Separation by promising to return as soon as possible; but nothing could prevail with them to think of staying in the Desart without him. Some Authors tell us they accompanied him to *Rome*; while others say they follow'd him to that City; but all agree that the *Chartreuse* was quite deserted on this Occasion, and the poor Buildings recommended to the Care of *Seguin*, Abbot of *Chaise Dieu* in *Auvergne*, the former Proprietor of the Place.

The Saint was receiv'd by the Pope in a Manner that sufficiently express'd his Holiness's Sense of his Merit, and Esteem for his Person. His Companions were allow'd a House in the Town; but soon found the Difference between their present Situation and what they had left in *France*. The Noise of the Streets, the perpetual Hurry and Confusion of a large and populous Place, and a Number of troublesome Visits disturb'd their Repose, and broke in upon the Spirit of Retirement which had been their first Motive for leaving the World. This unhappy Change, the manifest Result of their own ill Conduct, open'd their Eyes, and made them wish to recover their former Peace and Solitude. *Bruno*, glad of this Disposition, sent them back to the *Chartreuse* and made *Landuin* their Prior; for the Pope would not allow our Saint to leave his Court.

The

Oct. 6 The Saint while thus detain'd did not forget what he ow'd his Disciples; but sent them most excellent Advice for their Conduct and Advancement in their State in several Letters. Upon receiving an Account of their Difficulties and Scruples in the Practice of Penance, he answer'd them in a Manner suitable to their respective Cases, comforted them under their Mortifications, and encouraged them to Patience and Perseverance. Upon the Pope's going for *France*, *Bruno* obtain'd Leave to return to his favourite Desart; but, considering that if his Holiness made any Stay in that Country, he should be involved in all the Difficulties with which he had so long struggled at *Rome*, he retired to a convenient Place in the Diocese of *Squillace* in *Calabria* in Company with some Disciples whom he had gain'd since his Arrival in *Italy*. From this Solitude he wrote a fine Letter to *Raoul*, afterwards Archbishop of *Rheims*, in which he puts that Ecclesiastick in Mind of his Vow, and presses him to discharge the Obligation which still subsisted.

Bruno had not been long in his new Hermitage, when *Roger* Count of *Sicily* and *Calabria*, being carried that Way in Pursuit of Game, had the Curiosity to talk with him, and was so well pleased with the Saint's Behaviour and Manner of Life that he gave immediate Orders for building a Church, with a convenient Number of Cells, and annexing the Revenues of a neighbouring Monastery and some Land adjoining for the Maintainance of him and his Companions. Our Saint's settling in *Calabria* is by some dated in 1090, and by others in 1096; but all Writers, who have Occasion, to mention him place his Death in 1101. *Bruno*, finding himself near his End, sent for his whole Community, gave them a particular Account of his Life; and concluded his Discourse with an explicit Profession of his Faith, especially on the Articles of the Blessed Trinity, and the holy Eucharist, which was exactly conformable to the Belief of the Catholick Church at this Day. He died on the sixth of *October*, the Day kept by the Church in Memory of that great Servant of God, and excellent Model of Penance.

His Body was buried behind the Altar; where his Sanctity was manifested by Miracles.

Saint *FAITH* Virgin, and Saint *CAPRASIUS*, Martyrs.

ST. *Faith*, a Native of *Agen* in *Aquitain*, was from her Infancy instructed in the Principles of the Christian Religion, and educated in a Way suitable to the plentiful Circumstances of her Parents, and her holy Profession. As soon

soon as she became acquainted with the Merit of Chastity, as a Christian Oct. 6. Virtue, she consecrated her Virginity to God. About the Year 287 the Emperor *Maximian Herculius*, persecuted the Disciples of *Jesus Christ* in several Provinces of *Gaul*. *Aquitain* was govern'd by *Dacian*, a Man famous for Bigotry to Pagan Superstition, and blindly devoted to his Prince's Will. That Magistrate, being at *Agen* when the Emperor was in *Gaul*, was particularly active in searching for Christians, and pressing them to renounce the Faith. Several Martyrs suffer'd for refusing this Compliance; and Orders were issued out for seizing our Saint, whose Virtue made her in a particular Manner the Object of *Dacian*'s Aversion. Being inform'd of this Enquiry, and persuaded that she could not long remain conceal'd, she begg'd the Almighty to strengthen her, and inspire her with proper Answers on her Trial, and then hasten'd to the Tribunal before the Officers discover'd her. The Governor employ'd both Promises and Menaces; but finding her proof against both, he order'd her to be laid on a Gridiron over a slow Fire; which cruel and lingring Torment she endured with a Courage and Cheerfulness, that converted several of the Spectators, and encouraged them to meet Death for the same glorious Cause with Intrepidity.

Caprasius was one of those humble Christians who hid themselves when the Storm broke out; being apprized of St. *Faith*'s Conflict he address'd himself to God and begg'd she might obtain the Victory. As he grew warm in his Devotions he felt a strong Inclination to follow her Example; and, being persuaded the Motion came from Heaven, offer'd up an earnest Prayer for Resolution and Perseverance; after which he made his Way to the Governor, where he declar'd himself a Christian. Upon this open Confession, he was loaded with Chains, in Order to receive the Punishment due to his supposed Crime. The Governor perceiving him young and fit for Service, attempted his Constancy by the Profer of a considerable Post at Court; but *Caprasius* rejected every Proposal but that of dying for his Faith, with true Christian Generosity; and declared that his Imperial Majesty had nothing to bestow on his Favourites that could compare with what he hoped for at the Hands of the God he serv'd. *Dacian* then deliver'd him to Executioners, with Directions to try the Force of Torments on him; but his Courage and Fidelity under the most severe and barbarous Usage had the same Effect on the Spectators as those of St. *Faith*. The Governor, enraged to find all he had hitherto done, only increase the Courage and Number of the Christians, condemn'd the two Martyrs to lose their Heads, and extended that Sentence to some, who had embraced the Faith upon seeing their Manner of maintaining it.

The

Oct. 7. The Night after their Suffering, the Faithful carried off the Bodies and buried them as well as the unhappy Posture of Affairs would permit. About the Middle of the fifth Century *Dulcitius* Bishop of *Agen* built a Church in that Town, to which he removed the venerable Relicks with due Solemnity. The ancient Mrrtyrologes place S. *Faith*'s Name on the sixth of *October*, supposed to be the Day on which she glorified God; and in this they are follow'd by that of *Rome*. The Dutchy of *Aquitain* being annex'd to the Crown of *England* upon the Marriage of *Henry* II to Q. *Eleanor*, the Festival of that Saint was established in our Island; where it was observed till the Change of Religion, as appears by the Calendars used here before that Time.

According to the foregoing Account, *Caprasius* suffer'd on the same Day; and his Name was formerly join'd with that of S. *Faith* on the sixth of *October*; but most Martyrologes mention his Martyrdom on the twentieth of the same Month.

The VII Day.

St. *MARK*, Pope.

UPON the Death of St. *Silvester*, which happen'd on the last Day of the Year 335, *Mark*, a Native of *Rome*, was raised to the holy See, and consecrated on the eighteenth of *January* following. It pleased God to reward his good Intentions in Favour of the Flock committed to his Care, before he had Time to put them in Execution; for he died on the seventh of *October* 336. His Name occurs on that Day in the *Roman* Calendar drawn up in the Pontificate of *Liberius*, who was promoted to St. *Peter*'s Chair in 352; which will always pass for a Proof of the Veneration paid to his Memory soon after his Death; and shews the Sense of Antiquity in Regard to the holy Pope's Vertue and Sanctity, 'though we have none of the Particulars of his Life.

St. *SERGIUS*, and St. *BACCHUS*, Martyrs.

ACcording to the best Accounts we can find of St. *Sergius* and St. *Bacchus*, they were both commanding Officers in the *Roman* Army, and

attended

attended the Emperor *Maximian* into *Syria*. That Prince, being inform'd that *Sergius* and *Bacchus* profefs'd the Faith of *Chrift*, refolved to know the Truth of the Accufation, and do his utmoft to bring them over to the Religion of the Empire. He was near the River *Euphrates* when he undertook to put them to the Trial, which he did by propofing their joining with him in a Sacrifice to *Jupiter*, and eating what was offer'd to that Idol. Not being able to prevail with them to commit that Act of Apoftafy, the Emperor order'd their Helmets to be taken off, and the degraded Soldiers to be drefs'd in Womens Cloaths with iron Chains about their Necks. In this ridiculous Equipage they were lead through the Army, and conducted to the Palace. *Maximian* made them feveral ftrong Reproaches on the Subject of Religion, and then remitted them to *Antiochus*, Prefect of the Eaft, with Orders to force them to abjure the Name of *Chrift*, or difpatch them for their Contempt of the Gods. *Antiochus* follow'd the Emperor's Directions moft punctually, but without Succefs; upon which *Sergius* was thrown into Prifon; and *Bacchus* beaten 'till he expired. This Tragedy was acted at *Barbaliffa*; at his leaving that Town the next Morning *Sergius* was brought out, and obliged to walk nine Miles before him in Shoes full of Nails, with the Points toward his Feet; but neither this nor the other Torments which he endured making the leaft Impreffion on his Mind, the Prefect order'd him to be beheaded.

Oct. 7.

Bacchus's Body had been privately buried in a neighbouring Cave by the Chriftians of *Barbaliffa*: That of *Sergius* was depofited where he fuffer'd; but when the Church enjoy'd Peace the Relicks of the former were removed to the Place where thofe of the latter lay, that their Memory might be honour'd together. *Alexander*, Bifhop of *Hierapolis*, who was prefent at the general Council of *Ephefus* in the Year 431, raifed a ftately Church there, which was confecrated under the Name of *Sergius*; and the Town, where he finifhed his Courfe, being confiderably augmented in the fifth Century, was call'd *Sergiopolis*.

The Veneration of thefe two illuftrious Victims of *Jefus Chrift* was not confined to the Limits of *Syria*, but foon made it's Way into *Egypt*, as appears from the Monuments of the Church of *Alexandria*. *Ptolomaïs* in *Phenicia* paid an early Refpect to our Martyrs in a Church built in that City by the Emperor *Juftinian*, who came to the Crown in 527. That Prince, who had a particular Devotion to St. *Sergius* and St. *Bacchus*, raifed feveral Churches in their Name in other Provinces. Nor have the Chriftians in the Weft appear'd lefs fenfible of the Merit of the Saints of this Day than thofe of the Eaft; for in the seventh Age, at lateſt, they had a Chapel in *Rome*, which was repair'd and enlarged in 731 by Pope *Gregory* III. Both the *Latins* and *Greeks* place their Feſtival on the ſeventh of *October*.

The VIII Day.

Saint *BRIDGET*, Widow.

BIRGIT more commonly called *Bridget*, Daughter to *Birger* of the Blood Royal of *Sweden*, and *Sigridis*, deſcended from one of the firſt Families in that Kingdom, was born at the Beginning of the fourteenth Century. The firſt remarkable thing recorded of our Saint was that having never articulated one Word 'till ſhe was three Years old, ſhe then came to the free Uſe of her Tongue on a ſuddain, and ſpoke as plain as any Perſon of a more advanced Age. Not long after this Wonder ſhe loſt her Mother, a Woman of ſingular Piety and Devotion; and was then put into the Hands of an Aunt, whoſe Vertue and Prudence were well known to her Father. She was at ten Years of Age ſo ſenſibly affected by a Sermon on the Paſſion of our Saviour, that the following Night ſhe dreamt ſhe ſaw the bleeding Victim ſtretched on the Croſs, and upon enquiring who had brought him into this Condition, was anſwer'd, that thoſe were his Murtherers who neglected his Commandments, and took no Care to ſhew themſelves truly ſenſible of his Love for Mankind. This Viſion left ſo deep an Impreſſion on her Mind, that ſhe made the Crucifixion of *Jeſus Chriſt* the conſtant Subject of her Meditations, and never reflected on that melancholy Myſtery without a thorough Compunction of Heart, expreſs'd in Sighs and Tears.

At the Age of thirteen ſhe was by her Father's Direction married to *Ulfo* Prince of *Nericia*, then but eighteen. *Bridget* was more inclined to devote her Virginity to God; but her Obedience to a pious and wiſe Parent made her accept of the propoſed Match. It pleaſed God to bleſs this Marriage with eight Children two of their Sons died on their Way to *Paleſtine*, where they were to join the Chriſtian Army againſt the Infidels; two others departed in their Infancy; of four Daughters two engaged in a married State, one became a Nun; and *Catharine* the youngeſt is the Perſon whom the Church honours as a Saint on the twenty fourth of *March*. She made it her chief Care to bring her Children up in the Fear of God, and give them an early Acquaintance with the Truths of Salvation; form'd their tender Minds to ſuch pious Exerciſes as were most proportion'd to their Years; and frequently inculcated the Excellency of Works of Mercy, and the Necessity of Penance. Being now the happy Mother of a sufficient Number for supporting and continuing the Family, she prevail'd with her Husband to observe Continence the Remainder of their Lives. Her Exhortations on that and other Vertues work'd so strongly on *Ulfo* that he soon began to grow indifferent to the Court where he had spent his whole Time, and appear'd but seldom among those whose Happiness depended on the Smiles of their Prince. In short *Ulfo* entertain'd the same Contempt of the World, which had always made a conspicuous Part of *Bridget*'s Character; and gave into the same devout Practices which had been her Employment from her Infancy; with his Consent she undertook to treat the Poor and Sick as her own Children, built an Hospital for their Reception, made a handsome Provision for their Entertainment, Relief and Instruction, and served them with her own Hands.

Bridget, always solicitous for the eternal Welfare of her Husband, employ'd all the pious Arts in her Power to disengage him entirely from the Love of the World; to keep him for some Time out of the Way of such Temptations as were peculiar to his own Country, where his Birth and good Qualifications almost inevitably engaged him in Company, she prevail'd with him to undertake a Pilgrimage to *Galicia* in Honour of St. *James*, and accompanied him in that devout and difficult Journey. In their Return *Ulfo* fell dangerously ill at *Arras*; and his Recovery is by the Author of the Saint's Life attributed to the Force of her Prayers. At their reaching *Sweden*, which was in the Year 1343, he was so thoroughly disgusted of the World that he resolved to retire into a Monastery; but God, satisfied with that holy Resolution, took him to himself before he could put it in Execution.

Our Saint's Liberty being now complete by the Death of her Husband, she was resolved to live in a more retired, and perfect Manner than she could do before. To this End, she divided her Substance among her Children, disposed of every thing that could divert her from the Service of God, devoted her whole Time to Acts of Piety; and, upon going into Mourning, chose a Dress suitable to the penitential Life she design'd to lead the Remainder of her Days. This Step was censured and laugh'd at by the World; and the Court was particularly severe upon her; for the best Appellation they could afford this Part of her Conduct was that of Lowness of Spirit; but the Opinions of Men gave the Saint no Uneasiness, while her only View was to please the Almighty.

St. Bridget.

Oct. 8. *Bridget* was well acquainted with the Secret of joining the Duties of interiour Life with the exteriour Functions of Charity, Devotion and Penance. Her bodily Mortifications were many and severe; her Fasts frequent and strict; her Rest short, and such as scarce deserved that Name; her Sentiments of Devotion were particularly tender, and affectionate; and her Compassion for others was equal to the Severity with which she treated herself. The Poor were always secure of a tender Mother and bountiful Benefactress in her; for she fed twelve of those unhappy Objects every Day with her own Hands, and washed their Feet on *Thursday* Evening in Imitation of our Lord's Humility, who washed those of his Apostles before his Passion.

Before she divested herself of her Fortune, and perhaps in *Ulfo*'s Life Time, she founded a Convent of Nuns at *Wastein*, and gave them an excellent Set of Rules; which were also proposed to, and accepted of by a Body of Religious of the other Sex; which is the Origin of the *Bridgitans*, an Order confirm'd long since by the holy See. The Monastry of *Wastein* had been the Place of her constant Residence ever since the Division of her Substance among her Children; and after about two Years spent in that Retreat, she felt a strong Inclination to undertake a Journey to *Rome*, and pay her Devotions to the Almighty in a Place consecrated by the Blood of a numerous Army of Martyrs. During her Stay in that City she lead a very retired and penitential Life, and seldom went abroad but to the Church or Hospitals. By continual Application to the great Object of her Devotion, and a close Conversation with the Almighty, she acquired both Wisdom and Courage enough to enable her to advise and reprove Persons in the most exalted Stations, as appears from the many Letters she wrote to Popes, Bishops, Emperors, Kings, and Princes; and this Liberty was displeasing to none of those Powers, because every one was persuaded she acted by the Direction of the divine Spirit.

It pleased God to afflict our Saint with a very bad State of Health; but when ever she enjoy'd the least Respit, she employ'd the favourable Interval in making devout Pilgrimages in *Tuscany*, *Umbria*, the *Marca* of *Ancona*, the Kingdom of *Naples*, and *Sicily*. Those Journeys, which were always perform'd in the Spirit of Penance, reduced her to a very low Ebb; but she could not be easy 'till she had visited the Place of our Saviour's Sufferings. She had honour'd the Life and Death of *Jesus Christ* by an ardent Devotion at the several Places which he had favour'd with his Presence, and was upon her Return for *Europe*, when she was seiz'd with her last Sickness, which was a Fever, attended with a Weakness and violent Pain in her Stomach. This Indisposition

sition was considerably encreased before she reached *Rome* ; but did not set her Oct. 8. pious Soul at Liberty 'till the twenty third of *July* 1373 in the seventy second Year of her Age.

Her Body was buried at *Rome*; but removed a Year after into *Sweden*, and deposited in her Convent at *Wastein*. The many Miracles perform'd there and in the Church at *Rome* where her Arms was left confirm'd the Opinion the World had long entertain'd of her Sanctity ; and she was canonized by Pope *Boniface* IX in 1391. The *Roman* Martyrologe mentions her on the eighth of *October*, which it owns was neither the Day of her Death nor that of the Translation of the venerable Relicks.

St. *THAIS*, Penitent.

THAIS a young Lady famous for her loose Life, whose Conversion is recorded for the Encouragement of Sinners, and whose Penance is to be remember'd as an excellent Proof of a real Change of Heart, lived toward the Middle of the fourth Century ; but we have no Account of the Place of her Nativity, nor the Scene of her Debaucheries. We are inform'd, indeed, that she excell'd in Beauty, and was possess'd of several engaging Qualifications, which not being under the Conduct of Religion led her into those Extravagancies from which the Divine Grace afterwards rescued her, and that her own Mother had a consierable Hand in her Ruin. *Thaïs* had been instructed in the first Principles of our most holy Religion ; she believed in God, and knew this Life would be succeeded by an Eternity happy or miserable, according to our different Behaviour here. But then these important Truths were stiffled by an unbridled Love of Pleasure, and a Desire of making a Figure in the World at the Expence of her Vertue, so that her Faith was dead and barren ; and she retain'd only the Name of a Christian.

This thoughtless Prostitute was posting to eternal Destruction when the Divine Mercy interposed in her Favour, and employ'd *Paphnutius* an Anchoret of *Thebaïs* as an Instrument of the great Work. That holy Man, having receiv'd an Inspiration from Heaven to endeavour her Conversion, dress'd himself in a Manner suitable to the Part which he was to act, and went in Quest of the lost Sheep, with the charitable View of bringing her to the Fold. Upon finding *Thaïs* he seem'd inclined to converse with her in a criminal Way, gave her what Money he had brought, and was conducted to a handsome Room. *Paphnutius* told her he could not think they were private enough there ;

and

Oct. 8. and defired to be accommodated with a more retired Place. *Thaïs* replied that she was ready oblige him; but, said she, *what do You apprehend here? If* "*you would avoid the Sight of Men, I can assure you we are safe enough here;* "*but if your Caution proceeds from our being seen by God, where is it possible to* "*find a Shelter from his all-penetrating Eye? What*, return'd *Paphnutius*, *do* "*you know there is a God? Yes*, replied *Thaïs*; *and that Heaven or Hell will be* "*the eternal Lot of all Mankind. Is it possible*, said the holy Hermit, *you should* "*know all this and yet go on in this miserable State, damning yourself, and others* "*without Remorse?*" *Thaïs* was now convinced that the Person who made her this stinging Reproach was a true Servant of God; and, soften'd by the divine Grace which began to work in her Heart, threw herself at the holy Man's Feet, burst into a Flood of Tears, begg'd he would interceed to the Almighty in her Favour, desired only three Hours to settle her Affairs, and assured him she submit to any Penance he should enjoin.

Paphnutius, pleased with the Conquest, promised to receive her; in the mean Time *Thaïs* got together all her ill-gotten Wealth, which consisted of Jewels, magnificent Furniture, and rich Cloaths, carried the whole into one of the pubblick Streets, burnt them in the Face of the Town, and invited her Lovers to feast their Eyes on the Sacrifice. She then took her Leave of the World, and repair'd to the Place appointed by *Paphnutius*; and after some Stay there was removed to a Monastery of her own Sex. Her holy Master shut her up in a Cell, fasten'd the Door, and left her nothing but a little Window open, at which she was to receive a daily Supply of Bread and Water. *Thaïs*, thus enclosed, desired the holy Anchoret's Instruction for praying; who told her she was not worthy to pronounce the sacred Name of God, or raise her Hands to Heaven; that all the Direction he could give her on that Article was to turn her Face to the East, and only say, *You who created me, have Mercy on me*. The Convert complied punctually with his Orders; and had remain'd three Years in that State when *Paphnutius* went to consult St *Anthony* about her, and beg his Advice for continuing, or ending her Penance. The Saint spent that Night in Prayer with his Disciples, and *Paul* one of that Number was favour'd with a Revelation assuring him that *Thaïs* should receive a Place in Heaven. At his Return *Paphnutius* releafed his penitential Prisoner, who profess'd a great Desire to pass the Remainder of her Life there; but the holy Anchoret, assured of the Remission of her Sins, would not allow it. *Thaïs* then told him that during her Confinement she had constantly consider'd the Crimes of her past Life as a terrible Heap always before her Eyes, and bewail'd them in the Bitterness of her Soul, which had been her

whole

whole Employment. About a Fortnight after her Releafe fhe enter'd on Pof- Oct. 9. feffion of the Happinefs which God had prepared for her.

The *Greek* Church honours our Penitent's Memory on the eighth of *October*; the *Latins* are not unanimous in the Day, but generally venerate her for the Wonders God perform'd in her Favour.

The IX Day.

St. *DENIS* the *Areopagite*, Bifhop and Martyr.

THE Converfion of the illuftrious Saint of this Day has been related in our Account of St. *Paul*, Vol. 2. pag. 555. Some Authors fuppofe him born in *Thrace*, while others fpeak of him as a Native of *Athens*; but he was certainly a Citizen of that Seat of Learning and Politenefs, as appears from his Character of Senator, or Counfellor of the *Areopagus*. His appearing in that Poft is a ftrong Proof of his being a Man of good Morals, great Probity, and well qualified for the Adminiftration of Juftice. All thofe good Qualities were fanctified by the Grace of Baptifm; and no Man was judged more capable of governing the Faithful of *Athens* in the Capacity of a Bifhop than this valuable Convert. Thofe, who make him different from the famous Apoftle and firft Bifhop of *Paris* of the fame Name, fuppofe he fuffer'd for the Faith at *Athens*, or not far from that City, either under *Domitian*, or *Adrian*. But thofe, who are of Opinion that the *Areopagite* and the Bifhop of *Paris* are one and the fame Perfon, tell us that after he had ruled the Church of *Athens* fome Years, and brought it to a flourifhing Condition, he made a Journey to *Rome*, and found St. *Clement* in St. *Peter*'s Chair, who fent him into *Gaul* to preach the Gofpel; that he founded a Church at *Paris*, and laid down his Life for the Faith. This is the Account we have of the Matter in the *Roman* Martyrologe; which *Baronius* undertakes to maintain againft thofe who are for making two different Saints of *Dionyfius*. According to the fame learned Author, he was join'd in that Apoftolical Commiffion by *Rufticus* a Prieft, and *Eleutherius* a Deacon, the Companions of his Martyrdom, as well as of his Labours. Such Writers as are inclined to affert a Difference between the Senator of *Athens*, and the Apoftle of *France*, tell us the latter came into that Country at the Beginning of the III Century, or at lateft toward the Middle of the fame Age, had his Miffion from *Rome*,

and

Oct. 10 and after forming a Body of Clergy, and raising a handsome Edifice for the publick Service of God, was put to Death in Company with *Rusticus*, and *Eleutherius*. Both these Parties, however, agree in this that *Dionysius* and his two Ecclesiasticks already mention'd, were carried before *Fesceninus*, Prefect of *Paris*, who applied Threats, Persuasions, and Tortures to make them abjure the Name of *Christ*; and, finding them an Overmatch for all he could do, order'd them to be beheaded. This the *Roman* Martyrologe applies to the *Areopagite*; whereas, those, who contend for a Distinction, confine the Account to the first Bishop of *Paris*. The *French*, who pretend to be best acquainted with their own Eclesiastical History, venerate the holy Bishop of *Athens* on the third of *October*, and the Apostle of their own Country on the ninth. The stately and rich Abbey near *Paris*, which bears our Saint's Name is a standing Monument of the Veneration of both Prince and People to their Apostle. The Kings of *France* have always look'd on him as their Protector and Patron, had Recourse to his Intercession in all publick Calamities, and begg'd the Assistance of his Prayers upon their engaging in any hazardous Enterprize; and the Church dedicated in his Honour has long been the Repository of the Royal Ashes.

The X Day.

St. *FRANCIS BORGIA*.

THE Saint of this Day was Son to *John Borgia* Duke of *Gandia*, and Grandee of *Spain*, and *Joanna* of *Arragon*, Daughter of *Alphonso* natural Son to *Ferdinand* V, and born at the City from which his Father receiv'd his Title, on the twenty eighth of *October* 1510. His Parents were particularly careful of instilling Principles of Virtue and Piety into his tender Mind as soon as he was capable of any Impression; and, that nothing might be wanting for making him worthy of his illustrious Birth, and the Religion in which he was educated, he was furnished with a Governor and Preceptor of known Prudence, Experience, and Learning, who directed all their Thoughts and Labours to forming his Sentiments, and regulating his Passions; which was no hard Task; for God had bless'd our Saint with virtuous Dispositions, an excellent Capacity and great Docility.

Francis

Francis lost his Mother, when but ten Years old; and was scarce twelve Oct. 10. when his Father carried him to *Saragossa*, where he was put into the Hands of his Uncle, Archbishop of that City. That Prelate, who undertook to finish his Education, provided him with Masters to instruct him in the Languages, History, and other Branches of School Learning. Those Studies proved no Obstacle to our Saint's pious Exercises; and he had not been long at *Saragossa* when he was so touched with two Sermons on the last Judgment, and our Saviour's Passion, preached by his Director, that nothing but his not being of an Age to dispose of himself could have detain'd him one Moment in the World.

One Reason of our Saint's Removal to *Saragossa* was to avoid the Fury of the Rebels, who made their Advantage of *Charles* the fifth's Absence, took up Arms against the Regency, and thus became Masters of several Towns in the Kingdom of *Valencia*, among which was *Gandia*. The same Calamity obliged several of his Relations to leave the Monastery in that City, and retire to *Baëza* in the Kingdom of *Granada*. *Francis* went thither to visit them, was taken ill before he left the Place, and kept his Bed almost half a Year; during which Time he gave excellent Proofs of a Mind deeply affected with a Sense of God's Right to govern his Creatures as he pleased, and submitted to the Scourge with an admirable Patience, and Humility. Upon the Marriage of the Infanta *Catharine*, Sister to *Charles* V, with *John* III King of *Portugal*, he was made Page of Honour to that Princess. But his Father, who had more exalted Views for him in *Arragon*, soon recalled him from the Court of *Portugal*, and engaged the Archbishop of *Saragossa* to reassume his Care of his Nephew. He was about eighteen Years old when his Inclinations ran very strong toward a Cloister; upon which his Father and Uncle thought proper to send him to the Court of *Charles* V, where they hoped his Thoughts would soon take a different Turn; nor were they mistaken; for *Francis*, 'though still full of tender Sentiments of Religion, had a Heart not insensible to the Glory of the World. The Ripeness of his Judgment and Prudence were such as seldom appear even in a more advanced Age; and his unaffected Complaisance, and Assiduity could not fail of gaining the Emperor's Favour. 'Though he willingly accepted of every Mark of his Prince's Regard for him, he was a Stranger to Gaming, Debauchery, and the other Vices which are but too commonly practised, and authorized in Courts.

The Empress had so just an Idea of the young Courtier's Merit, that she proposed a Match between him and *Eleanor de Castro*, a Lady whom she had brought out of *Portugal*. The Emperor was well pleased with the Proposal;

and,

Oct. 10 and, as an Acknowledgment of his first Services and Encouragement to his active and aspiring Temper, made him Marquis of *Lombay* and Master of the Horse to the Empress. This Marriage was favour'd with the Blessing of God, and a numerous Offspring; the happy Couple lived together in a Manner sufficiently expressive of their Regard for a Sacrament, which was design'd by the Almighty to represent the Union of *Jesus Christ* with his Church; and his whole Family was regulated by the Precepts of the Gospel. Without any Violation of his Duty to God, he studied his Prince's Inclinations; was allow'd to share his Diversions, particularly that of Hunting; and had the Honour of studying the Mathematicks with him, especially those Branches that are necessary for fortifying Towns. From these Engagements the Emperor proceeded to give him more substantial Proofs of his Opinion of his Wisdom, and Fidelity by letting him into his most important Designs, and desiring his Advice in the most difficult Undertakings.

Francis attended his Imperial Majesty in his Expedition to *Africa* in 1535; and at his Return from that Campaign, fell into a violent Fit of Sickness, which shew'd his Patience and Resignation to great Advantage. A second Affliction of the same sort, the Death of *Garcilas de Vega* a famous Poet, and his intimate Friend, with that of his imperial Mistress were so many Means employ'd by divine Providence to disengage his Affections from the World, and cure him of all Inclination to the shortlived Pleasures, and precarious Grandeurs of this Life. That great Princess died at *Toledo* in 1539; the Sight of that beautiful Lady's Corpse preached strongly the Vanity of Beauty; but her funeral Oration pronounced by the famous *D'Avila* completed his Disgust of all the World admires, and idolizes. This was the Situation of his Mind, when he applied himself to that holy Preacher, begg'd his Direction, resolved from that Moment never to engage in the Service of one of whom Death could deprive him, retire into a Monastery if he survived his Wife.

'Though these Impressions were never worn out of his Mind, he complied with the Will of his Sovereign so far as to accept of the Government of *Catalonia*, and the Command of the Order of St. *James*. Upon taking Possession of his Post, the Face of the whole Province was changed; several inveterate Abuses were removed, and Justice and Religion flourished. The great Duties of a Post, which made him at once the Father and Judge of a numerous People, were no Impediments to his beginning the Practice of a Religious Life in his Palace. Four or five Hours every Morning were spent in Prayer, without any Prejudice to Publick Affairs, or Neglect of his Family;

mily; and what Time seem'd to be lost by private Exercises of Piety was suf- Oct. 10
ficiently made up by his Fasts and other Mortifications; for his Meals and Sleep
were short, and his Supper entirely banished. He was constantly attended by
two *Dominicans*, and a *Franciscan*, Men of great Reputation for Sanctity and
Learning. By their Advice he confess'd his Sins once eyery Week; communicated in publick all great Festivals, and privately every Sunday in the
Year. This was the Life of our excellent Viceroy, when *Anthony Aroaz*,
the first profess'd Member of the Society of JESUS after the ten concern'd in
the first Project of that holy Order, came to *Barcelona*, and preached in
that City. By his Means *Francis* became acquainted with this new Institute
and the Character of it's great Founder, to whom he wrote upon the Question
of frequent Communion, which then divided the ablest Doctors in *Spain*. *Ignatius*'s Answer was so prudent and satisfactory that the Viceroy resolved to
consult him alone in all his Doubts and Difficulties for the future, and do all
in his Power toward establishing the Society in his Dominions. Pursuant to his
Direction, *Francis* continued his weekly Communion.

Our Saint was about thirty two Years old when his Father's Death gave him
the Title of Duke of *Gandia*; but he was so far from any Thoughts of making a more considerable Figure in the World by his Accession to that Honour; that he petition'd the Emperor to be allow'd to resign his Government and retire. That Prince granted the former Part of his Request; but obliged him to repair to Court immediately; and accept of the Office of Master of the Houshould to the Infanta *Mary* of *Portugal* Daughter to King
John III, then upon the Point of being married to *Philip*, the Emperor's Son.
His Dutchess was at the same Time declared Lady of Honour to the said
Princess, and their of her Daughters allow'd honourable Employments under
her. But the Death of the Infanta, which happen'd before the intended Marriage,
broke all these Measures, and providentially left Our Saint at Liberty to follow
his own Inclinations to a private Life. The Emperor going about that Time
for *Italy*, *Francis* return'd to *Gandia*; where his Presence consoled the People
under the Loss of the late Duke. He fortified the Town against the Insults
of the *Moors* and *Corsairs*, repaired the Hospital, encreased it's Revenue, and
made considerable Advances toward settling the *Jesuits* there. The Dutchess
had her Share in that and other good Works, and enter'd into all his Designs
for promoting the Glory of God, and procuring the Good of Mankind.

Francis was thirty six Years old when his Lady died, and left him Father
of eight Children; all of which were afterwards married to Persons of the
first Rank in *Spain*, except one Daughter, who consecrated herself to God
among

Oct. 10 among the *Poor Clares* at *Gandia*. Our Saint had now no Obstacle to the Performance of his Vow in it's utmost Extent; so that, after some Time spent in providing for his Children, he had nothing to do but choose the Order in which he would spend the Remainder of his Days. His Affection for the Society of *Jesus*, for whose Reception he had then built a handsome College at *Gandia*, soon determin'd him on that Article. In Order to qualify himself for that solemn Engagement he perform'd *the Spiritual Exercise*, as prescribed by S. *Ignatius*, under the Direction of *Peter le Fevre*, that Saint's first Companion, who was then in *Spain*, but died soon after at *Rome*; his Concern at the Death of that Servant of God, who had assisted him in his first Steps toward a Religious Life, led him into serious Reflections on their Conversation on that Subject, and produced two small Treatises on Humility, which were judged very solid and edifying; and those are not the only Pieces he composed before he quitted the World.

Being now confirm'd in his Resolution of entring the Society of *Jesus*, he signified his Mind to the holy Founder, who receiv'd the Proposal with Joy. *Ignatius* answer'd his Letter in the fullest and most satisfactory Manner, approved of the Motion; but advised him to make the best Provision he could for his Children before he left the World, and finish all the Houses he had begun for the Use of the Society before the Publick was acquainted with his Design; he told him he could wish he would apply to the Study of Divinity, and take his Doctor's Degree before he engaged in the Order; but desired all this might be managed with the utmost Secrefy, 'till a proper Season for making the Discovery, because the World would be startled at so extraordinary a Change, and attempt to divert him from the Execution of his pious Designs. *Francis* complied exactly with every Article of the Saint's Advice, and endeavour'd to procure a sufficient Stock of Learning for instructing others according to the Aim of that excellent and charitable Society.

Ignatius, considering the many Ties our Saint had and how difficult it would be to break them at once, obtain'd the Pope's Permission for his spending four Years in the World after he had taken the Vows. Upon the Arrival of his Holiness's Brief for that Purpose, *Francis* was profess'd in the Chapel belonging to the College of *Gandia* in as private a Manner as was consistent with the Rules of the Society. After this he left his Castle to his eldest Son, and retired to another House where he might pursue his Studies, and practice the Obligations of his new State without Interruption. One of the first Orders he received from his holy Superior was to moderate his Austerities, that he might have Strength enough to perform what he had recommended

commended to him; upon which he made an excellent Diſtribution of his whole Time in the following Manner; he left his Bed at two in the Morning: ſpent ſix Hours in Prayer: and then made his Confeſſion, heard Maſs, and receiv'd the Bleſſed Euchariſt every Day. The Reſt of his Time till Dinner was devoted to the Study of Divinity, except one Hour, which was employ'd in ſuch temporal Affairs as were inſeperable from his appearing as a Grandee of *Spain*. After Dinner, he ſpent an Hour in talking to his Servants and giving them neceſſary Directions; which being done, he return'd to his former learned and laborious Enquiries. After a convenient time ſpent in that Manner, his Door was open to all who had Buſineſs with him 'till the Cloſe of the Day; and then he retired to pray and read the Word of God; theſe pious Exerciſes concluded in a rigorous Examination of his Conſcience, and ſhort Repoſe on a Carpet ſpread on the Ground: and it is eaſy to imagine that one ſo regular as our Saint took Care that his whole Family ſhould obſerve much more Order, than is uſual in the Houſes of Perſons of Quality. His Way of living made ſo deep an Impreſſion on thoſe who were Eye-witneſſes of it that ſeveral of the firſt Rank propoſed him to themſelves as a Model of a true Chriſtian Life.

Oct. 10

In the Year 1549 the Duke of *Gandia*, having finiſhed all the Affairs which obliged him to appear in that Character, made his Will like a dying Man, and ſaw it executed before he left his own Country. He then ſet out for *Rome*, where he arrived on the thirty firſt of *Auguſt* 1550, attended by *John* his ſecond Son, thirty of his own Servants on Horſeback, and ſome *Spaniſh* Jeſuits ſummon'd to aſſiſt at a general Chapter of the Order. In the Beginning of the next Year by the Direction of St. *Ignatius* he wrote to the Emperor, acquainted him with his Reſolution, and deſired his Leave to renounce all the Titles and Employments which he then held under that Prince. Our Saint ſhew'd his Zeal for the Increaſe of the Society by founding a large College at *Rome*, and building a Church for the Uſe of the profeſs'd Houſe in the ſame City. Two of theſe new Religious having been dignified with a Cardinal's Cap, *Francis* apprehenſive of receiving the ſame Mark of the Pope's Favour, poſted back to *Spain*, and ſpent ſome Time incognito in *Guipuſcoa*. As his Veneration for St. *Ignatius* had determin'd him to that Province, he made a Viſit to *Loyola*, the Place of his Birth, and retired to *Ognata* about four Leagues from that Caſtle, where he receiv'd his Imperial Majeſty's Anſwer containing a full and free Conſent to his Requeſt, high Commendations of the Saint's Virtue, and Aſſurances of acknowledging his Services by protecting his Family. A few Days after the Arrival of

this

Oct. 10 this Letter he sent for a publick Notary, and renounced all he had in the World in Favour of his eldest Son, according to the legal Forms provided in that Case.

Thus divested of all that detain'd him in the World, he cut his Hair, and put on the *Jesuits* Habit. All this was done in 1551; on the first of *August* the same Year he was ordain'd Priest, and said his first Mass in the Chapel at *Loyola*. He then retired to a little Hermitage near *Ognata*, where he gave heartily into the Practice of Humility and Mortification; catechised the Children and ignorant Persons of more advanced Years; and preached in a Stile suitable to the mean Capacities of his Country Audience. His Example had a happy Influence over several of the Nobility; some of whom left the World, and consecrated the Remainder of their Days to God in different Places; while others hasten'd to *Ognata*, to enjoy the Advantage of his Coversation and Direction.

John III, who was strongly inclined to give the most signal Proofs of his Sense of our Saint's Merit, design'd to dignfy him with the sacred Purple at the next Promotion of Cardinals; to which he was warmly solicited by the Emperor *Charles* V. As soon as *Ignatius* was apprized of the Matter, he employ'd all Means in his Power to divert his Holiness from it, and his Application on that Subject met with the wished for Success. Not long after this happy Escape *Francis* receiv'd his holy Superior's Orders to leave *Biscaye*, and labour for the Salvation of others in a more enlarged Sphere; his Instructions were to visit several Persons of the first Quality in different Parts of *Spain*, who were desirous of regulating their own Lives and those of their Families by his Advice. He obey'd; and the Sacrifice which he made of his Inclination to Solitude was rewarded by prodigious Success in *Castile*, particularly at *Burgos*, and *Valladolid* where the Emperor kept his Court, in the University of *Salamanca*, and at the Court of *Joanna* Daughter to the Emperor, design'd to marry *John* only Son to the King of *Portugal* the third of that Name. His Labours were rewarded and encouraged in the same Manner in *Andalousia*, and *Portugal*; to which Country he was invited by the King, one of the chief Patrons of the Society. While he was at that Court he had the Satisfaction of seeing his pious Counsel follow'd by the most considerable of the Princes and Nobility. Don *Lewis*, the King's Brother carried his Zeal and Devotion so far as to desire to engage among the *Jesuits*; but our Saint and St. *Ignatius*, considering that Prince's Age, his ill State of Health, and the Necessity his Majesty had of his Assistance in the Administration of his Kingdom,

dom, defired he would not think of making that unfeafonable Step, but Oct. 10 fatisfy himfelf with reducing his Family to an exact Regularity. *Ignatius*, perceiving the Bleffing of God attend all the Endeavours of our Saint, named him Superior of the Society for *Spain* and *Portugal*, and foon after put the *Jefuits* of the *Eaft-Indies* under his Direction. *Francis*'s Activity and Succefs in his Station was fuch that in lefs than two Years the Society had Houfes and Colleges in above twelve of the moft confiderable Towns under his Jurifdiction, which he vifited frequently.

In the Year 1557, *Francis* wrote a Letter of Condoleance and Confolation, to the Queen of *Portugal* on the Death of her Royal Confort; after which he was deputed by the Emperor to make his Compliments on that melancholy Occafion, and treat with her about fome private Affairs of great Importance. At his Return from the Court of *Portugal*, he was preparing for a Journey to *Rome*, where his Prefence and Affiftance were required for the Choice of a General, when he was feiz'd by a violent fit of the Gout; which he look'd on as a double Providence, both as it kept him out of the Way of farther Promotion, and allow'd him to remain where his Order wanted the Support of his Authority. The Saint met with no fmall Oppofition from Perfons, whofe Station enabled them to be very troublefome to him in the Difcharge of his Duty; but his Patience and indefatigable Induftry carried him through all thofe Difficulties. He went on to found new Houfes of *Jefuits* in feveral Parts of *Spain*, and undertook the Miffion of *Granada*, *Afturia*, and *Africa*.

In the Year 1560 *Francis* made a Journey into *Portugal*, vifited all the Houfes founded there by the late King, the chief Protector of the Order; preach'd the Lent at *Evora*, and then went to *Brague* to facilitate the founding a College in that City, which had been much oppofed. He was at *Porto* and employ'd in concerting Meafures for raifing a Houfe of *Jefuits* there, when he heard that the Inquifition had forbid the Reading of the Pieces which he had compofed before his Profeffion; and his Silence and Modefty gave his Adverfaries an Opportunity of concluding him guilty of fome Errors in thofe pious Writings. They did not fcruple loading him with the moft extravagant and mortifying Calumnies, and gave an odious Turn to his Friendfhip for *Bartholomew Caraanza* Archbifhop of *Toledo* who, having affifted *Charles* V at his Death, was thrown into the Inquifition on Sufpicion of favouring fome Errors imputed to that Prince.

By Vertue of an Order from Pope *Pius* IV, and *Lainez* General of the *Jefuits*, he made a Journey to *Rome* in the Year 1561. At his Arrival there he

underftood.

understood that *Lainez* was gone to *France* with the Cardinal of *Ferrara*, and
Oct. 10 that his Obedience was due to *Alphonsus Salmeron*, one of the most learned Men of the Society. The Saint had not been many Months at *Rome* when that Father was dispatched to the Council of *Trent* with the Character of the Pope's Divine; and the General being obliged to assist in the same venerable Assembly, *Francis* was entrusted with the Government of the whole Society during the Absence of those great Men. *Lainez* returning to *Rome* in 1564 made our Saint one of his four Assistants in the Government of the Order; *Spain* and *Portugal* fell to his Share in the Division; and that General dying the next Year, *Francis* was chosen in his Place, in Spight of all the Opposition his Humility could make on that Occasion.

The whole Order was soon sensible of the Blessing which attended his Administration, and increased prodigiously both in *Europe* and the *Indies*. Being sensible that the true Beauty of all Religious Bodies consists in a strict Observance of the Rules left by their Respective Founders, he took a particular Care to enforce the rigorous Poverty prescribed by St. *Ignatius* in all the profess'd Houses, Noviceships, and Seminaries of his Order. The new General gave fresh Vigour to the Constitutions in Being, supplied what was wanting, and put the last Hand to the Discipline of the Society; so that it has been justly observed, that the Body of *Jesuits* owes it's Perfection to our Saint; for, 'though *Ignatius* must be allow'd the Honour of laying the Foundation of this noble Edifice, *Francis* may challenge that of finishing the Building. His Infirmities, Inclination to Retirement, and a deep Sense of the Weight of his Post, which he had fill'd to the Satisfaction and Admiration of the whole World five Years, put him upon desiring his Discharge from that Obligation in 1570; but his Request was not granted. *Pius* V then in St. *Peter*'s Chair, gave him Leave to retire to *Tivoli* for some Weeks, after which he was order'd to accompany Cardinal *Alexandrini*, that Pope's Nephew, into *France*, *Spain*, and *Portugal*; in which Kingdoms his Eminence appear'd with the Character of Legate from the holy See. After he had executed the Commissions lodged in his Hands with universal Applause, and to the manifest Prejudice of his Health, he return'd to *Rome* soon after the Election of *Gregory* XIII; but was so ill that he could give his Holiness no Account of his Negotiations. The Fathers of the Society, convinced that they should soon be deprived of their holy General, begg'd he would name his Successor, and allow them the Satisfaction of taking his Picture; but he would do neither; which Resolution he maintain'd to his last Moment, and left his sorrowful Children on the Night between the last of *September* and first of *October*.

His

His Body was buried in the old Church of the profess'd House near those Oct. 10. of the two preceeding Generals; and in the Year 1617 removed to *Madrid* by the Cardinal and Duke of *Lerma*, first Minister of State to the King of *Spain*, and Grandson to the Saint, where it is honour'd at this Day. *Francis* was beatified by *Urban* VIII in the Year 1624; canonized by *Clement* X in 1671; and his Festival fixed on the tenth of *October* by *Innocent* XI in 1683.

✦✦

Saint *PAULINUS*, Bishop of *YORK*, afterwards of *ROCHESTER*.

PAULINUS, an *Italian*, was sent into *England* in the Year 601 to assist the Missionaries employ'd there for the Conversion of our *Saxon* Ancestors, and labour'd many Years in that Part of the Lords Vineyard with great Zeal and Success under the Direction of St. *Augustin*, St. *Mellitus*, and St. *Laurence*, the first Bishops of *Canterbury*. He was carrying on that Apostolical Work with his usual Vigour when *Edwin* King of *Northumberland* made a Proposal of marrying *Edelburg*, Sister to *Edbald* King of *Kent*, and Daughter to the holy King *Ethelbert*. As *Edwin* was still a Slave to Superstition and Idolatry, it was not thought proper to accept of the Offer without making some Terms in Favour of Religion; the King of *Northumberland*, understanding this Difficulty, replied that *Edelburg* should be allow'd to bring as many Christians as she pleased into his Dominions, assured them of Protection and Toleration, and promised to embrace the same Religion, if upon a candid and thorough Examination it appear'd to him more holy and worthy of the supreme Being. This Profer facilitated the Match; the Princess was sent to the Court of *Northumberland* in 625, and our Saint, whom *Justus* then Archbishop of *Canterbury*, had invested with the Episcopal Dignity, was chosen to accompany her thither.

The chief Design of the King of *Kent* in putting *Paulinus* in his Sister's Retinue was to preserve her from the Corruptions of a Pagan Court; but the holy Prelate had a farther View in that Journey, and design'd to do all in his Power for propagating the Kingdom of *Jesus Christ* among the *Northumbrians*. In the following Year the Queen being deliver'd of a Daughter, *Edwin* was going to thank his Gods for the Favour; upon which Occasion our Saint undertook to prove to him that his Gratitude was due to the God of the Christians, and reason'd so strongly on that Subject that the King allow'd him to baptize the new born Princess, and promised to embrace the Faith, if he
return'd

Oct. 10 return'd victorious from his War with the King of the *West Saxons*, who had made an Attempt on his Crown and Life.

Edwin had all the Success he could wish, and the Satisfaction of seeing his Enemy fall in the Field of Battle; but did not immediately perform what he had promised. He relinquished the Worship of his Idols; but desired to discourse with *Paulinus* more at large on the several Articles of the Faith, and hear what the wisest and best Part of his Council had to say to each Particular, before he profess'd himself a Christian. While he was thus employ'd, Pope *Boniface* V, being inform'd of his good Dispositions, wrote to the King, and exhorted him to receive the Faith of *Jesus Christ*; he dispatched a Letter to the Queen at the same Time, in which he congratulated her on the Prospect of her Royal Consort's Conversion, and put her in Mind of her Obligation to do all in her Power for advancing that good Work. *Edwin*'s Declaration was deferr'd 'till Easter in the Year 627; having then surmounted all his Difficulties, he conven'd the chief of his Nobility, his Council, and several Officers of his Household and Army, whom he was resolved to sound and endeavour to engage them to accompany him to the sacred Font. Having gain'd them, he built a Church of Wood at *York*, which *Paulinus* consecrated in Honour of St. *Peter*, and then baptized the King, his two Sons, and great Numbers of all Ranks.

Paulinus who was now look'd on as the Apostle of that Kingdom, and Bishop of all *Edwin*'s Dominions, thought proper to fix his See at *York*, the usual Residence of the Kings of *Northumberland*. The Saint, however, did not confine his Labours to that City, but consider'd himself under an Obligation of propagating Christianity in all Parts of his royal Convert's Dominions, who was then the most powerful Prince in this Island. The divine Seed, which the holy Bishop sow'd under his Protection, produced such a plentiful Harvest that he was harldly able to confer the Sacrament of Regeneration on all who offer'd themselves. Nor was *Edwin* less active in his own Court, where he became an Instrument in the Hand of the Almighty for gaining a considerable Number to the Faith; and his Zeal carried him to undertake the Conversion of *Carpwald* King of the *East-Angles*, which he happily effected. *Honorius*, who succeeded *Boniface* in the holy See, hearing what Progress the Gospel made in the North of *England*, wrote a congratulatory Letter to the King, and sent the *Pallium* to *Paulinus*, and *Honorius*, whom that Saint had lately consecrated Archbishop of *Canterbury* at *Lincoln*.

Edwin had reign'd seventeen Years, when *Ceadwalla*, tributary King of the Oct. 11. ancient *Britons*, then confined to *Wales* took up Arms against him, and being join'd by *Penda* the formidable King of *Mercia*, gave *Edwin* Battle and left him dead in the Field, with his Son *Osfrith*. This melancholy Blow which was struck on the fourteenth of *October* 633, changed the whole Face of Religion in the Kingdom of *Northumberland*, and entail'd a violent Persecution on the Church of that Country; for *Penda* was a profess'd Pagan; and *Ceadwalla*, 'though a pretended Christian, was not inferiour to his Ally in Barbarity, but treated the Faithful there as so many Hereticks on the Account of the Difference about the Observance of *Easter*. In this Distress *Paulinus* seeing no Way left to secure his own Person and that of the Queen, but leaving the Place, made the best of his Way into *Kent* with that Princess and her whole Family. At his Arrival King *Edbald* and *Honorius* the Archbishop, well acquainted with the Saint's Merit, receiv'd him very handsomely, and press'd him to accept of the See of *Rochester*, vacant by the Death of the last Incumbent. *Paulinus* accepted of that Preferment, and discharged his Duty in that Post with his usual Zeal, Vigilance and Charity 'till his Death, which happen'd on the tenth of *October* 644, the Day appointed in the *Roman* Martyrologe for honouring his Memory.

The XI Day.

Saint TARACHUS, Saint PROBUS, and Saint ANDRONICUS, MARTYRS.

UPON the Publication of the Imperial Edicts for a Persecution at the Beginning of the IV Century, *Maximus*, Governor of *Cilicia* being at *Pompeiopolis*, *Eutolmus* and *Palladius* presented three Christians of different Ages and Countries to that Magistrate; and at his coming to *Tarsus* the Metropolis of the Province the same pretended Criminals were brought before him a second Time in Order to be tried in Form. *Demetrius*, an Officer in the Army, placed them before the Governor's Tribunal, and open'd the Charge against them, which set forth that the Persons at the Bar were of the impious Sect of Christians, and disobedient to the Emperor's Orders.

Maximus, addressing himself to *Tarachus*, observed that he began with him as the first in Rank, and the eldest of the Company, and then ask'd him his Name. The venerable Confessor answer'd he was a Christian. "Let me not

Oct. 11. "hear that impious Appellation, replied the Governor, but tell me your "Name." *Tarachus* repeated his former Answer; upon which *Maximus* order'd him to be struck on the Face, and at the same Time admonished not to give such cross Answers. *Tarachus* then assured the Judge that he had already told him his real and essential Name; but, if he was desirous to know that which he had made Use of in several Circumstances of Life, he would be pleased to understand that *Tarachus* was the Name he receiv'd from his Parents, but *Victor* what he bore in the Army. The Governor's next Enquiry was concerning his Station; to which the Martyr replied he was a Soldier; and, being born at *Claudiopolis* in *Isauria*, enjoy'd the Privileges of a *Roman* Citizen; but had quitted the Service upon the Account of his Religion. *Maximus* gave an odious Turn to his last Words, told him he was dismiss'd from the Army because his abominable Principles had made him unworthy to draw a Sword for the Emperor, and asked who gave him his Discharge; *Tarachus* assured him he had obtain'd that Favour from *Fulvio*. The Governor then put on a mild and insinuating Look, profess'd a Compassion for the Saint's grey Hairs, invited him to sacrifice to the Gods, as a sure Way to Promotion and Honour and urged the Example of their Imperial Majesties for what he recommended to him. *Tarachus* replied, that those Princes were misled and deceived by the Devil. *Maximus*, resenting this Affront to the Emperors, gave Orders for striking him again and breaking his Jaws; upon which *Tarachus* declared that "he had said; and always would say that they were deceived and mistaken, "like other Men." Come, said the Governor, sacrifice to the Gods of our Fa-
"thers and take your Leave of these idle Whims, and obstinate Adherence
"to your own Opinion." "No, replied the Saint, I worship the God of
"my Fathers not with the Blood of Victims, but the Sacrifice of a pure Heart;
"Well, said *Maximus*, my Regard for your Age obliges me to advise you
"to lay aside these wild Notions, obey the Emperors, shew a due Deference
"for Me their Representative, and comply with the Laws of our Ancestors.
Tarachus answer'd that he never oppos'd the Laws of his Ancestors. "Draw
"near then, and sacrifice, replied the Governor. "No, said the Saint, my Regard
"for the Laws of my Ancestors, will not allow me to commit that wicked
"Action. How! asked *Maximus*; is there then any Law but that which I
"press. Yes answer'd *Tarachus*; and you transgress it by worshiping Stocks
"and Stones, the Works of Men's Hands." The Governor, resenting the
"Freedom of this Reproach, directed his being struck on the Neck with this Admonition, *cease to talk and act foolishly*; but the courageous Martyr assured him he should not quit the Means of saving his Soul, 'though he was pleased

to

to call his Perseverance Folly. Upon the Governor's telling him he would undertake to cure him and bring him to his Senses, *Tarachus* calmly replied he might do what he pleased with his Body, which was entirely in his Power. *Maximus* then order'd him to be stript, and lashed severely. "Yes, said the "Saint, now you have really made me wise; for the Blows I receive will but "inspire me with fresh Strength, and inhance my Confidence in God, and his "*Christ*." These Words gave the Governor an Opportunity of accusing the Saint of worshipping two Gods, and consequently being inconsistent with himself; to which Charge he replied he confess'd but one true God; upon which *Maximus* bid him remember he had given that Appellation to *Christ*. This Appeal to the Martyrs Words put him upon professing the Divinity of our Redeemer, calling him the Son of the Living God, the Hope of the Christians, and declaring him the Author of Salvation to such as suffer for his Sake. He would probably have enlarged on that Subject had not the Governor interrupted him by bidding him drop that rambling Discourse, and offer Sacrifice to the Gods. *Tarachus*, answer'd that what he had said deserved a better Title, being no more than strict Truth; to which he added that was then sixty five Years old, had been brought up in the Faith, and was not disposed to abjure it. *Demetrius*, who was present during the whole Trial, went up to the Saint, and advised him to sacrifice for his own Security. "Be gone, thou "Minister of Satan, said the invincible Martyr, and keep thy Advice for thy "own Use. *Maximus* then order'd him to be loaded with Chains of the largest Size, and thrown into Prison; and call'd for the second of this illustrious Company.

Demetrius brought his Prisoner to the Bar, and *Maximus* ask'd him his Name. "My chief and most valuable Name, said he, is *Christian*; but I "am distinguished in the World by that of *Probus*." The Governor's next Question was concerning his Family and Country; to which he replied "his "Father was a *Thracian*, that he was born at *Sida* in *Pamphylia*, that he "could not not boast of noble Descent, but gloried in the Appellation of "*Christian*". "That Denomination, said *Maximus*, will do you no Service; "take my Advice therefore; sacrifice to the Gods, and thus you may pro- "cure the Favour of their Imperial Majesties, and engage my Friendship". *Probus* immediately answer'd that he neither wanted to recommend himself to the Esteem of those Princes, nor desired the Governor's Friendship, adding that "he had left a considerable Fortune for the Service of the Living "God, 'through *Jesus Christ*". *Maximus* then commanded the Officers who attended the Court to see him stript, bound, and severely whipt. This

sanguinary

sanguinary Order was executed as soon as given; and the Martyr had bore the Lash some Time, when *Demetrius*, desired he would have some Regard for his own Flesh, and observe how the Blood stream'd from his Body. "My Body, "said the patient Sufferer, is in your Power, and the Severities which you "inflict on it are as agreeable to me as Perfumes. What, said *Maximus*, "do you still persist in your Madness"? *Probus* answer'd that reproachful Question by observing to the Governor that Character was ill bestow'd on one, who refused to worship Devils. He had hitherto been beaten only on the Back; but now by the Judge's Direction he was turn'd in Order to receive the same Correction on his Belly. While this was doing the Martyr invoked the Assistance of the Almighty; upon which the Persons employ'd in torturing the Saint were order'd to ask him where was his Assistant, when they laid on the Lash. *Probus*, full of Courage and Confidence in God, declared he was always ready to help him, and that all the Arts of Cruelty the Governor could employ should never stagger his Resolution. That Magistrate desired he would consider what his Obstinacy had brought on him, and how much Blood he had lost. "Know, replied the undaunted Soldier of *Jesus Christ*, "that the more my Body suffers for my Saviour the more vigorous my Soul "grows." *Maximus*, finding he could make no Impression on the Martyr at that Time, endeavour'd to reduce him to a Compliance by farther Hardships; and in this View order'd him to be carried off, loaded with Irons, his Hands and Feet to be streched in the Stocks; with a strict Prohibition of using any Means for the Cure of his Wounds.

Upon the third appearing at the Bar, *Maximus* begun with the usual Interrogatory, and was answer'd in the same Manner, as before. The Governor then observed to him that the Apellation of Christian had been of no Use to his Companions, and therefore commanded him to answer without Circumlocution. "If then you would know the Name I bear among Men, said "the Saint, it is *Andronicus*". The second Question was as in the former Trials; to which he replied he was a native of *Ephesus*, and descended of one of the first Families in that City. "Well, said the Governor, wave all idle "and senseless Speeches, and be ruled by one, who is disposed to treat you "with all the Tenderness of a Father; those who have already appear'd here "on that Subject do not find their Accounts in the Folly and Extravagance "of their Discourses and Principles; honour the Emperors therefore, and "sacrifice to the Deities, whom our fore Fathers own'd and thus you shall be "consider'd, and receive the Reward of your Obedience". *Andronicus* replied; "it is with Justice you call them the Gods of *your Fathers*; for you
"are

"are no better then Sons of the Devil, and even Devils, while you do the
"Works of that evil Spirit". *Maximus*, incensed at this unexpected and
galling Retortion, told him the Warmth of his Youth inspired him with
Insolence; to which the Saint answer'd that, 'though he appear'd Young, his
Soul was full of Robust Manhood, and prepared for the most severe Trial.
"Leave babling, and haranguing, said the Governor, and sacrifice, that you
"may avoid the Punishment due to the Refusal." Upon which *Andronicus* assured him his Sentiments and Resolutions were the same with those of his Predecessors in the Course, and that he was ready to meet any Sufferings on that Score with Pleasure. Immediately after this Declaration he was sentenced to share the Fate of those whom he seem'd so fond of imitating. As the Executioners were preparing for the Work, *Demetrius* desired him to comply with the Imperial Orders; and the Governor advised the same; but *Andronicus* declared he never had sacrificed to Devils, and was resolved never to be guilty of that sacrilegious Impiety; upon which the Word was given for beginning the Execution. *Athanasius*, and Officer belonging to the Jayl, applied next to our Saint, urged the Authority of his superior Age, which he supposed would pass for a Presumption of more Wisdom, and with the Gravity of a Father press'd him to obey the Governor. "Be gone, replied
"*Andronicus*, keep your Advice for your own Use; 'though you are old,
"your Understanding is weak, as appears by your persuading me to sacri-
"fice to Stones and Devils." *Maximus*, hearing this courageous Answer, asked him whether he was insensible to the Torments, and resolved to continue in his Folly, without the least Compassion for himself. "This Folly, said
"*Andronicus*, is necessary for us who place our Hope in *Christ*; whereas
"temporal Wisdom entails eternal Death on its Possessors." *Maximus* asked the Saint who taught him this boasted Folly; "I learnt it, replied he, from
"the saving Word, in whom we live, and shall live, our Hopes of a Re-
"surrection being built on God, who is in Heaven." The Governor assuring him that if he went on in that Strain, he should feel the Weight of more severe Torments; *Andronicus* calmly replied that, as his Body was in his Hands, he might do what he pleased with it. *Maximus* then order'd his Legs, and Sides to be torn, Salt to be thrown in his Wounds, and his Sides to be scraped with Bits of broken Pots; but *Andronicus* triumphed over all this Cruelty, and assured him his Body receiv'd fresh Strength from the Hands of his Tormentors; that he fear'd not his Threats, and despised all he could do to him. After this truly Heroick Speech the Martyr was chain'd and conducted to Prison.

Some

Oct. 11 Some Days after, *Maximus*, being at *Mopsuesta*, order'd the three glorious Champions of *Jesus Christ* to be brought before him for a second Trial, and begun with observing to *Tarachus* that old Age was generally honour'd, and supposed to be accompanied with good Sense, and Prudence, and therefore he had Reason to expect a Change in his Sentiments and Resolutions, which could not fail of recommending him to the Esteem, of his Superiours. *Tarachus* answer'd; " I am a Christian, and heartily wish that both you and their Im-
" perial Majesties would open your Eyes, and correct your mistaken Notions,
" that the true God may give you Life and Strength." This charitable wish provok'd the Governor to order his Mouth to be struck with Stones, with this Admonition, *quit your Folly*. But the Execution of this Sentence could not hinder him from telling that Magistrate the Character of Fool would better suit Him. Upon *Maximus* bidding him observe his Teeth were loossen'd, and consider what he brought upon himself by persisting in his Confession, *Tarachus* assured him he could not hurt him, 'though he cut off all his Limbs; for he should still stand his Ground by Virtue of the Strength he receive from *Jesus Christ*. After this the Martyr was silent; but such was the Cruelty of the Magistrate that he order'd him to be struck, with a Command to Speak; upon which *Tarachus* urged the Loss of his Teeth, and the Blows he had reeceiv'd on his Jaws as a sufficient Excuse for his Silence; " and
" yet, said *Maximus*, you remain obstinate; come to the Altar, and sacrifice
" to the Gods. No, replied the Saint, 'though I have almost lost the Use
" of my Speech, you shall never move my Resolution, which grows stron-
" ger by my Sufferings". When *Maximus* told him it was in his Power to conquer his boasted Strength, the Martyr declared he was ready for the Attack and did not Doubt of *Victory* in the Name of God who fortified and supported him in the Conflict. The Governor then order'd the Saint's Hands to be held open, and Fire applied to the Palms. He was under this Torment when he told his Judge, " he did not fear his temporal Fire, but was resolved to
" avoid eternal Flames by refusing to worship false Gods." *Maximus* bid the Martyr consider what he had suffer'd for his Folly, and resolve to sacrifice. Upon another formal Refusal, he was sentenced to be hung up by the Feet and smoaked. " Do you imagine, said he, that I, who have proved an Overmatch for
" your Fire, am afraid of your Smoke." He was in that Posture when the Governor called to him, and required his Compliance; to which he replied;
" You may sacrifice to Men, as you used to do; but God forbid I should be
" guilty of such a Crime." The Governor then order'd a Mixture of Salt and the sharpest Vinegar to be pour'd into his Nostrils; but the Martyr told

him

the Executioner his Vineyar was sweet to him, and his Salt insipid; upon Oct. 11 which the Governor directed the Addition of Mustard. The Martyr was so little affected with this Prescription that he called the Judge by his Name, and let him know that his Servants had given him Honey instead of Mustard. *Maximus*, finding all his Attempts fall to the Ground, could only assure *Tarachus* that he would make it his Business to invent fresh Tortures against his next Appearance, to cure him of his Folly; " and it shall be mine, replied " the Martyr, to prepare for the Attack".

Tarachus being chain'd and carried to Prison, *Probus* was asked whether he had given the Matter a second Thought, and was disposed to follow the Emperor's Example in sacrificing. " I come, replied the Saint, better prepa-
" red to Day: for what I have suffer'd already has only confirm'd and strength-
" en'd my Resolution. Employ your whole Power on me, then; and You
" shall find that neither You, nor your Masters the Emperors, nor the Gods
" whom you serve, nor even your Father the Devil shall oblige me to adore
" Gods, whom I know not." After a short Dialogue between the Governor and the Martyr concerning the Dignity of the Pagan Divinities, the latter concluded with declaring he would not own a Plurality of Gods, but was resolved to adhere to the Worship of the one supreme Being, who alone deserved that Appellation. *Maximus*, endeavouring to make his Advantage of this Profession, invited him to sacrifice to *Jupiter*, whom he stiled the great, invincible God. " How! replied *Probus*, shall I pay divine Honours to one, who
" married his own Sister; that infamous Debauchee, as he is described even by
" your own Poets." The Governor, shock'd at the History of his great and invincible God, order'd his Mouth to be stopt with Blows, with a Caution against Blasphemy. *Probus* could not forbear complaining of the Injustice of this Proceeding, observed once more that *Jupiter's* Character had been drawn in the same Colours by those who profess to worship him, and appeal'd to his Judge for the Truth of what he had said. The Governor, instead of reasoning with his Prisoner, order'd Bars of Iron to be heated and applied to his Body. His Direction was follow'd most exactly; but the Martyr declared the Fire had lost it's Force, and did not affect him. *Maximus* commanded the Bars should be heated again, and *Probus* press'd close to the Instrument of Torture. But the Fire in the Saint's Opinion was as weak as before; upon which he was order'd to be bound, stretched out, and whipp'd into Obedience; but neither that, nor shaving his Head, and putting live Coals on it, nor any other Acts of Cruelty, which the Governor could direct, or his Officers inflict

had the least Influence on the Martyr's Constancy; whereupon, he was order'd to Prison, and *Andronicus* call'd to his Trial.

Maximus endeavour'd to gain *Andronicus* by assuring him that the Martyrs, who had been tried before him, had at last, 'though with much Difficulty, own'd the Gods of the Empire; told him their Obedience would be soon rewarded by the Prince, who enforced the Worship of those excellent Beings; advised him to prevent the Stroke of Justice by a ready Compliance with his Duty; and swore by the Gods and the Lives of the invincible Emperors he would make him a terrible Example, if he refused what was required. "Lay "not such a Weakness to the Charge of those who have appear'd here on "the same Subject, said the Martyr; nor imagine it in your Power to shake "my Resolution with artful Speeches. I cannot believe that They have dis- "obey'd the Law of their Fathers, renounced their Hopes in our God, and "obey'd your extravagant Orders: nor will I ever fall short of them in "Faith and Dependence on our common Saviour. Thus arm'd I neither "know your Gods, nor fear your Authority; fulfil all your Menaces, exe- "cute your most sanguinary Inventions, and employ every cruel Art in your "Power on me." Upon this Defiance he was by the Governor's Order stretched out at full Length, and whipp'd unmercifully. His Body was one continued Wound, when the Martyr asked the Governor whether this was all he could do to him, pursuant to his solemn Oath; and assured him this was nothing to those, who love the living God. *Maximus* then order'd his Wounds to be rubb'd with Salt, and his Body to be turn'd, that every Part of it might bear the Marks of his Hatred to the Christian Religion. *Andronicus*, supported by the Power of God, observed that he who had heal'd his former Wounds in an expeditious Manner, would take the same Care of him a second Time. The Governor, hearing of his Cure, reproached his Guards with acting contrary to his express Orders in that Point. *Pegsiaus*, Keeper of the Prisons solemnly assured him no Man had been admitted to see the Prisoners, and offer'd his Head as a Punishment of his Neglect, if it could be proved on him. *Andronicus* now thought it Time to declare the Author of that Favour, and let the Court know that the God whom he and his Companions served was a powerful Physician, and could perform the greatest Cures by his bare Word. This Session ended with the Governor's Orders for putting the invincible Martyr in Irons, and a strict Charge to let no Man see him.

Not long after, *Maximus* being at *Anazarbum* call'd for the three illustrious Martyrs. Upon understanding they waited his Pleasure, he order'd *Tarachus* to be brought in, and asked him whether what he had already suffer'd had

let

let him see his Error, and disposed him to comply with his Duty to the Gods, Oct.11 whom he called the Governors of the Universe. "Woe be to You and Them, "replied the Martyr if the World is under the Direction of such as are de- "stined to eternal Torments, a Fate which will attend all who adore them." This Speech was follow'd by a Repetition of his former Professions, and declared he would maintain the Faith inviolably in Spight of all the Torments that could be inflicted on him. The Martyr was then bound, the Proposal of sacrificing to the Pagan Deities urged to him again, and upon his persisting in the Refusal, he was threaten'd with a lingring Death. *Maximus*, enraged at the Intrepidity of the Martyr, order'd him to be struck on the Face, and his Lips to be cut; upon which *Tarachus* assured him that while he disfigured his Body, he gave fresh Vigour to his Soul. The Governor surprized, and confounded, imputed his Insensibility of this cruel Usage to Magick. To which the Saint replied that he never was engaged in those diabolical Arts, having never worshipped Devils, but adhered to that God, who gave him Patience under his Sufferings, and furnished him with what he was to say at that Time. Upon the Governor telling him all he could say would prove useless to him, and advising him to procure his Relief by sacrificing, *Tarachus* replied that he was not Fool enough to renounce his God, from whom he expected eternal Life, and obey a Man, who could only give him a few Moments bodily Ease, follow'd by an everlasting Death. As soon as he had ended this Declaration, *Maximus* order'd red hot Spits to be applied to his Breast and Sides; his Ears cut off; his Head close shaved, and flead; and burning Coals laid on the bare Skull. *Tarachus* assured his cruel Judge that 'though he should Order his whole Body to be excoriated, he should not force him from his God. After threatning to burn his Body and scatter the Ashes in the Air to prevent the Christians paying their Respect to his Relicks, and preserving them as Trophies of his Victory, the Governor remanded him to Prison, with a Promise of exposing him to the Beasts the next day.

Probus, being call'd to his third Examination, was bid to consider the melancholy Consequences of persisting in his former Resolution, remember what he had already felt, and the Condition to which his Obstinacy had reduced *Tarachus*, and think of making his Way to Preferment by an Act of Religion. "No, said *Probus*, we are all one Opinion in the present Affair, and have all "form'd the same Resolution. Imagine not that I shall change my Language "on this Occasion; for neither Tortures, nor Threats can shake me. My "Courage is proof against all you can do, and I wait the Discharge of your "whole Rage on me with Impatience." The Governor observed that he was

sensible

Oct. 11 sensible he and his two Companions had agreed to refuse the Honours due to the Gods; and advised him with an affected Tenderness to prevent the Sroke that was ready to fall on him by a dutiful Compliance with the Imperial Orders; but the Martyr's Reply was a Repetition of his own and their Resolution to persevere in their Fidelity to the Almighty. Upon which the Governour gave the Word for hanging him up by the Feet, and applying red hot Spits to his Body. While he was in this Posture some Meat and Wine, that had been offer'd to the Idols, were forced into his Mouth. The Martyr could only appeal to Heaven, and protest against the Violence which was offer'd him; and then, addressing himself to the Governor, let him know that his Soul would receive no Damage where his own Will was not concern'd, as in the present Case, in which he was merely passive. His Legs were then burnt with the hot Spits; and *Maximus* expressing his Surprize at the Saint's Perseverance, after all he had suffer'd by his Direction; He replied, " I freely give my Body to be treated as you please for the Preservation of my Soul." Upon the Governor ordering his Hands to be pierced with sharp Nails made hot for that Purpose, *Probus* express'd his Gratitude to the Almighty for allowing him this Conformity with the Sufferings of *Jesus Christ*. But neither that Act of Cruelty nor the Loss of his Eyes, which soon follow'd it, could make the least Abatement in our holy Martyr's Courage; whereupon he was sent back to Prison loaded with Chains, and a strict Charge given that no one should be permitted to visit him or his Companions, to which was added an Assurance that he should be thrown to the Beasts on the first Occasion.

Upon *Andronicus* appearing, according to the Governor's Order, he was ask'd whether he was inclined to save his Life by acknowledging the Gods of the Empire; his Answer was that he was ready to bear the utmost Effects of his Aversion to the sacred Name of *Jesus Christ*, and would with the divine Assistance give him substantial Proofs of the Vigour of his Soul. *Maximus* had once more Recourse to the same vile Calumny which was employ'd to deceive the Martyr at his second Examination, and assured him that *Tarachus* and *Probus* had sacrificed to the Gods, in Obedience to the Imperial Edicts. The Martyr declared as before, that he would not give Credit to what he said to the Disadvantage of those glorious Soldiers of *Jesus Christ*; whereupon his Belly was burnt, and hot Irons thrust between his Fingers; but *Andronicus* triumphed over the Cruelty of his Judge, and declared that his Union with *Jesus Christ* would make him an Overmatch for all he could invent. *Maximus* observed to him that the Person on whose Assistance he depended was no better than an infamous Malefactor, who suffer'd on the Cross; and asked him

what

what he could hope for from one of that Character. This contemptuous Way Oct. 11. of speaking of the Saviour of the World fired the Martyr with new Zeal, who told the blaspheming Governor he was not worthy to mention that venerable Name, which would be of no Use to him, while he persecuted the Servants of God; and profess'd that all his Sufferings would turn to his Advantage, and be rewarded in Heaven. *Maximus* used the same Violence to *Probus* in regard to the detestable Offerings of the Pagans; against which the Saint protested in the same Manner, as had been practised by that Martyr. Upon the Governor threatning to cut out his Tongue, *Andronicus* begg'd he would be as good as his Word, and do the same Execution on his Lips, which had touched the idolatrous, abominable Food. After this and some other Speeches which the Governor resented as so many Affronts to the Powers whom he represented, he order'd his Tongue to be cut out, and all his Teeth forced from his Jaws; to which he added a Caution that must pass for a strong Proof of the Christians reserving and venerating the Relicks of those who suffer'd for the Faith. " *Go*, said that Magistrate in the Transports of his Zeal against our holy Religion, and it's Votaries, *burn the Teeth and Tongue of that wicked*
" *Head; and scatter the Ashes so that none of his impious Associates may take*
" *them up and keep them as somewhat valuable and holy.* After this Charge the Saint was remanded to Prison, where he was to expect the first favourable Opportunity of finishing his Course with his two Companions.

The *Trials* of the three Martyrs being thus concluded, *Maximus* sent for a proper Officer, and gave him Orders for a publick Show the next Day. The Governor's Will being notified to those who had the Care of the Beasts, and the whole Town invited to the Amphitheatre, which was about a Mile from *Anazarbum*, the Scene of this barbarous Diversion was crouded with Spectators at the Time appointed. The cruel Sports had lasted some Time, and several were kill'd, when the Governor dispatched a Message to the Prison for bringing the Martyrs to the Amphitheatre. What they had suffer'd made them unable to walk, so that it was necessary for the Guards to carry them to the Place design'd for their last Combat. The Appearance of such melancholy and shocking Objects spread a confused Murmur among the Spectators; some of whom could not forbear expressing their Concern and Resentment at the Governor's Proceedings, and left the Amphitheatre. Several Beasts were let loose, but would not touch the Martyrs; which incensed *Maximus*, who, full of Rage at the Disappointment of his Malice, order'd the Keeper to be severely chastised, and then in an angry Tone bid him immediately bring out a Beast that would execute his Design on the

Criminals

Oct. 11 Creminals in Question. The Keeper, half dead with Fear, let loose a fierce Bear, that had dispatched three Men that Day; but neither That nor a terrible Lioness, which afrighted the whole Company, could be provoked to hurt those faithful Servants of God. *Maximus* laid the Blame of the whole Miscarriage on *Terentianus*, the Officer whom he had entrusted with the Affair, and order'd the holy Martyrs to be kill'd with the Sword which was done accordingly.

Upon leaving the Place, the Governor posted ten Soldiers there to guard the Bodies of the Saints, which lay mixed with those of the Gladiators and Malefactors, who fell for the Diversion of the People. Some Christians, who had observed all that had passed from a neighbouring Mountain, took the Advantage of the Night, came down, fell on their Knees, and begg'd the Almighty would assist them in carring off the venerable Relicks. They then went on; and coming near the Amphitheatre, found the Soldiers at Supper, and a good Fire blazing near the Bodies. They retired some Steps, and made a second Prayer on the same Subject; soon after which a terrible Storm of Rain, and Thunder, attended with an Earthquake, quenched the Fire and forced the Soldiers from their Posts. The Weather growing Calm on a suddain, the Christians made a third Address to Heaven, and then ventured to the Amphitheatre; but it was so dark that it was impossible to distinguish what they sought. In this Distress, they raised their Hands and Voices to God; and immediately were directed to the desired Treasure by a Stream of Light, which pointed out the holy Bodies. Transported at their Success, they carried the precious Remains off, and by the Help of the same Light, which made the Discovery, lodged them in the Hollow of a Rock.

The three Martyrs finished their glorious Course on the eleventh of *October* in the first Year of *Dioclesian*'s Persecution, as appears from the Account of their Sufferings; a Piece deservedly esteem'd one of the most valuable Monuments of Ecclesiastical Antiquity. The Christians, who carried off the Bodies of our Saints, purchased a Copy of their Trial; added the Rest upon the Credit of their own Senses, and sent the whole to the Church of *Iconium*, desiring it might be communicated to the faithful of *Pisidia* and *Pamphylia*, for their Edification and Instruction.

The

The XII Day.

Oct. 12

St. *WILFRID*, Archbishop of *York*.

WILFRID was born in the Kingdom of *Northnmberland* about the Year 634, in the Reign of *Oswald* whom the Church honours as a Saint on the fifth of *August*. His Parents, who were Persons of Distinction, were particularly careful of his Education in the Principles of the Christian Religion and the Rudiments of Learning. But his Mother dying when he was about thirteen Years old, and his Father marrying again soon after, he left the House, and went to *York*, where the Court was kept while this Island was divided between seven Kings. At his Arrival he was introduced to Queen *Eanfled* Wife to *Oswy*, then in Possession of the Throne. That Princess seeing the young Stranger handsome, polite, and of a very promising Appearance in every Respect, made him an Offer of a Place worth his Acceptance. *Wilfrid* modestly declined the Favour, letting her Majesty know his Inclinations led him to Retirement; and the Queen, pleased with that Declaration, promised to do all in her Power to facilitate the Execution of his Design. In this View she put him into the Hands of one of the chief Officers of the King's Houshould, who was bound for the Monastery of *Lindisfarne*, with a Resolution of engaging in that Religious Community. *Wilfrid*, glad of this Opportunity of leaving the World, accompanied that Gentleman to the Monastery, where he spent some Years in Study, and the Exercise of Christian Piety. This House, which stood in a Peninsula between *England* and *Scotland* was full of Irish Monks, placed there by the late holy King of *Northumberland*; and *Wilfrid* had observed some Difference between them and other Churches in Relation to the Feast of *Easter*, and other Particulars; which gave him an Inclination to travel to *France*, take an exact View of Ecclesiastical Discipline in that Kingdom, and visit the most regular and celebrated Monasteries there.

Taking his Leave of the Abbot and Monks at *Landisfarne*, he went to *Canterbury*, with Letters of Recommendation from *Eanfled* to *Ercombert*, King of *Kent*, her Cousin German. *Wilfrid* reached that City toward the Close of Archbishop *Honorius*'s Life, where he had an Opportunity of seeing the Practice of the *Roman* Church, which was introduced there with the Gospel. After some Stay at *Canterbury*, he went for *France* with St. *Benedict Biscop*, about six Years older than himself, who was going abroad with the same View. The two Travellers met with a kind Reception at *Lyons* from the Bishop of that City; who was so much charm'd with *Wilfrid*'s Behaviour, and Capacity that

he

Oct. 12 he detain'd him, while his Companion pursued his Journey to *Rome*. Among other Means which that Prelate employ'd to engage his Stay, he made him an Offer of his Niece, and a handsome Establishment at *Lyons*. *Wilfrid*, 'though form'd to please, and engage the Affections of Mankind, could not think of fixing in the World, and therefore declined that honourable, and advantageous Alliance, and let the Bishop into his Design of devoting himself to the Service of God; who thereupon furnished him with all that was necessary for carrying him to *Rome*, but would not let him go 'till he had obtain'd his Promise of taking *Lyons* in his Way home.

Thus accommodated *Wilfrid* went for *Rome*, where he contracted an Intimacy with *Boniface*, Archdeacon of that Church, a Man of great Reputation for Learning and Vertue, who undertook to give his new Friend a Light into Ecclesiastical Discipline, and such Branches of Literature as would best answer the Design of his leaving *England*. Having spent near a Year under that excellent Master, he made a second Visit to *Lyons* in 654; where the Bishop receiv'd him with great Joy, gave him the Tonsure, obliged him to accept of an Appartment in his House, and resolved to make him his Heir, and press his succeding him in the Episcopal Chair. During his Residence at *Lyons*, *Wilfrid* enjoy'd the Conversation of several Persons of eminent Qualifications, who were instrumental in forming him to the Vertue and Knowledge his State required. He was still at that City when *Clovis* II died and left his Queen *Bathilda* the Tuition of three young Princes. 'Though that Lady acquitted herself of all the Duties of her Station with admirable Prudence, she had no small Disturbance from some of the Nobility who made their Advantage of *Clotaire*'s Weakness, for the Gratification of their own irregular Passions; and one of their Number, who made it his Business to persecute all such as opposed his irregular Motions, employ'd a Set of Ruffians to assassinate our Saint's great Patron. *Wilfrid*, having paid his last Duties to that venerable Prelate, return'd to *England*; where he was well receiv'd by *Alfrid*, *Oswy*'s eldest Son and his Associate in the Kingdom of *Northumberland*. That Prince took a singular Pleasure in hearing our Saint's Account of the *Roman* Rites, and express'd a great Desire to see them introduced in his Dominions. Knowing *Wilfrid*'s Inclination to Retirement, and to secure his Assistance more effectually, he gave him a Piece of Land called *Rippon* in the Diocese of *York*, on which he design'd to found a Monastery, and had already laid the Foundations of that Building. The Saint, acting in Concert with that Prince, finished the House, and was made first Abbot of the same. He had been some Time in that Post, when

when it was thought proper to raise him to the Dignity of Priesthood, which Oct. 12 was perform'd by *Ailbert* a *Frenchman*, Bishop of *Dorchester*.

The Dispute about keeping *Easter* began now to run very high; as the *Northumbrians* had received their Christianity from the Missionaries of *Ireland*, some of them were for adhering to the Practice of that Country, where the Feast of our Lord's Resurrection was celebrated on the fourteenth Day of the Moon, when it fell on a *Sunday*; while others, understanding the Rest of this *Island* and the whole Church observed that great Solemnity on the first *Sunday* after the fourteenth of the Moon, according to the Regulation of the *Nicene* Council, were as warm in asserting this Practice. This Difference caused no small Confusion in the moveable Feasts, and made a Sort of Schism. *Oswy*, sensible of the Inconveniency of this Division, resolved to do all in his Power for uniting his Subjects on that Article. To this End in 662 he assembled a Council at *Strenshall*, now called *Whitby*, where he assisted with his Son. *Colman*, Bishop of *Lindisfarne*, was at the Head of those who defended the *Irish* Custom, in which he was seconded by *Hilda* Abbess of the House, where they met. *Ailbert*, Bishop of *Dorchester*, was to explain the Sentiments of the opposite Party; but not being well versed in the Language of the Country, deputed *Wilfrid* to perform that Task, for which he was very well qualified. Our Saint acquitted himself of that Commission so well that the two Kings and *Ced*, Bishop of *London* declared loudly for the *Roman* Custom, and resolved to join the whole Catholick Church in the Point in Debate. *Colman* could not be prevail'd with to quit the Party which he had espoused; who, rather than conform in that Particular, quitted his Bishoprick and went for *Ireland*.

Paulinus, Bishop of *York* having left that City in 634, as has been related in our Account of that holy Prelate on the tenth of this Month, the Episcopal See remain'd vacant about thirty Years; in which Time the large Diocese of *York* labour'd under such Difficulties as called aloud for Relief. *Oswy* and *Alfrid*, taking the distressed State of that Church into serious Consideration, named *Wilfrid* to the Bishoprick of *York*. The Saint accepted of that Post with much Difficulty; and went to *France* for Consecration; for at that Time there was but one Bishop in all *England*, which was not sufficient according to the Canons. The Ceremony was perform'd at *Compiegne* by *Ailbert*, who had left our Island and was then Bishop of *Paris*. During his Absence, those whom he had opposed so successfully in the Synod of *Strenshall* made the King believe that his Return was uncertain, and, the Necessities of the ruin'd Church being very pressing, prevail'd with him to place *Chad* in

Oct. 12 the Episcopal Chair, who was consecrated by an *English* Bishop, assisted by two *British* Prelates.

Wilfrid, coming back to take Possession of his Bishoprick, found it disposed of in the Manner already related. He could not but be surprized at this uncanonical Proceeding; but, rather than create the least Disturbance, retired to his Monastery at *Rippon* 'till a more convenient Opportunity should present itself. About three Years after, *Theodore*, who had been consecrated at *Rome*, came over with the Character of Primate of *England*; by Virtue of which Authority *Chad* was deposed, as has been already observed on the second of *March*, and our Saint put in Possession of his Right.

King *Oswy*, who survived *Alfrid*, died in the Year 670, and was succeeded by *Egfrid* his second Son. The Beginning of the new King's Reign was favourable to the Church of *York*, as it allow'd it's excellent Pastor the peaceable Exercise of his Functions. The Cathedral built by *Paulinus* being now fallen to Ruin, and scarce fit for the Service of God, *Wilfrid* repaired that Edifice, cover'd it with Lead, glazed the Windows, a thing at that Time far from Common in this Island; and made a considerable Addition to the Revenue of that Church. Several other Buildings sacred to the Worship of the Almighty were by his Direction beautified, and supported; and a new Church at *Rippon* acknowledged him it's sole Founder. He built that of *Hagustald*, now call'd *Hexham*, which was look'd on as a most curious and surprising Piece of Architecture, and became the See of a new Bishoprick in his Time. Several other charitable Foundations in different Parts of his Diocess, encouraged by Queen *Etheldreda*, proclaim our Saint's Concern for his Flock and that Princess's excellent Dispositions for advancing the real Good of her Subjects. *Etheldreda* did nothing of Consequence without our Saint's Advice, who negotiated her Seperation from the King, gain'd his Consent for her retiring into a Monastery; gave her the Veil in the Abbey of *Coldingham*. The Queen had not been long there when *Egfrid*, had Thoughts of making her leave the Cloister and return to Court. Being apprized of his Design, she fled to the Kingdom of the *Eastangles*, where she could depend on more Security. This drew the King's Anger on our Saint, which was not appeased 'till he took another Wife.

Eromberga the new Queen, not being able to bear one in the Kingdom so powerful as our Saint's Dignity and personal Merit had made him, resolved to destroy the King's good Opinion of the holy Prelate; and found Means to execute her Malice by surprising *Theodore* Archbishop of *Canterbury* into her Measures. She urged the Necessity of dividing that populous Kingdom

among

among several Bishops; and this pretended Zeal for the Church prevail'd with Oct. 12 the good Primate to depose *Wilfrid*, and establish *Bosa* and *Eata* in his Room. Some time after three new Bishopricks were erected within the Diocese of *York*; but *Wilfrid* was quite excluded in the Division. *Bosa*, as Pastor of the *Deiri*, was placed at *York*; *Eata*, as Bishop of the *Bernicians*, fix'd his See at *Lindisfarne*; *Tunbert* was settled at *Hagustald*; and *Trumwin* entrusted with the Church of the *Picts*, or Inhabitants of the Southern Parts of *Scotland*. Our Saint, thus displaced, carried his Complaint to Court; but could get no other Answer than that nothing was laid to his Charge, but no Alterations would be made in this new Regulation.

Finding no Redress, he came to Resolution of leaving *England* about the Year 679 attended by *Eddi*, formerly Chanter of *Canterbury*, whom he had employ'd in reforming and settling the Choirs at *York* and *Rippon*. That Priest, was his inseperable Companion in all his Travels from that Time, wrote his Life; and it is from that Piece we have borrow'd our Account of the Saint. *Wilfrid* embark'd for *Friesland*, where he preached the Faith with the Zeal and Success of an Apostle; converted and baptized Prince *Algisius* and great Numbers of his Subjects; and then set forward for *Rome*, taking *France* in his Way to that City. *Dagobert* II was then on the Throne of *Austrasia*; and as he ow'd the Recovery of his Father's Crown to our Saint's Assistance and Advice, he receiv'd him in a Manner expressive of his Gratitude, acknowledged the Favour before the whole Court, and endeavour'd to engage his Stay in his Dominions by an Offer of the Bishoprick of *Strasbourg*. But nothing could divert him from his intended Journey, because he hoped for that Relief from the holy See which he could not find at home.

Wilfrid reached *Rome* toward the Close of *September* 679, where he found *Agatho* in St. *Peter*'s Chair; who espoused his Cause in a Manner becoming the first Bishop, conven'd a Synod in *October* the same Year, and in Conjunction with that venerable Assembly pronounced him free from all Censures, and rightful Bishop of *York*. His Holiness held a Council of 125 Prelates against the *Monothelites* in 680, in which our Saint was present and subscribed in the Name of the Archbishop of *Canterbury*, and the whole *English* Church, pursuant to a Deputation from the Primate, and other Bishops of this Island. This Commission was sufficient to persuade *Wilfrid* that *Theodore*'s Mind was changed in his Regard, and that he would make no Difficulty of promoting his Re-establishment; and in this Persuasion he set out for his own Country. As he pass'd through *France* he was very near being involved in the Calamity which had taken off *Dagobert*. That Prince, being

Oct. 12 War with King *Thierry*, was basely assassinated by the Direction of *Ebroïn*, prime Minister to his Enemy. The two Armies lay on the Frontiers of the Dioceses of *Langres* and *Toul* when *Wilfrid*, whose Road lay that Way, fell into the Hands of the Ruffians, who had massacred the unfortunate King of *Austrasia*. The Head of them, well acquainted with our Saint's History so far as it regarded the deceased Prince, reproached him with the Service he had done that King, and laid all the Miscarriages of his Reign to *Wilfrid*'s Charge; but the Saint reason'd the Case so well with a Bishop in *Ebroïn*'s Army, that he escaped with his Life and pursued his Journey to *England*.

As soon as he landed, he went to the Archbishop of *Canterbury*, and shew'd him the Pope's Order for his re-assuming the Government of his Diocese. Meeting with no Opposition from his Primate, or the other Bishops, he made his Way to *York*, where he was but coldly receiv'd by *Egfrid*, still prejudiced against him by the Queen. Upon attempting to enter on his Pastoral Functions, pursuant to the Direction and Decrees of the holy See, he was thrown into Prison, where he suffer'd much Hardship; for his Enemies gave out that he had either imposed on the Pope by a false Account of the Matter, or bought his Favour and Protection. *Eremburga*, who raised this Storm against the Saint, was taken dangerously ill soon after his Commitment, and, apprehending her Indisposition was the Effect of the divine Justice for her Proceedings against that Prelate, order'd he should have his Liberty; which he employ'd in preaching the Gospel among the *South-Saxons*, great Numbers of those People being still Slaves to Idolatry. *Edilwach* King of *Sussex*, according to our Saint's Historian, receiv'd him as a Person sent from Heaven for his Instruction, listen'd to his Doctrine with great Docility, and was initiated in the Faith by Baptism. Under the Protection of that Royal Convert he continued his Apostolical Labours, and gain'd several Thousands to the Faith of *Christ*. *Edilwach*, as a small Return for the ineffable Favour he had receiv'd by his Ministry, gave him several Parcels of Land, which enabled him to build and endow the Monastery of *Selsey*, afterwards a Bishop's See, and then translated to *Chichester*.

This Monastery was his usual Residence during his Stay in that Kingdom. *Nothelm*, who succeeded *Edilwach*, embraced the Faith upon hearing our Saint; in which he was follow'd by *Nothgida* his Sister. That Princess founded a Monastery and built some Churches with what was design'd for her Dowry; this was with the a View of divesting herself of all she had in the World, and retiring from it, which she perform'd soon after under the Direction of our Saint. When he had established Religion on so good a Foot in *Sussex*, he

made

made an Apostolical Journey to the Country of the *West Saxons*, where he laid Oct. 12 the first Foundations of the Christian Religion in King *Ceadwalla*, who was baptized at *Rome* by Pope *Sergius* I in 689. Having obtain'd a Grant of a fourth Part of the Isle of *Wight*, he sent a Priest thither to instruct the deluded Natives and rescue them from Idolatry.

Since our Saint left the Kingdom of *Northumberland* his Behaviour had been irreproachable in the Eyes of the whole World, and God had rewarded his Evangelical Labours with prodigious Success, wherever he preached. The Reputation of his Vertue, and Success of his Ministry affected *Theodore* so strongly that he could not but reproach himself with Weakness in consenting to his being deposed, and a criminal Negligence in not making him publick Satisfaction for that Injury. This was the Posture of the Archbishop's Mind, when he let *Wilfrid* know he was heartily sorry for what had pass'd, and would assured him he employ all his Authority in doing him Justice against his malicious Enemies. This Message was follow'd by an Interview, in which *Theodore* ask'd the Saint's Pardon before another Bishop. After the Death of King *Egfrid* in 685, the Archbishop of *Canterbury* gave a sufficient Proof of his Sincerity by applying to *Alfrid* his Successor in Favour of the injured Prelate; whom that Prince was pleased to allow to return to his Flock. *Wilfrid*, thus in Possession of his Diocese, asserted his Jurisdiction over the Churches of *Rippon*, and *Hagustald*, which were thus reduced to Monasteries, their Condition before his Expulsion. St. *Cuthbert*, Bishop of *Lindisfarne*, dying in 687, our Saint was under a Necessity of taking Care of that Diocese, 'till a new Bishop could be chosen. He supported the Weight with exemplary Patience and Courage, and exercised all the Functions of that extensive Charge with an active Zeal, constant Vigilance, and indefatigable Industry. *Wilfrid* had not enjoy'd the Pleasure which a true Pastor feels when employ'd in procuring the Salvation of those committed to his Care above five Years, when a new Storm arose; his Enemies insinuated to the King that it would be expedient to erect an Episcopal See at *Rippon*, and convert the Revenues of that Monastery to the Use of the new Bishop and his Successors; and that our Saint was obliged to submit to the Regulation which had been made, and approved of by the Primate of *England* upon his Deposition. The holy Prelate would not consent to this Usurpation; he did not pretend an Exemption from such Mandates as *Theodore* had published for the Reformation of Ecclesiastical Discipline, conformably to the Canons; but was of Opinion that those which he had granted to the Prejudice of the See of *York*, were either originally null and void; or, at least tacitly revoked by his

repenting

Oct. 12 repenting of his Conduct in that Point, and making his Reconciliation in a solemn Manner. These were his Sentiments of his own Case; but finding Enemies too formidable, and perceiving that his Stay could be of no Service to his People, he left the Kingdom once more, and fled to *Ethelred* King of *Mercia*, who receiv'd him very graciously, and committed to his Care the See of *Litchfield*, vacant by the Death of *Saxulf*. That Prince, whom History stiles our Saint's faithful and constant Friend, made no small Advantage of his Conversation; and it is observed by the Author of *Wilfrid*'s Life that *Ethelred*'s Resolution of ending his Days in a Cloister, which he executed in 704, was the Result of the holy Bishop's pious Discourses on the Vanity of the World and the Importance of Salvation.

Wilfrid had labour'd in the Work of the Lord near twelve Years under the King of *Mercia*'s Protection, when *Brithwald*, Successor to *Theodore*, and several other Prelates meeting about six Miles from *Rippon*, invited him to that Synod. The Saint, imagining his Affair would be handled there in an equitable Manner, and some Accommodation offer'd, set out immediately; but was surprized at his Arrival to find the greatest Part of the Bishops prejudiced against him, and ready to give a Sanction to the Calumnies of his implacable Enemies. Several Articles were urged against him in that Assembly; but 'though he confuted them to the Confusion of his Persecutors, *Wilfrid* was still press'd to make a free Resignation of his Title to the See of *York*. Upon refusing to comply with their Proposal, he was confin'd to his Monastery at *Rippon*; and some Steps were taken toward degrading him. But the Saint broke the Course of their Proceedings by appealing to the holy See; nor could his Age and Infirmities divert him from undertaking a Journey to *Rome*, where he hoped to find that Justice which was denied him at home. The Matter was examin'd by Pope *John* VI in a Synod in the Year 704; where *Wilfrid* was absolved and declared innocent; but as the other Claimant of the See of the *York*, and the Bishop of *Hugustald* were not present, it was order'd that a Synod should meet in *England*, where they should urge their several Pleas before our Saint, and Measures be taken for bringing the Dispute to an amicable Conclusion; but if no Accommodation could be made on the Spot, all the Parties concern'd should apply to the holy See for a final Determination of the Affair.

Wilfrid reached *England* in the Year 705, and upon coming to *York* solicited the Execution of the Decree pass'd at *Rome*. The Archbishop of *Canterbury*, glad of this Opportunity of making some Amends for his Conduct in the late Synod, readily consented. But King *Alfrid* did not comply so easily.

ly. He had stood out some Days when he was seized with a violent Fit of Oct. 12 Sickness; in his Extremity he made a Promise to Almighty God that if he recover'd, he would forward the Execution of the Decisions of the holy See in Favour of our Saint; and if he died, charged his Successor to do him that Justice. He had scarce ended this Declaration of his Disposition in Regard of the injured Prelate when he became Speechless, and died in a few Days. *Eadulf*, who seized on the Crown, was so far from acting conformably to the last Will of his Predecessor, that he sent our Saint Word that if he did not quit the Kingdom in six Days after that Notice, both He and all his Adherents should suffer Death. But the Usurper sate but two Months in the Throne of *Northumberland*, and was then deposed to make Room for *Osred*, Son to the late King. This Revolution brought *Brithwald* toward *York* in the Close of 705, where he found Things in a very good Posture for terminating this troublesome Affair. *Bosa* dying about that Time, the Saint was restored to his own See; but it was thought necessary for the Peace of the Church to prevail with him to resign the Bishoprick of *York*, and content himself with *Hagustald* and *Rippon*. From that Time *Wilfrid* divided his Days between those two Monasteries, and lived in the Practice of such Mortifications as seem'd not well suited to his Years, and bad State of Health. Two Years after his Re-establishment, he was taken with his last Sickness, which being long and violent gave him a glorious Opportunity of shewing a true Christian Patience and Resignation to the Will of God. During his Illness, he put all his Affairs in Order; and distributed his whole Substance among the Poor, except what he devoted to other pious Uses, such as endowing, or adding to the Revenues of Churches. He was in a very languishing Condition when the Abbots of two Monasteries in the Kingdom of *Mercia*, deputed by *Cenred*, Successor to *Ethelred*, brought him that Prince's Invitation to his Court, where he was desirous of modeling his Life by the holy Bishop's Advice. *Wilfrid*, 'though scarce able to travel, could not decline a Work where Salvation was concern'd. After several Conversations with *Cenred*, and some excellent Regulations of the Monasteries which he had founded in that Kingdom under his devout Predecessor, he expired at *Oundle*, at present a Town in *Northamptonshire*, on the twenty fourth of *August* 709, being then in his 67th Year.

His Body was removed to *Rippon*, and buried at the Foot of St. *Peter*'s Altar. That Monastery being demolished by King *Edred*'s Army, in 948 our Saint's Relicks lay buried in the Ruins, 'till *Odo* Archbishop of *Canterbury* order'd them to be dug out, and deposited in his Metropolitan Church in the Year 959; leaving some of them at *Rippon* for the Comfort of the Inhabitants

Oct. 13 bitants of the Country where the Saint had spent a considerable Part of his Life. *Landfranck*, who was raised to the Metropolitan See in 1070 put the the valuable Treasure into a new Shrine, and about the Year 1080 removed it with great Solemnity on the twelveth of *October*, the Day on which the *English* Church kept his Festival, as also that on which his Name occurs in the *Roman* Martyrologe.

The XIII Day.

St. *EDWARD* the Confessor, King of *ENGLAND*.

*E*DWARD, whose exemplary Piety has given him the Title of Confessor, was Son to *Ethelred*, who came to the Crown of *England* in the Year 978. The *Danes*, who had been very troublesome to this Island ever since the Foundation of the Monarchy in the Beginning of the IX Century, landed in such Numbers in that weak and unfortunate Prince's Reign, that he was obliged to rescue his Dominions from those bold Invaders by the Stipulation of forty thousand Pounds a Year; a Tribute, which in the Language of our *Saxon* Ancestors was called *Danegelt*. Our Saint being born in those troublesome Times was by his Royal Father's Direction carried over to *Normandy*, where it was presumed his valuable Life might be secure. During his Exile *Emma* his Mother, who attended him took care to educate him in a Manner suitable to his Birth, and Baptismal Obligations; and that excellent Princess had the Satisfaction of seeing early Inclinations to Vertue, and a Horror of Vice as it were interwoven with his Nature. The admirable Sweetness of his Temper was accompanied with uncommon Purity of Heart, and solid Piety. Those good Qualities join'd with a general Benevolence recommended him to the Esteem, Respect, and Love of all who knew him.

Upon the Death of *Hardicnute*, which happen'd in the Year 1042, *Edward* was placed on his Father's Throne, and made it his whole Study how to re-establish that Felicity and good Order in his Dominions, which had been destroy'd by a Usurpation of three successive Kings of the *Danish* Race for above twenty Years together; and his first Care was to see *Jesus Christ* reign in the Hearts of his Subjects. He was crown'd on *Easter* Day 1043; and, at the Solicitation of his affectionate Nobility, married *Editha*, Daughter to Earl *Godwin*, the richest, and most considerable of their Number. That Lady was perfectly agreeable to our Saint; but what recommended her most to his

Esteem

Esteem was her Love of virginal Chastity, which they agreed to observe their whole Lives.

Oct. 13

Earl *Godwin*, a Man of a warm Temper and naturally ambitious, was puff'd up with this honourable Alliance, and depended on the King's Weakness too much. *Emma*, our Saint's Mother, had long entertain'd a Suspicion of his being the principal Actor in the Tragedy of her eldest Son's Death, and consequently was not inclined to favour his Pretensions, or promote his Designs. That Earl presuming on the Credit he had with his Son in Law, whisper'd several Things to her Disadvantage, advanced a strong Accusation against her Chastity; and was so successful in his diabolical Attempts that the Queen Mother was stript of all she possess'd in *England*, and her Person confined; an unhappy Instance of the Misfortune of Princes, who seldom hear or see Things as they are in themselves, but are under a Necessity of taking them as represented by their Ministers, who are not always remarkable for Honesty, and a generous Concern for their Master; but too often make the Man, whom they call their Sovereign, the Tool of their own Passions. *Emma* had now no Way left to clear her Innocence, but that of an *Ordeal* Trial, in which it was expected that God should visibly interpose in Favour of the injured Person; that Princess was willing to put the Matter on that Issue, and walk'd over nine red hot Plowshares blindfold in the Cathedral of *Winchester*, before a numerous Assembly of the Nobility and Gentry of the Kingdom. Her miraculous Preservation on that Occasion was acknowledged an authentick Justification of her Vertue, and affected the King so that he immediately fell at his Mother's Feet, begg'd Pardon for his Credulity, and underwent a rigorous Penance for his Fault in the Face of the whole Company.

Edward was favour'd with the Gift of Prophesy, as appear'd from several Predictions concerning the miserable End of Earl *Godwin*, the Death of the King of *Denmark*, the Ruin of his Fleet, and several Calamities which fell on this Nation after his Decease. Nor was he less famous for Miracles; one of which is acknowledged hereditary to the Kings of *England*, and the Distemper which is cured upon their Touch is therefore called the *King's Evil*. The many Wonders perform'd at his Tomb recommended him to the Veneration of our pious Ancestors soon after his Death, which happen'd on the fifth of *January* 1066. *William* the Conqueror, who came to the Crown in *October* the same Year, order'd his holy Predecessor's Coffin to be inclosed in a rich Case of Gold and Silver; and in 1102 his Body was taken up entire. Pope *Alexander* III canonized our Saint in Form at the Request of *Henry* II in the Year 1161; and two Years after the venerable Relicks were translated with great

I   Solemnity

St. Callistus, Pope and Martyr.

Oct. 14 Solemnity on the thirteenth of *October*, the Day on which the Church of this Island celebrated his Memory in a more particular Manner than on that of his Death; and, though the *Roman* Martyrologe places his Name on the latter, the Breviary of that Church keeps his Festival on the former.

✣✣

The XIV Day.

Saint *CALLISTUS*, Pope and Martyr.

UPON the Death of *Zephyrinus* toward the Close of the Year 218, *Callistus*, or, as most Latin Writers call him, *Callixtus*, was placed in St. *Peter*'s Chair. He was a *Roman* by Birth, the Son of *Domitius*, and consecrated to the holy See about the Beginning of the Year 219. Since the Persecution raised by the Emperor *Severus*, which ended with his Life in 212, the Church had enjoy'd Repose. *Heliogabalus*, a Prince of an infamous Character had been some Months on the Imperial Throne when our Saint was promoted to the papal Dignity; but his Debaucheries employing his whole Time, and engrossing all his Thoughts, the Christians receiv'd no Molestation in the Practice of their Religion. *Callistus* made the best Use possible of that happy Calm, which was complete when the World was deliver'd of that Monster in the Year 222; for *Alexander*, who succeeded that Prince was so favourably disposed to the Disciples of *Jesus Christ*, that he allow'd them more Liberty than they had ever known since the first Foundation of the Church. The Author of that Emperor's Life, a profess'd Pagan, gives the following Instance of his Regard for the Professors of our most holy Religion; A Dispute happening between the Inn-keepers of *Rome* and the Christians of the same City about Piece a of Ground, the Emperor decided it in Favour of the former, 'though their Adversaries accused them of entring on Possession of it to the Prejudice of the Publick. Those who tell us our Saint built a Church on that Spot of Ground advance nothing but what is extremely probable, if we may believe what some Authors of great Credit have said, *viz.* that the Christians began to erect publick Edifices for divine Worship in *Alexander*'s Reign. But the most considerable Work that has been ascribed to our Saint is a Burial Place, which he made on the *Appian* Road, the largest and most celebrated of the Kind, for the Reception of the Bodies of Martyrs.

Alexander's

Alexander's Inclination to favour the Christians did not prove a perfect Security for those People, while the Laws of the Empire against Innovations in Religion stood unrepeal'd, or the Populace lay under no particular Restraint in that Particular. Several Christians fell a Sacrifice to the blind Zeal of the Rabble, or the Malice of Men in Power; and our Saint is usually reckon'd one of those who suffer'd for the Faith at that Time; 'though some Place his Death in 233, others in the following Year. The fourteenth of *October* is universally allow'd to be the Day of his Martyrdom, and is that on which the *Roman* Martyrologe honours his Memory.

The XV Day.

Saint *TERESA*, Virgin.

TERESA, a Native of *Avila* in the Kingdom of *Castile*, was born on the twelfth of *March* 1515. Her Parents were both of ancient and noble Families, and such as made a very considerable Figure in the World; but their Personal Merit was what distinguished them much more than the illustrious Names of their Ancestors. *Alphonso* our Saint's Father had several Children by a former Wife, and by *Beatrix* her Mother. *Teresa*, the youngest of three Daughters, was happy in Parents who made it their first Principle in the Education of their Children to commend and favour nothing but Vertue in their Presence. *Alphonso*, who had the Character of Honour, Probity, Sincerity, Integrity, and Charity, was particularly fond of good Books, and took Care to be always furnished with a considerable Stock of them in the vulgar Tongue for the Improvement and Instruction of his Children. The Use which *Teresa* made of this favourable Opportunity, join'd to her Mother's Care of her religious Education, inspired her with the first Sentiments of Devotion, which were very warm when she was scarce seven Years old. She was her Father's chief Favourite, a Distinction founded on the excellent Dispositions which the Almighty had form'd in her; and the same Motive made the Saint herself prefer *Rodriguez* to her other Brothers, 'though she loved them all. He was about four Years older than *Teresa*; and, as their Inclinations seem'd to point the same Way, they sate down to read the Saint's Lives together. 'Though our Saint was very young when she enter'd on that Task, she had then so exalted an Idea of the inestimable Value of the Kingdom of Heaven that upon perusing the Account of the Sufferings of the Martyrs, she concluded they had procured eternal Happiness at a small Expense, and wished she might be immediately allow'd the same Favour at the same Price. *Rodriguez* and *Teresa*, full of such Thoughts and Desires, began to consider of proper Means for obtaining the desired Happiness, and came to a Resolution of going among the *Moors*, where they might reasonably hope for an Opportunity of laying down their Lives for the Name of *Jesus Christ*. Our Saint tells us that while they were employ'd in perusing the Pieces which had inspired them with an ardent Desire of Martyrdom, nothing touched them more than to observe that the Writers of those edifying Accounts frequently inculcated the Eternity of the Pains and Pleasures of the World to come ; *How* ! said they one to another, *for ever? what! will they never end?* and the frequent Repetition of those amazing Words made such a deep Impression on *Teresa*'s Mind, that her whole Thoughts were turned to the narrow Way, which as our Lord assures us leads to Life.

Their Attempt to visit the Infidels in Quest of Martyrdom being defeated by the Authority of their Parents, who did not think either Prudence or Piety would privilege that extraordinary Step, their next Thought was to retire into some Desart ; but that Project had no better Success than the former. These Disappointments could not divert our Saint from the Practice of all the Vertues in her Power, and such Exercises as had the same Tendency with her desired Retirement. She lived as privately as possible in her Father's House, spent a considerable Share of her Time in Prayer, and disposed of her little Allowance to the Poor. *Teresa* was but twelve Years old when she lost her Mother, a Lady of an unblemished Character in Regard of the World, and exemplary at home. But, as the best of People are subject to Failings, that excellent Woman was too fond of Romances, and made no Difficulty of putting those dangerous and monstrous Compositions into the Hands of her Children. *Teresa*, spending much of her Time in her Mother's Company, contracted a Habit of reading those pernicious Books ; which, as she tells us herself, was the first Cause of her Coldness and Indifference to divine Entertainments, and gave her a Taste for the World. Thus corrupted, her whole Thoughts were bent on appearing to Advantage in the World, and attracting the Eyes of Crouds, 'though with no farther View than that of being admired ; but her Vertue never was in more Danger than from her Conversation with a Female Relation of a bad Character, which banished all her good Thoughts, and pious Inclinations, and was very near engaging her in the same vicious Course of Life. The Saint assures us she had then lost all Sense of the Fear of God, and that a Concern for her Honour was her only Restraint. She was

was about fourteen Years old when she stood on the Brink of this Precipice, Oct. 15 and in all human Probability would have been lost, had not her vigilant Father snatched her from the Danger, and placed her in a Convent.

Teresa had not been a whole Week in that religious Retreat when Grace began to arise above the bad Impressions she had receiv'd from her late Companion; her Relish for the World decay'd, and her Aversion to a monastick Life was soon worn out by the frequent Repition of Lessons of Piety, and the Conversation of that holy Community. Never did the Influence of Conversation appear in a stronger Light than in the whole Behaviour of our Saint; for in less than a Year and a half, as her Heart was inflamed with the Love of God, and Eternity the sole Object of her Thoughts and Desires, Prayer was her chief Employment; and her constant Attendance at all the Exercises of the House, to which a Boarder could be admitted, was matter of Edification to that religious Family, who glorified God, for the Victory his Grace had obtain'd. Our happy Convert, remembring the Dangers to which Virtue is inevitably exposed in the Word, and touched with a Sense of her own Weakness, desired to spend the Remainder of her Days in a Cloister; but could not resolve to engage in that Community, which she thought too strict, and austere. Her Mind was floating in this Manner when she fell ill, and her Father took her home. Upon her Recovery she was sent into the Country for the Air, which gave her an Opportunity of visiting her Uncle, who after the Death of his Wife had left the Town with a Resolution of ending his Days in Retirement. That Gentleman's Discourse on the great Truths of Salvation, his solid Reflexions on the Vanity of the World, and the Importance of Eternity sunk deep in her Mind, and inhanced her Inclination to a Monastick Life; but it was above three Months before she could overcome her Aversion to the Fatigues of that State, which Difficulty was encouraged by the Weakness of her Constitution. During that Interval she enjoy'd but little Health; but her Resolution was so strengthen'd by the Perusal of good Books, particularly St. *Jerom*'s Epistles, that she was now entirely bent on flying from the World. Her Father's Affection was the only remaining Obstacle in her Way; for, upon asking his Consent, he opposed the Motion, and press'd her to suspend the Execution of her Designs 'till his Death; *Teresa* on her Side was so urgent for Leave to follow what she was persuaded was a Call from Heaven that he granted her Request, and she enter'd the Convent of *Carmelite* Nuns at *Avila* on the second of *November* 1535, being then in her twenty first Year. Till that Time the Saint observes her best Motions were full of Imperfection; but, as the same holy Woman

informs

Oct. 15 informs us, she had no sooner taken the Religious Habit, but the miserable Remains of Concupiscence were expell'd by a predominant Charity; and all the low and unworthy Views which had entertain'd her Mind or raised her Passions, vanish'd and made Way for Love of God. The Conquest of her corrupt Inclinations, and the Courage with which she had trampled on every thing that opposed her Union with the Almighty were rewarded with a plentiful Supply of such Graces as were necessary to support her in her present Station. The Dryness and Coldness of her Soul were now changed into a rapturous Warmth and Tenderness that cannot be described even by those who are favour'd in the same Manner. Penetrated with the divine Flame she found no Difficulty of complying with the most difficult and mortifying Exercises of that Community; and had no other Trouble upon her but that of not attending to the Call of her Heavenly Spouse much sooner.

Our Saint's Fervour might make her less tender of her Health; but could not render her quite insensible to her natural Infirmities, which receiv'd a considerable Increase from her Change of Diet, and new Way of Living. She had always been subject to fainting Fits, which began now to visit her more frequently than ever, and being attended with violent Pains in the Stomach and several other Disorders, reduced her to a very low Ebb. As the Inclosure of Nuns was much less strict before the Council of *Trent* than we see it at present, her Father, finding her Case too hard for all the Means used in the Convent, took her out a few Days after her Profession, and left her in the Hands of a celebrated Physician at *Beceda*. The Season of the Year not allowing her to begin her Course of Physick, she resolved to pass some Time with her eldest Sister, a Lady of an exemplary Life, who was married in the Country; In the Beginning of the following Spring she enter'd on proper Measures for the Recovery of her Health, which however did not succeed; for it was the Will of God to exercise her Patience by a long and violent Indisposition. She had been three Months under the Doctor's Hands when it was very evident that his Medicines were too violent for her Constitution, and endanger'd her Life instead of giving her Relief. In this Condition she was carried to her Father's House, and several Physicians consulted, who agreed in pronouncing her Case desperate. Thus she lay almost three Months in racking Pains without any other Remedy but what she found in a perfect Conformity her Will to that of God; and on the fifteenth of *August* fell into a Swoon, which lasted four Days. Her Father, concluding she would never come to herself, procured her the Sacrament of Extreme Unction, and order'd the Ground to be open'd for her Burial; but before his Directions could be put in Execution *Teresa*, recover'd her Senses, made her Confession, and thank'd Oct. 15 the Almighty for not taking her off in a State so dubious as her Humility made her think her's was.

The Force of our Saint's Distemper had contracted her Nerves, and reduced her to a mere Skeleton; all her Joints seem'd dislocated; and scarce one Limb was capable of performing it's Office. In this miserable Condition she was by her own Direction removed to the Convent, where she continued a Cripple three Years, but an edifying and instructive Example of Patience and Submission to the divine Will. 'Though she had Resignation enough to be contented with her Infirmities, she frequently petition'd for a Cure with the sole View of serving God with more Vigour and Alacrity than she had done before. Several particular Devotions were perform'd by the Saint and others by her Direction to this End; all which consisted in the Celebration of Masses, and the Use of other approved Prayers. She then put herself under the Protection of St. *Joseph*; and was convinced of the Force of his Intercession by several Favours both spiritual and corporal. Gratitude to her Patron, and a Sense of his being particularly dear to the Almighty, were her Motives for recommending the Veneration of that great Saint to others with a charitable and religious Zeal.

Upon the Recovery of her Health it would be reasonably expected that she should consecrate it without Reserve to the Being from whose Bounty she receiv'd that Favour. But, for her more effectual Humiliation, it pleased God to permit her to fall into a surprising Relaxation in her Devotions, and pious Exercises. Finding her Soul divided by Distractions, and her Mind disturbed with vain and useless Discourses, she was ashamed to approach the Almighty, or attempt a Conversation with him by Prayer, while in that imperfect Way. Upon her leaving God in this Manner, she lost all those spiritual Comforts which attend a close Familiarity with that excellent Being and inexhaustible Fountain of Joys; and the Devil took this Opportunity to prevail with her to leave off mental Prayer, under a Pretence of Humility and Unworthiness. *Teresa* continued, however, to join with the Community in vocal Prayers, and her Exteriour was perfectly regular; which procured her the Affections and Esteem of the whole House. As a Proof of their Confidence in our Saint, she was allow'd at least as much Liberty as the eldest Member of that devout Family, which exposed her to continual Distractions in a House where secular Visitants were too freely admitted. In the Year 1542 she left the Convent, and paid her last Duties to her Father; after which she return'd with a full Resolution of re-assuming the Practice

Oct. 15 of mental Prayer, according to the Advice of a pious *Dominican* to whom she had made her Confession; but found it no easy Task. The Struggle between Grace and Nature upon this Occasion, 'though it lasted several Years, was not to be perceived by any but the Person who felt it; for how imperfect soever she might seem in her own Eyes, even the most clearsighted of those who conversed with her look'd on her as a Model of Perfection, which few could attain to. The Frailty of her Nature, amidst the innumerable Favours which the Almighty heaped on her, was the common Subject of her Grief, and the Cause of many Tears. The Want of a good Director was a sensible Affliction to the Saint; for, as she tells us, it was long before she found one who understood her Dispositions, and had both Knowledge and Charity enough to conduct her in a Way suitable to the Situation of her Interiour. She continued near twenty Years in perpetual Anxiety, and labouring under such Afflictions of Mind as might justly give her the Character of a living Martyr to the Love of God. Nothing was more instrumental in restoring her Peace of Soul than the Example of the Convert in the Gospel, *whose many Sins were forgiven, because she loved much*; she had a particular Confidence in the Intercession of that illustrious Penitent, and hoped her Prayers might procure her the same Comfort from *Jesus Christ*. St. *Augustin*'s Confessions were of great Use to our Saint on this Occasion; and she professes that she felt the same Struggle in her Soul which that great Man describes as preceeding his entire Conversion.

Teresa, thus happily reinstated in the Possession of those spiritual Comforts, which result from a close Union of the Soul with it's Author, soon became the Subject of the publick Discourse. The Raptures she felt at the Time of mental Prayer, and the Suspension of all the Operations of the Soul by a strong Attention to God were of so extraordinary a Nature that several Persons of the strictest Piety express'd their Dislike of what they did not yet understand, and interposed their charitable Endeavours to preserve her from what they thought an Illusion. The Characters of those excellent Spiritualists gave our Saint no small Uneasiness; and she was so apprehensive on that Head that she was ready to quit the Practice of mental Prayer, which she began now to suspect might not be agreeable to, nor encouraged by God; but was advised to continue that seraphical Commerce with Heaven by a Priest of the Society of *Jesus*, who clear'd up her most material Difficulties on that Article. About the same Time *Teresa* had the Happiness to converse with St. *Francis Borgia*; and upon consulting that holy and judicious Man, was confirm'd in her Prayer, for he assured her it proceeded from the Spirit of God. Upon that Father leaving *Avila*, Providence directed her to another able and pious Priest
of

of the same Society, who led her on to a farther Degree of Perfection with a happy Mixture of Prudence and Severity. In Order to fix her Mind entirely on the great Object of her Devotions, that excellent Director let her know she must divest herself of all particular Friendships; a Lesson that sounded very harsh in the Ears of one, whose generous Temper strongly inclined her to make a Return of Affection to all who profess'd a particular Regard for her, which 'till then she had thought no less than an Act of strict Justice. But the Saint was resolved to sacrifice all to God, and tear every thing from her Soul which could prove an Impediment to the Perfection after which she aspired. When she had gain'd this Victory over herself, she could truly say she loved no Creature but in God, and for God.

From that happy Day *Teresa* was by the Power and Goodness of the Almighty transform'd, as it were, into another Person. She was so sensible of the Change, that she look'd on herself as a new Creature and pour'd out her Soul in Expressions of Gratitude for this miraculous Deliverance from the Clogs of the World. A particular Enumeration of the Favours, which our Saint receiv'd from Heaven, and the many Visions which encouraged her Perseverance would rather amaze than edify our Readers; and, as we propose in the Course of this Work rather to instruct than surprize, we shall remit the curious to her own Account of her Commerce with *Jesus Christ*, and observe that Vanity had no Share in the Publication of it. Those, who had the Direction of her Conscience, judged it proper to communicate it to the World as a glorious Proof of the Power of God, and an Admonition to weak and imperfect Christians not to despair of surmounting the greatest Difficulties, or give over their Labours, 'though they do not immediately gain their Point. The Saint in Obedience to God's Vicegerents, and out of Zeal for the Glory of her great Benefactor, drew up an exact Description of her Manner of praying, and with Humility and Gratitude gave the whole History of her wonderful Conversation with the Author and Rewarder of those Vertues. This first Piece of her writing, begun in the Year 1561, was composed entirely by our Saint without the least Assistance or Alteration, and submitted to the Examination of the most learned Professors among the *Dominicans*, who were unanimous in approving the Book, and thankful to God for the Favours he had done his Servant, as there set forth. *Bannez*, one of those whose Names appear'd on that Occasion, obliged her some Time after to write her Treatise *Of the Way to Perfection*, and, by the Order of *Jerom of Ripalda*, another of her Directors, she undertook to give the History of her several *Foundations*, which was not finished 'till

Oct. 15 the Close of her Life. We have several other admirable Pieces of sublime Spirituality penn'd by our Saint, and a Collection of her Letters.

When she first took her Pen in Hand in Order to give the World an Account of the Wonders which God had done in her Favour since her Engagement in the *Carmelite* Order, she wished to see that Religious Body shine in it's primitive Beauty, and uniformly established in the rigorous Observance of their Rule; which Desire she communicated to the Nuns among whom she lived, and proposed the Execution of her Design in Favour of the Order. The greater Part of the Community gave into the Proposal immediately; and some Ladies of distinguished Piety in the World proferr'd their Assistance on that Occasion; the former were ready to give their Advice and Interest in promoting the good Design: the latter to contribute considerable Sums toward carrying on this useful Project. Thus powerfully assisted, and depending on the Blessing of Heaven on her Endeavours, she enter'd on the Reformation of the Carmelites, and laid the first Plan of it in the Convent of St. *Joseph*, which she built at *Avila*. She met with much Opposition from several Quarters; but God, who governs the Hearts of Men, inclined the Pope, her Diocesan, and the General of the Order to promote the good Work, which she had undertaken. *Pius* IV granted a Brief for enforcing, or at least authorizing, the aforesaid Reformation; but the Bishop of *Avila* made some Difficulty of putting that Instrument in Execution, because our Saint would neither have Revenues for the House, nor allow her Nuns to bring in their Fortunes, a Scheme which he thought almost impracticable. St *Peter* of *Alcantara*, who had lately made a Regulation of the same Nature in the Order of St. *Francis*, and given our Saint a helping Hand toward drawing up her Scheme, had Credit enough with that Prelate to engage his Approbation of *Teresa*'s Plan, so that on the twenty fourth of *August* 1562 the Affair was concluded to her Satisfaction; the Church dedicated in Honour of St. *Joseph*, and the new Convent inhabited by our Saint and eight Nuns, four of which Number follow'd her from the House in which she took the Habit.

The Saint was scarce settled in this House when she was obliged to leave it and return to her former Monastery; but, when the Storm blew over, she went back to S. *Joseph*'s, and soon found that the late Disturbance was only an Effect of the Divine Goodness which design'd her Sanctification by Patience and Perseverance. The Number of those who enter'd that Convent soon made it necessary to enlarge the Building; and in a few Years a considerable Number of Houses were built for the Reception of such as were disposed to embrace this Reformation; all which was done with the General's Consent, who coming

into

into *Spain*, and examining into the Matter was convinced of the Sanctity and Prudence of *Teresa*, and edified at the Revival of the first Rigour of his Order. Thus authorized she appointed a Prioress, and Subprioress in the new Monastery, with a View of obeying them with as punctual a Simplicity as could be expected from the youngest Nun in the House. But the Superiors of the Order opposed that Regulation, being of Opinion that the same Hand, which had planted, should be employ'd in cultivating; and obliged her to undertake the Government of the Convent at *Avila*, and all others which should receive the same Reformation. *Teresa*, being now irresistably engaged in the great Work, form'd the Monastery of St. *Joseph* in such a Manner as to qualify it for a Model to all other religious Communities of that Sort. The ancient Spirit of the *Carmelite* Rule revived under her Conduct; Silence, Prayer, Meditation, and rigorous Abstinence were prescribed to, and practised by our Saint's small Family; who were to go barefoot in all Seasons of the Year, wear no Linen, never meddle with curious Works, employ themselves in Spinning in their own Cells, and very seldom go to the Grate. The Foundress prevented all Objections and Complaints of the Rigour of these Regulations by her own Example; which convinced them that she exacted nothing from others which she did not practise herself.

Teresa had spent five Years in this Convent when, animated with the Success which God had bestow'd on her Endeavours, she entertain'd Thoughts of reforming the Friars of the same Order. The Bishop of *Avila* shew'd his Approbation of her Design by communicating it to the General, still in *Spain*, desiring his Concurrence in the Affair, and offering to bear the whole Charge of an Essay in his Diocese. The Saint likewise wrote to the General on the same Subject, who readily granted her an unlimited Commission. She had not been long in Possession of this Power, when Providence directed two *Carmelite* Friars to her. She was then at *Medina del Campo*, where she had lately founded a Nunnery; and those Fathers were upon the Point of leaving their Convent in Order to enter among the *Carthusians*.

Teresa, being apprized of their Design, begg'd to speak with them before they put it in Execution; and upon hearing their Reasons for that extraordinary Step, which turn'd chiefly on their Desire of living in the Practice of more severe Mortifications than they could find at home, she advised them to consider the Danger of quitting their first Vocation; assured them they need only comply with her Directions, and might depend on meeting with what they wanted, without altering their former Obligations. In the Conclusion she let them know she had Leave from his Holiness and the General of the Order to do all in her Power toward re-eſtabliſhing the Practice of the Rule in it's primitive Vigour. This Propoſal was perfectly agreeable to the two Friars, who put themſelves into her Hands, and attended her to *Valladolid*, where they took the new Habit, and then carried the Rules, which the Saint had drawn up, to *Durnello*, a ſmall Town in the Dioceſe of *Avila*, where they were ſecure of the Biſhop's Protection, and form'd the firſt Community of Barefooted *Carmelite* Friars on the thirtieth of *November* 1568. About the ſame Time *Tereſa* founded her third Houſe at *Malaga*: the fourth was erected at *Valladolid* the ſame Year; and almoſt every ſucceeding Year of her Life was remarkable for ſome new Eſtabliſhment of that Sort, ſo that ſhe had the Satisfaction of ſeeing ſeventeen Convents of Women, and fifteen of Men, which own'd her their Foundreſs.

Never was any Enterprize more vigorouſly oppoſed, or carried on with more Prudence, Moderation and Reſolution than that in which our Saint was engaged; for the more Oppoſition ſhe met with in the Execution of her Project, the more her Vertue appear'd to Advantage. She was obliged to make frequent Journeys to the ſeveral Places where ſhe eſtabliſhed her Reformation; but her Recollection, Tranquility of Mind, and Obſervance of the Rule were as complete and regular as in the moſt profound Solitude. In the Midſt of theſe pious Labours *Tereſa* fell ſick at *Alva*; where ſhe died on the fourth of *October* 1582

The venerable Body was buried the next Day, which according to the Reformation of the Calendar, begun that Year, was the 15*th*. The Reputation of her Vertue, conſiderably increaſed by ſeveral Miracles perform'd at her Interceſſion made our Saint the Object of univerſal Veneration before ſhe was canonized in Form, which was done by *Gregory* XV in the Year 1622. The Kingdom of *Spain* acknowledges her their Patroneſs, and places her next to St. *James* the Greater.

The XVI Day.

Saint GALLUS, Abbot.

*G*ALLUS, a Native of *Ireland* was born after the Middle of the ſixth Century of Parents conſiderable both for their Birth and Vertue, who put him into the Hands of St. *Colomban* in his Infancy. That holy Monk, of whom we ſhall give a particular Account on the twenty firſt of *November*, found

found him full of excellent Dispositions, which he improved, and had the Happiness of seeing him make a considerable Progress in Vertue and Learning in a little Time. The Abbot of that House was so well pleased with his Skill in expounding the holy Scriptures, that he desired to see him dignified with the Sacred Character of Priesthood; but it is most probable that he did not execute his Design; for the Saint did not receive holy Orders 'till his Journey to *France*, nor then without much Resistance from his Modesty. St. *Colomban* having form'd a Design of leaving his Country, and aiming at a greater Perfection in the penitential Life, chose twelve Monks to accompany him on that Occasion, of which *Gallus* was one. About the Year 589 this devout Body went for *England*, from whence they cross'd over to *France*, and built the Monastery of *Anegray* in the Diocese of *Bezançon*. The Place which they chose for that End was barren, wild, and exactly such as those Penitents could wish. They staid there almost two Years; after which at the Intreaty of some Persons of eminent Piety, who were desirous of enjoying their edifying Conversation, they removed into *Burgundy*, where St. *Colomban* founded the Monastery of *Luxeu* in 592, which soon grew very considerable for Regularity and the Number of it's Inhabitants.

Oct. 16

Gallus spent several Years in that House in all the Tranquility he could desire in a religious Life; but had afterwards his Share in the Mortification which *Thierry* King of *Burgundy*, gave St. *Colomban*. While that Prince exercised the Patience of the Abbot of *Luxeu* by frequent Banishments, our Saint was obliged to fly to *Theodebert* King of *Austrasia* for Protection, where he was soon after join'd by his holy Superior. *Theodebert* receiv'd them as Angels from Heaven, and express'd great Satisfaction in being allow'd to entertain such faithful Servants of God. After some Stay at his Court, *Colomban* desired Leave to go into *Italy* upon some Business with *Agilulf* King of the *Lombards*; but *Theodebert*, could not think of losing so valuable a Person, and therefore begg'd he would choose what Place he pleased in his Dominions, where he might serve God peaceably and instruct his Subjects. The Saint accepted of the Profer, and, after much Opposition from the Idolaters in *Switzerland*, came to *Arbon* on the Lake of *Constance*, where he and his Companions were kindly receiv'd by *Willimar*, a holy Priest of that Town.

Upon Enquiry for a Place proper for the Reception of him and his Monks, *Colomban* was directed to a Desart near *Bregentz*, where he went attended by our Saint and another, and found an old ruinous Chapel, once devoted to the Service of the true God, and since profaned by Superstition and Idolatry. *Colomban*, full of Zeal for the Salvation of Mankind, could not bear to see the

Natives.

Natives of that Country Slaves to the Devil, and therefore order'd our Saint to preach the Gospel to them, because he was well acquainted with their Language. Those deluded People had fix'd three brazen Statues in the Wall of the aforesaid Chapel, which they worshiped as the ancient Gods of their Country to whom they ow'd all they enjoy'd. Upon the Day appointed for the solemn and publick Adoration of those Idols the Concourse of People was very considerable, and St. *Gallus* took that Opportunity of signalizing himself in the Cause of God. When he had reason'd for some Time in a strong and invincible Manner against their abominable Religion, he grew warm, and in the Transports of his Zeal broke the Idols, and threw them into the Lake. Several of his Auditors embraced the Faith; while others, remaining in their Errors, resented the Indignity done to what they esteem'd sacred. But nothing could hinder our Saint from pursuing the good Work, which he had so happily begun. *Columban* sprinkled holy Water in the Chapel, dedicated that Building to the Service of the Almighty, consecrated an Altar, and from that Time Divine Service was regularly perform'd there.

St. *Colomban*'s other Companions, whom he had left at *Arbon*, hearing what had pass'd at *Bregentz*, came thither soon after, built themselves Cells about the Chapel, and join'd the Work of the Hands to their pious Exercises. While every one was employ'd for the Maintainance of the whole Community, it was *Gallus*'s Business to make Nets for Fishermen, or provide Fish for the Rest of that industrious Family of true Monks.

The Infidels, incensed at the Loss of their false Gods, carried their Complaint to Duke *Gunzon* Governor of the Place, which set forth that these Strangers had done nothing since their Arrival but create Disturbances, and hinder the Original Inhabitants from hunting in the Neighbourhood; but, being too much enraged to wait the Decision of the Judge, they stole some Cattle that belong'd to the Monastery, and murther'd two of the Monks. The Governor, who was probably a Christian, but more influenced by politick Reasons than Religion, order'd *Columban* and his Disciples to leave the Country. The Saint, instead of offering any thing in Justification of himself and his Religious Family, obey'd immediately; which he judged most prudent, as things then stood; for *Thierry* had defeated and kill'd his Brother *Theodobert*, and thus made himself Master of *Austrasia*, in which Kingdom the new Monastery lay. *Columban* and his Companions went for *Italy*; but *Gallus* being very ill at that Time was left behind. His Sickness increasing, he was carried to *Arbon*, where *Willimar* receiv'd him with true Christian Charity, gave him two of his Clergy to attend him during his Ilness, and took particular Care to supply him with all

that

that was necessary or convenient for him, while in that Condition. Upon his Recovery, he applied himself to *Hiltibod*, a Deacon of *Arbon*, who was well acquainted with that Country, and desired he would direct him to some convenient Place where he might spend the Remainder of his days in Retirement. *Hiltibod* was so well pleased with our Saint's Design that he engaged to accompany him to a Desart well provided with Water, and the frugal Necessaries of Life, and share the holy Pleasures of Solitude and Piety with him.

Oct. 16

Gallus was too well known in that Part of the World to remain long alone; the Reputation of his Vertue and Miracles soon brought him a great Number of Disciples; and the Magistrate, who had banished him and his Brethren from their former Retreat, being inform'd of his whole Conduct, changed his Mind so far as to promise him all the Service in his Power. We are told that a Daughter of that Governor being miraculously cured of a dangerous Distemper by our Saint, he loaded him with Presents and offer'd him the Bishoprick of *Constance*, then vacant by the Death of *Gaudentius*. *Gallus* accepted of that Nobleman's Presents with a View of bestowing them on the Poor at *Arbon*, but declined the proferr'd Dignity with a becoming Modesty. The Duke, not satisfied with the Refusal, assembled the Bishops of that Province; who, being directed to proceed to the Choice of a Pastor for the Church of *Constance*, were unanimous in naming our Saint to that Post. *Gallus* still persisted in his Resolution of remaining in his humble State; and by Way of Excuse let the Electors know it was his Opinion that he could not accept of the vacant See without his Abbot's Permission; adding that it was not probable that *Columban*, who had forbid him to say Mass when he left him, would consent to that Promotion. Finding him invincible on that Article, the Bishops desired he would at least oblige them so far as to recommend a proper Person to their Choice. *Gallus* named *John*, a Deacon and one of his religious Family, who was placed in the Episcopal Chair without any farther Enquiry into his Morals, and Capacity; and the Saint made a Sermon at his Consecration, which is extant at this day among other valuable Pieces in a Book intituled *The Library of the holy Fathers*.

After some Days Stay with the new Bishop, which were employ'd in furnishing him with Directions for his Conduct in that exalted Station, he return'd to his Desart, where he built a Church, and raised twelve Cells for his Monks. This was the humble Beginning of the famous Abby of St. *Gall*, which is still standing in the Diocese of *Constance*, surrounded by a Town of the same Name. That House is now govern'd by St. *Benedict*'s Rule, and among

others

other Privileges annex't to it, the Abbot is a Prince of the Empire. *Gallus* had pass'd above two Years without approaching the Altar; but, as the Prohibition reached only to the Time of *Colamban*'s Death, being inform'd of that Event in a Vision, he reassumed the Exercise of his Functions, and said Mass for the Repose of his dear Master's Soul. When he had finished the tremendous Sacrifice, he dispatched his Deacon, whom the Author of his Life calls *Magnoald*, to a Monastery in the Territories of *Milan*, where St. *Colomban* had resided since he left *Switzerland*, to inform himself of the Truth; where he was assured of what the holy Abbot had declared. This happen'd in 615 and ten Years after the Monks of *Luxeu*, having lost their Superior, deputed six of their Number to entreat our Saint to undertake the Government of that Monastery. *Gallus*, who had refused to accept of the Bishoprick of *Constance*, declined the Proposal on the same Motives of Humility; for that Abbey was then grown very considerable for it's large Revenues and the Honours annex'd to it by the Benevolence of temporal Princes.

Gallus, always maintain'd a close Union with *Willimar*, his old Friend, and Benefactor. Being now both well advanced in Years, and seldom meeting, that Priest, he complain'd of the Seperation in such Terms as express'd his Value for our Saint, and thinking his End near, earnestly entreated him to make one Journey more to *Arbon*, and allow him the Satisfaction of embracing him once more before he left the World. The Saint complied with his Request, reached *Arbon* some few days before the Feast of the Dedication of the Church in that Town, and preached to a numerous Congregation assembled on that solemn Occasion. This is the last Act we find recorded of the holy Abbot, who fell ill three days after that Festival, and died there after four days Sickness on the sixteenth of *October*. Authors are divided on the Year of his Passage to Immortality; but the most probable Opinion is that he finished his Course in 646.

John, whom our Saint's Interest had placed in the See of *Constance*, was then alive, and removed his Body to his Hermitage, where God manifested the Sanctity of his Servant by Miracles. The *Roman* Martyrologe honour, his Memory on the Day of his Departure.

The

The XVII Day.

Saint *HEDWIGIS*, Dutchess of *Poland*.

THE Princess, whom the Church honours this day among her Saints, was Daughter to *Berthold*, Duke of *Carinthia*, Marquis of *Moravia*, and Count of *Tirol*, and *Agnes* Daughter to the Count of *Rotlech*, and happy in an Innocence and Integrity which made her much more confiderable than her illustrious Birth. All her Inclinations were turned to Vertue as soon as she was capable of distinguishing Good from Evil, and she discover'd no Marks of Levity even in her Infancy. She was placed very young in the Monastery of *Lutzingen* in *Franconia*, and there instructed in the holy Scriptures, which proved her greatest Comfort in the whole Course of her Life. At twelve Years of Age she was married to *Henry* Duke of *Silesia* and *Poland*, a Match in which she engaged more out of Compliance with her Parents than any Inclination to that State. After the Birth of her sixth Child she engaged her Husband to perpetual Continence; to which they obliged themselves by an express Vow in the Presence of their Bishop; and after that Solemnity, which could not be kept private, lived apart, and never met but before Company, to avoid giving Scandal to the Weak.

Hedwigis undertook the Education of her Children, whom she form'd to the Service of God with a religious Care, and had the Pleasure of seeing her Labours crown'd with Success. She was particularly diligent in regulating her whole Family by the Maxims of the Gospel; established the Service of God in her House; banished Lies, Detraction, and every thing contrary to Modesty and Decency wherever she had any Authority. At her Persuasion the Duke founded a Monastery for *Cistercian* Nuns at *Trebnitz* near *Breslaw* in *Silesia*. This Building was begun in the Year 1203, the Church dedicated in 1219, and the House so liberally endow'd that it was capable of holding and maintaining a thousand Persons. The holy Foundress furnished it with a great Number of Widows and Maids, among which was *Gertrude*, her own Daughter, afterwards Superior of that Community. The Convent of which we are speaking, was also made a Nursery of Piety for young Ladies, especially such as were reduced by the Misfortunes of their Parents, or other Casualties; those who were disposed to a monastick Life were profess'd in that or any House which they preferr'd; and such as were inclined to the married State were by her Charity placed advantageously in the World.

Oct. 17   The Saint had always entertain'd a contemptible Opinion of all the World calls great, or admires; she carried her Digust of the Vanities of this Life so far as to strip herself of all the gaudy Ornaments, which amuse the greatest Part of her Sex, and wear nothing that could distinguish her from Persons of a lower Rank. Always mindful of St. *Peter*'s Lesson of Modesty and Simplicity to the Women, she had never given into the Practice of setting herself off to Advantage by the little Artifices of Dress, and Decorations which that great Apostle condemns, but directed all her Cares to adorning her Soul in such a manner as might engage the Affections of her Heavenly Spouse. The Simplicity which she had observed, while with her Husband, was upon that Seperation converted into somewhat still more ordinary; for from that Time her Historian tells us she wore only plain gray Stuff. Her Desire of advancing in Perfection put her upon leaving the Palace; and fixing at *Trebnitz* near the Monastery in Company of some devout Persons of her own Sex. While she was there she frequently retired into the House, lay in the Dormitory, complied with all the penitential and pious Exercises of that Community; and nothing but a Desire of continuing her Assistance to the Poor hinder'd her from embracing a Religious State. The Duke, her Husband, was so far from being dissatisfied with her Conduct, that he made it his Business to copy her Example as far as his Station in the World would allow. His whole Thoughts were directed to administring Justice to his Subjects, and making Religion flourish in his Dominions by Christian Laws. He observed the Modesty and Recollection of a Monk in the Midst of a Court, and was acknowledged by all the Father of his People, the Support of the Weak, and a complete Model for his Subjects in all that related to Piety. We should have thought the Duke's Panegyrick unseasonable when we undertake to speak only of the Dutchess, if we did not consider that his Commendation has a direct Tendency to inhance her Character in the Minds of our Readers, whose excellent Example incited that Prince to the Practice of such Vertues as seldom appear on the Seat of sovereign Power.

  Hedwigis was remarkable for a happy Equality of Temper, and a Tranquility which seem'd proof against all Disturbance. Upon receiving the News of her Husband being wounded in Battle, and taken Prisoner by *Conrad* Duke of *Kirn*, she said without the least Emotion that she hoped to see him at Liberty, and in good Health in a little Time. The Conqueror rejected all Terms that could be offer'd for *Henry*'s Freedom; which untractable Obstinacy obliged his Son of the same Name to raise an Army, and attempt his Rescue. *Hedwigis* had a Soul too tender and full of Humanity to hear of the

Effusion

1.Ep.3.3

Effusion of Christian Blood without doing all in her Power toward diverting Oct. 17 that Evil; which inspired her with a Resolution of going in Person to *Conrad*, and soliciting her Husband's Delivery. The very Appearance of that vertuous Lady struck the haughty Duke with Terror, disarm'd him of all his Rage, and awed him into a Compliance with her Demands.

In the Year 1238 the good Duke of *Poland* died; and the Nuns of *Trebnitz* express'd their Sense of that Loss by Tears, and other Marks of Grief, while *Hedwigis* was the only Person who could think of the deceased Prince with dry Eyes; she urged Resignation to the Will of God, and the Unreasonableness of such an ungovern'd Grief, with a Serenity of Mind, and Composure of Features which shew'd her a great proficient in the Vertues which she recommended. Three Years after her Patience was put to another severe Trial by the Death of *Henry the pious*, her eldest Son, who fell in an Engagement with the *Tartars*. His Widow and Sister, then Abbess of *Trebnitz* were inconsolable upon hearing of that Misfortune; but *Hedwigis* in the same uniform Spirit of Resignation, enforced that excellent Disposition of Mind to the two young Ladies, and taught them to join her in adoring, and submitting to the impenetrable Decrees of God, who is absolute Master of his Creatures.

The remaining Part of our Saint's Life was one continued Series of Pennance, Devotion, and Charity. Ever since the Year 1203 she had abstain'd entirely from Meat; her Brother the Bishop of *Bamberg*, and several others, whom she esteem'd, had endeavour'd to prevail with her to treat herself with less Severity; but in vain. She never broke through this Rule which she had imposed on herself, but once, in Compliance with the Commands of *William of Modena*, Legate from the holy See, who employ'd all the Authority of his Character to obliged her to eat Meat, when much indisposed. Her usual Method since the aforesaid Year had been to live on Bread and Water on *Wednesdays* and *Fridays* and all the Fasts of the Church: on *Mondays* and *Saturdays* Herbs and Roots were her only Food; and on *Sundays*, *Tuesdays*, and *Thursdays* she allow'd herself Fish, and Whitemeats; she wore a coarse Haircloth next her skin; walk'd barefoot in the roughest Roads; and took a short Repose on the Floor cover'd with a Skin.

It is impossible to express the exact Recollection, which she observed when at Prayers; and much more so to convey a just Idea of the Transports of her holy Soul while thus conversing with her God. Her Attendance on the publick Service of the Church was constant, and her Behaviour there particularly edifying. Her Charity had no other Bounds but the Necessities of her Neighbours; and not only her Fortune, but all the Gifts with which Heaven had

Oct. 18 favour'd her, were employ'd for the Relief and Comfort of the Miserable; of this Sort was the Power of Miracles, with which the Almighty had entrusted her.

The Author of our Saint's Life tells us she had the Gift of Prophesy, which enabled her to foresee her own Death some Days before she fell into her last Sickness. It conducted her to the Port of eternal Rest on the fifteenth of *October* 1243. Her Body was deposited in the Church belonging to the Convent of *Trebnitz*, where her Sanctity and Glory were manifested by a great Number of Miracles, which hasten'd her Canonization. That Ceremony was perform'd with due Solemnity by *Clement* IV on the Anniversary of her Decease in 1267, the Day on which the Roman Martyrologe mentions her Name; but *Innocent* XI, who was raised to the holy See in 1676, placed the Office of our Saint on the seventeenth of *October*.

The XVIII Day.

St. LUKE, Evangelist.

Rom. 16, 21. ST. *Luke*, was a Native of *Antioch* in *Syria*, and Relation of St. *Paul*, but educated in pagan Superstition. He was brought up to Learning from his Infancy; and his own Writings are a sufficient Proof of his thorough Acquaintance with the *Greek* Tongue; which has led some to conclude him a *Grecian* by Birth. Some Authors suppose he became a *Jew* before he profess'd the Faith of *Christ*; but others are of Opinion that he pass'd from Paganism to Christianity; and the Title of *Proselyte*, which is given him by the Ancients, may be applied to our Saint 'though he never receiv'd Circum-

Col. 4. 14 cision, or practised the Law of *Moses*. He was a Physician before his Conversion; and in all Probability profess'd the same Art after he engaged in the School of *Jesus Christ*; for St. *Jerom* assures us he was very eminent in his Way.

Our Saint was the inseperable Companion of the Apostle of the Gentiles;
Acts 16. but it is not certainly known when he began to follow him. We find, indeed, that he was with him when he travell'd from *Troas* to *Macedonia* about the Year fifty one; and we have good Reason to believe he never quitted his Master for any considerable Time 'till his last Imprisonment at *Rome*. He
v. 12. spent some Days with St. *Paul* at *Philippi*, according to his own Account of
the

the Matter; but has not told us how he was employ'd or where he went from that Time to the Apoſtles Journey to *Jeruſalem*, which happen'd about ſix Years after. During this Interval it is ſuppoſed he wrote the Goſpel, which bears his Name. St. *Matthew* and St. *Mark* had already publiſhed their Account of our Saviour's Life and Actions; but other pretended Goſpels appearing at that Time, from which the Truth ſuffer'd very much, our Evangeliſt thought proper to inſtruct his illuſtrious Friend *Theophilus* and the whole Chriſtian Church in the aforeſaid Particulars, as he receiv'd them from the Apoſtles, and others who had attended our Lord during the whole Courſe of his publick Miniſtry. It is uſually thought, that whenever S. *Paul* uſes the Phraſe *my Goſpel*, he means this Piece; but then the Meaning of that Way of ſpeaking, according to St. *Irenæus*, is, that *Luke* wrote the ſame Doctrine which the Apoſtle had taught and preached, or that he ſet him on that Work.

Oct. 18

Luke. 1.

About the Year 56 St. *Paul* ſent our Saint with *Titus* to *Corinth*; for St. *Jerom*, who is follow'd by all Commentators in that Point, expreſsly, ſays *Luke* is the Man whom the Apoſtle commends ſo highly in his ſecond Epiſtle to the *Corinthians*. He tells that People the Church had aſſign'd him that excellent Perſon as a Companion in his evangelical Labours. Not long after they arrived at *Corinth*, St. *Paul* went to that City; and from thence wrote his Epiſtle to the *Romans*, in which he mentions our Saint by the Name of *Lucius*, and calls him his Kinſman. But we have already ſaid, after S. *Jerom*, that the Evangeliſt was St. *Paul*'s inſeperable Companion 'till his Death; and conſequently the Travels of that Apoſtle were thoſe of our Saint.

c. 8. v. 18. &c.

c. 16. v. 21.

The *Acts of the Apoſtle* are by St. *Jerom* and moſt antient Writers attribubuted to St. *Luke*; whoſe chief Deſign in that Work ſeems to have been to give the Hiſtory of his Maſters Labours and Sufferings for the Goſpel, which he had done in a plain and unaffected Manner, 'though in an elegant Stile, and brought his Account of that great Apoſtle down to the ſecond Year of his Stay at *Rome*, the Time when he compoſed that Piece. Some have believed him the Author of the Epiſtle to the *Hebrews*; and others made him only Tranſlator of that Book from the Language of that People; both theſe Opinions are founded on the Semilitude of the Stile.

We know but little of St. *Luke*'s Hiſtory after St. *Paul*'s Martyrdom. According to St. *Epiphanius*, he undertook to preach *Jeſus Chriſt* in *Italy*, *Gaul*, *Dalmatia*, and *Macedonia*. The moſt feaſible Account of his Death places it in *Patras*, a City of *Achaia*; and St. *Jerom* ſays it happen'd in his eighty fourth Year, without ſpecifying the Manner of it. The Emperor *Conſtantius* removed the venerable Relicks to *Conſtantinople* in the Year 357, where they

were

Oct. 19 were receiv'd with great Solemnity, and laid in the Church built by *Constantine* the Great in Honour of the twelve Apostles. Our Saint's Festival is observed on the eighteenth of *October* by the Churches of the East and West; and his Name stands among those of Saints of the first Rank in the Calendar of the Church of *England*.

The XIX Day.

St. *PETER* of *ALCANTARA*.

THE Saint, whose Memory we celebrate this Day was born at *Alcantara* a small Town in the Province of *Estramadura* in *Spain* in the Year 1499. *Alphonso Garavito*, his Father, was a Lawyer by Profession, and entrusted with the Government of that Town: *Mary Villela de Sonabria* his Mother, a Lady of good Extraction; but both more valuable for their Piety and personal Merit than the Rank they bore in the World. Upon the first Dawn of Reason, *Peter* discover'd such happy Dispositions to Virtue, and was so constant and indefatigable in his Addresses to Heaven as soon as he understood his Dependence on God, that his Parents had good Reason to hope for all in him that could be desired in a Child. He had not finished his Philosophy in his own Country when his Father died; but that Loss was supplied in some Measure by a worthy Gentleman, who married his Mother, and sent him to study the Canon Law at *Salamanca*. During the two Years, which he spent in that University, his Life was perfectly regular, and his whole Time divided between his Closet, the publick Schools, the Church and the Hospital.

In 1513 he was recalled to *Alcantara*, where the Devil attack'd him with ambitious Thoughts, and insinuated how considerable a Figure he might make in the World, if he would but pursue what seem'd within his Reach. But God supported him with his Grace, gave him the Victory over his subtle and vigilant Enemy, and inspired him with a Resolution of embracing a religious Life, where he might have no Concern but that of securing his own Salvation. The Order of St. *Francis* was *Peter*'s Choice; and he took the Habit in the Convent of *Manjarez* situated in the Mountains which run between *Castile* and *Portugal*. The Saint was but sixteen Years of Age when he enter'd that House; but his Zeal, and the extraordinary Marks of a true Vocation facilitated his Admission; and his Behaviour during his Noviceship

was

was such as left no Room to doubt of his being directed thither by the Spirit of God. His Fasts were rigorous; his Meals and Rest short; the most mortifying Austerities had nothing frightful or difficult for him; his Disengagement from the World and Union with his Creator suffer'd nothing from his various Employments in the Monastery. He had first the Care of the Vestry; then, of the Gate, and afterwards of the Cellar; all which Offices he discharged with uncommon Exactness, and without the least Dissipation.

A few Months after his Profession, *Peter* was sent to a remote and solitary Convent at *Belviso*; where he built himself a Cell at some Distance from the rest, with Mud and the Branches of Trees, in which he spent the Day, and practised his Mortifications without Interruption or being seen; a Pleasure which he enjoy'd some Time without Discovery, and about three Years after was sent to *Badajoz* by his Provincial. His Business there was to appear at the Head of a new Community lately established in that City, the Metropolis of *Estremadura*; and we may easily judge what were his Superiors Sentiments of our Saints Prudence, and other Qualifications, when we consider him in that Situation before he was twenty one Years of Age. When he had spent three Years in that Post, the Time fixt by the Rules of the Order for holding the Office of Guardian, he receiv'd his Provincial's Command to prepare for holy Orders. All the Excuses and Objections, which his Humility could form on that Occasion did but confirm his Superior's Resolution of being obey'd; so that he was obliged to receive Priesthood in the Year 1524, and was soon after employ'd in Preaching. The ensuing Year our Saint was made Guardian of the Convent of *Our Lady of the Angels*; in which Station he consider'd himself as a Servant to the whole Communnity, and would be distinguished from them only by the indispensible Obligation of encouraging them in the Practice of Penance by his own Example.

Upon quitting that Post Preaching was his chief Employment, and the Word of God in his Mouth produced surprizing Effects in the Hearts of his Auditors. The Success of his Labours in that Way encouraged him to continue them six Years together, after which he made it his earnest Petition to be placed in a Convent, where he might enjoy the Pleasures of religious Solitude, and divine Contemplation. In Complyance with his Request, *Peter* was sent to that of *Lapa*; but at the same Time was commanded to undertake the Government of that House. While he was there he composed a small Treatise *On Prayer and Contemplation*, at the Instance of a particular Friend, who had often heard him discourse on that Subject, and was desirous of seeing his excellent Rules in Writing. The Reputation of the Author made every

one

Oct. 19 one eager to peruse that Piece; and in a little Time it found it's Way to the most distant Parts of *Spain*. All the Franciscan Monasteries, and some others receiv'd it as a Rule for the Conduct of their Novices in the Practice of Prayer; and it procured him the Friendship and Esteem of the most celebrated Masters of spiritual Life. The Publick, upon reading this Treatise, conceived so exalted an Idea of the Saint, that he had pressing Invitations from all Parts to preach the Word of God. *John* III, King of *Portugal*, being acquainted with his Character, desired to see him at *Lisbon*. *Peter* could not decline that Journey, enforced by the Command of his Provincial, when he was assured that his Presence might promote the Glory of God, and be instrumental in the Salvation of his Neighbour; but made it on Foot. He appear'd a second Time at that Prince's Court soon after; and, during his stay there, converted several Persons of the first Rank. The Infanta *Mary*, Sister to the King, did all in her Power to retain him there; but *Peter* had no Relish for the Splendour, and Noise of a Palace; and the Superiors of his Order, who design'd him for a more extensive Mission, were not well pleased at his being confin'd to so narrow a Corner of the World. While the Saint was in this uneasy Situation the Inhabitants of *Alcantara*, being divided, came at last to a Resolution of referring their Case to him, and acquiescing in his Determination; which made it necessary for him to hasten to that City; and the King of *Portugal*, and his devout Sister were too good to oppose so charitable a Work.

As soon as *Peter* had restored Peace among the Inhabitants of *Alcantara*, he was chosen Provincial of *Estramadura*. His Age was then inferiour to what was required for that Post; but that Difficulty, 'though warmly urged by himself, was allow'd no Weight; all being persuaded that he was old enough, because full of Vertue and Prudence. His Conduct sufficiently justified their Choice; for he acquitted himself of all the Duties of that Station with universal Applause and, when his Time was expired, made a Journey into *Portugal* in Company with some of the most vertuous of his Brethren, where he laid the first Foundations of the reform'd Province of *Arabida*. The Place which bore that Name was a Cluster of barren Mountains, and consequently very well suited to the Design of our Saint and his Companions. Upon their Arrival to this Scene of Penance, they applied to the Duke of *Aveiro* for Leave to settle there; who not only granted their Request but assisted them in raising Cells in the habitable Parts of the Place. The new Hermits led a very austere Life in the Mountains: they wore nothing on their Feet; lay on

Bundles

Bundles of Vine Twigs, or the bare Ground: Neither Meat nor Wine were admitted to their Table; and Fish appear'd only on Festivals. *Peter* undertook to awake the rest at Midnight; at which Time they said their Mattins together, and continued in Prayer 'till break of Day. Then they repeated *Prime*, which was follow'd by one Mass only, according to the original Regulation of their holy Founder St. *Francis*; and the Afternoon was divided between Acts of Devotion and Labour. They had not been long in that Desart when they obtain'd the General's Leave to admit Novices; and a Grant of the Convent of *Palbaës* for their Reception and Trial. *Peter* was obliged to undertake the Government of this new House, and the Direction of such as presented themselves.

The intended Reformation being now on a good Foot, our Saint was in the Year 1544 recalled into *Spain*. His Provincial's Design in that Order was to engage him in the Service of the several Churches in his own Country, who desired nothing more than to receive the great Truths of Salvation from his Mouth. But *Peter's* Love of Retirement, which was now his predominant Passion, carried him to the most retired Convent he could find; and, after four Years spent in that Manner, he was allow'd to return to *Portugal*, at the Request of Prince *Lewis* the King's Brother, and his old Patron the Duke of *Aveiro*. During the three Years, which *Peter* remain'd in that Kingdom, he raised his new Congregation to a very flourishing Condition; but his Reputation for Sanctity drew so many Eyes on him, and gave so much Interruption to his Retirement that he hasten'd back to *Castile*, where he hoped to enjoy more Quiet.

In the Year 1554 our Saint form'd a Design of establishing a Body of Friars in the rigorous Practice of St. *Francis's* Rule, as given by himself; and upon offering his Plan to *Julius* III, then in St. *Peter's* Chair, he obtain'd a Brief from his Holiness; which was receiv'd by the Provincial of *Estremadura*, and approved of by the Bishop of *Coria*, who gave him an Hermitage in his Diocese; where he and one Companion might make an Essay of what they proposed. After some Trial, *Peter* went to *Rome*, where he was favour'd with a second Brief from the Pope, and Letters from his General empowering him to erect a new Convent, according to his Scheme. At his Return he executed his Project with the Assistance of some Persons of Quality, who were glad to contribute to that good Work. The House was built near *Pedroso*; and by his Direction it was but thirty two Feet long, and twenty eight wide. The Cells were so small that it was impossible his Disciples should forget their Engagement in a penitential Life, while lodged there.

Oct. 19. When *Charles* V began to entertain serious Thoughts of resigning the Crown of *Spain* to his Son *Philip*, and the Imperial Scepter to his Brother *Ferdinand*, and end his Days in a Monastery, he desired to put his Conscience under the Direction of our Saint; but could not prevail with him to undertake that Charge. *Peter* had not the same Success when his General named him Commissary for reforming the Order in the whole Kingdom of *Spain*. Being invested with that Authority, he made Use of it for promoting the particular Reformation, which he had begun with universal Approbation. About that Time the Saint, going to *Avila*, contracted an Acquaintance with St. *Teresa*, and was very serviceable to that holy Woman in solving her Doubts, and dispelling some Clouds which then hung on her Mind. He examin'd into her Manner of praying, spoke much in it's Commendation, and at his Leisure sent her in Writing his Reasons for approving of her Conduct in that Point; which *Teresa* look'd on as so many weighty Decisions in Favour of her Practice, and Rules of Spirituality, on which she might safely depend.

Some Disputes arising between the Houses which had embraced our Saint's Reformation, and those which retain'd their former Discipline, he was obliged to make a second Journey to *Rome*, where *Paul* IV granted him two very considerable Briefs for the Support of his new Institute. At his Return to *Spain*, he had the Satisfaction of observing the Blessing of God attend his Endeavours in so signal a Manner that in less than six Years after he began to execute his Design, there appear'd nine Houses, which own'd him their Founder and Superiour. *Peter* had no small share in St. *Teresa*'s Reformation of the *Carmelite* Order; he removed several Obstacles in that Saint's Way, and was very serviceable to her in pursuing the Work for which that holy Woman is so justly commended.

Peter exerted himself with the utmost Vigour in Favour of his penitential Family 'till the Year 1562. He was seiz'd with a Fever in his Convent of *Viciosa*; from thence he was removed to the Duke of *Orepesa*'s Country Seat; but soon after at his own Request carried to *Arenas*, where he had the Satisfaction of expiring in the Arms of his Brethren on the eighteenth of *October* in the 63d Year of his Age. St. *Teresa* assures us that she was favour'd with a glorious Appearance of her holy Friend and Director after his Death; and that he broke out into this Extasy: *O happy Penance, that is rewarded with so much Glory!*

His venerable Body was buried in the Church belonging to the House in which he died. Some Years after, the Friars with the Bishop of *Avila*'s Permission, took it up, put it into a Coffin, and fixt it in the Wall of their Church.

The Reputation of the Miracles perform'd at his Interceſſion prevail'd with Pope *Gregory* XV to beatify him in 1622; and *Clement* IX canonized him in 1669. His Office is transferr'd to the nineteenth of *October*, becauſe the Day of his Death is taken up with the Feaſt of St. *Luke*.

The XX Day.

St. *ARTEMIUS*, Martyr.

ARTEMIUS, whoſe Memory the Church venerates this Day, was Commander of the Forces in *Egypt*, when *Julian* the Apoſtate came to the Imperial Crown in the Year 361. In that Quality he was to aſſiſt the Prefect or Governor of the Country in keeping the Peace among that mutinous People. The Pagans of *Alexandria*, hearing of the Emperor's Diſpoſition in Regard to Religion, thought this a favourable Opportunity of purſuing their Revenge for what they pretended they had ſuffer'd from him during the two preceeding Reigns. *Julian* coming to *Antioch* in 362, their Complaint was drawn up in Form and laid before that Prince; which turn'd chiefly on two Points, *viz.* his having demoliſhed ſeveral of their Idols in the Time of *Conſtantine* the Great; and aſſiſted *George* the *Arian* Biſhop of *Alexandria*, in plundering the Temples of their Gods. Upon reading their Accuſation the Emperor order'd *Artemius* to repair to *Antioch*, and anſwer to what was urged againſt him by his Enemies. It appear'd at his Trial that the General had really been particularly active in deſtroying Idolatry, and removing the Objects of Pagan Worſhip under *Conſtantine* and his Son *Conſtantius*; a Crime which the Apoſtate could not pardon, and which could be expiated only by the Blood of the Offender. *Artemius* was firſt deprived of his Commiſſion, ſtripp'd of all he had in the World, and then beheaded.

The Sedition at *Alexandria* after the General's Death was a ſufficient Proof of the Intention of the Pagan Inhabitants of that City in taking him off; and his Power was ſo conſiderable that the Apoſtate ironically ſtiled him *the King* of *Alexandria*. The Church has conſecrated his Memory, and honours him among her Martyrs. Both the *Greeks* and *Latins* place his Feſtival on the twentieth of *October*, as appears from the Menologe of the former, and *Roman* Martyrologe.

Julian, writing an Account of his Proceedings againſt *Artemius*, lays the Death of his Brother *Gallus* to our Saint's Charge; but that it is well

Oct. 21 known that that artful Prince usually forged imaginary Articles against such as he persecuted on the Account of Religion, and that *Gallus* lost his Head by the express Order of *Constantius*, who look'd on him as no better than a hot-headed insolent Commander, ripe for Rebellion; and we may judge of the Sense of the Christian Church in Regard of our Saint by the Honour paid to his Memory in the first Ages.

The XXI Day.
St. *HILARION*, Abbot.

HILARION, the Founder of the Monastick Life in *Palestine*, was born toward the Close of the III Century in a small Town about five Miles South of *Gaza*. His Parents, who were Pagans, sent him to take his first Rudiments of Learning at *Alexandria*; but we are not told how he became acquainted with the Christians in that City nor from whom he receiv'd his Instruction in the Faith. St. *Jerom*, his Historian, begins the Account of his Life with a Commendation of his Capacity for Learning, his happy Progress in his Studies, and the Purity and Innocence of his Morals, which procured him the Esteem and Affection of all who conversed with him. He was a great Proficient in the Art of speaking; but his most substantial Commendation is that, being full of Faith and the Love of God, he preferr'd religious Assemblies to profane Shows, and always chose rather to pray than divert and amuse himself.

Hilarion, having heard of St. *Anthony*, whose Name was than well known all over *Egypt*, made a Visit to that holy Man in his Desart about the Year 306. Upon the Sight of that excellent Solitary, he was struck with a Veneration for his Virtue, which appear'd in every Feature; but his Conversation was so delightful, that *Hilarion* staid with him two Months; during which Time he was very exact in observing every Particular of that Saint's Conduct; but not being able to bear the Crouds that resorted to St. *Anthony* on different Accounts, some for Instruction, others for Cure, he took his Leave of the Desart attended by some of that Great Masters Disciples, who join'd him in the Resolution of fixing in a Way like that of S. *Anthony* in his Youth.

At his Return to his Country, finding his Father and Mother dead he made over Part of his Substance to his Brothers, and gave the other among the Poor. *Hilarion* was not above sixteen Years old when he made this extraordinary Step; after which he retired to a solitary Place about six Miles

from

from *Majuma*, which *Constantine* the Great made a City in Consideration of the Readiness with which it's Inhabitants embraced Christianity in his Reign. His Friends and Relations could not but blame his Choice, and endeavour'd to dissuade him from settling in a Desart, which they assured him was infested with Robbers, and Assassins; but no Danger could deter him from the Prosecution of his Design, and all the Answer he made to their Advice was that he fear'd Nothing but Eternal Death. This Resolution in one so Young and tender as our Saint was both surprizing and edifying to all who knew him; his Constitution was so weak that the least Excess of Heat or Cold affected him very sensibly; and yet his whole Cloathing consisted only of a Piece of Sackcloth, a Leather Coat which St. *Anthony* gave him, and an ordinary short Cloak. At his first entring on that penitential Life he renounced the Use of Bread, and for six Years together his whole Diet was fifteen Figs a Day, which he never took 'till Sunset. When he felt the Attacks of any Temptation he retrenched Part of his scanty Meal; and sometimes spent three or four Days without eating. His Employments in the Desart were digging, and making Baskets; the latter of which provided him with the frugal Necessaries of Life.

During the first four Years of his Penance he had no other Shelter from the Inclemencies of the Air than a sort of Arbor composed of Rushes, and other Greens which he found in a neighbouring Marsh; after that he raised himself a small Hermitage, which was to be seen in St. *Jerom*'s Time; where he Slept on a Rush Mat, and sometimes on the bare Ground. He cut his Hair but once a Year and that at *Easter*; never washed the Sackcloth which he wore next to his Skin; nor put off his Coat while it would hang on his Back. At the Age of twenty one he made some Alteration in his Diet, but not in Favour of his Appetites; for three Years together he lived on a small Quantity of Lentils steep'd in cold Water; and his whole Food for the three next Years was Bread, Salt, and Water. From his twenty seventh Year to his thirty first he eat only wild Herbs, and raw Roots; and from thirty one to thirty five he confined himself to six Ounces of Barley Bread a Day, to which he added a few boil'd Herbs without Oil; which he used afterwards upon finding his Sight decay, and other Inconveniencies resulting from his Manner of living. Thus he went on 'till his sixty fourth Year, when, thinking his Departure not far off, he retrenched his Bread, and from that Time his whole Meal never exceeded five Ounces.

Any one, who knows the Malice and Industry of the Enemy of our Salvation, will easily believe that our Saint did not pass his Days in the Desart without some Disturbance from that infernal Spirit. The Warmth of *Hilarion*'s

Oct. 21 Youth was the first thing that the Tempter employ'd against him; but the holy Hermit reduced the irregular and violent Motions of the Flesh by severe Mortifications and hard Labour. The Adversary, thus worsted, renew'd the Attack, and assaulted the Saint in several Shapes; sometimes that subtle Spirit alarmed him with great Variety of Noises; at others he endeavour'd to afright him with hideous Appearances, and monstrous Spectres; and when all this terrible Artillery proved too weak, he shifted the Scene, and presented him with all that could delight and charm the Senses.

According to St. *Jerom*, our Hermit had spent twenty two Years in his Desart, before it pleas'd God to make him famous for the Gift of Miracles. The first that is recorded is the Cure of Barrenness, which follow'd his Prayers for that Favour; but the miraculous Relief which a young Gentleman of Fashion receiv'd by his Ministry was what considerably inhanced his Reputation. *Elpidius*, who afterwards bore a considerable Office in the Empire, attended by his Wife and three Sons, had lately made a Visit to St. *Anthony* in his Desart; and at his Return his Children were all taken ill of a Fever and Ague, which detain'd the whole Family at *Gaza*. Their Distemper seem'd superior to the Physician's Skill; and the afflicted Mother, a Lady of great Virtue, concluded herself deprived of the Blessing she enjoy'd in them, when upon hearing of our Saint's Character, whose Desart lay near *Gaza*, she set out immediately, attended according to her Quality by some Servants of both Sexes, and found the Servant of God. It was some Time before the Lady could prevail with *Hilarion* to go with her, for he had made a Resolution never to enter any Place that was inhabited; but, conjuring him by the God whom he worship'd, by the sovereign Physician of our Souls, by the Cross and Blood of *Jesus Christ*, she at last engaged his Company to *Gaza*. Coming near the Beds where the Children lay, he called on the Name of our Redeemer with his usual Fervour; and had not been long there when the Children fell into a violent Sweat, which refreshed them so that they were able to eat, knew their Mother, and kiss'd the Hand of their Benefactor. This Miracle, being noised abroad, drew great Numbers from *Syria* and *Egypt* into St. *Hilarion*'s Desart, proved the first Motive to the Conversion of several Heathens, and engaged some Christians to embrace a Monastick Life under our Saint's Direction. 'Till that Time neither *Syria* nor *Palestine* were acquainted with that penitential State, so that he was the first Founder of it in those Countries.

Hilarion was the Instrument in God's Hand for delivering several possess'd Persons from the Power of the Devil. St. *Jerom* mentions two of that Sort,

whose

whose Relief was universally talk'd of in his Time. One of them, whose Name was *Orion*, express'd his Gratitude for the Favour by carrying his whole Family to the Monastery, and laying several rich Presents at the Saint's Feet. " Know " you not, said the Saint, what happen'd to *Giezi* and *Simon*; the former of which " was punished for taking Money for the Gift of the Holy Ghost; the latter " for buying the same Power ? *Orion*, continuing to press the Saint to accept of somewhat at least for the Use of the Poor, was answer'd that He would find more frequent Opportunities of disposing of his Money in that Manner.

Oct. 21

4. King 5
Act. 8,18

A Christian named *Italicus* kept Horses at *Majuma* for the Publick Diversions of the *Circus*, and was engaged in a Match against a Heathen Magistrate of *Gaza*. Being well assured that his Adversary depended on unlawful Arts for Victory, he made his Way to *Hilarion*, and begg'd his Assistance against the superstitious Means that Pagan employ'd. The Saint told him with a Smile that his best Way would be to sell off all his Horses, and bestow the Money on the Poor for the Good of his own Soul. *Italicus* replied that he was obliged by the Laws to appear at the ensuing Games; and that, being a Disciple of *Jesus Christ*, and consequently not allow'd to make Use of Magick, he could not but think he had done well in applying to him on that Subject. The Monks join'd the Petitioner, and urged his Request so warmly that *Hilarion* pour'd some Water into an Earthen Vessel out of which he drank, and bid him sprinkle it in his Stable, on his Horses, their Drivers, and the Barriers of the *Circus*. *Italicus* having punctually complied with the Saint's Directions, and the Affair taking Air, the whole Town was full of Expectation of the Event. The Signal being given, the Horses started; those of *Italicus* seem'd to fly, and those of his Adversary appear'd Leaden-heel'd. This remarkable Difference surprized the Spectators, and even the Pagans cried out, " *Christ* has worsted *Marnas*; for that was the Name of the Idol of *Gaza*. But as they had no Notion of any Power superior to that of Magick, they imagined the Victory owing to a more eminent Skill in that diabolical Art, and therefore in the Transports of their Fury demanded the Delivery of the Christian Magician *Hilarion*, in Order for Punishment; but that Motion was over-ruled by the wisest of their Number; and this remarkable Accident was follow'd by the Conversion of several Infidels.

St. *Hilarion*'s Reputation for Sanctity and Miracles was not confined to the Bounds of *Palestine*, *Egypt*, and *Syria*, but reached the most distant Provinces of the Empire. *Candidatus*, an Officer of the Guards under *Constantius*, who had been troubled with an evil Spirit from his Infancy, made a Journey to his Desart for Relief. At his reaching *Gaza*, he enquired where he might find our holy Monk, and was conducted to his Hermitage by a commanding Offi-

cer

Oct. 21 cer in the Troops attended by the Heads of the Town. *Hilarion*, who was at his Devotions when that numerous Company came up to him, receiv'd them civilly, gave them his Blessing, and after an Hour's Conversation dismis'd all but *Candidatus* and his Retinue, which was very large; for the Saint knew by his Looks, what had brought him thither. The Officer was an entire Stranger to any Language but *Latin* and that of his own Country, which lay beyond the *Rhine*; but, upon the Saint's speaking to him in *Syriack*, and *Greek*, he answer'd in both those Tongues, and pronounced them with the utmost Propriety. The Devil, who had taken Possession of *Candidatus*, offer'd to give an Account how he enter'd, and pretended he had been forced into his Body by Magical Operations. The Saint told the infernal Spirit it was not material how he got Admission into his present Habitation; and commanded him in the Name of *Jesus Christ* to quit it immediately. The Officer, thus deliver'd, desired his Benefactor would accept of a large Sum in Token of his Sense of the Favour; upon which *Hilarion* presented him with a barley Loaf, and observed to him that those, who lived on such Food, valued Gold no more than Dirt. This and many more Miracles of the same Nature drew the Eyes of the whole World on our Saint.

Hilarion began to admit Partners of his Solitude soon after Heaven placed him in so strong a Light by the Gift of Miracles; and in less than twenty Years the Number of his Disciples and Monasteries was such as lead him to complain of the prodigious Extent of his Religious Family as an insupportable Burthen; and the Crouds, which resorted to him for Cure and Relief, made him frequently languish after the Tranquility he enjoy'd in the former Part of his Life.

He visited all those Houses once a Year; on which Occasion he was always join'd by the whole Body that lived under his immediate Direction. He was on one of those Journeys, when he chanced to come to *Elusium* in *Idumea* on the Day devoted by the Idolaters of that Place to the solemn Worship of *Venus*. Being apprized of the Saint's Arrival, who had deliver'd several possess'd Persons in that Country, the People met him in large Companies, and begg'd his Blessing. *Hilarion* spoke to them with all imaginable Sweetness, conjured them to worship the true God, and promised to see them often, if they would receive the Faith of *Jesus Christ*. The divine Grace work'd very powerfully in Favour of that deluded People; for they would not let him leave the Town 'till he had traced out the Plan of a Church; and the very Priest, who was dress'd for the profane Sacrifice, begg'd to be instructed, and admitted to Baptism.

Nothing

Nothing could console our Saint under the Loss of his lovely Solitude, which Oct. 21 was render'd impracticable by his present Situation; and the Monks, apprehending he would leave them for the Pleasures of Retirement, watched all his Motions very narrowly. At last he came to a Resolution of making his Way to some distant Desart, and order'd an Ass to be brought for the Journey; for he was then about sixty three Years old, and his Strength had suffer'd such a Diminution from his rigorous Fasting that he was not able to walk. His Design taking Air, the whole Country was alarm'd, as if threaten'd with with some publick Calamity; and above ten thousand Persons arose to prevent his Journey. The Saint declared his fixt Resolution of removing; and assured them he would neither eat nor drink, while thus detain'd; to which he added, as a Reason for his Departure, that he could not bear to see Churches demolished, the Altars of *Jesus Christ* trampled on, and the Blood of his Children spilt. After seven Days Opposition, finding *Hilarion* inflexible, they consented to his pursuing his own Inclinations, and attended him as far as *Bethel*, where he took his Leave of those Crouds, and continued his Journey with forty Solitaries, all furnished with Provisions, to avoid being burthensome to the Country through which they travell'd. In his Way he visited several holy Solitaries, Bishops and Confessors banished by the *Arians*, and after much Fatigue reached the Monastery of St. *Anthony*, who had then been dead near a Year. After a particular Enquiry into the Particulars of that holy Abbot's Life, *Hilarion* made his Way into the higher *Egypt*, attended only by two Monks, and took up his Habitation in a Desart of that Country, where he practised Abstinence and other Mortifications with a Fervour equal to that of Persons, who are in the first Zeal of their Conversion. After St. *Anthony*'s Decease the Country had been three Years without Rain, a Calamity, which gave Occasion to the Inhabitants to say that the very Elements mourn'd the Loss of that holy Abbot. They came in great Numbers to our Saint, whose Reputation made them hope for Relief by his Intercession, and desired he would offer his Prayers in their Favour. He complied with their Request; and the desired Blessing was granted; but at the same Time a prodigious Multitude of Serpents, and other venomous Creatures appear'd, and infested the Country so that it was once more necessary to have Recourse to *Hilarion* for their Removal or Destruction, and the Cure of such as had been wounded by them. The Honours paid him by the Natives on that Score were so offensive to his Modesty that he left them soon after, and directed his Course to the vast Wilderness of *Oasis*. In his Way thither he visited the Monks of *Brutium* in the Suburbs of *Alexandria*; but left that devout Community the same Evening.

ning. The Monks press'd his Stay among them with all the Arguments in their Power; but he assured them it was necessary for their Security that he should leave them, and therefore persisted in his Resolution of pursuing his Journey. The Sequel shew'd he had the Spirit of Prophesy, and that he spoke by divine Direction, both then, and when he quitted the Desart of *Palestine*, as already related. The Empire was then in the Hands of *Julian* the Apostate; and the Pagans of *Gaza* made Use of his Aversion to the Christian Religion to prosecute their Revenge for the Affront our Saint had put on their Idol *Marnas*, and the Conversions which follow'd that miraculous Defeat. In this View they had destroy'd his Monastery, lodged a Complaint against him, and obtain'd an Order from that Prince for executing him and his favourite Scholar *Hesychius*. The Day after *Hilarion* left *Brutium*, a strong Party from *Gaza* reach'd that Monastery, upon Intelligence that the Object of their Hatred might be found there; and, upon being disappointed said one to another that he well deserved the Character of a Magician, because he foresaw their Pursuit and had provided for his own Security.

The Desart of *Oasis* could not screen him from the Notice and Conversation of Mankind; so that after about a Year spent there he resolved to seek Shelter from the World in the desart Islands. This was his Disposition, when he receiv'd the News of the Apostate's Death and the Succession of a Christian Emperor; which was press'd to him as a favourable Conjuncture for returning to *Palestine*, and rebuilding his Monastery there; but *Hilarion* would not listen to the Proposal, and embark'd for *Sicily* with one Companion. When they were at Sea the Son of the Master of the Vessel, seized by an evil Spirit, cried out to our Saint, mentioning his Name, asked that Servant of God why he pursued him through all the Elements; and begg'd to remain unmolested 'till the Ship reached the Port. *Hilarion* replied that he might stay where he was if God permitted it; and advised him not to impute his Disturbance to a poor Sinner, if he was dislodged by the Almighty. The Child was soon after freed from the Power of the Devil; but the Saint engaged his Father, and the whole Company not to mention him on that Account. Upon landing in *Sicily* the holy Abbot offer'd to pay his Passage and that of his Companion with a Book of the Gospels, written with his own Hand; But the Master, observing their whole Stock consisted in that Manuscript, and the Cloaths on their Backs, would not accept of it.

Hilarion apprehending he should be discover'd by the Eastern Merchants who traded to *Sicily*, if he settled on the Coasts of that Island, went six or seven Leagues up the Country, where he found a wild Place fit for his Purpose.

Purpose. Nothing can be imagined more truly penitential than the Manner in which he and his Companion undertook to live in this new Desart; for beside their Devotions, their Custom was to gather Wood, make a Fagot every Day, and fell it in the Neighbouring Villages for their Maintainance. *Hilarion* had not long enjoy'd the Pleasure of absolute Solitude when a possess'd Person at *Rome* discover'd the Place of his Retreat. The Devil, who was doom'd to destroy his own Kingdom, having declared where the holy Hermit might be found, the unfortunate Man in his Power made his way to his Hut, and receiv'd immediate Relief. From that Time he was visited by great Numbers of infirm People, and others 'till he soon became as famous in *Sicily*, as he had been in *Palestine*. From thence his Reputation was carried into *Greece*; and a *Jew* in *Peloponnesus*, now call'd the *Morea* falling into Conversation with *Hesychius*, then in Quest of his old Friend and Master, told him that the whole Discourse of that Part of the World turn'd on a Christian Prophet, famous for Miracles. This was Mark sufficient for the Discovery of our Saint, and engaged him to cross to *Sicily*, where, finding *Hilarion* resolved to remove to some barbarous Country, where his want of the Language would make his Acquaintance and Conversation with Mankind impracticable, he conducted him to *Epidaurus*, now *Ragusa* in *Dalmatia*; but his Miracles soon defeated his Design of remaining there unknown, the most remarkable of which is what follows, as related by St. *Jerom*. The Earthquake in 365, mention'd by all Writers both sacred, and profane, swell'd the Sea so that *Epidaurus* was in imminent danger of being swallow'd up by the Waves. The Inhabitants of that Town, who were no Strangers to the Gift, which the Saint had receiv'd from God, and had been more than once employ'd in their Favour, went in a Body, and brought the Saint within Sight of the angry Waters. *Hilarion* made three Crosses on the Sand, and then stretched his Hands toward the Sea, which immediately retired and subsided.

This Miracle raised him so many Admirers, and drew such Crouds to him, that he could not think of staying there any longer. He embarked in the Night, made the Island of *Cyprus*, and stopp'd about two Miles from the Ruins of *Paphos*. The Repose, he enjoy'd there, was but short lived; for the possess'd Persons published their Sense of his dreaded Presence so loudly through the whole Island that in less than a Month after his Arrival he was surrounded by no less than two hundred of the Inhabitants. *Hilarion*, thus discover'd once more by the Enemy of his Rest, exerted the Power which God had given him so vigorously and successfully, that in a Week's Time the evil

Oct. 21 Spirits were obliged to quit their Hold, and give Glory to the Being, who acted by his Ministry.

Hilarion spent two Years in *Cyprus*, during which Time his Escape from that Island was his only Thought and Desire; but *Hesychius*, who was still with him, found him a Place there, where he might probably enjoy his Wish without the Fatigue of another Voyage. It was a pleasant Spot of Ground situated between the Mountains about four Leagues from the Shore; where he perform'd several miraculous Cures. The neighbouring Inhabitants were very happy in such a Guest; but, understanding he did not usually remain long in one Place, guarded all the Passages so carefully that they secured that Blessing for the remaining Part of our Saint's Life, which lasted not quite five Years after his last Choice. The Saint, foreseeing his Dissolution, and speaking of it to some, who visited him in his Retreat, the Inhabitants of *Paphos* and other Places flock'd to him, and desired to see the last Moments of so holy a Life. When the Time of his Departure was near, he address'd himself to his own Soul in the following Terms with a perfect Tranquility; *Depart, my Soul,* " said the holy Abbot, *depart: Why this Delay? Do you fear Death after al-* " *most seventy Years spent in the Service of* Jesus Christ? He had scarce finished these remarkable Words when he expired in 371 or the following Year, being then eighty Years old.

Hesychius was in *Palestine*, when *Hilarion* died; but, upon hearing that News he made a Journey to *Cyprus*. After ten Months spent in that Island, he found Means to carry off the Saint's Body privately, and buried it in his Monastery at *Majuma*. St. *Jerom* assures us that the Almighty honour'd the Saint's Memory in his Time with several Miracles both at *Cyprus* and in *Palestine*. The Churches of the East and West keep his Festival on the same Day, which is the twenty first of *October*.

Saint URSULA, and her Companions, Virgins and Martyrs.

THE Learned are not agreed on the Time when *Ursula* and her Companions suffer'd; some placing their Martyrdom toward the End of the fourth Century, others in the middle of the V. They are generally allow'd to have been Natives of our Island, to have fallen into the Hands of the *Huns* in *Germany*, and died by the Sword of those Barbarians rather than comply with Proposals prejudicial to their Virgin Purity. But it is still disputed whether they

they were settled in that Country, and what was the Occaosin of their lea- Oct. 22
ving their own. The *Roman* Martyrologe honours them as Martyrs on the
twenty first of *October*, without mentioning their Numbers, and says that several of their Bodies were buried at *Cologn*.

The XXII Day.

Saint PHILIP, Bishop of *HERACLEA*, and his two Companions, Martyrs.

PHILIP, according to the Acts of his Martyrdom, had for some Time appear'd to great Advantage in the Characters of a Deacon and a Priest; and was in an advanced Age raised to the Episcopal Dignity by the united Voices of all concern'd in their Election. *Severus*, and *Hermes*, the former a Priest, the latter a Deacon, the chief of his Disciples, were so excellently form'd by his masterly Hand that they were ready to join him not only in the Pro-fession of the Faith, but also in laying down their Lives for the same. The holy Bishop had govern'd the Church of *Heraclea*, the Metropolis of *Thrace* with the utmost Prudence and Vigilance for some Time, when the Imperial Orders for persecuting the Christians were issued out. The Dangers, which then arose to his View, gave him not the least Disturbance; several of his Flock, solicitous for the Safety of their valuable Pastor, advised him to retire, and a-void the Storm, which was then ready to be discharged on his Head; but *Philip* would not listen to the Proposal, and exhorted his People to Patience, assuring them that thus they might defeat the most malicious Designs of the Enemy, and convert what was intended for their Destruction into the Means of improving their Vertue and enhancing their Merit. He was entertaining them with such Discourses about the Feast of the *Epiphany*, when *Aristomachus*, an Officer of the Town, undertook to execute the Governor's Order for shutting up the Churches. Upon which the Bishop endeavour'd to convince him that the Christian Religion could not be destroy'd by that Act of Violence, as long as the living Temples of the holy Ghost were in Being; assuring him that Al-mighty God, dwelt not in Houses made with Hands, but in the Hearts of those who love and worship him. *Aristomachus*, however, proceeded according to his Commission, and seiz'd all the sacred Vessels and Books; which proved a sen-sible Mortification to the Christians. *Philip*, 'though, not allow'd to enter the Place of Worship, took his Station at the Door, where he instructed and en-

couraged

couraged his People, and deliver'd himself in a Manner suitable to their respective Necessities.

Bassus, Governor of the Province, finding the Faithful thus assembled with their Bishop, order'd them all to appear before him, and then desired to know which of the Company was the Master and Instructor of the Christians. *Philip* immediately replied He was the Man; upon which the Magistrate took Occasion to repeat the Tenour of the Imperial Edict forbidding the Disciples of *Jesus* to meet, and directing their being put to Death, if they refused to sacrifice to the Gods. " Now therefore, continued he, bring all the Vessels used
" in your Worship, and the Scriptures, which you read and teach the Peo-
" ple, and give them into my Hands before you are forced to it by Tor-
" ments. *If*, replied the Bishop, *you take any Pleasure in seeing us suffer,*
" *we are prepared for the worst you can do. This infirm Body is in your Power;*
" *use it as you please. The Vessels, you demand, shall be deliver'd up; for God*
" *is not honour'd by Gold or Silver, but by the Fear of his Power; and the Orna-*
" *ments of the Soul are more pleasing to Christ than the Decorations of Churches.*
" *But, as to the sacred Books, it is neither proper for Me to part with them, nor*
" *You to receive them.*

This Answer incensed the Governor, who immediately order'd a convenient Number of Executioners to attend the Court; among whom *Muccapor* stood distinguished for Inhumanity, and was employ'd to torture the holy Prelate. When he had bore the Torture for some Time with edifying Courage, *Hermes*, who was present, had Zeal enough to assure the Governor it was not in his Power to destroy the Word of God, which would be preserved by Tradition, 'though all the Books which contain the sacred Treasure were lost. This Speech drew the Judge's Indignation on him; who commanded him to be whipp'd; after which he accompanied *Publius*, the Governor's Assistant to the Place where the Church Plate and the Scriptures were kept. That Officer, attempting to put some of the Vessels by for his own Use, the holy Deacon oppofed the Motion, and suffer'd for his Freedom. *Bassus*, being inform'd of what had pass'd, gave *Publius* a severe Reprimand, and order'd some Care to be taken of *Hermes*, who had receiv'd a Wound on his Face from the Assistant's Hand; but gave Directions at the same Time for bringing in all the Plate and Books, that could be found; while *Philip*, and his Congregation were carried to the Market Place under a strong Guard, with the double View of diverting the Pagans with their Disgrace, and deterring the Christians from following their Example.

To render the Meeting of the Faithful impracticable, the Governor order'd Oct. 22 the Church to be laid open at Top, which was immediately executed; and then a Fire was made by his Directions, and the sacred Volumes thrown into the Flames. The News of this sacrilegious Act being brought to *Philip*, the Saint, who was still in the Market Place surrounded by a Crowd of Spectators, address'd himself to them in a set Discourse, tending to shew how little Apprehension we ought to have of any temporary Fire, and what should be our Horror of that which is eternal, and kindled by God's Justice. The holy Prelate had scarce finished his Speech, when *Cataphronius* a Pagan Priest, attended by his Assistants, appear'd with the Instruments of Sacrifice, and the Meat that had been profaned by Idolatrous Worship. This detestable Sight provoked *Hermes* to declare aloud that what was design'd as an Entertainment for Men was no better than a diabolical Meal, and was brought thither to pollute the Souls of the Faithful. On which Occasion *Philip* only said, *God's Will be done*. Soon after, the Governor came to the Market Place attended by a prodigious Multitude of both Sexes, and all Ages, some of whom express'd great Compassion for the suffering Christians; while others, especially the Jews, clamour'd more loudly against them, and declared that the Persons before them ought to be obliged to offer Sacrifice.

As soon as *Bassus* could be heard, he press'd the Bishop to sacrifice to the Gods, to their Imperial Majesties, and the Fortune of the City; to which he replied that the Christians were instructed to give divine Honour to the true God only; that their Sovereign had a Right to civil Obedience, but not to Religious Worship; and that nothing made by Man's Hands should divert him from terminating all his Views in the Almighty. The Governor then pointing at the large and beautiful Statue of *Hercules*, advised him to consider what Veneration was due to that excellent Piece. " *Alas!* replied the Saint,
" *how unhappy are you, who are so grosly mistaken in the Nature of the Deity,*
" *and ignorant of the Truth, as to worship your own Workmanship: what Value is*
" *there in Gold, Silver, Brass, Iron, or Lead, which are dug out of the Bowels*
" *of the Earth? You are unacquainted with the Divinity of* Jesus Christ, *which*
" *is incomprehensible to human Capacities; but what Power can your Idols boast,*
" *which are made by a paltry Mechanick, a drunken Statuary? And yet these*
" *are your Gods.*" After some other Observations on the Absurdity of the Pagan Religion, he concluded that it appear'd from what he had said that the Heathens worship'd what may be lawfully trod on, and made Gods of what Providence had design'd for their Use.

Bassus

Oct.22. *Baſſus*, who could not but admire the Reſolution, which our Saint expreſs'd, and deſpair'd of perſuading him to offer Sacrifice, turned to *Hermes*, and in an angry Tone exacted that Proof of his Obedience; but the holy Deacon urged his Religion as an Impediment. Upon the Governor aſking what was his Station in the World, *Hermes* told him he was an Officer, and punctual in following the Directions of his Maſter. *Baſſus* laid hold of this Profeſſion, and aſked him whether he would follow the Example of his Biſhop, if he could be induced to honour the Gods of the Empire. " *I would not*, anſwer'd the " Saint; *but I am ſatisfied He will never do it ; for our Perſuaſion and Reſolu-* " *tion is the ſame.* After ſeveral uſeleſs Threats, and preſſing him to ſacrifice, at leaſt to the Emperors, he and his Biſhop were carried to Priſon; in their Way thither the venerable old Prelate was inſulted by the Rabble, and thrown down ſeveral Times ; but ſhew'd neither Grief nor Reſentment at this Uſage. After a few Days Confinement, the Martyrs were removed to a Houſe near the Jail, where they were allow'd the Liberty of converſing with their Brethren, whom they entertain'd with pious Diſcourſes, and Exhortations to Courage and Perſeverance. The Converſion of ſome Heathens, whom Curioſity drew thither, taking Air, the Saints were remanded to the Priſon, which being contiguous to the Theatre, and having a Door into that Building, they had ſtill the Opportunity of receiving their Friends, who reſorted thither from all Parts, threw themſelves at *Philip*'s Feet, and begg'd the Aſſiſtance of his powerful Prayers.

Baſſus's Time expiring, he was ſucceeded by *Juſtin*, a Man of a violent, and inhuman Temper. Upon the Arrival of the new Governor, *Zoilus*, a Magiſtrate of *Heraclea*, carried *Philip* before him. *Juſtin* aſked the Saint whether he was the Biſhop of the Chriſtians? to which he readily anſwer'd, *He was*. The Governor then let him know under what ſevere Penalties the Emperors enjoin'd all their Subjects to ſacrifice to the Gods, and adviſed him to comply with the Order in Compaſſion to his own grey Hairs. " *I am a Chriſtian*, " ſaid *Philip, and therefore cannot do what you require ; your Commiſſion is to* " *puniſh our Refuſal, not force our Compliance.* When *Juſtin* told him he ſhou'd feel the Weight of his Authority, the holy Biſhop replied, " *You may rack* " *and torture me ; but can never conquer me ; for it is not in the Power of Man* " *to induce me to ſacrifice.* *Juſtin* aſſured him he ſhould be dragg'd through the Streets by the Feet ; and, if he ſurvived that Execution, thrown into Priſon again to ſuffer freſh Torments. *Philip* declared he was ready to bear that or any thing for the Religion which he profeſs'd ; upon which his Feet were tied

together

together; the Saint dragg'd through the Town, very much wounded with the Oct.22. Stones, and then carried back to Prison. The enraged People had long been in Quest of *Severus*; who, by the Direction of the holy Spirit, surrender'd himself, and was carried before the Governor. *Justin* urged every thing that he thought capable of intimidating that holy Priest, and, finding him insensible to all he could say on that Subject, committed him to Prison. Upon his representing the Punishment due to his Disobedience in strong Colours to *Hermes*, the Martyr replied, " *You will never gain your Point. I have been educa-*
" *cated in this Faith; my holy Master has instructed me in these Principles from*
" *my Cradle. I can never renounce my Religion, nor act in Contradiction to the*
" *Obligation it lays on me. This is my Confession; use me as you please.*" Upon this Declaration the Martyr was remanded to his Confinement; where he and his two Companions lay seven Months, and were then removed to *Adrianople*, and kept in a private House there 'till the Governor's Arrival. The Day after *Justin* reached that City, *Philip* was brought before him, and asked why he had not made the intended Use of the Time which had been allow'd him for changing his Mind. Upon his declaring that he persisted in his former Profession, the holy Bishop was whipp'd unmercifully, and then conducted back to Prison. *Hermes*, being order'd to appear, was attack'd with Promises and Threats, but remain'd invincible.

Three days after, *Justin* order'd them before him again, and asked *Philip* why he acted so rashly and continued in his Disobedience to the higher Powers; to which the Saint replied; " *My present Behaviour is not the Effect of Rash-*
" *ness; but proceeds from the Love and Fear of God, who made the World, and*
" *will judge the Living and the Dead; and whose Commands I dare not trasngress.*
" *I have hitherto done my Duty to the Emperors, and am always ready to comply*
" *with their just Orders, according to the Doctrine of our Lord, who bids us* Matt. 22
" *give both* Cesar *and God their due. But I am obliged to prefer Heaven to*
" *Earth, and obey God rather than Man.*" The Governor then directed his Discourse to *Hermes*, and advised him to consult his own Safety by sacrificing, 'though *Philip*'s great Age made him think his Life not worth preserving. The holy Deacon undertook to shew the Reasonableness of his Refusal by discovering the Absurdity of the Pagan Worship; but *Justin* interrupted him, and in a Rage told him he talk'd as if he would persuade him to embrace the Christian Religion; to which *Hermes* answer'd, " *I heartily wish you and all*
" *present that Happiness;*" but desired the Governor would not imagine it in his Power to draw him over to Idolatry. *Justin*, full of Confusion at the invincible Courage of the two glorious Combatants, advised with his Assistant,

O and

Oct. 22 and some others, and then condemned them to be burnt alive; which Sentence was executed soon after. The Martyrs expired with the Praises of God in their Mouths. Their Bodies, remaining entire, were thrown into the River; but taken up by the Christians, and deposited about twelve Miles from *Adrianople*.

Severus, being thus left alone in the Prison, look'd on himself as a Ship floting on the Waves without a Pilot; but at the same Time was full of Joy and Gratitude to the Almighty, who had crown'd his Companions. Transported with the Prospect of the Glory that attends Martyrdom, he fell on his Knees, and earnestly begg'd he might be admitted to share the Happiness; which was granted him the next Day; but the Manner of his Death, and other Particulars of his Sufferings are not recorded.

Baronius in his Notes on the *Roman* Martyrologe places the Death of our Saints under *Julian* the Apostate. Others are inclined to believe it happen'd under *Decius*; but the Order for burning the holy Scriptures, and destroying Churches, which seems peculiar to *Dioclesian*'s Persecution, has induced several Learned Men to date their Triumph in the Year 304. The twenty second of *October* is universally observed in their Honour.

The XXIII Day.

Saint IGNATIUS, Patriarch of *Constantinople*.

THE great Patriarch, whose Memory we venerate this Day was Son to the Emperor *Michael*, who resign'd the Crown to *Leo* the *Armenian*, in the Year 813, and originally named *Nicetas*. When his Father quitted the Imperial Throne, our Saint, then fourteen Years old, embraced the Monastick Life, and from that Time was called *Ignatius*. *Leo*, whose Treachery and Ambition had obliged *Michael* to retire, disposed of him and his Family in several distant Islands, and castrated his three Sons, 'though he was their Godfather; and all this to secure the Crown to himself and his Posterity. But that Rebel was deposed and murther'd at *Christmass* in the Year 820; and his four Sons served in the same Manner. During the Troubles of the Empire under that Prince's Successors, our Saint enjoy'd true Repose and solid Pleasure in his Religious Retreat. The holy Community in which he lived was so sensible

sible of his Merit, and great Proficiency in his State that upon the Death of their Abbot they were unanimous in chosing him to succeed to that Post.

All the Gifts he had receiv'd from Heaven appear'd now to Advantage; for he govern'd his penitential Family with such masterly Prudence, and form'd them so excellently to Perfection that the House, 'though very large, soon became too narrow for the Reception of such as crouded to it, and begg'd to be placed under his Direction. This prodigious Increase put the Saint on building three new Monasteries in so many different Islands; and toward the Close of his Life he founded a fourth on the Continent, which bore the Name of St. *Michaël*. The Orthodox Prelates, who had suffer'd much from the powerful Party of *Iconoclasts*, being apprized of his great Vertue and other Qualifications for the Ministry, were of Opinion that God design'd to honour the sacred Character in his Person, and therefore resolved to promote him to holy Orders. *Basil*, one of their Number, executed their Resolution, and ordain'd him Priest, after he had first pass'd through the lower Degrees in the Clergy. His Reputation for Sanctity and Purity of Faith, was such that great Numbers from *Constantinople*, the neighbouring Towns, and even from *Bithynia* resorted to his Monastery for Instruction; and Parents brought their Children to him to receive Baptism, and the first Rudiments of Christian Learning from the holy and orthodox Abbot.

The Persecution, which the Catholicks suffer'd from the Enemies of sacred Images continued 'till the Death of the Emperor *Theophilus* at the Beginning of the Year 842. The Church then assumed a new Face, and the Veneration for those Representations of the great Servants of God was asserted, and established by *Theodora*, Widow to the late Emperor, and Regent during the Minority of her Son *Michaël* III, assisted by the Patriarch *Methodius*, whom that Princess had placed in the See of *Constantinople*. The Death of that excellent Prelate was no small Loss to the Eastern Church; and the Empress and orthodox Bishops directed their whole Care to find one worthy of that exalted Station, that is one both willing and able to carry on the good Work which the deceased Patriarch had begun, and *Theodora* had so much at Heart. All Persons of eminent Piety and Wisdom were consulted on this Article, and the general Voice declared for *Ignatius*, who was consecrated on the fourth of *June* 846, or the following Year.

It was easy to see this was in every Particular the Man desired; for he was possess'd of all the Qualities of a good Pastor; but none was more remarkable than the generous Liberty he used in opposing Vice, wherever he found it, and reprimanding publick and scandalous Offenders, 'though seemingly pro-

Oct. 23 tected by the Dignity of their Birth or Station; of which vertuous Impartiality the following is recorded as a glorious Inſtance. *Bardas*, Brother to her Imperial Majeſty, was a Man of Parts, and well verſed n State-Affairs, on which Account he was admitted to a conſiderable Share in the Government; but his Morals were deteſtable, and he carried his Paſſions ſo far as to diſmiſs his Wife, and allow himſelf Criminal Converſation with his Daughter in Law. *Ignatius*, full of Zeal for that unhappy Man's Soul, endeavour'd to reclaim him, and perſuade him to expiate his Sins. *Bardas* gave no Attention to his charitable Remonſtrance, but added Sacrilege to his Crimes, and attempted to receive the Bleſſed Euchariſt on the Feaſt of the *E. piphany*, in the Year 858. The holy Patriarch, reſolved not to admit of that Profanation of the venerable Myſteries, refuſed him Communion; but the debauched Prince, provoked at this truly Epiſcopal Courage, threaten'd to kill him on the Spot. *Ignatius* ended the Service without any Concern, being ready to lay down his Life rather than ſuffer ſuch an Outrage on the ſacred Body and Blood of *Jeſus Chriſt*. *Bardas* from that Moment made it his whole Study to ruin the Patriarch; to which End he prevail'd with the young Emperor to remove his Mother from any Share in the Government; not only becauſe that Princeſs was the chief Protectreſs of *Ignatius*, but alſo becauſe ſhe ſtood in his Way, and proved an intolerable Check to his Ambition. *Michaël*, whoſe natural Diſpoſitions were exactly ſuch as *Bardas* could wiſh, eaſily gave into a Propoſal, which ſeem'd to make him independent. At the Inſtigation of his artful Uncle, he ſent for the Patriarch, and order'd him to cut the Hair of his Mother and three Siſters, as a Mark of their engaging in a Monaſtick Life. His Refuſal was by his malicious Enemy repreſented in the moſt odious Colours, and the Emperor was made to believe this was not the only Inſtance of his rebellious and ungovernable Temper. His Imperial Majeſty's Judgment being thus corrupted by this evil Counſellour, *Ignatius* was baniſhed to *Trebintbus*, one of thoſe Iſlands, where he had formerly built a Monaſtery; and this violent Step was taken after the Patriarch had filled the See of *Conſtantinople* eleven Years.

A corrupt Prince, who has the Power of puniſhing ſuch as oppoſe his Will, and rewarding thoſe who can ſacrifice all to Intereſt, ſeldom wants proper Inſtruments for purſuing his moſt criminal Inclinations; and the unhappy Affair before us is a melancholy Proof of this Obſervation. Much the greater Part of the Biſhops, reſolved to change with the Times, and keep their Place in the Emperor's Favour at any Rate, were eaſily prevail'd with to make two Viſits to our illuſtrious Exile, and preſs him to a voluntary Reſignation of his

See

See; but he continued deaf to the Proposal, 'though enforced with the powerful Rhetorick of Threats and Promises. The Bishopss thus moulded to the Will of *Bardas*, made no Difficulty of placing *Photius* in his Room. That Usurper was a Man of Birth, and great Qualification; well versed in all Branches of useful Learning, happy in a prodigious Genius, well improved, and deservedly esteem'd the most considerable Person of the Age; but his Sincerity and Honesty were not equal to his Judgment and Capacity, as will appear from the Sequel of our Story. When he was named to the aforesaid Dignity he was possess'd of the Office of Secretary of State; and in six Days Time pass'd from the Tonsure to the Episcopal Character.

Photius could not be satisfied with his own Situation without forging such Calumnies against the banished Patriarch, as would privilege his Deprivation. In that View he engaged some of his Party to impeach him of treasonable Designs against the Emperor. *Bardas*, pleased with the Thought, dispatched Officers to *Terebinthus*, with Orders to do all that was necessary for bringing the Saint to the Condition of a Criminal. At their Arrival they executed that Commission with all possible Exactness, and tortured the injured Prelate's Servants to oblige them to confess the pretended Conspiracy; but, finding no Proof, they carried *Ignatius* to another Island; and from thence removed him to a small Town near *Constantinople*, where *Leo Lalacon*, Captain of the Troops beat him unmercifully on the Face, and then threw him into a close Prison loaded with Irons like a Malefactor. While in this wretched Situation, he was told nothing would purchase his Liberty but a Declaration in writing that he had resign'd his Bishoprick voluntarily. Being fully persuaded of his own Right to the See of *Constantinople*, he was resolved to bear any thing rather than give up his Flock into the Power of the Wolf by such a formal Act. *Ignatius*, remaining firm in that Resolution, was carried to *Numera*, and afterwards to *Mitylene* in the Island of *Lesbos*.

Photius, despairing of bringing the Saint to his Terms, conven'd the Bishops of his Party, and pronounced the holy Patriarch depos'd and excommunicated; but, finding his Conduct did not please all, he sent a Deputation to *Rome*, desiring *Nicholas* I, then in S. *Peter*'s Chair, to dispatch Legates to *Constantinople*, whose Presence he pretended would be necessary for entirely reducing the *Iconoclasts*, and establishing Ecclesiastical Discipline in the Eastern Church; but his true Motive for this Request was to get his Right acknowledged by the Representatives of the Church of *Rome*. His Holiness sent two Legates, but let *Photius* know he could say nothing to his Ordination 'till their Return. In the mean Time *Ignatius* was removed to *Terebinthus* in *Febr.* 861,

where

where his Usage was at least as barbarous as what he had met with in other Places since the Beginning of his Troubles.

Upon the Arrival of *Rodoaldus* and *Zachary* Legates from the holy See, *Photius* call'd a Council of 318 Bishops, who summond our Saint to appear, but let him know it was the Emperor's Will that he should not presume to wear the Episcopal Ornaments before that Assembly, and at his entring he found a formidable Party prepared to oppress him. After repeated Solicitations to resign his Post, and as many Refusals from the holy Patriarch, no less than seventy two Witnesses were produced against him, who being well instructed in the Part they were to act on that Occasion, the Saint was formally deposed. The Pope's Legates, aw'd into a Compliance with the Measures of the Court, were so far from opposing the Proceedings of that Council, that they consented to all ill Treatment the Saint met with after their factious Sentence.

Photius, flushed with the Success of his late Enterprize, grew wanton in Cruelty, and studied how to mortify his Competitor in the most effectual Manner. By that Intruder's Direction *Ignatius* was put into the Hands of three merciless Villains, with Orders to ply him with all manner of Torments 'till he should subcribe the Decree of his own Condemnation. Those Instruments of the false Patriarch's Revenge and Malice executed their Commission with great Fidelity; and after several barbarous Indignities, one of them seiz'd on his Hand, and forc'd him to trace a Cross on a Paper which he had prepar'd for that Purpose, containing an Acknowledgement of *Ignatius*'s uncanonical Promotion, and Tyrannical Administration. This pretended Subscription was transmitted to the Emperor; who, believing it genuine, order'd the Saint his Liberty and Leave to retire to a Country Seat, left him by his Mother.

The sanguinary Usurper, who could not think himself secure while *Ignatius* was in a Capacity of ever regaining his Right, consulted the Heads of his Party, and came to a Resolution of cutting off his Hand, and plucking out his Eyes. On *Whitsunday* in the Year 861 the holy Patriarch, who suspected nothing of that Nature, was surprized to see his House beset with Soldiers; without any farther Enquiry into their Business, he put on the Cloaths of one of his meanest Servants, and thus made his Escape, attended only by *Cyprian*, his favourite Disciple. Finding a Vessel bound for *Propontis*, he went on board, and landed in an uncultivated, and almost uninhabited Island; where he lay conceal'd for some time, and subsisted on Charity. *Photius* order'd strict Search to be made for him in all the Towns and Monasteries near

Constantinople;

Constantinople; and then obtain'd the Emperor's Consent for dispatching six Oct. 23 Vessels to the neighbouring Islands, and Coasts in Quest of the Saint, with Directions to execute him as a Traytor and Rebel, wherever they found him. The Persons thus commission'd met him frequently; but his Disguise screen'd him from their Notice. In *August* following the Imperial City felt a violent Shock of an Earthquake, which continued near forty Days. The People rouzed by that Calamity cried out that divine Vengeance was now fallen on them for what *Ignatius* had suffer'd at their Hands. The Emperor and his Uncle, alarm'd at the Danger, and the Clamours of their Subjects, order'd publick Notice to be given that the Saint might retire to his Monastery in Peace.

The Pope had exact Informations of all that had pass'd at *Constantinople*, and in order to provide a speedy Remedy against what he had but too much Reason to apprehend, would follow from those violent and uncanonical Proceedings, called a Council at *Rome*, in which he declared the Acts of the Council of *Constantinople* null, disown'd all his Legates had done there; and, excommunicated *Photius* and all who had had any hand in depriving and persecuting *Ignatius*. The Invader of the See of *Constantinople* was now grown so powerful that he resolved to stand his Ground, 'though both the Pope and Emperor should be united against him. *Bardas* continued to persecute our Saint 'till the Year 866, when he was put to Death for a Design against his Nephew's Life; and the Death of that Prince, which happen'd in the ensuing Year, made a happy Change in Affairs. *Basil* was no sooner in sole Possession of the imperial Throne, which he had before shared with *Michaël*, but he banished *Photius*, gave Orders for conducting *Ignatius* to the Imperial City in a Manner suitable to his Character, and on the twenty third of *November* 867 reinstated him in his Church after nine Years unjust Seperation from his Flock.

The holy Patriarch, thus restor'd to his Dignity, suspended the Usurper, with all who had receiv'd Orders from his sacrilegious Hands, or communicated with him; and then desired the Emperor would endeavour to procure a General Council, as the only Remedy for the many Abuses which had been admitted during the late Troubles. That Prince readily consented to the Proposal, and sent Embassadors to *Rome* on that Subject. *Adrian* II, then in the holy See, sent three Legates to represent his Person at *Constantinople*, where the Council was open'd on the fifth of *October* 869. The twelve Bishops, who had all along espoused our Saint's Cause and shared his Sufferings, sat near him, and the Patriarch held the next Place to the Legates of the holy See. This Synod, after considering the Case of such Prelates as had

been

Oct 23. been consecrated by our Saint or his immediate Predecessor *Methodius*, but had been either deceived or forced into the Usurper's Party, and finding them full of Compunction for what was passed, desirous to be receiv'd to the Catholick Communion, and disposed to submit to any canonical Penance, their Petition was granted, and they allow'd to take their Places in that venerable Assembly. They then proceeded to examine the Particulars of *Photius*'s irregular and violent Conduct; and finding him, obstinate, pronounced *Anathema* against him.

The Prudence, Vigilance, and Sanctity of our holy Patriarch appear'd to so great Advantage after his Re-establishment, that it was evident his Sufferings had improved his Experience, and carried his Virtue to a higher Pitch, than when he sat quietly in his See; though even then he was an excellent Pattern for his Flock. While *Ignatius* was wholly employ'd in the Functions of his Character, his Enemy was plotting his Disgrace and Expulsion. *Photius* had been eight Years in Exile before he could think of proper Means to execute his malicious Designs; at last, finding the Emperor's weak Side, he endeavour'd to gain his Favour by flattering him with a most illustrious Descent, deduced his Genealogy from the famous *Tiridates* King of *Armenia*. This agreeable Forgery succeeded to his Wish, and *Photius* was order'd to repair to the Imperial City, where he soon established himself in that Princes Favour. His Attempts on the Patriarchal See fell to the Ground; but he took upon him to officiate as a Bishop, an Usurpation which our Saint could only bewail.

The Saint did not long bear that Mortification; for his great Age, and Infirmities brought him to a happy Death on the twenty third of *October* 878. His Body, inclosed in a wooden Coffin, was first carried to St. *Sophia*'s Church; where the usual Prayers were offer'd for his Soul: it was then removed to St. *Mennas*'s, where two Women possess'd by the Devil were deliver'd in the Presence of the venerable Relicks; but it was afterwards buried at S. *Michaël*'s at some Distance from the Town, built by our Saint. Both the *Greeks* and *Latins* observe his Festival on the Day of his Passage to Eternity.

The XXIV Day.

Saint *MAGLOIRE*, BISHOP.

ST. *Magloire*, a Native of great *Britain*, and born toward the Close of the fifth Age, was Cousin German to St. *Samson*, of whom we have spoken at large

large *July* twenty eight, and S. *Malo*, whose Life may be seen on the fifteenth of *November*. In his very Infancy he was put into the Hands of St. *Eltut*, Abbot of a Monastery in *Glamorganshire*, which afterwards bore his Name. That holy Superior, who had an excellent Talent at forming Children to Piety and giving them an early Sense of their Duty, employ'd his utmost Skill in the Education of young *Magloire*, and sent him back to his Parents as soon as he was grounded in the Principles of Religion and put in the Way of improving his Mind by Study. *Magloire* staid at home 'till St. *Samson*'s Visit to his Father, then dangerously ill, was follow'd by the Conversion of the whole Family.

Magloire, then about seventeen Years old, was by a Cousin's Care placed in a neighbouring Monastery; where he was so fervent and exact in observing all the Practices prescribed by the Discipline of that School of Pennance and Devotion, that he soon became perfect in all the Virtues recommended or required in that State. His Superior, perceiving his Progress in every thing that could qualify him for the sacred Character, procured him the Order of Deacon; in which Station he shew'd an excellent Example of Purity of Heart, Humility, Mortification, Abstinence, and Devotion. *Samson* being consecrated Bishop, and going for *France*, as has been related in our Account of that Saint, was so charm'd with *Magloire*'s Character that he engaged his Company in that Apostolical Voyage. They landed on the Coast of *Armorica*, now call'd *Britany*, and began their Mission near *Aleth*, a Seaport in that Providence, at present known by the Name of S. *Malo*'s. Having secured the Protection of *Childibert*, King of *Neustria*, in whose Dominions that Country was situated, they preached along the Coast with great Success; and *Samson*, the Head of that Mission, was soon enabled to raise several Monasteries for the Reception of his Disciples. The chief of those Religious Houses was at *Dol*, then in the Diocese of *Rennes*, the Place of that Prelate's ordinary Residence. Our Saint spent the greatest Part of his Time at the Head of a Community not far from that of his Cousin, who ordain'd him Priest, and afterwards consecrated him Bishop, without assigning him any particular See.

In whatever Character our Saint appear'd, his Mortifications and Austerities were still the same. His usual Food was Barley Bread, with the Addition of a few Legumes; and on great Festivals he sometimes eat Fish, but then more out of Complaisance to others than any Inclination to Variety or Change of Diet. He never took his Meal 'till Sunset; and eat nothing on *Wednesdays* and *Fridays*. He always wore a Haircloth next his Skin, and practised every other Severity on his own Body which he could do without seeming to affect Singularity.

St. Magloire, *Bishop.*

Oct. 24. The Death of St. *Samson* in 564 or the following Year left *Magloire* the Care of the Monastery of *Dol*; and, according to those Writers who hold that *Samson* erected an Episcopal See at that Town, our Saint succeeded him in that Post. *Magloire* was now near seventy Years old, and his Infirmities, the inevitable Consequence of his evangelical Labours, had reduced him to so low an Ebb, that it seem'd necessary to allow him to end his Days in Silence and Retirement. This indeed was his only Wish; but his Reputation in that Country proved a powerful Obstacle to the Pursuit of his Inclinations; and finding a Retreat absolutely impracticable in *Britany*, about three Years after the Decease of his holy Predecessor, he put his Religious Family into the Hands of a Monk, whom he could trust with that important Charge, and cross'd over to *Jersey*, an Island lying between *Britany* and *England*; where he spent seven Years. We are told he built a Monastery in that Island, and found the Inhabitants ready enough to contribute to its' Maintainance out of Gratitude for the Pains he took for their Salvation. He breath'd his pious Soul into the Hands of his Redeemer on the twenty fourth of *October*, 575.

His Body was removed to the Priory of *Lebon*, near *Dinan* in the Diocese of St. *Malo*'s in the Year 857; but his Relicks were translated to *Paris* in the X Century, and lodged in the Collegiate Church of St. *Bartholomew* in that City. *Hugh Capet*, who came to the Throne of *France* in 987, enlarged St. *Bartholomew*'s Church, made a considerable Addition to it's Revenue, converted the House into a *Benedictin* Abbey, which from that Time bore the Name of our Saint. Those Monks were removed to another Part of the Town in the twelfth Age; but in the sixteenth the Pope made a Grant of that House to the Archbishop of *Paris*; and in the same Century the Religious, being transplanted to St. *James*'s-*Street*, brought the Remains of St. *Magloire*, to their new Habitation; where they are honour'd at this Day; 'though the House is now in the Hands of *Oratorians*, and is employ'd as a Seminary to the Diocese of *Paris*. The *Roman* Martyrologe honours his Memory on the Day of his Death.

The XXV Day.

St. *CHRYSANTHUS*, and St. *DARIA, Martyrs.*

THE two Saints, whom the Church this Day proposes to our Veneration, are better known by the Respect paid to their Memory than by the History of their Lives, or Circumstances of their Deaths. It is certain that they suffer'd Martyrdom together at *Rome*; which is usually dated in the Reign of *Numerian*, who came to the Imperial Throne in 283, and sat but eight Months.
But

But some, observing that History has left us no Account of that Prince's persecuting the Christians, have placed their Sufferings under *Valerian*.

S. *Gregory* of *Tours*, who quotes the Acts of their Martyrdom, tells us that great Numbers of the Faithful, meeting at their Tombs soon after their Death, to celebrate their Memory by offering the venerable Mysteries, the Emperor or the Prefect of *Rome* in his Name, order'd the Cave to be stopp'd up with Stones, and Sand, while they were at their Devotions; and thus the whole Congregation was buried alive. The same Author tells us that the Cave being thus stopp'd remain'd unknown 'till the Time of *Constantine* the Great, and that then God was pleased to discover it. Since that Time the Names of *Chrysanthus* and *Daria* have been well known in the Church, and publickly honour'd by her devout Children. The *Roman* Martyrologe mentions them on the twenty fifth of *October*; but does not tell us whether it was the Day of their Martyrdom, or that of the Discovery of their Relicks.

St. GAUDENTIUS Bishop of *Brescia*.

UPON the Death of *Philastrius* the holy Bishop of *Brescia* in *Italy*, which happen'd about the Year 386, the Bishops of the Province, with St. *Ambrose* their worthy Metropolitan at their Head, met to consider of the Choice of a Successor to the vacant See, and soon came to a Resolution of naming *Gaudentius* to that Post; who, 'though young, had so fair a Character for Virtue and Learning that he was recommended by the united Voices of the Clergy and People on this Occasion. *Gaudentius* was then in the East; and the Prelates, who knew his Humility, apprehending that the News of his Election would prove an Impediment to his Return, not only deputed proper Persons to press his leaving the East, but at the same Time wrote to the Bishops of that Country, and desired they would not admit him to their Communion, if he refused to hasten to his new Flock. This Message found our Saint at *Cesarea* in *Cappadocia*, where the Church was in a flourishing Condition, and such as sufficiently spoke the pastoral Vigilance and Activity of the great St. *Basil* it's late Pastor. He would willingly have spent the Remainder of his Days in that City; but the Demands of St. *Ambrose* and his Collegues, and the Compliance of the Eastern Prelates with their Request obliged him to return for *Italy*, and undertake the Government of the Church of *Brescia*. At his Arrival he was consecrated by St. *Ambrose*, assisted by other Bishops of the Province; and in a Sermon preached immediately after that Ceremony, complain'd of the Violence offer'd to his Inclinations.

Thus unavoidably engaged in the Episcopal Office, his whole Study was how to discharge every Obligations of that Character to the Honour of God,

Oct. 25 and the spiritual Advantage of those under his Care. In this View he govern'd his Flock with all the Vigilance, Zeal, and Charity, which are the Marks of a truly pastoral Spirit. *Benevolus*, one of the most considerable Men at *Brescia*, who had been Secretary of State to the Emperor, but quitted that Post to avoid being drawn into any thing against his Conscience in Compliance with *Justina*, Mother to *Valentinian* II, a great Patroness of the *Arians*. That excellent Man, being a constant Hearer of his holy Bishop, 'till hinder'd by Sickness, desired he might enjoy the Pleasure of persuing his good Instructions at home, since he could not attend the Church. *Gaudentius* could not refuse so reasonable a Request, and it is to *Benevolus*'s Regard for his Discourses that we owe almost all that is extant under our Saint's Name.

It is commonly thought the Church of *Brescia* continued long in Possession of our good Pastor; but we have but few of the Particulars of his Conduct in that Station. All we know of that Sort is that he was one of the Deputies from the Council of *Rome* in the Year 405 to *Constantinople*, charged with Letters in Favour of St. *Chrysostom* from Pope *Innocent* I, and the Emperor *Honorius* to *Arcadius* who govern'd in the East; of which Commission and it's Success the Reader may see our Account toward the Close of St. *Chrysostom*'s Life *January* the twenty seventh. *Gaudentius* refused to hold Communion with *Atticus*, who had usurped the See of *Constantinople*, and persisted in his Resolution so vigorously that he acquired the glorious Title of a Confessor for that Part of his Conduct; and almost deserves that of a Martyr for what he suffer'd from St. *Chrysostom*'s Enemies. It is not certain how long our Saint lived after that Embassy: some place his Death in 420, others in 427. His Name occurs in the *Roman* Martyrologe on the twenty fifth of *October*.

The XXVI Day.

Saint EVARISTUS, Pope.

EVARISTUS, according to the best Account extant, was a Native of *Greece*, of a Jewish Family; but we are not told from whom he receiv'd Christianity, or what brought him to *Rome*. We find him there, however, in the last Year of the first Century, and at the same Time hear of his Promotion to the holy See on the Demise of St. *Clement*. *Trajan* gave the Church much Disturbance during our Saint's whole Pontificate. We cannot have a more just, and advantageous Idea of the holy Pope's Labours for his Flock, and the Blessing that attended his Endeavours than by considering what St. *Ignatius* of *Antioch*

tioch says of the Church of *Rome*, after *Evaristus* had govern'd it seven Years. The holy Martyr commends the Christians of that City for their Charity, which had made them a Model to all of that Denomination; for the Purity of their Doctrine, and the strict Union which subsisted among them. This ought to be consider'd as no less than a Panegyrick on *Evaristus*, by whose pastoral Hand these Vertues had been cultivated at *Rome*. Some Writers are of Opinion that the Division of the City into distinct Parts, and fixing the Titles of Parishes there was the Work of our Saint.

Evaristus, according to the most probable Calculation, died toward the End of *October* in the Year 109. The Church honours him as a Martyr; an Appellation usually bestow'd on the first Popes, who struggled with many Difficulties under the Pagan Emperors, 'though they did not end their Lives by the Sword of the Persecutors; and his Name appears on the twenty sixth of *October* in the *Roman* Martyrologe.

Saint LUCIAN, *and Saint* MARCIAN, *Martyrs.*

LUCIAN, and *Marcian* were brought up in the Errors of Paganism, and gave into all the Extravagancies of which Persons in those unhappy Circumstances are capable. They lived in the open Profession and Practice of Magick, which they employ'd either to execute their Malice on their Neighbours, or engage the Affections of vertuous Women. These Libertines having conceived an irregular Passion for a young Lady of strict Vertue, who had consecrated her Virginity to God, practised every unlawful Art to corrupt her Mind, and prevail with her to gratify their vicious Inclinations; but their Attempts proved unsuccessful upon a Virgin, who counterworked all their Charms by constant Prayer. In vain they invoked the Assistance of their infernal Friends, in vain they multiplied their diabolical Charms; for the Powers whom they served, according to the Acts of our Saints, were forced at last to confess they had no Influence over such as acknowledged the true God, and were under the Protection of *Jesus Christ*. This Declaration shock'd *Lucian* and *Marcian*, who began to conclude that *Jesus Christ*, who was so much superior to their Apostate Correspondents, and defeated all their Endeavours, must certainly be invested with extraordinary Power. By the Assistance of the divine Grace, they pursued this Hint so far as to conclude it necessary to renounce the Devil who had deceived them, and embrace the Religion of him, who had gain'd the Victory over their Art and it's Author. The Sincerity of their Conversion appear'd by the burning of their Books in the Face of the whole Town, generally supposed to be *Nicomedia* in *Bithynia*, and declaring publickly

publickly that for the future they neither knew, nor hoped in any Being but the God, who had convinced them of their former Folly and Impiety.

After this Confession they made their Way to the Church, gave a full Account of what had pass'd, and receiv'd Baptism. Being now strengthen'd by the Grace of Regeneration, they left their Friends, their Fortune, and all their Expectations in this World, and retired to a Place where Penitential Works became the whole Employment of their Lives; they were so sensible of the Enormity of the Faults, which had engross'd their whole Thoughts 'till that Time, that Bread and Water was their whole Food, and whole Days were frequently spent without any Nourishment.

This was their Way of living 'till the same Spirit, which effected the Change of their Hearts, inspired them with the charitable Resolution of appearing again in the World, and instructing their deluded Acquaintance in the Faith which they had embraced. Their Discourses on that Subject receiv'd no small Weight from the Consideration of their former Opposition to the Religion which they now press'd with so much Zeal. Nothing could stop the Progress of their Evangelical Labours but the Persecution which broke out in the Beginning of *Decius*'s Reign, who came to the imperial Throne in the Year 249. As soon as the sanguinary Edict was published, the two Converts were seized and carried before *Sabinus*, Proconsul of *Bythinia*, who began with asking *Lucian* his Name and Station in the World. The Saint satisfied both his Questions, and declared he was now a Preacher, and Defender of the venerable Law, which he once opposed and persecuted. Upon the Judge enquiring by what Authority he undertook to preach, he replied that the Laws of Humanity and Charity obliged all Men to endeavour the Conversion of their Neighbours, and do all in their Power for rescuing them from the Snares of the Devil. *Marcian*'s Reply to the Proconsul's Interrogatories was not different from that of his Companion; whereupon *Sabinus* reproached them both with Ingratitude to the Gods, from whom they had receiv'd so many Favours. *Marcian*'s Answer was that their Conversion was the Effect of the same Grace which was given to St. *Paul* who from a Persecutor of the Church became a Preacher of the Gospel. The Judge then advised them to consult their own Security by returning to what he called their Duty, and assured them that nothing but their Compliance with what he exacted could gain them the Favour of the Gods, and their Prince. To which Remonstrance *Marcian* replied that He and *Lucian* could never be sufficiently thankful to God who had deliver'd them from Darkness, and favour'd them with the glorious Light they now enjoy'd. *Sabinus*, observing the Martyr magnify the Power of their Redeemer, asked them why he had not preserved them from the Hands of the Magistrate?

strate; and why he did not rescue them from the Sufferings which threaten'd them. "*The true Glory of a Christian,* said *Marcian, is to lay down
" what you call Life, and obtain eternal Life by Perseverance in the Faith. We
" heartily wish,* continued the Saint, *that God would give you Grace and Understan-
" ding, that you might know the Dignity and Power of the Being, whom we serve,
" and how much he does in Favour of such as believe in him.* The Proconsul
laughed at their Expectations of future Happiness; and desired they would
obey the Imperial Orders, and sacrifice to the Gods before he proceeded to Severities, "*We are ready to bear the worst you can inflict,* replied *Marcian*;
" *and resolved to undergo any Torments rather than incur the Displeasure of the
" true and living God.*

The Proconsul, convinced that he lost his Time and Labour on the two excellent Persons before him, condemn'd them to be burnt alive. Upon their
Arrival at the Place of Execution, they address'd themselves to the Almighty
in the following Manner; " *Our Praises, O Lord* Jesus, *must fall short of what
" we owe for our Deliverance from Pagan Errors, the Happiness of suffering for
" your Name, and the comfortable Prospect of being join'd with your Saints for
" ever. To you be Praise and Glory, and into your Hands we commend our Souls.*"

Their Martyrdom is dated on the twenty sixth of *October* and placed at *Nicomedia* in the *Roman* Martyrologe, and others of good Reputation.

Oct. 26

✛✛

The XXVII Day.

Saint *FRUMENTIUS,* Apostle of *Ethiopia.*

BEfore *Constantine* the Great could effect his Designs in Favour of the
Christian Church, *Metrodorus* a Philosopher undertook several Journeys
out of Curiosity and a Desire of seeing the World, and travell'd to the farther
India, for so the Antients called *Ethiopia.* At his Return he presented the
Emperor with a Quantity of Pearls, and other Curiosities which he had collected in his Travels, assuring that Prince his Present would have been much
more valuable, had not *Sapor* King of the *Persians* seiz'd on the best Part of his
Treasure. His Success was *Meropius*'s Encouragement for undertaking the
same Voyage; he was a Philosopher too and a Native of *Phenicia,* and was
accompanied in that Expedition by two Boys, his near Relations, with whose
Education he was intrusted; *Frumentius* was the Name of the elder, *Edesus* that
of the younger.

In the Course of that Voyage homeward the Vessel which carried our Travellers, touched at a Port belonging to the Barbarians, to take in fresh Water,

or

Oct. 27. or Provisions for the Company. It was the Custom of those People to kill all the Subjects of the Empire, they could find upon hearing that the *Romans* had violated their Treaties with them. This either really was the Case, or they were so inform'd when *Meropius* landed in the aforesaid Port. The Ship was stopt, and the whole Crew, and Passengers put to the Sword, except the two Children, whose tender Years and Innocence pleaded so strongly in their Favour that they were carried to the King of that Country. The Prince was so well pleased with the young Captives that he gave Orders for their Education, and when they grew up, made *Edesus* his Cup bearer; and *Frumentius*, being possess'd of a much better Capacity, was entrusted with all his Writings and Accounts, that is in our Way of speaking made Secretary of State and Chancellor of the Exchequer. From their first appearing in publick Business they engaged the Affections and Esteem of all who knew them, and were honour'd as the first Subjects in the Kingdom during the Life of their Royal Protector, and Benefactor. Upon that Prince's Death his Widow took Possion of the Throne; and, thinking it impossible to employ two Persons of more Honour and Fidelity than the two Favourites of the deceased King, begg'd their Assistance in the Management of Affairs 'till her Son, then an Infant, should be in a Capacity of acting.

Rufinus, a Priest of *Aquileia*, who flourished in the IV Century gives us all the foregoing Particulars, and adds that, while the Brothers were thus employ'd, God inspired *Frumentius* with a Desire of enquiring for Christians among the *Roman* Merchants, who traded to that Country, some of whom were settled among the Barbarians. Upon finding some of that Denomination, *Frumentius*, who had now a considerable Share in the Government, allow'd them all convenient Power in all Parts of the Kingdom; and advised them to meet publickly, choose what Houses they pleased for the Performance of religious Worship, and serve God according to the *Roman* Way. That great Man encouraged the Practice of what he recommended by his own Example, applied to the Duties of the Christian Religion with an edifying Fervour, and made the planting of Christianity in that barbarous Country his chief Employment and first Care.

The King coming to Age, and taking the Reins of Government into his own Hands, *Frumentius* and *Edesus* laid an Account of their Administration before him, resign'd their Posts, and set out for their own Country, 'though that Prince and the Queen Mother used all Manner of Entreaties to engage their Stay. *Edesus*, eager to see his Relations went directly to *Phenicia*; but *Frumentius* took the Rout of *Alexandria*, where he found St. *Athanasius* the holy Bishop of that City, gave him the History of his own

Life, and desired that Prelate would send a Pastor to the numerous Body of Oct. 28 Christians, which he had left among the Infidels. *Athanasius* was very attentive to the Proposal, and desired him to repeat it in an Assembly of Bishops. They being unanimous in naming *Frumentius* to that Office, *Athanasius* consecrated him Bishop, and sent him back with that Character to *Axuma*, then the Metropolis of *Ethiopia*, where he gain'd Great Numbers to the Faith by his Discourses and Miracles. Our Historian assures us he had this Account from *Edesius*, who was afterwards ordain'd Priest at *Tyre*.

Our Saint continued his Apostolical Labours with great Application and Success for many Years, and had the Satisfaction of seeing the King, his Brother and the greater Part of the Nation receive the Doctrine of *Jesus Christ*. He always maintain'd a strict Correspondence with the Great Bishop of *Alexandria*, which made him odious to the *Arians*, and particularly to *Constantius* the Patron of that impious Sect, who demanded him of the King of *Ethiopia*, in order to be examined and instructed by *George* the Invader of St. *Athanasius's* See; but we do not hear of his being sent into *Egypt*. The *Roman* Church honours the Memory of St. *Frumentius* on the twenty seventh of *October*; the *Grecians* keep his Festival on the thirtieth of *November*, which the *Ethiopians*, particulary those whom we call *Abyssins*, observe on a Day that answers the eighteenth of our *December*, and reverence our Saint as the Apostle of their Country.

The XXVIII Day.

St. *SIMON*, Apostle.

SIMON one of the twelve Apostles was a Native of *Galilee*, and is in the Gospel distinguished by the Title of *Zealot*. We are in the Dark as to the Time of his becoming a Disciple of *Jesus Christ*; and his Election into the Apostolical College is the first and only thing recorded of our Saint. Some modern Greek Writers affirm that he carried the Light of the Gospel into *Egypt*, *Libya*, *Africa*, *Mauritania*, and the British Islands. But, according to the best Accounts we can gather from the Antients, he preached and suffer'd Martyrdom in *Persia*.

Luke 6. 15.

St. *JUDE*, Apostle.

JUDE, whom St. *Matthew* and St. *Mark* call *Thaddeas*! was also one of the Twelve, and Brother to St. *James the Less*; but in what Sense both he and our Saint are called our Lord's Brothers may be seen in our Account of St. *James*, *May* first. According to *Hegesippus*, as quoted by *Eusebius*, *Jude* was married and had several Children; but the other Particulars of his

Oct. 28. Life are unknown 'till we hear of his Labours for the Propagation of the Gospel, which St. *Paulinus* Bishop of *Nola* in the V Century tells us were employ'd in *Libya*. He is usually honour'd as a Martyr; but the Time and Place of his Suffering are uncertain; the current Opinion in the Western Church is that he seal'd the Gospel with his Blood in *Persia* in Company with St. *Simon*.

Among the inspired Writings we have an Epistle address'd by our Saint to all *the beloved in the Father, who are called and preserved by* Jesus Christ; in which he strenuously opposes, such as endeavour'd to corrupt the Faith in those early Times of the Church, and draws them in proper Colours. It is usually thought that the Innovators, against whom the Apostle inveighs were the first Disciples of *Simon* the Magician, whose Morals were not more pure than their Doctrine.

The *Grecians* observe the tenth of *May* in Honour of St. *Simon*, and the nineteenth of *June* is by them dedicated to the Memory of St. *Jude*; but the *Latins* join them in one Festival on the twenty eighth of *October*.

The XXIX Day.

St. *NARCISSUS*, Bishop of *Jerusalem*.

NARCISSUS, born toward the Close of the first Century, was well advanced in Years when he was placed at the Head of the Church of *Jerusalem*, and is reckon'd the thirtieth Bishop of that City since the Apostles. 'Though he is with good Reason supposed to have been near fourscore Years old, when he undertook the Government of that ancient Church, he acted in the Episcopal Character with the Vigour and Courage of a young Man. About the Middle of the second Age we find our holy Prelate in a Council at *Cesarea* in *Palestine*, conven'd on the Question of keeping Easter; which then began to make a great Noise in the Church. Our Saint, and *Theophilus* Bishop of the Town where that Assembly met, are mention'd as presiding in it; and consequently *Narcissus* must be allow'd the Reputation of a considerable Share in drawing up the Synodical Epistle attributed to all present, for observing the Feast of our Lord's Resurrection on *Sunday*.

Eusebius, in his Ecclesiastical History assures us that in his Time the Christians of *Jerusalem* preserved the Memory of several Miracles done by the Hands of our holy Bishop; one of which is as follows. While he possess'd that See, the Deacons, whose Business it was to light the Lamps in the Church on Easter Eve, were unprovided with Oil at that solemn Time. The People were sensibly afflicted

afflicted at this Deficiency; upon which *Narcissus* order'd the proper Offi- Oct. 29 cers to fetch some Water from a neighbouring Well, and bring it to him. After some devout and fervent Prayers pronounced over the Water, he directed them to pour it into the Lamps. They had no sooner obey'd his Commands but the Element was by the Omnipotence of God converted into Oil, to the unspeakable Surprize of the Faithful.

This Miracle recommended the holy Bishop most powerfully to the Veneration of all good Men; but there is no Security against the Malice of such as find their Account in blasting the Character of those who declare open War against their Vices. This was the Case of *Narcissus*. Three incorrigible Persons, who look'd on the Episcopal Severity and Exactness of the Saint as an insupportable Yoak, and apprehended the Lash of Ecclesiastical Discipline, resolved to prevent the Stroke of Justice by destroying his Reputation. To this End they forged a false Accusation against him, and laid a detestable Crime to his Charge; but *Eusebius*, who has given us the Account of this Matter, does not specify the Nature of that imaginary Crime. To gain the Credit of the World more effectually they had Recourse to solemn and dreadful Perjury. One wished he might perish by Fire, if what he urged was not true: the second that he might be struck with some loathsome Disease on the same Condition; and the third that he might lose his Sight, if the Saint was not really guilty of what was alledged against him. But *Narcissus*'s Virtue was so well known that those Imprecations made little or no Impression on the People to his Disadvantage. *Narcissus*, however though innocent in the Opinion of his Flock, could not stand the Shock of that bold Calumny; or rather made it a plausible Excuse for leaving *Jerusalem*, and spending some Time, in Solitude which had long been his Wish.

Narcissus spent several Years undiscover'd in his Retreat, where he enjoy'd all the Pleasure that a good Conscience, and close Conversation with Heaven can bestow. While he remain'd conceal'd from the most inquisitive Eye, divine Justice overtook the Villains who had conspired against his Reputation, and aspersed his Virtue; for each of them was punish'd as they had wished. The first was burnt in his own House with his whole Family; the second was cover'd with such a Disease as he had call'd for: the third, seeing the miserable Ends of his Partners in Iniquity, and apprehending the like exemplary Punishment, made a publick Declaration of the whole Plot against the Saint; but his Grief for his Crime produced such continual Floods of Tears, that he lost the Use of his Eyes.

Our Saint having disappear'd for some Time, the Bishops of that Province thought their Concern for the Christians of *Jerusalem* obliged them to provide a Pastor for the Church of that City. *Dius* was their first Choice; but, he dying soon after his Election, *Germanio* was placed on the See, which appear'd vacant, and was soon after succeeded by *Gordius*. The Person last mention'd had been some time in quiet Possession of the Bishoprick, when *Narcissus* appear'd like one from the Dead. The whole Body of the Faithful, transported at the Recovery of their holy Pastor, whose Innocence had been so authentickly vindicated, conjured him to reassume the Administration of his Diocese. Authors are not agreed whether *Gordius* left the See of *Jerusalem*, or shared the Government of it with *Narcissus*; but it appears from the Sequel of the Story, as deliver'd by *Eusebius*, that our Saint survived him.

Narcissus was in sole Possession of the Bishoprick, when Providence in Consideration of his great Age and Infirmities, directed *Alexander* to his Assistance, of whom we have spoken on the eighteenth of *March*; and it appears from a Letter of that Prelate, that He and *Narcissus* govern'd the Church of *Jerusalem* together. Our Saint, according to that Epistle, was above one hundred and sixteen Years of Age when it was written; but we do not know how long he survived the Date of it. The *Roman* Martyrologe honours his Memory on the twenty ninth of *October*.

St. MARY, the PENITENT.

THE Saint, whose Penance is proposed this Day as an Encouragement and Model to unhappy Sinners, was Niece to *Abraham* a famous Hermit either of *Syria* or *Mesopotamia* in the V or VI Century. That holy Man had left his Country, and Fortune to indulge the heavenly Pleasures of Prayer and Solitude; but was some Time after employ'd by his Bishop in converting a whole Town of Pagans. That difficult and glorious Work being completed, the Anchoret return'd to his former Solitude, which was never interrupted again but by his Concern for *Mary*, the Person of whom we are to speak in this Place.

Mary was left an Orphan at seven Years of Age, and by some Friends of her deceased Father recommended to the Care of her Uncle, who had then spent some Time in the Desart. *Abraham*, who had too much Charity to make his present State an Excuse for neglecting his Niece in that Distress, built a Cell contiguous to his own for her Use, open'd a Window of Communication in the Wall that divided them, and there instructed her in the Holy Scriptures. *Mary* spent several Hours of the Night in singing the Praises of God with her devout Uncle; endeavour'd to imitate his Austerities;

Austerities; and made a considerable Progress in Virtue under that excellent Master. *Abraham*, believing her sufficiently confirm'd in such a Disengagement from the World, as he had profess'd so many Years, made no Difficulty of disposing of her Fortune among the Poor, as he had done of his own upon engaging in his present State. His Niece gave her free Consent to the Act, and spent a considerable time in the sincere and faithful Practice of Religion and Penance. But no Virtue is proof against the Malice of the Devil, unless guarded by Humility, and Vigilance; and our Saint was an unhappy Instance of that Truth.

An artful Hypocrite, who had nothing but the Dress of a Hermit, found his way to *Mary*'s Cell, pretending to be drawn thither by his Opinion of her Virtue. After some Visits he prevail'd with her to open her Window and thus allow him the Satisfaction of seeing the Person whose Discourse was so engaging and edifying. Their Conversation at first turn'd on pious Subjects, but by Degrees other Topicks less innocent were admitted; which encouraged the Hermit to discover a criminal Passion for the innocent young Woman That disguised Libertine employ'd every Artifice in his Power to seduce her; but she held out a whole Year, and probably might have conquer'd the Temptation entirely, had she been diffident enough of her own Strenth to let her Uncle into the Affair, and beg his Advice. For want of that necessary Precaution, *Mary* yielded at last, left her Cell, and consented to all that Agent of Hell had proposed for her Ruin. As she ran headlong down the Precipice, she was at the Bottom before she gave her Case one cool Thought. But she had scarce sacrificed her Virtue, when she was touched with a quick Remorse for what she had done; full of Horror at her Crime and despairing of Pardon she tore her Cloaths like a Madwoman, beat herself unmercifully, and had dispatched herself, had it been in her Power. When the first Transports of Rage against herself were over, instead of thinking of suing for Pardon, she concluded there was none for her, changed her Cloaths and made her way to a Town, where she was not known, with a Resolution of stiffling all Sense of Guilt by plunging deeper in Debauchery.

About this time St. *Abraham* dreamt he saw a Dragon devour a Dove; and, when he awaked, imagining what he had seen a Presage of some violent Persecution of the the Church of *Christ*, he imploy'd his Prayers and Tears for averting that Calamity. Two Days after, he had the same Dream; and thought he kill'd the Dragon, open'd it, and found a Dove whole and alive in his Belly. Upon waking he called *Mary*, whom he imagined still in her

Cell,

Oct. 29. Cell, and complain'd that he had not seen her of two Days; but, receiving no Answer, he made a farther Enquiry, and found Part of the Dream verified by the Loss of his Niece. It is impossible to express the venerable Hermit's Grief on this Occasion.

After two Years spent in fervent Prayer for the Recovery and Salvation of one, whose Education and spiritual Welfare had long been his chief Concern, he heard where she was, and what Life she had lead; upon which, being persuaded the two Years absence were represented by the two Days Interval betwixt his Dreams, he began to entertain Hopes of rescuing her from the Power of the Devil. In Pursuit of this good Work, he left his Hermitage, disguised himself, and rode in Quest of his lost Sheep. Coming to the Inn, where he was inform'd his Niece practiced Prostitution, he alighted, and after some Hours Repose asked the Master of the House for the Young Lady under his Roof, of whose Beauty he had heard, before he reached that Place. In Compliance with this Request, *Mary* was introduced to the supposed Galant, who received her with a Gaiety suitable to the Character which he assumed, though his Heart was ready to break at the Sight. *Abraham*, who had eat neither Meat nor Bread for forty Years together, order'd a handsome Supper, and behaved himself with a Cheerfulness that proved as effectual a Disguise as his Dress; for he had but too much Reason to fear he should lose his Labour, if he discover'd himself before he was secure of her. In this View he submitted to be conducted to the Chamber, where she proposed to spend the Night with him; *Abraham* desired her to fasten the Door, and then, catching her by the Arm, and throwing off his Hat, which cover'd great Part of his Face, " Look on me " Mary, said the holy Anchoret, *see if you know this Face; am not I the* " *Person from whom you received your Education? What is become of your coarse* " *penitential Dress; and the austere Practices, which you learnt under my Di-* " *rection? Or rather what is become of yourself since you left your Father?* " *Tell me, what Villain has torn you from these poor Arms, and plunged you* " *into this miserable State.*"

This unexpected Address struck her Dumb, and fixt her to the Place without Sense or Motion. *Abraham* employ'd very innocent Art to recover her from the Surprize, begg'd she would not despair of Mercy, and mention'd several Instances of Sinners, received to God's Favour after some Years spent in the most criminal Excesses. So much Goodness, and the Tears of a tender Parent had the desired Influence on *Mary*'s Heart, who declared herself ready to attend him to the Desart; which she did early the next

Morning.

Morning. *Mary*, thus delivered from the Jawes of Hell, lamented her paſt Oct. 30 Folly, and puniſh'd her Sins with a Severity expreſſive of a true Senſe of her Enormity. The Sincerity of her Converſion, and the Puniſhment which ſhe inflicted on her guilty Body were ſo pleaſing to the Almighty, that three Years after her Return to that Scene of Penance ſeveral miraculous Cures were perform'd by her Prayers. St. *Abraham* continued his ſpiritual Aſſiſtance to our Penitent, till it pleaſed God to reward his Labours by a happy Death. She ſurvived her excellent Director five Years; which Time was ſpent in Prayers, Tears, and incredible Auſterities. The *Greeks* honour her Memory with that of her Uncle on the twenty ninth of *October*: But the *Roman* Martyrologe places the holy Hermit's Name on the ſixteenth of *March*.

The XXX Day.

St. *MARCELLUS*, a Centurion, Martyr.

MARCELLUS, whoſe glorious Victory the Church this Day commemorates, was a Centurion, or Captain in the the *Trajan* Legion in the Reign of *Dioclefian*, and *Maximian*, a Profeſſor of the Chriſtian Religion, and poſted with his Company at *Tangier* in *Africa*. The Anniverſary of the Emperor's Birth-Day being in the Year 298 celebrated in that Town with great Solemnity, and Sacrifice to the Pagan Deities making a conſiderable Part of that Solemnity, all the Subjects of the Empire were expected to conform to the blind Religion of that Prince on that Occaſion; but *Marcellus*, well inſtructed in the Duties of his Profeſſion, expreſs'd his Deteſtation of thoſe profane and ſacrilegious Practices by throwing away his Belt, the Badge of his Military Character, at the Head of his Company, and declaring aloud that *he was a Soldier of* JESUS CHRIST, *the eternal King*. He then quitted his Arms, and added that *from that Moment he ceaſed to ſerve the Emperor; and thus expreſs'd his Contempt of the Gods of the Empire, which were no better than deaf and dumb Idols*. "If, continued he, *their Imperial Majeſties impoſe the Obligation of ſacrificing to them and their Gods, as a neceſſary Condition of their Service, here I throw up my Commiſſion, and quit the Army*."

The Soldiers, ſurprized to hear *Marcellus* deliver himſelf in this Manner ſeiz'd him, and carried him before *Anaſtaſius Fortunatus*, Judge of the Legion,

Oct. 23 gion, who committed him to Prison. When the idolatrous Entertainment was over, that Magistrate order'd *Marcellus* to be brought in, and asked him what he meant by quitting the Service so abruptly. Our Saint answer'd him with a brief and plain Account of what he had done, upon which *Fortunatus* told him it was not in his Power to connive at his Rashness, and must therefore lay his Case before the Emperor.

On the thirtieth Day of *October Marcellus* was by *Fortunatus*'s Direction carried to *Aurelian Agricolanus*, Vicar to the Pretorian Prefect, then at *Tangier*, who upon hearing what had been alledged against him, asked him whether he had really done as the Judge's Letter set forth. His own free Confession mader farther Examination unnecessary; and the Vicar proceeded to give Sentence of Death against him, which was immediately executed by Beheading; a Punishment inflicted on him for Desertion, and what they call'd Impiety, as it is express'd in the Acts of his Martyrdom taken on the Spot.

Cassian, whose Business it was to attend the Court, and write down the Trials, was so affected with the Intrepidity of the Saint, that he threw down his Books, and declared against the Injustice of the Proceedings. The Vicar, shock'd at what he saw and heard, asked the Notary with some Emotion what he meant. *Cassian* was bold enough to repeat his Protest against the Sentence; and *Agricolanus*, apprehending he might go on in that offensive Strain, order'd him to be hurried away to Prison. *Cassian*, being examined, and persisting in his Opinion, receiv'd the Crown of Martyrdom on the third of *December* following.

The *Roman* Martyrologe has given us the Names of the two Martyrs on the respective Days of their Suffering; but we thought it could not be amiss to Speak of them together on the thirtieth of *October*, and that we were privileged in so doing by the Connexion between the Acts the said glorious Victims.

The XXXI Day.

St. *QUINTIN*, Martyr.

ST. *Quintin*, of whom the *Roman* Martyrologe speaks as a Native of *Rome*, and descended of a Senatorian Family, is by his Historian called the Son of *Zeno*; but no Particulars of his Life are recorded 'till we find him employ'd in the Labours of an Apostle. Full of Zeal for the Kingdom of of *Jesus Christ*, and desirous of making that powerful Name known among the Infidels, he left his Country, renounced all Prospects of Preferment, and, attended by *Lucian*, his Companion in the Evangelical Work, made his Way to *Gaul*. *Lucian* and our Saint preached the Faith together 'till they reached *Amiens* in *Picardy*; where they parted. *Quintin* choosing to pursue his Mission in that Country, his Companion undertook to plant the Faith at *Beauvaris*, where he received the Crown of Martyrdom.

We are not acquainted with the Particulars of St *Quintin*'s Actions and Sufferings; all we know of the Matter is that God made him equally powerful in Words and Works; that his Discourses were authorized, and strongly recommended by great Numbers of Miracles; illustrated and enforced by a most holy and mortified Life, and that he receiv'd the Reward of his charitable Labours about the Beginning of the Reign of *Dioclesian* and *Maximian*; the former of which Princes ascended the Imperial Throne in the Year 284; The latter in 286. *Maximian* had constituted *Rectius Varus* Prefect of the *Prætorium*, who being equal to his Sovereign in Superstition and Cruelty, executed his Designs against the Christian Religion with Ardour and Fidelity.

Rectius, who probably resided at *Treves*, the Metropolis of the *Belgick Gaul*, but was then employ'd in what was called the *second Gaul* not far from *Soissons*, having Intelligence of the prodigious Success which attended St. *Quintin*'s Endeavours, was so incensed at the Progress of the Christian Religion that he immediately form'd a Resolution to take off the holy Preacher; but deferr'd the Execution of it 'till his Business carried him to *Amiens*, which happen'd soon after. Upon his Arrival there; he order'd the Saint to be seized, thrown into Prison, and loaded with Chains. The next Day he was brought before the Prefect, who attempted his Constancy with such Promises and Threats as could not but affect any Man who was to be influenced by Motives of Hope or Fear; but, finding him proof against both, he order'd him to be whipp'd unmercifully, and then confined to a close Dungeon, without the Liberty of receiving either Comfort or Assistance from the Faithful. The Author of this Account tells us that *Quintin* was miraculously deliver'd that Night, and found preaching to the People the next Morning. This Prodigy, according to the same Writer, proved the Conversion of several; but the Prefect, looking on it as an Effect of some Magick Power, issued out a second Order for apprehending him, and endeavour'd by several violent Methods to stagger his Resolution; but with as little Success as before. His Limbs were stretched with Pullies, 'till all his Joints were dislocated: his Body was torn with Scourges of Wire: boiling Pitch and Oil were pour'd

Oct 31. on his Back; and lighted Torches applied to his Sides. The holy Martyr, strengthen'd by him whose Cause he Defended, remain'd Superior to all the cruel Arts of his barbarous Persecutor, and preserved a perfect Tranquility of Mind in the Midst of such Torments, as fill'd the Spectators with Horror.

After some Time spent in torturing the Saint, *Rectius* was obliged to leave *Amiens*, and direct his Course to the Territory of *Vermandois*; upon which he order'd *Quintin* to be conducted thither under a strong Guard, where he died under the Hands of his Executioners. The common Opinion is that he finished his Martyrdom on the thirty first of *October*, in the Year 287. The venerable Body was carefully watch'd till Night, and then thrown into the River *Somme*; and discover'd to the Faithful some Time after his Death; The Town where his Relicks now lie bears the Name of the holy Martyr.

St. *WOLFGANG*, Bishop of *Ratisbone*.

*W*OLFGANG a Native of *Swabia*, descended from Parents remarkable neither for Riches nor Poverty, was put into the Hands of a Neighbouring Ecclesiastick, when but seven Years old, and afterwards removed to the Abbey of *Richenow* near *Constance*, a House at that Time famous for the Education of Youth; where *Wolfgang* distinguish'd himself by Modesty, Devotion, and every thing that cou'd recommend him to the vertuous Part of Mankind. During his Residence in that Monestery he contracted an Intimacy with a young Person of Quality, named *Henry*; and, when he had finish'd his Studies, accompanied him to *Wurtzbourg*, where that Gentleman's Brother was then Bishop. In that City he learnt the holy Scriptures under *Stephen* an *Italian* Professor, who growing Jealous of his Scholar's superiour Skill in classick Learning, quarell'd with him and forbid him his School. Before that Rupture our Saint had but little Relish for the World, and he thought this a proper Opportunity for putting his Design of Retiring in Execution. *Henry*, who loved *Wolfgang*, alarm'd at the Notion opposed it most Vigorously, and had Power enough over him to detain him at *Wurtzbourg*; being chosen Archbishop of *Treves* in 956, he obliged our Saint to accompany him to that City, made him several advantageous Profers; but could prevail with him to accept of nothing in his Diocese, but the Care of a School for Children. He acquitted himself of the Duties of that Post so well that *Henry* obliged him to undertake the Government of a Community

of

St. Wolfgang, *Bishop.*

of Ecclesiasticks, with the Title of Dean, which flourished so well under his Direction that the most regular Monastery gave not more Edification than that Body of secular Canons.

Upon the Death of the Arch Bishop of *Treves*, which happen'd in the Year 964, *Wolfgang* resolved to return to his own Country; but *Bruno*, Archbishop of *Cologn* and Brother to the Emperor, prevail'd with him to spend some Time in that City. That Prince was very pressing with our Saint to accept of a Bishoprick, or any other Preferment which his Interest could procure; but he declined those advantageous Offers, and went for *Swabia* where he enter'd the Monestery of *Enfilden*, governed at that time by *George* an *Englishman*, who had left his own Country to serve God in Silence and Mortification. The Abbot, who was no Stranger to his Character before he received him into his Community, soon found that his Reputation for Virtue was much inferiour to his Merit. He had not been long in that Monestery before he was entrusted with the Direction of the Students; and all the Neighbouring Convents sent their young Monks to him for Instruction in Piety and Literature.

The Diocess of *Ausburg*, in which his Monastery stood, was then govern'd by St. *Ulrick*, whose Life may be seen on the fourth of *July*. That Prelate coming to visit the House, according to Custom, was so charmed with *Wolfgang*'s Virtue and Capacity that he was resolved to consecrate that Saint's excellent Talents to the Service of God in the Ministry; with this View he ordain'd him Priest, in spite of all the Opposition his Humility could form on that Occasion. Having received an Apostolick Spirit at his Ordination, he applied for his Abbot's Leave to preach the Gospel, among the Infidels, which he obtain'd, left his Monestery in the Year 972, attended by a select Number of Monks, and made his Way to *Panonia*, where he knew the *Hungarians* would find sufficient Employment for him and his Companions. Those *Barbarians* made such obstinate Resistance to the Endeavours of our Saint, that he gain'd but little Ground in that Country; whereupon *Piligrin*, Bishop of *Passaw*, dissuaded him from prosecuting his Enterprize, and engaged him to spend some Time with him. That Prelate became so sensible of our Saint's Merit, that he resolved to solicit his Promotion to the See of *Ratisbone*, which became vacant about that Time. *Wolfgang*'s Character, faithfully drawn, being privately sent to the Emperor *Otho* II, that Prince dispatched an Order for carrying him to *Ratisbone*, where *Frederick* Archbishop of *Strasbourg*, his Metropolitan, should consecrate him. The Saint could not avoid accompanying the Emperor's Officers to *Ratisbone*, where the

Clergy

Oct. 31 Clergy and People were unanimous in his Election; but he declared loudly against the Proceedings, and protested against the Violence which was offer'd him. The Chucrh of that City knew his Value too well to listen to his Remonstrances, and put him into proper Hands to conduct him to *Frankfort* for the Emperor's Approbation. *Wolfgang*, arriving at Court, threw himself at *Otho*'s Feet, assured him he was mistaken in the Choice, and begg'd Leave to return to his Monestery; but the Prince was deaf to all he could say on that Subject, invested him with the Temporalities of the Bishoprick, and sent him back to *Ratisbone*, where he was consecrated and inthroned amidst the Acclamations of his Flock. The Author of his Life observes that he never quitted the Monastick Habit, but practiced all the Austerities of a Religious Life, when in Possession of the Episcopal Dignity. He reform'd his Clergy, made excellent Regulations for Monasteries of both Sexes; instructed the inferiour Pastours in their Duty to God and their Flock, and thus introduced an edifying Change in the Morals of his whole Diocess. *Wolfgang* had an excellent Talent at touching the Hearts of his Auditors, and was indifatigable in Preaching; in short, after discharging all the Duties of his Station twenty Years with the utmost Vigilence and Fidelity he was favour'd with a Passage to a glorious Immortality on the last Day of *October* 994. He was buried at *Ratisbone*, where his Sanctity was attested by many Miracles; and the Day of his Death is by the *Roman Martyrologe* consecrated to his Memory.

The End of *October*.

THE
LIVES
OF
SAINTS;

COLLECTED FROM

AUTHENTICK RECORDS,

OF

CHURCH HISTORY,

With a full Account of

THE OTHER

FESTIVALS throughout the YEAR.

The whole Interspersed with

Suitable REFLECTIONS.

Number XI. *for* NOVEMBER.

LONDON:

Printed for THOMAS MEIGHAN, in *Drury-Lane*, MDCCXXIX.

Advertisement.

THE following Work is collected from such Authorities, as are universally acknowledged to be unexceptionable. And therefore what is omitted, and might by some be expected here, is not judged or declared false and spurious by such Omission; but only not inserted, because doubted of by some.

AN Alphabetical TABLE OF The Saints in *November*,

And other Festivals in the same Month.

A	Day	F	Day
ALL SAINTS,	1	Felix, of *Valois*,	20
All Souls,	2	Flora and Mary, *Martyrs*,	24
Andrew *Apostle*,	30		
C		**G**	
Catharine, *Virgin and Martyr*,	25	Gregory Thaumaturgus,	17
Cecily, *Virgin and Martyr*,	22	**H**	
Charles, *Archbishop of* Milan,	4	Hugh, *Bishop of* Lincoln,	17
Chrysogonus, *Martyr*,	24		
Clement, *Pope and Martyr*,	23	**I**	
Columban, *Abbot*,	21		
Crown'd *Martyrs*,	8	John the Almoner,	11
D		**L**	
Didacus,	13	Laurence *Archbishop of* Dublin,	14
Dionysius, *Bishop of* Alexandria,	17	**M**	
E		Malachi, *Archbishop of* Armagh,	3
Edmund, *Archbishop of* Canterbury,	16	Malo, *Bishop*,	
Edmund, *King and Martyr*,	20	Marcellus, *Bishop of* Paris,	
Elizabeth, *Widow*,	19	Martin *of* Tours,	
Eucherius, *Bishop of* Lyons,	16		

An Alphabetical Table.

	Day
Martin, *Pope and Martyr*,	12
Maximus, *Confessor*,	25
Maximus, *Bishop of* Riez,	27
Moses, *Martyr*,	25

N

Nympha, *Virgin*,	10

P

Peter and Paul, *the Dedication of Churches in their Honour*,	18
Peter, *Bishop of* Alexandria, *Martyr*,	26
Philemon,	22
Presentation *of the* Blessed Virgin,	21

R

Romanus, *Martyr*,	18

S

	Day
Saturninus, *Bishop and Martyr*,	29
St. Saviour's *Church, its Dedication*,	9
Stanislaus Kostka,	13
Stephen, *Martyr*,	28

T

Theodore, *Martyr*,	9
Trypho *and* Respicius, *Martyrs*,	10

V

Vitalis, *and* Agricola, *Martyrs*.	4
Virgilius *Bishop of* Saltzbourg.	27

W

Winock, *Abbot*,	6
Willibrord, *Bishop of Utrecht*,	7

Z

Zachary *and* Elizabeth,	5

NOVEMBER the First.

The Feast of ALL SAINTS.

THE Design of the Church in this Day's Festival is to honour God in all his Saints; some of whose Names are written only in the Book of Life, and are not specified in the Course of her holy Year, either because their Sanctity was known to God alone, or because the Calamities of the Christian Church, or other Accidents have deprived us of the Particulars of their Lives. The Veneration of Saints, or holy Persons in Possession of the Glory, after which we all aspire, is not founded on a Persuasion of their Independence on the Almighty, or any essential Excellency of their Nature, but is given them in Consideration of what God by his powerful Grace has made them; so that the Supreme Being is still the last Object of our Respect to the most perfect of his Creatures; or rather, the whole of our Veneration for the Citizens of the Heavenly *Jerusalem*, is no more than an Act of Worship directed to God, *who is wonderful in his Saints*; and our Addresses to them, in whatever Terms they may appear, are by the constant Doctrine of the Catholick Church understood only as so many Petitions to our happy Fellow Creatures for the Assistance of their Prayers for obtaining the same Graces which have carried them through the Dangers and Temptations of this Life, and raised them to their present State of Glory. This Representation of the Article before us is exactly conformable to the Language of the Council of

Nov. 1. *Trent* which in the twenty fifth Session directs the Bishops, and all who are employ'd in instructing the Faithful, to teach them *that the Saints reigning with* Christ *offer Prayers to God for Men: and that it is good and profitable to invoke them, and have Recourse to their Prayers for obtaining Favours from God, through* Jesus Christ *our Lord, who is our only Redeemer and Saviour.*

After having premised thus much concerning the Spirit of this Day's Devotion, we proceed to an Account of the Institution of the Festival. Under the Emperor *Augustus*, some Years before the Birth of our Saviour, M. *Aprippa* in his third Consulship raised a magnificent Temple, which as *Dio*, a Pagan Historian observes, was called *Pantheon*, either because it's Founder had there placed the Symbols of several Gods in the Statues of *Mars*, and *Venus*; or, as that Author is rather inclined to think, because its convex Figure represented the Heavens; and in either of these Senses it might be called the *Residence of all the Gods*, which is the Interpretation of the *Greek* Name. This Masterpiece of Architecture, as *Pliny* informs us, was dedicated to *Jupiter the Revenger*, a Compliment paid him under that Denomination on the Account of *Augustus*'s Success at *Actium* against *Anthony* and *Cleopatra*. When the Masters of the *Roman* Empire became Christians, they enacted several Laws for abolishing Idolatry, and levelling Temples in their Dominions. *Theodosius* the younger, who came to the Imperial Throne in 408, publish'd an Order for demolishing all Buildings dedicated to the Service of Idols; but *Honorius*, that Prince's Uncle, who governed in the West, though no less an Enemy to Pagan Superstition than He, strictly forbid all Sacrifices in the Heathen Temples, but declared for their being preserved as so many Ornaments to the City of *Rome*; and the Preservation of the beautiful, and bold Structure in Question is owing to this Order. Those Edifices remain'd useless, and shut up, till Christianity was so well establish'd in the World that the Church seem'd to be in no Danger from Idolatry; they were then open'd, cleansed from their former Defilement, and converted into Places for the Worship of the true God, who thus triumphed over those pretended Deities in their own Temples. This appears from St. *Gregory*'s Conduct in Regard to our converted Ancestors; upon the Conversion of King *Ethelbert*, that holy Pope wrote to him and exhorted him to destroy the Temples of the Idols; but, giving the Matter a second Consideration, thought proper to allow the establishing of God's Worship, where the Idols had once been adored; as may be seen in St. *Gregory*'s Letter to *Mellitus*, Bishop of *London* on that Subject.

About

About three Years after the Deceafe of that great Pope, *Boniface* IV was Nov. 1. placed in St. *Peter*'s Chair, and undertook to open the *Pantheon*. When he had banifh'd all Remains of Idolatry from that Temple, he confecrated it to God with due Solemnity, in Honour of the bleffed Virgin and all the holy Martyrs. This Ceremony was perform'd on the thirteenth of *May*, on which Day it is mention'd in the *Roman* Martyrologe. The Church, for fo we muft now ftile it, was call'd *St. Mary's at the Martyrs*; but is at prefent better known by the Title of the *Rotonda*, or round Church; to which the Bleffed Virgin's Name is fometimes added.

The Feaft of that Dedication, though annual, could not be properly called the *Feaft of all Saints*, as appears from the very Form of the Title; but muft be allow'd to have prepared the Way for it. The firft, who fpoke with that Latitude was Pope *Gregory* III, who in the VIII Century built a Chapel in St. *Peter*'s Church in Honour of our Saviour, the Bleffed Virgin, the holy Apoftles, and all the holy Martyrs and Confeffors; from that Time it is probable a Day was kept at *Rome* in Honour of *All Saints*: *Gregory* IV, going into *France* in the Year 835, advifed *Lewis the Pious*, to appoint the Feaft of *All Saints* in his Dominions, according to the Practice of *Rome*. The Emperor liften'd to the Propofal, and with the Confent of his Bifhops pubifh'd an Order for obferving the firft of *November* in Honour of *All the Saints*, in *Germany* and *France*; and from thefe Countries the faid Feftival foon made it's Way through the whole Weftern Church. The *Grecians* commemorate the Glory of the Members of the Church Triumphant on the *Sunday* after *Whitfunday*.

St. *MARCELLUS*, Bifhop of PARIS.

ST. *Marcellus* is by the *French* Hiftorians reckon'd the firft Saint known among them for a Native of *Paris*. He was born in the IV Century, of a Family which was to receive Honour from him; brought up in Sentiments of Piety; and fo happily prevented with the Grace of God, that his Infancy was remarkable for fuch Virtues as are look'd on with Veneration in a more mature Age. Humility, Meeknefs, Charity, Mortification, Modefty were the Ingredients of his Character, as foon as he came to the Ufe of Reafon. The uncommon Gravity that appear'd in his Conduct in his firft Years recommended him fo ftrongly to the Bifhop of *Paris*, that he engaged him to enter among
the

Nov. 2. the Clergy of that City, and gave him the Order of Reader in his Church at his first Admission. The Author of our Saint's Life assures us that his Ministry in that Station was attended by Miracles. His Sanctity was so conspicuous to the whole Town that the Bishop, pursuant to the Judgment and Desire of his People, promoted him in due Time to the higher Orders, and at last invested him with the Priestly Dignity.

The Inhabitants of *Paris* had so profound a Veneration for our holy Priest, that upon the Decease of that Pastor, the general Voice declared *Marcellus* his Successor. The Saint made what Objections his Humility suggested on that Occasion; but they were over-ruled, and he obliged to accept of the weighty Charge, which he did with Trembling. In his Person were to be seen all those Virtues which should adorn the Episcopal Character, and might make him a Model for all who should be placed in that See. A Life so holy concluded in a happy Death on the first of *November*, at the Beginning of the V Century. His Feast is observed on the third of *November* in the Church of *Paris*, because the two preceeding Days are otherwise taken up; but his Name occurs in the *Roman* Martyrologe on the Day of his Decease.

The Body of the holy Prelate was buried about a Quarter of a League from *Paris*, in a Village, which has been since much enlarged, and join'd the Town, and is reckon'd one of it's Suburbs; but now the Canons of the Cathedral of *Paris* are in Possession of his venerable Relicks.

The II Day.

The Commemoration of all the Faithful Departed, commonly called All Souls *Day.*

THE Being of a Purgatory has by several able Pens been so largely proved that it will not be necessary to say much here in Confirmation of that Article of our Faith. We shall only observe that the Necessity of admitting such a State arises from the Inequality of Sins, and the Punishments due to them; some destroying Grace, and being therefore call'd *Mortal*: Other less heinous, and not so prejudicial to the Soul; and yet not the least Impurity can be admitted into Heaven. The holy Council of *Trent* has strictly forbid the Pastors of the Church meddling with curious Enquiries, nice Speculations, and doubtful Points on this Head, when

employ'd

employ'd in teaching the People committed to their Care; and reduces the whole Doctrine of a middle State after this Life to this plain and modest Definition, viz. *That there is a Purgatory: and that the Souls there detain'd are assisted by the Suffrages of the Faithful, but chiefly by the acceptable Sacrifice of the Altar.* And, indeed, a State of Temporary Suffering, or Punishment in the other World once admitted, both Reason and Charity unite in Favour of the pious Practice of offering Prayers for the Relief of such as are in that State; for the same Arguments that are urged for applying to Heaven for the Sick and Afflicted in this World, which to them is a Sort of Purgatory, are equally strong for our Addresses to the Almighty, for such as are under his correcting Hand in the other. We are to consider the Church of *Christ* as composed of three different Parts, *viz.* The Triumphant, the Suffering, and the Militant; and that Catholick Charity embraces all the Members of *Jesus Christ*. Our Love for Him should engage and bind us, as it were, to his whole Body, and teach us to share the Miseries and Afflictions of it as well as it's Comforts and Blessings; so that, as we are obliged to interest ourselves in the Joy and Glory of the Saints by commemorating their Triumps, congratulating their Happiness, and recommending ourselves to their powerful Intercession, so we are to take Part in the Afflictions of the Suffering Part of the Church, and assist the Sufferers in the best Manner we are able; and thus only the Communion of Saints, or Communication of good Works among all the living Members of *Christ* will be complete.

It is evident from the Writings of the Primitive Fathers and the ancient Liturgies of all Christian Churches that Prayers for the Dead were always Part of their publick Worship; St. *Crysostom* and St. *Augustin* seem to be unexceptionable Evidences in the present Case. The former in his third Homily on the Epistle to the *Philippians*, says, " *It was not in vain that* " *the Apostles ordain'd a Commemoration of the Deceased in the venerable and* " *dreadful Mysteries; they were sensible of the Benefit and Advantage of* " *that Practice; for*, continues that holy Doctor, *when the Congregation* " *stands with open Arms, as well as the Priests, and the tremendous Sacrifice is* " *before them, how should our Prayers for their Relief miscarry? But this is* " *said of such as depart in Faith.*" The latter in the one hundred and seventy second Discourse, *on the Words of the Apostle*, declares that the Church in his Time pray'd for the Dead in the great Sacrifice, and founded that Practice on the Tradition of their Ancestors; the Effect expected from this Devotion is by that Father thus expres'd: " *That God deals with them more* " *mercifully*

Nov. 2. "*mercifully than their Sins deserve.*" This was the Sense of the purest Antiquity; but the Institution of a general Commemoration of all the Faithful departed, as now practiced, is owing to the devout Care of St. *Odilo*, Abbot of *Cluny*, who died in the Year 1049. That holy Person publish'd a Decree obliging all the Monasteries of his Order to pray for all the Faithful Departed on the second of *November*. It is dated in 998, and was soon after adopted by the whole Western Church. At the Beginning of the XIII Age this Devotion was well established in our Island; as appears from a Council held at *Oxford* in 1222, where the second of *November* is on that Account placed among the Feasts of the second Rank, that is such as allow'd only Works of most Importance and Necessity: and a College founded at *Oxford* under the Title of *All Souls* by *Henry Chichley* Archbishop of *Canterbury* in 1437 is a standing Proof of the Sense of our religious Ancestors on that Point in the XV Century.

The III Day.

St. MALACHI *Archbishop of* Armagh.

THE Saint of this Day, whose Vertues engaged the Admiration of St. *Bernard*, and employ'd the Pen of that excellent Writer, was born toward the Close of the XI Century, in the County of *Armagh* in *Ireland*. His Parents were Persons of the first Rank; and his Mother, whose Virtue was much Superior to her Quality, was particularly careful to teach him the Law of God preferably to all other Branches of Knowledge; but as *Malachi* was happy in most excellent Dispositions to both Learning and Piety, he acquired human Literature under the Direction of able Masters, while he learnt the Principles of Religion from the Example and Instructions of his Parents. His Infancy was distinguished by a Modesty, Docility, and Sweetness of Temper which gain'd him the Love of all who saw him; and the uncommon Gravity of his Youth encouraged the largest Hopes that could be form'd of his future Life. His Application to Study was constant and indefatigable; and, by retrenching such Diversions as employ'd his Companions, he exceeded them all in his Progress in Learning.

But the Cultivation of his Mind was not the only, or the chief Employment of our Saint in his first Years. His Inclinations to converse with God made him seek Retirement, where Prayer, and all the Exercises of true

Piety

Piety were his Entertainment and Delight. The Increase of his Age made no Alteration in the Purity of his Morals and the Simplicity of his Heart; in Order to secure the Treasure with which God had entrusted him, he left his Father's House, and put himself under the Direction of *Imarius* a holy Recluse, who lived in a Cell near the Church of *Armagh*, where he spent his Time in Fasting, Prayer, and the Practice of such Austerities as that excellent Master judged most proper for keeping his Body and Mind in due Subjection. This extraordinary Step in a young Man, who had all the Conveniencies and Pleasures of Life in his Power, made no small Noise at *Armagh*; but *Malachi*, equally indifferent to the several Opinions of the World on that Occasion, stood his Ground bravely against all Attempts to tear him from his penitential Retreat. The eminent Sanctity of his Life, the Simplicity of his Obedience, his Mortification and Silence were so edifying, that several Persons desired to form themselves by his Example. *Malachi*'s Concern for the Salvation of his Neighbour prevail'd with him to apply to *Imarius* on that Subject, and he succeeded so well with the holy Hermit that the Petitioners were received, and soon became a considerable Community. The Saint always look'd on himself as the least, and most unworthy of that religious Society; but *Celsus*, then Archbishop of *Armagh*, had different Sentiments of his Merit, and therefore with the Concurrence of his Superior obliged him to accept of Deacon's Orders. The Fervour, and Purity, with which he discharged all the Duties of his Ministry in that Station, were sufficient to encourage his Diocesan's Hopes, that he would do Credit to the Priesthood; and accordingly he was invested with the sacred Character at twenty five Years of Age, in Spight of all the Objections his Humility and Modesty could form against that Promotion. Thus qualified he was immediately imploy'd in Preaching, and, the Sanctity of his Life being an irresistible Proof of the Truth of his Doctrine, made incredible Progress in the Reformation and Conversion of his Auditors. He rooted out several inveterate Vices; corrected a great Number of Abuses; and re-established Purity of Faith and Morals among the People. He made several useful Regulations in Ecclesiastical Discipline, which were encouraged and authorized by his Bishops; settled the regular Reherfal of the Canonical Hours in all the Churches in the Diocese, which was soon after follow'd by the other Churches of *Ireland*; enforced the Practice of auricular Confession, the Use of Confirmation, and the Observation of the Canons in Regard to Matrimony; for, as St. *Bernard* assures us, all these Particulars were either

not

Nov. 3. not known, or much neglected in *Ireland* before our Saint exerted his Zeal on that Occasion.

While *Malachi* was thus employ'd in restoring the Worship of God to it's primitive Beauty, and establishing the constant and due Administration of the Sacraments, his Humility made him diffident of his own Skill in Ecclesiastical Affairs, and put him on visiting *Malachus*, Bishop of *Lesmor* in what was then called the Kingdom of *Momonia*, a Prelate well versed in things of that Nature, and remarkable for great Erudition and solid Virtue. After some Years spent under that venerable Person, he return'd to his own Country; where he had the Satisfaction of finding his Uncle, who held the Abbey of *Bangor* in Commendam, resign his Pretensions to the Revenue of that House, put it into his holy Nephews Hands, and desire to be admitted a Monk there under his Direction. The Saint, with the Consent of *Imarius*, undertook the Reformation of that famous Monastery, placed a convenient Number of Religious there, and soon recover'd the Character it formerly bore for Regularity, and strict Discipline; which he was more effectually enabled to do by the Miracles God perform'd by his Hand at his entring on that Task.

Malachi had not been long at the Head of his Religious Family, when the See of *Connor*, now in the Country of *Antrim*, becoming vacant, he was named to that Dignity. The Resistance he made on that Occasion did but inflame the Desires of the People to see him placed in the Epicopal Chair; in which they were join'd by *Imarius*, and the Archbishop his Metropolitan, who would hear of now Excuse. The Saint was but thirty Years old when he was obliged to accept of the said Bishoprick; and his holy Historian tells us that upon beginning the Eercise of his Functions, he found his Flock consisted of Men, who had nothing Christian but the bare Name. Their Customs were barbarous; their Manners Savage; their Vices numerous and shocking; the Sacraments were scarce known among them; the Ministers of the Altar were few, and those idle, and little better in their Morals than the Laity; so that Preaching and the regular Performance of Divine Service were almost universally neglected. This was the unhappy Face of the Diocese of *Connor*, as described by St. *Bernard*, when *Malachi* was raised to that Bishoprick. But this dreadful Prospect was so far from discouraging our good Pastor that the Calamitous Condition of the People committed to his Care proved an effectual Spur to his Zeal, and made him particularly active, and vigilant. He press'd the great Truths of Religion, and the holy Maxims of the Gospel in his publick Discourses with an Apostolical Vigour; and gave Advice suitable to every Man's Case in private with a sweet Mixture of Tenderness, and
wholsome

wholsome Severity; and when all those Means fell short of the desired Effect, Nov. 3. he pour'd out his charitable Soul in Tears in the Presence of God, and spent whole Nights in soliciting Heaven in their Favour. It is impossible to describe the Fatigues of his Ministry, or tell what he suffer'd from his ungrateful Flock while in Pursuit of their Salvation; but the Saint's Perseverance was at last rewarded with Success; the rebellious Hearts of his People were conquer'd by the Grace derived to them at the Intercession of their Bishop; the Savages soften'd into Humanity and a Sense of Religion; the Churches were fill'd; the Sacraments frequented, and Discipline restor'd in the whole Diocese.

Celsus, Archbishop of *Armagh*, being dangerously ill, named *Malachi* to succeed him in the Metropolitan See, declaring that he knew no Man fitter for that Post than He. The Saint's Establishment in that Post was opposed by *Maurice*, a Relation of that late Bishop, who claim'd a Right to it by Virture of a long Prescription in Favour of his Family, which had been in Possession of the See of *Armagh* near two hundred Years. During that Time, the secular Power supporting their Claim, several Lay-Men, some of them married, had been acknowledged Archbishops of that See; an Abuse, which gave Birth to the Corruption of Discipline, and Morals already mention'd. *Celsus*, who was a Man of Probity and Zeal for the House of God, had recommended our Saint to the Choice of his Flock on his Death-bed; but *Maurice* kept Possession of the Metropolitan See five Years. *Malachi* was press'd by all such as had any Concern for the Church of *Christ*, to take Possession of his Diocese, pursuant to the known Will and Desire of *Celsus*; but could not be prevail'd on to make one Step that might Occasion the least Disturbance. He had spent three Years in a Monastery when two holy Prelates, who could not bear to see the Church of *Armagh* suffer Violence from the Wolf, who bore the Character of Pastor, obliged him under Pain of Excommunication to accept of the Bishoprick in Question; but the Saint could not be prevail'd on to enter the Town, while the Usurper was alive; a Caution which he observed for preventing the worst Effects of *Maurice*'s Ambition, and Avarice, which he fear'd would put him on violent Measures for maintaining his Ground. That pretended Bishop, being at the Point of Death, directed the Choice of *Nigellus* to succeed him. But no Regard was paid to his Nomination; for the King, Bishops, and the whole Body of the Laity declared for *Malachi*, who was thereupon acknowledged the only lawful Metropolitan of *Ireland* in the Year 1133.

Nov. 3. The three first Years of his Pontificate were full of Troubles; for, upon his Expulsion, *Nigellus* had carried off a Book said to have belong'd to S. *Patrick*, and a Crosier adorn'd with Gold and Jewels, called the Crosier of *Jesus*, because, as was then believed, it had been in the Hands of our Saviour. These Relicks, which had long been in the Possession of the Archbishops of *Armagh*, being shown to some ignorant People, were look'd on as giving a good Title to the exiled Usurper, a Mistake; which pursued with the Warmth of indiscreet Zeal, inspired great Numbers with a thorough Aversion to the Saint, and gave him much Disturbance. When this Breach was heal'd, *Malachi* proceeded to such Regulations as were wanting in his Diocese; after which he resign'd his Bishoprick into the Hands of *Gelasius*, a Man of singular Merit, and every Way qualified for the Post, and retired to *Connor*. That Diocese had formerly been divided between two Bishops, and our Saint thinking the antient Institution preferable to what he found established, placed a Bishop at *Connor*, and fix'd his own Residence at *Down*; where he form'd a Community of Regular Canons; and soon after made a Journey to *Rome* to gain the Approbation of the holy See for what he had done, and obtain the *Pallium* for the new Archbishop of *Armagh*, and another for an Archbishoprick restored by *Celsus*.

Malachi left *Ireland* in the Year 1139; and in his Way to *Italy* made a Visit to St. *Bernard*, which was follow'd by a strict Friendship. Pope *Innocent* II, then in St. *Peter*'s Chair, received our Saint with all the Respect due to his Virtue, confirm'd all he had done in *Ireland*, promised him the *Pallium*; and made him his Legate for *Ireland*; but would not hear of his Petition for quitting his Bishoprick and spending the Remainder of his Days at *Clairvaux*, On his Way home he made a second Visit to the holy Founder of that House; express'd a deep concern at being deprived of the Satisfaction of ending his Life in that religious and penitential Retreat; and after a short Stay there pursued his Journey, leaving four of his Disciples with St. *Bernard* to be form'd by his Rule and Example. These, and others sent with the same View, returning into their own Country propagated St. *Bernard*'s Reformation of the *Benedictine* Order in *Ireland*.

Our Saint had obtained the Promise of the *Pallium* for the Archbishop of *Armagh*, as has been said already; but *Innocent* II died before the necessary Ceremonies could be observed for gaining that Favour. *Celestin* II, and *Lucius* II, who succeeded him died in less then a Year and a half; and *Eugenius* III was raised to the holy See on the Decease of the latter in 1145. Upon hearing that his Holiness was in *France* three Years after his Promotion,

tion, he conven'd the Bishops of *Ireland*, as Pope *Innocent* had directed Nov. 4 him, and undertook to be their Deputy to *Eugenius* on the same Errand, which had carried him to *Rome*. At his Arrival at *Clairvaux* he was received with great Joy and Respect by the holy Superior of that Monastery, but understood that the Pope was at *Rome* by that Time; and design'd to go on after some shortRepose with his holy Friend. *Malachi* reached *Clairvaux* about the thirteenth of *October*, and said Mass for the Community on S. *Luke*'s Day; but had scarce left the Altar when he was attacked with a Fever, upon which he took his Bed; and seeing the Monks very active in assisting him, assured them that all the Pains they took for his Food or Physick were unnecessary, because he was satisfied he should not recover. After some Days Illness he desired extreme Unction; and, to give the less Trouble to those about him, would receive it in the Church: that Sacrament was follow'd by the *Viaticum*; after which he return'd to his Chamber, still declaring his End was near, 'though his Looks gave no Encouragement to others to believe his Prediction. But the Event justified what he had said; and he expired peaceably in the Night between the second and third of *November* 1148, in the sixty fourth Year of his Age.

The Saint's Body was carried by a Number of Abbots, into the Chapel belonging to the Monastery, where the tremendous Sacrifice of the Mass was offer'd, and the Funeral perform'd with religious Solemnity. St. *Bernard* pronounced a Panegyrick on his departed Friend; and afterwards wrote his Life in Order to preserve the Memory of such excellent Qualifications as composed his Character. The *Roman* Martyrologe places his Feast on the third of *November*.

The IV Day.

St. CHARLES BORROMEO, Archbishop of *Milan*.

ST. *Charles*, the Glory of his Age and Reviver of Ecclesiastical Disciplince, was born in the *Milanese* on the second of *October* 1538. His Father was Count of *Arona* in the same Country; his Mother was of the Family of *Medicis*, which has long made so considerable a Figure at *Florence*; and both remarkable for more Humility and Piety, than is commonly to be found in Persons of that exalted Birth. After this Character it will be unnecessary to tell our Readers that they took particular Care of his Education

Nov. 4. Virtue. Our Saint in his very Infancy gave excellent Proofs of his future Sanctity; what Time was not employ'd in the necessary Application to his Book, was dedicated to God by Prayer and other pious Exercises; and, while his School-fellows were diverting themselves in a Manner suitable to their Age, *Charles*'s usual Amusement was to adorn an Oratory, or build little Chappels. His Father, perceiving which Way his Inclinations carried him, and judging from his whole Conduct that divine Providence design'd him for the Service of the Church, initiated him in the Clergy as soon as his Age would allow him to receive the Tonsure; and when twelve Years old, he was put in Possession of the Abbey of St. *Gratignan* upon his Uncle's resigning that Benefice, which had been long in the Family. The Saint 'though not then sensible of the Abuse of putting those Benefices into the Hands of such as were incapable of answering the pious Intent of the Founders; was convinced that the Poor were to be fed out of the Revenues of the Church. In Order to comply with his Duty in that Point he desired his Father, who undertook the Management of his Abbey, not to employ any of the Profits arising from it to the Uses of his Family, but leave him at full Liberty to dispose of them for the Relief of the Necessitous; and the Author of his Life, well acquainted with every Circumstance of it, tells us, that he was so exact in that Point, that if his Father had Occasion to make Use of some of the Money upon any pressing Demand, the Saint was as careful to urge the Payment of it, as if he was accountable to another for the Disposal of the Rents of his Abbey.

When *Charles* was qualified for the higher Studies, he was sent to *Pavia*; where he learnt the Civil and Canon Law under *Francis Alciat*, a celebrated Professor. The Students of that University were famous for Debauchery, and Libertinism; but our Saint preserved his Inocence in the Midst of Corruption, like *Lot* in *Sodom*; and, 'though several Snares were laid for his Virtue, the Grace of God made him victorious, and carried him through Difficulties of that Sort which seem'd invincible. Retirement and Prayer were his only Arms against the Assaults of the Devil, and his Agents; and he was content to bear the Reproach of Insensibility and what other Appellation was bestow'd on his Virtue rather than violate the Temple of the holy Ghost at the Instigation of the Companions of his Studies. While *Charles* was at *Pavia*, Cardinal *de Medicis*, his Uncle, gave him another Abbey, and a rich Priory; but the Poor were the only Gainers by the Increase of his Fortune; for his private Expences, and Manner of Life were still the same.

His

His Father's Death interrupted his Studies, and brought him to *Milan* in Nov. 1558; but when he had settled the Affairs of the Family to the Satisfaction of all concern'd, he went back to *Pavia*, took his Doctor's Degree, and then return'd to *Milan*; where he soon after receiv'd the Compliments of the Nobility and Gentry upon his Uncle being promoted to St. *Peter*'s Chair.

The new Pope, who took the Name of *Pius* IV, was scarce seated in his Post when his Concern for the Church made him call our Saint to *Rome*. Before he was twenty three Years old, he gave him a Cardinal's Cap, and the Archbishoprick of *Milan*; and employ'd him in the most important Offices. His new Dignity seem'd to require some Alteration in his Way of Living, and oblige him to appear in a Manner which might do Credit to his Uncle; he therefore took a magnificent Palace, furnished it in the best Manner, hired a great Number of Servants, kept a splendid Table, and was attended by several Men of Family, and Learning; but the Death of his elder Brother open'd his Eyes, and let him see how little real Grandeur he receiv'd from Titles and Attendance. All the World expected to see the Cardinal resign his Cap, and marry, as being the only Person remaining capable of supporting the Honour of his Family; but, to the great Surprize of all who knew him, he then enter'd into holy Orders, and consecrated himself to God in the Priesthood. He was preparing himself for the faithful Discharge of the Duties of that Character, when his Holiness, well acquainted with his Virtue and Capacity, made him Great Penitentiary of the Church of *Rome*, and Archpriest of S. *Mary Major*'s; put several Kingdoms and Religious Orders under his Protection; and employ'd him as his Legate at *Bologna*, in *Romagna* and the *Marca* of *Ancona*. 'Though his Thoughts were divided among so many Employments, his Heart was always the same; for the Glory of God, and the Good of the Church were the only Springs of all his Actions. He was happy in an uncommon Presence of Mind, which made him equal to the most difficult Affair; and it is not easy to determine whether his Diligence or Integrity was greater.

The Council of *Trent* was open'd in *Dec.* 1545; but the Shutting of it was reserved for Pope *Pius* IV, or rather was owing to our Saint's Administration under his Uncle; for all Writers, who have Occasion to speak of the Conclusion of that venerable Assembly, and the many Difficulties to be conquer'd on that Occasion, allow the holy Cardinal the Credit of being the chief Instrument in accommodating Affairs, and hastening the End of the Council. *Charles* began to put it's Decrees for Reformation in Execution on himself; he retrenched much the greatest Part of his Retinue; neither wore Silk, nor

allow'd

Nov. 4. allow'd any in his Family to do it: banished all Superfluities from his House and Table: and fasted on Bread and Water once a Week. He would have gone farther, and quitted the Administration of Church Affairs, had not *Bartholomew de Martyribus*, the holy Bishop of *Braga* in *Portugal*, whom he deservedly honour'd as a Father, and Master, interposed and diverted him from that Step by representing the Advantage the whole Church receiv'd from his remaining in his Post. The Saint complied with that excellent Prelate's Advice, but found it no easy Task, especially when he consider'd his present Situation would not allow him the Satisfaction of residing on his Bishoprick. He made the best Provision in his Power for his Flock during his Stay at *Rome* by sending them a grand Vicar of consummate Prudence, exemplary Piety, and a large Capacity. The Diocese of *Milan* was then in great Disorder, and that excellent Priest exerted all his Zeal and Courage for it's Reformation; but met with so much Opposition, especially from the Clergy, that St. *Charles* was convinced nothing but his own Presence could reduce them. He represented the Affair so strongly to the Pope, who had often refused him Leave to reside at *Milan*, that it was now impossible for his Holiness to detain him; and he reached that City in *September* 1565.

The holy Archbishop had been there only a Month when he call'd a Provincial Synod, in which several Cardinals appear'd, and all the Bishops of his Province, either in Person, or by their Deputies: where the first Steps toward Reformation of Manners, and Restoration of Ecclesiastical Discipline were taken. As soon as that Assembly broke up, our Saint undertook to visit his whole Diocese; but was interrupted in that Employment by a Journey to *Rome*, occasion'd by his Uncle's Sickness, who receiv'd the last Sacraments from his Hands, and expired in his Arms on the ninth of *December* following. *Charles*'s Behaviour in the Conclave was such as convinced his Collegues that he had nothing but the Glory of God and the Good of the Church at Heart in the Choice of a Pope. His Prayers were continual, his Fasts rigorous while that important Affair was in Agitation; and he offer'd the great Sacrifice of the Mass every Day to implore the divine Direction. By these Means, and the solid Reasons which he offer'd to the other Cardinals, they placed one at the Head of the Church, who did Credit to his Post, and is at present acknowledged a Saint in our publick Calenders. *Pius* V, being thus advanced to the holy See, did all in his Power to engage the Saint's Stay at *Rome*, and prevail with him to accept of the same Employment under him which he had enjoy'd under his Predecessor. But the holy Archbishop press'd his

his Return to his People with such an Apostolical Zeal, that his Holiness Nov. 4. dismiss'd him with his Blessing.

St. *Charles* arrived at *Milan* in *April* 1566, went vigorously to Work for the Reformation of his Diocese, and found Employment enough for all his Zeal, and Resolution. The great Truths of Salvation were almost universally unknown; and such as remain'd among them were obscured by gross Errors, and disgraced by Superstition. The Sacraments were generally neglected, and the Priests scarce knew how to administer them; the Clergy were debauched; and Monasteries of both Sexes full of Disorder. To remedy these Evils, he published the Decrees of the Council of *Trent*, and those of his own Synod through the whole Diocese; and encouraged the Execution of them by reforming his own Family into a Model of Ecclesiastical Simplicity. He dismiss'd all his secular Officers, and several of his Servants, and fill'd his House with Divines and Canonists, who were capable of serving him in the Government of his Church. He sold the most valuable, and less necessary Parts of his Furniture and Equipage: resign'd all his Benefices but such as he thought might be converted to useful Foundations, and gave the whole Income of them among the Poor. He disposed of Part of his Estate for the Use of the indigent Members of *Jesus Christ*, and lodged almost all the Remainder in the Hands of his Uncles, who were obliged to allow him somewhat Yearly for the Maintainance of Seminaries, Charity Schools, Hospitals, and poor Convents. His Family was composed of almost an hundred Ecclesiasticks, each of which had his particular Employment: the Hours of Prayer were settled so that no one could plead any Excuse for absenting himself from his Duty. Examination of Conscience, Meditation, Reading good Books, and other devout Practices had their stated Times. The Priests confess'd their Sins once a Week at least, and said Mass every Day; those who were not honour'd with that Character were constant in their Attendance at the great Sacrifice, approached the Tribunal of Penance at least once a Month, and receiv'd the holy Eucharist at the Hands of our Saint. The whole Family dined together, like a Religious Community; and was always entertain'd with a spiritual Book during their Meals. All *Wednesdays* and the whole Time of *Advent* were observed with Abstinence; and they fasted very strictly on *Fridays*, the Eves of the holy Bishops of *Milan*, the Patrons of that City, and several other Days of voluntary Devotion. Such as were initiated in the Clergy always wore long Cloaths, and imitated their Master in the Plainness of their Dress; and what Laymen were admitted into his House for such Employments as were not suitable to the Ecclesiastical State,

Nov. 4. State, wore Black, and were taught to make Simplicity their only Ornament. Virtue, and Piety were the beſt Recommendations to the holy Biſhop's Houſe; and all who were happy enough to be admitted under his Roof might depend on a tender Father, and a conſtant Friend in the Perſon of our Saint. In ſhort, the Archbiſhop of *Milan*'s Palace was under as good Regulations as any Religious Community, ſo that it is not to be wonder'd that it produced a great Numbers of excellent Perſons for the Service of the Church, among which were one Cardinal, and above twenty Biſhops, moſt of whom were employ'd by the holy See as Nuncios at the chief Courts in Europe.

Theſe were the firſt Advances toward the deſign'd Reformation of the Dioceſe of *Milan*; a Taſk that would be much eaſier when all he could preſcribe for others was already practiſed at home. His next Buſineſs was to rectify what was amiſs in his Chapter, where he ſoon reſtored the Service of God to it's original Splendor and Beauty; and converted ſeveral large Prebends into ſuch Diſtributions as might engage the Canons to quit their Benefices, and give conſtant Attendance in the Choir. Our Saint founded three new Prebends in his Metropolitan Church, each of which proved ſingularly uſeful: one was given to a Divine who was to preach every *Sunday*, and read Lectures in Divinity twice a Week to ſuch as were deſign'd for the Miniſtry: the ſecond was deſtin'd to the Maintainance of an able Prieſt, whoſe Buſineſs it was to give Abſolution in reſerved Caſes, and hold Conferences on Points of Morality and Caſes of Conſcience: the third was beſtow'd on a Doctor of the Canon Law for inſtructing young Eccleſiaſticks in the Cuſtoms, Practices, and Deciſions of the Catholick Church. He erected Schools in all Parts of his Dioceſe for the Chriſtian Education of Children, and took Care that the low Circumſtances of their Parents proved no Hindrance to their Admiſſion. The Monaſteries under his Juriſdiction were unwilling to part with the Liberty they had long enjoy'd to the manifeſt Prejudice of their Rule; ſo that the Reformation of thoſe Houſes was a Work of much Time and Labour, and coſt the holy Prelate many Prayers and Tears.

In the Year 1567, our Saint had a Diſpute with the Officers of civil Juſtice, who infringed his Epiſcopal Juriſdiction; and the Governor and Senate of *Milian* were engaged in the Conteſt. As that City was then in the Hands of the King of *Spain*, the Magiſtrates laid their Complaint before him, while the Archbiſhop appeal'd to the Pope's Judgments for the Deciſion of the Affair, which concluded in Favour of the Church; but *Charles* uſed the Advantage he got in that Affair with ſo much Modeſty that the Governor and chief Citizens made it their whole Study to cultivate a good Underſtanding

with

with him, and leave him no Room to complain of the least Attempt or Design on his Jurisdiction. This troublesome Affair was not quite concluded when the Saint set out for the Northern Part of his Diocese, which went a considerable Way in the *Alps*. He found Ignorance and Immorality reign there without Opposition, and the Priests more corrupt than the Laity. They kept Concubines in the Face of the World, left their Churches to their Sons, made their Benefices allow Portions for their Daughters, and sold the Sacraments, and other holy Things with Impunity; for they had long been used to look on the *Swiss*, under whom they lived, as their only Superiors, who never disturb'd them on any Account where they were not immediate Sufferers. The holy Pastor travell'd through Places which seem'd inaccessible in Quest of his stray'd Sheep; displaced the ignorant and vicious Priests; and established such in their Room as were capable of restoring the Faith, and Morals of the People to their original Purity. Some of those remote Corners of his Diocese being infected with the Heresies of those Times, he made his Way to them through incredible Difficulties, preached among those unhappy Persons, catechized their Children, attended the Sick in their last Moments, and heard the Confessions of such as were desirous of returning to the Almighty by his Means.

After these truly Apostolical Labours, which were crown'd with much Success, the holy Prelate conven'd his Clergy; and, remembering what Disorders he had met with in the Course of his Visitation, made several most excellent Regulations for the People committed to his Care; and had the Satisfaction of seeing those Co-operators in the Ministry resolved to execute them very punctually. In the Year 1569 he held a second provincial Synod, where he engaged the Bishops, his Suffragans, to undertake a like Reformation in their Respective Dioceses, and assured them of all the Assistance in his Power for promoting so necessary a Work. As he profess'd a profound Veneration for the Council of *Trent*, he on all Occasions enforced it's Decrees, and squared his whole Conduct by it's Directions. In this View he provided for the regular Education of Pastors by erecting and endowing three Seminaries in the City of *Milan*. The first of those Houses, design'd for the Education of his Clergy in such Studies as were necessary for their Station, was frequently honour'd with the Presence of it's holy Founder, who enquired into their Progress in Learning and Piety, talk'd to them about their Vocation, and assisted at all their publick Exercises. The second was fill'd with Persons, whose Capacity would scarce reach the more difficult Studies of Philophy and Divinity; and they were there instructed in Cases of Conscience,

Nov. 4. and the Rules of Christian Morality. The third was raised for the Reception of such as Age, or Infirmities had render'd incapable of their Functions. He founded the same Number of Seminaries out of Town, which produced a great Number of holy and learned Pastors for the Use of his whole Diocese.

S. *Charles* founded several Communities of Religious famous both for Virtue, and great Abilities, who were employ'd in Assisting his Clergy in gaining Souls. The Company of *Oblati*, or Persons devoted to the Service of God by a particular Obligation, was erected by our great Prelate, with the View of having a Number of worthy Ecclesiasticks always ready to go into any Part of his Diocese, and labour for the Conversion and Reformation of the People. He receiv'd the *Theatins* and *Jesuits*; gave the latter Leave to settle at *Lucern* and *Fribourg* in *Switzerland*; and the Establishment of the *Capucins* in that Country was the Work of our Saint.

Nor was he less Active in inspecting the Orders already establish'd in his Diocese, of which that of the *Humiliati* seem'd to want the most Reformation in his Time; his Endeavours in that Way were successful, and the most Part came readily into his Measures. But some old Members of that corrupted Body could not bear to see themselves stripp'd of what they had long possess'd, reduced to the Laws of a Community, and divested of an usurped Authority, which they had abused to the Detriment of the Order; and therefore resolved to have their Revenge on the holy Archbishop. To that End they hired one of their Number, a Man of an infamous Character, and ready to engage in any thing rather than submit to Regularity, to assassinate the Saint. On the twenty sixth of *October* 1569 the Villain found Means to Post himself at the Door of a Chapel, where the holy Prelate was performing his Devotions, and discharged a Pistol at him. The Ball reached the Saint; and was shot at so small a Distance that he must have fallen, had not Providence visibly interposed in his Favour; it fell at his Feet, and only singed his Rochet; upon which St. *Charles's Rochet* became a Proverbial saying in *Italy* for a thing impenetrable. This extraordinay, and miraculous Protection made such an Impression on the most rebellious and unreasonable Persons in his Diocese that they strove who should give strongest Proofs of Submission to the holy Bishop; and his Holiness resented the Attempt on our Saint so far as to suppress the whole Order of the *Humiliati*, who had thus notoriously deviated from their Institution.

In the Year 1570 the excellent Archbishop of *Milan* visited the Northern Parts of his Diocese a second Time with good Success; and at his Return
to

to the Episcopal City undertook to reform the Abuses practised there in the Nov. 4. Time of *Carnaval*. It happen'd very opportunely at that Time that Christendom was engaged in a War with the *Turks*, and the holy Prelate press'd the Necessity of imploring the Divine Assistance against the Infidels so successfully that on the three Days before *Lent* the whole Town deserted their extravagant and absur'd Diversions, and flock'd to the Church in Obedience to their Pastor's Voice. The Devotion of the People on that Occasion was so general, that the Saint, 'though assisted by two of his Canons, spent six Hours on *Sunday* Morning in giving Communion; and in the succeeding Years he always found some new Method of diverting them from their Masquerades, and fixing them to their Duty.

Upon the the Death of *Pius* V, which happen'd on the first of *May* in the Year 1572, the Saint, as Cardinal, was obliged to repair to *Rome*, and assist at the Choice of his Successor. He was then in a very indifferent State of Health; and nothing but a Desire of contributing to the Good of the Catholick Church could have prevail'd with him to undertake that Journey. He was so much out of Order that he was obliged to travel in a Litter, and take his Physician's Directions in Writing, and proper Medicines, according to his Prescription. He was crossing a River near *Bologna* when the Mule, that carried those necessary Provisions, fell, and his whole Load was carried down the Stream. St. *Charles* smiled at the Accident, would not allow his Servants to go back for a fresh supply, but told them he took this as a favourable Presage that he should have no farther Need of such Assistance. While at *Rome*, he found himself under a Necessity of taking Advice; but observing the Contrariety of Sentiments between the Physicians of that City, and those of *Milan*, he resolved to take another Course, consult their Art no more, and try what a rigorous Temperance would do toward the Recovery of his Health. This Project succeeded to his Wish, and in a little Time he acquired that Strength which carried him through the Labours of his Post in a Manner that surprized all who had known his lingring Ilness.

Gregory XIII was raised to St. *Peter*'s Chair on the thirteenth of *May*; but our Saint stay'd six Months at *Rome* after that Promotion. During which Time he gave the new Pope some excellent Advice for the Government of the Church, and resign'd all those Preferments and Titles which could draw him from his dear Flock. At his Return to *Milan*, he called his third Provincial Council, which confirm'd all his former Regulations. *Alvaro* lately made Governor of that City, acted by Jealousy, and an indiscreet Zeal for

Nov. 4. his Royal Master, fell out with the holy Prelate, and carried things so far that he was excommunicated. Some of the Magistrates, who had long waited for a favourable Opportunity of revenging the Affront which they imagined they had receiv'd by the Saint's suppressing several idle and prejudicial Diversions, hoped they might find their Accounts in this Rupture; but the Governor's Death disappointed their malicious Expectations, and brought them to a Sense of their Fault.

About the same Time *Henry* III, who had been crown'd King of *Poland* was on his Way to *France* to take Possession of that Throne which devolved to him by the Demise of his Brother *Charles* IX. Upon his reaching *Monza* in the *Milanese* Territories, our Saint went to that Town, had an Interview with the Prince, and gave him some important Rules for his Conduct in Regard of the *Calvinists*, who were very troublesome in the Kingdom of *France*.

In 1574 the Pope call'd St. *Charles* to *Rome*; and, to engage him more effectually to that Journey, put him in Mind of the Jubilee which was to be open'd the following Year. The holy Prelate, however, would not leave his Flock 'till he had obtain'd a Dispensation in Form; which he insisted on that his Example might not be pleaded by other Bishops for their Non-residence, how specious soever their Pretence for leaving their Diocese might be. During his Stay at *Rome*, he gave surprizing Proofs of a profound Humility, great Mortification and strict Piety; and return'd to *Milan* in February 1575. He had not been there long when he gave the Necessities of his Diocese a fresh Review; published the Jubilee for the ensuing Year pursuant to his Holiness's Permission, and spent a considerable Time at *Cremona* and *Bergamo*, where he thought his Presence most necessary at that Juncture.

The Plague raged in *Milan* in the Year 1576, and gave our Saint a glorious Opportunity of shewing the true Spirit of a Pastor, whose Character obliges him him to lay down his Life for his Sheep. He was very warmly solicited to leave the Town; and those who urged his Removal grounded their Advice on the Reasonableness of preserving so valuable a Life for the Use of such Parts of his Diocese as were not yet visited by that Calamity. St. *Charles* was deaf to those Remonstrances, resolved to remain at *Milan*, 'though he died in the Execution of his Ministry, and order'd all necessary Assistance for the unhappy Persons, who felt the afflicting Hand of God on that Occasion. As the Sickness multiplied those miserable Objects, the Saint had Recourse to new Means for relieving them, sent his Plate to be changed into

Money

Money for their Use, sold all his Goods with the same charitable View, and employ'd proper Officers to gather Alms for them through the whole Diocese. The excellent Example of our holy Prelate, enforced by strong Exhortations to Compassion for the Sufferers, animated considerable Numbers of the Clergy and Laity to serve them according to their several Stations, and Abilities. The Saint's Care for the Bodies of his People being always attended with a true Concern for their Souls, he heard their Confessions, and gave them the Viaticum and extreme Unction with his own Hands. Publick Prayers were perform'd by his Direction with a Fervour equal to the Danger; the Archbishop preached Penance to his afflicted People almost every Day; assisted constantly at the Processions which he had order'd, and walking barefoot with Rope about his Neck seem'd to offer his own Life, as an Expiation for the Sins of his Flock. After the infectious Distemper had raged with the utmost Violence four Months together, it began to abate in *November*, and in the Beginning of the ensuing Year quite ceased. The Saint appointed a publick Thanksgiving for this Relief, directed three Days Prayer for such as had died in the late Calamity, and instructed those who survived it how to make a Christian Use of what had happen'd by divine Direction.

Nov. 4

A Conduct so heroick and truly Christian, which was spoke of all over *Europe* with Admiration, seem'd to claim a grateful Acknowledgement from all who had been Eye Witnesses of it, and felt the Benefit of his charitable Assistance; but his Services met with no other Recompence than what usually attends the best Actions of holy Men in this World, his Charity was repaid with fresh Persecutions which God permitted for the Trial and Improvement of his Virtue. The third Governor of *Milan* since our Saint's Promotion to the See of that City was one of those unhappy Men who cannot bear the Lustre of Virtue in others, and imagine the Integrity of their Neighbour a strong Reproach to themselves. With this corrupt Disposition that Magistrate revived the old Quarrel about Jurisdiction, accused the Archbishop of having exceeded his Commission during the Plague, abolished the innocent Diversions of the Town, and introduced dangerous Novelties. These Complaints, sign'd by the most considerable Persons at *Milan*, were transmitted to the King of *Spain*, to whom the Saint was represented as an ambitious, enterprizing Man, and an Enemy of the Royal Authority. His Majesty, thus imposed on, granted an Order for seizing some of the Officers of the Episcopal Court, and stopping all Proceedings there. The Governor was empower'd to take Possession of his Estate at *Arona*, a strong Guard set upon his Palace, several abusive Manifestos were publish'd against him, and Letters sent to *Rome* to misrepresent

Nov. 4. present his Conduct to his Holiness. The Saint, satisfied with the Innocence of his own Intentions, enjoy'd a perfect Tranquility of Mind in the Midst of this Storm; but, observing his Enemies made a bad Use of his Patience, and put a Malicious Construction on his Silence, he thought himself obliged to depute proper Persons to *Rome* and the Court of *Spain* to inform the Pope and King of the whole Affair. The Dispute ran so high at last that the Saint was obliged to make a Journey to *Rome*, where he gave his Holiness a particular Account of all he had done for reforming the Manners of his Flock, remedying Abuses, and maintaining the Rights of his See. The Pope, full of Admiration at the Wisdom and Apostolical Spirit that appear'd in his whole Conduct, approved of all his Regulations, and commended his Zeal; but could not then determine the Question about the Extent of his Jurisdiction.

The Saint left *Rome* in the Beginning of the Year 1580, a few Days after the Arrival of the Deputies from the Governor and Magistrates of *Milan*. He reached that Town soon enough to hinder the Extravagancies which his Adversaries threaten'd to revive in the Carnaval, and from that Time met with little or no Opposition on that Head. The Death of the Governor, which happen'd soon after, removed all the Difficulties that remain'd; and both the King of *Spain* and the Pope did Justice to the holy Bishop. In 1581 he held his fifth Diocesan Synod; and after *Easter* the following Year his sixth and last Provincial Council. It is remarkable that we have no Account extant of a Bishop convening so many of those Assemblies in so short a Space of Time, and with such Success. We have the Decrees of those venerable Bodies in the *Acts of the Church of Milan*; which may, not improperly be called a Collection of the Sentiments and Episcopal Labours of our Saint. We there find excellent Rules made in his Diocesan Synods, admirable Instructions, and Remedies against all Disorders, and Immoralities. The holy Prelate always open'd those Assemblies with a large Discourse full of an Apostolical Spirit, and animated with a Fire that kindled the Hearts of his Clergy into a generous Ardour to imitate that great Pattern. In the Year last mention'd the Saint made another Journey to *Rome* to consult his Holiness, about proper Measures for Stopping the Progress of Heresy in the Extremities of his Diocese; where he obtain'd a second Approbation of all he had done for the Maintainance of Ecclesiastical Discipline, and in a particular Manner of of such Canons and Decrees as related to the Sacrament of Penance, which he had restored to a Severity, that, though much short of what had been practised in the first Ages of the Church, came as near it as those corrupt Times would allow.

At

At his Return, he found it necessary to make his Appearance in the Country of the *Grisons*, where the Errors of *Zuinglius* were propagated with but too much Success; that Country was full of Persons, who seem'd to have shook Hands with all Religion; for they practized Sorcery, and all the Crimes of which Human Nature is capable, when destitute of the Fear both of God and Man. Those Barbarians were so fond of their Supperstition, and so averse to all in Communion with the Pope, or under the King of *Spain*, that nothing but a particular Providence could have protected the Saint from their Attempts on his Life, while on the Road. But the holy Prelate, resolved to endeavour the Salvation of those ungrateful and brutish People at any Rate, began his Mission among them with the Catholicks who had been long neglected, and decreased considerably every Day. The greatest Part of that Number lent a willing Ear to their Pastor's Voice, and resolved upon a Reformation. Several Hereticks were afterwards converted, and some Apostates, who had taken Shelter there, reclaim'd. This Apostolical Journey is dated in 1583; and the following Year, which was the last of his Life, he endeavour'd after Perfection with the Vigour of one in the first Warmth of his Conversion, for he made a considerable Addition to his corporal Austerities, which in every ones Judgment had already ruin'd his Health. It was his Custom to make a General Confession once a Year; and, to do it with less Disturbance, he undertook a Pilgrimage to Mount *Varallo*, a Place of Devotion in the Diocese of *Novara*; where he spent six Hours every Day in mental Prayer, contemplating on the Exellency of the Deity, and the Sufferings of *Jesus Christ*, and the rest of his Time was taken up with pious Exercises. He was seiz'd with his last Sickness, while thus employ'd, and reached *Milan* with much Difficulty; where he receiv'd the Reward of his Labours on the third of *November*.

Nov. 4.

The News of our Saint's Death spread a general Consternation through the whole Town, and every one lamented the Loss of a tender Father. His Body was, according to his own Directions, laid under the Steps to the high Altar in his Cathedral. His Will, which was made in the Time of the Plague, constituted the Poor of the great Hospital his sole Legatees; but his Library given to his Chapter, his Writings to the Bishop of *Vercelli*, and some Pictures, and Houshold Goods to his Friends. The Solemnity of his Canonization was perform'd by Pope *Paul* V on the first of *November* 1610; and since that Time several Churches and Chapels have been built in his Honour; and his Festival is universally observed in the Western Church on the Day after his Decease.

The

Nov. 5.

St. VITALIS *and* St. AGRICOLA, Martyrs.

ALL the Account we have of the two Martyrs before us, is owing to St. *Ambrose*, who tells us that *Agricola*'s Behaviour in the World was such as engaged the Affection of the very Pagans among whom he lived, and that *Vitalis* his Servant learnt the Christian Religion from Him. They were both seiz'd, probably in the Year 304, carried before the Magistrate, and upon making a formal Profession of their Faith, allow'd the Honour of Suffering for it. *Vitalis* was tortured first; and died under the Hands of his Executioners. *Agricola*'s Martyrdom was deferr'd for some Days, in Hopes that, Reflecting on what his Servant had suffer'd, he might secure his own Life by renouncing his Religion; but they were soon convinced that *Vitalis*'s Example had confirm'd him in the Resolution of adhering to his Saviour 'though with the Expence of his Blood; upon which he was fasten'd to a Cross with several large Nails, and receiv'd the Crown of Martyrdom. The Instruments of his Passion were buried with him at *Bologna* in *Italy*, the Place of their Sufferings.

The venerable Bodies were buried among the *Jews*; and, after the Spot where they lay had been forgot for some Years, miraculously discover'd and taken up by St. *Ambrose* in the Year 392, who left some of the Relicks in a Church, which he dedicated at *Florence* soon after. The *Roman* Martyrologe proposes these two holy Martyrs to the Veneration of the Faithful on the fourth of *November*.

The V Day.

St. ZACHARIAS, *and* St. ELIZABETH.

THIS holy Couple is by the *Roman* Martyrologe placed at the Head of the Saints of this Day, who are honour'd by the *Greek* Church on the fifth of *September*. *Zacharias* and *Elizabeth* the Parents of St. *John* the *Baptist* were of the House of *Aaron*, the Source of the *Jewish* Priesthood. The Holy Spirit has left us their Character in Words which give us a most exalted Idea of the Persons before us; they were not only happy or prudent enough to avoid giving Men Offence or Occasion of Complaint against them, but were also *Just before God*, and most punctual in the Observance of *all his Commandments*. All the Particulars of their Lives are recorded in the Gospel

Luke 1. 6:

have

have been already mention'd in our Account of the holy Baptist's Nativity, Nov. 6. and the Visitation of the *Blessed Virgin*; we shall here consider the Sentiments of Antiquity in Regard of *Zacharias*.

Several of the most considerable among the *Greek* Fathers tell us that *Herod*, King of *Judea*, put *Zacharias* to Death for concealing his Son when the Innocents were destroy'd by his Order; they speak of this as a current Opinion in their Times, and add that He he was the Person meant by our Saviour, as the last of the Prophets whom the *Jews* had kill'd, and consequently that he fell between the Temple and the Altar, i. e. between that Part of the Temple where the Priests only enter and the Altar of Burnt-Offerings. This was the uniform Tradition of the *Greek* Church in the first Ages, and is mention'd as such by *Origin*, St. *Basil*, St. *Gregory* of *Nyssa*, St. *Cyril* of *Alexandria*, and St. *Peter*, Bishop of the same See and Martyr. St. *Jerom* has taken the Liberty to dissent from those great Lights of the East, and declare that the Opinion is grounded on some Apocryphal Pieces, which he affords no better Appellation than that of Dreams. Cardinal *Baronius* was the first who join'd St. *Elizabeth* in the same Festival with her holy Husband, and seems to say that her Name had 'till then never appear'd in any Martyrologe. His Words are these, ELIZABETH *is placed on the same Day with* ZACHARIUS *her Husband, not because we have any Assurance of their dying on the same Day; but considering that her Name had been omitted, for want of being acquainted with that Circumstance, it has been thought proper to comemorate them together;* for, continues the Cardinal, *it seem'd shameful to forget a Woman of so much Sanctity, so highly commended in the Gospel, and by the holy Fathers.*

Matt. 23 35.

The VI Day.

St. WINOCK, Abbot.

WINOCK, a Native of *Britany* in *France*, and probably descended from the antient *Britons*, who took Shelter in that Province when this Island was seized by the *Angles* and *Saxons* to the Prejudice of the Natives, was born in the VII Century, but in what Year is not known. As his Heart was touched with an early Grace, and his Inclinations to Virtue grew stronger with his Years, as soon as he was able to choose for himself, he came to a Resolution of treading in the Steps of those holy Persons, who had left the World, renounced all the Advantages of their Birth and Station in it, and spent the greatest Part of their Lives at a Distance from every thing that could interrupt their Conversation with Heaven. In this View he set out with three Companions, who employ'd some Time in Journeys of Devotion. Coming into the Diocese of *Terouenne*, they made a Visit to the Monestery of *Sithiu*, since called St. *Bertin*'s, and famous at present by that Name in the Town of St. *Omer*'s. The holy Abbot, from whom it receiv'd that Appellation, was then at the Head of that religious Community, and had acquired great Reputation for Wisdom and Sanctity. Strongly affected with the admirable Patterns of Virtue and Penance, form'd by the Saint's masterly Hand, they petition'd for Admission into his holy Family. *Bertin*, always ready to improve the good Dispositions of such as Providence directed to him, receiv'd them without Difficulty, and observing the Fervour, with which they urged their Demand, promised himself the Satisfaction of seeing them equal those whose Example had inspired them with a Desire of living under his Direction. The holy Abbot was not deceived in his Hopes; for the new Monks enter'd into all the Obligations of that State with so much Cheerfulness, and observed all the Rules of the House so punctually that they soon did Credit to their Profession. St. *Bertin* was so well pleased with their Conduct that after some Time spent in his Abbey, they were commission'd to leave *Sithiu*, and form a new Community in a Place, which he named for that Purpose. *Winock* and his Companions raised themselves Cells, pursuant to their Abbot's Direction, where they lived some Time in the Practice of such Severities as are suggested by a Heart full of Horror for Sin, and Apprehension of the Arts of the common Enemy; but they still professed a Subjection to, and Dependence on S. *Bertin*.

Their Lives were so edifying in that new Situation that *Heremar*, one of the first Men in that Country, thought he should promote the Glory of God by bestowing a more commodious Piece of Ground on them. In this View he settled his Estate of *Wormhout* upon them, where our Saint and his Associates built a Monastery and an Hospital, that thus they might constantly be employ'd in Prayer, Penance, or Charity to the Poor, especially such of them as labour'd under the additional Affliction of Sickness, or were destitute of Habitation. The Lustre of *Winock*'s Virtue, who was placed at the Head of this small Community, soon encreased the Number of Monks, who always found an excellent Rule for their Behaviour in every Particular of the Life and Actions of their holy Superior. His appearing above the rest made no Alteration in his Humility; for when ever they wanted his Assistance he was

ready

ready to stoop to the most laborious and mortifying Employments for their Relief and Instruction.

After several Years spent in this Manner, our Saint was favour'd with a happy Passage to a glorious Eternity about the Year 717, and buried in the Church at *Wormbout*, where the People's Veneration for his Memory was inhanced by Miracles perform'd at his Tomb. When the *Danes* made a Descent into *Flanders* in the Middle of the IX Century, the holy Relicks were removed to *Sithiu*; but in the Year 900 *Baldwin* Count of *Flanders*, ordered them to be translated to *Berg*, and deposited in a Church which he had built there in Honour of our Saint and St. *Martin*. That Place is now become a considerable Town, known by the Name of *Winoxberg*, where the Remains of our Saint are still preserved with due Respect. The *Roman* Martyrologe places him on the VI of *November*, generally supposed to be that of his Death.

The VII Day.

St. WILLIBRORD, Bishop of *Utrecht*.

WILLIBRORD, a Native of our Island, was born toward the Year 658 in the Kingdom of *Northumberland*. His Parents took a singular Care of his Education; and, to keep him more effectually out of the Reach of Corruption, placed him in a Monastery before he was seven Years old. The House they chose on this Occasion was the famous Abbey of *Rippon* in the Diocese of *York*, then happy in the Presence and Direction of St. *Wilfrid* its holy Founder; whose Life we have written on the twelfth of *October*. *Wilibrord* was brought up in that excellent Seminary of Virtue and Learning 'till he was old enough to choose his State of Life; and then engaged in the Monastick Profession. It soon appear'd that the Spirit of God had directed him in that Resolution; for, 'though his Constitution was weak, his Fervour and Exactness was equal to what made the Character of the best and most exemplary in the House. He was humble, modest, and of an easy obliging Temper; his Actions, Discourse and whole Conduct were grave, regular, and uniform; his Application to Books of Spirituality indefatigable; the sacred Oracles of God's written Word were his favourite Entertainment; and it was remarkable that he express'd much more Concern for the Nourishment of his Soul than of his Body. When he was twenty Years old he conceived a strong Desire of making a Journey to *Ireland*, which at that Time was generally look'd on as *the Island of Saints*, and the common Retreat of such devout Souls as were disposed to quit the Conversation of Mankind most effectually. What chiefly determin'd *Willibrord* to that Change of Place was the great Reputation of *Egbert* and *Wigbert*, two *English* Priests who had made that Step upon the same pious Motive. Having obtain'd his Superior's Permission, he set out, and arrived safe to the desired Place; where he put himself under the Direction of *Egbert*, and made such Progress in Virtue and Christian Knowledge that after about ten Years spent there he was promoted to the Priesthood at the Request of all who had been Witnesses of his Behaviour.

Our Saint's excellent Director had long entertain'd an ardent Desire of labouring for the Conversion of the Infidels on the Borders of *Friesland*; but had been diverted from that Apostolical Design by some Persons of known Piety and Zeal, who persuaded him to employ his Talents in the small Islands between *Ireland* and *Scotland*; he was confirm'd in his Inclination of following their Advice by the bad Success of *Wigbert*, who had undertaken that Expedition, and return'd to *Ireland* without any other Satisfaction but that of a charitable Intention. *Egbert*, however, full of Concern for the Northern Idolaters, and finding our Saint every Way qualified for the Task, prevail'd with him to undertake that Mission, which he believed was reserved for him. *Willibrord*, then about thirty one Years of Age, undertook the great Work, with a Cheerfulness which sufficienty spoke him prepared to encounter all Difficulties in the Prosecution of it; and was join'd by eleven Evangelical Labourers of distinguished Zeal, and Virtue.

Willibrord landed in *Freisland* in the Year 691, and engaged the Protection of *Pepin* Maire of the Palace, then very powerful in that Country, who assured him of all Manner of Assistance, and sent him to *Rome* for the Apostolical Blessing and the Sanction of the holy See. At his Return, he and his Companions undertook to preach to the Inhabitants of South *Freisland*, which comprehended what is now call'd *Holland* and *Zeland*. After three Years continual Labour, and suitable Success, he went to *Rome* a second Time with Letters from *Pepin* to Pope *Sergius* I, giving an Accont of the Saint's Conduct since his Arrival in that Country, and begging that he might receive the Episcopal Character, which wou'd allow a greater Weight to his Mission, and enable him to furnish his numerous Converts with inferior Pastors. His Holiness was so well Satisfied with *Willibrord*, that he consecrated him on the twenty second of *November* 696, gave him the Title of Archbishop, presented him with the *Pallium*, the usual Mark of that Dignity, though sometimes bestow'd on other Prelates, gave him the Name

St. Willibrord, *Bishop*.

Name of *Clement*, and empower'd him to fix his See in what Part of *Freisland* he judged most proper.

Nov. 7.

After a Fort'night's Stay at *Rome*, the Saint made his Way to the Court of *France*, where his old Patron *Pepin* received him very graciously, and gave him fresh and substantial Assurances of his Favour and Protection. By his Means *Willibrord* attain'd the Grant of a Settlement in *Utrecht*, which enabled him to make that the Center of his Mission, and the Place of his ordinary Residence. Thus authorised he built a Church in that Town dedicated to *Jesus Christ*, under the Title of *The Saviour*, which he made his Cathedral; and repair'd another which then bore the Name of S. *Martin*, and afterwards enjoy'd the same Honour. The holy Bishop's indefatigable Application to the glorious Work was such as seem'd to prove that with the new Obligation he had received at his Consecration of enlarging the Kingdom of his Divine Master, he had acquired fresh Strength, and a considerable Augmentation of his Zeal. After *Ratbod* Duke of *Freisland* had been worsted by *Pepin*, he retired into the Western Parts of that Country. Our Saint had too much Courage to be deterr'd from visiting those Parts by the Consideration of that Prince's Religion, or the Enmity which subsisted between him and the Maire of the Palace. He preached vigorously there against Paganism, and God govern'd the Heart of *Ratbod* so much in Favour of the Gospel that; though not disposed to receive the important Message, he shew'd our apostolical Missionary all Manner of Respect, and gave him free Leave to make what Conquests he cou'd among his Subjects. His next Journey was to *Denmark*; but *Ongend* their Sovereign remaining proof against all the Attempts of our Saint for his Conversion, his Example had so powerful an Influence over the Barbarians, that he could do no good in that Country. At his quitting the Place he carried off thirty young Persons, whom he instructed and baptized on the Road.

Willibrord was on his Way to *Friesland*, when he was thrown on an Island between that Country and *Denmark*, which bore the Name of *Fositus*, the God which the Pagans of that Place adored. The Island was consecrated to that false Divinity in so solemn and awful a Manner that the Natives dared not touch the Cattle that grazed on it, nor speak one single Word while they were drawing Water from a Fountain there. The Saint, touched with a tender Concern for the deluded Wretches, was resolved to do his best for undeceiving them; in this View he killed some of the Cattle for the Use of himself, and Company; and baptised three Persons in the Fountain pronouncing the Words aloud. The Idolators, according to their own superstitious

Nov. 7. stitious Notion, expected every Moment to see the Christians, who had ventured to eat of the consecrated Beasts, run mad or die suddenly. But, finding no such Judgement fall on the supposed Criminals, they could not well determine whether the Impunity of the Saint and his Friends was to be attributed to the Patience of their God, or his Want of Power. In this Perplexity, they laid the Affair before *Ratbod*, who transported with Zeal for the Idol, and resolved to assert his Honour against the bold Offenders, order'd Lots to be cast three Times a Day for three Days together, and their Fate to be determin'd by them. But God, who over-rules the seeming Chance of such Decisions, directed the Lot so that it fell constantly on one Person, who was sacrificed to the Rage of the Idolaters, and honoured as a Martyr of *Jesus Christ*. *Ratbod*, vexed at the Miscarriage of his sanguinary Design on our Saint, sent for him and reproached him with Want of Respect for what was by the Natives of the Country esteem'd most venerable and sacred; but, finding him invincible on that Article and not inclined to make any Reparation for the pretended Affront of his God, and being under some Apprehension from the *French* Power, he thought fit to dismiss him without any farther Proceedings.

'Though the Inhabitants of *Freisland* seem'd our Saint's peculiar Care, his Concern extended to the Pagan *Saxons*, among whom he sent some of his Disciples, when he was not in a Capacity of going to them in Person; and, upon leaving *Ratbod* he directed his Course to *Warckeren*, one of the chief Islands belonging to *Zeland*, where we at present see the two flourishing Cities of *Middlebourg* and *Flessingues*, ; his Patience and Charity made considerable Conquests in Favour of the Christian Religion, and establish'd Churches there for it's Continuance and Preservation. *Charles Martel*, Maire of the Palace, and Son to our Saint's Patron who had fill'd the same Post, took all Opportunities of expressing a particular Regard for his Merit, and engaged him to baptize his Son *Pepin*, afterwards King of *France*.

Radbod Duke, or, according to some Authors, King of *Freisland*, dying in the Year 719, *Willibrord* was at full Liberty to preach in every Part of that Country; and about the same Time was join'd in his Apostolical Labours by *Winfrid* an *English* Priest, commonly known by the Name of *Boniface*, Apostle of *Germany* and Bishop of *Mentz*, whose Life may be seen *June* fifth. That excellent Missionary spent three Years in *Freisland* in the same Labours which employ'd our Saint near fifty; for the most probable Opinion is that *Willibrord* died in 739. His Body was carried to the Monastery of *Epternach*, which he had founded about two Leagues from *Treves*, according to his own

Will

Will and Direction, and depofited in a Marble Tomb; where as *Alcuin* the Nov. 8. Author of his Life, who wrote about fifty Years after, affures us Miracles were then perform'd daily at his Interceffion. The fame Writer gives us the fixth of *November* as the Day of the Saint's Death; but the *Roman* Martyrologe places his Feftival on the feventh of the fame Month.

The VIII Day.

The four Crowned Martyrs at ROME.

THE Martyrs of this Day, known at firft by the Title of *Crowned*, and fince diftinguifhed by the Names of *Severus, Severianus, Carpophorus* and *Victorius*, are become very famous by the Publick Veneration fhewn them by the Church; but we have very little of their Hiftory remaining. All we know of them is that they were Brothers, employ'd in Offices of Truft and Honour at *Rome*; that in *Dioclefian*'s Perfecution they declared loudly againft the Worfhip of Idols, which drew the Rage of their Pagan Countrymen on them; that they were whipp'd with Scourges loaded with Leaden Plumets, and expired under the Hands of their Tormenters. St. *Gregory* the Great mentions a Church at *Rome* dedicated in Honour of our Saints, which Cardinal *Baronius* believes the fame that now bears the Title in that City.

Saint WILLEHAD *firft Bifhop of* Bremen.

WILLEHAD, one of thofe holy Perfons, who do honour to this Ifland, was born in the Kingdom of *Northumberland* toward the Middle of the VIII Century, and educated from his Infancy in Learning and Piety. He had no fooner learnt the Maxims of the Gofpel, but he reduced them to Practice; and, when capable of forming a Refolution, confecrated himfelf to the Service of God. The Aufterity of his Life, his conftant Attendance on Prayer and the many Virtues that fhone out in his whole Conduct, made him the Object of univerfal Efteem, and engaged his Bifhop to confer the Order of Priefthood on him. Underftanding that the Natives of *Freifland*, and *Saxony* had given the Gofpel a favourable Reception, he was infpired with an Inclination to vifit thofe Countries, and affift in the Propagation of *Chrift*'s Kingdom there. The Saint applying to King *Alchred* for leave to profecute his Defign,

that

Nov. 8. that Prince confulted the Bifhops in his Dominions, and other Perfons remarkable for Piety, who all approved of his Zeal; whereupon he was allow'd to follow the Divine Call.

Willebad began his Miffion at *Dockum* in *Weft Friefland*, made his Way through the Country now called *Over-Iffel*, and feveral other Parts. His Preaching, fupported and illuftrated by an exemplary Life, was attended with extraordinary Succefs among fuch as were Strangers to the Truth at his Arrival. The Barbarians, who remain'd obftinate in their Infidelity, fired at the Affront he put on their Gods, and the contemptuous Manner in which he treated what they had been ufed to look on as facred and venerable, came to a Refolution of killing him. One of the Confpirators, more calm and reafonable than the reft, propofed deciding his Fate by Lots, which they imagined directed by the Powers they worfhip'd: but the Almighty interpofed in Favour of his Servants and determin'd what Men look on as Chance for his Prefervation. The Chriftian Religion making a confiderable Progrefs in the Country, fome of our Saint's Difciples, full of Zeal for the Glory of the true God, proceeded to demolifh the Places dedicated to Superftition and Idolatry; which incenfed the Pagans fo that they refolved the Death of our Saint and his Companions. *Willebad* felt the Weight of their Indignation; one of them directed a Sword to his Neck, which muft have cut off his Head, had not Providence diverted the Stroke; the Saint got no Damage, for all the Execution was cutting the String of a Reliquary which he wore about his Neck. This Deliverance furprized the Enemies of the Chriftian Religion, and ftruck them with a profound Veneration for *Willebad*.

In the Year 780 *Charlemagne*, being in *Saxony*, heard the Saint's Character, and was defirous of feeing fo extraordinary a Perfon; finding his Merit exceeded his Reputation, he affign'd him the Canton of *Wigmode*, which lay between the *Wefer* and the *Ebb*, for the Scene of his Labours, and fupplied him with what was neceffary for the building Churches there. *Willebad* had made a confiderable Number of Converts, when *Witikind*, Prince of *Saxony*, ftirr'd up the Inhabitants of that Country againft *Charlemagne*, which obliged the Saint to fly for his own Security; but all fuch of his Difciples, and Companions in the Miffion as fell into the Hands of the Barbarians were put to Death. *Willebad* put to Sea, and went for *Friefland*, where he ftaid 'till he was convinced that his Return to *Saxony* was impracticable; and then made a Journey to *Rome*. Pope *Adrian* I receiv'd him very gracioufly; and at his Return the Saint retired to the Abbey of *Epternach* in the Diocefe of *Treves*, where he was join'd by feveral of his Difciples who had been difperfed persed by the *Saxon* Persecution. He spent two Years in that House, where his whole Employments were Prayer, Meditation and transcribing Books.

Nov. 9.

After several bloody Battles, *Charlemagne* entirely reduced the *Saxons* in the Year 785, and thus made Way for the Gospel among that barbarous People. Upon this favourable Change of Affairs *Willehad* left his Monastery, waited on the victorious Prince at *Ersburg*, and desired his Orders for preaching the Gospel in *Saxony*. The King receiv'd him with all Marks of Respect for his Zeal and Virtue, directed him to return to *Wigmode*, and gave him the Revenue of a small Monastery in *France* for his Support. The Saint, thus authorized and protected, reassumed his Mission, preached the Faith publickly, rebuilt the Churches which had been demolished in the late Times of Confusion, and employ'd proper Persons for the Instruction, and Direction of the People.

Charlemagne, being at *Wormes*, had the Satisfaction of hearing what Wonders the Almighty perform'd by the Ministry of his Servant; upon which he procured his Consecration, and gave him *East-Friesland* and Part of *Saxony* for his Diocese. He receiv'd the Episcopal Character on the fifteenth of *July* 787, and fixt his Seat at *Bremen*. This new Dignity served only to make the Saint more vigilant and active; his Austerities were still the same, as before his Promotion; and nothing but an Express Command from his Holiness could prevail with him to indulge himself so far as to eat Fish, when his Infirmities seem'd to call for a Relaxation; for 'till then he had lived on Bread, Honey, Fruite and Herbs. The Dedication of his Cathedral is the last Action we find recorded of his Life; and a Week after that Ceremony, he receiv'd the Reward of his Labours, on the eighth of *November* 789. The Church honours his Memory on the Day of his Death.

The IX Day.

The Dedication of St. Saviour's Church *at* ROME.

THE *Roman* Church this Day commemorates the Dedication of the Edifice, which is still their Cathedral, and has been in all Ages known by different Names. From it's being built in the *Lateran* Palace, it is still known by that Appellation with the Addition of St. *John*, because join'd by two Chappels, one of which bears the Name of *John the Baptist*, the other of *John the Evangelist*. The *Roman* Martyrologe mentions the said

Church by the Title of it's Dedication, *viz:* St. *Saviour*'s; but it has been frequently ſtiled *Conſtantine*'s *Baſilick*, becauſe, as we are told, it was built at the Charge of that excellent Prince, who endow'd and adorn'd it.

※※※※※※※※※※※※※※※※※※※※※※※※※※※※※※※※※※

St. THEODORE, Martyr.

THE holy Martyr, whoſe Memory the Church celebrates this Day was a Native of *Syria* or *Armenia*, engaged in the Army, and ſent into his Winter Quarters in the Province of *Pontus* at the Beginning of the IV Age. *Theodorus* reſided at *Amaſea*, when *Galerius Maximian* publiſhed an Edict for continuing the Perſecution, raiſed by his Predeceſſor *Dioclesian*; on which Occaſion 'though but newly liſted in the Emperor's Service, he ſhew'd all the Courage and Experience of an old Soldier in *JeſusChriſt*; and was ſo far from concealing his Faith for Fear of Danger, that, according to S. *Gregory Nyſſen*'s Expreſſion, he ſeem'd to carry it written on his Forehead. Being ſeized and carried before the Magiſtrate, he was aſked how he dared profeſs a Religion ſo diſagreeable to the Emperor; or neglect a Manner of Worſhip practiſed by his Sovereign. *Theodore* ſhewing the inflexible Reſolution of his Soul by the Calmneſs of his Look, anſwer'd, " *I know not your Gods; nor indeed do* " *they deſerve that Name. 'Tis abſurd to beſtow the Title of Divinity on Devils;* " *but* Chriſt *the only begotten Son of God, is my God. Welcome Blows, Wounds,* " *and Fire, while I ſuffer for adhering to him; and if theſe Words offend you, cut* " *out my Tongue; for every Part of my Body is ready when God calls for it as* " *a Sacrifice.*" The Governor of the Province, and a commanding Officer of the Army were on the Bench, when the young Soldier deliver'd himſelf in thoſe ſtrong Terms; ſhock'd at his Courage they began to deliberate on the Matter, and conſider what they ſhould do in the preſent Caſe. An Officer, diſpoſed to ſhew his Wit, and divert himſelf with what the Martyr had ſaid, aſked him whether his God had a Son; and whether he was produced in the ſame Manner with Mortals? " *My God,* replied Theodore, *is not ſubject to* " *the Paſſions on which Men act; but I repeat it that He has a Son, who was* " *born in a Manner worthy of God. But I am ſurprized that you do not bluſh* " *at holding a Female Deity, the Mother of twelve Children.*

His Judges were now come to a Reſolution, and with a pretended Compaſſion allow'd him Time to give the Affair a ſecond Thought; upon which he was diſmiſs'd, and employ'd the Interval in Prayer for Perſeverance. In the Middle of *Amaſea* ſtood a Temple dedicated to *Cybele*, the fabulous Mother

ther of the Pagan Deities; *Theodore*, full of a holy Indignation at the Su- Nov. 9. perstitious and Idolatrous Worship of that Goddess, finding a favourable Opportunity, set that Fabrick on Fire, and destroy'd it. The Martyr was so far from denying the Fact, that he gloried in it; and when Information was given against him to the proper Magistrate, he declared had done nothing but what might challenge the highest Commendation. He was carried a second Time before the Governor and his Assistant, who examined him, and found him ready to prevent their Questions by his Confession of the Fact. They then endeavour'd to terrify him with Threats of the most violent Torments; and finding him proof against every thing of that Nature, changed their Stile, and resolved to see what Profers of Honour and Preferment would do; but all those glittering Trifles had no Influence on *Theodore*, who rejected the Proposal with so much Contempt, that his Judges threw off the Disguise of Kindness, and order'd him to be whipp'd severely as an impious Adversary of the Gods, and a disobedient Subject to the Emperor. 'Though the Sentence was executed with as little Mercy as the Persecutors could desire, the Saint maintain'd his former Tranquility, and Greatness of Soul, and seemingly insensible to the Blows, sung those Words of the Psalmist, *I will* Pf. 33. 1. *bless the Lord at all Times, his Praise shall always be in my Mouth.* When the Governor's Cruelty was tired out by the Patience of the Martyr he was sent to Prison, where the Almighty did Wonders in his Favour; for, according to S. *Gregory Nyssen*, in the Night the Voices of a great Company singing were hear'd, and the Prison was lighted as if a great Number of Lamps had been placed there on Purpose. The Jaylor, alarm'd at what he saw and heard, ran to the Dungeon; where he found the Saint, and the other Prisoners asleep.

After a third Examination, and Defeat of all Attempts to shake his Constancy, *Theodore* was condemn'd to be burnt alive; which Sentence was executed immediately. His Death is usually placed in the Year 306; and his Festival observed by the Eastern Church on the eighteenth of *February*, commonly supposed to be the Day of his Victory; but the ninth of *November* is sacred to his Memory in the West.

Nov. 10

The X Day.

St. TRYPHO, and St. RESPICIUS, Martyrs; and St. NYMPHA, Virgin.

TRYPHO and *Respicius* were Countrymen, and probably Relations; their Acts mention them as Natives of *Bithynia*, and born at *Apamea*, or near that Town, where their Ancestors settled some Time before. They made so considerable a Figure among their Neighbours that upon the opening of *Decius*'s Persecution they were immediately seized by Order of *Aquilinus* Governor of *Bithynia*, loaded with Irons, conducted to *Nice*, where that Magistrate resided, and thrown into Prison 'till he was at Leisure to try them. After some Days Confinement they were brought into Court, where they appear'd full of the Fire of the holy Spirit, which animated them, and made them an Overmatch for all the Attempts of the Persecutors. The Governor's first Questions, as usual in those Cases, were about their Names, and Station in the World: to which they answer'd that one of them was called *Trypho*, the other *Respicius*; that they were in the usual Stile well born, but that the Christian Religion allow'd what they call'd Fortune no Consideration, because all things were govern'd by divine Providence. One of the Assistants on the Bench hoped to intimidate the Saints by telling them the Emperor had directed all such to be burnt alive, as should refuse to sacrifice to the Gods. To which *Respicius* replied that he and his Companion only wished they might be thought worthy to suffer in that Cause, and desired the Court would proceed to the Rigour of their Commission. *Aquilinus* then endeavour'd to persuade them to that Act of Pagan Religion by observing that they were at Years of Maturity, and must certainly understand the Resonableness of what was urged. "*Yes*, said *Trypho*, *we understand what we do perfectly well; for which Reason we are determ'd to remain true to* Jesus Christ; *and desire to fight for that Name to the last Drop of our Blood.*

The Governor press'd them again to conform to the Religion of the Empire; and, finding them persist in the Refusal, order'd them to be put on the Rack. That Sentence was scarce pronounced when they express'd their Readiness to undergo all that the most ingenious Cruelty could invent or inflict by stripping themselves, and stepping forward with a surprizing Alacrity. They bore the Torture with admirable Patience and Tranquility near three Hours; during which Time they spoke strongly of the Power of the Almighty,

mighty, and the Punishment due to Idolaters. *Aquilinus* then order'd the Martyrs to be exposed naked in the open Air. It was Winter, and the Severity of the Frost was such as disabled them from walking, or even standing without exquisite Pain. When they had born that Mortification some Time, they were presented to the Governor again, who asked them whether they were now inclined to repent of their Conduct. " *Yes,* answer'd " *Trypho, that is the whole bent of our Inclinations and Desires, and the grand* " *Design of our Religion*". *Aquilinus* then order'd them to Prison, assuring them that, if they did not comply with his Proposal, they should be treated with the utmost Rigour.

[Nov.10]

Soon after their Commitment, the Governor made the Tour of the other Cities under his Jurisdiction, and at his Return to *Nice* call'd for our illustrious Prisoners, whom he attempted to gain by Words which seem'd to express a Tenderness for the Persons before him, and begg'd they would consider their own Good before it was too late. *Trypho* answer'd that their own real Good was the only Object of their Thoughts, and that they could not follow his Advice better than by remaining firm in their Profession. *Aquilinus,* finding all his Endeavours defeated, commanded their Feet to be pierced with large Nails, and in that Condition they were dragg'd through the Streets. But he who is the Strength of Martyrs supported them under their Sufferings, and gave them a Courage superior to the utmost Malice of the Enemy. The Governor, surprized and confounded at their Patience, order'd them to be whipp'd; which was done 'till the Executioners were tired with the Task. This Conquest enraged that Magistrate so that he directed the Officers of the Court to tear their Flesh with Hooks, and apply lighted Torches to their Sides. The Saints remaining the same in the Midst of all these violent Attacks, the Governor call'd out to the Tormentors, and desired they would exert the utmost of their Skill on the Persons in their Hands; but the Martyrs were still superior to the Storm; upon which he address'd himself to them, and advised them to grow wise, and consult their own Security. *Respicius* assured the Judge it was not in the Power of Words or Blows to divert them from their Duty to God, and engage them in the Worship of senseless Idols.

The next Day they were examined a third Time, and press'd, as before, to obey the Emperor's Edict; but upon *Trypho*'s assuring the Court that he and his Companion were not to be moved from their Resolution of serving and fearing the Living God, the Governor pass'd Sentence of Death on them, and they were immediately beheaded on the first of *February* in the

Year

Nov. 10 Year 251, the Day on which the *Grecians*, among whom they suffer'd, honour the Memory of St. *Trypho*; but He and *Respicius* are mention'd together on the tenth of *November* in the *Roman* Martyrologe, in Conjunction with St. *Nympha*, who is there supposed to have glorified God by Martyrdom at the same Time. The Account we have of her makes her a holy Virgin of *Palermo* in *Sicily*; but the rest of her History is universally allow'd to be very obscure.

The XI Day.

St. MARTIN, *Bishop of* Tours.

HISTORIANS are very much divided about the Year of St. *Martin*'s Birth; it is not our Business in this Place to examine the Reasons alledged for each particular Calculation, or decide in Favour of one to the Prejudice of the rest; but we hope we may be allow'd to follow the Chronology of S. *Gregory*, one of his Successors in the See of *Tours*, who places it in the Year 316. The Saint was a Native of that Part of the antient *Pannonia* which now bears the Name of the *Lower Hungary*, and educated at *Pavia* in *Italy*, where his Parents were then settled. His Father served in the Imperial Troops, and arose to the Commission of a Milatary Tribune, which was not much different from that of a Brigadier amongst us. The Laws of the Empire obliged the Saint, as an Officer's Son, to bear Arms; but his Inclinations could never be taught to agree with that Profession; from his Infancy he seem'd animated with the Spirit of God, and seem'd to have no Relish for any thing but the Service of God, 'though his Parents were Slaves to Idolatry. *Martin* was but ten Years old, when the divine Grace working powerfully in his Soul, he made his Way to Church, and desired to be admitted among the Catechumens. His Request was granted; and after two Years Instruction he conceived so ardent a Love of God that nothing but the Tenderness of his Age could have hinder'd him from retiring into the Desart. His Heart, however, was always in the Church, and Monasteries; and he then laid the first Foundation of that eminent Sanctity to which the Almighty design'd to raise him.

Martin was just fifteen Years old when their Imperial Majesties issued out an Order for inlisting such of the Veterans Children as were able to bear Arms; and our Saint was one of that Number. Being discover'd by his Father,

ther, he was forced from his religious Retreat, took the Military Oath and Nov. 10. was enter'd in the Cavalry. Upon his March our young Soldier was attended by one Servant, whom he treated like his Friend and Equal; and all the Time he remain'd in the Army, he was a Stranger to the Vices and Extravagancies, which ufually attend that Profeffion. His Patience, and Humility gain'd him the Efteem of all who faw him, and the Innocence of his Life engaged the Admiration even of thofe who would not be at the Trouble of copying his Example. 'Though he had not receiv'd Baptifm, he perform'd all the Works of a perfect Chriftian; the Neceffitous were fecure of Affiftance while he had any thing to beftow; and he was reduced to his Arms and one Coat when he met a poor Man near *Amiens*, naked and begging Relief; it was then Winter, and the Seafon very rigorous, and feveral had pafs'd that miferable object without Notice. *Martin*, whofe Heart was not proof againft the poor Man's Diftrefs, divided his Coat betwixt the Beggar and himfelf. Some of thofe who faw this Action diverted themfelves with the Figure of a Soldier half cloathed; while others admired his Conduct and were concern'd that they had not prevented that generous Act. The following Night the Saint dreamt he faw *Jefus Chrift* drefs'd in what he had beftow'd on the poor Man, and heard him delare that *Martin*, 'though then but a Catechumen, had given him that Piece of a Coat.

This Acknowledgment infpired the Saint with frefh Courage and Confidence in the divine Goodnefs, and determin'd his Refolution of being baptized. He was favour'd with the Sacrament of Regeneration at eighteen Years of Age, and had Thoughts of quitting the Service immediately; but his Colonel, who had a fingular Regard for him, engaged his Stay two Years longer; at the End of which Term the Officer expected his Difcharge, and then promifed to bear him Company in renouncing the World. During that Interval *Martin* was fo entirely taken up with the Obligations of his Baptifm, that he had little more than the Name of a Soldier, and exprefs'd much Impatience at being detain'd one Moment from the Service of God. After about five Years Service in the Army, therefore, according to the moft feafiable Account, *Martin* quitted the Camp; after fome Years fpent in Retirement he made his Application to St. *Hilary* Bifhop of *Poitiers*, who was raifed to that See about the Middle of the IV Century, and was look'd on as one of the moft confiderable Prelates in *Gaul*. That great Man foon knew the Value of our Saint, and after a few Months offer'd to ordain him Deacon for the Service of his Church. *Martin*'s Humility made a vigorous Oppofition to that Propofal; upon which the Bifhop of *Poitiers* thought proper to

place

place him in a lower Station, and in that View made him an Exorcist. He had been some Time employ'd in the Functions of that Order when he had a Dream in which the Will of God was signified to him, and directed him to make a Visit to his Parents, and endeavour their Conversion. St. *Hilary* allow'd him to undertake that Journey on Condition that he should return to *Poitiers*, which he promised. On the Way he fell into the Hands of Highwaymen; who seem'd resolved to murther him; but, one of the Gang opposing the Motion, he was bound, and stripp'd; and upon that Person asking him whether he had not been in much Apprehension from the violent Death which seem'd to threaten him, he answer'd that as he was a Christian, and put his whole Trust in God, he had nothing to fear while under his Protection; but that indeed he could not but be under a great Concern for Him and his Associates, who hazarded their eternal Salvation by their wretched Course of Life. He pursued his Discourse on that Subject, and spoke so strongly on the Necessity of Faith in *Jesus Christ* and a Life conformable to the great Precepts of the Gospel, that he converted the Highwayman, who endeavour'd to efface the Crimes of his former Life by Penance in a Monastery, and took a singular Pleasure in acknowledging the Favour he had received from Heaven by the Means of our Saint.

Martin continued his Journey into *Pannonia*, where he had the Satisfaction of rescuing his Mother from the Danger that attends the Profession of Idolatry; but his Father remain'd in his Infidelity. While he was there great Numbers were induced to embrace Christianity by the invincible Force of his exemplary Conduct; and the *Arians* in *Illyricum* found a formidable Adversary in the Person of our Saint, who suffer'd much from that Sect, and was driven out of the Town for opposing their Tenets. *Martin*'s next Journey was into *Italy*, where he had the Mortification to hear that the Church of *Gaul* was very much disturbed by those Hereticks, and that his holy Master S. *Hilary* was banished by the Faction. Upon this melancholy News he found a Retreat near *Milan*, where he enter'd on a Monastick Life; but was soon molested by the active Malice of *Auxentius* Bishop of that City, one of the Heads of the *Arian* Party, who obliged him to leave the Country. *Martin* was persuaded that he could not do much Good by continuing the Contest with one so powerful and resolute as that unhappy Prelate, and therefore retired to a small Island on the Coast of *Liguria* in Company with a Priest of consummate Virtue, where he lived on the Produce of the Place 'till he understood that *Constantius* had consented to St. *Hilary*'s Return to his Bishoprick. Under his Protection he settled near *Poitiers*, with a View of leaving the World and

enjoying

enjoying the useful Conversation of that holy Prelate. The Bishop of *Poi-* Nov.11 *tiers*, willing to encourage the devout Disposition of his Disciple gave him a Piece of Land about two Leagues from that City, where he built a Monastery, which is usually reckon'd the first that was founded in *Gaul*, and was standing in the Middle of the VIII Century.

Our Saint had spent some Time in his Monastery and gather'd a numerous Family there when the See of *Tours* became vacant by the Death of S. *Lidorius* the second Bishop of that Church. *Martin*'s Virtue and Miracles had spread his Reputation through the whole Country, and the Clergy and People of *Tours* united in desiring he might succeed that deceased Pastor; but they were so well acquainted with the Saint's Humility and Love of Retirement, that they were obliged to have Recourse to a Stratagem to draw him from his Monastery. *Ruricius*, one of the Citizens of *Tours*, went and threw himself on his Knees before the holy Monk, begging he would favour his sick Wife with a Visit; *Martin* yielded to his Importunity, put himself under the Conduct of his Petitioner, was seized by great Numbers of the People who lay in Ambuscade on the Way, and conducted him to *Tours*, where he was consecrated in the Year 371 amidst the Acclamations of all concern'd in the Election.

Martin's Promotion made no Alteration in his Way of Living; but the same Poverty of Spirit, Plainness of Dress, Humility of Heart, and Mortifications were continued which had been the distinguishing Parts of his Character, while in the Monastery. At his first Accession to the See of *Tours* he lived in a Cell near the Church; but, finding great Inconveniency from the Crouds of Visitants that resorted to him there, he built a Monastery two Miles from the City; where the holy Prelate had a wooden Cell, but most of the Monks lodged in Holes of the Rock; and this was the humble Beginning of the celebrated Monastery of *Marmoutier*, which subsists at present under S. *Benedict*'s Rule. The Blessing of Heaven was pour'd on this new Establishment in so plentiful a Manner that the holy Founder was accompanied by eighty Religious upon his first retiring to that Place. They were form'd by his Example, and had no other Contention but that of approaching nearest to that excellent Model of Austerity, Mortification, and Devotion; their whole Life there was not much better than a continual Fast; only the Sick were allowed Wine; none of the Community was permitted to call any thing his own, or buy and sell; the younger Members were employ'd in transcribing Books; and such as were incapable of that Work by Age or Infirmities had no other Business but Prayer; they never quitted their Cells but when the

Nov. 11 Publick Service called them to the Chapel; their Dress was one coarse Garment of Camels Hair, and, if like that of their Superior, black. This Monastery was afterwards the fruitful Parent of several others in the Diocese of *Tours*, and proved an excellent Seminary for such as were to be placed in the most conspicuous Stations in the Church.

The Saint had not been long in Possession of his See, when he was obliged to go to *Valentinian*'s Court, then in *Gaul*; we are not told what Affair carried him thither, but are assured, that the Emperor being apprized of his Journey and Business, and resolved to refuse his Request, gave Orders for not admitting him into the Palace. After twice attempting to enter, and still finding the Gate shut against him, *Martin* had Recourse to his usual Weapons; put on a Hair-shirt, strew'd Ashes on his Head, fasted and prayed seven Days together; after which time an Angel appear'd to him and encouraged him to make a third Trial; whereupon the holy Bishop went directly to the Palace, where he found all the Doors open; pass'd the Guards without the least Opposition; and made his Way to the Emperor's Apartment. That Prince, seeing the Saint come toward him, sat still, and in a very haughty and angry Tone asked who had dared to let him in. He had scarce pronounced the furious Words when his Seat was surrounded with Flames which obliged him to leave it. *Valentinian*, struck with Awe for the holy Prelate, embraced him, and assured him of all he could ask. *Martin* had several Audiences after that, was entertain'd at the Emperor's Table, and at leaving the Court desired to accept of some rich Presents, which he declined, out of Love to the Poverty he profess'd.

The Circumstance last mention'd is related by *Sulpicius Severus*, who was personally acquainted with our Saint; and whom the Church honours as a Saint; and the same Author gives us the following Story. Near *Marmoutier* was a Place consecrated to the Memory of a pretended Martyr by a popular Mistake, and graced with an Altar, as if the Ashes of some Victim of *Jesus Christ* lay buried there. St. *Martin*, who was not so credulous, made strict Enquiry among the oldest of his Clergy for the Name of the Person, whose Relicks were supposed to be deposited there; but, not being able to trace the Original of this Tradition, he absented himself from that Place for some Time to avoid giving any Encouragement to Superstition. Going thither one Day attended by a small Number of his Monks, and standing on the Sepulchre, he begg'd the Almighty would let him know who had been buried there. He had scarce ended his Prayer when, turning to his Left, he saw an Apparition with a very disagreeable and frightful Aspect; upon being

ing commanded to discover the Name of the Person whom it represented, and his Condition in the other World, the Spectre obey'd and declared he was a Highwayman, who had been executed for his Crimes, and was then suffering in Hell. The whole Company heard the Voice; but the Apparition was visible to St. *Martin* only, who immediately order'd the Altar to be demolished, and undeceived the People.

Nov. 11

No Man exerted himself more vigorously against Idolatry, than our Saint, who seem'd to be raised up by a particular Providence in an Age when their Imperial Majesties did in a Manner countenance Pagan Superstition by allowing all their Subjects to follow the Religion of their Ancestors. Scarce a Day passed which was not Witness of some Conquest gain'd by him over the Power of the Devil; and he frequently hazarded his Life in the Destruction of Places and Objects of Idolatrous Worship. Having demolished an old Temple, he was giving Orders for felling a tall Pine Tree, which stood near that Building, and was held sacred, when the Heathen Priest, join'd by great Numbers of Idolaters, opposed him; and after some Discourse on the Difference between the God of the Christians, and the pretended Deities which the Pagans adored, the latter told our Saint that since he reposed such Confidence in his God, they would cut down the Tree in Dispute upon Condition that he should stand under it when it fell. *Martin* agreed to the Proposal, and submitted to be tied where it seem'd impossible for him to avoid the Blow. This Sight drew great Crouds to the Place, and the Monks, who attended the holy Bishop, were full of Apprehension for their Master. The Tree began to fall on the Saint, and every one concluded him a dead Man, when lifting up his Hands, and making the Sign of the Cross it was driven violently toward the other Side, and alarm'd the Spectators, who thought themselves most secure. This miraculous Deliverance was follow'd by the Conversion of the greatest Part of those who had been Witnesses of it. *Sulpicius Severus*, who relates this Passage, sets down several other Favours of the same Nature, which were deservedly look'd on as so many authentick Proofs of a divine Protection, and the Vanity of Idols. The same excellent and holy Writer assures us that Threads drawn out of his Cloaths, and Letters written by his Hand were known to cure Distempers; and it would be an endless Labour to attempt to enumerate all the Miracles which God perform'd by his Means.

While St. *Martin* was thus employ'd in propagating the Kingdom of *Jesus Christ*, the Western Empire was in Confusion by the Usurpation of *Maximus* who had made his Way to the Crown by the Death of his Master *Gratian*;

tian; and the Church of *Gaul* was disturb'd by the *Priscillianists*, who began to come thither from *Spain*, where their Errors, consisting of a Mixture of several condemn'd Heresies, were first broached. Those Hereticks had been condemn'd in a Council held at *Saragossa* in the Year 380; but *Ithacus*, a Catholick Bishop, carried the Affair to the secular Court; and upon *Maximus*'s coming to *Treves* presented him with a Petition full of Complaints against *Priscillian* and his Followers. That Prince, whose chief Fault was Ambition, and who was otherwise a Man of some Probity, and pretended a Concern for Religion, referr'd the Matter to a Council, which he order'd should meet at *Bourdeaux*. *Priscillian* would not hear of the Judgment of the Bishops, and appeal'd to the Emperor; the Catholick Prelates condescended to plead their Cause before *Maximus*, then at *Treves*. Our Saint was at that City before the Arrival of the Parties, where he had been soliciting the Emperor's Pardon for some who had the Misfortune to incur his Displeasure; and observing the Heat, and Passion, with which *Ithacus* proceeded in the aforesaid Affair, and which he thought both a Violation of Charity, and a Disgrace to the Church, undertook to moderate the Matter by dissuading *Ithacus* from proceeding as he had begun, and begging the Emperor to spare the Lives of the Criminals, who were already cut off from the Church, and thus sufficiently punished in a regular Way. *Maximus*, out of Respect to the Saint, stopt all Proceedings as long as he staid in the Town; and, when he left it, promised he would shed no Blood in the Case before him; but broke his Word at the Instigation of evil Counsellors, and referr'd the Affair to *Evodius*, a Man of strict Justice without the least Mixture of Compassion. *Priscillian* was convicted by his own Confession, and executed with some of his Accomplices by the Emperor's Order.

The next Year, which was 386, St. *Martin*'s charitable Concern for the distress'd carried him to *Treves* a second Time. The cotemporary Author of his Life tells us that several Bishops made their Court to *Maximus* with servile Flattery, but that our Saint always preserved an Apostolical Authority at Court. The Emperor, full of an awful Respect for *Martin*'s Virtue, spent some Time in importuning him to eat at his Table, before he would comply with the Invitation, and was bold enough to let that Prince know he did not think he ought to allow himself that Freedom with a Man who had deprived one Emperor of his Life and another of his Kingdom. *Maximus* assured the holy Bishop he had not accepted of the Imperial Purple willingly, but was obliged to it by the Army; that the incredible Success of his Enterprizes seem'd a Declaration of Heaven in his Favour, and that his

Enemies

Enemies were all fairly kill'd in the Field. *Martin* was at last prevail'd on Nov.11 to eat with the Emperor, who was so well pleased with the Favour that he invited the most considerable Persons of his Court, among whom where his Brother and Uncle, both Counts of the Empire, and *Evodius*, who was Consul that Year, to share it with him. About the Middle of the Entertainment the proper Officer presenting the Cup to the Emperor, according to Custom; who order'd it to be given to our Saint, expecting to receive it from him; but the holy Bishop express'd his Sense of the Dignity of the sacred Character by giving it to a Priest, who attended him. *Maximus* and the whole Company were agreeably surprized at that Action, which grew the common Topick of Discourse at Court; and *Martin* was admired and commended for his Courage and Sincerity. From that Time the Emperor frequently sent for the Saint, and had the Satisfaction of hearing him talk on the Glory of the Saints, and the Difference between this Life and the next. The Empress was still more constant in her Attendance on the holy Bishop, and sat at his Feet Night and Day to imbibe the excellent Instructions which flow'd from his venerable Mouth.

St. *Martin*, perceiving that Passion had a much larger Share in the Conduct of *Ithacus*, and his Companions, than Zeal for Religion, refused to hold Communion with them; but that hot-headed Faction, being supported by the Emperor, became very troublesome and formidable. The Prelates, who join'd *Ithacus* in a pretended Zeal against the *Pricillianists*, being assembled at *Treves* for the Choice of a Bishop of that City, obtain'd the Empeor's Promise for sending Officers into *Spain* with a Commission to search for Hereticks there, seize their Goods, and put them to Death; on which Occasion several Catholicks would probably have suffer'd; for those of *Ithacus*'s Party took the Liberty of fixing the Charge of Heresy on such as lead a retired Life, or were distinguished from their Neighbours by an eminent Degree of Virtue, and pretended to discover a Heretick by his Exterior. This Order was granted the Day before our Saint went to *Treves* to solicit the Pardon of some Persons of Distinction, who had fallen into Disgrace for espousing *Gratian*'s Cause. The Party, alarm'd at his Approach, and apprehending he might defeat their Design by setting it in it's true Light, prevail'd with *Maximus* to send him Word, while on the Road, that he was to come no farther, unless he would promise to keep Peace with the Bishops, whom he should find at *Treves*; but the Messenger being, satisfied with the Saint's saying he would enter the Town in the Peace of *Jesus Christ*, he met with no farther Molestation; and at his Arrival made his Way to Court, where he press'd the Emperor very strongly to

recal

Nov. 11 recal his Order for diſtreſſing the Hereticks in *Spain*; and declared that their Converſion was to be endeavour'd by Means more conformable to the Spirit of the Goſpel. While that Prince was conſidering of the Saint's Petition, the Faction, incenſed at his refuſing to communicate with them, applied to the Emperor, and begg'd he would conſider how low their Credit in the World would be if *Martin* was allow'd to keep that Diſtance from them; and conjured him with Tears to employ all his Power to oblige the holy Biſhop to join them.

'Though the Emperor's Affection for the Remonſtrants would have put him upon violent Meaſures, he did not judge it ſafe or prudent to follow his Inclinations in Regard to a Man, whoſe Sanctity engaged the Eſteem of all who knew him; for which Reaſon he appointed him a private Audience, and endeavour'd to gain him by obſerving to him that the Hereticks had been condemn'd by the Civil Power, independent of the Judgment of the Biſhops; that, ſince *Itbacus* and his Adherents were allow'd to be Catholicks, he could not ſee why the Saint ſhould withdraw himſelf from their Communion; that *Theognoſtus* was the only Prelate who had ſeperated from them; and that *Itbacus* had been declared innocent in a Council lately held. *Maximus*, finding theſe Conſiderations made no Impreſſion on our Saint, gave a Looſe to his Paſſions, left him abruptly, and diſpatched an Order for executing the Perſons, in whoſe Favour he had undertaken that Journey. After ſome Struggle between his Zeal for the Credit of Religion, which he thought diſgraced by the Party's violent Proceedings, and Charity for thoſe whoſe Lives he had begg'd, he determin'd in Favour of the latter, and let the Emperor know he was ready to communicate with *Itbacus* upon Condition that the Officers diſpatched to *Spain* were recall'd, and the ſuppoſed Traitors pardon'd. *Maximus*, glad to make ſuch a Conqueſt on any Terms, granted him all he aſked without the leaſt Heſitation; the next Day the Saint appear'd among the Biſhops, as required, and aſſiſted at the Conſecration of *Felix*, a Man of ſingular Piety, but could not be prevail'd with to ſign this Act of Communion.

As ſoon as his Buſineſs was done, *Martin* haſten'd back to his Flock, full of Remorſe for his Compliance, which, 'though the Reſult of Charity, did not appear perfectly innocent upon Reflection. He was in this Diſpoſition when he ſtopp'd in a Wood, and let his Companions go on before him, where he was comforted by an Angel, who told him that, 'though he had indeed committed a Fault, the Almighty was inclin'd to make ſome Allowance for the Motive on which he had acted, and the Streight to which he was reduced; but adviſed him to take Care he did not endanger his own Salvation by indulging

ging his Grief 'till it lead him to defpair. St. *Martin* continued his Journey Nov.11
to *Tours*, where he was receiv'd like an Angel of Peace; and from that Time
had no farther Communication with *Ithacus* and his Party. S. *Sulpicius Severus*
who has recorded this Fact, tells us, he had often heard the Saint mention it
with the utmoft Concern, and own that his Power of working Miracles was
much weaken'd fince his countenancing the Faction by what he had done
at *Treves*.

S. *Martin* was fourfcore Years old when he told his Monks, whom he alaways call'd his Brothers, that his End drew near; for he was favour'd with a Forefight of the Period of his Labours, and fpoke of the approaching Change in a Manner which exprefs'd more Hope than Fear. Being inform'd of a fcandalous Difference among the Clergy of *Cande* at the Extremity of his Diocefe, he made a Journey to that Town attended, as ufual by a great Number of his Difciples. After fome Stay there, and bringing Matters to an amicable Conclufion, he was preparing for his Return, when he was feiz'd with his laft Sicknefs. As foon as he was taken ill, he call'd his religious Retinue about him and declared that the Time of his Departure was come. Their Tears, and folemn Intreaties of his Stay among them affected the Saint fo ftrongly that he repay'd their Charity with Tears, and Addreffing himfelf to the Almighty, profefs'd his Readinefs to undergo the Fatigues of his Poft longer, if the divine Wifdom judged his Continuance in this World neceffary for his Flock; but his Victories were complete, and after fome Days fpent in conftant Prayer, he expired on a Heap of Afhes, which he judged the moft proper Bed for a Chriftian. According to the Calculation which we have follow'd, the Saint died in the Year 397; but Authors are far from being unanimous on that Article.

The News of the holy Bifhop's Death drew great Crouds from feveral Parts of his Diocefe, and the People of *Poitiers* and *Tours* difputed the Poffeffion of his Relicks with fome Warmth; but the latter carried them off, while the former were afleep, and depofited that Treafure, where the Church and Monaftery that bear his Name ftand at prefent. The venerable Relicks were honour'd with many great Miracles, and remain'd the Object of univerfal Devotion 'till the *Huguenots* in a Fit of frantick Zeal burnt them and fcatter'd the Afhes in the Wind. It has been obferved that our Saint is the firft Inftance of publick Veneration to what we call Confeffors in the *Weft*; a Cuftom which it is fuppofed begun in the Eaft with S. *Meletius* Bifhop of *Antioch* in the IV Century.

St. JOHN

St. JOHN the ALMONER.

ST. John, whose extraordinary Charity to the Poor has acquired him the Surname of the *Almoner*, was a Native of *Cyprus*, and raised to the Patriarchal See of *Alexandria* at the Beginning of the VII Century. As soon as he was placed in that conspicuous Station his first Concern was to get an exact Account of the Necessities of his Flock, in Order to provide them with a suitable Relief. He begun with taking a List of all the Poor in the Town, whom he usually call'd his Masters; and, finding their Number amount to above 7500 settled a daily Allowance on them. The Day after his Consecration he regulated the Weights and Measures through his whole Diocese; and thus provided a speedy Remedy for the most crying Injustices in Trade, and prevented the Ruin and Oppression of his People.

Being sensible that such as were placed above others by Riches or Titles of Dignity, made no Scruple of distressing the Weak, who were often hinder'd from applying to proper Persons for Relief, by inferior Officers, he resolved to redress this Grievance as soon as he was raised to the Episcopal Chair. In this View he gave publick Audience twice a Week before the Church Door, where he receiv'd all his Petitioners with a most engaging Sweetness, and dispatched every Man's Business with an Expedition that much enhanced the Favour. When he observed any of his Friends surprized at his Conduct, or ready to commend him for opening so easy a Way to his Tribunal, " *If* " said he, *We Mortals are allow'd the Liberty of entring the House of God, and* " *there offer our Prayers, and tell our Necessities; if the Almighty suffers us to* " *press our Petitions to him, and conjure him to give us speedy Relief; how easy* " *ought We to be of Access, and how ready to serve our Brethren. We, who* " *are but fellow Servants with Them, and acknowledge one Master; an* " *Obligation which we should never decline did we but remember that our Sa-* " *viour has assured us of the same Treatment at his Hands which we give* " *our Neighbour.*" The holy Bishop had not been long employ'd in this charitable Manner before he found the good Effects of his Endeavours, He was one Day sitting in the usual Place, but was surprized to find no Business, and went home full of Grief, fearing some unforeseen Accident had defeated his Design of being serviceable to the Distressed; but *Sophronius*, a Man of singular Piety near his Person comforted him by observing to him that he ought rather to rejoice at the Success of his Administration, and thank God who by his Ministry had established such a good Understanding among the People that

all

all Disputes were banished from among them, and their Union was like that of the heavenly Spirits.

St. *John* possess'd the other Eiscopal Virtues in an eminent Degree. He had an inviolable Affection for the Orthodox Faith, and the Unity of the Church; and was frequently heard to say that 'though a Man should have the Misfortune to be exteriourly cut off from the Catholick Communion, he would still have no Inducement or Excuse for joining Hereticks; " *for,* said " he, *if a Man is forbid both by divine and human Laws to marry another* " *while his own Wife is alive, even 'though his living with her is impracticable;* " *how shall We, who have been united to God by Faith in* Jesus Christ *and Bap-*" *tism, venture to violate this holy Union, and join his Enemies*". Full of such excellent Sentiments he applied vigorously to restoring the Church of *Alexandria* to that Purity which it receiv'd from its Apostolical Founder, and purge it from the reigning Heresies of those Times. His Concern for the Orthodox Doctrine and Ecclesiastical Discipline made him particularly careful in his Choice of Pastors, whose exemplary Lives, and Skill in the Conduct of Souls qualified them for the important Work in which they were to be employ'd.

The holy Bishop could not bear to see any of his Congregation leave the Place of divine Worship 'till the whole Service was ended; and, observing one Day that several went out immediately after the Gospel, and spent that Time in idle Discourses which should have been employ'd in preparing for Communion, he quitted the Altar, follow'd them, and sat down among them. Perceiving them surprized at his Conduct, he told them with all imaginable Calmness, that the Shepherd must not be seperated from his Flock, that he was ready to return to the Altar, if they would accompany him, but would stay there if they were resolved on the same; " *for,* said the holy Prelate, " *my only Motive of offering Sacrifice publickly is to serve You.* This Practice was so successful that the Author of our Saint's Life assures us it produced a thorough Reformation in that Point upon being repeated once more.

The Saint took a particular Care to avoid all Superfluities in Discourse, especially such as were criminal; of this Sort are Rash Judgment, Slander, and Detraction; and when he found the Conversation turning on his Neighbour's Faults, he had always the Art of shifting the Subject. He prescribed the Use of much Tenderness even for the greatest of Sinners, being persuaded that several, whose Crimes were publick, might repent of them, and recover God's Grace, 'though few were Witnesses of their Repentance. This Way of thinking inspired him with that admirable Sweetness which appear'd in his Conduct toward Sinners, even when obliged to correct them; for his

A a only

only Aim being the Change of their Hearts, he never endeavour'd to give them Confusion. But when all soft Means fail'd, he had Resolution enough to employ others of a stronger Nature, which were more likely to produce the desired Effect; of which the following Story is an Instance. He had taken some Pains to persuade a Man of Quality in his Diocese to be reconciled to one who had offended him, but found him obstinately deaf to the Proposal; the Saint then proceeded to reprove him in the strongest Terms; but to no Purpose; at last he invited him to hear Mass in his Chapel, where he was to be join'd only by the Bishop, and his Clerk; when they came to the Lord's Prayer they repeated the four first Petitions together; but the Bishop and his Clerk left the Nobleman to pronounce the Words, *Forgive us our Trespasses, as we forgive them who trespass against us*, alone. When he had ended that Petition, the Saint turn'd to him, and desired he would be pleased to reflect on what he had asked of the Almighty and consider that he had solemnly protested he forgave all who had offended him, as an Inducement for God to treat him with the like Compassion. Those Words, 'though deliver'd with all the Sweetness Charity could inspire, were like a Clap of Thunder to the Nobleman; he threw himself at the Bishop's Feet, profess'd his Readiness to follow his Directions, and declared he was heartily reconciled to his Enemy.

The holy Prelate's Practice on such Occasions was exactly conformable to what he had prescribed to others. He once left the Altar, according to the Precept of *Jesus Christ*, and went to offer a Reconciliation with an Ecclesiastick, whom he had been obliged to excommunicate, and who had not Humility enough to submit and ask his Peace. That unhappy Person was so surprized at the Charity of his Bishop, and the Anxiety which he expressed for his Salvation, that, full of Confusion, he enter'd into himself, and desired the Saint would receive him to Penance. *Nicetas*, the Governor of *Alexandria* professed a particular Veneration for the Patriarch, and had been very active in his Promotion, but was once by some malicious Persons work'd into a Quarrel with him. Our Saint, satisfied of his own Innocence, and concern'd for his misinform'd Friend, sent to him in the Evening, and let him know *the Sun was almost set*. This Expression struck *Nicetas* to the Heart, and put him in Mind of the divine Precept of Reconciliation; he made his Way to the Episcopal Palace, and with Tears begg'd the holy Prelate's Pardon; who received him joyfully, and told him the Way to cut off a considerable Number of Sins was to shut his Ears against busy Informers, and never form a Judgment 'till he had heard both Sides. *Nicetas* listen'd to this

excellent

excellent Advice, and assured the Patriarch he would never suffer himself to be prejudiced against any one, nor enter into private Differences, without the utmost Necessity and a View to heal the Breach.

Nov 11

Though our Saint's Charity was universal, and extended to every Condition in human Life, it seem'd in a more particular Manner employ'd in the Relief of the indigent and miserable Part of Mankind, so that this Branch of Charity has ever been look'd on as the distinguishing Part of the Saint's Character; for he reduced himself to the lowest Ebb of Poverty in Favour of those distressed Members of *Jesus Christ*; of which we have the following remarkable Instance. A Gentleman of a plentiful Fortune, knowing the Quilt of the Patriarch's Bed was scarce fit for Use, purchased a new one of considerable Value, which he sent him, desired it might be laid on his Bed, and assured him he should think himself honour'd by his Acceptance of that Present. The Saint, in Compliance with his Benefactor, used the Quilt that Night, but could not sleep while he consider'd himself cover'd with what would procure the same Comfort for a great Number of Poor. As soon as it was Day, he sold the Quilt, with a Design of disposing of the Money according to the Dictates of his own charitable Heart. The Donor, being inform'd of what the Holy Bishop had done, purchased the Quilt a second Time, and sent it to him, begging he would favour him so far as to convert it to his own Use; but the Saint sold it again, saying, he was resolved to try who should be weary first.

John had govern'd the Church of *Alexandria* six Years, when the *Persians*, after making themselves Masters of *Syria* and *Palestine*, sacked *Jerusalem*, and carried off the Holy Cross, with a great Number of Christians. This Calamity drove prodigious Crouds to *Alexandria*, where they hoped to be at a convenient Distance from the victorious Enemy; and the Patriarch's Charity convinced them that divine Providence had directed them to that City. Though the Misery of those unhappy Persons was very great, the Saint's Goodness to them was still greater; and it was Matter of Wonder to the whole World, how he found Means to support an Expence, which seem'd to exceed the Power of Crown'd Heads; but God, whose Steward he always profess'd himself, multiplied the Gifts of his Charity in his Hands, and the wealthiest Persons of *Egypt*, *Africa*, and *Cyprus* were by his Exhortations and Example encouraged to make him the Depositary of large Sums for the Relief of the distressed Christians.

The Taking of *Jerusalem* by the Infidels is dated in 614; and a Famine, which oppress'd *Egypt* the ensuing Year, stopp'd the Hands of such as had before contributed very plentifully to the Support of the Miserable under his

Protection. This was the unhappy Situation of Affairs at *Alexandria*, when a very rich Man, who had been twice married, and consequently was excluded from Holy Orders by the Canons, hoped to make his Advantage of the present Calamity, and gain Admission to the sacred Ministry. In this View, he let the holy Patriarch know that all the Money and Corn he had in the World should be freely given to the Poor, for which he desired no other Return but to be allowed the Satisfaction of serving the Church in the Quality of Deacon. *John*, full of Compassion for the Man, told him his Offering was defective and impure, because made on a Motive which could never be agreeable to God; assured him no Consideration should prevail with him to violate his Fidelity to the Almighty, who could, if he pleased, multiply the small Quantity of Provision which remain'd, so as to feed his numerous Family; and that the Example of *Simon* the Magician, who desired to buy Holy Things, was sufficient to deter him from accepting of his Offer on those Terms. This Resolution, and Confidence in God, was soon rewarded; for he had scarce dismiss'd the Gentleman, when News was brought that two of the largest Ships, which he had sent to *Sicily*, were enter'd the Port of *Alexandria*, loaded with Corn.

The Famine was follow'd by a great Mortality, which found fresh Employment for our Saint's indefatigable Charity; and he attended the Sick with as much Assiduity as he had fed the Hungry. At the Beginning of the Year 616, the Mortality ceasing, the Saint's Presence was not so necessary at *Alexandria*, as during the late Calamities; this Consideration, join'd to a Foresight of what that City had to suffer soon after from the *Persians*, made him resolve to retire to *Cyprus*, where he might have no other Business, but that of preparing for his approaching End. He had not been many Days in that Island, when he died the Death of the Just, being then in his sixty fourth Year. The eleventh of *November* is universally allowed to be the Day of his Departure, 'though his Name appears on the twenty third of *January* in the *Roman* Martyrologe, which *Baronius* believes to be the Day of his Consecration.

The XII Day.

St. MARTIN, *Pope and Martyr*.

THE holy Pope, whose Memory we celebrate this Day, was born at *Todi* in *Italy* about the Beginning of the seventh Century. His Parents provided

vided him with the best Masters that Country afforded; and, as he had a Mind Nov. 12 turn'd to Vertue, as well as a good Genius for Study, he made great Progress in both in a little Time. Having acquired a sufficient Stock of Philosophy and Eloquence to appear to Advantage in the World, the divine Grace, ever watchful for his Sanctification, led him to consider that the Knowledge of a Philopher, and the Rhetorick of an Orator are not only vain, but dangerous Accomplishments, when not accompanied with solid Piety, founded in Humility, and taught to contribute to the great End of improving Vertue, and directing our Lives. This Consideration made him more diligent than ever in seeking true Wisdom, and making his Salvation his only Care; in which View he renounced all Worldly Hopes, and consecrated himself to God in the Ecclesiastical State. He enter'd among the Clergy of *Rome*, and had been in Priest's Orders some Time, when Pope *Theodore* died on the twentieth of *April* 649.

Martin's Behaviour had been such, that on the first Proposal of filling the Holy See with one who would do Honour to that exalted Post, all concerned in the Election unanimously declared for our Saint, and published his Character with universal Applause. As soon as he was placed in St. *Peter*'s Chair, the World had the Satisfaction of seeing their largest Hopes encouraged by his Conduct; for every Action of his Life was visibly animated with an ardent Love of God, and a tender Concern for all committed to his Care. His Compassion for the Poor appeared in large Contributions for their Relief, and the Offices of Hospitality which he perform'd in Favour of Strangers. His Fasts were rigorous and frequent; and Prayer employ'd a very considerable Part of his Time. He was always ready to receive returning Sinners; took no small Pains to lead such through the Paths of Penance, as testified their Sorrow by Tears; and comforted them by letting them see what Reason they had to confide in God's infinite Goodness. He loved his Clergy with a Brotherly Tenderness, had a particular Regard for the Monks, and honoured the Episcopal Character wherever it was found.

At our Saint's first appearing at the Helm, the Ship enjoy'd a Calm; but the Hereticks and Schismaticks of the East soon raised a Storm, which employed all his Vigilance and Courage to save the People committed to his Care from making Shipwreck of their Faith. The *Monothelites* were the original Authors of these Disorders; a Sect, which, not daring to maintain the Unity of Nature in *Jesus Christ* in express Terms after the Decisions of the Council of *Chalcedon*, asserted that he had but one Will and Operation of Mind. This Heresy was favour'd and protected by the Emperor *Heraclius*; and *Sophronius* Bishop of *Jerusalem* was the first, who undertook to stop it's Course. That

Prelate

Nov. 12 Prelate held a Council about the Year 634, and sent it's Decrees to Pope *Honorius*, and *Sergius* Patriarch of *Constantinople*. *Sergius*, who was then infected with the Errors in Question, and desirous of engaging others in the same, wrote an artful Letter to *Honorius*, insinuating, that the only Way to preserve Union in the Church, would be to drop all Discourse about *One or Two Operations* in *Jesus Christ*; and the Pope, not seeing into his Design, approved of the Proposal. Soon after his Holiness's Death, the Patriarch persuaded *Heraclius* to publish an Edict, strictly prohibiting the Use of the Terms on which the whole Dispute turned. *Severinus*, who succeeded *Honorius*, did not sit long enough to do any Thing in this Affair; but *John* IV condemn'd the Errors of the *Monothelites*; which, however, gain'd Ground at *Constantinople* under the Patronage of *Pyrrhus* and *Paul*, the two succeeding Patriarchs of that City. *Pyrrhus*, who had been forced from his See, went into *Africa*, where he was vigorously attack'd by *Maximus*, an orthodox Monk; and, upon being worsted, promised to lay his Recantation before the Pope. *Theodore*, then in St. *Peter*'s Chair, received him very graciously, and upon retracting his Errors, paid him the Respect due to the Patriarch of *Constantinople*; but *Pyrrhus* relapsed about two Years after, and *Paul* continued obstinate; whereupon they were condemn'd by the H. See, as the chief Favourers of Heresy.

This was the State of the Catholick Church, when *Martin* was placed at the Head of it; and his Zeal for the Faith, encouraged by *Maximus*, then at *Rome*, put him upon calling a Council in that City, which consisted of 105 Bishops, who condemn'd and rejected the *Ecthesis* and the *Type*, i. e. the Exposition and Formulary prescribed by *Heraclius*, and *Constans*, then on the Throne, which tended to the forbidding the Mention of *One or Two Operations in Jesus Christ*, and anathematiz'd *Cyrus* Patriarch of *Alexandria*, *Sergius* Patriarch of *Constantinople*, and his two Successors in that See. The Emperor, incensed at their Proceedings, sent an Order to *Olympius*, Exarch of *Ravenna*, or his Lieutenant in *Italy*, to repair forthwith to *Rome*, press the Reception of the Imperial Edicts, and seize the Pope, provided he had no Reason to apprehend any Opposition from the Army. The Exarch perform'd that Journey; but found the Church of *Rome*, and the whole Clergy of *Italy* ready to act in Concert in Defence of the Faith, and so strongly united, that he was convinced he could never carry his Point by violent Measures; for which Reason he had Recourse to Treachery, and directed one, who attended him to Church, to assassinate our Saint at the Time of Communion. But the divine Providence interposed for the Safety of the Holy Pope; for the Person employ'd in the black Work declared upon Oath, that as he was preparing to execute his Commission,

mission, he was struck blind, or at least his Sight was suspended for some Time, so that he did not see his Holiness at the Moment appointed for striking the sacrilegious Blow. *Olympius*, sensible of his Fault, in attempting the Life of one thus visibly under the Protection of Heaven, made his Peace with our Saint, and marched his Forces against the *Saracens* in *Sicily*, where he died soon after.

Calliopas succeeded *Olympius*, and at entring on his Office was order'd to seize St. *Martin*, upon a Charge of high Treason in corresponding with and assisting the Enemies of the Empire, and conduct him to *Constantinople*. The holy Pope was at his Devotions in St. *John Lateran*'s, when *Calliopas* arrived; and at his leaving that Church to meet that Magistrate, the Clergy and People who attended him on that Occasion, with a loud Voice pronounced *Anathema* to all who should say or think the Saint had made any Change in the Faith, and all such as should not persevere in the same to the last Moment of their Lives. This Declaration intimidated the Exarch so that he made a publick Profession of holding the same Faith with the Church of *Rome*, and thought it necessary to proceed no farther at that Time; but some Days after enter'd the Church, where our Saint was, gave his Soldiers free Leave to commit what Extravagancies they pleased within those sacred Walls, and shew'd the Clergy the Imperial Order for seizing on the Pope's Person, depriving him of his Bishoprick, and carrying him Prisoner to *Constantinople*. To avoid the unhappy Consequences of opposing this Attempt, St. *Martin* surrender'd himself, declaring he had rather die, if possible, ten times, than see any Blood shed on his Account; and was hurried away in the Night attended only by six of his Servants. The Vessel reach *Messina* in *Sicily* in eleven Days; and he was obliged to spend three Months in that and other Islands without convenient Rest or Refreshment; but he had much better Treatment at *Naxos* the largest of the Islands call'd *Cyclades* in the *Archipelago*, where he pass'd a whole Year; and in the mean Time *Eugenius* was placed in St. *Peter*'s Chair by the Authority of the Emperor.

Upon the Arrival of fresh Orders from *Constans*, Saint *Martin* was carried from *Naxos*, and used with the utmost Inhumanity on his Way to *Constantinople*; but amidst all his Sufferings he expressed more Concern for the Damage his Enemies did themselves than what he felt from their Hands. The holy Pope reached the Imperial City on the seventh of *September* 654, and was thrown into Prison, where he lay 'till the nineteenth of *December*. His two Letters to *Theodore* were probably written during this Confinement; in the former of which he refutes the Calumnies forged against him; both in

Regard

Nov. 12 Regard of his Faith and Loyalty. For a Proof of the Soundess of the former, he appeals to the Testimony of the whole Clergy in the Presence of the Exarch, as already specified, and his own solemn Protestation to defend the Truth as long as he lived. In Answer to such Objections as had been made against the latter, he declares he never sent either Money, Letters or Advice to the *Saracens*, but only remitted a Sum for the Relief of poor Christians among that People; he concludes with saying that nothing could be more false than what the Hereticks had alledged against him concerning the Blessed Virgin, whom he firmly believed to be the Mother of God, and worthy of all Honour after her divine Son. In his second Letter he gives a particular Account of his being seiz'd at *Rome*, as already related, and his Indisposition and ill Usage since he was dragg'd from that City; and ends with wishing and hoping his Persecutors would repent of their Conduct, when the Object of their Hatred was removed from this World.

On the Day appointed for the Trial of our Saint he was brought out in a Chair; for the Fatigues of his Voyage, the Hardships of his Prison, and his long Infirmities had made him unable to Walk. Upon his appearing before the Senate, the Person, who presided on that Occasion, commanded him to stand up, and being told his Legs would not support him, order'd him to be held up by two Men; which was done accordingly. Twenty Witnesses were produced against the holy Pope, who were all suborned to Urge the pretended Crimes against him with the Appearance of legal Depositions. *Dorotheus*, one of the Number, declared that if the Person before them had fifty Heads, he deserved to lose them all for disturbing the Peace of the West, and entring into a Conspiracy against the Emperor with *Oylmpius*. *Martin* began his Defence, and was going to give a plain Account of his Proceedings in Regard to the Imperial Orders, and such Formularies as had been offer'd to Subscription by the Direction of the Court of *Constantinople*; but was interrupted by *Troïlus*, one of the Senators, who told him he was examined on Civil Affairs, and that Religion was quite out of the Question. After which the Court broke up, and the President went and made his Report to the Emperor of what had pass'd.

In the mean Time *Martin* was carried into one of the most publick Places in the Town, and exposed to the View and Ridicule of the People; he was then removed to a Terrace, where the Emperor might have a Sight of him from his Window. There the President return'd to him, insulted him upon his Misfortunes, which he pretended were but so many just Judgments fallen on his guilty Head; order'd the Soldiers to divest him of the Marks of the

Episcopal

Episcopal Dignity, and deliver'd him into the Hands of the Governor of Nov. 12 *Constantinople*, as a Traytor with Direction to execute him immediately. He was stripp'd to his under Garment, which being torn by the rude Violence of the Executioners exposed his Body to the Severity of the Weather; and dragg'd to Prison, with a Chain about his Neck, and a naked Sword before him, which was to cut him in Pieces, according to the Tenor of the Sentence. He had suffer'd all the Hardships of a Prison for some Days without Refreshment, but what had been convey'd to him privately. The Emperor sent a Commissary to sound him, but the holy Pope prov'd an Overmatch for all the Art and Violence employ'd to shake his Constancy, and persisted in his Resolution of never communicating with the Church of *Constantinople*, 'till it renounced *Monothelism*.

The Saint lay almost three Months in Prison, and on the tenth of *March* 655 was removed to the House of one of the Publick Registers. Two Days after he was put on board a Vessel bound for *Chersonesus*; he was set on Shore in that Island on the 16th of *May*; where he languished four Months, and consummated a slow and painful Martyrdom on the sixteenth of *September*. The *Greek* Church honours our Saint under the Title of a Confessor on the fourteenth of *April*, the Day on which they suppose he reach'd the Place of his Exile; but the *Latins* venerate him as a Martyr on the twelfth of *November*, the Day on which it is believed his Body was removed to *Rome*.

St. THEODORE the STUDITE.

THEODORE, descended of an antient and honourable Family, was born at *Constantinople* in the Year 759; and, 'though his Birth and Education were such as qualified him for appearing in the World to Advantage, he consecrated himself early to God in the Monastick State. In 781 he retired to the Monastery of *Saccudion* in the Suburbs of *Constantinople*, then under the Direction of St. *Plato* his Mother's Brother, whose Life may be seen *April* the Fourth; where he soon became a Model of Fervour and Exactness to the whole House. After some Years spent in a constant Application to all the Duties of a Religious Life, and cultivating his Mind with Study, his Uncle fell dangerously ill, and, believing his End near, named our Saint to succeed him in the Government of the Monastery. *Theodore* was too humble to accept of that Post without much Opposition; and upon *Plato*'s Recovery

covery begg'd to be eas'd of the Burthen. But the holy Abbot, who had long desired a favourable Opportunity of leading a private and contemplative Life, would not listen to the Proposal; and the whole Community, who had heartily concurr'd to the Choice, declared they were satisfied that the present Establishment was directed by divine Providence.

Constantine, Son to *Leo* IV, then on the Imperial Throne, had been carefully educated in the Principles of the Catholick Religion by the Empress *Irene*, his Mother, who had got the whole Power and Authority into her own Hands. Her aspiring Temper render'd her odious to the Army, so that the Emperor when twenty Years old found Means to be declared sole Sovereign. *Constantine* had not been long in entire Possession of the Throne, before his Morals suffer'd from his Elevation; for he was no sooner Master of his own Actions, but he forgot his Duty to God, became a Slave to his Passions, divorced his Wife, and married *Theodota*, one of her Attendants. This scandalous Action rouzed the Zeal of our Saint and his holy Uncle, who resolved to oppose it, 'though the Favourite Lady was their Relation, and the Patriarch *Tarasius* prudently declined proceeding to Extremities. Our Readers may see the holy Patriarch's Conduct justified on the 25th of *February*; and that of our Saint is sufficiently recommended by the large Commendations bestow'd on him by several Writers. *Theodore* and *Plato*, therefore, were so far from entring into *Tarasius*'s Measures at that critical Juncture that they quitted his Communion, and declared the Emperor excommunicated. That Prince, dreading the Authority which their Virtue gave them over the Minds of the People, tried all Means for gaining them or prevailing with them to be silent at least on that Subject. After almost a Year's Solicitation the holy Monks remain'd inflexible; whereupon *Plato* was thrown into Prison, and his Nephew banished to *Thessalonica* in 796, with eleven Monks, who adhered to that Abbot's Opinion.

The following Year, *Irene* reassumed the Reins of Government upon the Death of her Son, 'though he fell a Victim to her Ambition. God, who knows how to bring Good out of Evil, made this Revolution serviceable to his Church; for the Empress recall'd all who had been banished by her Son; our Saint and his Uncle were allow'd to return to their Monastery; and upon hearing the Patriarch's Reasons for his Conduct, and having the Satisfaction of seeing the Priest who married the late Emperor to *Theodota* degraded, were reconciled to that holy Prelate and from that Time maintain'd an inviolable Union with him.

Theodore

Theodore and *Plato* had not long enjoy'd the Religious Pleasures of the Nov. 12 Monastery, when the *Saracens*, headed by *Abdimeleck*, pour'd down upon them, and obliged them to seek Shelter in a House within the Walls of the City, call'd *Studa*; and this is the Original of that Appellation by which he stands distinguished from other holy Men of the same Name. That Monastery which had been quite unpeopled by the preceeding Emperors, and particularly by the violent Proceedings of *Constantine Copronymus*, was now once more happily filled with Monks under the Direction of S. *Theodore*. *Michaël*, one of that Number, who has left us the History of the holy Abbot's Life, tells us that this new Community flourished incredibly by his Care, that it was encreased to a thousand Persons, that the pious and wise Superior made several excellent Regulations for Devotion, Study, and Labour; and that the whole Burthen lay on his Shoulders; for *Plato* had then renounced all Share in the Government of the Monastery, and profess'd the same Obedience to his Nephew, which was practised by the lowest Monk in that Religious Society.

This was the Posture of Affairs at *Studa*, when *Nicephorus* made his Way to the Imperial Dignity by the Deposition of *Irene* toward the Close of the Year 802. *Theodore*, however, enjoy'd the same Repose under the new Emperor till the Death of *Tarasius*, which happen'd four Years after. That Prince and the Bishops of the Province, sensible of the Influence which our Saint's Merit and that of his holy Uncle gave them over the Minds of all who knew them, desired their Opinion about the Choice of a Patriarch; which they gave with their usual Ingenuousness and Freedom in Favour of *Nicephorus*, a Man perfectly agreeable to the Emperor; and, if they made any Objection against that Choice, it was only because the Person in Question was not then in Orders; but the Messenger employ'd on this Occasion made such Additions and Misrepresentations, that the Emperor order'd them to be confin'd for opposing his Inclinations; but nothing could make them change their Opinion; so that, after almost a Month's Imprisonment, they were released. In the Mean while a Monk, related to the Emperor, who headed the Party against our Saint and his Uncle, employ'd all his Skill and Malice for ruining their Characters in the Opinion of that Prince; in which Work they were heartily join'd by *Joseph* the Priest, who had been degraded for the Adulterous Marriage of the late Emperor. That Ecclesiastick had insinuated himself so far into his Sovereign's good Graces, that he undertook to negotiate his Peace with the Patriarch; who, thinking a nine Years Pen-

Nov. 12 ance a sufficient Punishment of his criminal Complaisance, restor'd him to his Functions.

This Step answer'd the Ends of our Saint's Enemies most effectually; for He and St. *Plato* made strong Remonstrances against it, and affirm'd that this Facility was no better than an open Violation of Church Discipline. The Emperor, who had been particularly active in the Affair, resented that Liberty, and used all Means in his Power to bring them to hold Communion with *Joseph*. When neither Threats, Promises, nor ill Usage could move the two holy Monks, a Guard was set on the Monastery, which thus became a real Prison to them. The Courage and Resolution of our Saint and his Uncle alarm'd the whole World, and their deserved Reputation for Piety and Wisdom drew Numbers of holy Person to their side, among whom was *Joseph*, Bishop of *Thessalonica*, Brother to St. *Theodore*. This Division gave the Patriarch *Nicephorus* no small Uneasiness; upon which the Emperor for his Satisfaction call'd a Council at *Constantinople* in the Year 808, to put an End to this Dispute. The Assembly was composed of Bishops and Officers entirely devoted to the Emperor, and disposed to model their Decisions by his Directions; so that they not only confirm'd the Restoration of *Joseph*, but ventured to declare the Marriage of *Constantine* and *Theodota* valid. *Theodore* and *Plato*, still the same, opposed this irregular Decree with their usual Vigour, and refused to communicate with the Patriarch, whose Weakness on this Occasion they blamed and detested.

As the late Council had excommunicated all who would not communicate with *Joseph*, the Emperor took Occasion to punish the Refusal of our Saint his Brother, and Uncle, and several of their Monks with Banishment. They were dispersed into several different Islands, and suffer'd many Hardships; but all this ill Usage made no Abatement in the great *Theodore*'s Courage. He wrote to *Leo* III, then in S. *Peter*'s Chair, desiring him to oppose the new Heresy of the *Mœchians*, or *Favourers of Adultery*, a Title which he bestow'd on all who either approved of or tolerated *Constantine*'s second Marriage. The Pope thought him too warm on this Subject, and therefore express'd some Dislike to his Conduct; which drew many bitter Strokes from our Saint's Pen. Cardinal *Baronius* makes no Difficulty of saying that his Letter to *Basil* Abbot; of S. *Sabas*'s in *Rome*, which is full of Complaints and Reflexions on his Holiness, was dictated by Passion rather than Reason. Hence that learned Writer takes Occasion to observe that, " the Saints have their " Eclipses, like the Sun and Moon; but then they are but of a short Dura- " tion; and those glorious Lights shine afterwards with greater Lustre".

Several

Several of his best Friends, who had join'd him in condemning the Adul- Nov.12 terous Marriage, being of Opinion that he ought to moderate his Zeal, begg'd he would consider that Heresy was not a proper Appellation for an Opinion which had no Relation to Faith. This Remonstrance put him upon asserting that the Fact in Dispute naturally produced a Doctrine, which might justly be stiled Heresy, and gave Occasion to his writing a Treatise of *Dispensation* or *Indulgence*; in which he undertook to shew the Bishops, who composed the late Council, the Extent of their Power.

The Emperor *Nicephorus* was kill'd in a Battle with the *Bulgarians* in the Year 811, and succeeded by *Michael*, the first of that Name, an orthodox and pious Prince. As soon as he was seated on the Throne, he express'd his Esteem for Virtue by recalling our Saint, and the other illustrious Exiles; he negotiated a Reconciliation between them and the Patriarch *Nicephorus*, who being now free from all Restraint, and under no Necessity of complying upon prudential Motives, assured St. *Theodore* and his Adherents, that neither the restoring of *Joseph*, nor the Resolutions of the Council were the Result of his Opinion and Inclinations, but directed entirely by the late Emperor. And thus every Thing was once more upon a right Bottom, but did not long continue so; for in 813 *Michael*, after two Years Reign, retired to a Monastery, and was succeeded by *Leo* III, from his Country sirnamed *the Armenian*. *Leo* was scarce seated in the Imperial Throne, when he renew'd the War, which *Constantine Copronymus* had declared against holy Images; and from that Time *Theodore* had frequent Occasions of defending the Truth against such as attack'd the Honour due to *Jesus Christ* and his Saints, as express'd by a Veneration for their Images.

The new Emperor undertook to engage the Bishops and leading Abbots in his Party, and deposed the Patriarch *Nicephorus*, whom he look'd on as the chief Obstacle in his Way, plac'd *Theodotus* in his Room, and held a Synod at *Constantinople*, in which the Veneration paid to holy Images, and the second General Council of *Nice*, which had authorised the Practice, were condemn'd by a Faction of Court Bishops. All, who refused to set their Hands to the Decrees of this Cabal, were immediately banished; several worthy Prelates were driven from their Sees on this Occasion, and several holy Abbots torn from their religious Families. Among the latter none was reckon'd more considerable than our Saint, whom the Party look'd on as their most formidable Adversary. At his leaving *Constantinople*, he advised his Disciples to repair to what Places they thought would most effectually secure them from the Storm, which was falling on his Monastery, and went into Exile, attended only

by

by one of them. He was conducted into *Mysia*, and confined to an old Castle near the City of *Apollonia*: but nothing could stop his Pen; for from that close Prison he dispatched Letters to all Parts, with Exhortations to Perseverance, and Motives of Consolation for those who suffer'd for Truth. This Liberty was so disagreeable to the Emperor, that instead of recalling him with some who were allow'd the Favour of more commodious Prisons at *Constantinople*, he sent Orders for confining him still more closely, and inflicting several Torments on him. Conformably to this barbarous Direction, he was thrown into a Dungeon, which he was never allow'd to leave, but when he was to receive the Lash, or see his Companion and Disciple suffer the same Punishment.

After a whole Year's Hardships in this Prison, they were removed to another; and a Commissary sent from *Constantinople* to scourge them. That Officer, upon signifying his Order, was so struck at the Cheerfulness with which our Saint stripp'd himself for the Execution, that he had not the Heart to proceed. After this, St. *Theodore* wrote several Letters to encourage such as maintained the Catholick Doctrine, and bring those to a due Sense of their Fault, who had complied with the Emperor's Commands to the Prejudice of the Faith. One of them being intercepted, in which *Leo* was spoken of in a very free Way, the Saint was plied with fresh Torments; but bore them all with a surprizing Intrepidity. After three Years spent in this Prison, he was removed to a third in *Smyrna* in *Asia*, with strict Orders to let no Body see him.

Theodore had been close Prisoner at *Smyrna* above a Year and a half, when *Leo*'s Death, which happen'd in the Close of 820, gave a new Turn to the Affairs of the Church. As soon as *Michael the Stammerer* was seated on the Imperial Throne, he published an Edict for recalling and enlarging all who were banished or imprisoned for asserting a Veneration due to holy Images; but Historians tell us this favourable Disposition proceeded rather from a settled Aversion to his Predecessor than any Regard for Religion and Justice. *Theodore*, thinking the new Emperor orthodox in his Sentiments, and well disposed by Principle, wrote to him and several Persons of the first Rank, begging they would endeavour to settle a perfect Harmony between the Churches of the East and West; and then returned to *Constantinople*, where he had soon after the Satisfaction of seeing all his Monks together, who had been scatter'd into several Countries during the late Persecution. *Michael* allow'd Images to be placed in all Churches, but those of the Imperial City; for, as that Prince had not been used to pay them any Veneration, he declared he would not have such Objects in his View. Our Saint had no Regard to this Exception, but adorned the Church belonging to his Monastery with Images. *Theodore* was

afterwards

afterwards deputed by *Nicephorus* and the other Metropolitans to defire the Emperor would employ his Authority for removing the Scandal which Herefy gave. The holy Abbot acquitted himfelf of this Commiffion with his ufual Zeal; and, after thanking his Imperial Majefty in the Name of the Catholicks, offer'd to draw up an Expofition of the Orthodox Faith, which all his Subjects fhould be required to receive. That Prince, who was in Reality a bitter Enemy of holy Images, but had no Concern about Religion while he could preferve Peace in his Dominions, gave the Saint an Anfwer fufficient to convince the World, that nothing of that Sort was to be hoped for from him.

Nov. 12

Our Saint, finding his Labour loft on the Emperor, refolved at leaft to make the beft Ufe of the prefent Toleration, and employ'd all his Skill to recover Hereticks by Difcourfe and Writing. His Endeavours were crown'd with great Succefs; but no Conqueft was more confiderable than that of the famous *Theoctiftus*, who taught that the Bleffed Virgin exifted from all Eternity: that the Devils would be faved after the Day of Judgment: that *Jefus Chrift* was not crucified: and that a Monk had it in his Power to refcue an hundred and fifty Souls from Hell. This Zeal was difpleafing to the Emperor, who imagin'd it prejudicial to that Liberty of Confcience which he had allowed in Matters of Religion; and therefore took Occafion to order all who maintain'd the Veneration of holy Images to leave *Conftantinople*. It is fcarce neceffary to tell our Reader, that *Theodore* was one of the Exiles on that Occafion, after what has been faid of his Zeal and Courage on the Subject in Difpute. The Saint went into *Bithynia*, where he ftaid till he was fummoned to *Conftantinople* to anfwer to fome new Articles urged againft him by his Enemies, who endeavour'd to make him more odious to his Sovereign by a Charge of Treafon. *Theodore* found no Difficulty in wiping off the Afperfion; but his generous Soul was fo fhock'd at his Loyalty being fufpected, that he left the Imperial City, with a full Refolution of ending his Days at a Diftance from that ungrateful Prince and his wicked Inftruments. Attended by the fame Monk, who had fhared all his Sufferings, he retired to the Peninfula of St. *Trypho*, on the Coaft of *Bithynia*, where he died on the eleventh of *November*, in the Year 826.

His Body was carried into the Ifland *Princefs*, near the *Bofphorus*, and buried there; but removed to *Conftantinople* with great Solemnity in the Year 844. Both the *Greeks* and *Latins* obferve his Feftival on the twelfth of *November*.

Nov. 13

The XIII Day.

St. DIDACUS.

DIDACUS, commonly call'd *Diego* by his Countrymen, was born towards the Close of the fourteenth Century in the Diocese of *Seville*. His Parents were not in a Condition of giving him any Inheritance, but that of a religious Education; but the Almighty was his chief Master, and the holy Spirit his Guide from his Infancy, as it appear'd by his Love of Retirement in his tender Years, his constant Attendance in the publick Service of the Church, the Fervour of his private Divotions, his Modesty, Abstinence, and the Innocence of his Life. His Inclination to Piety lead him to a Priest, who lived in the Exercise of Penance and Contemplation in a small Hermitage near the Place of his Birth; from that holy Recluse he learnt to carry the Yoke of *Jesus Christ*, and spent several Years under his Direction. He subsisted on Alms, and what Time could be spared from Prayer and other pious Exercises was imploy'd in Working, so that but a small Part of the Night was allotted for Repose. The Wooden Porringers, Spoons, Cups, and Salts, the Produce of his Hours devoted to Labour, were disposed of as Presents to such as afforded him the Necessities of Life, but not given as a Motive for their loading him with any thing superfluous. His Affection for Poverty was so very sincere that one Day, seeing a Purse of Money lying in the Road, he would not be at the Pains of taking it up, but apprized the first Person whom he met of the Treasure, which he had discover'd; his Humility so perfect that he cheerfully embraced the most mortifying Employments, and joyfully gave into the Practice of whatever could tend to lessen him in the Opinion of the World; his whole Aim was to keep his Senses, his Mind, and Body in Subjection by continual Mortifications; and he was always on his Guard against the Surprizes of the common Enemy.

His Vigilance, and Concern for his own Salvation let him see several Dangers to which he was still exposed, and which he could not more effectually avoid than by retiring to a Cloister, as the best Asylum from the Corruption of the World. Being particularly affected with the Practice of the *Franciscans*, he offer'd himself at their Convent of *Arrezafa* in the Diocese of *Corduba*, where he was receiv'd upon the first Petition. As he was not furnished with Learning, and his Humility taught him to think meanly of himself, he enter'd as a Lay-Brother. From the first Moment of his engaging in a

Monastick

Monastick Life he resolved to observe the Rule of the holy Founder according to the Rigour of the Letter; which he perform'd so exactly and faithfully that he never admitted those Exemptions which others made Use of, and call'd Explications of the *Franciscan* Institute, but were by him esteem'd no better than so many specious Pretences for eluding the Design of their Founder, and weakening the original Severity of his religious Family; so that our Saint's Conduct might pass for the most perfect Observation of St. *Francis*'s Rule, and the Spirit of that holy Man appear'd more strongly in every Action of *Didacus*'s Life than was possible in the written Constitutions of his Order.

Nov. 13

The Superiors of the *Franciscan* Body, finding *Didacus* capable of Governing and directing others, sent him to the *Canaries*, and placed him at the Head of a Convent in one of those Islands. That Country abounded with Idolaters, whose Conversion gave our Saint's Zeal and Charity full Employment. The Dangers to which he was expos'd, the Fatigues which he bore, and the bad Usage he met with in the Prosecution of that Apostolical Work made him only more vigorous in seeking the Salvation of the deluded People; and his Labours that Way were so successful, that much the greater Part of the Infidels receiv'd the Faith. After this glorious Conquest he was recall'd to *Spain* in the Year 1449; where he became very considerable for the Gift of Miracles; but, 'though that Power recommended him to others, he still retain'd the same humble Sentiments of himself. In the following Year he was allow'd to make a Journey to *Rome*, where he was present at the Canonization of St. *Bernardin* of *Sienna* one of the Chief Ornaments of the Order of St. *Francis*, whose Life may be seen on the twentieth of *May*. Upon that solemn Occasion near 4000 *Franciscans* from different Provinces met in the Convent of *Ara-Cœli*; most of whom were afflicted with a malignant and contagious Fever. This Calamity open'd a new Field for our Saint's Charity; for nothing could be more agreeable to Brother *Didacus* than the Commission of attending the Sick; and he was so active, and successful in that Post, that 'though Provisions of all sorts were then very scarce and dear in the Town, none of his Patients wanted what was necessary or convenient for Persons in their Condition.

At his Return from *Rome Didacus* was sent into the Province of *Castile*, and placed in a Convent at *Saussay*; from which he was afterwards removed to *Alcala de Ilenares*, where the Almighty was pleased to give extraordinary Proofs of the divine Power by his Hands, and removed him to an eternal Habitation on the twelfth of *November* 1463. His Reputation for Sanctity ran so high, that the Crouds which resorted to the Convent strove to secure something that had belong'd to him as a Relick, and Mark of their Regard for that faithful Servant of God. The Miracles perform'd at his Tomb were, so numerous, that upon due Information Pope *Sixtus* V canonized him on the second of *July* 1588. Those of the same Order translate the Feast of St. *Martin*, to make Room for our Saint on the Day of his Departure, on which his Name occur'd in the *Roman* Martyrologe before *Innocent* XI order'd his Festival to be observed on the thirteenth.

St. STANISLAUS KOSTKA.

STANISLAUS Son of *John Kostka*, a Senator of *Poland* was born at *Rostkow* Castle on the thirteenth of *October* 1550. His Parents, resolved to educate their Son with no other View than that of making him serve his Creator, placed him under the Care of a Tutor in their own House, for the Cultivation of his Mind, and forming his Heart to Religion; and were not long without the Satisfaction of being convinced that God had happily prevented their Care by a particular Grace, and an Inclination to Virtue which appear'd at the first Dawn of Reason. He was affable, obliging, grave, and so nice in the Point of Chastity, that one immodest Word gave him a most sensible Mortification. This Love of Purity made him industriously avoid all Company, where there was the least Danger of being a Witness to it's Violation, and employ his whole Time in Study and Prayer; which prudent Conduct went farther toward the Preservation of his Virtue than all the Instructions of his Parents and Masters. When fourteen Years old he was sent to *Vienna* to finish his Studies in a Seminary of *Jesuits* in that City; where he corresponded faithfully to the divine Grace which had thus placed him at a secure Distance from the Corruption of the World, and perform'd all the Religious Exercises of that House with a Fervour, that would have been admired in the most Zealous of those whose solemn Profession had engaged them in those devout Employments. He was so recollected when at Prayer, and the divine Fire which enflamed his Heart was so visible in his Countenance, that it must have warm'd any Heart which was not Frozen. The same Spirit which animated him at his Devotions, directed him in the Choice of his Company, which consisted of a select Number of his Fellow-Students with whom he conversed on pious Subjects, while others were in Pursuit of their Diversions.

Upon the Death of the Emperor *Ferdinand* I, which happen'd in 1564, the Seminary in which our Saint resided was obliged to break up; for

Maximilian

Maximilian II, who succeeded that Prince, took away the Revenues of the House; upon which Occasion *Staniflaus* was placed in the House of a *Lutheran* by his Relations, where his Virtue was exposed to severe Trials. His Brother, two Years older than the Saint, was his chief Persecutor, and the superior Virtue of *Staniflaus* was the only Motive of all that was done to mortify him by one who look'd on his Conduct as a tacit Censure of his own. The ill Treatment, he met with from the Hands of his Brother, join'd to the secret Austerities which he practised on his own Body, threw him into a Distemper, which was very near proving Mortal. In this Situation he gave excellent Proofs of an holy Indifference to Life, and all it's Enjoyments; and, 'though the Person in whose House he lodged took effectual Care to deprive his devout Guest of the Sacraments of the Catholick Church, his Faith and Resignation secured him all the Advantages he could wish from those divine Institutions. Upon his Recovery he consider'd that the Almighty had restor'd him to enable him to consecrate the Remainder of his Days to his Service; which he therefore resolved to do in the Society of *Jesus*.

Staniflaus unbosom'd himself to his Director on that Subject, and let him know the State of his Soul ever since he had form'd that Design. Having gain'd his Approbation, he made his Application to the Provincial of the lower *Germany*, then at *Vienna*, who made no small Difficulty of receiving him without the express Consent of his Relations. Despairing of gaining the Consent insisted on, he begg'd the Interposition of the Cardinal's Legate at the Imperial Court; but, his Instances proving too weak, the Saint undertook a Journey to *Rome*, where he threw himself at the General's Feet, and humbly petition'd for Admission to the Society. He reached that City toward the End of *October* 1567, where S. *Francis Borgia*, then at the Head of that flourishing Body, gave him an handsome Reception and admitted him to the Noviceship on the Feast of St. *Simon* and St. *Jude*, he being then full seventeen Years of Age.

The Saint had not been long among the *Jesuits* when he received a Letter from his Father, full of Threats, which shew'd him disposed to revenge what he thought Disobedience in his Son, on that Part of the Society which was in *Poland*, where he bore a great Sway. *Staniflaus* answer'd this angry Epistle in a Manner which shew'd him thoroughly persuaded of the Obligation of renouncing all that was dear to him in this World, when in Competition with what he judged his real Vocation. Being now entirely free from Molestation he applied vigorously to all Exercises of the Noviceship, practised an exact Submission to his Superiors, and pray'd with uncommon Fervour, 'till

Nov. 14 'till it pleased God to remove him to a permanent State before he had pass'd ten Months in the Trial of a Religious Life. The holy Youth expired on the fifteenth of *August* 1568. The Preservation of his Body without the least Signs of Decay or Corruption above two Years, and some Miracles perform'd at his Tomb, engaged *Clement* VIII to beatify him in 1604. His Canonization was perform'd in the usual Forms by his present Holiness *Benedict* XIII.

The XIV Day.
St. LAURENCE *Archbishop of* DUBLIN.

LAURENCE, youngest Son to *Maurice*, a Man of the first Rank in *Ireland*, was born in the Province of *Leinster* in the XII Century, and made a voluntary Offering of himself for the Service of God in the Church, when but twelve Years old. Such a Resolution in a Child of that Age surprized all who heard of it; but his Father, being persuaded that the holy Spirit had directed the Choice, freely consented to it and put him into the Hands of the Bishop of *Glandelack*, then a distinct Diocese, and since united to that of *Dublin*. That Prelate educated him in every Branch of Learning that was necessary for his State of Life, and inured him to the Practice of such Virtues as would make him a worthy Minister of the Church.

Laurence's Behaviour was so edifying, that upon the Death of the Abbot of *Glandelack*, he was unanimously chosen Superior of the rich Monastery there, 'though then but twenty five Years old. The Saint made no other Use of the Authority and large Revenue annex'd to his Post, but what was directed by the Desire of promoting the Glory of God, and the Good of his Neighbour. During the four first Years of his Administration a great Scarcity of Provisions carried off the greatest Part of the Inhabitants of that Country, and multiplyed the Number of the Poor. This was a long Trial of our Saint's Charity, who was look'd on as another *Joseph*, the Preserver of his Country, and Father of the Poor. While thus beneficent to Persons abroad, he was not less attentive to the spiritual Necessities of his own religious Family, which he govern'd more by the Example of his Virtue than the Authority of his Station. *Laurence*, 'though his Life was irreproachable, could not escape Persecution from false Brethren, who employ'd all their Art and Malice to asperse his Character; but he overcame them by repeated Acts of unmerited Kindness, the only Revenge practised by Saints in such Cases.

The holy Abbot had not been above five Years in that Station when the Bishop of *Glandelack* died; upon which Occasion the united Voices of all concern'd in the Election of a Successor to that See fell on our Saint, who absolutely refused to accept of the Dignity, and alledged his Youth as an Excuse; which, however would have been easily over-ruled, had not divine Providence reserved him for a more numerous Flock, and greater Labours; as appear'd by his Promotion to the See of *Dublin* some Time after. Upon the Death of *Gregory* the Archbishop of that Metropolis, several Persons of the first Families in *Ireland*, and the most learned Men in the Country made all the Interest in their Power for the important Post. But God, who resists the proud, directed the Hearts of all concern'd in the Choice so that the humble Abbot of *Glandelack* was unanimously elected. *Laurence* could not be prevail'd with to think himself worthy of the Episcopal Character, made a long and vigorous Resistance, and submitted his Sholders to the tremendous Burthen in a Manner that shew'd him truly sensible of its Weight.

Nov.14

He was consecrated in his own Cathedral by *Gelasius* Archbishop of *Armagh* and Primate of *Ireland*, assisted by several other Prelates, amidst the Acclamations of the People. As soon as the new Bishop was placed in his See, he began to enquire into the State of his Diocese, and made it his Business to find out such as were best qualified for serving God in the Church; and thus the Altars were attended by Men whose personal Merit fix'd the Devotion of the People, and the Pulpits fill'd with such as preach'd both by Word and Example. At his Persuasion the Canons of his Cathedral receiv'd the Rule of Regular Canons. The holy Bishop enter'd into the same Engagements, and procured a Bull from *Rome* in Confirmation of what he had done. The Fatigues of his large and populous Diocese were not allow'd a sufficient Reason, for making any Abatement in his corporal Mortifications; on the contrary he made some considerable Additions on that Article upon becoming a Regular Canon; for from that Time he abstain'd entirely from Meat; and Bread and Water were his only Food on *Fridays*. What he retrenched from his own Table was bestow'd on the Poor, who received their daily Bread from his Hands in great Numbers.

Upon the Removal of St. *Laurence*, King *Dermith* placed an Ecclesiastick at the Head of his Monastery, who was so notoriously unworthy of the Post that the Clergy and People deposed him, and chose *Thomas* a young Man of Learning and Virtue, Nephew to the holy Archbishop, and brought up by him. After that Election our Saint made frequent Journies to *Glandelack*; and spent as much of his Time as was at his own Disposal in a wild and desolate Place about three Miles from the Town ; where rigorous Fasts, and continual Prayer where his whole Employment.

Laurence had appear'd to Advantage in the See of *Dublin* some Years, when the Affairs of his Church obliged him to go for *England*. At his landing in this Island, being inform'd that the King was at *Canterbury*, he went to that City, lodged in the Abbey of the holy Trinity, and spent the first Night after his Arrival in Prayer at the Shrine of St. *Thomas*, to whose Intercession he recommended the Business which brought him thither, and officiated solemnly the next Day. As he was going up to the Altar a Madman, who had heard much of *Laurence*'s Sanctity, imagin'd it would be a meritorious Act to kill him, and thus procure him the Glory of Martyrdom; full of this Extravagant Thought, he forced his Way through the Croud, and knock'd him down with a heavy Stick. The Monks and the whole Congregation concluded him mortally wounded, and express'd their Concern by Tears; but the holy Bishop coming to himself raised his Head, call'd for some Water, blessed it, and directed some who stood near him to wash the Wound with it. The whole Company was agreeably surprised at the Success of this Prescription; the Blood stopt immediately, and *Laurence* was able to say Mass. The Author of our Saint's Life assures us he was an Eye-Witness of this miraculous Cure. The King order'd the frantick Assassin to be hanged; but the holy Prelate interceeded in his Favour, and obtain'd his Pardon.

A Council was held in the *Lateran* Palace at *Rome* in the Year 1179; upon which Occasion our Saint, the Archbishop of *Tuam*, five or six other *Irish* Prelates, and four *English* Bishops went to that City. When *Laurence* had contributed his Vote and Labours in what regarded the whole Church, he laid the State of that of *Ireland* before his Holiness, and begg'd some Care might be taken for preserving the Liberties of that National Church, and reforming what was amiss there. This Application was made with so much Prudence, and the Petition urged with so regular a Zeal that *Alexander* III, then in St. *Peter*'s Chair, constituted our Saint Legate from the holy See in *Ireland*. As soon as he return'd to his own Country, he began to execute his Commission in the most effectual Manner, remedied several inveterate Abuses, made useful Regulations wherever he came, and was particularly active in reforming the debauched Lives of the Clergy.

While the Legantine Power was thus excellently employ'd, the whole Island was afflicted with a Famine, which gave fresh Exercise to the Saint's Charity.

St. Laurence, *Archbishop*.

This Calamy fell on the Country while he was abroad; at his Return he lay'd himself under an Obligation of giving Alms to five hundred Persons every Day; and furnished three hundred more with Cloaths, Victuals, and the other Necessaries of Life. Several Women, being reduced so low that they could not keep their own Children, laid them at the Bishop's Door, or in other Places, where they knew he would see them; *Laurence*, always glad of an Opportunity of doing good to the Necessitous, order'd the poor destitute Infants to be taken up, and educated at his Expence, and the Number of them amounted to about two hundred.

Henry II of *England*, and *Deronog* the most powerful King in *Ireland* had been long at Variance, when St. *Laurence* undertook to negotiate a Reconciliation between those Princes. To that End he cross'd to *England*, and made his Application to the King, who was deaf to all Proposals of Reconciliation, and dispatched strict Orders to all the Sea-ports of this Island for stopping the Saint if he attempted to take Shipping for *Ireland*. Not long after *Henry* went for *Normandy*, and *Laurence* retired to the Monastery of *Abbington*, in Hopes that Prince would be in a better Humour when he came back from *France*. After three Weeks Stay in that House the holy Prelate, weary of expecting his Return, came to a Resolution of following him, and embarked at *Dover*. He was on his Way to King *Henry*, when a violent Fever obliged him to stop short, and take up his Abode in an Abbey of Regular Canons at *Ecc*, where he died on the fourteenth of *November* 1181, after having receiv'd the *Viaticum* and Extreme Unction at the Hands of *Osbert* Abbot of that House. He was buried in the Canons Church at *Eu*, where his Body lay conceal'd above four Years, while his Sanctity was published wherever he had been known. Toward the Year 1186 the said Church was pull'd down in Order to be rebuilt; and then the holy Prelate's Body was found entire. This Discovery inhaunced the Devotion paid to his Memory, so that the Community in which he died began to think of suing for his Canonization, which was perform'd with the usual Solemnity by Pope *Honorius* III in the Year 1226, and the Saint's Name occurs in the *Roman* Martyrologe on the Day of his Death.

Nov 14

Nov. 15

The XV Day.

St. MALO, Bishop.

MALO, Cousin to St. *Samson* and St. *Magloire*, of whom we have spoken in their proper Places, was a Native of *Great Britain*, born toward the Year 487, and receiv'd his first Instructions from *Brendan*, an *Irish* Abbot of great Reputation for Learning and Virtue. His Monastery, which stood in that Part of this Island which now bears the Name of *Wales*, was one of the most celebrated Schools then in Being for Piety and Literature; and comprehended Scholars of all Ages. *Malo*'s Heart and Mind were so well prepared by the Grace of God that every one was surprized at his Progress in human Learning and the Knowledge of the Saints. As he was naturally complaisant, and obliging, as well as judicious and discreet, he accommodated himself to the particular Humours and Inclinations of those about him; thus he conversed with the younger Part of the House like a young Man; and wore all the Gravity and Sedateness of riper Years when among those of a more advanced Age. His Application to Study, the Fervour of his Prayers, his rigorous Mortifications, and profound Humility on all Occasions recommended him to the Esteem of all who knew him; made him a Model of Devotion, Regularity, and Diligence to the whole numerous Community; and gave him a more than common Share in his holy Superior's Affections.

The See of *Guic-castel*, supposed to be the Town which now bears the Name of *Winchester*, becoming vacant, the Inhabitants fully inform'd of our Saint's eminent Virtue, went in a Body to the Monastery, and demanded him for their Pastor: *Malo* made all the Resistance in his Power on this Occasion; but, finding no Excuses or Reasons would pass, protested loudly against their Proceedings, and endeavour'd to secure himself by retiring to his Cell; but they forced the Door, carried him off by Force, and got him consecrated at *Guic-castel* in Spight of all the Opposition he could make. At his stepping into the Episcopal Dignity he was seiz'd with Horror, and imagined himself on the Brink of a Precipice. The great Number of Children, who cried for spiritual Bread, the Complaints of the Poor, the Sighs of the Miserable of various Denominations and the Crouds of Friends and Relations who broke in upon his Devotions, and Studies, made him very uneasy in his new Situation; to which Grievances were added many insuperable Difficulties about the Weight of his present Burthen. He could find no Way of

freeing

freeing himself from these Hardships but by endeavouring to recover his for- Nov.15
mer Liberty; and therefore came to a Resolution of quitting his Bishoprick;
and to procure his Ease more effectually, endeavour'd to find that Solitude and Retirement among Foreigners, which he could not enjoy in his own
Country.

Having let some discreet and worthy Persons into his Design, and engaged
them to accompany him in his Travels, he left the Town privately, threw himself
entirely on the divine Providence, took Shipping, and landed near *Aleth*, in
Britany. At his Arrival on the *French* Coast he fell into the Conversation of
Aaron a holy Solitary, who gave him a Reception suitable to his Merit,
though he had no Knowledge of him. After some Days Acquaintance, the
two Servants of God contracted a Friendship which tended to promoting their
mutual Good, and assisting each other in the Way to Perfection. They lived
together in this holy Intimacy remote from the Commerce of the World,
making their Salvation their only Care. This happy Union form'd by
the Love of God made their penitential Exercises easy, and even pleasant.
Bread and Raisins were their only Food, and Water their only Drink, which
they used with much Moderation, that they might not violate the strict Abstinence which they had prescribed to themselves. The Place of their Retreat
was a Peninsula, and join'd to the Continent by a small Neck of Land; which
gave the Inhabitants of *Aleth* a favourable Opportunity of visiting the two
holy Solitaries, with a View of receiving Instructions from them, and engaging their charitable Assistance in Favour of the aforesaid Town, which was
then over-run with Idolatry; but they were particularly pressing with *Malo*
on that Subject. At his Arrival at *Aleth*, he found the few Christians of
that Place in Possession of a small Chapel, where they had been used to meet
privately, but without Sacrifice or Priest. Here he began to preach the Terms
of Salvation with the Zeal and Vigour of an Apostle; and his Evangelical Labours, attended by such Works as spoke the Dignity of his Mission, and Importance of what he deliver'd, were crown'd with incredible Success, so that
much the greatest Part of that populous and trading Town embraced the
Faith, and begg'd he would stay among them, and maintain his Conquests
there. His Humility and Indifference to Honours had a considerable Share in
in his declining a Bishoprick in his own Country; but Charity obliged him
to undertake the Government of the new Church of *Aleth*, which it had
pleased God to raise by his Ministry. The Contributions of the Faithful for
establishing Religion among them were by our Saint's Care employ'd in
forming a holy and numerous Clergy for their Use. In the same View he
made

Nov.15 made considerable Additions to the Revenue and Building of *Aaron*'s Monastery, and upon his Death took it into his own Hands.

But all the Saint's Zeal and Charity could not protect him from the Malice of some who made it the whole Study and Employment of their Lives to destroy the glorious Edifice which he had raised among them. Those Agents of Hell persecuted the holy Bishop most unmercifully, and left no Reason to hope for Amendment, so that he left the Town, put to Sea without any Design but that of following the divine Direction, and was providentially thrown on the Coast of *Xaintonge*. Understanding that *Leontius* Bishop of *Bourdeaux* was then at *Xaintes*, he went to that Town, where he was well receiv'd by the holy Prelate, and upon telling his Case, provided with a handsome Retreat, and a sufficient Maintainance. This was *Malo*'s Situation when such of the Inhabitants of *Aleth* as had had no Hand in persecuting him, impatient of his Absence, and convinced their infant Church could not subsist without it's holy Founder, undertook to solicit his Return; and several of his Enemies having had Leisure to reflect on their own Conduct united in the Petition. The Saint had been under the Protection of the Bishop of *Bourdeaux* about three Years when the Deputies from *Aleth* arrived, who were so well instructed, and so hearty in the Affair that they would not go back without him.

Malo, thus recover'd, found but little Difficulty in governing his Flock, and had the Satisfaction of seeing Peace and Religion flourish among them; but his late Retreat had such powerful Charms for his devout Soul that he sent for *Garwall* from St. *Brendan*'s Monastery, placed him at the Head of his Converts at *Aleth*, and return'd to *Xaintonge*, where he ended his Days soon after. His Death with most Probability is dated in the Year 565. The venerable Body was buried at *Archambray*, but carried to *Aleth* in the VII Age; and from that Time the History of our Saint's Relicks being the same with that of the Remains of St. *Samson* and St. *Magloire*, it would be needless to repeat what has been already said on the twenty eighth of *July*, and the twenty fourth of *October*. The Town where our Saint planted the Gospel has been known by his Name ever since the Year 1141.

The XVI Day.

St. EUCHERIUS, *Bishop of* LYONS.

*E*UCHERIUS, a Native of *France*, born toward the Close of the IV Century, made a very considerable Figure in the World before he engaged in the Service of the Church. He had been married, and was happy in two Sons, *Salonius* and *Veranus*, whose good Dispositions were improved in the celebrated Monastery of *Lerins* under the Conduct of it's holy Founder *Honoratus*, and afterward Bishop of *Arles*, and by the Labours of that excellent Master *Salvian*, a Priest of *Marseilles*. But without saying any thing derogatory to the holy School of *Lerins*, or that of *Salvian*, we may be allowed to observe after the Person last named that they were educated no where with more Judgment and Care than at home; they did Honour to the Church in the Episcopal Character.

The good Sense of our Saint, improved by the Grace, of God gave him an early Disgust of the World; and the most feasible Opinion is that about the Year 422 *Eucherius* divested himself of all that could engage his Stay, or retard the Execution of his Design of making his Salvation his only Care. The Island of *Lerins* was the Place of his Retreat on that Occasion, and the new Monastery, founded there by S. *Honoratus*, his *Asylum* from the Dangers and Temptations which surrounded him while in Possession of a plentiful Fortune, and honourable Employments. The holy Founder of that Seminary of Learning and Piety, and the other illustrious Solitaries treated our Saint not like a Novice, but as a complete Master of spiritual Life. The famous *Cassian*, then Abbot of St. *Victor*'s at *Marseilles* had a very exalted Opinion of *Eucherius*, when he addressed some of his Conferences to him and St. *Honoratus*; for, speaking of both in the same Strain, he says they were become two admirable and edifying Models to the whole Community.

Our Saint desirous of a more close Retreat, went over to *Lero* another Island, not far from that of *Lerins*, called at present St. *Margaret*'s. This Seperation made no Change in the holy Friendship between our Saint and *Honoratus*, which was continued by Letters. In this Desart he wrote a Letter to St. *Hilary*, then at *Lerins*, but afterwards Bishop of *Arles*, full of Commendations of a Religious and retired Life; and a Treatise on the Contempt of the World addressed to *Valerian* his near Relation. These two Pieces, which are vastly preferable to all that bear our Saint's Name, were penn'd in *Latin* in a Stile not much inferior to that of the most polite Ages.

Nov.16 The Author has there convinced the World that all the Beauties of Eloquence, as well as all the Strength of Reasoning were in his Power; for it is scarce possible to read the former Treatise, without conceiving an ardent Desire of conversing with God alone, or the latter without being warm'd into a Resolution of renouncing the World.

About the Year 434 *Eucherius* was forced from the Pleasures of religious Solitude, and placed on the See of *Lyons*; but we know little more of his Behaviour in that Station, than that he was at the Council of *Orange* in the Year 441. His known Character for Virtue and Learning leaves us no Room to doubt of his having contributed very much to the Advancement of God's Glory, and his Neighbour's Salvation. *Claudian Mamertus*, Brother to the holy Bishop, whose History we have given on the eleventh of *May*, was personaly acquainted with our Saint, and makes no Difficulty to call him the greatest Prelate of that Age. *Eucherius* died after the Middle of the V Century; but neither the Day nor Year of his Departure are known at present. The *Roman* Martyrologe, and others place, his Name on the sixteenth of *November*.

St. EDMUND, *Archbishop of* CANTERBURY.

EDMUND, eldest Son of *Edward Rich*, was born at *Abbington* in *Berkshire* toward the latter end of the XII Century. If his Parents bore an inferior Rank in the World, they were equal to the most considerable in Virtue. His Father, who was a Tradesman, growing weary of Business retired to the Monastery of *Evesham* in *Worcestershire*, where he ended his Days in the *Benedictin* Habit. This was done with his Wife's free Consent, who thereupon undertook the Education of their Children. That excellent Woman, whose House was almost as regular as a Convent, instructed them both by Word and Example; and it was from her that our Saint learnt to repeat the whole Psalter on *Sundays* and Holydays before he broke his Fast, to live on Bread and Water every *Friday*, and several other Exercises of Mortification. As soon as *Edmund* was old enough to live abroad he was sent to *Paris*, in Company with his Brother *Robert* to study.

Edmund had spent some Time in that Seat of Arts and Sciences when his Mother, falling dangerously ill, order'd him over to *England*, and, upon her Death-Bed recommended his Brother and Sisters to his Care, which would not allow him to return to *Paris* so soon as he wished; but nothing could make him

him forget his Obligation of improving his Mind with Learning, and pur- Nov. 16
suing the religious Practices which he had learnt from his Mother. Falling
into the Hands of a holy Priest, he submitted to his Direction with great
Simplicity, and by his Advice made a Vow of perpetual Chastity, which he
observed with the nicest Fidelity his whole Life. His Sisters were young
and handsome; and the Saint, considering the Danger to which they would
be exposed in the World, especially since their Fortunes were but small, proposed their entring into a Convent, to which they readily consented, and
left him the Care of chusing a proper House for their Reception. His first
Application proved unsuccessful; for the Nuns to whom he made the Offer,
insisted on a certain Sum at their Admission; upon which *Edmund* laid by all
Thoughts of leaving them there, and recommended the Affair to God. Being
told of a poor Monastery, famous for the Strictness of its Discipline, and the
Regularity of its Inhabitants, he made his Way to that House; where he
was surprized to hear the Prioress call him by his Name, assure him that she
knew his Business, and was ready to receive his Sisters; which was done accordingly.

Our Saint, being now entirely at Liberty, went back to *Paris* to finish his
Studies, where he proceeded Master of Arts, and was then employ'd in teaching Humanity and the Mathematicks, which he did with universal Applause.
He had been thus employ'd six Years when he dreamt his Mother came to
him, and finding him very intent on some Geometrical Schemes, asked him
what was the Use of those Figures which engaged his Eye and Thoughts; to
which Question *Edmund* made some Reply, but not such as satisfy'd his Mother, who closed the Conference with advising him to make Diviniy his only
Study for the Future. His Mind being now turn'd to more sublime and
worthy Objects, his Devotion was considerably encreased; one Instance of
which was his constant Attendance at St. *Merri*'s Church, where he always assisted at *Matins*; when the Office was over, he spent a considerable Time in
Prayer, heard Mass, and then repair'd to the publick School without taking
Food or Rest. He went to Vespers every Day; after which Devotion, Study,
and charitable Works were his whole Employment. After some Years spent
in this Manner he took his Doctor's Degree; but there is some Dispute about
the Place where he receiv'd that Honour; some Writers of our Nation affirm it was at *Oxford*; but the *French* Historians are very positive it was at
Paris.

Thus qualified to preach, and read Lectures of Divinity, he perform'd both
with surprizing Success; for several of his Auditors and Scholars embrac'd a
Monastick Life. After he receiv'd the holy Order of Priesthood, he made large

Additions

Nov. 16 Additions to his Prayers and corporial Austerities, and consider'd himself as a living Sacrifice for the Necessities of the Church. His uncommon Merit drew the Eyes of Princes and Prelates on him, who expressed their Respect for him by offering him several Benefices; but he never accepted of above one at a Time, and resign'd that, whenever his Divinity Lectures would not allow him to reside on it. Finding himself importuned on all Hands to employ his admirable Talent in preaching the Word of God, he took his final Leave of the Schools, and was made Canon and Treasurer of the Cathedral of *Salisbury*. He had not been long in that Post, when his Character being publish'd at *Rome*, the Pope sent him an Order to preach the *Croisade*, with a Commission to receve a Maintainance from the several Churches in which he should appear on that Occasion. The Saint discharged the Obligation laid on him by His Holiness; but would not accept of any Reward for his Pains.

Some Years after, *Gregory* IX, undertaking to name a Person to the See of *Canterbury* pitched on *Edmund* as the worthiest Ecclesiastick he could find in *England*, after a strict Enquiry. The Chapter of *Canterbury* was unanimous in concurring to the Pope's Nomination, and their Election was afterwards confirmed by His Holiness. Thus far the holy See, and the Metropolitan Church had proceeded, without thinking it necessary to ask the Saint's Consent; and then a Deputation was sent to *Salisbury*, with Directions to conduct him to his Flock. *Edmund*, surprized at the Message, declared against the late Proceedings, and protested loudly against the Violence offer'd him. The Deputies, thus repulsed, apply'd to the Bishop of *Salisbury*, who employ'd all his Authority over our Saint in engaging him to obey the Pope, and submit to the Choice which the Clergy of *Canterbury* had made. *Edmund* submitted after much Resistance, and had not quite conquer'd all his Difficulties when he was consecrated on the second of *April* 1234.

The Dignity of Archbishop and Primate of *England* made no Alteration either in the Sentiments or Behaviour of our Saint. He had still the same humble Opinion of himself, which had ever been the most conspicuous Part of his Character; and observed the same Simplicity and Modesty in his Dress, while other Prelates gave themselves more Liberty in that Particular. His chief Employment was to enquire into and relieve the corporal and spiritual Necessities of his Flock; and he soon got the Reputation of a true Pastor, a charitable Physition, a good Father, and an upright Judge. He took a particular Care to provide Portions for young Women, whose Cirumstances would otherwise have exposed them to many Dangers and Temptations. In all his

Courts

Courts Justice was administer'd impartially and freely; for it was impossible for any Man to have a more settled Abhorrence for the Practice of taking Bribes, than our holy Archbishop. He gave Vice no Quarter, remedied Abuses with a becoming Resolution, and maintain'd Church Discipline with a truly Episcopal Vigour.

While *Edmund* was thus employ'd, it pleased God to permit him to share the Fate of some of his holy Predecessors, who had been severely persecuted by the King and Nobility; with this Addition to our Saint's Mortifications, that his own Chapter did all in their Power to make him uneasy. The good Prelate's Behaviour on that Occasion was exactly conformable to the Precepts of the Gospel, and the Practice of our blessed Saviour, who was always willing to lay down his Life for his most inveterate Enemies. What occasion'd the Misunderstanding between the Saint, and *Henry* III, then on the Throne of *England*, was that Prince's Practice of placing only his own Creatures in the Episcopal Sees, and at the Head of Monasteries, and keeping those Posts vacant for the sake of converting the Revenues to his own Use. To remove this Abuse *Edmund* apply'd to *Rome* and gain'd a Bull empowering him to fill all Vacancies in six Months after the Death of the last Incumbent; but the King, complaining of this Commission as an Attempt on his Prerogative, his Holiness *Gregory* IX revok'd it. Some other Difficulties obliged our Saint to seek that Repose abroad, which he could not hope to enjoy at Home. In this View he left *England* privately, made his Way to the Court of *France*, where he was very graciously received by St *Lewis* and the whole Royal Family. From *Paris* he went to *Pontigny* in the Diocese of *Auxerre*, and retired into the Abbey, which was grown famous for sheltering St. *Thomas Becket*, and *Stephen Langton*, two of his Predecessors. During his Stay there, he preached in the neighbouring Parishes till his ill State of Health obliged him to change Air, and remove to a Monastery at *Soissy*; where he died on the sixteenth of *November* 1241. His Heart and Bowels were deposited at *Soissy*; and his Body removed to *Pontigny*. *Edmund* was canonized in the Year 1245. by *Innocent* IV, who perform'd that Ceremony on the ninth of *June*, the Day which the *English* Church before the Reformation kept in honour of his Translation; but the *Roman* Martyrologe mentions the Saint on the Day of his Death.

Nov. 17

The XVII Day.

St. GREGORY *Bishop of* Neocesarea, *Surnamed* THAUMATURGUS.

THEODORE, now known by the Name of *Gregory*, and the Title of *a Worker of Miracles*, was born at *Neocesarea* in the Province of *Pontus*, and descended from Parents considerable for their Fortune and Station in the World, but Slaves to Pagan Superstition and Idolatry. He lost his Father at fourteen; and, as he assures us himself, began at that Time to have some Inclinations to the true Religion; though, as he owns, his entire Conversion was not effected immediately, but was perform'd by slow and ineffable Degrees. In the mean Time his Mother, pursuant to her Husband's Intention of bringing him up to the Bar, apply'd him to *Rhetorick*; in which he made such surprizing Progress, that it was easy to foresee he would become one of the most considerable Orators of the Age. He had then such a Regard for Truth and Justice, that he could never be induced, even in his Declamations, and other Exercises, to attempt the Praise of what was not truly commendable.

As the whole Empire was then in the Hands of the *Romans*, the *Latin* Tongue was a necessary Qualification for Preferment; for which Reason he was allow'd a Master, who was acquainted both with the Language and the Laws of that victorious and powerful People. That Professor grounded his Pupil in the first Rudiments of the Civil Law, and gave him a Relish for that Study, by assuring him that Branch of Learning would be useful to him in whatever Profession he should embark. By his Persuasion, he resolved to go to *Berytus* in *Phenicia*, where the Law was taught in great Perfection, and proposed making a Journey to *Rome* on the same Account. While this was in Agitation the Governor of *Palestine* made Choice of our Saint's Brother-in-Law for his Assistant, and carried him to *Cesarea*, the usual Residence of that Magistrate; but, not willing to live at a Distance from his Wife, our Saint's Sister, that Lady was conducted to him at the publick Charge, with such as she was disposed to take with her. This proved an Occasion of *Gregory* accompanying her to *Cesarea*, together with his Brother *Athenodorus*, who was afterwards a Bishop, and suffer'd for the Faith of *Jesus Christ*. They reached that Town in the Year 231, a little after the Arrival of *Origen*, who had left *Alexandria* to avoid the Trouble which *Demetrius* gave him there. That great Man, at the first Interview with our Saint and his Brother, found them possess'd of an admirable Capacity for Learning, and excellent Dispositions to Virtue, which

encouraged

encouraged him to endeavour to inspire them with a Love of Truth, and Nov. 17 the chief Good of Man; he succeeded so well in that commendable Attempt, that they enter'd his School, and laid aside all Thoughts of studying at *Berytus*.

Origen began with the Praise of *Philosophy*, by which Term he understood *True Wisdom*; he observed to them, that Self-knowledge was the first Step to the true Life of a reasonable Creature; that they were then to carry their Enquiries to real Good and Evil, in order to embrace the former, and avoid the latter; and that such as lived in a Neglect of such necessary Searches, were no better than brute Beasts. He pursued this Method several Days, and talk'd to them in a Manner that could not fail to engage their Attention, and warm their Hearts. He did not put on the Air of a Disputant, who aim'd at convincing and confounding his Adversary; but in the whole Course of his Conversation behaved himself like one, who had no other View, but that of making them happy by bringing them acquainted with what truly deserv'd the Appellation of *Good*. As the Beginnings of all Things are difficult, our Saint did not presently give into his Master's Way of thinking; but *Origen* went on, and spoke with such a lovely Mixture of Sweetness and strong Reasoning, that it was scarce possible to hold out against the Attack; and the two young Men soon forgot their own Country, their Friends, and their Design of studying the *Roman* Laws, and resolved to stay at *Cesarea*, and attend the Lectures of that celebrated Person. *Origen*, having thus gain'd their Hearts, and engaged their Attention, made it his Business to search into the most intricate Folds of their Souls, sounded their Hearts, and penetrated into their Sentiments with a Judgment and Sagacity peculiar to that great Master. Having thus prepared his Scholars, and discover'd the Strength of their Genius, he undertook to give them a regular Course of Instructions. He began with Logick, which, as laid down by him, taught them neither to admit nor reject a Proof at a Venture, but examine an Argument to the Bottom, without being dazzled at, or amused with Terms. He then proceeded to Natural Philosophy, which, as managed by that learned Man, led them to consider and adore the infinite Power and Wisdom of God, and admire the various and beautiful Works of the Creation with a becoming Humility.

The Mathematicks were the next Employment of our Saint and his Brother, while under *Origen*'s Tuition; and, as Astronomy and Geometry are comprehended under that Article, the former was made to raise their Views above the Earth, the latter to lead them to Truth by the satisfactory Method of Demonstration. These Studies were succeeded by Lessons of Morality,

Nov. 17 which *Origen* made to confist in an actual Conformity of our Lives to Reason; and his regular Conduct gave both Light and Strength to his Instructions on that Subject.

Their Minds being thus prepared, and their Paffions put under the Conduct of Reafon, *Origen* let them know that the moft valuable Knowledge was that of the firft Caufe, and thus lead them on to Divinity. That judicious Mafter confidering the Age of his two inquifitive and ingenious Scholars, open'd to their View all that had been written on that Subject by the ancient Poets and Philofophers, whether *Greeks* or *Barbarians*, except only fuch as denied the Being of a God, and a watchful over-ruling Providence. He made them read the Opinions and Arguments of all Sects, and pointed out what was worthy of Notice in each; but his conftant Advice was to beware of a particular Fondnefs for any Philofopher, which would only betray them into Miftakes and Prejudices; and captivate their Underftandings to God and his Prophets only. This, according to our Saint's own Account, was the Manner in which he and his Brother were infenfibly led on to Truth; and thofe Studies, which but too often help'd to confirm Men in Paganifm, were, by the prudent Management of their great Mafter, made fo many Steps toward Chriftianity; for nothing went farther toward giving them an advantageous Idea of our moft holy Religion, than a View of the Weaknefs of the Light with which the moft confiderable among the Philofophers were endow'd on the moft important Article of Religion, and the little Certainty that could be expected in Opinions, which often deftroy one another. Having brought them thus far on their Way, he proceeded to expound the holy Scriptures to them, of which he is univerfally allow'd to have been the moft learned Expofitor in that Age.

Gregory was now well acquainted with the Myfteries of the Chriftian Religion, and well verfed in the holy Language of the divine Writings, fo charm'd with one, and fo well perfuaded of the other, that he was ready to quit every Thing that interfered with his Defign of making God his only Thought. *Firmilian*, Bifhop of *Cefarea* in *Cappadocia*, whom the *Greek* Church honours as a Saint on the twenty eighth of *October*, made frequent Journeys into *Palestine*, which gave *Gregory* an Opportunity of contracting an Intimacy with him, and unbofoming himfelf on that Article. The holy Prelate employ'd all the Force of Argument, and the Authority which his Friendfhip gave him in confirming and improving his good Difpofitions. In the mean Time the Perfecution broke out in the Eaft under the Emperor *Maximin*, which obliged *Origen* to leave *Cefarea* in 235, and continue at a Diftance from that City the two fucceeding Years. *Gregory* went to *Alexandria*, the Capital

of

of *Egypt*, and famous at that Time for a School of Philosophy, and another of Physick. He was not yet baptized, nor are we told that he had ranked himself among the Catechumens in Order to receive the Sacrament of Regeneration; but his Morals were so strict and regular that the young Students at *Alexandria* grew jealous of his Virtue, and look'd on his Behaviour as a tacit Censure of their own Irregularities. To be revenged, they instructed an infamous Prostitute to go up to him, while engaged in a grave Discourse with some of his Learned Acquaintance, and with her usual Impudence make a Demand of Arrears due to her upon Contract for criminal Familiarities. Those, who knew *Gregory*'s Virtue, were fired with Resentment at this vile Aspersion on his Character; but he, without the least Emotion, desired one of his Friends would dismiss her on her own Terms, that their Conversation might suffer no farther Interruption from her Importunities. Some Persons of equal Malice and Levity, observing his easy Compliance with the Wretch's Demands, began to conclude him guilty, and divert themselves at the Expence of his Reputation. But it pleased God to clear his Innocence to the World in a Manner as surprizing as unexpected; for no sooner had that Agent of Hell receiv'd the Money, but she was seized by an Evil Spirit, howled in a frightful Manner, and fell down tearing her Hair, foaming at the Mouth, and staring with all the Fury and Distraction of a Fiend. In all Probability the Devil would have stiffled her, had not *Gregory*'s Charity prompted him to call on God in her Favour; and the Effect of his Prayers was immediately seen by the Recovery of that unhappy Woman.

Nov. 17

It is not easily decided whether our Saint receiv'd Baptism at *Alexandria* or after his Return to *Cesarea*, where he found his old Master in the Year 237; and having spent eight Years abroad, five of which he had attended *Origen*'s School, he went back to his own Country. He could not think of leaving that great Man, without expressing his Gratitude in a Speech deliver'd before a numerous Assembly, full of the highest Commendations that can be bestow'd on Man. This Piece is still extant, and esteem'd one of the most complete Performances in it's Way in all Antiquity; it is from this we take our Account of his Studies, and the Progress of the Grace of God in his Conversion.

At his Return his Countrymen expected to see him make a Figure on publick Occasions, take all Opportunities of placing his great Accomplishments in an advantageous Light, and aim at the most considerable Posts as due to his Merit; and expres'd no small Surprize at his retiring into the Country, and renouncing all the Conveniencies of Life for Solitude and holy

Nov. 17 holy Poverty. *Gregory's* whole Employment in his Retreat was to purify his Soul by an uninterrupted Conversation with the Almighty, and hoped the World thought no more of him than he of the World, when *Phedimus* Bishop of *Amasea*, who was favour'd with the Gift of Prophesy, and was no stranger to our Saint's Character, undertook to engage him in the Service of the Church. Upon the first Mention of this Design, *Gregory* fled into the Desart, and changed Place so often that he defeated the most diligent Enquiries and close Pursuits. The holy Bishop, finding the strictest Search did not answer his Ends, follow'd the Dictates of the divine Spirit, resolved to elect him 'though absent, raised his Hands and Eyes to Heaven, and declared in the Presence of God that he consecrated *Gregory* to the Service of the Church, and appointed him *Neocesarea* for his See. *Gregory* was three Days Journey from *Phedimus* when this solemn Declaration was made; but, being inform'd of the Manner in which he had devoted him to the Work of the Ministry, was persuaded that God had spoken by his Mouth; for which Reason he acquiesced in the Choice, and receiv'd the Episcopal Character at the Hands of the holy Bishop of *Amasea*. As soon as he was consecrated he desired that Prelate would allow him some Time for a more complete Knowledge of the Mysteries of Religion, which he spent in fervent Prayer for obtaining that Favour in a Degree proportion'd to the Obligation of his Station in the Church, and then went to *Neocesarea*, a Town famous for it's Trade and Number of Inhabitants, but full of Pagans; for St. *Gregory* of *Nysse*, who wrote his Life, assures us there were but seventeen Christian in it when he was placed there.

Our Saint was on his way to *Neocesarea*, when a violent Rain obliged him to take Shelter in a Heathen Temple, the most famous Building of that sort in the Country upon the Account of an Oracle deliver'd there. At his Entrance he made the Sign of the Cross several Times to purify the Air which was infected by the Smoke of idolatrous Sacrifices, and then spent the Night there in Prayer according to his Custom. He pursued his Journey the next Morning, and the Heathen Priest begun his usual Superstitions in the Temple; but the Devils declared they could stay there no longer, being forced away by the Man who pass'd the last Night within those Walls. After several vain Attempts to bring those Powers back, the Priest hasten'd after our Saint, threatening to inform against him, and bring him to a Punishment due to his Boldness. *Gregory*, without the least Emotion, told him that with the Help of God he could drive away, or call the Devils when he pleased; upon which the Priest bid him command them to return to their Temple. The Saint
complied

complied with his Requeſt, and difmiſs'd him with a Note in which was written ; *Gregory to Satan, Enter.* The Prieſt then went back to the Temple, laid this Note on the Altar, offer'd the cuſtomary Sacrifices, and was viſited by the Devils, as uſual. Surpriſed at what he ſaw, he ran after the holy Biſhop, overtook him before he reached the Town, and begg'd he would give him ſome Account of that God, whom his Gods obey'd ſo readily. *Gregory* undertook to lay before him the Principles of the Chriſtian Religion : and finding the Prieſt ſhock'd at the Doctrine of the Incarnation, as unworthy of the Supreme Being, told him that great Truth was not to be enforced by Words, or human Reaſoning, but by the Wonders of the divine Power ; whereupon the Prieſt pointed to a large Stone, and deſired the Saint would command it to move to a Place which he named ; *Gregory* invoked the Name of God, and begg'd he would give the deſired Satisfaction, which was immediately granted. This Miracle completed the Pagans Converſion, who without any Heſitation left his Employment, his Family, and his Fortune, and follow'd the Saint.

Theſe wonderful Works were known at *Neoceſarea* before *Gregory* reach'd that City, and brought out great Crouds of People, who were ſurprized to ſee him walk on with as little Concern or Notice, as if he had been in a Deſart. As he had renounced all he had in the World, and conſequently was not Maſter of a Houſe in the Town, the Chriſtians, who accompanied him, were uneaſy about a Place for their Reception. The Saint reproved their Solicitude, and told them their chief Concern ought to be for their ſpiritual Habitation ; he had ſcarce finiſhed his Diſcourſe on that Subject, when one of the moſt conſiderable Men in the Town made him an Offer of his Houſe, which he accepted of preferably to that of ſeveral others, becauſe he was a Chriſtian. He had not ſpent one Night at *Neoceſarea* before a great Number of the Inhabitants receiv'd the Word of God which he preached, and the next Morning his Door was crouded with Sick and Infirm Perſons of both Sexes, and all Ages, who recover'd their Health and Strength by the miraculous Power lodged in his Hands. His Preaching being thus ſupported and authorized by Miracles, the Body of Chriſtians ſoon became ſo numerous that the Saint was enabled to build a Church for their Uſe, to which all contributed either Money or Labour.

Gregory was conſulted by the Inhabitants of *Neoceſarea* in all their Difficulties, and his Deciſion made up all their Differences. Upon two Brothers diſputing the Property of a Lake which belong'd to their Father, and ſeeming reſolved to decide the Matter by Blows, the Saint pray'd that the Subject of this ſcandalous Conteſt might be removed ; whereupon the ſaid Lake was immediately

mediately dried up. S. *Basil* the Great, who mentions this Miracle, tells us that our holy Bishop stopp'd or changed the Course of Rivers; of which he gives us the following Instance. The *Lycus* overflow'd the Plains, where it did much Damage; upon which great Crouds resorted to our Saint, and begg'd his powerful Assistance in their Distress. *Gregory* went with them to the Breach, and told them they were to expect Miracles from God alone; he then called on the Name of *Jesus Christ*, fixt his Stick in the Bank, and pray'd that the River might never more exceed its Bounds to the Prejudice of the Country. His Petition was granted; for the Stick took Root, and became a large Tree, where the Waters, when most swell'd, were from that Time observed to stop.

These and innumerable other Miracles, perform'd by our Saint's Hand, propagated the Faith with great Success, and enabled him to plant several Churches in that Country; an illustrious Instance of which Apostolical Employment at *Comana* has been given on the eleventh of *August*. Before he had been ten Years a Bishop, Idolatry was in a Manner banished from *Neocosarea*, and the adjacent Country; and Christianity flourished on its Ruins 'till *Decius* raised a Persecution in the Year 250, on which Occasion St. *Gregory* advised his Flock to provide for their own Security by retiring rather than expose themselves to the Danger of falling; and it appear'd by the Sequel that the holy Bishop spoke by divine Direction; for not one of his People renounced the Faith during that Storm. The Saint set them an Example of what he judged expedient at that Juncture, by making his Way to a desert Hill, attended only by his Deacon, the Person whom he had converted on the Road by his Power over the Devils, and obliging a large Stone to move, when insisted on as a Proof of his Doctrine. The Persecutors, whose chief Aim was at the holy Bishop, having Intelligence of his Motions, pursued him; and getting exact Information of the Place where he lay, some of their Number were posted at the Avenues, while others were employ'd in searching the Mountain. *Gregory*, knowing the Heathens were in Quest of him, order'd his Deacon to join him in Prayer, and put his whole Confidence in God. They then raised their Hands and Eyes to Heaven, and pray'd standing, but without the least Motion, so that they, who had been sent to scour the Mountain, at their Return to their Companions reported that they had seen nothing but two Trees. When the Persecutors had given over the Pursuit, the Man who had conducted the Party to the Mountain, considering he had not 'till then heard of any Trees there, went back, and finding the holy Bishop and his Deacon still fixt in Prayer, threw himself at the Saint's Feet,

declared

declared himself a Convert to Christianity, and engaged to accompany him wherever he should go.

In the mean while the Pagans, despairing of finding the Pastor, directed all their Rage against his Flock, which they hoped might be easily surprized into Apostasy in his Absence. In this View several Officers were commission'd to carry their Enquires wherever they suspected the Christians lay conceal'd, force them from their Retreats, and drag them to Prison. *Gregory*, 'though locally distant from the distressed Church of *Neocesarea*, assisted the Confessors with his Prayers; and their Perseverance was the Reward of his charitable Addresses in their Favour. One Day, when thus employ'd, his Companions observed he was much disturbed, turn'd his Eyes away, as if offended with some odious and frightful Object, and stopt his Ears; he then remain'd some Time in Silence, and without Motion; after which, as if recovering from a Swoon, *Blessed be God*, said the Saint, *who has deliver'd us from their Teeth*. Those who were with him begg'd he would let them know the Vision; upon which he told them that the Moment before *Troadius*, a young Man of Distinction and a Christian, had been carried before the Governor, and, after standing the Shock of a great Variety of Torments, gain'd the Crown of Martyrdom. This extraordinary Declaration put the Deacon on going to the Town, where he had the Satisfaction of being assured that the Saint had good Intelligence of what passed among his People.

The Persecution ending with the Life of the Emperor in the Year 251, *Gregory* return'd to *Neocesarea*, and appear'd at the Head of his Flock; and two Years afterward, *Valerian*'s Reign beginning very favourably for the Church, the holy Prelate undertook a general Visitation of the whole Country, where he made several excellent Regulations for repairing the Damage done by the late Storm. The Plague, which raged with great Violence in *Pontus* at that Time, proved the providential Occasion of several Conversions in the City and Territories of *Neocesarea*. That Calamity first appear'd there on a Day devoted to the solemn Worship of one of their principal Deities; the whole Country came in on that Occasion, and flock'd to the Theatre in such Numbers that several were heard to beg of *Jupiter* that they might not be excluded this great Festival. *Gregory*, being inform'd of their Petition, assured them they should have no Reason to complain of Want of Room. This Prediction was immediately verified in a most terrible Manner; for the infectious Distemper made such Havock, particularly among the Pagans, that finding the Force of Drugs, and the Power of their pretended Gods too weak to stop the Contagion, they made their whole Application to

the

Nov. 17 the Saint, and begg'd he would address his God in their Favour. The Success of his Prayers in that calamitous Extremity made the Infidels lay by all Thoughts of seeking Relief from any Hand but his. The holy Bishop was always ready to employ the Gift of God on them freely, and had the Satisfaction of seeing them all embrace Christianity.

While *Gregory* was thus active in propagating the Faith of *Jesus Christ*, he was not less diligent and exact in establishing good Discipline among his People; we have an authentick Proof of his Concern for regulating the Manners of the Christians in his Canonical Epistle still extant, which is full of an Apostolical Spirit, and truly worthy of our great and holy Prelate.

The time of our Saint's Death is not certainly known, but is fix'd with great probability in 270, or the following Year. Finding his End draw nigh, he order'd a strict Enquiry to be made into the State of his Diocese, and particularly desired to know how many Pagans were then remaining in *Neocesarea* and the adjacent Country. Upon being told their Number did not exceed seventeen, he express'd his Concern for leaving the great Work imperfect, but at the same Time thank'd the Almighty, who had so far bless'd his Endeavours, as to leave no more Infidels than he had found Christians at entring on that Post. With this Satisfaction he breath'd his pious Soul into the Hands of his Redeemer, and was buried in the Church which he had built, and afterwards bore his Name. The whole Christian Church is unanimous in venerating his Memory on the seventeeth of *November*.

St. DIONYSIUS Bishop of ALEXANDRIA.

DIONYSIUS, cotemporary with the Saint, of whom we spoke last, was born of Heathen Parents, and educated in all the Sciences of the *Grecians* and *Egyptians*. His Capacity and Progress in Learning soon made him considerable in the World; and his boundless Curiosity of reading every thing that came into his Hands proved the Occasion of his Conversion to Christianity; a Change which some attribute to St. *Paul*'s Epistles. He receiv'd Baptism from the Hands of *Demetrius* Bishop of *Alexandria*; and from that Time trampled on the Honours and Dignities of this World, and despised the Favour of the Great, which seem'd to court his Acceptance. Soon after his embracing the Faith he put himself under the Tuition of *Origen*, who then taught the Rudiments of the Christian Religion at *Alexandria* with universal Applause, and made so bright a Figure in his School that in the

Year

Year 231 *Heraclas*, Succeſſor to *Demetrius*, gave him the Care of it, being then *Paleſtine*, in which Poſt he behaved himſelf ſo well that in 248 he was placed in the Epiſcopal See of *Alexandria* vacant by the Death of *Heraclas*. *Philip*, then on the Imperial Throne, favour'd the Chriſtians, who therefore had no Diſturbance from thoſe in publick Offices; but it pleaſed God to exerciſe our Saint's Patience and Charity by a Diſturbance which happen'd in the Church of *Alexandria* ſoon after his Promotion. A hot-headed factious Poet, who pretended to Divination, and a particular Zeal for his abſurd Religion, made it his Buſineſs to incenſe the Idolatrous Populace againſt the Chriſtians of that City. Several of the Faithful fell Sacrifices to their Rage; and the Courage and Conſtancy of the Martyrs were no ſmall Commendation of our holy Biſhop, who animated them to the Combat.

Decius, who came to the Crown in the Year 249, began his Reign with a ſevere Perſecution of the whole Church. The Sanguinary Edict reached *Alexandria* at the Beginning of 250; upon which Occaſion *Dionyſius* was particularly active in arming his People againſt the Attack, and preparing the Soldiers of *Jeſus Chriſt* for the Battle. The holy Biſhop had the Satisfaction of ſeeing ſeveral fall gloriouſly; but was ſhock'd and mortified at the Weakneſs of others, whoſe miſerable Apoſtaſy verified our Saviour's Obſervation on the Difficulty the Rich have to be ſaved. The Emperor's Order for putting the Chriſtians to Death had not been long publiſhed when *Sabinus*, Governor of *Egypt*, diſpatched a Soldier in Queſt of the holy Biſhop; who ſtaid in his own Houſe, without being diſcover'd; for the Meſſenger never imagin'd he would ſtay at home when he knew an Order was out for apprehending him. At the End of four Days *Dionyſius* left his Houſe, as he aſſures, by divine Direction, with a View of ſeeking a Safe Retreat; *Caius*, *Fauſtus*, *Peter*, *Paul* and ſeveral of the Faithful accompanied the Biſhop on this Occaſion. They all fell into the Hands of the Perſecutors, who conducted them to *Tapoſiris* under a ſtrong Guard. *Timothy*, a Prieſt, whom ſome ſuppoſe our holy Prelate's Son, knew nothing of what had paſs'd 'till going to his Houſe he found it full of Soldiers, and was inform'd that the Saint was taken. Full of Concern and Amazement *Timothy* left the Town, without knowing where to provide for his own Security, or how to make his Way to *Dionyſius*. He was in this Diſorder when he was met by a Peaſant, who aſked him what was the Cauſe of it; and, being inform'd of the whole Affair, ran to a Country Houſe where the Neighbours were keeping a Wedding, and let the whole Company know what had happen'd. The Gueſts, who were all Chriſtians, left their Dinner immediately, and went in a Body to *Tapoſiris*, with a

F f Reſolution

Nov. 17. Resolution of rescuing the holy Bishop, and placing him out of the Reach of the Persecutors. At their Arrival they shouted, and the Soldiers quitted their Post in Confusion. *Dionysius*, who was then in Bed, imagining this Alarm given by Thieves, offer'd them his Cloaths, which were his whole Substance. The Peasants, zealous for his Preservation, bid him dress himself with all possible Expedition, and accompany them. The Saint, understanding what had brought them to *Taposiris*, begg'd they would quit the Place, and leave him there, or prevent the Executioner, and give him all the Liberty he desired by Death. The Peasants, who were resolved on the Business, would not waste their Time in reasoning him into a Compliance, but carried him off by Force, and then allow'd him the Choice of a convenient Retreat.

Dionysius, attended by *Peter* and *Caius*, made his Way to a Desart in *Libya*, where he remain'd 'till toward the Middle of the Year 251; but was not useless to his Flock, 'though distant from them. Several Priests went privately to *Alexandria* by his Direction, where they comforted such as were thrown into Prison, and exhorted all to persevere in their Fidelity to *Jesus Christ*. He employ'd several Deacons in giving the Suffering Christians all necessary Assistance; and wrote frequently to them on the Reward of Martyrdom, and the Necessity of Perseverance.

When the Fire of Persecution was extinguished at *Rome*, *Cornelius* was placed in the holy See, which had been vacant sixteen Months. Our Readers are referr'd to the Life of that holy Pope, *September* sixteenth, for a full Account of *Novatian*'s Schism. The Dignity of our Saint's See, and the Reputation of his Virtue and Learning engaged his Holiness to give him an Account of his Promotion; and the Intruder endeavour'd to strengthen his Interest by notifying his pretended Election, according to the usual Forms. *Dionysius*'s Answer to the Antipope gives us so just an Idea of the Saint's Capacity, and pious Dispositions that we could not but think our Readers would be pleased with seeing it at Length, which is as follows.

Dionysius to *Novatian* his Brother, Greeting.

"The best Proof you can give of your being placed in the See of *Rome* "against your Will, as you pretend, will be your quitting that Post of your "own Accord; for we ought to submit to any thing rather than make a "Schism in the Church. To die in Defence of Unity in *Christ*'s mystical "Body, would be as glorious, as laying down our Lives rather than sacri- "fice to Idols, and in my Opinion more glorious; for in the latter Case a
"Man

"Man suffers for the Security of his own Soul only; whereas in the former
"that of the whole Church is consulted. If therefore you establish Union a-
"mong the Brethren, the Goodness of that Action will over-ballance your
"present Fault, which will be forgot, and you receive universal Commen-
"dation. If you cannot gain others to their Duty, at least take Care to
"save your own Soul. I wish you Health, and the Peace of the Lord".

This is St. *Dionysius*'s Letter to the Antipope, in which we are to observe that the Title of Brother, which he bestows on that Schismatick, is to be consider'd only as a Term of Civility, and Expression of Charity, and can by no Means pass for a Mark of Communion; for, as *Eusebius* assures us, the Saint on all other Occasions spoke of *Novatian* with Horror and Detestation, as a Disturber of the Church's Peace, and Broacher of sacrilegious Doctrine, which tended to exclude Sinners from Repentance, and misrepresent the infinite Goodness of God. As the Confessors, who had signalized themselves by suffering in the late Persecution, were the chief Support of *Novatian*'s schismatical Pretensions, the holy Bishop of *Alexandria* wrote to them on that Subject three several Times, and had the Satisfaction of seeing them abandon the Party, and communicate with *Cornelius* before the End of the Year.

The Errors, which *Novatian* join'd to his Schism, and which were made his Pretence for urging his Title to the Prejudice of his Competitor, were not confined to *Italy*, but made their Way into *Gaul*, *Africa*, and *Asia*. *Fabius* Bishop of *Antioch* seem'd inclined to favour the Pretensions and Doctrine of *Novatian*; upon which our Saint wrote several Letters to that Prelate; in one of which he relates the following memorable Story. "We had here, says
"*Dionysius*, an old Man named *Serapion*, who had spent the greatest Part of
"his Life without Reproach, but had the Misfortune to fall in the Persecu-
"tion. He had often begg'd to be receiv'd to Communion; but could not
"gain his Point, because he had sacrificed. At last he fell ill, and lay speech-
"less and senseless three whole Days; recovering the Use of his Tongue on
"the fourth, he call'd his Grandson, and broke out into this Expostulation;
"*how long*, said he, *must I be kept here? I beg to be deliver'd without further*
"*Delay; go, Child, and fetch me a Priest.* He then relapsed into his former
"State of Insensibility, and the Boy went in Quest of a Priest, but it being
"Night, and the Priest indisposed, he could not go, as desired. As I had or-
"der'd the giving of Absolution to Penitents on their Death Beds, particularly
"as had earnestly desired it before, that Ecclesiastick gave the Child the
"holy

Nov. 17 "holy Eucharist, directing him to moisten it and give it his Grand-father. "He had scarce enter'd the Room where the sick Person lay, when, coming "to himself, he said, *the Priest cannot come; but do as be order'd you, and dis-* "*miss me immediately.* The Child then moisten'd the consecrated Particle, "and gave it *Serapion*, who expired with a gentle Sigh as soon as he had "swallow'd it". The holy Bishop observes in the Close of the Account that God had manifestly preserved the old Man's Life 'till his Penance was complete, and admitted him to partake of the holy Mysteries in his last Momentts in Consideration of his former Virtues. We may be allow'd to remark from this Instance that the Eucharist was in the third Century reserved for the Use of the Sick; and that Communion in one Kind was in those early Times allow'd to be entire and sufficient; for who will venture to say that divine Providence interposed thus visibly in Favour of *Serapion*, only that he might receive a half Sacrament, or communicate in a Manner forbidden by the Word of God?

The *Roman* Empire was severely visited by the Plague in 250, which continued to rage some Years. The Havock, which that Calamity made in *Alexandria*, and the adjacent Country, gave our Saint frequent Occasions of shewing his charitable Concern for his Flock. The Distemper was considerably abated at the Beginning of *Valerian*'s Reign, which for some Time proved favourable to the Professors of our most holy Religion. *Dionysius*, resolved to make Use of that Calm to the Advantage of the Church visited *Egypt*, as Metropolitan of that Country. While he was thus employ'd he found the *Millenaries* had occasion'd no small Disturbance by asserting the Reign of *Jesus Christ* after the Day of Judgment in a gross and scandalous Sense, and made the Glory of Christ's Kingdom on Earth little better than a *Mahometan* Paradise. *Nepos*, a Bishop, the chief Stickler for that absurd Opinion in *Egypt*, had penn'd a Treatise called *A Refutation of the Allegorists*, in which he pretended to shew that what is said on that Subject in St. *John*'s *Revelation* ought to be understood litterally. This Piece bore a great Character among the Party, and therefore *Dionysius* thought it necessary to answer it in a Manner entirely respectful to the Memory of its deceased Author. This was executed in a Treatise entituled *Promises*, divided into two Books; in the first of which he lays down his own Opinion on the Subject in Dispute, and tells us of a Conference he had held with the chief of the *Millenaries*; which being carried on without Heat, or the least Appearance of Obstinacy or Prejudice on both Sides, ended in the Conversion of his Antagonists. In the second Book he speaks of the *Revelation* with an edifying Modesty; "for "my

"my Part, says the Saint, I dare not reject a Book so much esteem'd by
"several of our Brethren, but rather look on it as above my Capacity, and
"full of important Truths, 'though deliver'd in a obscure Manner; for,
"'though I do not understand that excellent Piece, I am persuaded it con-
"tains a mysterious Sense. I am not for measuring such Things by my poor
"imperfect Reason; but am willing to captivate my Judgment where Faith
"is concern'd; and so far from condemning what I do not comprehend, that
"I admire and revere it the more on that Account."

After some Years spent in endeavouring to inspire the Churches of the East with a just Horror for *Novatian*'s Opinions and Practice, he had the Pleasure of seeing his Labours crown'd with the desired Success toward the Year 256, sent the agreeable News in a Letter to *Stephen*, then in St. *Peter*'s Chair, and employ'd all his Prudence and Erudition in bringing the Question about Baptism conferr'd by Hereticks to a happy Conclusion; 'though St. *Jerom* is of Opinion that our Saint gave into the Sentiments of St. *Cyprian*, and St. *Firmilian*.

A Persecution breaking out in the fifth Year of *Valerian*'s Reign, the two hundred fifty seventh since the Birth of *Jesus Christ*, *Emilian* Governor of *Egypt* banished *Dionysius*, and several holy Confessors to *Kephro*, a poor Village near the Desart of *Libya*. Great Crouds resorted to the holy Bishop from all Parts of *Egypt*, and form'd a numerous Church under his Direction. The Conversion of the Idolatrous Inhabitants of *Kephro* cost our Saint no small Pains, and his charitable Attempts in their Favour drew a severe Persecution on him for some Time. But his Labours and Sufferings produced the desired Fruit; and *Dionysius* had the Pleasure of seeing much the greater Part of that People renounce their Errors, and Superstition, and follow *Jesus Christ*. He had no sooner gain'd this glorious Victory over the infernal Parent of Idolatry, but He and his Companions were by the Governor's Order removed to that Part of *Egypt* call'd *Mareotis*, and disposed of in several Towns and Villages. During his Banishment to the Place last named, *Dionysius* wrote several Letters about Baptism, and appriz'd Pope *Xystus* of the Appearance of a new Heresy. *Sabellius* had lately taught a Unity of Person in God at *Ptolomaïs*; and some Pieces written by his Adherents and the Catholicks on that Subject coming into the Saint's Hands, he penn'd several Letters in Answer to those of the *Sabellians*; Copies of which were sent to *Rome*. Some Bishops under *Dionysius*'s Jurisdiction, having espoused the impious Doctrine, and propagated it with but too much Success, the Saint deputed proper Persons to exhort them to quit their Errors; but to no Purpose,

pose, for Opposition did but add to the Warmth, and Boldness with which they maintain'd their Blasphemies. This Obstinacy gave Occasion to our Saint's Letter to *Euphranor* and *Ammonius*, in which he insists particularly on such Passages in the Gospel as speak of the Humanity of our Saviour, in Order to shew that the Son, as a distinct Person from the Father, was incarnate for our Redemption.

The Persecution of the Church ending in the Year 260, *Dionysius* return'd to *Alexandria*; but *Marcian*'s Rebellion, and *Emilian*'s Revolt put things into a fresh Disorder; the latter possess'd himself of all the publick Granaries, which occasion'd a severe Famine in *Egypt*. The Disorders of those calamitous Times fell particulary heavy on *Alexandria* in the Year 263; for the Scarcity of Provisions and the War had then brought the Plague among the Inhabitants of that populous City, which carried off great Numbers of both Christians and Pagans; but, as the holy Prelate observes in a Letter on that Occasion, the Distemper proved a more severe Calamity to the latter, while the former look'd on it only as a Trial of their Virtue, and an Employment for their Charity; and the Saint makes no Difficulty of bestowing the Title of Martyrs on such as lost their Lives in attending their Brethren during that Visitation; in which he has been follow'd by the *Latin* Church, whose Martyrologe proposes those Victims of Charity to our Veneration on the twenty eighth of *February*.

Our Saint had not been long at *Alexandria*, when a Complaint against him was carried to *Dionysius*, Bishop of *Rome*. In the Course of his Dispute with the *Sabellians* our Saint had particularly insisted on such Texts of Scripture as spoke of the Human Nature of *Jesus Christ*, and endeavour'd to enforce and illustrate the Distinction of Persons in God by such Passages in the new Testament as spoke of him and his Father seperately, such as that where our Lord says *He is the Vine, and his Father the Husbandman*. This Way of speaking seem'd to encourage a Distinction in Nature and Substance between the Father and Son, and make the latter the Work of the former; and some Orthodox and pious Christians, being scandalized at those Expressions, made a Journey to *Rome*, and procured the Condemnation of the Doctrine which they apprehended was contain'd in them. The Pope then wrote to our Saint, desiring he would explain himself on the Articles urged against him, and give the World the Satisfaction of his Sentiments on that Subject. In Compliance with this Request, and to repair the Scandal which his Expressions had given, while the Design of using them was not known or consider'd, *Dionysius* composed a large Treatise which he entituled *A Refutation, and an Apology*, address'd to his Holiness; in which he shews the Mistake of his

Accusers;

St. *Dionyſius* Biſhop.

Accuſers; defends what he had already written on that Subject; and lets the World know that, though he had not uſed the Term *Conſubſtantial* when ſpeaking of the Trinity, becauſe not to be found in the holy Scripture, yet that his ſubſequent Proofs which had been ſuppreſs'd amounted to the Senſe of that World. This Piece is urged by St. *Athanaſius* in his Defence of our Saint againſt the *Arians*, who pretended to claim him as one of the chief Patrons of their Hereſy. It appears from the Application to the holy See and our Saint's Anſwer directed to the Pope that both he and his Adverſaries acknowledged the Supremacy of the Biſhop of *Rome*. St. *Dionyſius* was the Author of ſeveral other Pieces, and Epiſtles, which have not reached us; and what we have of his is owing to the Care and Zeal of *Euſebius* and St. *Athanaſius*. The only entire Work of our Saint extant is his Letter to *Baſilides*, a Biſhop who had conſulted him on ſeveral Points of Diſciple, which contains ſhort but ſolid Anſwers to the Queſtions propoſed, and has always been reckon'd a Part of the Canons of the Eaſtern Church.

Dionyſius was ſcarce diſengaged from the Trouble, which the Hereſy of *Sabellius* had given him, when he was call'd on to oppoſe another Heretick, not leſs dangerous to the Church. This new Adverſary was *Paul* of *Samoſata*, Biſhop of *Antioch*, who affirmed that *Jeſus Chriſt* had no Exiſtance before the Bleſſed Virgin, but was afterwards made God; taking that Word in a figurative and improper Senſe. This ſtrange Doctrine alarm'd the Eaſtern Prelates, who thereupon united their Forces againſt the Enemy of the Faith, and form'd themſelves into a Council at *Antioch* in the Year 264; our Saint was invited to this Aſſembly; but, his Age and Infirmities not allowing him to undertake the Journey, he ſupplied his Abſence in the beſt Manner in his Power, writing to the Church of *Antioch*, without taking Notice of the unhappy Biſhop of that City.

Our Saint did not long ſurvive that Council; and *Euſebius* ſeems to ſay he died before it broke up. There are ſeveral Opinions about the Day of his Death, which by ſome is placed on the thirty firſt of *Auguſt*, by others on the tenth or twenty third of *September*; the *Grecians* keep his Feſtival on the third of *October*, and honour him as a Martyr in Conſideration of his Sufferings for the Faith; but the *Roman* Martyrologe propoſes him to our Veneration on the ſeventeenth of *November*.

St. Hugh

Nov. 17

St. HUGH *Bishop of* LINCOLN.

THE holy Prelate, whom the Catholick Church honours on this Day, as one of the brightest Ornaments of this Island, was the Son of a Gentleman in *Burgundy*, who had served in the Army, and acquired a great Reputation in the World for Honour and Piety, and born about the Year 1140. *Hugh* lost his Mother before he was eight Years old, and was soon after put into the Hands of some Regular Canons, who lived near his Father's Seat, for Education. The Abbot of that House committed him to the Care of a venerable and prudent old Man, who did all in his Power toward giving his Thoughts a serious Turn, and frequently inculcated the Indecency of amusing himself with the Vanities and Pastimes of a giddy World, while he profess'd to live by the Spirit of *Jesus Christ*. Our Saint had spent some Years among those devout Servants of God, when his Father retired to the same House, where he ended his Days in Peace.

Hugh, being bless'd with a happy Genius, and good natural Parts, made great Progress in every Branch of Learning to which he applyed; and it pleased God to favour him with the Spirit of true Wisdom, which taught him to devote all his Faculties, and their largest Emprovements, to his Glory. His Behaviour soon engaged the Affections of the Community so effectually, that at the Age of nineteen he was ordain'd Deacon, at the earnest Request of the whole House; and discharged all the Obligations of that Character faithfully, and in a most edifying Manner.

The Saint had been some Time in this Situation, when his Prior engaged him to accompany him in a devout Visit to a Monastery of *Carthusians*, where he was so charm'd with the Practice of that holy Community, that he was very earnest in soliciting his Admission among them. His Application on that Subject being suspected by the Prior, that Superior hasten'd his Return, and when he came Home, let the whole House know his Fear of losing our Saint; which affected the Canons so sensibly, that they came about him, conjured him not to leave them, and made him promise to continue the Happiness they enjoy'd in his Presence. Reflecting afterwards on what he had done, he was very much troubled at having yielded to their Importunities, and concluded that a Promise so extorted and, as he thought, prejudicial to his Salvation, could not be obligatory, especially since he found such a strong Vocation to the Way of Life, which he had renounc'd at the Importunity of his Brethren. In this Persuasion he left his Monastery privately, and

made

made his way to that of the *Carthusians*, who receiv'd him with open Arms.

When *Hugh* was of Age to receive the Order of Priesthood, a good old Monk, to whose Care he was recommended, asked him whether he was desirous of the sacred Character; to which he replied with great Simplicity of Heart, that he wished for nothing so much in the World. " How! said the " Monk; dare you desire a Dignity, which the most perfect Christians accept " of with Fear and trembling?" *Hugh*, startled at this Reprimand, threw himself at the Feet of his Director, and with Tears begg'd Pardon for what he had said. The old Man, seeing his Confusion, was convinc'd that Ambition had no Share in his Answer, bid him arise, told him he knew his Heart, and assured him he should not only be a Priest, but in due Time a Bishop. The Behaviour of our Saint after his Ordination was an authentick Proof of his real Vocation; his Prayers were more frequent and fervent than before, and his corporal Mortifications were considerably encreased.

He had spent ten Years in his Cell, when the Prior of the House made him Procurator for the Community; in which Post he acquired a Reputation that exceeded the Limits of *France*, and inspired *Henry* II, then on the *English* Throne, with a Desire of engaging him to spend the Remainder of his Days in this Island. That Prince had founded a *Carthusian* Monastery at *Witham*; but the two successive Superiors of that House met with so much Opposition from their Neighbours, that they could not raise a tolerable Community there, and thus the royal Benefactor's Design was defeated. *Henry*, zealous for his new Foundation, desired *Hugh* might be allow'd to undertake the Government of the decaying House. The Monks, among whom he lived, thought themselves obliged to correspond with the divine Will in this Particular, 'though to their own manifest Disadvantage, and sent the Saint to *England*, according to the King's Request. The Event shew'd that this Demand was directed by the Almighty; for *Hugh* had not been there long before he became the Father of a numerous and flourishing Family; and the Sweetness of his Temper, join'd to the Purity of his Morals, gain'd the Hearts of the most savage, and inveterate Enemies of that holy Foundation.

The See of *Lincoln* had been vacant eighteen Years, when King *Henry* declared his Resolution of providing that Church with a Pastor. He sent for the Dean and the most considerable of the Canons, to whom he communicated his Design, and directed them to make Choice of one fit for that Post. After some Deliberation they named our Saint, who was perfectly agreeable to the King

King, and the Election was immediatly authorized by the Royal Confirmation, and that of the Archbishop of *Canterbury* as Metropolitan, who over-ruled all the Saint's Difficulties, and he was consecrated in *Westminster* Abbey on the twenty first of *September* 1186. Assoon as *Hugh* was raised to the Episcopal Chair, he made it his first Care to engage the Assistance of such, whose Learning and Piety qualified them to carry the Yoke with him; and immediatly employ'd all the Authority of his Station in restoring Ecclesiastical Discipline, which was very much neglected in that Age; so that a truly Pastoral Vigilence, an inflexible Resolution of preferring the Good of his Church to all other Considerations, an active and indefatigable Charity, and a regular and fervent Piety were the indisputable Characteristicks of our Saint.

Hugh had solicited all the Popes who sat in his Time for Leave to quit his Bishoprick and return to his Cell; but was so far from gaining his Point, that they obliged him to undertake Affairs of the greatest Difficulty and Importance, and such as most nearly concern'd the Good of the Church and State. The Peace concluded in *Normandy* between *Philip* King of *France* and *John* King of *England*, in which the Saint had a considerable Hand, was acknowledg'd an authentick Proof of the Influence his Wisdom and Sanctity gave him over the Minds of Princes. This is the last remarkable Action of the holy Bishop's Life, who fell ill soon after at *London*, in his Way home. He receiv'd extream Unction on St. *Matthew*'s Day, expired on the sixteenth or seventeenth of *November* in the Year 1200, and was buried in his own Cathedral seven Days after, according to his own Directions. Some Authors tell us *Hugh* was solemnly canoniz'd by *Honorius* III, about twenty Years after his Departure; while orhers attribute the Performance of that Ceremony to *Nicholas* III, or *Honorius* IV. The *Roman* Martyrologe and antient Calendars of the *English* Church place his Name on the seventeenth of *November*.

The XVIII Day.

The Dedication of the Churches of St. PETER and St. PAUL at *Rome*.

WE this Day commemorate the Dedication of the two most early Buildings which were raised at *Rome* in Honour of the two great Apostles, who

who finished their Course by Martyrdom in that City; and they are commonly ascrib'd to the pious Bounty of *Constantine* the Great. The Church, which bore the Name of the Prince of the Apostles, was built on the *Vatican* Hill; and that which was devoted to the Memory of the Companion of his Sufferings, out of the Walls on the Road to *Ostia*.

Nov. 18

The *Vatican* Church, 'though frequently repair'd fell to Ruin so that several Popes of the fifteenth Century had Thoughts of building it again from the Ground. *Nicholas* V dug for a new Foundation; but *Julius* II, who was raised to St. *Peter*'s Chair at the Beginning of the sixteenth Age, was the first who put a Hand to the new Edifice, and laid the first Stone on the eighteenth of *April* 1506. The new Church was dedicated with great Solemnity by *Urban* VIII, in the Year 1626.

St. *Paul*'s Church was given to the *Benedictine* Monks by *Martin* II, in the Year 943.

St. ROMANUS *Martyr.*

ROMANUS, a Native of *Palestine*, was brought up in the Christian Religion from his Infancy, and officiated as Exorcist and Deacon in the Church of *Cesarea*, the Metropolis of that Province, when *Dioclesian*'s Persecution broke out. He was at *Antioch*, when the Imperial Orders for demolishing the Churches were executed in that City; and saw great Crouds of all Ages, and both Sexes flock to the Idol's Temples, in Obedience to the Prince's Edict for that Purpose. The Number of those weak Christians, who hastned to the abominable Sacrifice, rather than bear any Thing for their divine Saviour, was so shocking a Sight to our Saint, that he could not forbear attempting to save such as were on the Way to Perdition; and his zealous Labours were rewarded with the generous Confession of several who had fallen, as well as the Preservation of great Numbers, who were on the very Brink of Ruin.

The Governor of the East, whom some call *Asclepiades*, then at *Antioch* with *Galerius Maximian*, being inform'd of *Romanus*'s Conduct, order'd him to be seiz'd, and brought before him. The Saint went cheerfully, and upon Examination own'd the Fact, protesting he was ready to submit to any Punishment for so glorious a Cause. The Judge then order'd him to be stretch'd out, and severely whipt, and his Body torn with Iron Hooks. While under the Hands of his merciless Executioners, *Romanus* still intrepid, and unalterable, repeated his Profession, and reproached the Governor with Cruelty. That Magistrate press'd his Obedience to the Emperor; to which the Martyr reply'd that he acknowledged *Jesus Christ* as his supreme King, and was under no Obligation of complying with the Commands of his Prince, when they clash with his Duty to God. His Body was laid open to the Bone. *Asclepiades* order'd his Face to be disfigur'd in the same Manner; but the Saint's Patience triumph'd over the Cruelty of the Judge, and the Strength of his Officers.

Romanus betray'd not the least Emotion at what he felt, nor any Apprehension from what the Governor threatned, but went on with his Discourse on the great Truths of Christianity with equal Solidity, and Clearness. *Prudentius*, who flourish'd in the latter Part of the fourth Century, and other Authors tell us, that the Saint offer'd to stand to the Decision of a Child newly wean'd, about the Excellency of our holy Religion; they add that *Asclepiades* accepted of the Proposal, and agreed to put the whole Merits of the Cause on that Issue; and that the Child declared in Favour of the Unity of God and Divinity of *Jesus Christ*, for which he was put to Death. The *Greek* Church calls him *Barila*, and honours him as a Martyr on the Day consecrated to the Memory of St. *Romanus*.

Romanus was then condemn'd to be burnt alive; and went to the Place of Execution with surprizing Cheerfulness and Courage. He was tied to a Post, and the Wood laid about him, when a suddain Shower of Rain hinder'd the Pile from taking Fire. This Accident, which was interpreted as an immediate Interposition of Heaven, alarm'd the whole Town; and *Galerius Maximian*, being inform'd of the Matter, sent Word to the Governor that it was but reasonable to give the Man his Liberty, who was visibly under the divine Protection. *Asclepiades* attributed this miraculous Deliverance to the Force of Magick, and insinuated the usual Calumny so successfully that he obtain'd Leave to proceed to fresh Tortures, and dispatch the Saint, as he should judge most proper; upon which the Governor order'd the Martyr's Tongue to be cut out to the Root. According to the Rules of Physick this Operation must have put an End to his Life; but *Eusebius*, his Cotemporary, assures us that he survived it, and spoke more distinctly than before; and this Miracle is the whole Subject of a Discourse pronounced at *Antioch* by St. *Chrysostom* in Honour of the holy Martyr.

The Saint being order'd to Prison, where it was expected he would soon expire, the Governor was surprized at what he heard, sent for the Surgeon, who

had

had been order'd to execute the cruel Sentence, and taxed him with favouring the Criminal either on the Confideration of a Bribe, or becaufe he was a Chriftian; for *Eufebius* affures us that Artift had profefs'd the Faith before the Perfecution. The Surgeon, who had kept the Martyr's Tongue out of Veneration for the valuable Relick, produced it in Court, and affirm'd that *Romanus* could not then be alive according to the ordinary Laws of Nature. The Experiment was then made on a condemn'd Malefactor, who died immediately; but the Governor, fteel'd in Cruelty, was not to be foften'd into Humanity by the Miracle; and *Romanus* lay feveral Months in Prifon. During his Confinement the twentieth Year of *Dioclefian*'s Reign was obferved with great Solemnity, according to Cuftom; on which Occafion all the Prifoners were releafed, and allow'd a Share in the publick Joy; but *Romanus*, obtained a more happy Deliverance, being ftrangled on the feventeenth of *November*, in the Year 303.

Our Saint's Name foon became famous all over the Eaft; and in St. *Chryfoftom*'s time the Church of *Antioch* celebrated his Victory in a publick and folemn Manner. The *Grecians* keep his Feftival on the eighteenth of *November* in which they are join'd by the *Roman* Martyrologe.

The XIX Day.

St. ELIZABETH Widow.

ELIZABETH, Daughter to *Andrew* the II King, and Gertrude Queen of *Hungary*, was born in that Country in the Year 1207. The Reputation of her Royal Parents enaged *Herman*, Landgrave of *Heffe* and *Thuringia* to folicit her Marriage with his Son *Lewis*, while in her Cradle. Having gain'd their Confent, he fent a fecond Embaffy to negotiate her Removal to his Court, and commited her to the Care of *Bertha*, a Lady of Age and Experience, who was to educate her in a Manner fuitable to her Birth, and Views in the World. The Infant Princefs was given into the Hands of the Landgrave's Deputies, and carried to the Court of *Thuringia*, when but four Years old, where fhe was receiv'd like one who was to be a publick Good. She had not been above five Years there when *Herman* died; and two Years after fhe loft her Mother.

It is was foon evident to all about her that God had great Defigns in Favour of our Saint; and the Grace, which fhone forth in her Infancy, fufficiently

ficiently encouraged the largeſt Hopes and Expectations from her encreaſing Years. She was ſo happily prevented with the Love of God, that no Room for the Creatures could be found in her Heart; and, 'though ſurrounded, and, as it were, beſieged by the Pleaſures, and Delights of the World in their moſt engaging Shapes, ſhe had no Reliſh for them. She was educated with *Agnes*, Siſter to the young Landgrave; and upon their firſt Appearing together at Church, they were dreſs'd alike, and wore Coronets ſet with Jewels. At their entring the Houſe of God, *Sophia*, the *Landgrave*'s Mother, obſerving our Saint take off her Coronet, aſked the Reaſon of that Action; to which ſhe replied that ſhe could not but think it indecent for her to wear Jewels on her Head, where ſhe ſaw that of *Jeſus Chriſt* crown'd with Thorns. *Agnes* and her Mother, who were Strangers to that Way of thinking, and particularly fond of what *Elizabeth* trampled on, conceived an Averſion for the young Princeſs, and ſaid that, ſince ſhe ſeem'd to have ſo little Reliſh for a Court, a Convent would be the propereſt Place for her. The Courtiers carried their Reflexions much farther; dazzled and confounded with the Luſtre of her Virtues, they did all in their Power to depreciate the Saint, by obſerving that neither her Fortune nor Perſon were ſuch as the Landgrave deſerved and might claim, that He had no Inclination to her, and that therefore ſhe would ſhortly either be ſent back to *Hungary*, or at beſt married to ſome Nobleman of the Country. The young Prince's Abſence from Court left *Elizabeth*'s Enemies at Liberty to give a Looſe to their Calumnies; but at his Return his Behaviour was ſuch as convinced the World of his Affection for her, and ſilenced her moſt malicious Enemies.

Elizabeth was in her fourteenth Year, when ſhe was married to the Landgrave with great Solemnity; all the Clouds which had ſo long hung over her Head were then diſperſed; and from that Time the whole Court expreſs'd a profound Veneration for our Saint, whoſe Virtues encreaſed daily. She ſubmitted her Conſcience to the Direction of *Conrad*, a holy Prieſt, and celebrated Preacher, whoſe chief Employment was to moderate her corporal Auſterities, which were ſuch as her Age and Conſtitution could ſcarce bear. The *Landgrave* was ſo well pleaſed with his Wife's Conduct and Choice of a Director, that *Conrad* was allow'd the Privelege of diſpoſing of all Eccleſiaſtical Benefices in that Prince's Gift. *Elizabeth* had three Children, *Herman*, who ſucceeded to his Father's Honour and Eſtate, 'though not immediately; *Sophia*, who married the Duke of *Brabant*; and another Daughter, who ended her Days in a Monaſtery.

Our

Our Saint was remarkable for great Simplicity in her Dress, but so far from affecting Singularity in that particular, that she complied with the Fashions of the Court, when ever the Landgrave required or expected her to appear, as became her Rank. She sat very loose to all the Pleasures of this Life, and accepted of the Honours due to her exalted Station, with a Reluctancy equal to the Mortification which others feel upon being neglected and dispised. It was some Time before the Saint's Example produced any Change in the Ladies about her, who could not easily comprehend that the World, with all its Satisfactions, deserved so little Regard, as she express'd for it. At last, however, several of them were warm'd into an Imitation of that excellent Princess, retrench'd all Superfluities in their Dress and Table, devoted their Time and Thoughts to Works of Mercy; and some made Vows of perpetual Chastity. But, whatever Efforts those Ladies made to tread in the Steps of the Saint, they could only follow her at a Distance, and thought her inimitable in that profound Humility which made her comply with, and even court the most mortifying Tasks. She submitted cheerfully to wash the most disgusting Sores, and perform'd that act of Charity in a Manner which sufficienty express'd her Sense of approaching her Saviour in the Persons of his afflicted Members.

Elizabeth, convinced that nothing is more opposite to the Spirit of Christianity than Idleness, employ'd all the Time, that could be spared from her devout Exercises in Work; but then took Care that her Labours of that Sort tended more to promote Charity than improve or encourage Vanity; for which Reason, leaving Embroidery, and curious Works to such as made Ornament and Superfluity their Care, she sate down to spin Woollen, which was afterwards made into Cloth for the Use of Religious Communities or the Poor.

In the Year 1225, *Germany* was severely visited by a Famine; on which Occasion she distributed her whole Crop of Corn among those, whose Circumstances made that Calamity heavier to them. *Lewis* was then in *Italy* with the Emperor; and at his Return the Officers of his Houshold complain'd loudly of our Saint's Conduct, which they represented as an unnecessary and imprudent Profuseness; but the *Landgrave* was so well assured of our Saint's Prudence and Piety, that he declar'd himself satisfy'd with what she had done, without examining any farther into the Matter. In Consideration of such as were disabled by Age, or too weak to come for Relief to the Castle of *Marpurg*, the Place of her Residence, built on a steep Rock, she erected a large Hospital at the Foot of the said Rock for their Reception and Entertainment, where she frequently fed them with her own Hands, made

Nov. 19 their Beds, and attended them in the Heat of Summer, when that Place would have been infupportable to one of a lefs generous and indefatigable Charity. When any of thofe miferable Objects had the additional Incumbrance of Children, they were eas'd of them by her Order, and the helplefs Infants provided for at her Expence. *Elizabeth* was the Foundrefs of another Hofpital, in which twenty eight Perfons were conftantly relieved; fhe fed nine hundred daily at her own Gate, befide an incredible Number in different Parts of the Province, fo that fhe was generally called the Mother of the Poor, and her Revenue reckon'd the Patrimony of the Diftreffed. We muft not forget to obferve that our Saint's Charity was excellently temper'd with Difcretion; and that, inftead of encouraging fuch, as were able to work, in Idlenefs, fhe employ'd them in a Way fuitable to their Strength and Capacity.

In the Year 1227, the Landgrave fet out for the Holy Land with a numerous Retinue, join'd the Emperor *Frederick* in the Kingdom of *Naples*, and died at *Otranto* in *Calabria* on the 11th of *September* the fame Year. *Elizabeth*, who put on the Drefs of a Widow at that Prince's Departure, was moft fenfibly afflicted at the melancholy News; but it pleafed God to fupport her under this Lofs, and referve her for farther Trials. *Henry*, Brother to the late Landgrave, being put upon taking Poffeffion of his Dominions, to the Prejudice of *Herman*'s Title, who was then but four Years old, our Saint was ftript of all fhe poffefs'd in the World, forced from Court, and obliged to take Shelter in a poor Inn in the Neighbourhood; for the rebellious Party was fo formidable, that no body durft entertain the injured Princefs. As an Addition to her Affliction, her three Children were fent to her, while in that miferable Situation; and fhe was reduced to the loweft Ebb, when fhe applied to a Prieft for Relief, who was willing to receive her into his Houfe; but her Enemies forced her from thence, and fhe returned to the Inn, where only fhe could find Admittance. Thus, for her greater Perfection, a King's Daughter, and Wife to one of the moft confiderable Princes in *Germany*, fell from the Height of temporal Grandeur in a Moment, was reduced to fubfift on Charity; and fhe, who had fhew'd the Tendernefs of a Mother to the Children of others, was now obliged to accept of Bread for her own.

The Abbefs of *Kitzingen* in the Diocefe of *Wurtzbourg*, our Saint's Relation, hearing of her Misfortunes, gave her an Invitation to her Monaftery; and then took Care to put her into the Hands of her Uncle, the Bifhop of *Banberg*; who entertain'd her very handfomely, and fettled her in one of his own Houfes. Soon after a Perfon of the firft Rank, taking the Saints Caufe ferioufly to Heart, made the new Landgrave fo fenfible of the Indignity offer'd

fer'd to his Sister-in-Law, which was aniversally laid to his Charge, that, en- Nov.19
tring into himself, he expres'd a hearty Concern for what was past, and, as a
a Proof of his sincere Repentance, order'd her to be conducted to his Palace,
where she was treated in a Manner suitable to her Birth, and personal Merit.
Elizabeth had not been long in that Situation when her Enemies gave her all
the Uneasiness in their Power; but the Saint receiv'd that ill Usage as a new
Favour granted by the Almighty, for the Trial and Improvement of her Virtue, and made a truly Christian Use of all that domestick Persecution.

Pope *Gregory* IX, being inform'd of her Sufferings and Patience, sent her
a Letter of Consolation, and declared that he receiv'd her into the immediate
Protection of the holy See; on which Occasion *Conrad*, her former Director,
was commission'd to be particularly careful of her, watch all the Motions of
her Enemies, and made a faithful Report of their Attempts to his Holiness.
Some Time after *Conrad* went for *Marpurg*, the Place of his usual Residence,
and Scene of his pastoral Functions; to which City the Saint follow'd him,
without reflecting on the Number of her Enemies there, and lived upon the
Labour of her own Hands, as cheerfully as if she had been inured to it from
her Infancy. This was her Situation when her Father, being apprized of
her unmerited Disgrace, sent a Nobleman to invite her to his Court, and
assure her of a Reception suitable to her Birth; but *Elizabeth* was deaf to the
Proposal, and declared her fixt Resolution of continuing in a State of Humiliation and Povery.

After some Time spent in this Manner, *Conrad* and the few Friends, who
dared espouse the Cause of the distressed Princess, prevail'd with *Henry* to refund her Fortune for her Maintainance; but, as soon as the Money came into
her Hands, it was distributed among the Poor. After four Years of continual Mortification, it pleased the Almighty to reward her Patience by a
happy Death on the nineteenth of *November* 1231. The Reputation of her
Virtue was such that the first News of her Death brought great Crouds to the
Place where her Body lay; and, after their Curiosity and Devotion to the deceased were gratified, the venerable Relicks were with great Solemnity deposited in a Chapel near the Hospital which she had founded. Her known Sanctity and several Miracles perform'd at her Tomb prevail'd with *Gregory* IX
to canonize her in 1235; and the Day of her Departure is devoted to her
Memory in the *Roman* Martyrologe.

H h St. Pon-

Nov. 20.

St. PONTIAN, Pope and Martyr.

PONTIAN, a Native of *Rome*, and Son of *Calphurnius*, was on the Demise of St. *Urban*, placed in St. *Peter*'s Chair in the Year 230, and govern'd the Church without Disturbance 'till the Death of *Alexander Severus*, which happen'd about five Years after his Promotion. That Emperor was succeeded by *Maximin*, whose Cruelty soon made him odious to the Senate and People. He began his Reign with persecuting the Disciple of *Jesus Christ*, particularly the Clergy, supposing the whole Building must fall when it's Foundations were removed. Our Saint, whose Station made him the chief Support of the Church, was therefore one of the first who felt the Effects of that Prince's Aversion to our holy Religion. *Maximin* banished him and *Hippolytus* a holy Priest to *Sardinia*, where the Badness of the Air and other Hardships gave him the Glory of Martyrdom on the twenty eighth of *September*, in the first Year of *Maximin*'s Reign; or on the nineteenth of *November*, as the *Roman* Martyrologe seems to insinuate by placing his Name on that Day.

The XX Day.

St. FELIX of VALOIS.

FELIX, surnamed *Valois* from the Place of his Nativity, was born on the nineteenth of *April* 1127; and when grown up had so perfect an Aversion to the World that he retired into a Wood, lived there in the Practice of a rigorous Penance 'till he was sixty Years old, and seem'd to depend on finishing his Days in Obscurity, when it pleased God to draw him from his Solitude, and make him instrumental in the Relief of the most miserable Part of Mankind.

John of *Matha* had form'd a Design of erecting a new Order for the Redemption of Captives; having heard much of our Saint's Virtue, he went in Quest of him and desired his Advice and Concurrence in that noble Charity. The Particulars of that Establishment may be seen at large in the Life of the holy Founder *February* the eighth. In 1211 *John* made his last Journey to *Rome* where he died two Years after, and thus the Care of the new Order devolved on our Saint, whose Endeavours were crown'd with a Success equal to the Purity of his Intention, and a great Number of Houses were built for the Reception of such as were disposed to embark in that excellent Undertaking.

Felix

St. EDMUND, King and MARTYR.

Felix died, full of Years and good Works, on the fourth of *November*, Nov. 20 1212; but his Feast was translated to the twentieth of the same Month by Pope *Innocent* XI.

EDMUND, descended from the old *Saxons* whom the Natives of our Island called to their Assistance in the V Century, was raised to the Throne of his Fathers, and became King of the *East-Angles* on *Christmas* Day 855. The excellent Qualities of his Heart and Mind sufficiently spoke him design'd for a Station where the publick Good should be his whole Concern. Never were larger Hopes conceiv'd from the Administration of a Prince, than when *Edmund* took the Reins of Government into his Hands, nor were Subjects Expectations ever better answer'd than in the Conduct of this holy King. The Peace and Happiness of his People were his whole Concern, which he endeavour'd to establish and secure by excellent Laws, impartial Justice, and religious Regulations in his Dominions. His Life was free from Reproach; he was modest and humble; and a declared Enemy to Flatteres and Informers; for which Reason he would see with his own Eyes, hear with his own Ears, and do all in his Power to avoid being surprized into a wrong Judgment, or imposed on by the Passions and ill Designs of others. *Edmund* was acknowledged the Father of the Poor, the Protector of Widows and Orphans, the Support of the Weak, and, in a Word, a pubilck and extensive Good.

Higwais, or, as some call him, *Ingwar*, a *Danish* Prince had landed a formidable Army of Pagans in this Island in the Year 867, who, after three Years Stay and great Havock made in the Kingdoms of *Northumberland* and *Mercia*, pour'd down on *Edmund*'s Dominions, burnt the first Town they reach'd, and laid all waste before them. *Higwais*, depending on the Strength and Numbers of his Men sent a haughty and insulting Message to our Saint, and insisted on Terms, which that Prince was convinced neither Honour nor Conscience would allow him to accept of. The *Barbarian* was not disposed to make any Abatement in his Demands, and consequently *Edmund* had no Way left to secure his own Person but that of Flight; which he would not hear of, though press'd very warmly by his Friends, resolving to sacrifice his own Life cheerfully for the Preservation of his Subjects rather than intimidate them by his Absence. The Pagan Deputies were sent back with Directions to let their Prince know, that *Edmund* acknowledged no Superior but God; and that he was resolved not to submit to the Will and Laws of a Stranger, who had no Shadow of Pretence for that Attempt on his Dominions.

The Barbarian, incensed at this Answer, order'd Part of his Army to march forward, and bring the King of the *East Angles* to him. *Edmund* not being in a Capacity of holding out against the *Danes*, was taken, loaded with Chains, and conducted to the *Pagan* General. That Prince treated our Saint with all the Rudeness and Barbarity of an insolent Conqueror; but could not force one Complaint, or Mark of Resentment from the Royal Sufferer. *Edmund* maintain'd the Character of a King and a Christian to the End, and protested that the Desire of Life should never prevail with him to give up his People into the Hands of a Tyrant and an Infidel. *Higwais*, transported with Rage at the Saint's Resolution, and Greatness of Soul, order'd him to be beaten like a Slave, to let him know he was no longer in Possession of a Throne. He was afterwads tied to a Tree, and whipp'd, 'till the Barbarians were tired with the Execution; and, finding he remain'd inflexible, they placed him on an Eminence tied him to a Post, and shot at him. *Higwais*, enraged at his Constancy, and observing him very fervent in Prayer, and Invocation of the sacred Name of *Jesus*, thought that Death too slow, and finished the Tragedy by cutting off the Saint's Head with his own Hand.

The Royal Trunk was left on the Spot; but the *Danes* buried the Head in another Place. It pleased God to direct the Discovery of that Relick, which was laid with the Body as soon as the Pagans left the Country, and the Saint honour'd as a Martyr, because he fell by the Hands of Infidels, who probably insisted on some Terms prejudicial to our holy Religion. God gave frequent Proofs of the Sanctity and Glory of his Servant; and the Miracles perform'd at his Tomb prevail'd with the leading Men of the Country to build a Church in Honour of the Saint, and lodge his Relick in it. The Town of St. *Edmundsbury* in *Suffolk* takes it's Name from our Saint, and probably stands on the Ground where the Martyr died, or where the Church already mention'd was built; before the Reformation it was famous for a stately Abbey, said to be founded by *Canute*, who became Master of this Kingdom in the Year 1017. The *Roman* Martyrologe mentions the Royal Martyr on

the

the twentieth of *November*, and his Name appears on the same Day in all Calendars used in *England* before the pretended Reformation; from the Year 1222 to the said Period his Festival was reckon'd among those which we call holy Days of Obligation.

The XXI Day.

The PRESENTATION of the Blessed Virgin in the TEMPLE.

CARDINAL *Baronius* in his Learned Notes on the *Roman* Martyrologe observes that *the Presentation* was a Term formerly used to express the Action of the Blessed Virgin when she *presented* the Infant *Jesus* in the Temple; and the Menologes of the Modern *Greeks* seem to mean the same Thing by that Word at present; for on the twenty first of *November* they have *The Mother of God*'s *Entrance into the Temple*; and on the second of *February* they celebrate the same under a different Denomination, viz. CHRIST's *being found or met* (by old *Simeon*) *forty Days after his Birth*. It is not easy to fix the Time when *the Presentation* began to signify the Blessed Virgin being presented in the Temple by the Hands of her holy Parents. St. *John Damascen*, who died in the Middle of the VIII Century, mentions this Circumstance of her Life; from that Time at least it has been a constant Tradition that the Blessed Virgin, consecrated to God before her Birth, was solemnly offer'd to him in her Infancy. The Intention of the Church in this Festival seems to be to honour the Innocence and Sanctity of the Blessed Virgin's Life from her Birth to the Moment of the Incarnation of her divine Son, and set a holy example to all Parents of consecrating their Children to the Service of God, and begging his Grace to lead a pious and Christian Life.

St. COLOMBAN, ABBOT.

COLOMBAN, or *Colomb*, was born about the Year 560, in the Province of *Leinster* in *Ireland*, and educated from his Infancy in such Sciences as enlarge the Understanding and prepare the Mind for higher Studies. Being bless'd with a good Capacity, he made a consider Progress in Grammar, Rhetorick, and Geometry, in which Arts he was equall'd by few of his Age;

Nov. 21 nor was his Proficiency in Virtue less considerable. Having run through those first Exercises of his Youth, the Grace of God let him see that the extraordinary Qualifications, of which he was Master, would prove so many Enemies to Innocence, and expose him to several dangerous Temptations, especially while he remain'd among his Friends and old Acquaintance; for which Reason he came to a Resolution of leaving his own Country. The Motion was vigorously opposed by his Mother; but nothing could divert the Saint from following what he believed the divine Call. *Colomban* made his Way into a distant Province in the same Island, where he put himself into the Hands of *Silenus*, a venerable old Man, deservedly famous for an uncommon Degree of Piety, and a thorough Acquaintance with the holy Scriptures. That excellent Person, finding his Pupil well prepar'd to his Hand by great Penetration and a solid Judgment, took a singular Pleasure in his Instruction, and had the Satisfaction of receiving Satisfactory Answers to the most difficult Questions which he could propose. Some Authors assure us that the Saint composed several Treatises on the Scriptures, and among the rest one on the Psalms, while Under the Tuition of that able and holy Master.

The Fervour of his Devotion encreasing with his Learning, *Colomban*, after some Years spent with *Silenus*, enter'd the celebrated Monastery of *Bangor* in the Province of *Ulster*, now a Borough Town in the County of *Down*, and the Title of an Earl; where he lived under the Direction of *Congal*, Founder and first Abbot of that House. The Fasts, Watchings, and other pious and penitential Exercises, which were the whole Employment and chief Beauty of that flourishing Community, qualified him to govern others by the same Rules, which he practised with Vigour and Fidelity.

Colomban, whose whole Endeavours were after Perfection, always went on from one Degree to another; and, after a long Experience of the Monastick State at *Bangor*, resolved to leave *Ireland*, and spend the Remainder of his Days at a Distance from all that could fix his Thoughts to this World. Upon laying the Matter before his Superior, he found no small Difficulty to obtain his Leave for travelling; but urged his Request so warmly, and at the same Time so seriously that the Abbot, persuaded his Petition was directed by the Will of God, dismiss'd him with his Blessing, and allow'd him to choose twelve Monks out of the House who should accompany him. *Colomban*, thus attended, crossed over into *Great Britain* and from thence to *France*, resolving to go still farther if that Country would not afford him an Opportunity of labouring for the Salvation of his Neighbour, aud promoting ting the Glory of God. The Saint observed that Religion had suffer'd much

in

much in several Places from the Inroads of the Enemy, and the Negligence of the Pastors; Christian Piety was quite banished, and little more than the bare Name of Religion remain'd. Here now was a large Field for *Colomban*'s Charity and Apostolical Zeal; the Saint preach'd the Necessity of Penance, and a good Life arising that neglected People with incredible Success; and his Discourses on the Morality of the Gospel were the more persuasive, because explain'd, illustrated and enforced by a Life exactly conformable to the Precepts, which he had laid down; and indeed the Behaviour of his Companions was not less edifying, and instructive; their profound Humility, invincible Patience, and indefatigable Charity gave no small Weight to what they advanced for the Use of others.

Gontran, King of *Burgundy*, being acquainted with the Character of these excellent Strangers, invited them to his Court; and, upon hearing our Saint discourse on the great Truths of the Gospel, was so well pleased with him that he desired him to settle in his Dominions, and accept of a handsome Maintainance for himself and his Companions. The Saint express'd a grateful Sense of the proffer'd Favour; but assured that Prince he desired no other Accommodation than what would enable him to prrctise the Evangelical Precepts, which direct Self-denial, taking up the Cross, and following *Jesus Christ*. The King then desired he would chuse any Place in his Dominions, which he should judge most proper for the Execution of his Design. The Saint, thus commission'd, led his devout Family into a mountainous Desart, that lies between *Lorrain*, *Alsatia*, and *Francheconté*; where he found an old ruinous Castle, called *Anegray*, converted the Remains of that Building into a Monastery, and made what Additions were necessary for the Reception of his Companions. It was some Time before they could find any other Food than Herbs, and the Barks of Trees; but, when their Resignation and Patience had been sufficiently tried, Providence visibly interposed in their Favour; for *Caramtock*, Abbot of *Saulx*, being apprized of their Necessities in a Dream, sent them a large Supply of Provisions, and took effectual Care that they should never be reduced to their former Extremity for the future.

Colomban and his Companions, being thus discovered, where they hoped to live unknown to the whole World, great Numbers of sick and infirm Persons were brought to the Saint, who received their Cure by his Prayers; and several begg'd to share the Pleasures of a religious Retreat. His Community grew so numerous before he had spent three Years in his Desart, that he was obliged to look for a more commodius Place for their Reception and Entertainment. About three Leagues from *Anegray*, he discovered another Castle

stle, named *Luxeü*; and having obtain'd a Grant of that Building and a Piece of Land about it, raised the famous Monastery which is standing to this Day, and in the Hands of *Benedictin* Monks. This new House was soon filled with Persons of the best Families in *Austrasia* and *Burgundy*, and it was not long before the Saint was obliged to found another Monastery at *Fountaines*, for the Reception of his Disciples. He placed able and pious Superiors at the Head of that Community, and annex'd it to the Monastery of *Luxeü*. Nor were the Monks of *Anegray* neglected by their holy Founder, who gave them, and his other spiritual Children a Rule drawn up by his own Hand, which was long practised in *France*, and is still extant. It is short, and consists chiefly of Maxims relating to Monastick Virtues; such as Obedience, Poverty, Disinterestedness, Humility, Chastity, interior and exterior Mortification, Silence, and Discretion; which the Saint tells us he had received from his Fathers, i, e. the Monks of *Ireland*.

Colomban undertook to observe the Customs of his own Country, particularly that of keeping *Easter* on the fourteenth Day of the Moon, when it fell on a *Sunday*; a Practice, which had been expresly condemn'd and prohibited by the Council of *Nice*. His steady Adherence to that Singularity engaged him in several troublesome Contests with the Pope, and the Bishops of *France*. He wrote to *Gregory* the Great in Justification of the *Irish* Custom, but his Letter miscarried; about the Year 603 he sent his Reasons for differing from the rest of the Church in that Particular, to a Council then assembled in *France* on that Subject; begg'd every one allow'd to celebrate our Lord's Resurrection, according to the Discipline established in his own Country; desired the Protection of those Prelates for his religious and penitential Family; and declared that if the Storm, which this Question had raised, could not be laid without forcing him from his Desart, he was ready to imitate *Jonas* in offering himself as a Victim for the publick Peace.

Childibert, King of *Austrasia*, came to the Crown of *Burgundy* by the Death of *Gontran* his Uncle; and dying in the Year 596, left his two Sons in the Hands of *Brunehaut* their Grandmother. *Theodebert*, the elder, reigned in *Austrasia*, and *Burgundy* fell to the Share of *Thierry* or *Theodorick*, the younger. The latter of those Princes express'd a singular Satisfaction in having St. *Colomban* in his Dominions, made him several Visits at *Luxeü*, and recommended himself to his Prayers with much Respect and Affection. But no Civilities were capable of checking our Saint's Freedom in laying his Faults before him, especially his scandalous Practice of keeping several Concubines. The King was so touched with the Remonstrance, that he promised to reform

in

in that Particular. This Resolution incensed *Brunehaut* against the Person Nov. 21 who had induced her Son to form it; for that ambitious Princess apprehended her Son would marry, and she should lose all her Authority over him. *Colomban* going one Day to Court on some Business, *Brunehaut* presented *Thierry*'s natural Children for his Blessing. The holy Abbot, thinking his Compliance with that Demand would seem to imply an Approbation of their Right to succeed their Father, refused it; which exasperated *Brunehaut* so, that she immediately dispatched an Order to the neighbouring Monasteries, to break off all Commerce with *Colomban* and his Monks, strictly charging them neither to harbour nor assist in any Manner the holy Abbot, or any who lived under his Direction. Not content with this severe Order, she was very active and industrious in engaging the Nobility and Bishops in her Quarrel, and exerting her Malice against the Saint in a Manner which should carry the Appearance of Justice. The Bishops might more easily be prevail'd with to disturb the holy Abbot upon the Account of the old Difference about *Easter*; and were on this Occasion made to believe, that his Rule was far from unexceptionable.

Thierry was so warmly importuned on that Subject by his Grandmother and her Tools that he went to *Luxeû*, and undertook to expostulate with our Saint on his Way of Living, which was extremely different from what was practised in other Religious Houses of that Country, and threaten'd to banish him if he did not make some Alterations in his Institute, especially in Regard to Strangers, whom the Saint entertain'd out of the Inclosure of his Monastery, whereas the King insisted on the House being open to all, who were disposed to visit the Monks. *Thierry*, finding *Colomban* resolved to hear of no Alteration in his Rule, left the Place, and order'd the Saint to be carried to *Bezançon* 'till he should send farther Directions. His Guards, full of a profound Veneration for their Prisoner, ventured incurring the King's Displeasure, and let him return to *Luxeû*; but he had not long enjoy'd his Rest there when *Thierry*, animated by *Brunehaut*, and her Creatures, sent a Party of Soldiers headed by *Baudulfe*, and *Bertaire*, two Men of Quality, with positive Orders to secure *Colomban*, and oblige him to return to his own Country. Those Noblemen were so sensible of the Saint's Virtue, and Innocence, and so awed by his Reputation for Sanctity and Miracles, that instead of using Force, or pressing his Departure in a Manner which their Commission would have priveleged, they begg'd he would consent to the Journey, and give them Leave to conduct him to *Nantes*. The Saint, considering that a farther Resistance might draw a Storm on the Heads of his innocent Disciples, consented to the Proposal, and left his Desart in 610, after twenty Years Residence in it.

We are assured by the Author of our Saint's Life, that he perform'd several Miracles on the Road, and told *Leuparius* Bishop of *Tours* that in a short Time *Thierry* would loose the Crown of *Burgundy*, which should fall to *Clotaire* II, upon the Death of that Prince. This Prediction seem'd highly incredible to the Officers, who attended the Saint, because *Clotaire* was at that Time in a very weak Condition, and had been obliged to accept of the Conquerors Terms though extremely dishonourable and disadvantageous; but was justified by the Event; for three Years after, *Thierry*'s whole Race was cut off, and *Clotaire*, uniting the *French* Monarchy, became one of the most powerful Kings that ever reign'd in that Country. *Colomban* made some Stay at *Nantes*, and it was from that Town that he wrote his excellent Letter to the Monks of *Luxeü*, exhorting them to Patience, Union, and Regularity. The Saint, and such of his Companions as were allow'd to attend him, took Shipping, but were driven back by opposite Winds, which made the Master of the Vessel, and the King's Officers conclude that Heaven oppos'd his Departure; for which Reason they not only gave him his Liberty to go were he pleased, but furnished him with Money. The Saint, being now Master of his own Motions, made his Way to *Clotaire*, who receiv'd him in a Manner suitable to his Merit, and offer'd him a Settlement in his Dominions; but the holy Abbot declined the Favour, being unwilling to be the Cause of any new Misunderstanding between that Prince, and the King who had banished him; and rather inclined to attempt the Conversion of Infidels in some distant Country. After having given that hospitable Monarch some Directions for his Conduct, assured him that all *France* would in a little Time own his Power, and thank'd him for his Protection, he made his Way to *Austrasia*, hoping that King *Theodebert* would assist his Journey into *Italy*. That Prince receiv'd the holy Abbot, and some of his Disciples very favourably, and gave them free Leave to settle in any Part of his Dominions. *Colomban*, attended by a sufficient Number of his Monks, among whom was St. *Gallus*, spoken of at large *October* the sixteenth, went into what is now called *Switzerland*. *Gallus* having burnt a Pagan Temple, and broke the Idols, the Infidels pour'd down in such Numbers that *Colomban* and his Companions were obliged to fly to *Arbon* on the Lake of *Constance*, and from thence retired into a Desart near *Bregentz*, called by the *Romans Brigantium*, where he spent about three Years; during which Time he converted great Numbers of his Idolatrous Neighbours, reclaim'd

St. Colomban, Abbot.

claim'd several vicious Christians, and built a little Monastery for his Disciples, where each of them was employ'd in some useful and laborious Work.

Thierry becoming Master of *Austrasia* by the Defeat and Death of his Brother, our Saint could not think himself and his Monks safe in that Country, and therefore came to a Resolution of going for *Italy*, where they hoped for Protection from *Agilulph* King of *Lombardy*, who received him and his religious Retinue with all Marks of Respect, and left them the Choice of any Spot of Ground in his Kingdom. *Colomban*, thankful for the favourable Offer, pitched on a Desart at the Foot of the *Apennine* Hills near the River *Trebia*, where he found an old ruinous Church which he repair'd, and built Cells, which in Time were improved into a large Monastery.

The victorious King did not long enjoy his illgotten Advantage; for he died before he had been a Year in Possession of his Brother's Dominions. His Death is placed in 613; and *Sigebert*, his eldest Son, was placed on the Throne; but had not sate many Months before *Clotaire* march'd a formidable Army against him, and verified our Saint's Prediction; and thus all *France* obey'd one Monarch. As soon as that Prince was settled on the Throne he sent for *Eustasius*, who then govern'd the Monastery of *Luxeü*, desiring him to make a Journey into *Italy*, and intreat *Colomban* in his Name to return to *France*, where every thing should be done that could make him and his devout Family easy. *Eustasius* acquitted himself of his Commission; and our Saint charged him with a Letter of Thanks and Excuse, in which he gave the King some important Instructions for his Conduct. *Clotaire* receiv'd the Letter with a Joy which shew'd his Value for the Author, was pleased with the Saint's Advice, took the Monastery of *Luxeü* under his immediate Protection, and made considerable Additions to it's Revenue.

Colomban spent the Remainder of his Days in *Lombardy*, where he employ'd both his Tongue and Pen against the *Arians*, with great Success, and died on the twenty first of *November* in the Year 615. He was buried in his Monastery, where his Memory became glorious by several Miracles; and his Name occurs in the *Roman* Martyrologe on the Day of his Death.

Nov. 22

The XXII Day.

St. CECILY, Virgin and MARTYR.

THE Acts of St. *Cecily*'s Martyrdom tell us she was a young Lady of a good Family, a Native of *Rome*, and educated in the Principles of the Christian Religion from her Infancy. Having observed what Commendations the Word of God bestows on Purity and Continence, she made a Vow of Virginity; but her Parents had so little Regard to that Obligation that they forced her to Marry *Valerian*, a young Gentleman, whose Birth and Fortune were at least equal to hers; and who was prevail'd with to renounce Idolatry, and allow our Saint the Liberty of performing what she had promised to the Almighty. *Valerian*'s Conversion was follow'd by that of his Brother *Tiburtius*, which drew the Anger of the Civil Magistrate on them; we have already given an Account of the Martyrdom of *Valerian* and *Tiburtius* on the fourteenth of *April*. The Acts already mention'd place that of our Saint on the twenty second of *November*, in the Reign of *Alexander Severus*, who came to the Throne in the Year 222; 'though several Authors, considering how much that Prince favour'd the Christians, date St. *Cecily*'s Death in the Reign of *Marcus Aurelius* and *Commodus*, joint Emperors from 176 to 180. The *Grecians* are persuaded she suffer'd in *Dioclesian*'s Persecution, and keep her Festival on the same Day with the *Latins*.

St. PHILEMON, and St. APPIA, Disciples to St. PAUL.

PHILEMON was a Citizen of *Colossæ* in *Phrygia*, and converted to the Faith of *Christ*, but by whom and at what Time is uncertain. He was robb'd by *Onesimus* his Slave, who rambled to *Rome* where St. *Paul* persuaded him to a Change of Life and Principles, and sent him back to his Master. The Apostle was then a Prisoner; but had Leave to go abroad chain'd to his Keeper. When *Onesimus* left *Rome*, the Saint sent a Letter by him to *Philemon*, who was so well satisfied with his Slave's last Step, and allow'd the Apostle's Application in his Favour so much Weight, that *Onesimus* was pardon'd and, with his Master's Consent, went back to St. *Paul*.

Phil. v. 2. *Philemon*, as appears from St. *Paul*'s Epistle to that holy Man, had converted his House into a Church; His Faith, and Charity were thought worthy

the

the Commendations of that great Apostle; and from St. *Paul's* telling our Saint he ow'd himself to Him, some have concluded *Philemon* receiv'd the Gospel at his Hands, and was by him taught the first Principles of the Christian Religion.

Nov. 23
v. 5, 6,
7. v. 9.

As all we know of our Saint is included in the History of St. *Paul*, we are left in the Dark as to the Sequel and Conclusion of *Philemon*, who survived his Friend. The *Roman* Martyrologe tells us that he and his Wife *Appia* were put to Death by the Heathens on a Day dedicated to *Diana*, and places their Martyrdom under the Emperor *Nero*. Both the Eastern and Western Churches celebrate their Memory on the twenty second of *November*.

The XXIII Day.

St CLEMENT Pope and MARTYR.

THE Order and Manner, in which the three first Bishops of *Rome*, after the Apostles succeeded to that Post, is still disputed among the Learned; our Reader may see what we have said on that Subject on the twenty sixth of *April*, and twenty third of *September*. *Clement*, one of those early Bishops, was a *Roman* by Birth, and Son of *Faustinus*. He was converted to the Faith by the Apostles, and was so constant in his Attendance on those Evangelical Labourers, so attentive to their Doctrine, and active in assisting them in their Ministry, that the holy Fathers of the first Ages have stiled him the Disciple and Coadjutor of the Apostles, and sometimes given him the Title of Apostle. According to Pope *Zosimus*, he was educated in the School of St. *Peter*, under whose Direction he corrected his former Errors, and made a considerable Progress in the Paths of Truth and Virtue. St. *Chrysostom* is of Opinion that he was afterwards one of the constant Companions of St. *Paul* in his Apostolical Journeys. He is the Person mention'd by that great Apostle in his Epistle to the *Philippians* by the Name of *Clement* among such as had labour'd in the great Work with him, and had their Names recorded in the Book of Life; which Sentiment is authorised by *Origen*, *Epiphanius* and St. *Jerom*; from whose Writings we may therefore conclude that our Saint was at *Philippi* about the Year 52, when St. *Paul* preached in that City; that he was employ'd by that Apostle in the Ministry, and shared his Sufferings for the Faith there.

Cap. 4.
v. 3.

St. Clement, Pope.

Nov. 23. In his Pontificate the Church of *Corinth* was unfortunately disturbed by a scandalous Division among it's Members. This Disorder was occasion'd by a few turbulent Persons, who were bold enough to attack the Clergy, and to stir up the Laity depose some of that Number whose Behaviour was unexceptionable and might justly have secured them from that irregular Attack. This Schism had been the unhappy Cause of much Mischief among the Corinthians, some of whom through Weakness came to doubt of the Truth of their new Religion from the Conduct of those who affected to pass for the most zealous Patrons of it; and the Infidels did not fail to make their Advantage of this Faction, and asperse the whole Church for the Faults of some of it's Members; a mistaken Way of Reasoning that still subsists among the Enemies of our most holy Religion. This gave Occasion to that celebrated Epistle of our Saint to the Faithful of *Corinth*, which the primitive Fathers have commended, and spoke of as excellently adapted to the distress'd State of that Church. All Christian Churches, however divided on other Articles, agree in declaring this Piece one of the most valuable Remains of Ecclesiastical Antiquity, and placing it next to the holy Scriptures; it was universally receiv'd and admired in the first Ages of the Church, and read at the Time of divine Service not only at *Corinth*, but also in several other illustrious Churches even in the fourth Age as we learn from *Eusebius* and St. *Jerom*.

We have still extant a large Fragment of another Letter ascribed by some to the same masterly Hand, which seems to have been an Exhortation to Virtue in general. History has not left us any other undoubted Particulars of St. *Clement*'s Life, nor given us the Circumstances of his Death; which probably happen'd in *Trajan*'s Reign; the common Opinion is that he laid down his Life for the Faith under that Emperor; which according to the best Accounts must have been about the Year 100. The *Roman* Martyrologe mentions our holy Pope on the twenty third of *Noevmber*, and the *Grecian* Menologe on the twenty fourth of the same Month.

✤✤

The XXIV Day.

St. CHRYSOGONUS, Martyr.

ALL we know of St. *Chrysogonus* is to be found in the Acts of St. *Anastasia*'s Martyrdom, of whom we shall speak *December* the twenty fifth. According to that Piece, He had the Care of that Saint from her Infancy, and

from

from her Cradle brought her up in the Fear of God, and the Principles of the Christian Religion, *Chrysogonus* continued his Care of *Anastasia* 'till her Father, who was a Pagan, married her to one of his own blind Religion. That Engagement or the Persecution raised by *Dioclesian* tore him from his holy Pupil; for he was then seized and imprison'd for the Faith; and our Saint is said to have written a Letter to her during their Seperation, which has been preserved and is worthy of the Character of a Martyr, 'though the Learned are not agreed on it's Author.

Dioclesian being at *Aquileia* in 304, we are told he sent an Order to the Prefect of *Rome*, where our Saint was then confin'd, in which that Magistrate was required to send him and some other Prisoners for the same Cause to the Emperor. After several Trials to stagger his Resolution with Threats and and Promises, *Chrysogonus* was condemn'd to lose his Head, and glorified God by Martyrdom. The *Grecians* join our Saint with St. *Anastasia*, and keep their Feastival together on the twenty second of *December*; but the *Latin*'s universally devote the twenty fourth of *November* to his Memory.

St. FLORA, and St. MARY, Martyrs.

THE Saints, of whom we undertake to speak at present, 'though united in their Victory over the Enemy, and the Glory which crowns the Conquerors in that Engagement, were born in different Places, and educated in different Manners. *Flora* was Daughter to a *Mahometan* of *Seville* in *Spain*, a Man of a considerable and antient Family, who afterwards removed to *Corduba*, where the King of the *Saracens* kept his Court. Her Father's Death, which happen'd while she was young, proved an Advantage to her, as it left her entirely in the Disposal of her Mother, who being a Christian educated her in the Principles of Religion, and inspired her with Sentiments of Piety.

Eulogius a Priest of *Corduba*, an Eye Witness of what he relates concerning our Saint, and well inform'd of the rest, tells us he had her Character from her excellent Mother, who assured him that *Flora* was a great Proficient in the spiritual Life, at an Age when nothing is usually thought of, but the World and its Vanities; that her whole Thoughts seem'd turn'd to *Jesus Christ*; her whole Discourse was enflamed with the divine Love; God was her sole Care; her Fasts were rigorous; her Devotion full of Fervour; her Concern for the Poor most surprizing and edifying; and Precepts of the Gospel were her constant Study. Her Brother being a profess'd Enemy to Christianity, with

the

the Addition of a barbarous and savage Temper, *Flora* was for some Time obliged to use no small Caution in the Practice of such Virtues, as must have exposed her to a domestick Persecution at least. She was too zealous to bear this Restraint long; for which Reason about the Year 845, she left *Corduba*, in Company with her Sister, with a Resolution of making her Way to some Christians, where she might serve God with less Danger and more Freedom.

Our Saint's Brother could easily guess at the Motive of her hasty Journey, and in the first Transports of his Rage, used all his Authority and Interest in disturbing the Christians at *Corduba*; several Ecclesiasticks were thrown into Prison on his Information, and strict Enquiries made for the Disciples of *Jesus Christ*. *Flora*, being informed of what had happen'd since her Departure, began to consider herself as the Cause of what the Christians suffer'd at *Corduba*; having an interiour Conviction that God called her to fight for her Faith, she return'd to that City, and made her Way directly to the Persecutors, among whom she found her Brother "If, said our glorious Martyr, I am the Ob-
" ject of your Enquiry, if the Servants of God are tormented on my Ac-
" count, I now freely offer myself to your Disposal. I declare I believe in *Je-*
" *sus Christ*, glory in his Cross, and profess the Doctrine which he taught. This
" now is my Confession; and I hope through the divine Mercy that nothing
" you can do to me, will be able to make me retract or alter it." None of the Company seem'd so much enraged at this Declaration as the Saint's Brother, who, after some Threats, struck her; this violent Proceeding was followed by Attempts of a softer Nature; for he endeavour'd to gain her by Expressions of Concern, and pretended Kindness. Finding her equally insensible to all he could say, he then inform'd against her, and undertook to prove her a Christian before the Judge. He insinuated that *Flora* had been educated in the Religion of *Mahomet*, but had renounced it at the Suggestion of some Christians, who inspired her with the utmost Contempt for the great Prophet. When the Saint was call'd on to answer to the Charge, she declared she had never own'd *Mahomet*, but suck'd the Christian Religion with her Milk, and was so entirely devoted to the Author of that holy Profession, that she had consecrated her Virginity to him. The Judge, incensed at these Words, order'd her to be seiz'd by the Executioners, and Whips to be laid on her Head, which tore the Skin and Hair off, and cover'd her with Blood.

The *Mahometan* Magistrate, finding her persist in confessing *Jesus Christ*, deliver'd her into her Brother's Hands, with Directions to take Care of her, and

and instruct her in what he called the true Religion. *Flora* was conducted to Nov. 24 her Brother's House, where nothing was forgot that might influence her to the proposed Change; but as soon as she was able to move, she made her Escape over a Wall in the Night, and took Shelter in the House of a Christian, where she lay some Time undiscover'd, and then retired to a small Vilage near *Martos*, then call'd *Tucci*, in *Andaloufia*, where she was join'd by her Sister, who staid with her 'till her Martyrdom. *Eulogius*, the Author of this Account, visited her in that Place, and had the Satisfaction of kissing the Marks of the Wounds which she had received for *Jesus Christ*.

Mary was Daughter to an honest Tradesman at *Nieble* in *Estramadura*, who being a Christian had married a *Mahometan*, but converted her to the Faith, 'though with much Difficulty. The Badness of the Times obliged them to leave their own Country; and, after several Attempts to settle elsewhere, they resolved to stay at *Frognan*, about four Leagues West of *Corduba*; where they made a poor Shift to live, and educate our Saint and her Brother, in Sentiments of Piety. They lost their Mother soon after their Arrival in that Country, whereupon their Father provided for the Security of his Children by placing them in a Monastery. *Mary* spent several Years in that Religious Retreat, an edifying Patern of Humility, Obedience, holy Simplicity, and Fervour to the whole Community.

In the Year 851, the Persecution was renewed by *Abderrama* King of the *Saracens* in *Spain*, and *Walabonzus*, *Mary*'s Brother, was one of those who fell Victims to the Rage of the Infidels on that Occasion. *Mary*, hearing of his Victory, and full of a generous Confusion at being left behind by one so much younger than herself, gave a free Loose to her Grief, which proceeded not so much from the Loss of her Brother, as her not being allow'd to enjoy the Happiness, then in his Possession. This was the Saint's Disposition, when a Woman of great Piety, assured her she had been favour'd with a Vision, in which *Walabonzus* order'd her to tell his Sister she should shortly follow him, and die in the Manner she wished.

Mary, inflamed with an ardent Desire of Martyrdom, and depending on the Truth of this Vision, left the Monastery, and hastned to *Corduba*, where she was assured she could not remain long unobserv'd. Going into a Church in that City, she found St. *Flora*, who had left her Retreat on the same Motive, and was there recommending herself to the Author, and Rewarder of such Victories as Christians then gain'd over Infidels. Upon conversing together, and finding they acted on the same heroick Principles, and proposed the same glorious End of their Labours, they agreed to go together, and declare

Nov. 24 clare their Faith before the Judge. *Flora*, fortified with what she had formerly suffer'd for the Name of *Christ*, spoke first to the Magistrate; put him in Mind of his Cruelty to her five or six Years before; own'd and condemned her own Cowardice in making her Escape, instead of returning to the Field of Battle; repeated her former Protestations; and declared she look'd on *Mahomet* as no better than a false Prophet, an Adulterer, and a Magician.

Flora's Speech ending in that severe, 'though just, Reflection on the Impostor, *Mary* address'd herself to the Judge, and let him know she was Sister to *Walabonzus*, who was put to Death for declaring his Sentiments of *Mahomet* and his deluded Followers; to which she added that her Thoughts of their pretended Prophet were exactly the same, and that she was no less united in Faith than Blood with that holy Martyr. The Judge, surprized and enraged at their Boldness, committed them to a close Prison, with strict Orders to admit none to see them, but such Agents of the Devil as he should direct to employ their whole Skill in perverting them. The divine Grace carried them through all the Snares laid for their Souls; and the Judge, finding them inflexible, sentenced them to lose ther Heads, which was executed accordingly. Their Bodies remain'd that Day and the following Night exposed to the Beasts and Birds, and were next Morning thrown into the River; that of *Mary* was afterwards taken up, and buried in the Convent; but that of *Flora* was never discover'd, as we can learn; but the Heads were carried to St. *Acisilus*'s Church in *Corduba*. The twenty fourth of *November*, the Day of their Martyrdom, is that on which the *Roman* Martyrologe places their Festival.

The XXV Day.

St. CATHARINE *Virgin and* MARTYR.

THE Christians of *Arabia*, then under the *Mahometan* Yoke, discovering a dead Body on Mount *Sina* towards the Close of the eighth Century, supposed it once animated with the Soul of a Martyr, and expressed their Veneration for the Sufferer, who, as we are told, proved to be St. *Catharine*, a holy Virgin who had suffer'd Martyrdom in the fourth Century, at or near *Alexandria* the Metropolis of *Egypt*. The History of her Life gives her the Character of great Learning, and introduces her disputing with, and confounding the ablest Philosophers of that City, in Defence of the Christian Religion. Both the *Greek* and *Latin* Churches keep her Festival on the twenty fifth of *November*.

Nov. 25

St. MOSES *Martyr*, and St. MAXIMUS and other *Confessors*.

IN the Pontificate of *Fabian*, *Moses* was look'd on as the chief Ornament of the *Roman* Clergy; and the Character of *Maximus* was not much less considerable at that Time. They were both Priests, and did honour to that Character by the Sanctity of their Lives, and their Zeal for the Glory of *Jesus Christ*, and the Salvation of their Neighbour. The Persecution rais'd by the Emperor *Decius*, toward the close of the Year 249, prov'd a favourable Opportunity for shewing their Fidelity and Constancy. They were seized and thrown into Prison immediatly after the Death of the aforesaid Pope, in Company with several other illustrious Confessors. Those excellent Persons, with *Moses* at their Head, bore up bravely against the first Efforts of the Enemy, and their Behaviour went a great Way toward fortifying the Christians at *Rome* in the Faith, and inspiring them with a fixt Resolution of suffering any Thing in its Defence.

The Confessors were some Time confin'd, without any other Punishment but the Loss of their Liberty, and the Inconveniencies inseparable from a Jayl; as appears from a Letter written in the Name of that glorious Company to St. *Cyprian* Bishop of *Carthage*, in Answer to one from that great and holy Prelate. Not long after the Date of that Epistle, they were put to severe Trials, and felt the Force of a barbarous Variety of Torments; on which Occasion, *Maximus* and *Urban* triumph'd twice over the Malice of their Persecutors. Several Proposals were made for their Enlargement, a whole Year together; but, as Conformity to the Idolatrous Worship was always one, they strenuously refused to purchase their Liberty at the Expence of their Fidelity to *Jesus Christ*. For which Reason, St. *Cyprian* writing to them toward the End of the Year 250, observes, that every Time they declined the profer'd Favour, they made a fresh Confession of their Faith.

It appears from this Letter, and that mention'd before, that our holy Confessors and St. *Cyprian* were closely united in Sentiments and Affections. That worthy Prelate seems to feel the Weight of their Chains, and bear a considerable Share in their Sufferings; he recommended them to the divine Protection in his private Devotions; and order'd them to be remember'd in a particular Manner at the Altar. The Confessors at *Rome* made all the Return in ther Power for the Charity and Affection of that Saint, interested themselves in every Thing where he or his Flock was concern'd, and omitted no Opportunity of expressing their Veneration for him. Their Conduct in regard to such as had apostatiz'd in the Time of Persecution, was an excellent Proof of this Observation. Those unfortunate Persons, sensible of their Fault, and the Danger of their Situation, while excluded from the Church, were very pressing to be admitted to Communion with the Faithful without the least Delay. The Confessors at *Carthage* yielded so far to their Importunities and Tears, as to solicit their Reception very warmly, to the manifest Prejudice of Ecclesiastical Discipline. *Moses* and *Maximus*, with other Confessors, at *Rome* wrote to those of *Carthage*, and in very strong Terms let them know the pernicious Consequences of their mistaken Compassion.

In the Year 251, the illustrious Prisoners of *Jesus Christ* received their Liberty, of which some did not make so good Use, as they had done of their Chains; being imposed on by the artful Discourses of *Novatus* a Priest of *Carthage* then at *Rome*, and very active in disturbing the Church of that City. That factious Ecclesiastick was the great Promoter, or rather the principal Author of *Novatian*'s Schism, spoken of at large in our Account of St. *Cornelius, September* the sixteenth. The chief Article urged by the Antipope against that holy Bishop to make him odious was his too great Facility in receiving those who had fallen in the late Persecution; and *Novatus*, the Intruder's indefatigable Agent, undertook to talk to the Confessors on that Subject, and bring them over to his Party. *Maximus* and several others were decoy'd into the Schism, by a specious Profession of Zeal for Church Discipline. *Moses* was one of those who stood his Ground, was Proof against all their Solicitations, exerted himself vigorously for the Unity of the Church, declared he would not hold Communion with *Novatian* and his Adherents; and was prticularly active in discovering and defeating the Artifices of that Invader. The Persecution, 'though perhaps not so violent as when *Decius* was at *Rome*, was continued, and took off St *Moses* toward the Close of the Year 251. Pope *Cornelius* in an Epistle to St. *Cyprian*, is very large in the Commendation of his Behaviour under the Hands of the Executioners, and his Name occurs on the twenty fifth of *November* in the *Roman* Martyrologe.

The

The Confessors continued some Time in their Infatuation, and supported Nov. 25 Novatian's Title with much Zeal 'till St. Cyprian's Letters and his Treatise of the Unity of the Church opened their Eyes; and the Grace of God, who saw the Sincerity of their Hearts, dissolved the Charm, and laid open to their View the black Designs, Perjury, and Ambition of the Anti-pope. *Maximus, Urban, Sidonius,* and *Macarius,* the Chief of those who had been imposed on by *Novatian,* apply'd to *Cornelius,* acknowledg'd his Title to the See of *Rome,* and desired to be received to his Communion. Upon which, the holy Pope conven'd his Clergy to consider of the Petition; and the Confessors, attended by great Numbers who had been led away by their Example or Persuasion, and were desirous of following them back to the Church, appear'd before that reverend Assembly, own'd their Fault with great Humility and Compunction, and begg'd their Conduct during the Schism might be forgot. This Request was easily granted; and the News of their Return being communicated to the People, they ran in Crouds to give publick Thanks for the Recovery of those excellent Members of the Church, and embraced the Confessors with the same Transports of Joy, as if they had been just then set at Liberty. *Cornelius* gave St. *Cyprian* an Account of his whole Proceedings in this Affair; to which the latter replyed that, the Reunion of the Confessors had given the Church of *Africa,* sensible Pleasure, not only as that Act restored the Glory of their Confession which they had lost by engaging in Schism, but as their Example could not fail of giving a deadly Blow to the Schism itself. The Names of the four illustrious Penitents do not occur in any Martyrologe; but, as their History had some Connexion with that of St. *Moses,* and the Return of *Maximus* and his Companions was celebrated by the whole Catholick Church, as a publick Blessing, we thought an Account of their Conversion would be both edifying and instuctive.

The XXVI Day.

St. PETER Bishop of *Alexandria,* MARTYR.

*P*ETER succeeded *Theonas* in the See of *Alexandria,* in the Year 300, and, 'though the Church of that City had been govern'd by several very learned and holy Bishops, our Saint equall'd most of them in the former Advantage,

Nov. 26 vantage, and was inferior to none in the latter. St. *Jerom* and *Eusebius* reckon him the sixteenth Bishop of *Alexandria* after the Evangelical Founder of that Church. The Historian in his Commendation observes that the Fervour of his Piety, and Rigour of his Penance increas'd with the Calamities of the Church. This appears to have been his just Character from his Conduct in *Dioclesian*'s Persecution, which began three Years after his Promotion. That violent Storm, which affrighted and disheartned several Bishops and inferiour Ministers of the Church, did but awaken his Attention, inflame his Charity, and inspire him with fresh Vigour. He on all Occasions gave incontestable Proofs of his Concern for the Interest of the whole Church, and during the Time of the Persecution took a particular Care of those Parts of it under his Inspection, which extended to *Egypt*, *Thebais*, and *Libya*.

All under our Saint's Direction did not make the same Advantage of his excellent Instructions and Example. The Persecution had raged above three Years, and several within his Jurisdiction had renounced the Faith, during that Calamity; some had endured severe Torments from the Hands of the Pagans, but, 'though they enter'd the Combat with good Dispositions, and excellent Resolutions, had been weak enough to yield at last: others had been imprison'd, and bore the Loss of their Liberty, and all the Inconveniencies of a Jayl with true Christian Courage, but deserted their Colours when the Battle was near: a third Sort prevented the Enquiries of the Persecutors, and ran over to the Enemy, without suffering any Thing for the Faith. Some had sent Heathens to sacrifice in their Name, or had accepted of Attestations from the Magistrates setting forth that they had complied with the Imperial Edict, 'though in Reality they had not; these were look'd on however as a sort of Apostates, because these Artifices had drawn in several to Acts of Idolatry, who imagin'd they had really conformed. These and some other Degrees of Apostasy were distinctly consider'd by the holy Bishop of *Alexandria*, and a proper Penance prescribed for each.

Among those who fell during that Storm, none was more considerable than *Meletius* Bishop of *Lycopolis* in *Thebais*. That Prelate was charged with several Crimes, but Apostasy was the chief Article alledged against him. St. *Peter* called a Council, which after a full Hearing of the Matter, and finding *Meletius* guilty, deposed him. The Apostate had not Humility enough to submit to that canonical Sentence, or make a regular Appeal to some other Council, but immediatly headed a discontented Party, which was ready
to

St. Peter *Bishop Martyr &c.*

to follow him to any Lengths, declared against the holy Bishop of *Alexan-* Nov. 26
dria, and form'd a Schism, which subsisted above 150 Years. To justify this
extraordinary Step, he published several Calumnies against our Saint and his
Council, and declared to the whole World, that he had left that Prelate's
Communion, because he was too indulgent to those who had fallen. From
that Time *Meletius* laid several Snares for *Peter*'s Life, which were render'd
ineffectual by an overruling Providence. He disturb'd the whole Church of
Egypt with his factious and violent Proceedings; for he had the Assurance
to infringe our Saint's Patriarchal Authority, ordain Bishops within his Jurisdiction, and even place one in the Metropolitan See. The Historian *Sozomen*
tells us, these Usurpations were carried on with less Interruption and Opposiriti-
on, because the Bishop of *Alexandria* was obliged to retire, to avoid the Fury of
the Persecution. *Arius*, whose Name became famous some Years after, on
an Account well known to the whole World, was then among the Clergy
of *Alexandria*, and espoused *Meletius*'s Cause as soon as the Breach was open,
but quitted the Party after some Time; and *Peter* was so well satisfy'd of the
Sincerity of his Repentance, that he ordain'd him Deacon. *Arius* had not
been long in Possession of that Character, when he return'd to the *Meletians*,
and pretended to blame our Saint for excommunicating the Schismaticks,
and forbidding them to baptize. The holy Bishop convinc'd that that turbulent Ecclesiastick had no other View in this Complaint, than to foment
Divisions, and disturb the Peace of the Church, excommunicated him, and
could never be prevail'd with to revoke that Sentence.

Maximin Daia, Cesar in the East, renew'd the Persecution in 311, which
had been considerably abated by a Letter written the same Year by the
Emperor *Galerius* in Favour of the Christians. This was the Time design'd
by divine Providence, for crowning St. *Peter*'s Labours in the most glorious
Manner. The holy Prelate was seiz'd when he least expected it, and beheaded
without being told his Crime; 'though every one knew what made him odious
to the Pagans. His Death is usually dated on the twenty fifth of *November* but
the twenty sixth of the same Month is dedicated to his Memory by the *Latin* Church.

The XXVII Day
MAXIMUS *Bishop of* RIEZ.

MAXIMUS a Native of *Provence* in *France*, was born near *Digne*, toward the Year 380. His Parents, who profess'd the Christian Religion,
and lived up to its Principles, saw him baptized in his Infancy, and were
particularly

particularly careful of his Education. Their Endeavours on that Head succeeded to their Wish; *Maximus* even in his Childhood was an excellent Example of profound Humility, and an absolute Conquest of his Passions; and his Virtue encreased with his Years. He was affable and courteous to all, full of Compassion for the Miserable, liberal to the Poor, remarkable for Sobriety, and so charm'd with the heavenly Advantages of Chastity, that he made a Resolution of observing a perpetual Continence. His Mind and Heart were so entirely enaged by more valuable Objects that he trampled on the Honours and Pleasures, which amuse and employ the greatest Part of Mankind; and knew no other Use of Riches but that of relieving *Jesus Christ* in the Person of his distressed Members. He remain'd some Years in the World without living by it's Maxims or seeming to belong to it; and, 'though among his Friends and in his own Country, had no more Relish for his Situation than if he had been in Exile, and surrounded by Strangers. At last he broke the Chain which seem'd to fix him to the World, and retired to the Monastery of *Lerins*, so often mention'd in the Course of this Work, where his Virtues made him appear to Advantage, 'though in a Family of Saints.

Honoratus, the Founder of that excellent Nursery of Piety and Learning being in the Year 426 made Bishop of *Arles* no one was thought so worthy to succeed him in the Government of that House as *Maximus*, who was accordingly chosen unanimously. The new Abbot behaved himself so prudently in that Station, that the Monks scarce felt the Severities of the Rule, and obey'd with Cheefulness and Alacrity. His charitable Labours were not confined to the Limits of his Monastery, but extending to such as were not immediately under his Care, made several Converts, some of whom chose to end their Days at *Lerins*. The Gift of Miracles, with which he was favour'd, contributed very much to the Success of his Endeavours in that Way, and drew great Crouds to his Monastery from the Continent, which broke in on his Retirement, and oblig'd him to quit the House, and retire into a Forest in the Island, where he was discover'd in a few Days, and brought back to his Monastery.

Maximus had spent about seven Years at the Head of that holy Community, when the See of *Riez* in *Provence* became vacant, and those concern'd in providing a Successor immediately pitched on the Abbot of *Lerins*. They then gave the neighbouring Bishops an Account of their Choice, and deputed proper Persons to the Saint to acquaint him with the Matter, and press his Compliance. Upon the first News of their Proceedings *Maximus* went privately aboard a small Vessel, and made his Way to the Coast of *Italy*, where he hoped he might be secure; but he was mistaken; for either the Reputation of his Miracles, or the providential Falseness of some

trusted

trusted with the Secret, betray'd him. He was seized, carried to *Riez*, and Nov. 27 consecrated there amidst the loud Acclamations of the People. If the Episcopal Character, or the Grace receiv'd at his Consecration did not encrease the Number of our Saint's Virtues, his present Situation gave them a greater Lustre, and render'd them more generally useful. His Life at *Riez* was exactly the same as at *Lerins*; his Humility in that exalted Station was not different from what he had practised in his Cloister; he still retain'd the same Love of Poverty, the same Spirit of Penance, and the same Indifference to the World and it's Enjoyments, as when particularly obliged to those Virtues by his State of Life. His Patience and Charity now found more Employment than ever; for he was under an Obligation of being at once the Physician, the Judge, and the Pastor of a numerous People, all which Characters he fill'd in the most edifying Manner.

Our holy Bishop had a considerable Share in the Decisions of all the Provincial Councils held in that Part of *France* in his Time; and it is not easy to determine whether his Peity or Capacity was more conspicuous on those Occasions. After twenty seven Years spent thus in the Service of the Church, *Maximus* received the Reward of his Labours on the twenty seventh of *November*, and was buried in S. *Peter*'s Church, which he built. His Funeral was attended by a prodigious Concourse of People from all Parts, some of whom came to glorify God in his Servant, others to ask Favours and Blessings by his powerful Intercession.

St. VIRGILIUS, Bishop of SALTZBOURG.

*V*IRGILIUS was born in *Ireland*, at the Beginning of the VIII Century, and had the Advantage of rich and virtuous Parents, who gave him a pious and liberal Education; their Care in that Particular succeeded so well that he was look'd on as one of the most learned of his Country in that Age; but his Proficency in Virtue was much more valuable. He was courteous, obliging, modest and humble, and thus gain'd the Affections of all who knew him.

Virgilius went to *France*, when about thirty Years old; and, as he was then in Priest's Orders, it is probable his Business there was to find an Opportunity to serve God and the Church in that Character. By the Assistance of *Charles Martel Maire* of the Palace in *France* the evangelical Labourers had free Access to *Germany*; and the Reputation, and Example of St. *Boniface* and other Apostolical Missionaries drew great Numbers thither, who engaged in the same glorious Work, among whom were our Saint and his Countryman *Sidonius*, who employ'd their Zeal and Charity in *Bavaria*

Nov. 27 under Duke *Odilo*. After some Time spent there *Virgilus* was made Abbot of a Monastery at *Saltzbourg* founded by St. *Rupert*, first Bishop of that City about thirty Years before. The necessary Obligations of that Post did not divert our Saint from continuing to preach the Gospel in several Parts of *Bavaria*. In those Apostolical Journies he found great Numbers of Christians, who had been baptized by a Priest so little versed in the *Latin* Tongue that he gave a wrong Termination to some of the Words which compose the Form of that Sacrament. This Blunder produced a Dispute about the Validity of Baptism thus conferr'd; and St. *Boniface* was of Opinion that the Ceremony ought to be repeated; whereupon *Virgilus* and his Companion, appplied to the holy See for a Resolution of this Difficulty. *Zachary*, then in S. *Peter*'s Chair, wrote to *Boniface* on that Subject and declared the Baptism in Question valid, because the Priest's Intention was good, his Faith in the holy Trinity orthodox, and the Alteration complain'd of in the Form merely literal.

In the Year 752 *Pepin*, Maire of the Palace, was chosen King of *France* and consecrated by St. *Boniface*; and, our Saint who was endeavouring the Conversion of Infidels and Sinners with his usual Activity, imagining the young Duke of *Bavaria*'s Protection in that Work not sufficient, resolved to pay his Compliments to the new King, and beg his Assistance, when necessary. That Prince receiv'd him very graciously, and finding him a Man of great Virtue and more Learning than he had usually met with, detain'd him at his Court almost two Years for the Satisfaction of his edifying and instructive Conversation. *Pepin* had wore the Crown of *France* about twelve Years when he gave a publick Proof of his Regard for our Saint by naming him to the See of *Saltzbourg*, vacant by the Death of *John*, who had likewise been Abbot of the same Monastery, which own'd *Virgilus* for it's Superior. The Saint was obliged to accept of the Title, and Inspection of the Church of *Saltzbourg*; but it was near two Years before the neighbouring Prelates and People could prevail with him to receive the Episcopal Character.

Virgilius discharged all the Duties of his Station with great Exactness, was particularly courageous in defending the Rights of his Church on all Occasions, and at the same Time as active in maintaining and enforcing Ecclesiastical Discipline. His Pastoral Charity was not to be confined within the Limits of one Diocese; the *Sclavonians* were allow'd a Share in his Thoughts and Labours. *Chetimar*, who commanded those in *Carinthia*, having been initiated in the Faith by Baptism, was so devoted to our Saint as to do nothing of Consequence without his Advice; and *Virgilius* supplied him with Priests from his Monastery and Seminary, who were employ'd in Instructing the Subjects of that Prince. *Watung*, the worthy Successor of Duke *Chetimar*, receiv'd the Priests and others, whom our Saint sent into *Carinthia*, as favourably as his Predecessor had done; and the Progress which the Gospel made in their Hands has procured *Virgilus* the Title of Apostle of *Carinthia*.

The holy Bishop had sat about fourteen Years in the See of *Salatzbourg*, when his Zeal prompted him to visit his whole Diocese, and endeavour the total Extirpation of Idolatry among his People and others who had receiv'd some Light by his Means. *Carinthia* was not forgot on this Occasion; he consecrated several Churches, ordain'd some Ecclesiasticks in that Dukedom, and continued his Journey to the most remote Corners of *Sclavonia*. At his Return to *Saltzbourg* he was taken ill, and died in a few Days, on the twenty seventh of *November*, 780. His Body was buried in S *Peter*'s Church, and the Saint canonized by Pope *Gregory* IX.

The XXVIII Day.
St. STEPHEN, MARTYR.

THE holy Man, whose Life and Sufferings we venerate this Day, was born at *Constantinople* in the Beginning of the VIII Century; and dedicated to God in a particular Manner by his Parents as soon as he came into the World. When *Stephen* was thought capable of receiving Instructions, he was provided with proper Masters and inured to pious Sentiments from his Infancy. The Saint's Inclination leading him to prefer the holy Scripture to all other Books, he undertook to treasure up the Maxims of those sacred Writings in his Memory; and St. *John Chrysostom*'s Works were in his Opinion the most valuable Pieces of sacred Antiquity.

While our Saint was employ'd in the Improvement of his Mind, and acquiring a Stock of Virtue sufficient to carry him through all the Troubles and Persecutions, which Providence design'd for him, *Leo* the *Isaurian* form'd an impious Project for disturbing the Peace of the Church, by opposing the Respect paid by the Faithful to the Images of *Jesus Christ* and his Saints; by which they meant no more than to adore their Saviour in the Presence of what presented him to their View, and revived the Memory of his Sufferings; and honour those whom the divine Grace had raised to an eminent Degree of Sanctity while the Images of those great Servants of God were before their Eyes. This was the Practice of the Church in those early Times, which the Council of *Trent* has explain'd in the twenty fifth, and last Session in the following Words. " *The Images of* Christ, *the Blessed Virgin and other*
" *Saints are to be had and retain'd, particularly in Churches*; *and due Honour*
" *and Veneration to be given them. Not that we believe any Divinity or Virtue*
" *lodged in them, which can challenge Worship, or that we are to make any*
" *Petitions to them; or place our Confidence in Images, like the Heathens of old*
" who

Nov. 28

p. 134.

" *who put their Hope in Idols: but because the Honour, done to them, is re-*
" *ferr'd to the Prototypes, which they represent; so that when we kiss such Ima-*
" *ges, and kneel before them bear-headed, we adore* Chrift, *and venerate his*
" *Saints, whose Likeness they bear.*

The Emperor began the Persecution with deposing *German* Patriarch of *Constantinople*, who undertook the Defence of holy Images against that Prince's first Attack. Several Catholicks left the City, and retired into distant Provinces, where they hoped the Storm would not reach them; our Saint's Parents were of that Number; but before they provided thus for their own Security they thought themselves obliged to dispose of their Son in a Way suitable to his pious Inclinations, and their own Views in his Education. He was placed in a Monastery two or three Leagues from *Chalcedon*, which bore the Name of *Auxentius*, it's holy Founder; the Abbot of that House made no Difficulty of receiving him, and after some Days spent in giving him a general Idea of the Labours, and Hardships of a Monastick Life, cut his Hair, and gave him the Habit, though then but sixteen Years old.

Stephen enter'd into all the penitential Exercises of the Community with incredible Ardour, and his first Employment was to fetch in the daily Provisions for the Monastery. The Death of his Father, which happen'd some Years after, obliged him to make a Journey to *Constantinople*. When he had paid his last Duties to the Deceased, he sold his whole Fortune, gave the Money to the Poor, carried his Mother and one of his Sisters into *Bithynia*, and with the Advice and Assistance of his Superior placed them in a Monastery. That holy Abbot, drawing near his End, and being well assured that the Voices of the whole Community would fall on *Stephen* after his Decease, sent for him and gave him some Instructions in Relation to that Post. *John*'s Eyes were no sooner closed than the whole Body of Monks was unanimous in placing *Stephen* at their Head, 'though then but thirty Years old.

The Monastery of *Auxentius* was only a Number of small Cells scatter'd up and down the Mountain, one of the highest in that Province; and the new Abbot succeeded his Predecessor in a Cave on the Summit, where he join'd Labour with his Prayer, employ'd himself in such Works as gave little or no Interruption to his Conversation with God, and thus not only avoided being burthensome to others, but was enabled to relieve the Poor. The Lustre of our Saint's Virtue, his Application to Devotion, and Penance, and the Prudence of his Conduct engaged great Numbers to resort to him, and beg to be admitted into his religious Family, which soon grew very large. After some Years spent in the Government of his Solitaries, he resign'd his Place to *Marinus*, being resolved on a closer Retreat than was compatible with that Post, and the Practice of such Austerities, as he would not undertake to prescribe to others. In this View he built himself a Cell on the Top of of the Mountain much narrower than his Cave, and so streight every Way that it was impossible for him to lie or stand at his Ease. *Stephen* was forty two Years old when he shut himself up in this Sepulchre; but no Place could screen him from the publick View; the Reputation of his Sanctity diffused itself through the whole Country, and drew great Crouds who desired to see and hear him. *Ann*, a young Widow of Quality, was one of that Number, and let the Saint know her Inclinations to a Monastick Life; whereupon *Stephen* gave her all necessary Instructions on that Head, and desired she would consider the Danger of deferring the Execution of her good Designs, which she had Reason to believe inspired by God. The Lady, who heard him as an Oracle, and Interpreter of the divine Will, went immediately, sold her whole Estate, distributed Part of the Purchase among the Poor, took her Leave of her Friends, made a second Visit to the Saint, and let him know she had reserved a considerable Sum. *Stephen* reprimanded her severely for the Reserve, and assured her that renouncing her Estate by Halves would never entitle her to the Character of a complete Servant of *Jesus Christ*. The Lady, extremely surprized, answer'd that what she had done in that Case did not proceed from Avarice, but a Desire of leaving the Disposal of the said Sum to his Discretion. The Saint then told her he never undertook to do Charity with other People's Money; but directed her to some Places in the Neighbourhood where she might lay it out to the Advantage of her Soul; at her Return he gave her the Monastick Habit, and sent her to a House which he had built for Women at the Foot of his Mountain, and was govern'd by a Superior of the same Sex, under his Direction.

Constantine Copronymus, who succeeded his Father *Leo*, carrying on the impious War against holy Images with a Vigour, at least, equal to that of his Predecessor, levell'd his Malice chiefly against the Monks, whom he fear'd as the most resolute in maintaining the Catholick Practice in that Particular. Having procured the Condemnation of the Use of Images in Churches, and other Places of Devotion in a Council of Bishops ready to execute whatever he should direct, he endeavour'd to engage our Saint's Subscription to that Decision; for he was sensible of the Influence of his Example, and the Weight which his known Sanctity gave to all his Actions. *Callistus*, a Patrician, being dispatched to *Stephen* on that Errand, used all the Arts in his Power to prevail with the Saint to close in with the Emperor, and consent to the Acts of the pack'd Assembly already mention'd, and was excellently qualified for that Task, being Master of a strong and persuasive Eloquence; but *Stephen* was proof against the Attack, and the Patrician was obliged to return full of Confusion at a Miscarriage where he was sanguine enough to depend on Success. *Constantine*, incensed at our Saint's Answer, as reported by *Callistus*, sent him back to St. *Auxentius*'s, attended by a Party of Soldiers

Nov. 28 with Directions to drag him out of his Cell, carry him to the Monastery at the Foot of the Mountain, and keep him Prisoner there 'till farther Orders. The Soldiers, who executed their Commission with a barbarous Punctuality, found him so wasted with Fasting, and his Limbs so much weaken'd by the Streightness of his Cell, that they were obliged to carry him on their Shoulders.

Callistus, who had promised the Emperor not to quit the Enterprize 'till he had reduced the Saint to a Compliance with his Will, or form'd an Accusation against him which should disgrace him and destroy his Authority in the World, finding him invincible, had Recourse to other Means, and endeavour'd to suborn Witnesses against him. In this View he address'd himself to *Sergius*, one of our Saint's Disciples, gave him a retaining Fee, and promised him a much larger Sum upon performing the diabolical Work. *Sergius*, dazzled with the Charms of Money and the Prospect of ingratiating himself with *Constantine*, left his Monastery, and with the Assistance of an Officer of the Costoms at *Nicomedia*, drew up a scandalous Libel, in which *Stephen* was charged with calling the Emperor Heretick and Tyrant; and engaged one of *Ann*'s Servants to accuse the Saint of a criminal Conversation with that virtuous Lady. These and several other Articles were forged against the Saint, and transmitted to the Emperor, then in *Scythia*; who mmediatly sent Orders to his Lieutenant at *Constantinople* for sending him the Lady mention'd in the Charge. The Soldiers, who assisted that Officer in the Execution of his Commission, committed several Extravagancies in the Monastery, 'till the Abbess deliver'd the supposed Criminal into their Hands. They conducted her to the imperial Camp; where *Constantine* let her know he had no Doubt of what he had heard to her Disadvantage, but desired to have the whole Affair from her own Mouth, and would fain know what Means the detestable Hypocrite had inveigled her into her present State, for his own infamous Use. The holy Woman then declared she was ready to suffer the utmost Consequences of that Prince's Anger, rather than violate the Truth, and accuse a Man, who had been so useful to her in her spiritual Concerns. The Emperor, shock'd and confounded at this unexpected Reply, deferr'd a farther Examination of the Affair to a more convenient Opportunity, and detain'd the Lady 'till his Return to the imperial City; where he threw her into Prison, and assured her she should not leave that Place, 'till she came to a Resolution of renouncing the Monastick State, and her Friendship with him who had decoy'd her into it. After several repeated Attempts to make her own the pretended Crime, as an Article against our Saint, the Emperor order'd her to be severely whipp'd; but she still persisted in declaring *Stephen* an innocent and holy Person; whereupon she was confined to one of the Monasteries in *Constantinople* where it is supposed she was starved to Death.

Constantine, bent on the Ruin of our Saint, was always employ'd in inventing

venting some new Method of making him appear criminal. To this End Nov. 28 he engaged *George*, a young Courtier, in whom he could confide, to make a Journey into *Bithynia*, perswade *Stephen* to receive him into his Community, and return to *Constantinople*, as soon as he had carried his Point. *George*, having receiv'd Instructions for his Behaviour, promis'd a punctual Compliance with each Particular. Reaching the Mountain, he hid himself among the Bushes 'till toward Midnight, and then made to the Monastery, and in a most pitieus Tone, begg'd to be saved from the wild Beasts, and consider'd as an Object of their just Compassion, who had lost his Way. The Story of his Distress, thus pathetically deliver'd, could not but move a Person of so much Tenderness and Charity as our Saint, who thereupon sent out one of his Monks to bring him in. As soon as the Impostor enter'd the House, he threw himself at the Abbot's Feet begg'd his Blessing, declared he belong'd to the Court, that he and his Companions, by an unhappy Complaisance for their Sovereign's Sentiments, had been very near falling into *Judaism*, that God had been graciously pleas'd to let him see his Danger, and conducted him to that Place, where he desired he might be admitted among the Saint's Disciples. *Stephen*, suspecting nothing of this Artifice, told him with his usual Simplicity, that since the Emperor had expresly forbid admitting Novices, he could not think it safe or prudent to receive him. *George* then conjur'd him to consider the Value of a Soul, and declared that if his was lost by returning to the World, the Saint should answer for it at the last Day. *Stephen*, full of Zeal for the Salvation of his Neighbour, being thus warmly press'd, resolv'd to postpone all human Considerations, and expose himself to any temporal Danger, rather than hazard the loss of a Soul, and gave him the Habit. *George* spent three Days in the Monastery of St. *Auxentius*, during which Time the Emperor receiv'd an exact Account of every Step he took in this treacherous Affair. That artful Prince began now to play his Part; he assembled the People in the Amphitheatre, declaim'd loudly against the Monks in general, as a pestilent and rebellious Set of Men, and with a well acted Concern complain'd of *Stephen's* Insolence, who had corrupted all his Courtiers, and forced his Favourite *George*, into his Monastery. In the mean Time that hypocritical Tool of his Masters Passions came back, according to his Directions, in the Monastick Habit; and the next Day, the People being conven'd in the Amphitheatre for that Purpose, *Constantine* produced him in that Dress, which had the desired Effect; *Stephen* and the whole Body of Monks were abused in very gross Terms, and the seemingly injured Courtier stripp'd of the detested Habit, and handsomely rewarded for his dexterous Management of this hellish Contrivance.

The Emperor sent a Party of Soldiers to Mount S. *Auxentius* with Orders to drive away the religious Inhabitants of that Desart; in Execution of which Commission

Nov. 28 Commiſſion our Saint's Diſciples were forced from the Place, and their Monaſtery burnt down to the Ground. *Stephen* was dragg'd out of his Cell, inſulted, beaten unmercifully, put on board of a ſmall Veſſel in the Port of *Chalcedon*, and carried to a Monaſtery at *Chryſopolis*, near *Conſtantine*; where he was by the Emperor's Order viſited by five of thoſe Biſhops, who had join'd in condemning the Uſe of holy Images in the falſe Council of *Conſtantinople*, and were accompanied on this Occaſion by the Patrician *Calliſtus*, a Secretary of State, and another Officer. *Theodoſius*, Biſhop of *Epheſus*, open'd the Conference in civil and reſpectful Terms, to which the Saint replied with a Mixture of Sweetneſs and Strength, which convince without diſpleaſing reaſonable Perſons. *Conſtantine*, Biſhop of *Nicomedia*, had no Title to that Character; he aroſe from his Seat and kick'd our Saint in the Face as he ſat on the Ground, which encouraged one of the Guards to inſult and ſtrike him. *Calliſtus*, 'though a violent Stickler of the Party, could not but interpoſe his Authority for ſilencing and ſeizing the furious Prelate, and then let *Stephen* know the Diſpute might be ſoon ended by his ſubſcribing to the Decrees of the late Council; which too would be the only Means for ſaving his Life, forfeited by Diſobedience to his imperial Majeſty. The Saint then made ſome Remarks on the impious Doctrine deliver'd by that pretended Council; which, as he ſaid, deſerved no better Name than that of a pack'd Aſſembly, aſſuming the Title of Œcumenical, 'though it was but too well known that neither the Biſhop of *Rome*, nor the Patriarchs of *Alexandria*, *Antioch* and *Jeruſalem* had any Hand in it's Deciſions. *Stephen* inſiſted on theſe and ſome other Objections, 'till the Deputies, full of Confuſion, return'd to *Conſtantinople*; and, when aſked what Succeſs they had met with, the Biſhops would willingly have conceal'd their Diſgrace; but *Calliſtus* frankly own'd the Saint victorious, and an Overmatch for all Attacks both by the Force of Reaſon, and Contempt of Life.

Conſtantine, confounded and enraged at *Stephen*'s Conſtancy, baniſhed him to *Proconeſus* an Iſland in the *Propontis*, where he found a Cave agreeably ſituated near the Sea and not far from a Chapel dedicated in honour of St. *Ann*, and the Herbs that grew wild in his Deſart were his only Food. The Place of his Exile being known, all his Diſciples, who had been driven from Mount S. *Auxentius*, except the wicked *Sergius* and another, joyn'd him there, lived under his Direction, and rais'd a Moneſtary for their Uſe. In 765, after the Saint had ſpent about two Years in *Proconneſtus*, the Emperor being inform'd of the many Miracles perform'd by his Hands, which had a direct Tendency to authorize the Veneration of holy Images, order'd him to be remov'd to *Conſtantinople*, where he was thrown into Priſon, and loaded with Irons. Some Days after his Commitment, *Conſtantine* ſent for him to the Palace, made him ſeveral bitter Reproaches of Raſhneſs and Obſtinacy, and preſs'd him to give a Reaſon for his Conduct. The Saint was inclined to Silence

lence; but the Emperor still urging him to speak, he was oblig'd; and by Way of Illustration of his Argument in Favour of holy Images, threw one of the Emperor's Medals on the Ground, and trod on it; which Action being resented by that Prince, and his Courtiers as an Insult to Majesty, *Stephen* was sent to another Prison to take his Tryal, for violating the Respect due to his Sovereign.

In this second Prison, which he forsaw would be his last, the holy Abbot had the Satisfaction of finding 342 Monks from different Quarters, all confined for the same Cause; some of them had lost their Hands, some their Ears, others their Eyes, or Nose cut upon refusing to subscribe the Condemnation of the Use of holy Images, as Idolatrous. *Stephen* thank'd the Almighty who had given them Patience under their Sufferings, and was sensibly mortify'd that he had not been thought worthy of the same Trials. Those living Martyrs, however, look'd on him as an illustrious Confessor, honour'd him as their Master, attended his Instructions, laid open their Consciences to him, and form'd themselves into a sort of regular Community under his Direction. *Stephen*'s Virtue was such as commanded Respect even from the Jaylors, Persons, who have never had the Reputation of much Humanity and Compassion.

Stephen had spent about eleven Months in Prison, when some malicious Informers complain'd to the Emperor that *Stephen* had converted it into a Monastery and that all the Inhabitants of *Constantinople* flock'd thither to hear his idolatrous Doctrine. *Constantine*, enraged at this Account, gave Orders for beheading the Saint immediatly. The Executioner had tied him to the Stake, and was ready to give the decisive Blow, when the Emperor remanded him to and Prison, reserv'd him for a more cruel and painful Death. The next Day he sent two Men of Quality to found the holy Abbot once more, with Directions to make him an Offer of his Life, if he complied, or murther him on the Spot, if he persisted in his former Resolution. They deliver'd the Message; but seeing the Saint still the same, and invincible, they kiss'd his Feet, receiv'd his Blessing, and then went and told the Emperor, that finding *Stephen* obstinate, they had executed their Commission so effectually, that he could not live many Hours. The next Morning our Saint, being assured he should die before Night, assembled his Fellow Prisoners, exhorted them to persevere in the Orthodox Faith, and took his Leave of them for the last Time. The Emperor, understanding how his late Orders were eluded, gave a free Loose to his Passion, storm'd like a Madman, and reproach'd his Courtiers with want of Concern for his Repose, and permitting one to live who had more Power than himself. Some then in waiting, understanding *Stephen* was the hated Rival,

M m.

Nov. 28 val, hasted to the Prison in a Body, rushed in, and demanded the Criminal. The Saint who was prepared for the Attack, stept forward, and with all imaginable Calmness let them know he was the Person. Upon this Declaration they seiz'd him, and dragg'd him through the Streets of *Constantinople*, while the Mob was allow'd and encourag'd to pelt him with Stones, and beat him with Clubs; 'till *Philomathus*, one of his Executioners, dispatched him with a Blow on the Head. That unhappy Person was immediatly possess'd with an evil Spirit, and expired in a frightful Manner; but the rest were so little affected at the dismal End of their Companion, that they continued their Insults on the dead Body of our Saint, 'till his Limbs were torn assunder, and his Brains and Bowels left on the Ground.

St. *Stephen*'s Martyrdom is dated on the twenty eighth of *November* in the Year 767; and the Day of his Death consecrated to his Memory by both the Eastern and Western Churches, who usually stile him St. *Stephen the younger*, to distingish him from the holy Deacon of the same Name, who suffer'd in the Infancy of the Church, at *Jerusalem*.

The XXIX Day.

St. SATURNINUS *Bishop of* TOULOUSE, *Martyr*.

THE *French* look on *Saturninus*, the Saint of this Day, as one of the most illustrious Martyrs that Kingdom can boast, and assure us that his History has been composed with great Exactness and preserved with as much Care. The Author of that valuable Piece, who places the Saint's Death in the Middle of the III Century, says, that the Christian Religion made but a very slow Progress in *Gaul* at that Time; by which Way of speaking, we are to understand that, though the Gospel had been preached in that Country long before, the Church of *Gaul* had suffer'd much from the Persecutions of *Marcus Aurelius* and *Severus*, and the Scarcity of Evangelical Labourers.

The Bishops of *Rome*, zealous for the Propagation of the Faith, and pitying the unhappy Condition of that Part of our Lords Vineyard, consecrated seven Bishops, and sent them into *Gaul*; viz. Gratian, Paul, Trophimus, Saturninus Dionysius, Stremonius and Martial. We cannot tell whither the whole Number was sent at once; but it is evident that our Saint began that Apostolical Work, about the Year 245, and consequently receiv'd his Mission from Pope *Fabian*. Each of them chose some Place for his constant Residence fidence, and *Saturninus* settled at *Toulouse*, with a View of endeavouring the Conversion of the Inhabitants of that City, and the adjacent Country. Nov. 29

Our Saint's Preaching, confirm'd by Miracles, made numerous Conquests in a short Time. He conven'd his increasing Flock in a small Church at *Toulouse*; and the Capitol or chief Temple of the City lying in the Way betwixt that Building and our Saint's Habitation, the Devils, who resided in that Receptacle of Superstition and Idolatry and pretended to foretel future Events, were frequently struck dumb as the Saint pass'd by so that the Pagan Oracles flagg'd and at last became entirely silent, and all the Impostures of the pretended Deities, 'though supported and improved by the Artifice of their Priests, were detected and defeated. The leading Men among the Idolaters, surprized at this Change, and confounded at the disgraceful Silence of their Deities, began to enquire the Cause of it; and one, whom the Acts of our Saint justly stile an Enemy of our Religion, told them there was then a new Sect in the World, whose Votaries were bent on the Ruin of their Religion; that *Saturninus*, a Bishop of that impious People, passing frequently by the Capitol awed the Gods into Silence. One would imagine a Confession of this Nature must have produced an immediate Change in the Principles and Belief of the deluded Pagans, and that they should renounce the Gods, thus overcome by a superior Power. But such was their unhappy Blindness, that they did not Act according to their own Conviction in this important Case, but proposed killing that holy Prelate as the most expeditious Way of opening the Mouths of the pretended Gods; upon which Occasion the Author of this Account asks what can be more foolish than to stand in Awe of Beings who are commanded by others; and not fear him who governs all with an absolute Power?

While the Priests and People were engaged in these Consultations, they saw the Saint taking his usual Walk to Church, and full of Zeal for the Honour of their Gods, resolved not to lose this favourable Opportunity of executing their Design. They seiz'd and dragg'd him to their Temple, declaring they expected he should immediately either appease the offended Deities by sacrificing to them, or expiate the Crime with his own Blood. *Saturninus* boldly own'd that he knew but one true God, to whom he would offer a Sacrifice of Praise; that he look'd on the Pagan Deities as mere Devils; and then ask'd them how they could insist on his sacrificing to those Beings, who, according to their own Confession, were afraid of Him?

The Infidels, incensed at this Reply, abused the Saint with all the Rage and Barbarity that a mad Zeal for their injuried Deities could inspire, and after a great

Variety

Nov. 30 Variety of Indignities, tied his Feet to a Bull prepared for their idolatrous Sacrifices, which being driven from the Temple ran violently down and dashed the Saint's Brains out on the Steps. The Time of *Saturninus*'s Martyrdom is uncertain; some supposing it might happen in *Valerian*'s Persecution, which began in the Year 257; others placing it in the Reign of *Decius*, who died in 251.

The small Number of Christians then at *Toulouse* had not Courage enough to carry off the dead Body; which was done at last by two Women, who laid the sacred Remains on a Bier, and hid them in a deep Ditch, to secure them from any farther Insult, where they lay honour'd by God alone 'till the Church was blessed with Peace under *Constantine* the Great; and then *Hilary* Bishop of *Toulouse* built a small Chapel over his holy Predecessor's Body. *Silvius* another of our Saint's Successors in that See toward the Close of the IVth Century, built a magnificent Church in his Honour, which was consecrated, and enrich'd with the venerable Reliks by *Exuperius*, in the Beginning of the Vth. The Church keeps the twenty ninth of *November* in Memory of the holy Martyr's Sanctity and Sufferings, which was probably the Day of his Death.

The XXX Day

St. ANDREW, Apostle.

ANDREW, who had the Honour to be called first of all the Apostles, was Brother to St *Peter*, and a Native of *Bethsaida*, a small Town in *Gallilee*; and it appears from St. *Mark*'s Gospel, that he and the Prince of the Apostles, had a House at *Capernaum*.

c. 1. v. 29.

Upon St. *John the Baptist*'s appearing in the World, our Saint became his Disciple, and was with his Master, when *Jesus* passing by, the holy Precursor declared him *the Lamb, of God who takes away the Sins of the World.* His Mind being enlightned by the divine Grace, he immediatly comprehended the Meaning of those mysterious Words, and follow'd our Redeemer, in Company with another of St. *John*'s Disciples, whom the Evangelist has not named. *Jesus*, turning about and seeing them, asked their Business; to which they replied with a Question sufficiently expressive of their Desire of attending his Person, and hearing his Instructions; *Rabbi*, said they, *where do you live?* Our Saviour, pleased with their Disposition, invited them

Jo. 1. 36.

to satisfy themselves by going home with him; which they did, and there spent the remaining Part of that Day, and perhaps the following Night, as St. *Augustin* on this Place supposes.

Nov. 30

Andrew, thus initiated in the School of *Jesus Christ*, went home, imparted the happy Discovery of the *Messias* to his Brother *Simon*, introduc'd him to the Saviour of the World; they from that Time frequently heard that divine Person's Instructions, without leaving their Calling which was Fishing. *Jesus*, returning into *Gallilee* toward the Close of the same Year, and finding the two Disciples already mention'd employ'd in their Profession, commanded them to follow him, and promised to make them *Fishers of Men*; whereupon they immediatly quitted their Nets, obey'd the divine Call, and never left him, while he remained on Earth. The following Year, which was the second of our Lord's publick Ministry, he form'd the College of Apostles; and both St. *Matthew* and St. *Luke*, place *Peter* and *Andrew* at the Head of the chosen twelve.

Some Authors of the V Century tell us, that after the Descent of the holy Ghost, our Apostle preached the Gospel in several Provinces of the greater *Asia*; *Origen*, a much earlier Author, as quoted by *Eusebius*, says he did the same in *Scythia*. Several of the Fathers speak of his Evangelical Labours in *Greece*, particularly in *Epirus*, *Peloponesus*, and *Achaia*; and S. *Paulinus*, Bishop of *Nola*, has left us an Account of his Dispute with, and Victory over some of the most eminent Philosophers and Orators of *Argos*. Coming at last to *Patræ*, the Metropolis of *Achaia*, he was crucified there; some place his Martyrdom under *Nero*, others under *Domitian*. The Acts of his Martyrdom, attributed to the Priests and Deacons of *Achaia*, tell us that as soon as he saw the Instrument of his Sufferings, he broke out into this pathetick Salutation; " O excellent Cross, that hast receiv'd Beauty from our Lord's Limbs, " thou long desir'd, ardently lov'd, and constantly sought for Instrument, receive " me from among Men, and present me to my Master, that he who redeem'd me on thee, may receive me from thee.

St. *Andrew*'s Body continued at *Patræ* 'till after the Middle of the IV Century, when it was removed to *Constantinople* together with that of St. *Luke*, the Evangelist; and all Christendom agrees in keeping the thirtieth of *November* in Honour of our Apostle.

The End of NOVEMBER.

THE LIVES OF SAINTS;

COLLECTED FROM
AUTHENTICK RECORDS,
OF
CHURCH HISTORY.

With a full Account of
THE OTHER
FESTIVALS throughout the YEAR.

The whole Interspersed with
Suitable REFLECTIONS.

Number XII. *for* DECEMBER.

LONDON:
Printed for THOMAS MEIGHAN, in *Drury-Lane*, MDCCXXIX.

Advertisement.

THE following Work is collected from such Authorities, as are universally acknowledged to be unexceptionable. And therefore what is omitted, and might by some be expected here, is not judged or declared false and spurious by such Omission; but only not inserted, because doubted of by some.

AN Alphabetical TABLE

OF

The Saints in *December*,

And other Festivals in the same Month.

	Day		Day
A		Eulalia, *Virgin and Martyr*,	10
ADO, *Bishop of* Vienne *in* France.	16	Eusebius, *Bishop of* Vercelli,	15
Alexander, *Martyr*,	12	Eustratius, *and his Companions Martyrs*,	13
Ambrose, *Bishop of* Milan,	7	**F**	
Anastasia, *Martyr*,	25	Francis Xaverius,	3
Asella,	6	**G**	
B		Gorgonia,	9
Barbara, *Virgin and Martyr*,	4	**I**	
Bibiana, *Virgin and Martyr*,	2	Innocents,	28
C		John, *Apostle and* Evangelist,	27
Cheremon, *Bishop and Martyr*,	22	Ischyrion, *Martyr*,	22
Clement, *of* Alexandria,	4	**L**	
Conception *of the* Blessed Virgin,	8	Lazarus,	17
D		Lucius, *King of* Britain,	3
Damasus, *Pope*,	11	Lucy, *Virgin and Martyr*,	13
Delphinus, *Bishop of* Bourdeaux,	24	**M**	
E		Melchiades, *Pope*,	10
Eligius,	1	Meuris, *Martyr*,	19
Emiliana, *Virgin*,	24	Nativity	
Epimachus,	12		

An Alphabetical Table.

N

	Day
Nativity of *Jesus Christ*, or *Christmas-Day*,	25
Nicholas, *Bishop of* Myra,	6

O

	Day
Olympias,	17

P

	Day
Paul, *the Simple*,	18
Peter Chrysologus,	2
Philogonus, *Bishop of* Antioch,	20

R

	Day
Romaricus, *Abbot*,	8

S

	Day
Sabas, *Abbot*,	5
Sabinus, *Bishop of* Assisium, *Martyr, and his Companions*,	30
Servulus,	23
Silvester,	31
Spyridon, *Bishop of* Trimithusa *in* Cyprus,	14
Stephen *the Proto-martyr*,	26

T

	Day
Thea, *and others Martyrs*,	19
Theodore, *Abbot*,	28
Theodulus, *and his nine Companions, Martyrs in* Crete,	23
Thomas *Apostle*,	21
Thomas, *Archbishop of* Canterbury *Martyr*,	29
Thrasilla, *Virgin*,	24

W

	Day
Winebald, *Abbot*,	18

DECEMBER the First.

St. ELIGIUS, *Bishop*.

ELIGIUS, whom the *French* call *Eloy*, one of the greatest Ornaments of their Church, was born about the Year 588, at a Village two Leagues North of *Limoges*, the Capital City of a Province in *France*, and educated in the Fear of God from his Infancy. His Father having observed his Genius turn to nice and curious Works, which he perform'd with great Exactness, put him into the Hands of *Abbon* a Goldsmith at *Limoges*, and Master of the Mint in that Town, who had the Reputation of an honest Man, and an excellent Artist. *Eligius*'s Capacity and Inclinations to the Business soon made him Master of it; and his Readiness to learn join'd to several virtuous Qualities gain'd him the Love and Esteem of all, who knew him. His Heart was full of Sincerity, his whole Conduct under the Regulation of an exact Prudence, and his Temper sweet and obliging; his Discourse was agreeable, easy, and graceful; and he fill'd all the Duties of civil Life, without omitting what he ow'd to God. His Attendance at divine Service was constant and edifying; but of all the Instructions which he receiv'd in the Church none pleas'd him so well as what he could draw from the holy Scriptures when read there; he laid up those divine Oracles in his Memory, and when he came home made them the Subject of his most serious Thoughts and profound Meditations in Order to apply the sacred Maxims to his own Use.

Dec. 1. The Saint was about thirty Years old when he left his own Country and travell'd to *Paris*, where *Bobbon*, Intendant of the Finances, or Chancellor of the *Exchequer*, employ'd him in the Mint, and other Works where Metals were concern'd. *Clotaire* II, then on the Throne of *France*, had form'd a Project for making a Chair of State, richly adorn'd with Gold and Jewels; but could find no Workman who would undertake to execute it. *Bobbon*, perceiving his Royal Master troubled at the Disappointment, let him know he believed he had found the Man whom he wanted; whereupon *Clotaire* immediately order'd what he thought a sufficient Quantity of Materials to be deliver'd into his Hands; which being transmitted to *Eligius*, he made two Chairs exactly such as the King desired. *Clotaire*, charm'd with the Beauty of the Work, and surprized at the Skill and Honesty of the Artist, gave him a handsome Reward, and engaged him in his Service.

The Grace of God preserved our Saint from the Corruption of the Court; and he had not been long there, when he form'd a Resolution of entring into a more devout and austere Way of Living than he had practised before, 'though his Virtue had always been such as gain'd the Hearts of all who conversed with him. He took a View of his whole Life, made a general Confession, and imposed a severe Penance on himself. From that Time his Fasts, Watching, and private Devotions were equal to those of the most mortified and pious Monks; and he made his Court to his Prince as successfully by the Innocence and Regularity of his Life, as others usually do by Flattery, and other low Arts.

In the Year 628 *Clotaire*, dying, was succeeded by his Son *Dagobert*, who entertain'd so just an Idea of the Saint's Virtue, and Wisdom, that he frequently consulted him preferably to all his Council about publick Affairs, and took Directions from him for his private Conduct; *Eligius* made an excellent Use of his Credit with his Sovereign, and employ'd every favourable Opportunity in inspiring him with Sentiments of Justice, Clemency and Religion. The King was so far from being offended at the Liberty, that he reform'd his Life by his Directions, and treated *Eligius* with a Respect which drew the Envy and Jealousy of the whole Court on him, particularly the vicious Part of the Nobility, who did all in their Power to blast his Character. But their Calumnies were too weak to do him any Prejudice, destroy'd one another, and served only to give his Virtue a fresh Lustre, and enhance *Dagobert*'s Veneration for him, who loaded him with Favours; but could not make him rich, because all he receiv'd from the Royal Bounty was immediately employ'd in relieving the Poor, redeeming Captives, or raising Houses

for

for the Reception of such as were disposed to lead a penitential Life. The Abbey of *Solignac* was the first Religious Foundation owing to our Saint's liberal Charity; it was built two Leagues from *Limoges* on a Piece of Ground granted by the King for that Purpose, richly endow'd, peopled with Monks from *Luxeu*, and made subject to the Inspection of the Abbot of that Monastery. This new Community encreas'd considerably in a little Time, and consisted of 150 Persons, who work'd at several Trades, and lived in admirable Regularity. *Dagobert* gave our Saint a handsome House at *Paris*; which he converted into a Convent, and placed 300 Nuns in it under the Direction of St. *Aurea*, whose Name occurs in the *Roman* Martyrologe on the fourth of *October*. This Monastery has since been given to *Barnabites*, and it's Revenue annex'd to the Bishoprick of *Paris*.

Eligius had a profound Veneration for a Religious Life; and, 'though his Vocation did not determine him to the Choice of that State, he encouraged a Disposition to Retirement in his own Servants, and all such as receiv'd any Relief from his Hands. Our Saint's House became the common Resort of distressed Strangers, was look'd on as a publick Hospital, and his whole Fortune the Poor's Inheritance. When he had rescued any Foreigners from Slavery, his usual Way was to solicit their Naturalization, and then give them the Liberty of returning to their own Country, or settling in *France*. Those who were inclined to stay were placed in Monasteries or entertain'd in his Family, pursuant to their own Choice; and several of them made such a Progress in Virtue, while under his Roof, that many Parishes and Monasteries were furnished with Pastors and Abbots out of his domestick Community, who did Honour to the Church, and died with the Reputation of great Sanctity. He still continued his Business; but his chief Employment was to make Shrines for the venerable Relicks of Saints; and several Churches of *France* were furnished with excellent Pieces of Workmanship in that Way.

St. *Eligius*, 'though a Layman, and engaged in a State of Life, which seems naturally calculated for inspiring Covetousness, or at least an Affection for Riches, was admired by Persons of the most holy Professions, as a perfect Model of Regularity, Penance, Humility, and Disinterestedness; and both Ecclesiasticks and Monks honour'd him as their Master, and Director. When he first went to Court he conformed to the Fashion so far as to wear silk Cloaths, and other Ornaments used by Persons in his Station; but even then he wore a Hair Shirt, and practised several private Mortifications. When he was pretty well advanced in Spirituality, and had engaged the Affections of the King, and Courtiers sufficiently to place him above the Apprehension of being thought singular, and whimsical, he reform'd his Exterior into a Simplicity suitable to the State of his Interior, and engaged several of the Nobility to follow his Example in that Particular. This Simplicity, supported by a certain Dignity peculiar to the Saint, made him the Object of universal Esteem; and it was a common Thing for Embassadors from foreign Princes to the Court of *France* to consult him before they went for Audience, and regulate all their Motions by his prudent Advice; but all the Applause which his Wisdom, and Virtue drew upon him, could not inspire him with the least Vanity or Self-complacency. S. *Owen*, Bishop of *Rouën*, who was well acquainted with the Saint, and has left us his Life, gives us a long and authentick Account of Miracles perform'd by his Hands in Favour of the Blind, the Lame, and the Sick; and tells us he was particularly industrious in avoiding the Glory which naturally attends such Works, always attributing them to the powerful Intercession of some Saint. The same Author assures us he was as remarkable for the Spirit of Prophesy.

These extraordinary Gifts, and the Integrity of his Morals gave him no small Authority in the Church of *France*, even while he was a Layman; the third Council of *Orleans*, which condemn'd the *Monothelites* was conven'd at his Request; and the holy Author, whom we follow in this Account was his inseperable Companion in Labours of this Sort. Upon the Death of *Acarius* Bishop of *Noyon* and *Tournay*, which happen'd in the Year 639, *Eligius* was chosen to govern that large and populous Diocese, and his holy Friend and Historian placed in the See of *Rouën* at the same Time. *Clovis* II, then on the Throne, being in his Minority, had great Need of two such able and virtuous Persons at Court; but was prevail'd with to deprive himself of their Assistance in Favour of the Church. The vast Diocese, to which our Saint was named, still abounded with great Numbers of Idolaters, of a very savage and untractable Nature, and if any thing could make him accept of the Episcopal Character it was the Prospect of suffering for the Faith in the Execution of his Ministry. His Regard for the Canons would not allow him to proceed with Precipitation in this important Affair; for which Reason he desired he might be allow'd some Time to prepare himself, and take all the Degrees of holy Orders regularly after proper Intervals. St. *Owen* used the same Caution; and they were consecrated together at *Rouën* on the twenty first of *May* 640.

The Grace, which our Saint receiv'd at his Consecration gave a new Lustre to those Virtues, which had long charm'd and edified the World, and his present Situation afforded him more frequent Opportunities of relieving the Poor,

comforting

comforting the Sick, and stooping to the meanest Offices, wherever Charity was concern'd. The remaining Part of that Year was spent in enquiring into the State of his Diocese, and visiting that Part of it which lay near *Noyon*; and the following Year he took a View of more remote Places, which were inhabited by Men little superior to Brutes. At his Appearance among those Barbarians they were so far from acknowledging his Charity, and listening to the divine Message, as deliver'd by his Mouth, that they thought no Treatment too bad for one who disturbed their false Peace, and urged the Necessity of Self-denial. But the Saint's excellent Life soon disarm'd them of their Rage, and converted those ravening Wolves into mild Lambs. The Territories of *Courtray* and *Ghent*, which made Part of his Charge, were miserably over-run with noxious Weeds, when *Eligius* was commission'd to cultivate that neglected Field; but his zealous Labours changed it into a fruitful and delicious Garden.

To secure the Conquests which *Jesus Christ* had made by his Ministry, the Saint built several Churches on the Ruins of Idolatrous Temples, furnished them with virtuous, and indefatigable Pastors, and founded Monasteries for the Reception of such as desired to leave the World. These exterior Regulations were not made without much Difficulty; but he found it a much harder Task to reform the Heart, and root out Superstition and Vice, when fortified by Custom and long Habits; but his constant Application to the great Work, his Patience, Humility, and invincible Courage conquer'd all Opposition, and he had the Satisfaction of seeing much the greatest Part of his Flock such as he wished.

The Instruction of his Cotemporaries was too narrow a Task for our Saint's generous Charity, who therefore has left Posterity some Sermons, or Homilies, 'though all which bear his Name do not belong to him. But we may be assured of the Genuineness of that large Abridgment of his Doctrine, as given us by S. *Owen*, which has been thought considerable enough to be attributed to St. *Augustin*. That Piece will always pass for a Proof of *Eligius*'s Acquaintance with the sacred Writings, and the Works of the best *Latin* Fathers; and his Affection for Church Discipline. Being favour'd with a Foresight of his own Death, he conven'd his Disciples, took his Leave of them in a pathetick Exhortation to a virtuous Life, and expired in their Arms on the first of *December*, 659, in the seventy first Year of his Age.

His Eyes were scarce closed when the whole Town of *Noyon* took the Alarm, and express'd their Sense of the Loss by Tears, and all the Marks of Grief for the Death of a Father and Protector. The next Day Queen *Bathilda*,

Dec. 2. *thilda*, Widow to *Clovis* II, attended by the Royal Children, and a splendid Retinue reach'd the Town; but nothing afflicted her so much as that she came too late to receive his Blessing. That pious Princess offer'd to carry the Body to the Monastery of *Chelles*; and some of her Court were for removing it to *Paris*; but the Inhabitants of *Noyon* opposed the Attempt so vigorously that they remain'd in Possession of the valuable Treasure. His Head was afterwards sent to *Chelles*, where the Nuns keep it to this Day with great Veneration. The *Roman* Martyrologe honours his Memory on the Day of his Death.

The II Day.

St BIBIANA Virgin and Martyr.

JULIAN the Apostate made *Apronianus* Governor of *Rome* in the Year 363, who, while on the Way to that City, had the Misfortune to lose an Eye. Being a Slave to Idolatry and a violent Enemy of our holy Religion, he imputed this Accident to the Power of Magick, and gave Orders for discovering and punishing all who dealt in that Art; which has been frequently observ'd, was a common Pretence among the Pagans for persecuting the Christians. This Account we have from *Ammianus Marcellinus*, a a Heathen Author of undoubted Credit; and finding *Apronianus* mention'd as a Magistrate in the Acts of St. *Babiana*'s Martyrdom, we may be allow'd to suppose she suffer'd under the Person mention'd by the aforesaid Historian. According to the most probable Account, our Saint was Daughter to *Flavian*, who had filled a considerable Post, but was disgraced for his Religion, and dying in Banishment is honour'd as a Saint on the twenty second of *December* in the *Roman* Martyrologe. *Dafrosa*, the Saint's Mother was confin'd to her own House for some Time, with a View of starving her to Death; but the Persecutor changing his Mind a few Days after, she was carried out of the City Gates, and beheaded; for which Reason the Church venerates her as a Martyr on the fourth of *January*. *Bibiana* and her Sister, whom the Acts call *Demetria*, fell into the Hands of the Pagan Governor after the Death of their holy Parents, and were stripp'd of all they had in the World. It was supposed that the miserable State, to which they were reduced, would prevail with them to renounce their Religion; but God supported

ported them with his Grace against the Temptations of Hunger, and Poverty; Dec. 2. and *Demetria* died suddainly in *Apronianus*'s Presence. That Magistrate finding his Labour lost in *Bibiana*, and that she was proof against both Threats and Promises, put her into the Hands of *Rufina*, a Woman of a wretched Character, but extremely artful, who undertook to bring her to another Way of thinking. That Agent of Hell employ'd all the soft Means she could invent, which were afterwards succeeded by Blows; but *Bibiana* remain'd invincible. *Apronianus*, incenced at the Saint's Courage and Perseverance, pass'd Sentence of Death upon her, and order'd her to be tied to a Pillar, and whip'd with Scourges loaded with leaden Plummets 'till she expired. The Saint remain'd the same to the last Moment, and died under the Hands of her Executioners. The Body was left in the open Air, a Prey to Beasts; but *John* a holy Priest, carried it off the following Night, and buried it near *Licinius*'s Palace, where a Church was afterwards rais'd in Honour of the Martyr, rebuilt by Pope *Urban* VIII, in the Year 1628, and the Relicks of our Saint and her Mother and Sister, placed under the high Altar. The *Roman* Church honours *Bibiana*'s Memory on the second of *December*, which probably was the Day of her Martyrdom.

St. PETER CHRYSOLOGUS, *Bishop of* RAVENNA.

PETER, whose Eloquence and beautiful Stile, have deservedly given him the Name of *Chrysologus*, was born at *Forum Cornelii*, now called *Imola* in *Romagna*, toward the Beginning of the V Century, and baptized and educated by *Cornelius* the holy Bishop of that City, of whom he speaks with the utmost Respect and Gratitude. That excellent Prelate's Endeavours for forming our Saint to Virtue and Learning being blest with the desired Success, he engaged his worthy Disciple in the Service of the Church by ordaining him Deacon. *Peter* had exercised the Functions of that Order to the general Edification, and with the universal Applause of the Clergy and Laity of *Imola*, when the See of *Ravenna* became vacant by the Death of *John* Bishop of that Church, about the Year 433. Those concern'd in the Choice of a Successor soon came to an Agreement, and desired *Cornelius* to go to *Rome* at the Head of their Deputies for his Holiness's Confirmation. That Prelate could not decline the Office, and undertook the Journey with the Representatives of the Church of *Ravenna*, attended by *Peter* his favourite Deacon. *Sixtus* III, then in St. *Peter*'s Chair, had according

Dec. 2. ding to the Author of the History of *Ravenna*, been directed in a Vision to place our Saint in the Bishoprick of that City, and therefore refused to confirm the Election already made, and proposed *Peter* as design'd by Heaven for that Post. The same Author adds, that the Deputies from *Ravenna*, made a vigorous Opposition to the Pope's Motion, but acquiess'd upon a full Account of his Vision.

It is most probable that *Peter* receiv'd the Episcopal Character at *Rome*, and from the Hands of the Pope, at least if the foregoing Account is admitted. Being conducted to the Church of *Ravenna*, he employed an extensive Charity, and unwearied Vigilance in Favour of his Flock, which he fed very liberally with the true Bread of Life, the Word of God; and we have 176 of his Discourses still extant. When he enter'd on his Charge, he found large Remains of Pagan Superstition in his Diocese, and several Abuses which had crept in among the People in several Places; the total Extirpation of the former, and the Reformation of the latter were reserved for our zealous and holy Pastor.

Toward the Middle of the V Century, the Eastern Church was disturb'd by the *Eutychian* Heresy, which consisted in denying the real Distinction of the two Natures in the Person of *Jesus Christ* after the Incarnation. The Author of that absurd Doctrine, having been condemn'd and excommunicated by a Council at *Constantinople* after a full hearing, endeavour'd to surprize the most illustrious Bishops of the West into a favourable Oppinion of his Cause and Intentions. *Peter*, one of the most considerable of that Number, both for the Dignity of his See, and his personal Merit, was not forgot on that Occasion; and his Reply to the Heresiarch's Letter is an excellent Monument of his Regard for Church Unity, and his Deference for the holy See. This is the last Time we find the Saint mention'd in History; but it is generally believed he died long before the Close of the fifth Age. The *Roman* Martyrologe places his Name on the second of *December*, and seems to suppose he died, or at least was buried, at *Imola*.

The III Day.

St. FRANCIS XAVERIUS.

THE great Saint of this Day, the Glory of his Age and the Society of which he was a Member, whom Pope *Urban* VIII stiled the Apostle

postle of the *Indies*, descended of a considerable Family in *Navarre*, was born on the eighth of *April* 1506 near *Pampelona* the Metropolis of that Kingdom. *Francis* was the youngest of a great Number of Children; and all his Brothers were engaged in the Army, while his peaceable Temper carried him to Study. He was instructed in the *Latin* Tongue at Home, and then sent to *Paris*, the common Resort of Students from almost all Parts of *Europe*, where he began his Philosophy at the Age of eighteen, and by the Help of a happy Genius, and great Application, soon distinguish'd himself in that famous University. *Francis* had scarce spent two Years at *Paris*, when his Father, finding the Education of his numerous Family too expensive for his Circumstances, had some Thoughts of recalling him; but changed his Mind at the Perswasion of *Margaret* his eldest Daughter, Superior of a Convent at *Gandia*.

The Saint being thus allow'd to pursue his Studies, proceeded Master of Arts; was thought capable of teaching Philosophy as soon as he had taken that Degree; and the Applause which he receiv'd in his new Profession flatter'd his Vanity very agreeably, and inspir'd him with large Hopes of raising his Fortune. He read Lectures in the College of *Beauvais*, but lived at that of St. *Barbara*, where he and *Peter le Fevre* became acquainted with St. *Ignatius* of *Loyola*. *Le Fevre* was soon gain'd by the holy Man last mention'd, but *Francis* made a long and vigorous Resistance; for being of a warm and haughty Temper, and extremely fond of his own Abilities and Qualifications, he despis'd and banter'd *Ignatius*'s Proposals for forming his Society, as so many Instances of a degenerate Lowness of Soul, and took a singular Pleasure in diverting himself at that holy Man's Expence. *Ignatius*, finding his Labours lost on that ambitious and conceited Professor, but still zealous for his Conversion, thought he might succeed better, and insinuate himself into his Favour more succesfully, by seeming to compliment him on his great Learning; he therefore made it his Business to commend him largely on that Score, and was particularly active in recommending him among his Acquaintance, as a most extraordinary Master. This succeeded; for *Francis* could not but entertain an advantageous Opinion of a Person who did what he thought Justice to his Character, and desire a closer Acquaintance with a Man, who took such an uncommon Revenge for his ill Usage. Our Saint, conversing familiarly with *Ignatius*, soon found he had been mistaken in him, and gave him a favourable hearing on Points which he had before rejected with so much Disdain and made the Subjects of his Raillery.

Dec. 3. *Xaverius* began now to be convinc'd of the Vanity of the World, the Emptiness of its boasted Grandeur, and Deceitfulness of its proferr'd Pleasures; and was satisfy'd that no created Thing had a Right to the Possession of his Heart. These were the first Impressions, which the Grace of God made on our Saint; but his entire Submission to the Yoke of *Jesus Christ* was a Work of Time, and cost him much Pains. In the Year 1535, he came to a Resolution of regulating his Life by the Maxims of the Gospel, and put himself under the Conduct of S. *Ignatius*, whom he respected as the happy Instrument of his Conversion. As a Love of Fame had been his predominant Passion, he knew it was his Duty to be particularly active and vigilant against it; he therefore industriously sought all Opportunities of humbling himself, and courted the meanest Employments, and most contemptible Offices, with an Earnestness equal to what he had shewn in Pursuit of Applause and Distinction. Toward the Close of the Year he enter'd into a Retreat, perform'd the *Spiritual Exercises* according to the Spirit and Direction of his great Master, and made such Progress in the School of the Cross, that he refused a large Benefice at *Pampelona*, that was offer'd him.

After having taught Philosophy three Years and a half, *Francis* enter'd on the Study of Divinity; but had not been long employ'd in that Manner, when *Ignatius* communicated his Design of visiting the holy Land to him and his other Disciples, who all promised to accompany him thither, and unite their Labours for the Conversion of the Infidels; or, if that was not practicable, they agreed to throw themselves at the Pope's Feet, and offer their Service wherever he thought fit to employ them. St. *Ignatius* and his six Companions made this Vow together at *Mountmartre* near *Paris*, in the Year 1534, as has been related on the last of *July* in the Life of that holy Founder of the Society of *Jesus*. *Ignatius*, who was obliged to go to Spain and settle his Affairs before he put the Vow in Practice, left *Paris* in Autumn 1535, and order'd his Disciples to meet him at *Venice* at the Beginning of 1537. *Xaverius* and the rest of the holy Company began their Journey on the fifteenth of *November* 1536, and reached the Place appointed on the eighth of *January* following, where our Saint's chief Employment was to attend the Hospitals, and serve the Sick, 'till the Arrival of *Ignatius*. After two Months Stay at *Venice*, he and his Brethren were order'd to *Rome* with Directions to solicit the Mission of the holy Land, and Leave to enter into holy Orders. *Paul* III gave them a favourable Reception, and granted their Request. Having dispatched their Business at *Rome*, *Xaverius* and his Companions returned to *Venice*, where they took the Vows of Poverty and Chastity; and
our

our Saint return'd to his Employment in the Hospital. A War between the Turks and *Venetians* about that Time broke all Commerce with the *Levant*, and consequently ruin'd their Design of going to the holy Land, which proved a sensible Mortification to *Xaverius*, as it deprived him not only of seeing the Places consecrated by the Blood of *Jesus Christ*, but also of an Opportunity of shedding his own for that divine Master. As soon as he was ordain'd Priest, he retir'd to a Village about four Miles from *Padua*, where he spent forty Days in a poor ruin'd Cottage, exposed to all the Injuries of the Weather, lay on the Ground, fasted most rigorously, and subsisted on what Scraps of Bread he begg'd from Door to Door. After this Preparation he said his first Mass at *Vicenza*, where *Ignatius* had assembled all his Disciples; and then fell sick. Upon his Recovery, he was sent to *Bologna*, where his Labours and Mortifications soon reduc'd him to a very low Ebb; but the Vigour of his Mind overcame the Infirmity of his Body, and, though afflicted with a quartan Ague, was indefatigable in visiting the Hospitals, instructing the Ignorant, and preaching during his Stay in Town. He was thus employ'd when St. *Ignatius* called him to *Rome*, where he had made a Tender of his new Society's Services to *Paul* III, who accepted the Offer, and declared his Will that those evangelical Labourers should begin to preach at *Rome*, under the immediate Protection of the holy See. In this View, they were placed in several Churches; that of St. *Laurence in Damasoo* fell to the Share of our Saint and *Le Fevre*, who were to instruct the People there by Turns; and 'though the whole Society, which then consisted of only ten Persons, was particularly active in every Thing where either the temporal or spiritual Welfare of their Neighbour was concern'd, no one distinguish'd himself by a more ardent Charity, or a more edifying Zeal than *Xaverius*.

John III, King of *Portugal*, had entertain'd a Desire of planting the Faith of *Jesus Christ* in the *East Indies*; and, hearing the Character of this new Society, hoped he had found Men both willing and able to undertake that glorious Task. He wrote to his Embassador at *Rome*, directing him to lay his Design before his Holiness, and desire at least six of those apostolical Preachers might be sent on that important Errand. The Pope applied to *Ignatius* on the Subject, but could not prevail with him to send more than two. *Rodriguez* a *Portuguese*, and *Bobadilla* a *Spaniard* were named to that Mission; but the latter falling dangerously ill, his Place was supplied by our Saint. *Xaverius* receiv'd the Pope's and his holy Superior's Order as a Commission from the Mouth of *Jesus Christ* to carry the Light of the Gospel among the Infidels

Dec. 3. Infidels, and was transported with Joy at the Prospect of falling a Sacrifice for the Name of his divine Saviour.

The Saint left *Rome* in Company with the Minister of *Portugal*, on the fifteenth of *March* 1540. Though allow'd a good Horse, he chose to walk great Part of the Way, and beside the Hardships of the Journey, sought all Opportunities of practising Mortification, and Humility. He was ready to serve his fellow Travellers in the meanest Offices on the Road, dress'd their Horses, and frequently resign'd his Bed to others, and lay in the Stable.

At *Lisbon* he was joyn'd by *Rodriguez*, the Companion of his Mission, who came thither by Sea; and upon the Embassador's Account of them they were both order'd to Court. The King gave Directions to the proper Officers for accommodating them with a handsome Apartment in the Royal Palace 'till they were ready to sail; but they declined the Offer, desiring Leave to reside in the Hospital, and live on Alms, according to the Design of their holy Founder. Men so full of Zeal and Charity as our Saint and his Companion, could not be unemploy'd, while Sin and Ignorance were in the World; they began with catechizing Children, which they perform'd so well, that they were soon invited to preach in several Churches at *Lisbon*, desired to assist the Pastors in the Confessional, and join their Labours for the Conversion of Sinners. They appear'd to such Advantage in those Functions, and the Work succeeded so well in their Hands, that the King applied to *Ignatius*, and begg'd they might be allow'd to stay in *Portugal*. *Ignatius* complied so far with his Majesty's Request, as to grant him *Rodriguez*, who was his Subject, but desired *Xaverius* might pursue his Journey to *India*, where God call'd him. The King, satisfy'd with this Concession, made no Opposition to our Saint's embarking, but did all in his Power toward rendring his Mission effectual. He gave the Saint an exact Account of the State of the Country to which he was going, and all necessary Instructions for his proceeding in his foreign Dominions; he then deliver'd him four Briefs from his Holiness; the first of which appointed him Apostolical Legate; the second conferr'd on him all the Power and Authority, which the Church can grant, for the Propagation of the Gospel in the East; the third recommended him to the Protection of *David* King of *Ethiopia*; and the fourth was address'd to all the Christian Princes and Governments from the Cape of *Good Hope* to the Peninsula beyond the River *Ganges*. The King order'd the Saint should be handsomly provided with all Necessaries for that long and difficult Voyage, but he accepted of nothing but a moderate Quantity of devout Books, which would be necessary in his Mission, and a coarse Suit of Cloaths. When *Xaverius* was

was press'd to take one Servant at least to wash his Linen, and dress his Victuals, and desired to consider that the Character which he bore required some
Decorum, he replied that he could not only do these mean Things for himself, but design'd to employ his Hands the same Way for others, without any
Affront to the holy See, from which he receiv'd his Commission; and that
the false Ideas of Decency and State were so many Causes of the Calamities of the Catholick Church.

Dec. 3.

After eight Months spent at *Lisbon*, *Xaverius* sail'd in a large Ship, provided
for *Alphonso de Sousa* Viceroy of the *Indies*, in which were near a thousand
Persons. The Saint, considering the whole Company as committed to his Care,
made it his Business to remedy all the Disorders usually committed on Board;
to facilitate the desired Reformation, he studied the particular Tempers of
the Persons with whom he was to converse, entertain'd them all in a
Manner suitable to their respective Professions, and by a cheerful and easy
Behaviour engaged the Affections of all. He catechised the Sailors at
stated Times, preached every *Sunday* before the Main Mast, took Care of
the Sick, converted his Cabin into an Infirmary, lay on the Deck, and
lived on Charity during the whole Voyage, 'though the Viceroy was very
urgent with him to eat at his Table, or accept of a regular Supply of Food
from his Kitchen.

On the VI of *May* 1542 *Xaverius* landed at *Goa*, the most considerable
Town in the East for Trade. It had been above thirty Years in the Hands
of the *Portugueze*, who made it a Bishop's See, and the constant Residence of
the Viceroy. That Nobleman invited him to lodge in his Palace, but the
Hospital was preferr'd on that Occasion. Before he attempted the Exercise
of his missionary Functions, he paid his Respects to the Bishop of the Place,
shew'd him what Powers he had receiv'd from the Pope and the King of
Portugal, and declared it was not his Intention to make Use of them without
his Lordship's Permission. The Bishop, edified at the Saint's Humility, embraced him most affectionately, took the Pope's Briefs, return'd them after having kiss'd them in Token of his Reverence for the holy See, and assured him
of his Protection, Assistance, and Friendship. The excellent Harmony
which subsisted from that Time between the Bishop and the Missionary contributed very largely toward encreasing the Number of the Faithful.

When the *Portugueze* enter'd the Country, they endeavour'd to revive that
Christianity which St. *Thomas* had planted there, but had since been destroy'd
by the Pagans and Mahometans. As this was attempted by Force, and the
new Masters of the *Indies* were more solicitous for extending their Conquests,

and

Dec. 3. and enriching themselves with the Spoils of the Natives than propagating the Kingdom of *Jesus Christ*, and gaining Souls to God, their Labours had met with but little Success; great Numbers of the *Indians*, who had embraced the Faith relapsed to their former Superstition and Immorality for want of Instruction and good Example; those, who persever'd in their new Religion, were cruelly persecuted by the *Mahometans*; and the *Portugueze* were not well enough settled to protect them from the Insults of those Infidels. The *European* Christians there were a Disgrace to their holy Profession, and lived in direct Opposition to the Gospel which they profess'd; Justice was sold; Usury, Debauchery, Revenge, and several other Crimes were practised with Impunity, and even receiv'd a sort of Sanction from the Conduct of Men in Power. The Authority of the Church was trampled on; the Bishop's Admonitions and Censures laugh'd at and despised, and few seem'd sensible of the Danger of dying without the Sacraments, or in a State of Excommunication.

This now was the State of Religion in the *Indies*, when our Saint reached that Country and would have disheartned any one not inspired with the same Spirit that animated the first Preachers of Christianity in their Undertakings. *Xaverius* consider'd that the present Situation of Things could not be worse than that in which St. *Thomas* found them, and hoped that, serving the same Master, and being embark'd in the same Cause, he should be favour'd with the same Assistance from Heaven. Having observed what Influence the Example of the *Portugueze* had over the converted *Indians*, he thought it would be best to begin with Them. He endeavour'd to gain their Attention to his Discourse by Acts of Mercy such as visiting the Hospitals and Prisons, and begging for the Relief and Support of the Indigent. When he had made himself known by such charitable Works, he walk'd through all the Streets of *Goa* with a Bell in his Hand to give Notice to the Masters of Families that they were desired to send their Children and Slaves to Catechism; hoping that the *Portugueze* Youth, being well grounded in the Principles of Religion, and the Maxims of the Gospel, Christianity would revive in the capital City, and from thence make it's Way more easily into the Country. This succeeded to his Wish, and the Reformation began with the Children. When he had acquired a tolerable Knowledge of the vulgar Tongue, he preached in Publick; and when he left the Pulpit made his Visits to private Houses, in Order to finish the Conversion of such as had been moved by the Word of God. The Sweetness of his Behaviour, and the charitable Concern which he express'd for the Soul of his Neighbour on those Occasions were irresistable. After

St. Francis Xaverius.

After our Saint had spent about half a Year at *Goa*, the Face of Religion Dec. 3. was so happily alter'd that he left that Town, and travell'd to the Coast of *Paravas*, or *the Pearl Fishery*, where he heard he should find a large Body of People, who had receiv'd Baptism out of Gratitude to the *Portugueze* for their Assistance against the *Saracens*, but had retain'd all their Superstitions and Vices, and scarce deserved the Name of Christians. Having reached Cape *Camorino*, which lay in his Way, he went into a Village full of Idolaters, where he made the first Essay of his Mission to the Gentiles; and it pleased God to manifest his Approrbation of the Saint's Labours by a great Number of Miracles. The extraordinary and suddain Deliverance of a Woman in Labour, which was attributed to the Force of his Prayers, affected the Inhabitants so strongly that they immediately declared they were ready to embrace the Faith which he preached, with the Permission of their Prince; they had no sooner obtain'd that Permission but they presented themselves to *Xaverius*, begg'd to be rank'd among the Disciples of *Jesus Christ*, and made a solemn Promise to square their Lives by the Rules of the Gospel. This happy Beginning inspired the Saint with Courage for pursuing his Enterprize; and upon his Arrival at the first inhabited Place on the Pearl Coast, he perceived he had not been misinform'd of the State of Religion in that Country, and that the People were real Infidels with the additional Guilt of having profaned their Baptism. He begun with instructing them in the Obligations which they had contracted at the Reception of that Sacrament, and translated the Catechism, and some devout Prayers into their Language which was that of *Malabar*. From thence he went on to other Villages in the Country, where the Name of *Jesus Christ* was entirely unknown; and the Progress which the Gospel made in his Hands was so very great that, according to his own Account of the Matter, the bare Fatigue of conferring Baptism frequently made his Arms so weak that he could not move them. The many miraculous Cures, which the Almighty perform'd by his Hands, contributed largely to the Success of his Labours; and he was as happy in this Point as *Elisha*, who sometimes 4 Kings made use of his Servant and Staff on the like Occasions; for the Authors of 4. our Saint's Life assure us that he frequently sent the young Neophytes with his Crucifix or some other Instrument of Devotion, and commission'd them to pronounce the Lord's Prayer, or the Apostles Creed over the Sick. His own Endeavours, assisted by the active Zeal of those Converts, soon produced a wonderful Change in the whole Country; the Temples and Idols were destroy'd, and Churches built in all the Towns and Villages on the Coast of *Paravas*. The Splendor of his Miracles and the admirable Innocence of his

Life

Dec. 3. Life recommended him to the Veneration of all who saw or heard of him; and the very *Brachmans*, i. e. the Pagan Priests, the Philosophers and Divines of the Country, seem'd disposed to believe upon his Preaching, if they could have been admitted to Baptism and all the Advantages of the Christian Religion, without prejudicing their Fortune, or forfeiting the People's good Opinion by a publick Profession of Christianity; but the Saint assured them that the Gospel, which he deliver'd, allow'd of no such Dissimulation, and that a Disciple of *Jesus* was obliged to postpone all Considerations to that of securing his Salvation by doing his Master's Will.

Toward the Close of the Year 1543, after above fifteen Months spent on the Coast of *Paravas*, *Xaverius* return'd to *Goa*, where he was join'd by two Companions whom he had left at *Mozambick* on the Eastern Coast of *Africa*, and several others who offer'd their Assistance in the Apostolical Work. He brought some young *Indians* with him, with a View of placing them in the new Seminary in that Town, where they might be qualified for the Mission of their own Country, which could never succeed so well in the Hands of Strangers. The following Year he return'd to the *Pearl Coast*, attended by a large Supply of Evangelical Labourers, as well *Indians* as *Europeans*; shew'd them the large Conquests he had made among that barbarous People; instructed them in the Way of gaining the Idolaters to the Faith; and laid down certain Rules for confirming the Converts in their new Profession. Having given the Missionaries proper Directions for their Conduct, he left some of them in the chief Towns, where they were employ'd as Pastors, or Catechists, and carried the rest with him into the Kingdom of *Travancor*. *Xaverius* had the same Success there as had attended his Labours on the Coast of *Paravas*; he baptized ten thousand *Indians* with his own Hand in one Month; and sometimes a whole Village receiv'd the Sacrament of Regeneration in a Day. He had not been long in that Kingdom before the King allow'd him to build forty five Churches and Chapels; and the Saint in one of his Letters adds, that nothing could be more agreeable than to see the converted Natives strive who should be most active in demolishing the Temples and breaking the Idols, which they had lately held sacred. That Prince was the more favourable to the Christian Religion, because he had experienced the Power of the true God in the Defeat of the *Badages*, a savage People, who lived upon the Spoils of the whole Country. The Saint put himself at the Head of a small Party of the Christians, marched up to the Enemy with his Crucifix in his Hand, address'd them with a commanding and masterly Air, which inspired such a Terror into the Barbarians that they retired in Disorder,

and

and quitted the Attempt. This memorable Action procured the Saint the Appellation of *the Great Father*.

Dec. 3.

While *Francis* was thus employ'd in the Kingdom of *Travancar*, Deputies from the Island of *Manar*, drawn thither by the Reputation of his Miracles, begg'd he would visit their Country, instruct them in the Religion which he profess'd, and put them in a Way of sharing the Advantages which the Christians expected. The Saint did not think it convenient to leave his new Conquests 'till they were better secured, and therefore sent one of the Missionaries of *Paravas* to *Manar*; whose Labours succeeded so well that the whole Island was baptized, and six or seven hundred of those Converts had the Courage to lay down their Lives rather than abjure their Religion, when press'd to it by their King, who resided in the North of *Ceilan*. The News of the Progress of the Gospel in that Island proved a fresh Incentive to our Saint to make farther Attempts for propagating the Kingdom of Christ farther among the Infidels. In this View he left the Church of *Travancar* under the Direction of one of his Companions, and went for *Meliapor*, where it pleased the Almighty to give him several sensible Proofs of his Approbation of his Apostolical Designs in Favour of the Inhabitants of that populous City. After some considerable Conversions there in Spight of all the Malice, and Power of the common Enemy, the Saint went to *Malacca* in Order to proceed to *Macassar*, a large Island in the *Indian* See above 950 Leagues from *Meliapor*. His whole Journey to *Malacca* was one continued Series of miraculous and charitable Actions in Favour of the Souls and Bodies of the Natives of the Country, and he reached that Town on the twenty fifth of *September*, 1545. As that Place was the Resort of several Nations on the Account of Trade, all the Vices that are committed by a great Concourse of People, where all the Pleasures of Life are before them, reign'd there without Controul. St. *Francis*'s Design at first was only to take that City in his Way to *Macassar*; but the Governor prevail'd with him to stay there 'till he could get an exact Account of the State of Christianity in that Island. He would accept of no other Accommodation but what the Hospital afforded; where he was visited by great Numbers, no Strangers to his Character. That Apostolical Man, much afflicted at the deplorable Condition of the Inhabitants of the Town, undertook to devote the Time of his Stay there to the Reformation of those infamous Debauchees. He practised his usual Method of attending and assisting the Sick, and spent whole Nights in Prayers, Tears, and incredible Austerities for obtaining the Conversion of that unhappy People. When he left the Hospital he appear'd in the publick Streets, like a true

Dec. 3. true Apostle, preached the Doctrine of Penance, and declared it the Duty of every one to pray for Persons in Mortal Sin, as for such as were really dead. The natural Sweetness of his Temper, and his ingenious Charity suggested a thousand engaging Arts for gaining all Sorts, and he had the Satisfaction of seeing the Success of his Labours in the Reformation of much the greatest Part of *Malacca*, 'Though most of the Inhabitants profess'd the Christian Religion, their Distance from *Goa* the Seat of the Bishop, and the Plenty and Variety of temporal Delights had made them forget their Obligations, and all Thoughts of Penance and Sobriety had been long banished from among them. *Xaverius* established the Use of Confession among them, translated the Catechism, and other useful Books into their own Language. These Means, and the irresistable Force of his Miracles not only reform'd the corrupt Christians, but converted great Numbers of Pagans and Mahometans.

In the mean Time St. *Ignatius* sent him a fresh Supply of able and zealous Missionaries, who came with *John de Castro*, Successor to *Alphonso de Sousa* Viceroy of the *Indies*. *Xaverius*, receiving no News from *Macassar* after above three Months Stay at *Malacca*, and finding no Ship going that Way, concluded it was the Will of God that he should defer that Voyage 'till a more convenient Opportunity should offer, and employ his Talent in some neighbouring Islands, which were entirely destitute of Evangelical Ministers; and accordingly on the first Day of the Year 1546, he went on board of a Ship bound for the Isles of *Banda*. The Master of the Vessel was the only Christian in the Company; the rest a Mixture of Infidels, and Mahometans; but the Saint gain'd them all to the Faith. After six Weeks Sail they landed at *Amboyna*, an Island very considerable for Trade, and about thirty Leagues in Circumference. In all that large Island were only seven small Villages of *Indian* Christians, who had lately lost the only Priest among them. *Xaverius*, who was directed thither by a particular Providence, began with baptizing the Children, renewing the Use of the Sacraments, and giving suitable Instructions. Having thus renew'd the Face of Religion in the Villages, he made his Way to the Caves and Mountains in Quest of such poor Families as had left their Habitations to avoid the Insults and Cruelties of Pirates and Barbarians who infested the Coast, and assisted them to the utmost of his Power. At his Landing the Pagans and *Saracens* were in Possession of much the most considerable Part of *Amboyna*, but most of them were converted to the Faith of *Christ* before our Saint left that Island. From thence *Xaverius* went to the *Molucca* Islands, situated nearer to *Macassar*, which were filled with barbarous and intractable People; but the Grace that

attended

attended our Saint's Ministry soften'd their Hearts, and brought great Numbers Dec. 3. to the Knowledge of the Truth.

About the Middle of the Year 1547 *Xaverius* return'd to *Malacca*, where he was met by three Missionaries of the Society, who were going to the *Moluccas*, pursuant to the Advice he had sent of the Necessity of leaving some Apostolical Labourers in those Islands. *Mansilla*, the oldest of our Saint's Companions, who had attended him from *Portugal*, receiv'd an express Order for going on the same Mission; but chose rather to do his own Will on the Coast of *Paravas*, than comply with that of his holy Superior; this Act of Disobedience was so displeasing to *Xaverius*, that he dismiss'd him from the Society, and spent a whole Month in forming the other three to the Business in which he employ'd them. In the Beginning of the Year 1548 he landed in *Ceylan*, one of the most considerable Islands in the *Indian* See, and divided into seven distinct Governments; where he converted great Numbers in a small Time, among whom were two of their Kings, and then return'd to *Goa*. When he had regulated the Affairs of the *Indian* Church, distributed his Companions into several Provinces and Islands, and left Directions for such as should come over from *Europe*, he put to Sea in the Month of *April* 1549, in a Ship bound for *Malacca*, from whence he proposed to go for *Japan*, having in his Company four Converts of that Country; and after a long and dangerous Voyage he landed at *Cangoxima* on the fifteenth of *August* following. *Paul*, one of his Retinue, a Native of that Town, pursuant to the Saint's Instructions, acqainted the King of *Saxuma* with their Arrival, and Design, and begg'd the Favour of his Protection. Receiving a favourable Answer from that Prince, *Xaverius* began to learn the Language of the Country, and made such Progress in a Month's Time that he translated his Exposition of the Apostles Creed, which he had composed in the *Indies*; and then waited on the King of *Saxuma*, who receiv'd him very graciously, and gave his Subjects free Leave to embrace the Faith; but as the only Motive for his Civility to our Saint and his Companions was a Prospect of Advantage which might arise to the Trade of his Kingdom from a free Conversation with Foreigners, he was afterwards easily prevail'd with by the *Bonzes*, or idolatrous Priests of that Country, to issue out an Order that all his Subjects should adhere to their old Religion under the most severe Penalties.

After a Year spent at *Cangoxima*, with his usual Success, the Saint went to *Firando*, the Capital City of another Kingdom, where he obtain'd full Power from the King to preach the Gospel in his Dominions. His first Sermons made so strong an Impression on his Audience, that in less than three Weeks he

Dec. 3. he baptized more of the Infidels at *Firando* than he had done in the Kingdom of *Saxuma* in a Year. After a short Stay there he left his Converts in the Hands of *Cosmus de Torres*, set out for *Meaco*, the Seat of the Empire of *Japan*, and took *Amangucium* the Metropolis of *Nangato* in his Way. *Amangucium* was one of the richest, and consequently one of the most debauched Cities in the whole Country. The Novelty of his Doctrine, and the Appearance of a Stranger raised the Curiosity of the Inhabitants, who gave him the Hearing, at his Arrival; but, the Seed of the Gospel took no Root among them, and the holy Preacher was treated as a Madman; nor had he better Success at *Meaco*, after a long and difficult Journey thither on Foot.

At the latter End of the Year 1551 our Saint went back to *Amangucium*; and, having observed that the Faith which he endeavour'd to enforce had been ridiculed and rejected upon the Account of his mean Appearance, bought a rich Suit, and hired two or three Footmen. In this Equipage he waited on the King, presented him with several Curiosities, which he had brought from the *Indies*, and begg'd his Protection, which he obtain'd, and preached for some Time with incredible Success; but the *Bonzes*, alarm'd at the Progress of the Gospel, and confounded at the Miracles perform'd by his Hands, incensed the King against the Saint, and prevail'd with him to recal his Permission; and thus *Xaverius* lost almost all the Advantage he expected from his Presents, and Conformity to the Fashions of the World. But he gain'd above three thousand to the Faith during his Stay at *Amangucium*, in Spight of all the Opposition and Intrigues of the *Bonzes*, and the Change of the King's Dispositions in Regard to him and the Religion which he preached.

Having recommended the Christians at *Amangucium* to the Care of *Cosmus de Torres*, and his Companion *John Fernandez*, he travell'd to *Bungo* the Metropolis of a Kingdom of the same Name, about fifty Leagues South of *Amangucium*, were he design'd to take the Opportunity of a *Portugueze* Vessel, and return to the *Indies*. The Captain of that Vessel, attended by the chief of his Countrymen, saluted him with the Discharge of eighteen Canon at his Arrival, and treated him with a Respect which made his Merit known to the King of *Bungo*, who thereupon sent some of his Officers to visit him in his Name, and invite him to Court. The *Portugueze* held a Consult about the Manner in which *Xaverius* should appear before the King, and all agreed that it should be with all possible Magnificence, to do honour to the Christian Religion, and confound the *Bonzes*, who made their Advantage of the Saint's Poverty for discrediting his Doctrine. *Xaverius* opposed the Motion for some Time, but at last submitted to their Reasons, accepted of a rich
Equipage

Equipage and numerous Retinue, and was handsomely receiv'd by the King Dec. 3. and the whole Court. His Majesty, after a long Conference with our Saint gave him Leave to preach the Gospel through all his Dominions, and the *Bonzes*, heartily mortified at what pass'd, made several Attempts to render the King's Protection useless; but his Reputation was too well established at *Bungo* to be hurt by Calumny, and those Idolaters were always worsted in in the Dispute, though they engaged with him frequently.

After above two Years spent in *Japan*, *Xaverius* took Shipping for *India* on the twentieth of *November*, with a Design of going from that Country to *China*, and had been seven Days at Sea when a violent Storm arose which forced the long Boat from the Ship, and endanger'd the Lives of fifteen Persons who were in it; but it was recover'd, and all their Lives saved by the Prayers of our Saint. About a Fort'night after he landed in an Island where the *Portugueze* had a Factory. On the twenty fourth of *January* 1552 *Xaverius* reach'd *Cochin*; and before he left that Place converted a Mahometan Prince. He arrived at *Goa* in the Beginning of *February*, communicated his Design of going for *China* to the Viceroy and the Bishop, who approved of it, and assured him of their Assistance in the Execution of it; and after some necessary Regulations in regard to those Countries, which had embraced the Faith, and disposing of the Members of the Society in a Manner most suitable to the Necessities of the infant Churches of *India* and *Japan*, he set Sail for *China* on the fourteenth of *April*; and after having weather'd several Dangers, came to *Sanchian* an Island about thirty Leagues from the Coast of *China*. The *Portugueze* Merchants there endeavour'd to engage his Stay among them by representing to him the extreme Difficulty of entring the Country for which he was bound, and the Impossibility of prevailing with the *Mandarins* to dispense with the rigorous Laws of *China*, which made it Death for a Stranger to appear there without Leave. *Xaverius*, bent on that Mission, would listen to no Advice on the Subject, and agreed with a *Chinese* Merchant to carry him over privately; but God was satisfied with his Intentions; for, before this Project could be executed, he was taken with his last Sickness, and breath'd out his pious Soul into the Hands of God, who was his only Comfort in his last Moments; for the Inhabitants of *Sanchian*, by a strange Negligence and unpardonable Ingratitude, deserted him in his Extremities, and he expired in a poor Hovel on the second of *December*, 1552.

His Body was buried near the Port without any Ceremony; and the Funeral attended only by four Persons. *Alvarez*, a *Portugueze*, who had accommodated the Saint with the Hovel in which he died, threw a sufficent Quantity

tity of unflaked Lime into his Coffin, that the Flesh being consumed the holy Relicks might be more easily carried to the *Indies* the following Spring. In that View the Body was taken up about the middle of *February* 1553, and to the great Surprize of all present, found as entire as when laid into the Earth. It was removed to *Malacca*, and deposited in a Church which bore the Name of the Blessed Virgin; but carried to *Goa* in *March*, 1554; where it was receiv'd with all the Pomp and Ceremony used on the most solemn Occasions; and has been since honour'd with innumerable Miracles.

Xaverius was beatified by *Paul* V in the Year 1619, and canonized by his Successor *Gregory* XV on the twelfth of *March* 1622. His Name occurs in the *Roman* Martyrologe on the second of *December*; but *Alexander* VII placed his Festival on the third of the same Month.

St. LUCIUS, King of BRITAIN.

ABOUT the Year 179 *Lucius*, one of the *British* Princes, who 'though Subject to the Emperor, retain'd the Name and Dignity of King, sent a Deputation to *Eleutherius*, then in St. *Peter*'s Chair, desiring to be favour'd with able Missionaries from *Rome* to instruct him in the Faith of Christ. The Proposal was joyfully receiv'd, and venerable *Bede* assures us that the *Britons* having thus receiv'd our most holy Religion, continued in peaceable Possession of that Blessing 'till *Dioclesian*'s Persecution. 'Though this is all we know of our Saint, we could not omit his Name in a Work of this Nature, especially when undertaken by those of the same Country that receiv'd the Light of the Gospel by his Means.

It is thought he died at the Beginning of the III Century, and was buried where the City of *Gloucester* now stands. His Name is to be found in the Martyrologe on the third of *December*.

The IV Day.

St. BARBARA, Virgin and Martyr.

ST. *Barbara* is better known at this Day by the Honours paid to her Memory by the Churches of the East and West than by the History of her Life.

Life. Some Authors date her Martyrdom in the IV Age, under *Galerius* Dec. 4. *Maximian*, or his Succeſſor *Maximian Daia*; while others tell us ſhe ſuffer'd in the III Century under *Maximin* I. Nor is the Place of her Death more certain than the Time. Some ſpeak of *Heliopolis* in *Egypt* as the Scene of her Victory; others declare for *Tuſcany*; while a third ſort with more Probability aſſure us ſhe ſhed her Blood for the Faith at *Nicomedia* in *Bithynia*. Her Name occurs in the *Roman* Martyrologe on the fourth of *December*.

St. CLEMENT of ALEXANDRIA.

ST. *Clement*, according to St. *Epiphanius*, was a Native of *Athens*; but other Writers of good Credit ſuppoſe him born at the City from which he received his Surname, about the Middle of the ſecond Century. His Parents, were Gentiles, and educated him in the Superſtition of their blind Religion; but at the ſame Time took Care to have him inſtructed in all the Sciences known in *Grece* and *Egypt*; the great Variety of Learning which appears in his Works is a ſufficient Proof that his Curioſity and enterprizing Genius carried him to every Branch of Literature then in Vogue. It pleaſed God to viſit him early with the Light of Truth, and let him ſee the Vanity of Knowledge, when not directed to a right End, before he had long abuſed the Advantages which he receiv'd from Nature and Eudcation.

We learn from our Saint's Works that he had ſeveral Maſters, of whom he ſpeaks with a Pleaſure at once expreſſive of his Senſe of their Value and his own Gratitude for their Endeavours in his Favour. He tells us he had two in *Greece*, and two more in the Eaſt, one an *Aſſyrian*, the other originally a *Jew*, whom he found in *Paleſtine*; but ſays he fell into the Hands of a fifth in *Egypt*; who far excell'd the reſt. *Eusebius*, having obſerved that among other Commendations of this extraordinary Perſon, *Clement* calls him the *Sicilian Bee*, concludes he muſt mean *Pantenus*, a Native of *Sicily*, of whom we have treated on the ſeventh of *July*. Our Saint could not have left us a more ſubſtantial Proof of his Affection for Truth, than by letting his Readers know what Pains he took in Queſt of that ineſtimable Jewel, as already mention'd.

Clement was ordain'd Prieſt at *Alexandria*, and thus engaged in the Service of the Church of that City; but we have no Account of the Time of his Ordination. When *Pantenus* was ſent to the *Indies* about the Year 189, our Saint ſucceeded him in the catechiſtical School of *Alexandria*; in which Poſt he gave great Proofs of profound Erudition, and conſummate Prudence;

for

Dec. 4. for in the Course of his Instructions, he suited his Subject and the Manner of treating it to the Capacity and Disposition of his Pupils, and was as cautious of throwing obscure, and intricate Questions in the Way of weak or perverse Minds, as a tender Father would be of putting a Knife into the Hands of a Child unacquainted with the true Use of that dangerous Instrument; a Comparison which he was pleas'd to make on that Occasion. *Clement* could not think he had done his Duty by those who attended his Lectures if he had only enlighten'd their Minds; and therefore took as much Pains to rectify the Motions of their Hearts, to teach them to square their Lives by what they heard, and regulate all their Actions by the important Truths which he taught. In this Way of thinking he first enquired into the Extent of their Capacities, and the Strength of their Genius, and then made it his Business to observe every Action, every Word, and every Motion, that he might form a Judgment of the Soil on which the Seed of Life was thrown.

The School of *Alexandria*, while under his Direction, produced great Numbers of learned Men; but none so famous as *Origen*, who succeeded him in that Post, and *Alexander* Bishop of *Jerusalem*, of whom we have spoken on the eighteenth of *March*, who calls our Saint his Father, and owns he had been singularly useful to him in the Search after Truth. But the Saint, zealous for the Kingdom of *Jesus Christ*, extended his Care beyond the Limits of his School, and undertook to instruct his Cotemporaries at all Distances and the latest Posterity. His *Exhortation to the Gentiles* is the first publick Proof we have of that sort of Charity; in which he lays open the monstrous Absurdities, and ridiculous Impieties of Paganism, and exhorts it's Professors in a strong and eloquent Manner to renounce their Errors, and embrace the Faith. This Work was follow'd by another, divided into three Books; the Design of which is to instruct those, who know the true God, how to form their Lives suitably to their Religion, and therefore he intitules this Piece *the Pedagogue*, or *Director*. His *Stromata*, according to the Purport of the *Greek* Word, is a mix'd Work, comprehends a great Variety of Matter, and is divided into eight Books. We have a Treatise, which bears our Author's Name, in which he shews our Salvation does not depend on quitting our Fortunes and Estates, but on a right Use of what God's Providence has trusted us with; it begins with asking *what rich Man can be saved?* These are all the entire Pieces of our Saint, which have reached us.

Clement appear'd in the Professor's Chair about twelve Years; and then his learned and pious Labours were interrupted by the Emperor *Severus*, who persecuted the Church in 202. He was too well know to the Pagans at *Alexandria* to stand his Ground there without exasperating the Enemies of our holy Religion, and exposing himself to a Danger which the Gospel allows us to avoid, when in our Power. It is not certainly known what became of our Saint after that Retreat; it is usually supposed that he left *Egypt* on that Occasion. About eight Years after he was in *Cappadocia*, where St. *Alexander*, formerly his Scholar, and then Bishop, was in Prison for the Faith. It is not improbable that he spent some Time with that Prelate; and his Death is with great Probability placed about the two hundred and twentieth Year, after the Birth of *Jesus Christ*.

Dec. 5.

The V Day.

St. SABAS, ABBOT.

SABAS, whom the Church proposes to our Veneration this Day, was born in *Cappadocia*, not far from *Cesarea* in the Year 439. His Parents were distinguish'd both by their Rank and Virtue, ; his Father was engaged in a considerable Post in the Army, which obliged him to remove toward *Alexandria*, when our Saint was but five Years old, and leave him in the Hands of his Uncle during his Absence. The Grace of God work'd so powerfully on the Heart of *Sabas* that three Years after he retired to a Monastery, about two Miles and an half from the Place of his Nativity, inhabited by seventy Monks, who own'd St. *Basil* for their Father and Founder. 'Though his Relations were very pressing with him to quit his religious Solitude, he was too sensible of the Happiness he enjoy'd to listen to any Solicitations on that Head. He enter'd into all the Practices of a Cloister with Pleasure, and perform'd them with the utmost Exactness; which was so satisfactory to his Superior, that, upon his desiring Leave to visit the holy Places in *Palestine*, it was easily granted. He undertook that devout Pilgrimage in the Year 457, and spent the Winter in a Monastery under the Direction of *Elpidius*; where his Virtue became so conspicuous that all the religious Houses in that Neighbourhood were ambitious of his Company; but his Love of Retirement made him desirous of being under the Conduct of St. *Euthymius*, to whom *Elpidius* recommended him. *Euthymius*, who had a long Experience in the Monastick Life, did not think so young a Man fit for the *Laura*, the usual Residence of such as had pass'd all the Exercises of a penitential State, and therefore placed him in the Monastery govern'd by St. *Theoctistus*. St. *Euthymius*'s *Laura* consisted

Dec. 5. sisted of a Number seperate Cells scatter'd on a Mountain about twelve Miles from *Jerusalem*, and inhabited only by such as had been form'd in the Monastery already mention'd, which lay about three Miles from those holy Solitaries.

Sabas, thus put into the Hands of *Theoctistus*, devoted himself so entirely to God that he seem'd to think of nothing but him. His Days were imploy'd in Labour, the greatest Part of his Nights in Prayer, and the Spirit of Penance and Devotion animated all his Actions. As he was large and strong he undertook more Work than most of his Brethren; took a singular Pleasure in attending the Sick; and, 'though particularly active and diligent wherever Charity or Mortification call'd for his Hand, was always a Model of Exactness at the Service of the Church.

One of the Monks, having obtain'd Leave to make a Journey to *Alexandria* to settle some family Affairs, desired our Saint might attend him thither, and his Request was granted. While *Sabas* was at that City, his Father and Mother, lately settled there, knew him, though he had been absent so long, and were very pressing with him to make the Remainder of their Days happy with his Company; but the Saint discover'd the Artifice of the Devil, which lay conceal'd under the specious Appearance of a tender and paternal Affection; and, in Order to affect his Father more strongly by a Comparison within the Compass of his own Profession, observed to him that if Deserters ought to be capitally punish'd, a Monk who quitted the Service of God, after most solemn Engagements, could not be innocent. His Parents, finding him true to his Obligation, desired at least that he would accept of a considerable Sum to defray the Charges of his Journey, and furnish himself with some of the Conveniencies of Life. The Saint, after much Entreaty, took some of the Money; but carried the whole to his Superior, and discharged himself of that unnecessary Burthen with the utmost Simplicity.

At the Age of thirty *Sabas* was so far advanced in the Way of Perfection, and so well acquainted with the Duties of his State, that *Euthymius*, who call'd him *The young old Man*, gave him Leave to spend five Days every Week in a Cave alone at a Distance from the Monastery. *Cyril*, our Saint's Disciple, assures us he spent that Time without eating, made ten Baskets every Day, which he brought home on *Saturday* Morning, and return'd to his Cave on *Sunday* Evening loaded with Palm Branches for the Work of that Week. *Sabas* lived five Years in this Manner; after which *Euthymius* chose him and *Domitian* to be the Companions of his Retreat from the fourteenth of *January* to

Palm-

Palm-Sunday; which Interval every Year was spent in the Wilderness of Rouba.

Euthymius dying in 473, Monastick Discipline decay'd very much, which was Motive sufficient for our mortified Saint to leave the Place. He made his Way to a Desart near *Jordan*, where he was violently and frequently attack'd by the Enemy of his Salvation and Repose; but Prayer and Humility made him victorious. *Sabas* had spent four Years in this Desart, when in Obedience to the Will of God signified to him in a Vision, he removed to a Hole in a Rock near the Torrent of *Cedron*, where he lived some Time on the Herbs which grew near the Place; but, being discover'd by some Peasants, they undertook to supply him with a sufficient Quantity of Bread, Cheese, and Dates, and took a singular Pleasure in being useful to the holy Solitary. *Sabas* had lived five Years alone in this Cave, when God inspired him with a Desire of labouring for the Salvation of his Neighbour. Great Numbers crouded to him from all Parts; those, who were disposed to renounce the World, were receiv'd and accommodated with all that was necessary for that State of Penance. He was forty five Years old when his Disciples forming themselves into a regular Community of seventy, chose him for their Superior; and in a little time the Cells were multiplied into a large *Laura*. *Sabas* raised a small Chapel for the Use of his religious Family, and when any Priest pass'd that Way, or made him a Visit, he was invited to offer the holy Sacrifice; for the Saint thought himself unworthy of the sacred Character, and inculcated the same humble Sentiments into those under his Direction.

The Daily Increase of his Disciples obliged him to extend his *Laura* on both Sides of the Brook, which he was enabled to do by what Money they deposited in his Hands at their Admission. Their Number arose to 150, when some Malecontents, growing weary of the Happiness they enjoy'd, complain'd to *Sallustius* Bishop of *Jerusalem*, that *Sabas* was too ignorant and rustick to govern so large a Family, and that he was so whimsically scrupulous that he would neither take holy Orders himself nor allow any of his Monks to receive the Priesthood. *Sallustius*, who was no Stranger to the holy Abbot's Merit, seem'd to listen to this Remonstrance, and told the Complainants the Affair should be allow'd due Consideration. The next Day the Saint, and his discontented Disciples were order'd to appear; the latter were sanguine enough to imagine themselves secure of their Point, and that their Journey to *Jerusalem* would ease them of their hated Superior; but were confounded and surprized to see the Bishop decide the Affair by conferring the Priestly Character

racter on our Saint, and hear him close that Ceremony with an Exhortation to Obedience.

From that Time our Saint's Reputation drew great Numbers to his *Laura* from the most remote Parts of the Empire. Among the rest were three *Armenians*, who were afterwards join'd by a considerable Number of their Countrymen. *Sophia*, our Saint's Mother, had been some Years a Widow, when she sold her Estate, made her Way into *Palestine*, and finished her Days under the Conduct of her holy Son. Part of the Money, which that Lady left in our Saint's Hands, was laid out in building two large Hospitals, one for the Reception of poor Travellers, the other for the Entertainment of such Monks, and Hermits as came that Way. With the rest he repair'd his *Laura*, erected an Hospital at *Jericho*, and founded a new Monastery about three Miles from his own Cell. This House was fill'd with a select Number of such as were farthest advanced in Monastick Perfection, and furnished the Church with several excellent Bishops. He built a small Convent about a Mile from the *Laura*, for the Instruction of Novices; and those who were very Young were put into the Hands of *Theodosius*, who had built a Monastery about four Miles from our Saint's Hermitage, and by him form'd to monastick Discipline, 'till they were thought fit for the *Laura*, where only such were admitted as had pass'd a long Trial, and given great Proofs of a religious Spirit.

Sallustius Bishop of *Jerusalem* fell ill in the Year 493, and his Life being in evident Danger, the Monks and Solitaries within his Diocese went to him in a Body, desiring he would be pleased to place *Sabas* and *Theodosius* at their Head. The Patriarch, very well pleased with an Opportunity of securing the Happiness of the Petitioners before he left the World, made our Saint *Exarch*, or general Superior of all the Anchorets, whether they inhabited the Deserts, Hermitages, or Lauras; and his holy Friend was entrusted with the Inspection and Government of all the *Cenobites*, or Monks living together in Communities. *Sabas* was active and vigilant in the Execution of his new Commission; and some, who could not bear his just Severity and religious Exactness, turn'd his very Virtues into so many Heads of Accusations against their holy Superior. The factious Party grew so loud and troublesome that he thought it prudent to leave his *Laura*, and the rest of his extensive Charge in safe Hands, and remove the Cause of their Discontent. After some Time spent in a Cave near *Scythopolis*, he return'd to his *Laura*, hoping his long Absence had soften'd their rebellious Tempers into Reason, and Obedience; but had the Mortification to find them more violent than ever, and the Faction supported by no less than forty. Rather then engage in a

conten-

contentious Dispute, which must give much Scandal, he retired into the Neighbourhood of *Nicopolis*, where the Branches of a Tree were his only Cover, and it's Fruit his only Food, 'till the Proprietor of that Piece of Ground raised him a Cell, and supplied him with the Necessaries of Life.

It having been given out that the Saint was dead, he thought himself obliged to destroy the Credit of the Report by appearing at *Jerusalem*, where *Elias*, then Patriarch of that City, detain'd him 'till he prevail'd with him to return to his *Laura*. That Prelate sent a Letter by *Sabas* requiring the Rebels to receive him as their Superior, and pay him all the Respect due to his Station or leave the Diocese immediately. The Party, finding themselves thus disabled from making any farther Opposition, chose rather to quit the Place than submit; but, wherever they went, they were look'd on with Contempt. Our Saint, though so grossly insulted, was the only Person who shew'd any Regard for them; upon hearing they were endeavouring to settle in some Cells, that were scarce habitable, but the best they could find, he was so full of Concern for his disobedient Children, who had left their Father's House, that he remitted them some Money, solicited a Grant of the Cells on which they had seiz'd, and built them a Church. Overcome with the truly Christian Arms of our Saint, the Apostate Monks threw themselves at his Feet, acknowledged their Fault, and begg'd he would take them into his Protection. *Sabas*, whose whole Endeavours were directed to the Good of their Souls receiv'd them with open Arms, gave them an Abbot; and that Establishment was afterwards known by the Appellation of *the New Laura*.

Anastasius, who came to the Imperial Crown in the Year 491, favouring the *Acephali*, a Branch of the *Eutychians*, displaced *Macedonius* Patriarch of *Constantinople*, for defending the Decisions of the Council of *Chalcedon*, and fill'd his See with *Timothy*, who solicited the Communion of *Elias* Patriarch of *Jerusalem* and the other Prelates of the East, and their Subscription to *Methodius*'s Deposition. *Elias* believed that artful Hypocrite Orthodox, and therefore made no Difficulty of complying with the former Branch of his Request; but refused the latter on the Account of the violent and unwarrantable Manner in which the injur'd Patriarch had been forced from his See. The Emperor, not satisfied with this Way of deciding the Dispute, insisted on an absolute, unreserved Approbation of all that had been done in that Affair. *Elias*, apprehensive that the Prince's Anger might fall heavy on his Flock, deputed a select Number of the most holy Solitaries in his Diocese to *Constantinople*, to dissuade his Imperial Majesty from disturbing the Peace of the Church. *Sabas* was at the Head of this Embassy; but his Appearance was so mean

Dec. 5. mean that, when the others were admitted to Audience, he was thrust back by the Guards, who took him for a Beggar. Upon opening the Patriarch's Letter, *Anastasius* found our Saint mention'd by his Name, and desired to know which was He. Whereupon, strict Search being made, *Sabas* was found saying his Prayers in a Corner, and introduced to the Emperor, who treated him with much Respect; but was too much prejudiced against *Elias* and the Council of *Chalcedon* to listen to what the Saint had to say in Favour of that Prelate. *Sabas* spent the Winter in the Suburbs of *Constantinople*, and in the following Spring applied to the Emperor for the Relief of great Numbers of the Poor in and near *Jerusalem*, who had suffer'd much from the heavy Taxes. That Prince was upon the Point of granting our Saint's Request, when an *Eutychian* Officer in Waiting assured him that the Persons recommended to his Consideration were *Nestorians*, and Jews, and consequently unworthy of his Concern. This Expedition was not entirely useless; for, 'though the Saint did not carry his Point, the Monasteries of *Palestine* receiv'd a considerable Sum of Money from the Imperial Bounty, which was deposited in his Hands for their Use.

At his Return, *Sabas* confirm'd the Patriarch of *Jerusalem* in his Resolution of defending the Council of *Chalcedon*; and the Prelate adhered so firmly to the Decisions of that venerable Assembly that he was banished in the Year 513, and *John* put in his Place. The new Patriarch of *Jerusalem*, who had anathematized the Council of *Chalcedon*, seem'd ready to comply with all the Emperor could expect from him at that Juncture. Our Saint, alarm'd at the Danger to which the Church of *Jerusalem* was exposed, went to that City, where he found *John* with his Clergy about him, and exerted himself so vigorously that the Bishop not only promised him not to hold Communion with *Severus* the Usurper of the See of *Antioch*, as the Emperor had required, but engaged his Word to stand by the Council of *Chalcedon*. *John* was so sincere a Convert to the Orthodox Faith that our Saint had the Satisfaction of hearing him pronounce a solemn Anathema against *Severus* in St. *Stephen*'s Church. The Governor of *Palestine* was present at the Ceremony; but, finding the Congregation unanimous in applauding the Conduct of that Patriarch, thought it most prudent to make his way to *Cesarea* with as little Noise as possible. The Emperor, being inform'd of what had pass'd at *Jerusalem*, seem'd resolved to employ Violence against the Patriarch, and the two Superiors of the Monks of *Palestine*. Those holy Abbots, being inform'd of his Dispositions, drew up a Request to his Imperial Majesty, in which they complain'd of the Insults which the Monks met with every Day in *Jerusalem*;

accused

accused *Severus* of *Antioch* as the Author of all the Disorder and Scandal in the Eastern Church, and declared in the Name of the whole Body of Catholicks that they were ready to shed their Blood in Defence of the four general Councils. The Emperor, who was preparing for an Expedition when he receiv'd this Letter, had not then Time to proceed in that Affair. *Sabas* was indefadigably vigilant in the Discharge of the Duties of his Post, and particluarly active in maintaining the Orthodox Faith in it's Purity, and preserving regular Discipline in all the Monasteries of *Palestine*, which the *Eutychian* Monks endeavour'd to corrupt, as they had done those in *Syria*.

Justinian came to the Imperial Throne in the Year 527; and the Extravagancies committed in his Reign by the seditious *Samaritans* in *Palestine* were maliciously imputed to the Christians. *Peter*, Patriarch of *Jerusalem* and his Suffragans, knowing what Deference all the World paid to St. *Sabas*, begg'd he would undertake a Journey to *Constantinople*, put the Affair in a right, light and desire some heavy Taxes might be taken off. The holy Abbot was then fourscore and ten Years old; but nothing could hinder him from performing this charitable Embassy. *Justinian* receiv'd the venerable Solitary as an Angel from Heaven, granted all he asked with a Cheerfulness that shew'd his profound Veneration for him, and sent Orders for driving the *Samaritans* out of *Jerusalem*, and executing the Authors of the late Troubles. That Prince, at the Instance of St. *Sabas*, founded an Hospital in *Jerusalem*, and gave Directions for repairing the Churches which had suffer'd from the seditious *Samaritans*. Having given the Emperor some excellent Advice about the Hereticks of those Times, and foretold the Success of his Arms against the *Goths* and *Vandals*, who had infected *Italy* and *Africa* with *Arianism*, the Saint return'd to *Jerusalem*, were he published the Imperial Orders; and, at the Intreaty of the Patriarch and his Bishops, did the same in *Cesarea* and *Scythopolis*; after which he made his last Visit to the holy Places, and fell ill in his great *Laura*. The Patriarch, being inform'd of his Sickness, went to see him; and finding him unprovided of the common Necessaries of Life, order'd him to be removed to *Jerusalem*, where he was well attended and furnished with all his Condition required. *Sabas*, being assured that his End was near, begg'd he might be allow'd the Pleasure of dying among his Monks; which was granted him; and he Expired soon after in his Cell on the fifth of *December*, 531. Both the *Greeks* and *Latins* honour his Memory on the Day of his Death.

THE

Dec. 6.

The VI Day.

St. NICHOLAS, Bishop of MYRA.

ACCORDING to best Accounts extant, St. *Nicholas* was a Native of *Patera* in *Lycia*, and born in the III Century, of honourable Parents. Conducted by the Spirit of God from his Cradle, he observed a regular Abstinence two Days in a Week with an Exactness that shew'd he would prove a Model of Penance and Mortification. He was educated in Principles of Virtue, studied with uncommon Success, and was ordain'd Priest by the Bishop of *Myra*, the Metropolis of *Lycia*. Upon the Death of his Parents, he became Master of a plentiful Fortune, most of which was freely distributed among the Necessitous; and the saving three young Women from Ruin by giving them Portions is by his Historian recorded in his Commendation. The same Author tells us that *Nicholas* was pointed out by divine Direction to govern the Church of *Myra* in the Reign of *Dioclesian*, that he suffer'd Imprisonment for the Faith under that Prince, return'd to *Myra* upon *Constantine*'s Accession to the Throne, was present at the Council of *Nice*, and died soon after.

St. *Nicholas* is honour'd by the *Grecians* as a Saint of the first Rank, and both they and the *Latins* keep his Festival on the sixth of *December*. His Body was removed to *Bari* in the Kingdom of *Naples* in the Year 1087, where God manifested the Sanctity of his Servant by many Miracles; and the aforesaid Town is still famous for the Resort of Pilgrims from all Parts.

St. ASELLA.

ST. *Jerom*, our Saint's Historian, tells us She was represented to her Father in a Dream before she was born by a clear and bright Vessel of Glass, as a Presage of her Purity and the Lustre of her Virtues. She was scarce ten Years old when her Parents consecrated her to God in a particular Manner; and she soon after gave glorious Proofs that she had not receiv'd his Grace in Vain. Her Abhorrence of the Vanities of this World appear'd by her tearing the Pearls and Gold from her Neck and Arms, which her Station seem'd to make only a decent Ornament; and her Indifference to the Pleasures of this Life was manifest from her daily Mortifications. At twelve Years of Age she confin'd herself to a small Cell, where she enjoy'd all the

Pleasures

Pleasure that attends a heavenly Conversation. Bread, Salt, and Water were her whole Diet; she wore a Haircloth next her Skin; and could never be prevail'd with to dress in a Manner that might attract the Eye, or speak the least Regard for appearing to Advantage. As she look'd on Idleness as the most dangerous Vice that could be admitted in Retirement, she was always employ'd either in Prayer or Work; nor did the Labour of her Hands prove any Interruption to her Conversation with her heavenly Spouse, for even then she repeated some of the Psalms with great Fervour and Attention.

When St. *Jerom* was ready to sail from *Italy* to *Palestine* he wrote to our Saint, appeal'd to the great Tribunal of *Jesus Christ* for his Justification, complain'd of the perverse Disposition of his Enemies, who so easily credited what had been said to his Disadvantage, but would not believe him innocent, 'though declared so by the same Mouth which had calumniated him; so irreparable is the Sin of Detraction! and concludes with desiring her Prayers for a good Voyage. After St. *Jerom*'s Departure, *Asella* lead as solitary a Life at *Rome*, as she could have done in the Desart; she never left her Chamber but to visit the Tombs of the Martyrs, or assist at the publick Service of the Church; her Mortifications could not but appear in her Face, but she was a Stranger to Ostentation; the great Severities, which she practised on her own Body, did not destroy the Sweetness of her Temper, which was a happy Composition of Seriousness, and Cheerfulness. *Paladius*, who was at *Rome* in the Year 404, tells us he saw her, and that she was then grown old in a Monastery in that City. The Time of her Death is not known; the *Roman* Martyrologe places her Name on the VI of *December*.

The VII Day.

St. AMBROSE, Bishop of MILAN.

THE great Saint, whom the Churches of the East and West honour this Day, was Son to *Ambrose*, Prefect of the *Pretorium* in *Gaul*, and born in that Country about the Year 340. His Father dying when he was young, the Saint went with his Mother to *Rome*, where She and his Sister were employ'd in forming him to Virtue; and the best Masters that City afforded entrusted with the Care of his Studies. *Ambrose* made an excellent Use of these Advantages; and became so famous for his Learning, Eloquence, and Integrity that *Probus*, *Pretorian*, Prefect for *Italy*, made him his Assistant.

Dec. 7. He gave such Satisfaction in that Post that the Prefect made him Governor of *Liguria* and *Emilia*, two Consular Provinces, which comprehend the Dutchies of *Milan, Parma,* and *Modena, Bologna, Romagna, Piemont,* and the Republick of *Genoa*, When he was sent to that Government, *Probus* took his Leave of him with this Admonition; *Go, and act rather like a Bishop than a Judge*; by which Words the Prefect seems to advise a mild and gentle Administration, such as becomes the Episcopal Character rather than the haughty Severity, practised by most Magistrates under *Valentinian*, who was always best pleased when his Subjects suffer'd most.

The Emperor *Constantius* had forced *Dionysius*, an Orthodox Prelate from the See of *Milan* in the Year 355, to make Room for *Auxentius*, a violent *Arian*, who distress'd that Church near Twenty Years. Upon the Death of that Heretick, which happen'd in 374, the People of *Milan* were divided about the Choice of a Pastor; for the *Arians* were but too numerous and considerable in that City, and insisted strenuously on one of their own Principles, while the Catholicks opposed the Motion with a becoming Vigour. The Contest ran so high at last that *Ambrose* found it necessary to interpose his Authority; he went to the great Church where the People were assembled, and made an excellent Discourse on the Necessity and Advantage of preserving the publick Peace, and proceeding with a Spirit suitable to the Affair in Hand. The Success of this Speech was little less than miraculous; the Minds of the jarring Parties were immediately united; and the general Voice delared *Ambrose* their Bishop, 'though then but a Catechumen. This unexpected Choice surprized and affrighted the Saint, who immediately left the Church, and order'd several Criminals to be put on the Rack; a Severity which he hoped would make the People drop the Election; but the whole Tenor of his Conduct convinced them this was an affected Piece of Cruelty, and they repeated their Resolution of placing him in the vacant See. Confounded and amazed at what had pass'd *Ambrose*, went home with a Design of spending his Time there in Privacy and Retirement; but all knew his Value too well to allow him to live for himself only. He was persuaded by a mistaken Humility that the most effectual Way of avoiding the Episcopal Dignity would be to ruin his own Reputation; and in that View admitted publick Prostitutes into his House in the Face of the whole World. But the People, thoroughly prepossess'd in Favour of his Virtue, persisted in their Choice, and declared they were willing to answer for his Sins.

The Governor, finding all his Artifices too weak, had Recourse to Flight as the only Means left; he stole out of *Milan* in the Night, with a Design

of

St. Ambrose, *Bishop.*

of going to *Pavia*; but lost his Way and at Break of Day found himself at one of the Gates of *Milan*. *Ambrose* falling thus into the People's Hands, was guarded very carefully; and an Account of What had pass'd sent to *Valentinian*, with a Petition for his Consent to consecrate the Saint. That Prince, who was then at *Treves*, express'd great Satisfaction at their Choice; and added that the wonderful Unanimity which appear'd on that Occasion was the Work of God, who seem'd to point out the Person in Question, and therefore desired he might be consecrated without Delay. Before the Emperor's Orders reached *Milan*, *Ambrose* found Means to make his Escape once more, and hid himself in the House of *Leontius*, a Man of the first Rank in that Province; but the Emperor's Lieutenant in *Italy* being charged with the Execution of the imperial Orders, forbidding his Concealment under severe Penalties, he was deliver'd up by his Friend, brought back to *Milan* under a Guard, and baptized. He did all in his Power to defer his Consecration; but the People, impatient of the Delay, over ruled all his Difficulties; obliged him to accept of a Dispensation of the Canons in Consideration of the pressing Necessities of that Church, and saw him consecrated a Week after he was baptized. Our Saint's Consecration, which was perform'd, as is believed, on the seventh of *December* 374, was approved of by the whole Christian World; and both the *Latins* and *Greeks* venerate his Memory on that Day in Gratitude for the great Blessing bestowed on the Church at that Time.

Dec. 7.

As soon as the Saint was seated in the Episcopal Chair, he divided all his ready Money between his Church and the Poor, reserved only the Use of his real Estate during his Sister's Life, put the Care of his Family into his Brother *Satyrus*'s Hands, and devoted all his Thoughts and Time to the faithful Discharge of his Functions. As he had till then conversed chiefly with Profane Authors, and had little or no Acquaintance with those Branches of Learning which were absolutely necessary in his present Station, he made it his first Business to enquire into the Doctrine and Discipline of the Church. His Application to the Study of the holy Scriptures, and the Writings of the Fathers was indefatigable, and St. *Basil* was his favourite Author. Not satisfied with knowing that great Prelate in his learned Works, he wrote to him, and desired the Favour of his Friendship. St. *Basil* answer'd his Letter by the first Opportunity, express'd an uncommon Satisfaction in being acquainted with so valuable a Person, thank'd God for committing the Care of his Flock to a Man so well qualified for the Post, exhorted him to exert himself strenuously against Vice and Heresy, and begg'd he would write to him frequently.

St. *Ambrose*,

Dec. 7. St. *Ambrose*, being invested with the sacred Character, was oblig'd to teach as well as study, and sow the divine Seed among his People, assoon as it came into his Hands. He preached every Sunday, and offer'd the great Sacrifice every Day. He was so constant at Prayer that he depriv'd himself of his Rest, for the heavenly Satisfaction of conversing with God; and his Fasts and corporal Mortifications were very rigorous. The Saint had not been long on the See of *Milan*, before he gave the World a Proof of his Courage, and let the Church see what it might expect from such a Bishop. Some Magistrates having exceeded their Commission, and been guilty of several irregular Practices, he complain'd of their Conduct to the Emperor *Valentinian*. That Prince though remarkably haughty and passionate, was so far from resenting this Liberty, that he only replied, he had long known his Freedom of Speech; which however prov'd no Impediment to his Promotion to the See of *Milan*; and desired he would continue to apply such Remedies to his Soul as the Law of God prescribed.

Valentinian, dying toward the Close of 375, left two Sons; *Gratian* the elder, was then about seventeen Years old, and had been declared Emperor at eight; *Valentinian* the younger, about four Years old receiv'd the Title of *Augustus* six Days after his Father's Decease. Our Saint had all the Tenderness of a Parent for the two young Princes, made it his Study how to serve them by promoting their Interest, and giving them good Advice, and receiv'd a grateful Return of Affection, and Respect. The late Emperor had on all Occasions declared himself in Favour of S. *Ambrose*, so that during that Prince's Life it was not possible for the *Arians* to give him much Trouble; upon *Valentinian*'s Death the Party was in Motion, and might have defeated the Saint's Labours for his Diocese, had not *Gratian* asserted the Catholick Faith, and protected the holy Bishop in his Endeavours against Heresy; and thus the Peace of the Church was happily restored, and the Party quite routed. Our holy Prelate employ'd his Interest with the Emperor for the Good of the Church, and particularly that Part of it committed to his Care. His Discourses on Virginity which he recommended in the most engaging Terms, produced surprizing Effects among his Auditors; and *Milan* was soon full of young Ladies from all Parts of *Italy* and even from *Mauritania*, who consecrated their Virginity to God under his Direction, and took the Veil from his Hands. Those on the Spot were not so easily gain'd; several complain'd that he was too large in the Commendation of Celibacy; and Mothers knew no Way to secure their Daughters and keep them in the World but that of confining them, and hindering their hearing the Saint on that Subject. *Marcellina* his Sister, of whom
we

have spoken on the seventeenth of *July*, had been long profess'd at *Rome*; hearing of his Discourses and their Success, she congratulated the Preacher, and desired him to favour her with a Copy of them. At her Entreaty therefore St. *Ambrose* collected them into the three Books *Of Virgins*, as they stand at present. That Work was soon follow'd by his Treatise *Of Widows*, in which he speaks of second Marriages as indecent, but takes Care to reject the Opinion of those who condem them as unlawful. His next Piece is a Book *Of Virginity*, in which he justifies his Conduct against such as accused him of too much Zeal in recommending that State.

While our Saint was thus employ'd, the Eastern and Northern Parts of the Empire felt the Weight of God's Anger; the *Arian* Emperor *Valens* had the Mortification of seeing his Armies worsted, and Provinces ravaged by an Inundation of *Goths*. That Prince was obliged to March all his Forces against them into *Thrace*; and was near *Adrianople*, when he receiv'd News that *Gratian* his Nephew had gain'd considerable Advantages over the *Germans*, and was bringing his victorius Forces to his Assistance; but, being jealous of that young Prince's growing Power and Reputation, he took no Notice of the Offer, and proceeded in his Journey. *Gratian*, who was perfectly Orthodox, and a warm Friend of the Catholick Faith, was desirous of being furnished with a Preservative against the pernicious Doctrines, which prevail'd in the East; for that Purpose he applied to our Saint, desired he would compose a Treatise on the Divinity of *Jesus Christ*, and establish that important Article with the strongest Reasons in his Power. In Compliance with the Emperor's Request, *Ambrose* drew up the two first of his five Books, *Of Faith*, in the former of which he shews in what the Catholick Faith consists; proves the Unity of the Divine Nature, a Trinity of Persons, and the Divinity of *Jesus Christ*, after which he refutes the principal Errors of the *Arians*: in the Latter he shews that all the Attributes of the Divinity are found in the Son; explains his Manner of being sent by, and inferior to the Father; and distinguishes between what is proper to him as Man, and what as God. The three additional Books which appear under the same Title, were penn'd some Time after in Answer to the Calumnies of the Hereticks, who gave out that he had abridged their Objections so far as to injure their pretended Arguments, and answer'd them in too concise a Manner. This Work soon made it's Way 'through the whole Church, was every where read with Admiration, and quoted with Honour by the general Council at *Ephesus* in 431.

Valens's precipitate Pride proved his Ruin; for he lost the Day and his Life in an Engagement with the *Goths* in the Year 378; and the Barbarians carried

Dec. 7. ried that victorious Arms as far as the *Alps*, without any confiderable Oppofition. This Calamity gave our Saint a favourable Opportunity of exercifing his Charity toward the Miferable; he ranfom'd great Numbers of Chriftian Slaves; on which Occafion he melted down fuch of the Church Plate as had not been confecrated; and referved that which had been ufed for fome more preffing Occafion. The *Arians*, always forward to carp at his Conduct, gave an odious Turn to this Action; to which Reproach he anfwer'd in his fecond Book of Offices that it was more glorious and advantageous for the Church to fave the Souls of her Children than preferve her Treafure; that the Church poffefs'd Gold only to diftribute it among the Neceffitous; and that the ranfoming Captives out of the Hands of the Barbarians had a Tendency not only to fave the Lives of Men, and the Honour of Women, but preferve the Faith of the younger and weaker of that Number which was endanger'd by their being in the Power of their Idolatrous, or Heretical Enemies. As the Natives of *Illyricum*, who fled before the *Goths*, made their Way into *Italy*, St. *Ambrofe* wrote to *Conftantius* a Catholick Bifhop in *Romagna*, caution'd him againft that People, who were infected with *Arianifm*, and advifed him to keep them, if poffible, from converfing with the Catholicks, as the only fecure Means of ftopping the Progrefs of the Contagion.

At his Return to *Gaul*, *Gratian* wrote to our Saint in a very refpectful and ferious Manner, defiring he would make a Journey to Court, give him farther Inftructions on fome Articles, of which he was already firmly perfuaded, and fend him another Copy of his Treatife *Of Faith*, with the Addition of the beft Proofs of the Divinity of the holy Spirit. *Ambrofe*, pleafed with that Prince's excellent Difpofitions, anfwer'd his Letter in the Stile of a Panegyrick, fent him the Book which he defired; but begg'd more Time for compofing a Treatife of the holy Spirit, and affured him he would wait on him with all poffible Expedition. It is extremly probable that the Emperor prevented him; for we find him at *Milan* foon after the Date of St. *Ambrofe*'s Letter, where he receiv'd full Satisfaction in every Point.

In the Year 379 the Epifcopal See of *Sirmium* in *Pannonia* became vacant; and the Calamities, which two Heretical Bifhops had entail'd on that Church required an able Hand. 'Though that City lay out of our Saint's Province, he undertook to provide it with a Paftor; in which Step he thought himfelf privileged by the Example of feveral holy Prelates on the like Occafion, and the Reafon there was to apprehend the Influence of the Emprefs *Juftina* in the Election, who was then at *Sirmium* with her Son *Valentinian*. At his Arrival he found that Princefs very active in promoting the *Arian* Intereft, tereſt, and employing all her Authority for placing one of their Party in the vacant See; upon his entring the Church ſhe incenſed the People ſo againſt him that they attacked him in a tumultuous Manner, and attempted to turn him out. A young Woman, full of Zeal of the Cauſe, had the Aſſurance to ſtep up to the holy Biſhop, lay hold of his Cloaths, and endeavour to drag him toward that Side where the Women ſat, who where ready to make their Court to *Juſtina* by abuſing our Saint. *Ambroſe* told the bold Aggreſſor, that though he was unworthy of the ſacred Character which he bore, it did not become her to lay violent Hands on him, and that ſhe ought to fear the Judgment of God for her Raſhneſs; the Death of that young Woman, which probably happen'd the ſame Day, perhaps on the Spot, and the Saint's charitable Attendance at her Funeral the next, work'd ſo powerfully on the *Arians*, that they made no farther Oppoſition, ſo that *Anemius* was choſen and conſecrated. From that Time the Empreſs conceived a thorough Averſion to St. *Ambroſe*, and took all Opportunities of perſecuting him as the moſt formidable Adverſary of the Cauſe which ſhe eſpouſed.

The Intrigues and Threats of that implacable Enemy of the Catholick Faith could not make the holy Biſhop leſs careful of his Flock, or leſs zealous in the Defence of Truth. He provided the Churches under his Inſpection with learned, virtuous, and orthodox Paſtors; reconciled Differences; and labour'd hard to remedy the many Diſorders occaſion'd by Vice and Hereſy. In the Year 379 *Palladius* and *Secundianus*, two *Arian* Biſhops in *Illyricum* complain'd to *Gratian* that they were unjuſtly look'd on as Hereticks, and begg'd his Imperial Majeſty wou'd give Directions for convening the Biſhops of the Empire, eſpecially thoſe of the Eaſt, from whom they expected moſt Favour and Protection. *Gratian* conſented to their Requeſt, and named *Aquileia* for the Place where the Council ſhould be held, without ſetting the Time. St. *Ambroſe*, obſerving to that Prince that it would not be neceſſary to trouble ſo great a Number of Biſhops, while he and the other *Italian* Prelates were very able to deal with the Petitioners, *Gratian* gave free Leave to ſuch as were diſpoſed to reſort to *Aquileia*, and diſpenſed with the Abſence of all whoſe Age, Infirmities, or Poverty would not allow them to travel thither. The Council was open'd above two Years after, and conſiſted of about thirty Biſhops, moſtly *Italians*. *Valerian*, the Biſhop of the Place preſided; but our Saint was the Soul of that venerable Aſſembly, propoſed all the Queſtions that were handled there, confounded the two Champions of Arianiſm, and collected the Voices of the Prelates. About the ſame Time St. *Ambroſe* finiſhed his Treatiſe *On the holy Spirit*, which *Gratian* had deſired him to write.

write three Years before. This Piece is divided into three Books, in which he produces the Arguments made Use of by the greatest Doctors of the *Greek* Church in Defence of the Divinity, and Consubstantiality of the third Person in the Blessed Trinity.

Toward the Close of the Year 382 St. *Ambrose* was obliged to go for *Rome*, where Pope *Damasus* held a numerous Council for putting an End to the Schism at *Antioch*, then divided between *Flavian* and *Paulinus*; 'though the Fathers of that Council could not bring the Affair to the desired Conclusion, they express'd their Opinion of *Paulinus*'s Title to the disputed See by directing their Synodical Epistle to him as Bishop of *Antioch*. While St. *Ambrose* was at *Rome* he was invited to the House of a Lady of the first Quality, where he offer'd the great Sacrifice; a poor Woman in the Neighbourhood confin'd to her Bed with the Palsy, hearing where he was, begg'd to be carried thither, and recover'd the free Use of her Limbs by his Prayers. *Paulinus*, the original Author of our Saint's Life, and his Secretary, tells us he had the Account of this Miracle from several Persons of known Virtue, who had been Eye-witnesses of it. Soon after his Return to *Milan*, our Saint composed his Treatise *Of the Incarnation*, in which that Mistery is defended against the Objections of the *Arians* and other Hereticks. It was the Result of a Challenge made him by two of the Emperor's Houshold who promised to attend his Discourse on that Subject, but had the Misfortune to fall out of a Chariot in which they went to take the Air, instead of appearing at Church according to their own Appointment, and died on the Spot. Our Saint is so far from insulting the Memory of those unhappy Persons, that he has no where mention'd their tragical End, so that we are obliged to his Historian for the Account of it.

The Emperor *Gratian* being murther'd at *Lyons* in the Year 383 by a Party of his own Soldiers, who had placed the Imperial Diadem on *Maximus*'s Head. That succesful Rebel fix'd his Residence at *Treves*; and soon let the World see that *Gaul*, *Spain*, and *Britain* which had obey'd the late Emperor would not content his Ambition, and was preparing to pass the *Alps*. The Court of *Valentinian*, alarm'd at the News, resolved to send an Embassy to *Maximus*, to divert him, if possible, from the Enterprize. This Expedient was no sooner mention'd but all Eyes were placed on the holy Bishop of *Milan*, as the properest Person to negotiate this difficult Affair; even *Justina*, 'though his implacable Enemy, was obliged to beg his Assistance in this Emergency, and put her Son's whole Interest into his Hands. *Ambrose* undertook that dangerous Journey at the Beginning of the Winter, and met

Victor

Victor at *Mentz*, who was deputed from *Maximus* to *Valentinian* to lull him Dec. 7. into a false Security under the specious Pretence of making Peace with the young Prince. Upon the Saint's Arrival at the Tyrant's Court he advised with his Council, who were of Opinion that nothing could be done in this Affair till *Victor*'s Return from *Italy*. This Delay obliged our Saint to spend the whole Winter at *Treves*; during which Time he refused to hold Communion with *Maximus*, whom he look'd on as no better than his Master's Murtherer. All we know farther of this Affair is that *Maximus* dropp'd his Design of passing the *Alps*; but we have no Account of the Terms on which the Peace was concluded.

The Pagans at *Rome*, who had been sufficiently humbled by the Laws made by *Gratian*, took their Advantage of *Valentinian*'s Nonage, and his Mother's weak Administration, and began to entertain Hopes of recovering the Ground which they had lost in some former Reigns. Upon *Constantius* going to *Rome* in 357, the Altar of Victory which stood near the Senate House, was levelled with the Ground; *Julian*, the Apostate, rebuilt it; and *Valentinian* I let it stand; but *Gratian* demolished it once more, confiscated the Lands belonging to the Pagan Temples, and the Revenues appointed for the Maintainance of the Priests, or set apart for other idolatrous Uses; and took away the Salaries of the Vestal Virgins. The Heathen Part of the Senate, very much disgusted at this Order, deputed *Symmachus* to the Emperor's Court with their Complaint, and conceived great Hopes of Success from the Eloquence and Address of their Embassador, who was instructed to speak as if commission'd by the whole Senate. Such of that House as profess'd the Christian Religion drew up a Petition at the same Time, protested against the Proceedings of their Pagan Brethren, and declared they would never sit again, if the former Application succeeded. Pope *Damasus* remitted this Request to our Saint with Directions to deliver it to *Gratian*, who gave it it's due Weight, and rejected that of the Pagans.

After the Death of that Prince *Symmachus*, being made Governor of *Rome* in the Year 384, penn'd a Decree in the Name of the Senate in the Form of a Complaint for the Loss of the Privileges which the Pagans insisted on, and desired might be restored; as his Post obliged him to give their Imperial Majesties an Account of all that pass'd in *Rome*, he drew up a formal Complaint on the same Head, directed to *Valentinian*, *Theodosius*, and *Arcadius*, who then divided the Empire, for Relief of the pretended Grievances; but it was presented only to the first of those Princes; and all imaginable Care taken that *Ambrose* should know nothing of the Matter. *Symmachus* employ'd all his Art at this critical Juncture; but Providence had furnished the World with an able Advocate for the Christian Religion, and a powerful Disputant against the Heathen Follies in the Person of our Saint; who, being apprized of the Proceeding, wrote immediately to *Valentinian*, to hinder his being surprized or imposed on by the Pagans; having obtain'd a Copy of *Symmachus*'s Petition, undertook to answer it, which he perform'd in a very masterly and beautiful Manner; and the Emperor confess'd the Force of his Reasons by refusing all the Pagans had asked.

The Empress *Justina* made a very bad Return for the Services which our Saint had done her and her Son in his Embassy to *Maximus*, as already related; and employ'd the Calm she enjoy'd by his Means in persecuting that excellent Prelate. A little before Easter in the Year 385 that ungrateful Princess sent to the Saint in her Son's Name to demand a Church for the Use of the *Arian* Part of her Family at the approaching Festival; but the holy Bishop's Answer on that Occasion was that he could not deliver up the Temple of God. The next Day the Pretorian Prefect went to the Church, where he found St. *Ambrose* attended by a numerous Auditory, and endeavour'd to persuade him to a Compliance with the Empress's Demand in a publick Manner. The People, without waiting for their Bishop's Answer to the impious Proposal, declared loudly against it, and the Prefect was obliged to leave the Place. On Palm-Sunday our Saint perform'd the usual Service of that Day without the least Apprehension, or Appearance of Concern, 'though severely threaten'd for his late Refusal. The Catechumens being dismiss'd after the Sermon, which follow'd the Gospel, he undertook to explain the Creed to the Competents, or such as were to be baptized the following *Saturday*. He was thus employ'd when News was brought him that proper Officers had receiv'd Orders from the Court to seize the *Portian Basilick* that lay out of Town, and now bears the Name of St. *Victor*, for the Emperor's Use; but the Saint finished his Exposition of the Articles of the Faith, and proceeded to the Offertory without the least Emotion. He was at the Consecration when he was told that *Castulus*, an *Arian* Priest, had been seized by the People in the Street. This Account drew Tears from the Saint's Eyes, who earnestly pray'd that no Blood might be spilt for the Church, and offer'd his own even for his Enemies, the Hereticks. He had no sooner made this generous Offer to the Almighty but he dispatched some of his Clergy with Orders to rescue the *Arian* from the Danger which threaten'd him.

The People, full of mistaken Zeal for Religion, made some Resistance on that Occasion, and disputed the Affair very warmly with the Messengers

gers of Peace and Charity. The Disturbance made on this Occasion was by Dec. 7. the Court term'd Sedition; and great Fines were laid on the whole Body of Merchants; several of them were seized, and thrown in Prison into the holy Week, a Time when it had been customary to release those under Confinement, and all who had any Interest with or Influence over the People were threaten'd with the worst of Usage, if they did not do all in their Power for gratifying *Justina* in the Possession of the Church in Question.

On *Tuesday* the Counts and Tribunes went to St. *Ambrose*, and required him to surrender the Church, insisting on that Compliance as an Act of Obedience to the Emperor, who, as they said desired nothing but what he might justly Claim as his own. The holy Prelate answer'd that if his Imperial Majesty demanded his Lands, his Money, or any thing at his Disposal, he was ready to part with all; but that what belong'd to God was not subject to any Temporal Authority. " *If* said the Saint, *my Estate is aim'd at, I give it up;* " *if my Body, I will prevent the Officers by meeting them; would they load me with* " *Chains, or even lead me to Execution, I submit to all this with Pleasure. I* " *shall make no Provision for my own Security, shall neither engage the People* " *to surround and defend me, nor fly to the Altars for Protection; no, I had much* " *rather be sacrificed on the Altar for the publick Peace*". The holy Bishop deliver'd himself in this Manner, because he had been inform'd that a Party of armed Men were sent to seize the Church, and was apprehensive that the Opposition which the Catholicks would make on that Occasion might prove the Cause of shedding much Blood; he was therefore ready to lay down his own Life rather than the Church should bear the Reproaches of her Enemies on that Score. He was then desired to appease the People; to which he replied that all he could do in the Case was not to raise or incense them, for God only could over-rule their Passions, when heated; *but* continued the Saint, " *if you think I am the Author of this Commotion, punish me as you* " *please.*" *Ambrose* spent the Remainder of that Day in the Church, but went home at Night, that if his Enemies were disposed to lay Hands on him, they might have no Difficulty to find him.

Before the Break of Day next Morning the Saint went to the Church, which was soon after surrounded by Soldiers; most of whom were Catholicks as well as the Citizens of *Milan*; and the *Arians* were so inconsiderable a Number that they never ventured to appear in Publick, except when in the Retinue of their Protectress. The Saint understood by the Sighs of his Congregation that the Church was surrounded; while the Lessons were reading he was apprized that the new Basilick was full of People, and that they wanted

ted a Reader. The Soldiers posted about the Church understanding that the holy Bishop had forbid his Congregation to communicate with them, resolved to run any Hazard rather than be cut off from the Church, and made their Way in. The Women, alarm'd at their Entrance, endeavour'd to make their Escape; but were stopt by the Soldiers assuring them, their only Business there was to join them in the Service. *Ambrose*, perceiving the greatest Part of the People were inclined to go to the new Basilick, and desired his Company thither, engaged their Stay by preaching on Part of the Book of *Job*, which had been read in the Service of that Day. The Saint applied the Particulars of that History to the present Occasion, commended the Patience of his People, compared it to that of *Job*, and drew a Parallel between the Temptations to which he was exposed, and those which attack'd that holy Patriarch. While he was in his Sermon, News was brought him that the Emperor had dropt his Claim to the *Portian* Church, and that it was full of People, who desired to be favour'd with his Presence. That tender Father of all committed to his Care could not bear that any of them should be unprovided with Persons to assist them in the Discharge of their Duty to God, and therefore, 'though he did not think proper to leave the Place where he was employ'd in the same Manner, he sent the Petitioners a sufficient Number of Priests, who where directed to comfort that Part of his Flock by telling them he trusted in *Jesus Christ* that the Emperor would not continue their Enemy. He then went on with his Discourse, but turn'd it to the present Occasion, and thank'd God that those who were sent to distress and guard them were now mix'd with the Congregation; that they who were posted about the Church to invade God's Inheritance were become Coheirs with *Jesus Christ*; and that the Men, whom he thought his Enemies, were now ready to act in his Defence.

St. *Ambrose* had scarce finished his Expressions of Gratitude for the happy Change of Affairs in his Favour when a Secretary came up to him with Orders from Court, and, taking him aside, let him know that the Emperor resented his sending Priests to the Church last mention'd as an Act of Tyranny, and an Attempt which ought not to pass unpunished. The holy Bishop assured the Officer he had done no more than his Duty in the present Case; that when he understood the *Portian* Basilick was invested by Soldiers, he had Recourse only to Sighs for it's Deliverance; that, being advised by some of his Flock to go to the Church in Question, he had answer'd that 'though he could not give up the Temple of God, it was not his Business to assert his Right to it by Arms; and that, even when the Emperor had withdrawn his Claim to

that

that Church, he had sent his Priests thither only on a reasonable Presumption that his Majesty was disposed to favour them. "*If this is what you call Tyranny*, added the Saint, *why is my Punishment deferr'd? for all the Arms I have are the Power of exposing myself to the Stroak.*" As the Church in which St. *Ambrose* officiated was still surrounded by Soldiers, he could not go home; and therefore spent the Night in singing Psalms with the Brethren in a Chapel contiguous to the great Church.

The next Day, which was holy *Thursday*, the Book of *Jonas* was read, according to the Custom of those Times; on which Occasion the Saint undertook to make a Discourse on that Passage which Promises the Return of Sinners. The People, struck with those seasonable Words, began to hope this Prophesy would be fulfill'd in their Favour; and while the holy Bishop was enlarging on that Subject, News was brought that the Emperor had sent Orders for drawing off the Soldiers, who besieged the Church, and restore the Merchants the Fines which had been exacted of them. The Saint, thus deliver'd and victorious, wrote an Account of the whole Affair to his Sister *Marcellina*, then at *Rome*, who, upon hearing the Beginning of this Persecution, was anxious to know where and how it would end. *Ambrose*, who knew *Valentinian*'s Weakness and *Justina*'s restless and implacable Temper, suspected the Reality and Duration of this happy Revolution; and in the Conclusion of his Letter to *Marcellina*, told her he was apprehensive of, and even foresaw, new and greater Troubles. The Catholicks had other Enemies beside *Justina*, and the Ladies of her Court; *Auxentius*, who took upon him the Stile of Bishop, and *Calligonius*, an Eunuch, high Chamberlain to the Emperor, were continually at Work on that weak Prince, and employ'd all their Influence over him against the holy Prelate and his Flock. The latter was insolent enough to assure the Saint that if he dared thus despise *Valentinian*, while He was alive, it should cost him his Head; to which *Ambrose* replied that if what that Courtier threaten'd came to pass He should die like a Bishop, and *Calligonius* act like an Eunuch. We learn from St. *Augustin* that *Calligonius* was soon after beheaded for what that Father calls an infamous Crime.

The following Year but too fully justified our Saint's Apprehensions of the Revival of the Persecution. The Empress and her Son *Valentinian* being then at *Milan*, that Princess resolved to employ all her Authority for establishing *Arianism* in that City, and the adjacent Country; she began with threatening to depose such Bishops as refused to receive the Decisions of the Council of *Rimini*, and prevail'd with her Son to make a Law for privileging the *Arians* to hold publick Assemblies, and bear the Face of a Church. *Benevolus*, Secretary

cretary of State, then a Catechumen, but strictly and inviolably Orthodox, chose rather to lose his Post, and Estate than be concern'd in drawing up the Law proposed; which however, was published on the twenty third of *January* 386, as contrived by the *Arian* Bishop at *Milan*, a *Scythian*, originally call'd *Marcurinus*; but his Crimes making him odious, he changed his Name for that of *Auxentius*, which he hoped would ingratiate him with the Party, whose Cause had been in a languishing Condition ever since the Death of *Auxentius*, our Saint's Predecessor.

Some Time after the said Law appear'd *Dalmatius*, a Tribune and Notary, went to the holy Bishop by *Justina*'s Direction, and told him it was his Imperial Majesty's Will that he should choose what Persons he thought proper to plead his Cause before that Prince, and let him know *Auxentius* had receiv'd the like Order; to which the Officer by the same Authority added that, if the Saint was not disposed to put the Affair on that Issue, he had free Leave to retire to what place he pleased, that is, was desired to quit his See and make Room for *Auxentius*. *Ambrose* consulted some Bishops then at *Milan* on this Matter, who were unanimous against his appearing before the Emperor, as Judge of the Point in Dispute. By their Advice he drew up a Remonstrance to the Emperor in which by Way of Excuse for not complying with his last Orders, he urges the Sentiments of *Valentinian* I, that Prince's Father, who had often declared both in a publick and private Manner that the Judge ought, at least, to be equal to the Parties before him; that is, that Bishops are to be judged by their Peers only; and insists on it as a known Piece of Church Discipline that where the Faith is concern'd the Emperors themselves are subject to the Judgment of the Bishops. He then assures the Emperor that he should have deliver'd his Sentiments on that Subject by Word of Mouth, had not the other Prelates, and the People dissuaded him from it; and declares himself ready to quit his See, could he but be satisfied the Church of *Milan* would not fall into Heretical Hands in his Absence; *for* says he, *according to the Sentiments of my Collegues, leaving my Flock, while Affairs are in this dubious Posture is no better than delivering it into the Hands of the Enemy.*

As soon as the holy Prelate had sent this Remonstrance to the Court, he retired to the Church, where the People guarded him Night and Day for some Time, being apprehensive of a Design of carrying him off by Force; nor were their Fears groundless, for the Emperor, at his Mother's Instigation, posted Soldiers near the Church with Orders to let who would go in, but permit none to come out. The Saint thus shut up with his Congregation, comforted them under their Sufferings; and endeavour'd to inspire them with

that

that Resignation and Patience which their Case required. He made several Discourses on that Subject, of which we have one remaining, deliver'd on Palm-Sunday, as appears from the Gospel of that Day, which is his Subject. It is full of Assurances that he will never leave his People; that, 'though he should be dragg'd out of his Church by Force, his Heart should still remain there; and that, 'though *Valentinian* should exert all the Power of his exalted Station, he was resolved to suffer like a Bishop. The Saint, ever studious of supporting and comforting his Flock under Persecution, introduced the Singing of Hymns, composed by himself, and the Practice of repeating the Psalms alternately in two Choirs, according to the Custom of the Eastern Church at that Time; so that the Churches in the West owe the present Manner of repeating the divine Office to our Saint; and several of his Hymns are at this Day used in our Breviaries. The Discovery of the Relicks of St. *Gervasius* and *Protasius* was one of the most considerable Consolations which God afforded the Church of *Milan*, while groaning under *Justina*'s Persecution; but our Readers are refer'd to the nineteenth of *June* for the Particulars of that Favour, and the Share which our Saint had in that Solemnity of their Translation. The Lustre of the Miracles perform'd on that Occasion fill'd the Empress and her Adherents with Confusion, and obliged her to give over persecuting the Catholicks.

S. *Ambrose* made his Advantage of the present Calm, and improved it to the Good of Posterity by composing his Commentaries on St. *Luke*, and other instructive Pieces. We have already told our Readers what particular Charms St. *Augustin* found in the Conversation and Sermons of the holy Bishop of *Milan*, and that he receiv'd Baptism at his Hands on Easter-Eve 387. It is commonly supposed that our Saint made his Instructions for such as are *initiated in the Divine Mysteries*, on this Occasion.

Such was the Dignity of our Saint's Virtue that even his greatest Enemies were forced to own his uncommon Merit in the most authentick Manner. *Justina* must certainly entertain an exalted Idea of his Generosity, and invincible Charity, when after all she had done against him, she desired him to undertake a second Embassy to *Maximus*, and found him ready to embark in it on the first Proposal, 'though thick set with Difficulties and Dangers. His Instructions were to desire a Grant of *Gratian*'s Body, and a Confirmation of the Peace, which he had negotiated four Years before; for *Maximus*'s Conduct gave but too much Reason to apprehend that he would not long remain Contented with the Extent of his Dominions, but make an Attempt on *Italy*. The Saint reached *Treves* about the Middle of the Year 387; and the Day

after

Dec. 7. after his Arrival went to the Palace, where *Maximus* refused him Audience, unless he would declare his Business before the whole Council; 'though in that Age Bishops were exempted from that Formality, and always heard in private. *Ambrose*, faithful to the Interest of his Prince, and more concern'd for the Success of his Commission than the Privileges annex'd to his Dignity, enter'd the Council, where he found *Maximus* seated at the Head of that select Number of his Subjects. The Emperor arose from his Throne, to kiss our Saint, according to the common Practice on such Occasions; but, 'though his Imperial Majesty call'd him and the Lords of the Council advised him to go up, *Ambrose* remain'd at a Distance. After some Discourse, *Maximus* reproached him with having diverted him from the *Italian* Expedition at a Time when he was capable of carrying all before him. The Saint told him he was now come to wipe off that Aspersion, 'though he could not but own at the same Time his Intention of securing a Royal Orphan might sufficiently plead the Excuse of a Bishop, whose Character obliged him to such charitable Acts. The holy Embassador then proceeded to speak of *Gratian*'s Murther in Terms expressive of *Maximus*'s Gilt in that Affair, and desired that at least his Body might be restor'd to his Relations. The Emperor, surprized at our Saint's Intrepidity, closed the Audience with telling him he would consider of the Matter; the Saint, at leaving the Place, declared he would not hold Communion with him, and advised him to do Penance for the impious Murther of his Master. *Ambrose* kept the same Distance from all the Bishops who communicated with *Maximus*, and such as prosecuted the *Priscillianists* with a View of taking away their Lives.

Maximus, provoked at the Freedom of our Saints Discourse, order'd him to leave the Court immediately, and return to *Milan*; *Ambrose* set out soon after, without any Regard for the Dangers to which he was told by several Persons he would expose himself on the Road. While on the Way he wrote to *Valentinian*, and gave him an Account of his Embassy, to prevent that Prince being prejudiced against him by false or malicious Reports; and concluded his Letter with advising him to stand on his Guard against a crafty Enemy, who conceal'd his hostile Designs under the Appearance of Peace and Friendship. The Event sufficiently shew'd the holy Embassadour's Penetration; for toward the Close of the same Year *Maximus* pass'd the *Alps* with so little Noise that he was very near surprizing *Valentinian*. That Prince and his Mother had only Time enough to embark for *Greece*, where they put themselves under the Protection of *Theodosius* at *Thessalonica*, who restor'd *Valentinian* to his Throne about the Middle of 388, and kill'd the Usurper at *Aquileia*.

From

From that City he marched to *Milan*, where he was receiv'd as the Deliverer of the Catholicks, who were secure of a Friend wherever he had any Command or Influence. *Ambrose* was at *Aquileia* when he heard the Emperor had order'd the Bishop of *Callinicus* in the Province of *Osroëne* beyond *Euphrates* to rebuild a Synagogue for the Jews of that Town which had been burnt by the Christians. Upon receiving this News he immediately wrote a long Letter to the Emperor to prevail with him to revoke the Sentence; which he could not obtain, 'though he urged his Request in the most pressing Manner imaginable. The Saint, not discouraged at the ill success of his Letter, return'd soon after to *Milan*, and when the Emperor came into the Church spoke to him on the same Subject before the whole Congregation; and would not go up to the Altar 'till he had obtain'd *Theodosius*'s Word for stopping the Prosecution.

Dec. 6.

During that Prince's Stay at *Milan*, he receiv'd several Deputations from the most considerable Bodies of the Empire; one of the chief of which was that from *Rome*. *Symmachus*, of whom we have already had Occasion to speak, had contrived Matters so dexterously, that the greatest Part of the Deputies were Pagan Senators, who were entrusted to petition the Re-establishment of the Altar of Victory, which *Gratian* had demolished. Our Saint, who had exerted himself successfully on that Subject before, was not less active on this Occasion, and had the Satisfaction of seeing the Petition rejected. *Theodosius* was at *Milan*, when *Jovinian* and seven or eight of his Adherents, who had been lately condemn'd at *Rome*, reached that City. That Heretick taught that such as have been regenerated by Baptism with a full Faith, can never after be conquered by the Devil: that all, who preserve their baptismal Grace shall have a like Recompence in Heaven: that Virgins have no Merit superiour to that of Widows, or married Women, except what is founded on their particular Actions: that there is no Difference between abstaining, and eating with Thanksgiving; and that *Mary* ceased to be a Virgin after the Birth of *Jesus Christ*. Pope *Siricius* being apprized of their Motions sent three Priests to *Milan* with a Letter to that Church, containing the Condemnation of those Hereticks, and a brief Confutation of their Errors. St. *Ambrose* called a Council of Bishops, who condemn'd and rejected the Hereticks, and wrote a Synodical Epistle to his Holiness; in which *Jovinian*'s Tenets are confuted by Texts of Scripture; the Advantages of Virginity insisted on; and the perpetual Virginity of the Mother of God proved.

Botherick, who commanded the Imperial Troops in *Illyricum*, and resided at *Thessalonica*, sent an able Charioteer to Prison for attempting to corrupt one of his Servants; not long after his Commitment, the People petition'd for

for his Enlargement, with a View of being better diverted by the publick Shows in the *Circus*; not obtaining their Request, they mutinied, several of the Emperor's Officers were kill'd, and *Botherick* lost his Life in that popular Tumult. *Theodosius*, naturally warm and hasty, was so incensed at this Account, that he declared he would have ample Satisfaction of that seditious People; but *Ambrose*, and some other Bishops then at *Milan*, undertaking to intercede for the Criminals, the Emperor promis'd their Pardon. The chief Officers of that Prince's Court, understanding his merciful Dispositions, urged the Necessity of punishing such Commotions with the utmost Rigour, as an Example to his other Subjects, and prevail'd with him to give the Inhabitants of *Thessalonica* up into the Hands of the Army; but they were particularly careful to keep this Resolution secret, and execute it before our Saint was apprized of the Design; which was done in the following Manner. The People of *Thessalonica*, being assembled in the *Circus*, were there surrounded by Soldiers, who had Orders to fall on all they found, without Distinction of Sex or Age, so that great Numbers of Innocent Persons were involved in this Massacre, which lasted three Hours, and took off about seven Thousand.

The News of this bloody Execution coming to *Milan*, St. *Ambrose* and his Collegues, then assembled in that City, were sensibly afflicted at what had happen'd; the Saint did not think proper to appear before the Emperor in the first Transports of his Grief, and was of Opinion that *Theodosius* might enter into himself when left to his own Thoughts; for which Reason he left *Milan* a few Days before that Prince return'd thither. From his Retreat he wrote a long Letter to the Emperor, excus'd his not waiting his Majesty's Arrival, insisted on the Obligation under which he lay to speak freely on the present Affair, represented the Enormity of his Fault, exhorted him to a proportionable Penance, and endeavour'd to engage him to efface his Sin by Tears and good Works, by Reason, and the Example of Princes in the same Circumstances. The Emperor could not read this Letter without feeling some Remorse, which was soon improv'd into a hearty Sorrow for his Weakness in consenting to the Massacre of *Thessalonica*. In this Disposition he hasten'd to *Milan*; and the holy Bishop return'd to that City about the same Time. *Theodosius*, thinking himself oblig'd to express his Repentance by publick Acts of Piety, made his Way to the Church, designing to assist at divine Service, and partake of the sacred Mysteries. The holy Bishop, being inform'd that the Emperor was coming, left the Chair, went out to wait his Arrival at the Door, and as soon as he approach'd, spoke to him with all the Authority which his Character allow'd him; laid before him all the shocking

Circumstances

Circumstances of the late Calamity; and told him, that his Attempt to enter Dec. 7. the Temple of the Lord, while his Hands were stain'd with innocent Blood, was no less than sacrilegious Rashness. *Theodosius* heard the Reproaches of our Saint with an edifying Modesty, acknowleg'd his Guilt, but said he hoped for Mercy, in which he thought himself encourag'd by the Example of King *David*, who was at once a Murtherer, and an Adulterer. To which the Saint replied, " *As you have follow'd him in offending God, immitate his Repentance.* " This Exhortation finish'd the Work; *Theodosius*, perfectly instructed in the Maxims of Religion and the Power of the Church, submitted without the least Reply, and lived a private and penitential Life eight Months. Thus he continu'd 'till the Night before Christmas Day, and was inconsolable at being denied a Share in that great Solemnity. *Ruffinus*, one of those who had been most forward in promoting the Massacre, coming into his Chamber, begg'd to know the Cause of his Grief. The Emperor told him, with a Storm of Sighs and a Flood of Tears, that he could know no Comfort, when he consider'd himself excluded from the Temple of the Lord, while the lowest of Mankind were freely admitted. After some Endeavours to make the Emperor easy by justifying or at least extenuating a Crime, which he had advised, *Ruffinus* offer'd to go to the holy Bishop and solicit his Absolution, which he was sanguine enough to believe no hard Task. *Theodosius* assured him he knew not what he undertook, " for continu'd that Prince, *we have to do with a Man, who will never be so complaisant to the Imperial Dignity as to transgress the Laws of God in my Favour; and I know the Justice of my Sentence.* " *Ruffinus*, however, begg'd he might be favour'd with his Majesty's Commission, and promis'd to return with good News. " Go then, said *Theodosius*; and being warm'd into some Hopes of Success, follow'd him at some Distance.

Ruffinus employ'd all his Rhetorick on that Occasion; but *Ambrose*, with his usual Freedom broke in upon his Discourse, and told him his present Application was a flagrant Proof of his Indiscretion, considering his evil Councils had pushed the Emperor to that Act of Cruelty; and, that if he had any Shame or Fear of God remaining, he would not mention the Massacre of *Thessalonica*, but with Horror and Detestation, and do Penance for the ill Advice which he had given his Master in that Affair. *Ruffinus*, not discouraged at this Reprimand, pursued his Petition with unwearied Importunity; and, finding all he could say too weak, told the Saint, *Theodosius* was coming to plead his own Cause. *Ambrose*, transported with Zeal for the House of God, assured him in a Manner expressive of his Intrepidity, that he would post himself at the Church Door and oppose his Entrance, being resolved rather to die than permit the Laws of the Church to be violated. *Ruffinus*, thunderstruck at this truly Episcopal Declaration, sent a Messenger to the Emperor advising him to return back, if he would avoid being affronted by the holy Bishop. *Theodosius*, who was not far from the Church when he receiv'd this Advice, went on, and declared he had deserv'd the worst Usage he could meet with. Coming within the Enclosure, he did not attempt to enter the Church but made his Way to St. *Ambrose*, then in a large Room near the Place of Worship, and desired Absolution and Admission to the Congregations of the Faithful. The Saint with a becoming Severity told him he rebell'd against God, and trampled on the divine Laws, if he came thither to force his Way into the Church. " *No*, reply'd the Emperor, *I respect those sacred Ordinances and will never offer to enter, in Defiance of the Rules established in the Church; but beg you will take off these Chains and not shut that Door against me which the Lord has open'd to all such as do Pennance.*" The Saint then asked him what Penance he had done for so great a Sin, and what Remedies he had applied to the Wounds of his Soul. "*I come, to you* replied Theodosius, *as to my Physician, and expect to be directed to a Cure by you.*" The holy Bishop, finding him in this excellent Disposition, prescribed him a publick Penance, according to the Canons; and insisted on his making a Law that no Person should be executed in less than thirty Days after Sentence, a Precaution which hinders the ill Effects of Passion, and gives Princes Time to reflect coolly on the Judgment they or their Vicegerents should pass. The Emperor readily complied with both these Injunctions; whereupon S. *Ambrose* took off his Excommunication, and allow'd him to enter the Church. That Prince quitted his Royal Ornaments during the Time of his Penance, and prostrate on the Ground implored the divine Mercy in the Words of the Royal Psalmist, *My Soul hath cleaved to the Earth, give me Life according to your Word.* His Sorrow shew'd it self in so moving and edifying a Manner, that the whole Congregation pray'd and wept with him.

Theodoret, from whom we have taken this Account, adds that after the Emperor had made his Offering, he took his Place within the Choir or Sanctuary among the Clergy according to the Eastern Custom. S. *Ambrose*, observing him there, asked whether he wanted any Thing of him; to which the Emperor replied he waited the Time of Communion; the holy Prelate then sent a Deacon to let him know that none but the Ministers of the Church were allow'd to appear in the Sanctuary, and that his Place was among the Laity. *Theodosius* was very easy under this Remonstrance, and

assured

assured the Saint that he had no Ambition or irregular View in what he had done, which was the usual Practice at *Constantinople*, and left the Choir immediately. Being some Time after at that City, he made his Offering withdrew, and placed himself among the Laity; the Patriarch *Nectarius* asked the Emperor why he did not stay within the Rails, to which he answer'd with a Sigh that he had lately learnt the Difference between a Bishop and a Prince, and knew none but *Ambrose* worthy of the Name of a Bishop.

Theodosius left *Italy* toward the Close of 391, after securing the Tranquility of the Western Empire, and establishing *Valentinian* on the Throne. The Prince last mention'd had the Happiness to lose his Mother, who had abused the Easiness of his Temper to the Prejudice of his Catholick Subjects, and particularly the holy Bishop of *Milan*. *Theodosius* let him see how he had been imposed on, and gave him such Instruction on the Point of Religion, that from that Time he took all Opportunities of expressing his Respect and Affection for the Saint, and regulated his Conduct by his prudent and pious Advice. *Ambrose* endeavour'd to make his Interest with their Imperial Majesties serviceable to the Church; and, taking his Advantage of the Peace which then reigned in the whole Christian World, contributed his charitable Labours toward extinguishing the Schism which was continued at *Antioch* by *Evagrius* and *Flavian*, the former of whom succeeded *Paulinus*, the latter *Meletius*; but the Success was not answerable to the Goodness of his Intentions.

Valentinian was so much changed since he was under our Saint's Direction, that his Virtue and Wisdom made him the Object of universal Admiration, so that we may justly say he was loved and honoured by all Mankind except the Pagans. Count *Arbogastus*, Generalissimo of all that Prince's Forces, and a Stranger to the Name of *Jesus Christ*, was our Saint's most formidable Enemy, and it was but too evident that he had a Design on his Master's Life. *Valentinian* was thinking on proper Means for humbling that ambitious Officer, and retrenching his Power, when he receiv'd the News of an Army of Barbarians being on the Frontiers of *Italy*. The Emperor, then about twenty Years old, resolved to put himself at the Head of his Troops, and march against the Enemy; but desired to make all due Provision for his Soul before he engaged in that War. In this View he dispatched an Officer of his Bed-Chamber to *Milan*, and desired St. *Ambrose* to come to him at *Vienne* in *Gaul* with all possible Expedition, where he resolved to receive Baptism at his Hands; but before the Messenger return'd *Valentinian* was strangled by some of his Guards corrupted by *Arbogastus* on Whitson Eve,

Dec. 7. in the Year 392. His Body was sent to *Milan*, and St. *Ambrose* was on the Road to *Vienne* when he heard of the tragical End of his Sovereign ; but return'd immediately, took Care of that Prince's Funeral, and pronounced an Oration, in which he bewail'd the Emperor's Death with all the Tenderness of a Parent, and declared himself fully persuaded that his ardent Desire of Baptism and the serious Preparation he had made on that Occasion would sufficiently supply the Want of actual Reception of that Sacrament ; and, pursuant to his Opinoin of the State of his Soul, proceeded to offer the holy Mysteries for his Repose.

The Discovery of the Relicks of St. *Vitalis* and St. *Agricola* has been mention'd on the fourth of *November*, where we said he left Part of that valuable Treasure at *Florence*. The Author of our Saint's Life, who was his Secretary, and is universally allow'd the Character of Accuracy and Sincerity, tells us that during his Stay in that City he deliver'd an eminent Citizen's Son from an Evil Spirit which had long tormented him ; and that the Child dying suddenly, in a few Days after, his Mother laid him on the Saint's Bed, and it pleas'd God to restore him to Life at the Intercession of the holy Bishop. *Ambrose*'s Journey to *Florence* is dated toward the Close of 393 ; he staid in that City 'till the following *August*, and did not return to *Milan* 'till *Eugenius*, whom *Arbogastus* had placed on the Imperial Throne in the Room of *Valentinian*, left that City and marched against *Theodosius*, who had enter'd *Italy* with a formidable Army. After the Defeat and Death of *Eugenius* and his General, the Emperor wrote our Saint an Account of his Success, and desired him to offer Thanks to the Almighty who had given him the Victory.

Ambrose went soon after to *Aquileia* where he found *Theodosius*, and interterceeded for the Pardon of several of the Rebels, which was easily granted ; and that Prince, throwing himself at the Bishop's Feet, acknowledged himself indebted to his Prayers for all the Advantage he had gain'd over the Enemy. The Saint, having gain'd his Point, return'd to *Milan* a Day before the Emperor, who abstain'd from the Sacraments for some Time because he had stain'd his Hands with Blood, 'though in a good and just Cause ; and it is probable that St. *Ambrose*, who commends his Conduct on that Occasion, advised him to that reverential Distance from the Altar. *Theodosius* sent for his Children to *Milan*, put them into our Saint's Hands, and begg'd he would be a Father to them as he had been to *Valentinian*'s two Sons, who being form'd under his Direction would have made their Subjects happy, had they lived long enough to practise the excellent Lessons which they had learnt from that great Master.

Theodo-

Theodosius was preparing for his Return to *Constantinople* at the Beginning Dec. 7. of the Year 395, when he was taken with his last Sickness, and died on the seventeenth of *January* at *Milan*, where St. *Ambrose* made his Funeral Oration in Presence of *Honorius*, who succeeded him in the West. The Discovery of the Relicks of St. *Nazarius* and St. *Celsus* which happen'd soon after, and what Share our Saint had in the Solemnity of their Translation may be seen on the twenty eighth of *July*.

In the Year 396 the Inhabitants of *Milan* were entertain'd with publick Shows at the Emperor's Expence; and one of the Criminals, who was to be expos'd to the Beasts for their Diversion fled to the Church for Shelter. *Stilico*, in whose Hands *Honorius* was left during his Minority, granted an Order for tearing him from the Altar, and bringing him back to the Amphitheatre, which was immediately executed without the least Regard to the Sanctity of the Place, or the Presence of the Bishop and his Clergy. The Faithful were sensibly afflicted at this irregular Act, and our Saint lay postrate before the Altar, bewailing this Violation of the holy Place with Tears. The Sports of the Amphitheatre were continued, 'till two Leopards broke loose and wounded some of those who brought back the Criminal. *Stilico*, struck at this Account, and believing it a Punishment for his late Order, made all due Satisfaction, and changed the Malefactor's Sentence into Banishment. This happen'd in 396; and the following Year S. *Ambrose* received an Embassy from *Fritigil* Queen of the *Marcomans*, who lived in what is now call'd *Bohemia*. That Princess had heard our Saint's Character from a Christian lately come from *Italy*, and was so charm'd with the Account of his Virtues that she entertain'd a favourable Opinion of the Religion which he profess'd. This was her Disposition when she desired the holy Bishop to give her some Instructions in Writing; which he did, and at the same Time advised her to persuade her Husband to keep Peace with the *Romans*. This Letter, which is mention'd with large Commendations by *Paulinus*, but has not reached us, produced the desired Effect; and the Queen made a Journey to *Milan* for the Satisfaction of seeing and hearing the Saint, but had the Mortification to find him Dead at her Arrival.

Ambrose fell ill in *February* 397; and *Stilico*, apprehending his Death would be follow'd by the Ruin of the Empire, engaged some of the most considerable Persons in the Town to go to the Saint in a Body and conjure him to beg a longer Continuance on Earth. As they were importuning him on that Subject with Tears, he told them, "He neither had lived in "such a Manner as to be ashamed to remain among them, nor was afraid "to

Dec. 8. "to die; when he consider'd the Goodness of his Divine Master". The Saint languished 'till the third of *April*, and remain'd in Prayer from the Close of that Day to Midnight. *Honoratus*, Bishop of *Vercelli*, whom he had consecrated the Year before, attended him during his Sickness; and was taking a little Rest in a distant Room when he heard a Voice saying to him distinctly three several Times, *Arise immediately; he is at the Point of Departure.* *Honoratus* obey'd, gave him the Body of our Lord, and saw him expire as soon as he had receiv'd that sacred Food.

The venerable Body was carried to the great Church before Break of Day, where it lay 'till the next Day, which was the Feast of our Saviour's Resurrection, and was then removed to the *Ambrosian Basilick*, where it was buried. We cannot better conclude our Account of this great Saint and Father of the Church than by telling our Readers, after his Historian *Paulinus*, that he extended his Care to the whole Flock of *Jesus Christ*, assisted the most distant Parts of it with his Letters and other excellent Writings; that he allow'd himself but little Time for Rest, never eat 'till Evening, but on *Saturdays* and *Sundays*; entertain'd Persons of the first Rank, but could never be prevail'd with to take a Meal at any Table but his own, when at *Milan*; and made it an inviolable Maxim to himself never to concern himself with Matches, or undertake to recommend any one to a Place at Court, to avoid being answerable for the Miscarriages of such critical Affairs.

The VIII Day.

The Conception of the BLESSED VIRGIN.

SEVERAL good Writers, among whom is the Learned *Baronius*, are of Opinion that this Festival was first observed in *England*, toward the Close the eleventh Century. That celebrated Author tells us it ow'd it's Original to a Revelation in which *Elfin*, an Abbot of this Island, who being in great Distress at Sea was assured of landing safe, if he would undertake to promote keeping a Day in Honour of the Blessed Virgin's Conception. S. *Anselm*, who died in the Year 1109, favour'd this pious Institution; and a Council held at *London* in 1328 professes to tread in the Steps of that holy Metropolitan, when it orders the Feast of the *Conception* to be celebrated in a solemn Manner. About the Middle of the twelfth Age, the Emperor *Manuël Commenius* order'd the Observation of this Festival on the ninth of *December*

through

through the whole Empire. About the same Time some Attempts were made for introducing the same Festival in several Churches in *France*; the Manner in which the Canons of *Lyons* endeavour'd to establish it in that City made much Noise in the World; but none was more offended at their Liberty in that Point than St. *Bernard*, who wrote a long Letter to the Chapter at *Lyons*, which concludes with observing that if they were disposed to add this new Festival to those already in the Calendar, they should have had Recourse to the holy See, to whose Judgment he declares himself ready to submit his Sentiments on that Subject.

It is not improbable that the Conception of the Blessed Virgin was only a Feast of Devotion, and not universally receiv'd in *Italy* and *France* 'till the Year 1439, when the Council of *Basil* undertook to renew it's Observation according to *the ancient and laudable Custom*. Sixtus IV published two Decrees on this Subject, one in the Year 1476, the other in 1483, which changed that Custom into a Law. That Pope, who had been a *Franciscan* Friar, was inclined to maintain the Immaculate Purity of the Blessed Virgin's Conception; but finding the Disputes run very high between his Order and the *Dominicans*, forbid all under Pain of Excommunication to brand with Heresy, or accuse of Mortal Sin such as held either side of that difficult Question, which he was pleased to leave undecided. It is certain, however, that the Church in this and other Festivals of our Blessed Lady intends to give God Thanks for that pure and holy Creature, who gave Flesh to our Redeemer, and who can never be forgotten when we speak of the Humanity of *Jesus Christ*.

St. ROMARICUS, Abbot.

*R*OMARICUS, a Native of *France*, of illustrious Descent, made a considerable Figure at the Court of *Theodebert* who reign'd in *Austrasia* toward the Close of the VI Century; but the Grace of God preserved him from the Corruption of the World even where it is priveleged by Custom and recommended by Example. His Equipage and Retinue were splendid and numerous, and such as suited his Rank; but he maintain'd the Character of a Christian by large Alms, and protecting the weak and defenceless. He was sober, chaste, regular, and as well acquainted with the Spirit of Mortification, while in that exalted Station, as the most retired Monk. While at Court our Saint contracted a close Friendship with St. *Arnoul*, whom *Baronius* calls *Arnulphus*, afterwards Bishop of *Mets*. After several Discourses together on the Vanity of the World, and the Insufficiency of it's Pleasures and Satisfactions, they concerted Measures for quitting what their Judgment led them to despise; but some civil Commotions hinder'd the Execution of their pious Designs. A War broke out between *Theodebert*, and his Brother *Thierry*, King of *Burgundy*, in which the former was defeated, taken Prisoner, and soon after put to Death by Order of *Brunebaud* his Grandmother, who espoused his Brother's Cause. *Romulfus*, our Saint's Father, shared his Royal Master's Fate; for his Life and Fortune were forfeited for no other Crime than his Loyalty; and *Romaricus*, was banished for same Reason.

Romaricus, thus reduced and disgraced, made his Way to *Aridus* a Bishop, who had a great Influence over *Brunebaud*, and begg'd he would intercede with that Princess for a Grant of his Estate which had fallen into the Hands of her victorious Grandson. That Prelate, made insolent by his Interest at Court, kick'd the Petitioner as he kneel'd before him, which was all the Answer he thought fit to give the distressed Nobleman. The Death of King *Thierry*, which happen'd soon after, made a considerable Change in the Face of Affairs. *Brunebaud* and the haughty Prelate her Favourite, whose Measures were quite disconcerted by this Accident, sent for *Romaricus*, put him in Possession of his whole Estate, and begg'd he would assist their Escape from *Mets*. The Saint, who had learnt of *Jesus Christ* to return Good for Evil, did them all the Service in his Power; but divine Justice soon overtook that ambitious, cruel Princess and her Family; for *Clotaire* II made War on *Sigebert* II, then on the Throne, took him, two of his Brothers and their great Grandmother, put them to Death, and thus in the Year 614 became sole Monarch of *France*. This Revolution was follow'd by our Saint's Promotion to the in what same Rank he had formerly held in the Court of *Austrasia*.

Romaricus was at a Country House in what now bears the Name of *Lorrain*, when *Amatus*, a Monk of *Luxeu*, sent by his Abbot to preach in the Towns and Villages, spent some Days under his Roof; during which Time that holy Person discoursed largely on the false Grandeurs and deceitful Riches of this World, and put *Romaricus* in Mind of the young Man in the Gospel, who had lived in the strict Observance of God's Commandments, but lost all the Advantage of his good Works by an unhappy Affection for his Estate; the Monk went on to observe that in order to avoid the Fate of that young Man, he ought to secure Treasure in Heaven by distributing his Money among the Poor, according to our Lord's Advice, and endeavour to follow *Jesus Christ*, in the Road of Perfection. *Romaricus*, who had long entertain'd a mean Opinion of the World, and all it's Enjoyments made no Difficulty of owing the

Force

Force of his Arguments and Justness of his Observations, by divesting himself of all and retiring to *Luxeu* with his holy Guest. His Goods, and the greatest Part of his Estate, being converted into Money, were divided between that Monastery and the Poor; and several of his Slaves engaged in a Religious Life in the same House, whom he caress'd as his Brothers and Equals. His Love of Poverty and Humiliation appear'd by his choosing the most mortifying painful and low Employments.

When he divided his Fortune between the Abbey of *Luxeu* and the distressed Members of *Jesus Christ*, he reserved a considerable Estate in the Diocese of *Toul*, with which he founded and endow'd a double Monastery, call'd by the *Germans* to this Day *Romberg*, and by the *French Remirement*. *Romaricus* was assisted in the Execution of this pious Design by *Amatus* whom *Eustasius* Abbot of *Luxeu* placed at the Head of the new Community, to govern it by St. *Colomban*'s Rule; and the holy Founder was allow'd to live there under the Direction of that holy Person. *Eustasius*, who had a general Inspection of all the Monasteries where St. *Colomban*'s Rule was practised, having observed som Negligences in the Conduct of our Saint and his Abbot, admonished them of their Fault. *Agrestis*, a turbulent Monk of *Luxeu*, who had undertaken to discredit and ruin the Discipline of that House, and those depending on it, imagining this a favourable Conjuncture for gaining them to his Party, went to their Monastery, and work'd the Monks into a thorough Dislike of the Rule, and their holy Superior. The Faction, thus strengthen'd, gave *Eustasius* no small Trouble; but the suddain and unhappy End of *Agrestis* and fifty of his Adherents rouzed our Saint and his Friend, open'd their Eyes, and made them sue for a Reconciliation with their Superior, and repair the Scandal of their late Conduct by Submission and Penance. This Cloud thus blown over, *Romaricus* and *Amatus* were more strictly united to S. *Eustasius* than before; and on the Death of *Amatus*, which happen'd in the Year 627, our Saint was obliged to succeed to the Care of the new Monastery, which he govern'd near twenty six Years, with great Prudence and Charity.

St. *Anoul*, his old Friend, resigning the Bishoprick of *Mets* in 629, *Romaricus* made a Journey to that City, conducted the holy Prelate into the Desart near his Monastery, where he raised a Hermitage for his Reception, and assisted him to his last Moments. Our Saint died the Death of the Just on the eighth of *December* 653, and was buried near *Amatus* in the Church belonging to his Monastery. Pope *Leo* IX, who sat in St. *Peter*'s Chair in the Middle of the eleventh Age, and held the Bishoprick of *Toul* some Time after his Promotion, visiting that Diocese made a strict and regular Enquiry the Miracles and other Proofs of *Romaricus*'s Sanctity, canonized him according to the plain Manner of those Times; which consisted only in taking up the venerable Relicks and placing them in a more honourable Part of the Church. The *Roman* Martyrologe mentions our Saint on the Day of his Death.

The IX Day.

St. GORGONIA.

GORGONIA, who is this Day proposed to the married Part of her Sex as an excellent Pattern of Christian Life, and the Sanctity of that State, was Sister to St. *Gregory Nazianzen*, and probably elder than him and his Brother *Cesarius*. She was married to a Man of Quality in the Province of *Pisidia*, whose Name is not known at present, and who in all Appearance was a Pagan. She had several Children by him, whom she carefully form'd to Virtue by her own Example and frequent Instructions, and fill'd all the Duties of her State with an edifying Exactness and Fidelity. Her Humility, Love of Mortification, and Watchfulness over her own Actions recommended her to the Esteem, and Veneration of all who saw her: she had no Relish for that luxuriant Variety of Ornaments which have most powerful Charms for the Generality of her Sex; but was never better pleased than when employ'd in adorning Churches. She had a singular Respect for the Clergy; a tender Compassion for the Afflicted, and was very liberal to the Poor, especially to indigent Widows. Her House was open to all such as profess'd Piety and Virtue, and those of that Number who wanted her charitable Assistance were relieved in an affectionate Manner. Except when it was necessary to converse with her Neighbours for their Good, she observed a close Retirement, and appear'd but seldom, 'though possess'd of all those Qualifications which engage the Eyes and Admiration of Mankind. Her Capacity was extensive, her Wisdom such as made her the Oracle of the whole Country; and she had acquired the thorough Knowledge of the Mysteries of our holy Religion, by an indefatigable Application to the sacred Writings. She was too sensible of the Weakness of human Nature and the Artifices of the subtle Enemy of our Salvation, to trust her own Thoughts and Inclinations where her Soul was concern'd, and therefore prudently regulated

all

all her Actions by the Advice of her Director, who was probably *Faustinus* Dec.10 Bishop of *Iconium*, the Place of our Saint's Abode.

Gorgonia was the same in Adversity and Prosperity, and nothing could ruffle a Soul so entirely submissive to the Will of God as hers. Her Prayers, which were her chief Employment, were offer'd with uncommon Fervour, and an uninterrupted Attention to the great Object of her Devotions. Her Fasts were rigorous, her Rest short, and nothing could be more edifying than her constant Attendance at Church; all which appear'd the more extraordinary in our Saint, because then but a Catechumen; and not baptized till the Close of her Life. *Gorgonia*'s excellent Example was not useless in her own Family, for she had the Satisfaction of gaining her Husband, and seeing him receive the Sacrament of Regeneration; a Favour which she procured for her Sons and Grand-children.

Having thus sanctified her whole Family and put them in the Way of Salvation, she had nothing to wish for but the perfect Enjoyment of God in a better Life. As she forsaw her End, she prepared for it by making a considerable Addition to her pious Acts, and ended her Days in a Manner suitable to the Sanctity of her Life. *Gorgonia* died after the Year 369, for we are assured she survived her Brother *Cesarius*; and all we have related of her in this Place is taken from her funeral Oration spoken by St. *Gregory*. The *Greeks* honour her Memory on two different Days, *viz.* on the twenty third of *February*, and ninth of *December*; the latter of which is kept in her Honour by the *Latins*.

The X Day.

St. MELCHIADES POPE.

MELCHIADES, whom some of the Antients call *Miltiades*, a Native of *Africa*, was admitted young among the Clergy of *Rome*, and had Virtue and Capacity enough to recommend him to the highest Station in the Church On the second of *July* in the Year 311. At his Promotion to the holy See the Christians in *Italy* enjoy'd Peace under *Maxentius*, who made himself Master of *Rome* five Years before, and endeavour'd to recommend himself to the People's Esteem by an affected Mildness; but several Churches were still shut up. The holy Pope, zealous for the House of God, began his Pontificate with obtaining Letters on that Subject from *Maxentius* and the Pretorian

Prefect

Prefect to the Governour of the City, which had their Effect. But that Prince's Debaucheries proved a fort of Persecution in *Rome*, especially to the Female Sex, several of whom would have lost their Lives rather than their Virtue. This proved a sensible Mortification to our Saint, and lasted 'till *Constantine* the great enter'd the City in 312, after the Defeat and Death of *Maxentius*.

At the beginning of the following Year that victorious Prince, in Gratitude for his Success which he had good Reason to attribute to *Jesus Christ*, enquired into the State of the Church, in order to redress its Grievances and secure its Interest. The *Donatists*, who began to form a troublesome Schism in *Africa*, laid before the Emperor their Complaints against *Cecilian* Bishop of *Carthage*, who thereupon referr'd the Matter to *Melchiades*, and three *Gallican* Prelates, viz. *Maternus*, Bishop of *Cologn*, *Rheticius*, Bishop of *Autun*, and *Marinus* Bishop of *Arles*, whom he required to come to *Rome* with all possible Expediton. Our Saint, in Execution of the Imperial Orders, assembled a Council consisting of 15 *Italian* Bishops and the Prelates already mention'd; which was open'd on the second of *October* 313 in the *Lateran* Palace. That venerable Assembly declared *Cecilian* innocent, and approved of his Ordination, but did not cut his Accusers off from their Communion. *Donatus* of *Casa Nigra*, the Author of all the Confusion which had happen'd in the *African* Church, was the only Person condemn'd on that Occasion; the rest were allow'd to keep their Sees, upon renouncing their Schism; so that, without entering into the Merits of the Question, which might create fresh Disturbances, it was order'd that wherever there were two Bishops, one consecrated by *Cecilian*, the other by *Majorinus*, the disputed See should remain in Possession of him who was first placed in it, and the other be provided with another Bishoprick. S. *Augustin*, speaking of this prudent and moderate Decision, and the Share which our Saint had in it, calls him an excellent Man, a true Son of Peace, and a true Father of Christians.

Melchiades died on the tenth of *January* 314, on which Day his Name occurs in the antient Martyrologes attributed to St. *Jerom*, and that of *Venerable Bede*; but the *Roman* Church honours his Memory on the tenth of *December*; and the Supposition of his having suffer'd much under the Pagan Emperor *Maximian* before his Promotion to the holy See, has gain'd him the Title of a Martyr in the *Roman* Calendar.

St. Eulalia,

St. EULALIA, Virgin, and Martyr.   Dec. 10

EULALIA, a Native of *Merida*, and descended from one of the best Families in *Spain*, was educated in the Principles of the Christian Religion and Sentiments of true Piety, and distinguished herself in her Infancy by an admirable Sweetness of Temper, great Modesty, and a Sedateness seldom found in such tender Years. Diversions, Dress, and other Amusements which fill the Minds of young Persons had no Charms for *Eulalia*, whose Heart was raised above the World before she was thought capable of knowing it. Every Day made some Addition to our Saint's Virtues, who resolved to serve God in a State of perpetual Virginity. She was but twelve Years old when *Dioclesian* and his Collegue published their Edict for persecuting the Christians, and order'd that all without Exception of Age, Sex, or Profession, should offer Incense to the Gods of the Empire. The young *Eulalia* took the Publication of this Order, for the Signal of Battle, and was impatient to engage in Defence of her Faith. Her Mother, observing the Ardour with which she languished after Martyrdom, and apprehending the Consequences of her great Zeal, carried her into the Country, to prevent her falling into the Hands of the Persecutors; but the Saint defeated all her Measures, and found Means to make her Escape by Night, and return to *Merida*, where she arrived before the Break of Day after much Fatigue.

As soon as the Court sat she presented herself before the Judge, and, priveleged by the extraordinary Motions of the same Spirit which directed her to court Death, reproached him in strong Terms with the Folly and Stupidity of the Pagan Religion. That Magistrate order'd her to be seiz'd immediately; and, 'though highly incensed at the Indignity offer'd to his Gods, endeavour'd to gain her by soft Language and large Promises. The Saint answer'd all his Questions in the same warm Way in which she had begun. St. *Prudentius*, from whom we draw this Account, tells us that in the Transports of her Zeal she spit in the Judge's Face; that Christian Priest commends that Action as truly heroical; and, 'though it may seem to exceed the Bounds of Decency and Prudence, we are to consider it as the Result of her Youth and rash Zeal.

The Judge, incensed at our Saint's Behaviour, order her to be tormented as a Criminal of the first Rank. The Executioners began with tearing her tender Sides with Iron Hooks; it was visible from the Courage and Joy with which she supported these first Attacks, that the Being, in whose cause she suffer'd, supplied her with supernatural Strength; and her Behaviour under

other

other Tortures, such as the Application of lighted Torches to her Breast and Sides, put the Matter beyond the Possibility of a Doubt. The Flame catching her Hair, surrounded her Head, and put an End to the glorious Spectacle.

Prudentius, who lived in the fourth Age, tells us that when the holy Martyr expired, her Soul's Flight to Heaven was manifested to all the Spectators by the Appearance of a white Dove, which came out of her Mouth, and winged it's Way upwards. The same Author adds that that the Body was left exposed in the open Air; but soon after intombed, as it were in a great Snow that fell, and cover'd the whole Place. This last Circumstance shews that *Eulalia* suffer'd in the Winter; and it is generally believed she finished her Course about the Middle of *December*. The *Roman* and other Martyrologes of the best Credit place her Festival on the tenth of that Month.

Our Saint's Body was afterwards deposited near the Place of her Martyrdom, and a spacious and beautiful Church raised over her Tomb before *Prudentius* wrote his Hymn on the holy Martyr.

The XI Day.

St. DAMASUS, Pope.

THE holy Pope, whom the Church honours this Day, was a Native of *Spain*, and born at the Beginning of the IV Century. He came to *Rome* with his Father, who after some Stay in that City was dignified with the Order of Priesthood, and educated him with a View of forming him to the Service of the Altar. *Damasus*, being admitted among the Clergy, was employ'd in the same Church, from which his Father took his Title, and S. *Jerom* assures us he observed a perfect Continence during his whole Life. Our Saint was a Deacon of the Church of *Rome* in the Year 355; and one of those who bound themselves by a solmen Oath never to suffer any one to possess the holy See while *Liberius* was alive, who was than banished by *Constantius* for adhering to the orthodox Faith, and Asserting the Innocence of *Athanasius* against the Enemies of our Lord's Divinity; *Damasus* attended him to the Place of his Banishment, and spent some Time with him at *Berea* in *Thracia*.

Liberius

St. Damasus, Pope.

Liberius dying on the twenty fourth of *September* 366, *Damasus* then above sixty Years of Age, was raised to St. *Peter*'s Chair; where he had not sate many Days before one of the oldest Deacons at *Rome*, thinking himself injured by the Saint's Promotion to that Dignity, while he was overlook'd, form'd a Party against the new Pope, and prevail'd with Paul Bishop of *Tivoli*, a Man of no Learning or Capacity to consecrate him Bishop of *Rome*. This Schismatick, whom some call *Ursinus*, others *Ursianus*, found Means to divide the People and strengthen his Faction by Misrepresentations, and malicious Suggestions against our Saint. The Dispute ran so high at last, that *Juventius* Governor of *Rome* was oblig'd to employ all the Authority of his Post to keep the Town quiet. *Julian*, Commissioner for the Provisions, joyning that Magistrate at this critical Juncture, the Antipope with his chief Adherents was banished. As those seditious Persons were leaving the City, under the Conduct of proper Officers, *Ursinus*'s Party rescued them from their Guards, and carried them to the Church which is now known by the Title of St. *Mary Major*'s. Those, who had appear'd for *Damasus* during the Contest, alarm'd at this tumultuous and illegal Proceeding, invested the Church last mention'd in a hostile Manner; but *Ursinus*'s Creatures, coming to his Assistance, the Matter was disputed in a warm Battle, in which the Pope's Party was victorious, and 137 Persons of both Sexes were slain in that Action. The Effusion of so must Blood did not however extinguish the Fire of Sedition; and the Governor, finding himself unequal to the Task on which he had enter'd retired, to his CountryHouse.

At the Beginning of this Schism the Emperor *Valentinian* order'd that the Bishop of *Rome* should sit as Judge over other Prelates, and that he should examine their Causes in Conjunction with his Collegues; but the Peace of the Church was long disturb'd by the Antipope. Since the Banishment of that Schismatick his Partisans had constantly importuned the Emperoror for his Return to *Rome*, and gain'd their Point about a Year after his being obliged to leave that City; but *Ursinus* behaved himself so ill there that in two Months after his Sentence was reversed, and he sent into *Gaul* with a considerable Number of his Associates; and thus our Saint remain'd at full Liberty to execute his Office. The Schismaticks thus powerfully discouraged, and deprived of their Head, were not disposed to submit, but held their factious Assemblies in the Burial Place of the Martyrs near *Rome*, and forcibly kept Possession of a Church, 'though they had none of the Clergy among them. This oblig'd our holy Pope, and *Pretextatus*, then Governor of *Rome*, to apply to his Imperial Majesty for fresh Orders in this troublesome Affair, who directed

rected that Magistrate to put the Church in Dispute into our Saint's Hands, which was executed, and the Schismaticks dispossess'd of it by Force of Arms. *Damasus* made Vows at the Shrines of the Martyrs for the Return of his rebellious Children, and having obtain'd his Request by their powerful Intercession with the God of Peace and Unity, he acquitted himself of the Obligation by composing Verses in Honour of those glorious Members of the Church Triumphant.

The strict Discipline which our Saint had enforced was what disgusted some of the Clergy, and prompted them to join his Adversary. The Emperor *Valentinian* in the Year 370 made a Law forbidding all Ecclesiasticks, and Religious going to the Houses of Orphans and Widows, and allow'd the Relations of those helpless Persons to sue them in a secular Court upon trangressing this Order. The same Law makes it Criminal for any of the aforemention'd Persons to take Money of any Woman on any Pretence of Religious Services, or enjoy any Legacy by Will from their female Devotes, unless they are otherwise Heirs at Law. This excellent Regulation was read publickly in all the Churches of *Rome*; and some good Authors have supposed it made at the Intreaty of our Saint. It is certain, however, that *Damasus* was particularly careful in pressing the Observation of this Law, which could not but make him many Enemies among such as were too fond of the Conveniencies of this World, and an unlimited Conversation with secular Persons; and we must believe this Character Applicable to some of the Clergy and Religious at that Time, unless we would suppose a wise Prince could be induced to make a Law against meer Phantoms, and Creatures of the Imagination.

About the same Time his Holiness conven'd a numerous Council at *Rome*, in Order to consider of proper Means for recovering such as had fallen into *Arianism* in the Reign of *Constantius*. The Eastern Parts of Christendom, and the Province of *Illyricum* were chiefly concern'd in this Affair; for much the greater Number of the western Prelates had adhered inviolably to the Decisions of the Council of *Nice*. This Assembly condemn'd *Ursacius* and *Valens*, two Ringleaders of the *Arian Faction* in *Illyricum*; and *Damasus* transmitted the Account of these Proceedings to St. *Athanasius*, the first Champion of the Orthodox Faith, and the grand Object of the Hereticks Aversion. The holy Bishop of *Alexandria*, having receiv'd the Pope's Letter, assembled the Bishops of *Egypt* and *Libya* to the Number of ninty, wrote to his Holiness in the Name of that venerable Company, and express'd his and his Collegues Concern that *Auxentius*, the Usurper of the See of *Milan*, and the greatest Patron of the *Arians* in the West was not condemn'd.

St. Damasus, Pope.

demn'd. Before this Letter reached *Rome,* St. *Basil* sent one to our Saint, Dec. 11 in which he was very pressing with him to act vigorously in Concert with St. *Athanasius,* and join his Endeavours with those of the holy Patriarch toward reuniting the Eastern and Western Churches, who stood divided on the Contest at *Antioch,* of which we have had frequent Occasion to speak in the Course of this Work.

Some Time after the Bishops of *Egypt* receiv'd the desired Satisfaction from the Pope, and the Prelates of the West; for a Complaint being preferr'd by the Bishops of *Gaul* and some others against *Auxentius* and his Adherents setting forth that they maintain'd the Errors of the *Anomeans,* a Sect who added several impious Tenets to those of *Arius* and *Macedonius,* *Damasus* conven'd a Council at *Rome* in the Year 373, consisting of ninety three Bishops from different Countries, in which *Auxentius* and his Associates were condemn'd and excommunicated; the *Nicene* Faith confirm'd; and all that had been done to it's Prejudice at *Rimini* declared null and void. The Determinations and Decisions of this Assembly were transmitted to the Eastern Prelates and those of *Illyricum* in a Synodical Epistle.

As soon as the News of St. *Athanasius*'s Death reached *Rome, Damasus* dispatched Letters of Communion to *Peter* his Successor, who had sent him an Account of his Election to the See of *Alexandria.* The Deacon, who was charged with this Commission, falling into the Hands of the *Arians,* who were supported by the Emperor *Valens,* was seiz'd by an Order from *Palladius,* Governor of *Egypt,* a Pagan and an outrageous Enemy of the Christian Religion, dragg'd 'though the Streets of *Alexandria* with his Hands tied behind him, expofed to the Infults of the Populace, beaten and abufed with a Cruelty not inferior to what the Martyrs fuffer'd from profefs'd Idolaters, and then fent to the Copper Mines, with several other Catholicks. The Bishop made his Escape with much Difficulty, and took Shelter at *Rome,* where he spent almost five Years under our Saint's Protection.

Ursinus was not in a Capacity to give our Pope any confiderable Disturbance while the Emperor *Valentinian* was alive; but the *Luciferians* found our Saint's Vigilance and Zeal full Employment. Those Schifmaticks receiv'd that Name from a Bishop of *Cagliari* in *Sardinia,* who feperated from the Catholick Prelates; becaufe they admittted those to their Communion, who had fubfcribed the Council of *Rimini,* and such as repented of their Apoftafy, to the *Arians* while perfecuted by that Sect. They held their Affemblies at *Rome*; and feem'd to be comprehended in an Imperial Refcript directed to *Simplicius* Lieutenant of *Rome* in the Year 374, which directs the Banishment

X x 2 of

of all such as should form unlawful Assemblies in *Rome* in Contempt of Religion. By Virtue of this Order, *Damasus* inform'd against *Macarius* a *Luciferian* Priest, who conven'd some Schismaticks in the Night Time in a private House; whereupon he and several of his Congregation were sent into Exile. But the holy and active Pope, though assisted by the supreme Civil Authority, could not hinder the Schismaticks from having a Bishop of their own at *Rome*; and the Donatists took the same Liberty. *Optatus*, Bishop of *Milevis*, who has preserved the Names of the three *Donatists*, who pretended to the See of *Rome*, during our Saint's Pontificate, wrote a considerable Treatise against those turbulent Schismaticks, in which he undertakes to shew the Unity of the Catholick Church by the Succession of the Bishops of *Rome*, who are the Center of Unity to the Faithful; and gives us a Catalogue of Popes from St. *Peter* to *Damasus*, with whom he says all the World then held Communion, and challenges the *Donatists* to shew the Origin of their Episcopal Chair in that City.

In 376, or the following Year, our Saint call'd a Council at *Rome* which condemn'd *Apolinarius*, and *Timothy* his Disciple, who stiled himself Bishop of *Alexandria*. That Heresiarch admitted no human Soul, or Understanding in *Jesus Christ*, but affirm'd that the Divinity alone supplied that Defect, with other Extravagancies of the same Sort; which may be seen in our Account of St. *Epiphanius*, *May* the twelfth; and it is remarkable that this is the first Time we find those shocking Tenets condemn'd in a publick Manner.

We have had frequent Subject to mention the Schism of *Antioch*, and and let our Readers know that the western Prelates with our Saint at their Head declared for *Paulinus*'s Title to that Bishoprick, preferably to St. *Meletius*. St. *Basil*, who had different Sentiments on that Subject, endeavour'd to divest our Saint of his Prejudices against *Meletius*, but did not succeed in the charitable Attempt; whereupon he wrote to *Peter* of *Alexandria*, still at *Rome*, and complain'd of our Saint's Conduct in this Affair in Terms, which sufficiently shew he was not acquainted with the Motives on which he proceeded; while the holy Pope was as hard on *Meletius* and *Eusebius* of *Samosata* for the same Reason; a melancholy Instance of the Weakness of Man, and a useful Lesson of Humility, Diffidence of ourselves, and Calmness in Enquiries, where our Neighbour's Reputation, or Repose are at Stake. While the Church venerates all the Persons already mention'd as Saints, 'though of different Opinions in Regard of certain Facts, which all were not equally inform'd of, she seems to insinuate that the Errors of our Judgments in such Cases will not be imputed to us, while our Hearts are sincere,

and

and our Intentions directed to the Preservation of Unity among the Members of *Jesus Christ*.

Valentinian dying toward the Close of the Year 375, *Ursinus* put himself into Motion, endeavour'd to rally his scatter'd Forces, and entertain'd some Hopes of making his Party considerable in *Rome*. He amused himself with these vain Hopes, and Attempts; but could not prevail with *Gratian*, who succeeded his Father in the Western Empire, to do any thing in Favour of his Pretensions. After the Demise of *Valens*, who govern'd in the East, and before *Gratian* had associated *Theodosius* in the Empire, *Damasus* held a Council at *Rome*, consisting of a great Number of Bishops from all Parts of *Italy*, in which properMethods were concerted for justifying the Saint, and defeating the Attempts of the Antipope. The Fathers of this Synod wrote to *Gratian*, and his Brother *Valentinian*; thank'd them for confirming the Law made by their Father in Favour of the Church; and complain'd that *Ursinus*, 'though long banished, still solicited the populace by his Emissaries, whom he had ordain'd in Defiance to the Canons; and that some Prelates who had either been actually condemn'd by Pope *Damasus*, or had good Reason to apprehend they should fall under his Censure, copying that Schismatick's Example, secured the lower sort by large Bribes, and thus, kept Possession of their Churches by Force. We learn from the same Epistle that *Ursinus* and his Party went so far as to subborn an Apostate Jew to attack our Saint in Person, and endeavour to bring Him to the Necessity of pleading before Men of no Authority or Character, who was constituted Judge of all others; and that their Imperial Majesties had done publick Justice to the Pope's Innocence by banishing the Tool of that restless Faction.

Theodosius, desirous of Uniformity of Sentiments in Religion through the whole Empire, made a Law in the Year 380, in Conjunction with *Gratian* and *Valentinian*, in which it is declared that only such as adhered to the Faith taught by our holy Pope and the Bishop of *Alexandria* should be look'd on as Catholicks. The following Year a Council was held at *Aquileia*; where *Arianism* was formally condemn'd, and a fresh Enquiery made into the Articles urged against our Saint by the Schismaticks, who had accused him of several enormous Crimes, and among the rest of Adultery; but had no better Foundation for this Calumny than that the Female Part of *Rome* had been almost unanimous in espousing hisCause against *Ursinus*. St. *Jerom* in his fiftieth Ep.calls him, *a Lover of Chastity, Virgin Doctor of theVirgin Church, an excellent Man, and one well versed in the holyScripture*; and his Virtue was so well known even in the East, that *Theodoret* in his History represents him as a Person of eminent

eminent Sanctity, and always ready to say and do every thing that had any Tendency to maintaining the Faith of the Apostles. This Character was of itself sufficient to destroy the Probability of what was alledged by the Saint's Enemies; but the Council thought fit to examine every particular Accusation in a legal and deliberate Manner, and give an authentick Testimony in Favour of his Innocence.

Damasus govern'd the Church eighteen Years with great Wisdom, and Integrity of Heart, and receiv'd the Reward of his Labours on the eleventh of *December* 384, the Day on which his Name occurs in the *Roman* Martyrologe.

The XII Day.

St. EPIMACHUS, St. ALEXANDER, &c. Martyrs.

THE Persecution set on Foot by *Decius* raged with the utmost Violence at *Alexandria* in the Year 250; and the two holy Martyrs, whom the Church proposes to our Veneration this Day, shed their Blood for the Faith on that Occasion. As the Magistrates were very industrious and active in searching for Christians in that City, *Epimachus*, and *Alexander* fell into their Hands; and upon confessing the Name of *Jesus Christ*, at their first Examination, were loaded with Chains, committed to Prison, and suffer'd all the Hardships of a long Confinement. Remaining the same after this severe Trial of their Faith and Patience, they were beaten with heavy Sticks, their Sides torn with Iron Hooks, and their Martyrdom consummated by Fire. St. *Denis*, Bishop of *Alexandria*, who was an Eye-Witness of their Sufferings, gives us this short Account of the Matter in his Letter to *Fabius* of *Antioch*, as quoted and preserved by *Eusebius*; and the same holy Prelate speaks of four glorious Martyrs of the other Sex, who were crown'd on the same Day, and at the same Place. *Ammonarium*, a Virgin of an irreproachable Life, stands first in that glorious List. Her Judge employ'd all the cruel Arts in his Power to draw somewhat from her in Favour of the Pagan Deities and to the Prejudice of her holy Profession; but the Saint had assured him he should never prevail with her to drop the least Word of that Sort, and kept her Promise inviolably; whereupon she was led to Execution; but the Manner of her Death is not specified. The second of those holy Women was named *Mercuria*, a Person venerable

for

for her Age and Virtue; the third was *Dyonisia*, who, though a tender Mother of many Children, preferr'd God to that and all other human Considerations; the fourth was another *Ammonarium*. The Judge tired out with the Courage and Constancy of the first Female Champion, and supposing the three before him would in all Probability give him as much Trouble, pronounced Sentence on them, and they were beheaded immediatly. The six Martyrs of *Alexandria* are mention'd in the *Roman* Martyrologe on the twelfth of *December*, which is supposed to be the Day of their Death.

The XIII Day.

St. LUCY, Virgin and Martyr.

LUCY, one of the brightest Stars of the Church of *Sicily*, was born at *Syracusa*, then the Capital City of that Island. She lost her Father in her Infancy, but *Eutychia* her Mother took a singular Care to educate her in the Principles of Christianity, and furnish her with Sentiments of Piety and sublime Morality. That Lady had Thoughts of marrying her Daughter who had, unknown to her, consecrated her Virginity to God, but as she was on the Point of pressing the Proposal, she was afflicted with a bloody Flux, which continu'd on her four Years, and providentially diverted her Thoughts from the Marriage of our Saint. *Lucy*, sensibly afflicted at her Mother's Distemper, and full of Faith in the Intercession of St. *Agatha*, made a devout Pilgrimage to *Catana*, where that holy Virgin's Relicks lay, and petition'd for the Cure of a Person so dear to her. Her Prayers were successful; and *Eutychia*, in Gratitude for the Favour she had receiv'd by her holy Daughter's Means, left her at full Liberty to pursue her Inclinations to a single Life, bestow her Fortune on the Poor.

The Acts of our Saint's Martyrdom tell us she was seiz'd in *Dioclesian*'s Persecution, at the Beginning of the IV Century, and by *Paschasius* Governor of *Sicily* condemn'd to Prostitution; but that God deliver'd her in a wonderful Manner; made her an Overmatch for all the Cruelty of the Persecutors, and gave her the Crown of Martyrdom, after a long and glorious Combat. The *Greek* and *Latin* Churches agree in placing her Festival on the thirteenth of *December*, which before the Change of Religion

in

Dec.13 in this Island, was a Feast of the second Rank, *i. e.* one of those which required the People's Attendance at Mass, but allow'd necessary Works, such as cultivating the Earth &c. and her Name stands in the reform'd Calendars to this Day.

✧✧✧✧✧✧✧✧✧✧✧✧✧✧✧✧✧✧✧✧✧✧✧✧✧✧✧✧✧✧✧✧✧✧✧✧✧

St EUSTRATIUS *and his Companions*, MARTYRS.

THE Martyrdom of these Saints is usually dated in the Reign of *Galerius Maximian*, who obliged *Dioclesian* to abdicate in the Year 305, and they stand distinguish'd from other glorious Victims under that Prince by their extraordinary Ardour for dying in the Cause of their Saviour. *Eustratius* had been employ'd as Secretary under the Governor of the lesser *Armenia*; and being order'd to bring several Christians to that Magistrate's Tribunal, exhorted them to Perseverance in their Profession. This Action was reckon'd a Violation of his Trust, and an Affront to his Sovereign, and therefore punish'd with the utmost Severity. After several violent Torments, born with a Patience and Courage truly Christian, he was thrown into Prison at *Sebaste*, where he was visited by *Blasius* Bishop of that City, of whom we have spoken on the third of *February*, and receiv'd no small Comfort and Advantage from the Discourse and Example of *Auxentius*, a Priest in the Neighbourhood. Our Saint's Conduct was such as made several Converts to the Faith, for which he suffer'd; *Eugenius* a young Man of his own Country was one of that happy Number; who, struck with the Intrepedity which appear'd in every Word while before the Judge, and his wonderful Constancy while under the Hands of his Tormentors, loudly declared himself a Christian.

Lysias the Governour going soon after to *Nicopolis*, another City in the lesser *Armenia*, order'd *Eustratius*, *Eugenius* and *Auxentius* to be brought before him there; and after they had given several glorious Proofs of an invincible Courage and divine Assistance, the two last were condemn'd and executed at the Gates of *Nicopolis*. *Mardarius*, who had left his Wife, his Children, and all that was dear to him in this World, to follow *Eustratius* from *Sebaste* to that City, with a View of sharing the Glory of Martyrdom with that excellent Person, had the Happiness to seal his Faith with his Blood before him; for he either was dispatch'd at the same Time when *Auxentius* and *Eugenius* suffer'd, or expired in the Hands of his Tormenters. The Governor upon reviewing his Troops observing *Orestes*, one of the Officers,

wear

St. Spyridon, *Bishop*. 347

wear a golden Cross on his Breast, knew him to be a Christian; and upon Dec. 14 a farther Enpuiry, found he was not the only Soldier of that Persuasion; whereupon he transmitted an Account of this Discovery to *Agricolaüs*, Governor of all *Armenia*, who resided at *Sebaste*, and *Eustratius* was sent back to that City together with *Orestes*. The latter had his Trial and Sentence as soon as he reached *Sebaste*, and expired on a large Gridiron, heated red hot for that Purpose. The Day following *Eustratius* consummated his Martyrdom in a fiery Furnace.

The *Grecians* honour the Memory of the five illustrious Martyrs on the thirteenth of *December*, the Day on which the *Roman* Martyrologe commemorates their Victory.

The XIV Day.

St. SPYRIDON Bishop of *Trimithusa* in *Cyprus*.

BEFORE *Spyridon* was dignified with the Episcopal Character he was employ'd in keeping Sheep, and continu'd the same rural Exercise after his Promotion. As we have no Account of his Education, we may be allow'd to suppose his Pastoral Labours and Vigilance in the Field were what prepar'd him for the Inspection and Government of a more valuable Flock, and the Simplicity and Innocence of his Heart engaged the Almighty to furnish him with all the Lights requisite for the faithful Discharge of a more important Trust. The holy Bishop, of whom we are speaking, flourished at the Beginning of the fourth Century; and *Sozomen* the Historian, who wrote at the Beginning of the fifth, tells us that a Gang of Thieves, attempting one Night to carry off some of his Sheep, were stopt by an invisible Hand, so that they could neither perpetrate the intended Theft, nor make their Escape. *Spyridon* coming early next Morning, and finding them thus miraculously secured, set them at Liberty by his Prayers, told them in a facetious Manner, that he was unwilling they should go away unrewarded for the Care they had taken of his Flock in the Night, and therefore desired them to accept of a Ram for their Pains. He then begg'd they would consider the Danger of their State, and amend their Lives; and observed to them that they had taken much unnessceary Pains, and run a great Hazard for what they might have made their own by asking for it.

'Though

Dec. 14. 'Though our holy Prelate had little or no Acquaintance with Letters, and had never employ'd his Time or Thoughts on human Sciences, he had made the Scriptures his daily Meditation, and learnt what Veneration is due to those sacred Oracles, even in the most minute Particulars, and such as seem of but little Importance. The Bishops of *Cyprus* being assembled, *Triphyllius* one of that Number, a Man of great Learning and Eloquence, was by them engaged to preach to the People ; having Occasion to mention that Passage in the Gospel where *Jesus Christ* says to the Paralytick, *take up your Bed and walk*, he made use of a Word to Express the Sick Man's Bed, which he thought more elegant and beautiful than that in the original Text. *Spyridon* full of a holy Resentment at this false Niceness, and Attempt to add Graces to what was already adorn'd with Simplicity, arose and interrupted the Preacher by asking him whether He was better than the Person who made use of the Term which he rejected, or alter'd?

St. *Spyridon* had been married, and was happy in a Daughter, named *Irene*, who lived with him and waited on him with all the Affection of a dutiful Child, and, all the Assiduity and Submission of an active and faithful Servant. She maintain'd a Virgin Chastity to her last Moment, and copied the Example of her Father's Virtue with great Exactness. *Irene* dying before our Saint, one who had lodged somewhat of Value in her Hands unknown to her Father, made a Demand of it. *Spyridon* made all possible Enquires for the Thing in Question, but without Success, for *Irene* had buried it in the Ground for the greater Security. The Man, to whom it belong'd, persisted in the Demand, with Tears, and all the Marks of a ruined and desperate Person, resolved not to survive the Loss. The holy Bishop touched with the poor Man's extravagant Sorrow, went to the Place, where his Daughter was buried, call'd her by her Name, and asked her where she had laid what such a Person had left in her Hands. Having receiv'd exact Directions from his Daughter, the Saint found what he wanted and deliver'd it to the Owner.

Sozomen, from whom we have taken this Account, tells us he divided his whole Substance into two Parts ; one of which was employ'd in Maintaining himself and a great Number of poor People, the other was lent to such as wanted a present Supply, and were expected to repay it when able ; on which Occasion he allow'd every one to serve himself and take what he judged necessary in his present Circumstances.

Rufinus, who died at the Beginning of the V Century, tells us that St. *Spyridon*, assisted at the Council of *Nice* in 325, which consisted of a glorious

ous Number of Saints and Confeſſors, who had ſuffer'd much from the Pa- Dec. 15 gan Enemies of our Faith; and the *Roman* Martyrologe tells us he was one of thoſe who loſt their right Eye, and had their left Ham cut in the Reign of *Galerius Maximian*, and were ſent to work in the Mines. The Time of our Saint's Death is not known; the *Greeks* honour his Memory on the twelfth of *December*, and keep his Feſtival with great Solemnity to this Day; but the *Latins* venerate him on the fourteenth of the ſame Month.

The XV Day.

St. EUSEBIUS, Biſhop of *Vercelli.*

THE holy Biſhop, whom the Church propoſes to our Veneration this Day, was one of the brighteſt Lights of the IV Age, was a Native of *Sardinia*, and deſcended from one of the moſt conſiderable Families in that Iſland. Upon his Father's Death, *Reſtituta* his Mother removed to *Rome*, where ſhe was attended by our Saint and his Siſter. *Euſebius* applied ſo ſeriouſly to his Studies in that City that Pope *Silveſter* admitted him among his Clergy, and initiated him in the Miniſtry by conferring on him the Order of a Reader. He proceeded to the ſuperior Degrees, and more exalted Functions at *Rome* and we are told that *Mark*, S. *Silveſter*'s immediate Succeſſor, ordain'd him Prieſt. *Julius* was in St. *Peter*'s Chair when our Saint appear'd firſt at *Vercelli*, then a City in the *Ciſalpine Gaul*, now in the Principality of *Piemont*. We are not told on what Occaſion he went to that City; but his Behaviour there was ſuch as gain'd the Affections and raiſed the Admiration of all who ſaw and converſed with him. Upon the Death of that Biſhop, the Church of *Vercelli* were unanimous in begging he would accept of the vacant See, 'though they were not unprovided of ſeveral excellent Perſons well qualified for the Poſt. According to St. *Ambroſe*, *Euſebius* was the firſt Prelate in the Weſt, who join'd the Practiſe of Monaſtick Diſcipline with the Life of an Eccleſiaſtick. He and his Clergy obſerved a Regularity not much inferior to that of the holy Inhabitants of the Deſart; their Faſts were rigorous; Reading, Study, Prayer, and Work divided their Time; they abſtain'd from the Converſation of Women; and united their whole Forces againſt ſuch Temptations as might break in upon them. The Clergy of *Vercelli*, under theſe Regulations, were in Reality a religious Community; and the Houſe where they lived bore the Name of a Monaſtery. This

Dec. 15. This School furnished the Church with several Illustrious Bishops, and here our Saint laid in a Stock of Virtue sufficient to make him an equal Match to the Persecutions which he was to encounter.

Liberius, who succeeded to the holy See in 354, sensibly afflicted at the Conduct of *Vincent* Bishop of *Capua* at the Council of *Arles* the preceeding Year, where he had been weak enough to subscribe the Condemnation of St. *Athanasius*, deputed *Lucifer* Bishop of *Cagliari*, *Pancratius* a Priest, and *Hilary* a Deacon to *Constantius*, to obtain his Imperial Majesties Assistance for calling another Council, in which the Questions in Dispute might be regularly discuss'd, and the Faith of the Church secured. As the Court was then at *Milan*, he wrote at the same Time to *Eusebius*, whose Bishoprick lay near that City; and, being well satisfied with his Capacity and Zeal, desired he would join his Legates in urging the said Request, and employ his strongest Arguments to convince that Prince of the Necessity of consulting the Peace of the Church. After *Lucifer* and his Companions had left *Rome*, *Liberius* dispatched a second Letter to our Saint, repeating the same Exhortation, and begging him to be particularly active in Defence of the Faith and St. *Athanasius*, whose Condemnation the *Arians* aim'd at against all Law and Reason. *Eusebius* receiv'd the Pope's Legates in a manner expressive of his Regard for the holy See, and Concern for the Purity of the Faith, assuring *Liberius* he would do his utmost in the important Affair, with which he had entrusted him. His Holiness wrote a third Letter to our Saint, thank'd him for the Readiness with which he undertook that Commission, and concluded with desiring him to exert all his Vigour in Favour of the Catholick Cause, and use all the Power his Virtue gave him at Court for the speedy assembling of the Bishops. As the Pope and the Eastern Prelates had been very urgent in desiring a Council, though with different Views, *Constantius*, who always favour'd the *Arians* conven'd one at *Milan* in the Beginning of the Year 355. 'Though the Eastern Bishops were not near so numerous in that Assembly as those of the West, *Eusebius* knew what Influence the Emperor had over them, and how dexterous the *Arians* were at deceiving well meaning Persons into their Measures, and therefore concluded his Presence in the Council would be of little or no Use to the Orthodox Cause. His Absence put both Parties in Motion, for all were desirous of engaging so valuable a Prelate in their Interest. Thirty famous *Arian* Bishops sign'd a Letter, which they sent by two of their Number, desiring the Saint to join them in procuring Unity and Charity among Christians, and condemning *Athanasius*. The Emperor wrote to *Eusebius* on the same Subject, and

and told him he had nothing to do but give his Consent to what had been Dec. 15 transacted and decreed by the Council. The holy Bishop, thus importuned, let the Council and Emperor know he would come to *Milan*, where he would do what he should judge just and agreeable to God's Will. *Lucifer*, and the two other Legates from *Rome* wrote to him at the same Time, and press'd his hastening to *Milan*, to detect and destroy the Artifices of the *Arians*, and resist *Valens* their Ringleader, as St. *Peter* had done *Simon* the Magician.

The Terms, in which our Saint had answer'd the Emperor's and Council's Invitation, alarm'd the Hereticks so, that, he was ten Days at *Milan*, before he could gain Admission into the Church where the Bishops met; but, when the Faction had put Things on what they thought a good Foot, he was sent for, and required to sign St. *Athanasius*'s Condemnation. *Eusebius*, with his usual Prudence, observed that it would be necessary to begin with subscribing the *Nicene* Faith, and promised to do whatever could be desired, when all present had given their Assurance of their Orthodoxy. *Dionysius*, Bishop of *Milan*, declared his Approbation of the Proposal, and was going to write his Name, when *Valens* forced the Pen and Paper from him; and the Dispute ran so high that the People were acquainted with it, and began to declare loudly in Favour of our Saint and his Associates. The *Arians*, apprehending they should be worsted if they continued in the Church, removed to the Imperial Palace where *Constantius* undertook to preside. That Prince order'd *Eusebius*, *Dionysius*, and *Lucifer* to appear, and sign *Athanasius*'s Sentence; upon their observing that the holy Bishop's Innocence had been acknowleged by *Ursacius* and *Valens*, his most inveterate Enemies, the Emperor, press'd beyond the Power of a reasonable Reply, declared himself ready to accuse the absent Prelate. *Eusebius* and his two Companions shew'd the Absurdity and Unreasonableness of the Emperor's Proceedings, and declared themselves firmly resolved never to condemn *Athanasius*, in his Absence. *Constantius*, incensed at their Refusal threaten'd to make their Lives pay for their Disobedience, and in the Transports of his Rage drew his Sword, as if resolved to execute the Sentence, with his own Hand. Growing somewhat cooler, he order'd the three invincible Champions for the Faith into Banishment. *Dionysius* was sent into *Cappadocia*, where he died: *Lucifer* to *Germanicia* in *Syria*, of which City *Eudoxus* a celebrated *Arian* was Bishop; and our Saint to *Scythopolis* in *Palestine*, to be treated according to the Discretion of *Patrophilus*, one of the Heads of the Heretical Party. These illustrious Exiles, thus maliciously seperated, were so many
Apostolical

Dec. 15 Apoſtolical Preachers ſcatter'd into different Provinces by a particular Providence, to eſtabliſh the Catholick Faith in Places, where the *Arians* ſeem'd to reign without Controul; and their very Chains ſpoke ſtrongly and efficaciouſly in Favour of the Cauſe for which they ſuffer'd. They were every where reſpected as Confeſſors of *Jeſus Chriſt*, viſited by Deputies from ſeveral diſtant Provinces, and ſupplied very plentifully with all Neceſſaries. *Liberius* wrote to our Saint and the two other Biſhops, aſſuring them he was divided between Sorrow for their Abſence, and Joy for the Glory attending their Baniſhment for the Faith.

Euſebius ſuffer'd a great Variety of Hardſhips from *Patrophilus* and his Creatures; but it pleas'd God to ſoften the Rigour of them by ſeveral viſible and inviſible Conſolations. *Syrus* a Deacon, and *Victorinus* an Exorciſt were deputed from *Vercelli* and the neighbouring Churches with Letters, and a conſiderable Sum of Money for the Saint's Uſe. *Syrus*, having acquitted himſelf of his Commiſſion, made a devout Journey to *Jeruſalem*; and in the mean Time the *Arians*, who could not bear to ſee *Euſebius* treated with ſuch Reſpect by diſtant Churches, dragg'd him from his Apartment half dreſs'd, and, after ſeveral Inſults and Indignities, ſhut him up in another, where they confin'd him four Days, during which Time they frequently reproached him with Obſtinacy and Diſobedience to his Prince, importuned him to enter into their Sentiments, and abuſed him in a moſt outrageous Manner upon his Refuſal; all which they pretended was done by Virtue of the Emperor's Order.

After four Days ſpent thus without any Food, our Saint was allow'd to return to his former Habitation, where he was receiv'd with all poſſible Demonſtrations of Joy, and the Houſe ſurrounded by Lights. His Enemies, gall'd at the Honours paid him at his Return, and enraged at the charitable and chriſtian Means, which he employ'd to engage the Hearts of the People, began to conſider how they ſhould deſtroy him without expoſing themſelves to a Legal Conviction of being concern'd in his Death. In this View, in leſs than a Month, they forced their Way into the Houſe, where he lived, hurried him away to a cloſe Priſon, where he was attended by *Tegrinus*, an orthodox Prieſt; and all who had viſited him or expreſs'd any Concern for him met with the ſame Treatment. Having thus ſecured the Saint's Perſon, they plunder'd his Lodgings, and ſet a Guard at the Priſon Door, with ſtrict Orders to hinder his Friends, or Servants from carrying him any Proviſions. After ſix Days ſpent without eating, *Euſebius* ſeem'd at the Point of Departure; but the People were ſo loud and preſſing in his Favour, that his Enemies were obliged for their own Security to allow one of his Servants, to attend him. *Syrus*, returning from his Pilgrimage, waited on the Saint, Dec. 15 who found Means to give him a Letter from the several Churches, in which he expres'd his Joy to hear they remain'd firm in the Faith, and gave them an Account of his Sufferings from it's Enemies. *Eusebius* was enlarged at last, and lodged in Count *Joseph*'s House, where he was visited by St. *Epiphanius*. *Joseph*, had renounced *Judaism* for the Faith of Christ, which he asserted in it's utmost Purity on all Occasions, and had a settled Aversion to the *Arian* Heresy. The *Arians* had employ'd all their Art to gain that Nobleman to their Party, and engage him to join them in persecuting our Saint; but, falling short of their Aim, they removed *Eusebius* to *Cappadocia*, and afterwards into the lower *Thebaïs*, where he remain'd 'till the Death of *Constantius*, which happen'd in the Close of the Year 361.

Julian who succeeded that Prince, hoped to pass for a Man of singular Clemency and Humanity, by recalling all the Exiles, who had been forc'd from their respective Countries in the late Reign; but, as the Hereticks were included in that Act of Grace, his real Intention was to sap the Foundations of the Christian Religion by encouraging all Sects, and thus fomenting an intestine War in the Church. *Eusebius* left *Thebaïs* in Company with *Lucifer* of *Cagliari*, who had been removed to that Country some Time before, and proposed to his Companion making a Journey to *Alexandria*, to consult with St. *Athanasius* about religious Affairs, and concert Measures for uniting the Church of *Antioch*, then divided between those who obey'd *Meletius*, and the *Eustathians*, who refused to acknowlege that Prelate for their Pastor. *Lucifer*, thinking it more proper to go directly to *Antioch*, dispatched two of his Deacons to *Alexandria*, with Instructions to act there in his Name, and give his Assent to the Transactions of the Council to be held in that City. Our Saint, however, went to *Alexandria*, where, in Conjunction with the holy Defender of the orthodox Faith, he procured the meeting of a Council, which, though not numerous, consisted entirely of such as had signalized themselves by a generous Confession during the late Persecution and Troubles. That venerable Assembly came to a Resolution of receiving all such as quitted their Heresy; but with this Restriction, that the Heads of the Heretical Party and their Abbettors should be excluded from the Clergy, while such as had been surprized or forced into Compliance with the Heterodox, were upon renouncing the Tenets and Communion of the *Arians*, allow'd to keep their former Rank in the Church. The Council transmitted an Account of their Proceedings to *Lucifer* and two

other

Dec. 15 other Bishops at *Antioch*; and the Letter was sent thither by our Saint, and *Asterius* Bishop of *Petra* in *Arabia*.

Eusebius left *Alexandria* soon after the Council broke up, and upon his Arrival at *Antioch* was most sensibly mortifiy'd at the unhappy Posture of Affairs in the Church of that City. *Lucifer* endeavour'd to reunite the Catholicks under one Bishop; but, meeting with a vigorous Resistance from the *Eustathians*, he thought it expedient to satisfy them by placing *Paulinus* in the See of *Antioch*, who had been ordain'd Priest by *Eustathius*, and was perfectly agreeable to those who bore his Name. This indiscreet Step was so far from healing the Breach, that it made it much wider, and the Schism subsisted 85 Years. *Eusebius*, finding Things in this Situation, would not communicate exteriourly with either of the Catholick Prelates, who appear'd on the disputed See, being apprehensive that his declaring for either would but increase the Division, which he wished to see remedied. His Prudence and Regard for *Lucifer* would not allow him to make any publick Reflections on that Prelate's Conduct; he therefore bewail'd this precipitate and unfortunate Consecration in private, and hoped a Council might put all on a right Foot. *Lucifer*, disgusted at our Saint's Caution, which he took for a tacit Reflexion on his Proceedings, carried his Resentment so far as to break Communion with him, which was no less than deserting that of the Catholick Church, to which *Eusebius* was firmly united. To give a tolerable Colour to this Rupture, *Lucifer* retracted his Approbation of what the Council of *Alexandria* had done in Favour of such as had been decoy'd into a Subscription of the Council of *Rimini*, or communicated with the *Arians*, and thus gave Rise to the Schism which was long known by his Name.

St. *Eusebius* left *Antioch*, with *Evagrius* a Priest of that City, who afterwards succeeded *Paulinus*; but before he turn'd to his own Church he visited some of the most considerable Cities in the East, where he strengthen'd those who were weak in the Faith, and had the good Fortune to recover several, who had been seduced, by the crafty *Arians*. The Churches of *Illyricum* shared his charitable Labours in the same Way; and he travell'd through that Province into *Italy*, where he was receiv'd with extraordinary Expressions of Joy by all the Catholicks. At his Return, he was transported to find St. *Hilary* Bishop of *Poitiers* in that Country, and join'd him heartily in endeavouring to restore the Peace of the Church. The *Italian* Prelates, being inform'd of the Success of our Saint's Apostolical Labours in *Illyricum*, wrote to their Collegues in that Country, and congratulated them on their Return to the Catholick Faith, which had suffer'd much from

Ursacius

Urfacius, Valens, Photinus, and *Germinius.* Our Saint acted in Concert with the holy Bishop of *Poitiers* till the latter left *Italy*; we find them both at *Milan* in the Year 365, and engaged together against *Auxentius* the Heretical Bishop of that City, the chief Support of the *Arian* Party in the West. That Enemy of the Catholick Faith was complete Master of the Arts of Dissimulation, and Shuffling, and had imploy'd his Skill very successfully on the young Emperor *Valentinian,* whom he gain'd to his Communion by a fallacious Profession of Faith, and made our Saint, and his Companion in the glorious Cause of the Church pass for two factious, and contentious Incendiaries. St. *Hilary* undertook to shew the Emperor that he was imposed on in the present Affair, but *Auxentius* had Influence enough on that Prince to continue the Delusion, and prevail with him to issue out an Order for his Adversary's leaving *Milan* immediately.

After this Contest, we have no farther Account of *Eusebius,* whose Name occurs on the first of *August* in the *Roman* Martyrologe, where he is mention'd as a Martyr, for the Catholick Cause; but the *Roman* Missal and Breviary give us his Festival on the fifteenth of *December,* which is probably the Day on which his Relicks were removed.

The XVI Day.

St. ADO, *Bishop of* VIENNE *in* France.

ADO, a Native of *France,* and descended of a noble and ancient Family, was born about the Year 800, and sent to the Monastery of *Ferrieres* in the Diocese of *Sens* as soon as he was susceptible of any Impressions. He was received into that School of Religion and Literature by the Abbot *Sigulphus,* where he soon exceeded all those of his own Age in Learning and Vertue. *Markward,* Abbot of *Prom* in the Diocese of *Treves,* who spent his first Years at *Ferrieres,* and still kept a strict Correspondence with the Monks of that Abby, having heard of our Saint's great Merit desired he might be sent to *Prom.* That Abbot's Request was granted, and *Ado* staid there till the Jealousy and restless Malice of such as had neither his Vertue nor Learning obliged him to quit the Place after the Death of his Friend and Protector *Markward,* which happen'd in the Year 853. *Lupus,* then Abbot of *Ferrieres,* had been so prejudiced against him by his Enemies that the Saint dared not venture back to that House, but went to *Rome,* where he spent

Dec. 16 five Years. From that City he removed to *Ravenna*, where he compofed his Martyrologe, by the Help of an ancient Piece of the fame fort which bore St. *Jerom*'s Name. This Work, much more methodical and full than any Thing of that Nature which had appear'd before his Time, made a confiderable Addition to *Ado*'s Reputation, and recommended him fo ftrongly to St. *Remigius* Bifhop of *Lyons*, that upon our Saint's going to that City foon after its Publication, that Prelate took more than ordinary Pains to engage his Stay in his Diocefe; and, as he was ftill reckon'd a Monk of *Ferrieres*, wrote to the Abbot of that Houfe for his Permiffion to employ him in the Service of the Church of *Lyons*. *Remigius*, obtaining his Requeft, gave *Ado* the Care of a Parifh near *Vienne*.

The Saint, thus entrufted with the Cure of Souls, behaved himfelf in fo edifying a Manner that he had not been above a Year there when the united Voices of the Clergy and People of *Vienne* named him to the Efpifcopal See of that City vacant by the Death of *Agilmar*; and the Choice was approved of and confirm'd by all the Bifhops of the Province; but, 'though exactly canonical oppofed by *Gerard*, a Man of Quality in that Country, who had been made to believe that *Ado* had left his Monaftery in an illegal and rebellious Manner. Upon Application to *Lupus*, that Abbot clear'd up the Matter beyond the Power of farther Cavil, own'd he had been impofed on to *Ado*'s Prejudice by his malicious Enemies, and declared he was glad of that Opportunity of doing Juftice to the injured Monk. The Objection againft his Election being removed in a Manner fo advantageous to the Saint's Character, he was confecrated by the Bifhops of the Province in the Year 860; and immediately after his Promotion wrote to *Nicholas* I, then in St. *Peter*'s Chair, fending him a Profeffion of his Faith according to the ecellent Cuftom of thofe Times. His Holinefs anfwer'd our Prelate's Letter, and approved of his Election; but let him know his Profeffion of Faith would have been more complete and fatisfactory, had it mention'd his receiving the fifth and fixth General Councils; whereas his fpeaking only of the four firft left Room to fufpect he had not the fame Regard for the other two. He therefore defired he would explain himfelf on that Subject; and in the mean Time fent him the *Pallium* and the Decrees of a Council lately held at *Rome*.

Ado's Promotion made no Change in his Behaviour; he was ftill the fame humble, modeft, mortified Man, as when in a Cloifter; and endeavour'd to infpire his Flock with the like Sentiments and Difpofitions. He was indefatigable in preffing the great Truths of Salvation, and labour'd hard for the

Reformation

Reformation of Manners, and establishing good Discipline among the People committed to his Care. He regulated the publick Service of his Church with much Zeal and Wisdom, and express'd a particular Tenderness for the Poor, who had Hospitals raised for their Reception and Entertainment at his Expence; to sum up his whole Character in two Words, *Ado* knew all the Obligations of his Post, and discharged them with the utmost Exactness and Fidelity. He was present at the Council at *Toufy* near *Toul* in *Lorraine*, which was held on the twenty second of *October* 860 against vagrant Monks and Clergymen; and assisted at several other Synods after that Time, always distinguishing himself by a superior Capacity, and an ardent Zeal for Purity of Faith and Manners. *Lothaire*, King of *Lorraine* would have employ'd him in soliciting a Divorce from his lawful Wife, and procuring Leave to marry another; but while several worthy Prelates betray'd too much Complaisance for their Prince's Passions, *Ado*'s Behaviour in this Difficult Affair was such as engaged the Pope to commend his Courage, Vigilance and Zeal, in opposing publick Sinners, though seemingly screen'd from Censure by their exalted Station. 'Though our Saint had his Share in all the publick Transactions of the Church, his Mind was as recollected, as if his whole Business lay within the Compass of his own House. The Multiplicity of Affairs never made him less constant in Prayer, or less rigorous in his Mortifications. He had spent sixteen Years in all the Labours of his Station, when it pleased God to reward him with a happy Death on the sixteenth of *December* 875. His Body was buried in St. *Peter*'s Church at *Vienne*; and his Name occurs in the *Roman* Martyrologe on the Day of his Passage to Immortality.

Dec. 17

The XVII Day.

St. LAZARUS, *Brother of* Martha *and* Mary.

NOT long before our Lord's Passion, as he was employ'd in his publick Ministry on the other side of *Jordan*, he receiv'd the News of *Lazarus*'s Sickness; and, knowing the Design of divine Providence in that Affair, answer'd, " *This Sickness is not unto Death, but for the Glory of* " *God, that the Son of God may be glorified by it.*" After two Days spent in the same Place, *Jesus Christ* declared his Resolution of returning to *Judea*; and, after replying to what his Disciples had urged to dissuade him from exposing his Person among his implacable Enemies, he told them their

Jo. ii. 4.

Dec. 17 Friend *Lazarus* was asleep, but that he would go and awake him. His Disciples, not understanding their Master's Meaning, endeavour'd to wave this Reason as insufficient, by observing that if he was asleep, he was in no Danger, and consequently that our Lord's Presence would not be necessary at that Time. *Jesus*, perceiving their Misapprehension of what he had said, told them in plain Terms *Lazarus* was Dead; adding that He was glad he was not there before, that what they should see him do might confirm and encrease their Faith in him.

Our Blessed Saviour coming toward *Bethany*, near two Miles from *Jerusalem*, the Place of *Lazarus*'s Habitation, he was told the Deceased had then been four Days in the Grave, and found great Numbers of the *Jews* from *Jerusalem*, who came to comfort his Sisters under their Loss. *Martha*, being apprized of our Lord's Approach, met him on the Road; but her Behaviour on this melancholy Occasion has been given at large on the twenty ninth of *July*. *Mary* also threw herself at his Feet, bath'd in Tears. *Jesus* seeing a deep Sorrow in every Face for the Loss of *Lazarus*, sympathiz'd with the Company, mingled his Tears with theirs, and asked where they had laid his Friend; whereupon He was conducted to the Place where *Lazarus* lay, which was a Cave closed with a large Stone, which he order'd to be removed. *Martha*, whose Faith seem'd yet imperfect, observed to him that her Brother's Corpse had lain there four Days, and consequently stunk; but *Jesus* reprimanded her with this strong Expostulation, " *Did I not tell* " *you*, said he, *that you should see the Glory of God, if you would but believe.*" The Stone being removed, according to his Direction, our Lord raised his Eyes towards Heaven, address'd himself, to the first Person of the Blessed Trinity in the following Words; " *Father, I thank you for having heard* " *Me. I know indeed that You always hear Me; but I say this for the sake* " *of the People who stand by, that they may believe You have sent me.*" When he had ended this Speech, he call'd aloud, *Lazarus, come forth*. Our Lord had no sooner given the Word of Command, but *Lazarus* arose, bound Hands and Feet, as usual then in such Cases; and the same powerful Voice which raised him, order'd him to be untied and set at Liberty. This Miracle gain'd several of the *Jews* there present, engaged their Belief in *Jesus* and put them upon communicating this wonderful Affair to the *Pharisees*, the most obstinate and incredulous Part of that People.

Our Saint's Resurrection alarm'd the chief Priests and *Pharisees*, who immediately enter'd into a Consultation against our Saviour, being apprehensive that if he was allow'd to go on in this Way, the whole People would follow.

low and believe in him. *Jesus*, knowing their Design, retired to *Ephrem*, Dec. 17 near the Desart of *Judea*, where he was accompanied by his Disciples; but six Days before the Feast of the Passover, he return'd to *Bethany*, where he supped in the House of *Simon the Leper*. *Lazarus* being one of the Company at that Entertainment the Place was much crouded by the *Jews*, curious of seeing a Man who had been raised from the Dead; and the chief Priests, seeing how efficacious this Miracle proved in the Conversion of great Numbers of the People, consulted about killing the Man, who was an incontestable Evidence of the Resurrection of the Dead, and the Mission of *Jesus Christ*. The Evangelist has not told us that this vain and criminal Design was executed; and it appears from St. *Epiphanius* that the ancient Tradition of the IV Century allow'd him thirty Years after our Lord's Resurrection.

Jo. xii.

The Place of our Saint's Death is still less certain than the Time. If we may depend on what the *Grecians* say on this Article, he ended his Life in *Cyprus*, and was buried at *Cytia* in that Island. This Opinion is confirm'd by several *Latin* Writers, who tell us that in their Time *Cyprus* could shew several Churches dedicated in his Honour. Some make him a Bishop in that Island, and give him the additional Title of a Martyr; others assure us he was Bishop of *Marseilles*, and died in that City. We leave the Discussion of this perplex'd Affair to the Criticks, and hasten to tell our Reader that the Memory of St. *Lazarus* has always been held in great Veneration both in the East and West. The *Grecians* keep three Days in his Honour, that of his Resurrection, on the Day before *Palm-Sunday*: that of the Removal of his Body to *Constantinople* in the IX Century, the seventeenth of *October*; and another Commemoration of his Relicks and those of St. *Magdalene* on the fourth of *May*. The *Roman* Martyrologe places his Festival on the seventeenth of *December*.

St. OLYMPIAS WIDOW.

OLYMPIAS, a Lady of illustrious Descent, and a plentiful Fortune, was left an Orphan in the Hands of *Procopius*, who is supposed to have been her Uncle. She had several Qualifications, which recommended her to the World, and made her one of the most considerable Matches in the whole Empire; for besides her Birth, and large Estate, she was possess'd of all the Beauties of Body and Mind which can engage Affection, and Respect

Dec. 17 spect. She was very young when married to *Nebridius*, who had been Governor of *Constantinople*; the Wedding was honour'd with the Presence of several holy Bishops, and a great Appearance of Persons of the first Rank. *Nebridius* dying in twenty Months after his Marriage, *Olympias* was address'd by several of the most considerable Men of the Court, but rejected all those advantageous Offers, and declared her Resolution of remaining single the Rest of her Days. *Theodosius* the Great, then Master of the Eastern Empire, hearing her Character, was very pressing with her to accept of *Elpidius*, a *Spaniard* and his near Relation; but *Olympias* excused herself in the most respectful and modest Manner imaginable. Upon the Emperor's going on to urge the Affair, after several decisive Answers, that Lady replied that had it been the Will of God she should live with a Man, she should not have lost her Husband so soon, but that his Death led her to conclude Providence had not design'd her for that State. *Theodosius*, provok'd at the ill Success of his Negotiation in Favour of *Elpidius*, put her whole Fortune into the Hands of the Governor of *Constantinople*, with Orders to act as her Guardian 'till she was thirty Years old. At the Instigation of the disappointed Lover, the Governor hinder'd her from seeing the Bishops, or going to Church, hoping thus to tire her into a Compliance with the Emperor's Proposal, who declared himself much offended at her Conduct. That excellent Widow told his Imperial Majesty, she was obliged to own his Goodness in easing her of the Trouble of disposing of her own Money, which she had long found a heavy Burthen; and that the Favour would be complete if he would order her whole Fortune to be divided between the Poor and the Church, and thus preserve her from the Danger of Vanity in the Disposal of it, or a worldly Spirit in keeping it. *Theodosius*, struck with this unexpected Reply, made a farther Enquiry into that Lady's Way of living, which gave him a more exalted Idea of her Virtue, and procured *Olympias* the free Disposal of her Estate.

It is not to be wonder'd that the Particulars of a Life like that of our Saint should prevail with the Emperor to recal his former Order. She eat nothing that had Life; seldom allow'd herself the Use of a Bath, which is thought a necessary Refreshment in hot Countries; and, when her Health obliged her to go into the Water, it was with her Cloaths on. Her Dress was mean; her Furniture poor; her Fasts frequent and rigorous; her Prayers full of Fervour; and her Charity without Bounds. She took a singular Pleasure in providing Churches with proper Ornaments, gracing the Altars with rich Plate, increasing the Revenues of Monasteries and Hospitals, relieving Prisoners and Exiles; and look'd on the Poor at all Distances

as

as Children of God's House, committed to her Care. She gave Millions of Slaves their Libery, instructed several of her own Sex in the Faith of *Jesus Christ*; was constant in her Visits to the Sick, the Aged, the Widows, Orphans, and all such as had no Friends or Means of Subsistence; in short, she applied with indefatigable Vigour to all good Works in her Power.

Such was her Virtue that the most eminent and holy Prelates of that Age were fond of her Acquaintance, and maintain'd a Correspondence with her which always tended to promote God's Glory, and the Good of her Neighbour. Of that Number were St. *Amphilochius* Bishop of *Iconium*, St. *Gregory Nyssen*, St. *Peter* of *Sebeste*, and St. *Epiphanius*. *Nectarius*, Patriarch of *Constantinople* often consulted her in Things relating to the Government of his Church; but the great S. *Chrysostom*, who succeeded that Patriarch, was more closely united to our Saint than the Rest. The honour'd him as a holy and useful Friend, and a wise Director, undertook the Administration of his temporal Affairs; and thus left him no Employment but that of his Ministry. Her Intimacy with St. *Chrysostom*, and the Relief which she gave to the Monks persecuted by *Theophilus* of *Alexandria* made her particularly odious to the Schismaticks who deposed the holy Patriarch, and procured his Banishment. *Olympias*, and several Ladies of Distinction, signalized their Zeal on this Occasion, and adhered inviolably to their lawful Pastor, 'though disgraced and absent. Several Attempts were made to gain our Saint's Approbation of these violent Proceedings, and induce her to own the Title of *Arsacius*, the Invader of St. *Chrysostom*'s See; but she remain'd inflexibly faithful to the injured Prelate. The Faction, desirous of revenging her Opposition to their Measures, accused her of setting the Church on Fire, when the holy Patriarch was forced from *Constantinople*, an Accident that was usually imputed to his Friends and Adherents. Upon appearing before the Governor of *Constantinople*, she was ask'd what induced her to the Act alledged against her; to which she replied, that this Accusation was destitute of all Probability, it having been her known Character to employ large Sums in building and repairing Places consecrated to holy Uses. The Governor, finding it impossible to support this Charge with any thing like legal Evidence, changed his Stile, affected a Concern for *Olympius*, and the other Ladies in the same Way of thinking, and advised them to purchase their own Ease and Security by embracing the Intruder's Communion. Several of her Companions came into the Schismatical Party out of Fear; but our Saint, with her usual Courage, declared it unjust to alter the Accusation, after advancing a Calumny against her in so publick a Manner; desired to be allow'd Council on her former Charge; and
assured

assured the Governor, nothing should engage her to hold Communion with *Arsacius*, which she was persuaded was unlawful. She was dismiss'd for that Time; but, brought into Court again some Days after; and without any farther Trial, sentenced to pay a large Fine for her pretended Crime.

Olympias paid the Money; but left *Constantinople* soon after, and retired to *Cyzicum*, where she receiv'd several Letters from St. *Chrysostom*, then at *Cacusus*, the Place of his Exile: It is usually thought our Saint survived that holy Bishop, who died in the Year 407; but neither the Time, Place, nor Circumstances of her Death are known. The *Greeks* honour her Memory on the twenty fifth of *July*, and the *Roman* Martyrologe places her Name on the seventeenth of *December*.

The XVIII Day.

St. PAUL the SIMPLE.

*P*AUL, before he embraced a solitary Life, had been employ'd in providing for his Family by Husbandry, in a Village of *Thebaïs*, which Business he follow'd 'till he was near sixty. He had several Children, and a Wife much more beautiful than vertuous, who had held criminal Conversation with a Neighbour some Time before *Paul* knew any thing of the Matter. Returning to his Cottage one Day, sooner than he was expected, he caught them in the Fact, and without betraying the least Emotion; " *All this goes well*, said " he, *and gives me no Uneasiness*; *I find*, continued he, addressing himself to " his Wife's Gallant, *that all here belongs to you*; *for which Reason I leave* " *the Woman and her Children in your Hands, and will retire into the Desart*". In eight Days he reached St. *Anthony*, told him his Inclinations to Solitude, and earnestly begg'd for Admittance in his holy Family. That Saint was persuaded; *Paul*'s Age would not bear the Severities of that State of Life, and therefore refused his Request, 'till overcome by his repeated Importunities, and was soon convinced that the Spirit of God had directed him thither. He was particularly pleased with his Simplicity and Patience, and took a singular Pleasure in giving him Instructions suitable to his new State. To try him thoroughly, that great Master frequently order'd him to do Things which nothing but Humility, and Obedience could make tolerable; such as making Baskets, pulling them in Pieces, and making them up again; spending a whole Day in drawing Water, and throwing it on the Ground.

After

After some Time spent with St. *Anthony*, and giving sufficient Proofs of his Vertue, *Paul* was allow'd a Cell about a League from that of his holy Master, where he was directed to practise the great Lessons, which he had learnt of him. Our Saint had not spent a Year in that Retreat, before the Almighty confirm'd St. *Anthony*'s Judgment of his Vertue, and rewarded his Docility and unreserved Obedience with a Power of driving out Devils, and curing the most desperate Distempers; so that in a little Time his Miracles exceeded those of St. *Anthony* both in Number, and Greatness; who frequently sent sick and possess'd Persons to our holy Solitary for Relief, owning that the Gift which *Paul* had received was more extensive than that with which he was entrusted. Our Saint was likewise favour'd with a Faculty of looking to the Bottom of Men's Hearts, and seeing the Dispositions and Motions of their Minds, which appear'd on several Occasions, but chiefly in one recorded by *Palladius*, who flourish'd in the Beginning of the V Age, and tells us he declared the Conversion of a Sinner, who came to Church, and received that Grace while he was hearing Mass there. It is probable that *Paul* lived till the Year 318, but the Day of his Death is unknown. The *Grecians* keep the seventh of *March* in his Honour, in which they are follow'd by the *Roman* Martyrologe; but the other western Churches place his Name on the eighteenth of *December*. The *Greeks* give our Saint the Surname of *Acacus*, i. e. *Innocent*, and the *Latins* distinguish him by that of *the Simple*, because his chief Vertue was Simplicity, and an undisguis'd Sincerity of Heart.

Dec. 18

The XVIII Day.

St. WINEBALD, *Abbot*.

WINEBALD was born in the Kingdom of the *West Saxons* about the Year 702, and educated in a Monastery of that Country 'till he went for *Rome* with his Father and *Willibald* his Brother, as has been related on the seventh of *July*, *Richard* the Father of our Saint, dying on the Road, was buried at *Lucca* in *Tuscany*; but *Winebald* and his Brother pursued their Journey and reach'd *Rome* in *November* 721. *Willibald* had received the Monastick Habit in *England*; but our Saint was initiated in the Clergy at *Rome*, where he consecrated the Remainder of his Days to the Service of God. They enter'd into a Cloister together soon after their Arrival in that City, where the Violent Heats threw them into a Fever in the Year 722. Upon his Recovery *Willibald*

bald made a devout Journey to the holy Land, but our Saint staid at *Rome*, where he studied the holy Scriptures, made great Progress in Vertue, and, after seven Years spent in the faithful Discharge of all the Duties of his Profession, return'd to *England*, and engaged several of his Relations to retire from the World, or at least make their Salvation their first Concern, and lead a Life conformable to the Evangelical Precepts.

In the Year 738 he obtain'd the Permission of his Superiors for making a second Journey to *Rome*, in which he was accompanied by a younger Brother. They had not been long in that City before St. *Boniface* Bishop of *Mentz*, their near Relation, came thither for the third Time; who was so well pleased with their Behaviour that he proposed their going to *Germany* and assisting him in the Apostolical Work, which he had happily begun in that Country. *Winebald* knew the Reward that attended gaining Souls to God, and therefore complied with the Invitation, and reached *Germany* in the Year 739, where he was soon after join'd by his elder Brother. Our Saint was employ'd in preaching the Gospel in *Thuringe*, then more extensive than at present; and as he practised his Monastick Rule with great Severity and Exactness, his Example was as efficacious as his Discourses in recommending the Doctrine which he deliver'd. *Boniface*, perceiving his Zeal, and the great Regularity of his Life, ordain'd him Priest, and put seven Churches or Parishes under his Direction, which he govern'd till the Country was better provided with Pastors.

About the Year 741, our Saint went to *Bavaria*, where he settled under the Protection of Duke *Odilo*. At his entring the Country he found great Numbers of it's Inhabitants still Slaves to Idolatry, and those who profess'd Christianity plunged into gross Superstitions, and Slaves to several detestable Vices. Having made the former acquainted with the Terms of Salvation, and rescued the latter from their inveterate Corruptions, he return'd to *Thuringe*, where he continued the Labours of his Mission with his usual Zeal and Activity. Going to *Mentz* to give the Apostle of *Germany* an Account of his Success, and consult him on some Difficulties which occurr'd in the Course of his Ministry, he was caress'd by all who had any Regard for the Kingdom of *Jesus Christ*, on the Account of his uncommon Merit and great Services. His Reputation for Sanctity was so well establish'd at *Mentz*, that several express'd an ardent Desire of putting themselves under his Direction. The Saint, full of a charitable Concern for his Neighbours, had once some Thoughts of building a Monastery in that City; but, considering that the great Plenty of Wine there might break in upon that rigorous Abstinence,

which

which he was resolved to prescribe his Disciples, he had Recourse to his Brother, then Bishop of *Aichstat*, with whose Assistance he built a double Monastery at *Heidenheim*; took the Direction of the Monks into his own Hands, and committed the Nuns to the Care of his Sister *Walburga*, of whom we have spoken on the twenty fifth of *February*. Our Saint's charitable Labours for the Salvation of his Neighbour suffer'd no Interruption from his rigorous Retreat; for he divided his Time and Thoughts between his Monks, and the rest of the World so exactly, that, without neglecting his own devout Family, he exerted himself with great Vigour against Vice in all Characters, ever suiting his Discourse to the Capacity and Necessities of the several Persons with whom he conversed.

Dec. 19.

His continual Fatigues reduced him to so ill a State of Health that he was obliged to discontinue his Apostolical Labours for some Time, and employ'd that Interval in visiting several holy Prelates, and well disciplined Monasteries in the Neighbourhood. His profound Veneration for St. *Benedict* made him desirous of ending his Days on Mount *Cassino*; and he had engaged the Abbot *Gratian* to receive him there; but *Willibald*, and other Persons of great Piety and Wisdom, over-ruled his Inclinations in that Point, and prevail'd with him to stay with the devout Community, which, he had form'd at *Heidenheim*. His Indisposition encreased daily; and, finding his End near, he desired his Brother would favour him with his Presence, and hear the last Dispositions of his Heart, in whose Arms he died on the eighteenth of *December*, in the Year 761, the Day on which his Name appears in the Martyrologes of our Country, and those of the *Benedictins*.

The XIX Day.

St. MEURIS, St. THEA and others, Martyrs.

THE City of *Gaza* produced a great Number of illustrious Martyrs of both Sexes during the Persecution raised by *Dioclesian* and his Collegue, and continued by *Galerius*, and *Maxamin*. Some died on the Spot, while others were sent to *Cesarea*, the Metropolis of *Palestine*, the usual Residence of the Governor of the Province. None were more conspicuous among the former than two holy Women, whom the Church honours this Day, who bore up bravely against all the Cruelty of Man, and Malice of the Devil, and triumphed over both to the last Moment,

Dec. 19 one of them named *Meuris* the other *Thea*. All we know in particular of these two Martyrs is that the former died under the Hands of the Persecutors, and the latter languished some Time after she had pass'd 'through a dreadful Variety of exquisite Torments. The Author of the Life of S. *Porphyrius* Bishop of *Gaza*, who lived toward the Close of the IV Century, tells us that their Relicks were deposited in a Church in that City which bore the Name of St. *Timothy*, who suffer'd in the same Persecution. The *Roman* Martyrologe honours them as Martyrs on the nineteenth of *December*.

It is the Opinion of some good and creditable Authors that *Timothy*, just mention'd, was the same whose Name occurs this Day in the *Greek* Menologes, and the *Roman* Martyrologe; others have taken the Liberty to suppose the Saint in Question the same of whom we have spoken on the nineteenth of *August*, on which Occasion they add that *Timothy* whom the *Roman* Church proposes to our Veneration on the nineteenth of *December*, was a Deacon in *Mauritania*, and suffer'd in *Thebaïs* with *Maura* his Wife about the same Time that *Meuris* and *Thea*, already mention'd, finished their Course at *Gaza*. This holy Couple had not been married three Weeks when *Timothy* was seiz'd by the Persecutors, and carried before *Arrianus*, Governor of *Thebaïs*, who endeavour'd to awe the Saint into an Act of Idolatry by the Fear of Punishment; but the Saint replied that the Spirit of *Jesus Christ* residing in him forbid him to comply in that Particular. *Arrianus*, knowing that *Timothy* had the keeping of the holy Scriptures, commanded him to give them up in Order to burn them, pursuant to the Imperial Edict. The Saint replied that had he Children, he would sooner give them into his Hands than the sacred Word of God. The Judge, incensed at this Answer, order'd his Eyes to be put out with red-hot Irons, that thus those Books might at least be useless to him; and, seeing him bear the Execution of this Sentence with the utmost Tranquility, he directed his being hung by the Feet, with a Stone tied to his Neck and a Gag in his Mouth.

All, who saw the Trial, were surprized at his prodigious Patience under such severe Tortures; some officious Persons let the Judge know the Saint was newly married, and insinuated that 'though he seem'd an Overmatch for all Attempts on his Constancy, he might not probably be proof against a tender Regard for his Wife. *Arrianus*, pleased with the Proposal, order'd *Maura* before him, endeavour'd to intimidate her by telling her the only Way to preserve her Husband's Life was to persuade him to sacrifice to the Gods, and promised her a handsome Gratification if she gain'd her Point. *Maura*, who was but weak in the Faith, and lov'd her Husband's Life beyond all

other

other Confiderations, attacked him with the moſt tender Expreſſions in her Power, and employ'd her ſtrongeſt Perſuaſives to engage his Conſent to what was required. The Gag was taken out of his Mouth that he might ſpeak his Sentiments on that critical Occaſion; but the Saint was no ſooner reſtor'd to the Uſe of his Speech, but he declared his Abhorrence for their miſtaſten Affection, and his Reſolution of preſevering in the Faith of *Chriſt*. *Maura* repeated her Importunities, 'till the Saint reproached her ſo ſtrongly with her Weakneſs and Infidelity that ſhe gave into his Way of thinking, and reſolved to imitate his Courage and Fidelity. *Timothy* adviſed her to repair her Fault by declaring her new Diſpoſition to the Governor, becauſe ſhe had undertaken that ſinful Commiſſion by his Orders. *Maura* had ſome Difficulty to comply with his Advice 'till his Prayers engaged the Almighty to inſpire her with a Reſolution equal to the difficult and dangerous Taſk; then making her way to *Arrianus*, ſhe told him ſhe was united with her Huſband in every Point, and ready to ſuffer any thing in Satisfaction for her late Crime. The Judge attempted her Conſtancy by ſeveral Means, and finding her invincible, order'd her to be tortured. *Timothy* and his Wife, thus happily one, defied the moſt ingenious Malice of their Perſecutors; whereupon they were condemn'd to be crucified within Sight one of another. As they were going to Execution, *Maura*'s Mother met her and endeavour'd to diſſuade her from perſevering in a Profeſſion, which brought her to ſo infamous an End; but the Saint was ſuperior to all ſuch Conſideratations, and met Death with the utmoſt Intrepidity. The Names of *Meuris* and *Thea* occur in the Roman Martyrologe on the nineteenth of *December*.

The XX Day.

St. PHILOGONUS, Biſhop of ANTIOCH.

*P*HILOGONUS, probably a Native of *Antioch*, was brought up to the Law, and made a conſiderable Figure at the Bar for ſome Time; where he on all Occaſions behaved himſelf like a Man of Honour and Conſcience. His Integrity in that Station, and the whole Tenor of his Life were ſuch as recommended him to the Epiſcopal See of *Antioch*, and proved a ſufficient Motive for diſpenſing with the Canons, which require ſome Time ſpent among the Clergy, and removing him from a ſecular Employment to the higheſt Station in the Church. He ſucceeded *Vitalis* in the Year 318; and St. *Chryſoſtom*, from whom we take this Account, mentions the flouriſhing State of the Church of *Antioch* in his Time, as an authentick Proof of the Saint's excellent Adiminiftration, especially when it is confider'd how difficult it was to reduce fuch Churches to good Order, and regular Difcipline, which lately felt the Weight of Perfecution.

The Eaftern Chriftians did not enjoy a perfect Peace when *Philogonus* was raifed to the See of *Antioch*; and when he hoped the Storm raifed by *Maximin* quite blown over, another gather'd under the Direction of *Licinius*, who join'd with *Conftantine* in the Beginning of his Reign in publifhing an Edict in Favour of the Profeffors of our holy Religion, but falling out with that Prince, took his Revenge on the Chriftians, whom he protected. This Perfecution gave the Saint a glorious Opportunity of fhewing his Zeal for Religion, and the Honour of his Divine Mafter; his Behaviour on that Ocfion procured him the Title of Confeffor, which in thofe early Times was ufually beftow'd on fuch as remain'd true to their Profeffion, though attack'd by Threats and Promifes.

The Fire kindled by *Licinius* in the Eaft was not extinguifhed, when a new Herefy appear'd which made infinitely more Havock in the Church than the moft violent Perfecutions fet on Foot by the Pagans. About the Year 319 *Arius*, a Prieft and Paftor in *Alexandria*, broached his impious and blafphemous Tenets in that City. *Philogonus* was one of the firft who took the Alarm, and one of the moft active in oppofing this Monfter at it's firft Appearance in the World; fo that when *Arius*, writing to *Eufebius* Bifhop of *Nicomedia*, bragg'd of the Concurrence of all the Prelates of the Eaft to his Sentiments, he excepted our Saint and two other Bifhops, whom he ftiled ignorant Hereticks, becaufe they maintain'd the Eternity of the Son, and his Equality to, and Confubftantiality with, the Father. *Alexander*, Bifhop of *Alexandria*, did all in his Power for ftopping the Progrefs of the Infection; he condemn'd the Herefiarch, obliged him to leave the Town, and wrote a Synodical Epiftle in the Name of the Council of *Egypt* to *Philogonus*, and other celebrated Defenders of the Apoftolical Doctrine, to caution them againft the Artifices of *Arius* and his Abettors and Followers.

If the holy Bifhop of *Conftantinople*, who has left us *Philogonus*'s Panegyrick, had been pleafed to defcend to the Particulars of his Life, we fhould have been able to entertain our Readers with a larger Account of our Saint. His Death is commonly placed in the Year 323; and his Memory is honour'd by both the *Greek* and *Latin* Churches on the twentieth of *December*, the Day on which his Feftival was obferved at *Antioch* in St. *Chryfoftom*'s Time, and probably that of his Death.

The

The XXI Day.

St. THOMAS, Apostle.

THE Apostle of this Day had two Names, or rather is call'd by the same in two different Languages; for *Thomas* and *Didymus*, the one in *Syriack* the other in *Greek*, signify a Twin. He was a Native of Galilee, and call'd to the Apostolical College when our Saviour had been employ'd about a Year in his publick Ministry. The Gospel gives us no Account of our Saint from that Time 'till *Lazarus*'s Sickness, which brought our Lord into *Judea*, 'though his Life had been in Danger there very lately. The Disciples endeavour'd to dissuade him from that Journey; but upon his declaring his Resolution, *Thomas* exhorted the Company to attend him cheerfully and share his Fate; John 11. 16. " *Let us go, and die with him,*" were the Words of our Apostle on that Occasion.

The Evening before his Passion, *Jesus Christ* undertook to comfort his Disciples against the approaching Scene of Woes, which would shock and discourage them, by several Promises and Instructions. Among other Things c. 14. he assures them there were several Mansions in his Father's House, and that he was going to prepare a Place for them there; to which he adds that they knew where he went, and were not unacquainted with the Way which he was to take. St. *Thomas* took Occasion from this Declaration to tell our Lord that he and his Collegues knew not whither he was going, and ask'd " *How then can we know the Way?* *Jesus*, without reproaching our Apostle with the Slowness of his Understanding, replied that He was the Way, the Truth and the Life; that no Man goes to the Father but by Him; and that, if they had known Him, they must necessarily know his Father too.

Our blessed Saviour appear'd to the Apostles toward the Close of the John 20. Day on which, he arose from the Dead, but *Thomas* was not one of the Company at that Time. Those chosen Disciples telling him what they had seen, He declared he would not believe his Lord's Resurrection unless he saw and felt the Marks of the Nails in his Hands and Feet, and the Wound in his sacred Side. Eight Days after, the Apostles being together in the same Place and *Thomas* among them, *Jesus* made a second Appearance and saluted them with a Wish of Peace, and then, turning to our Saint, invited him to take the desired Satisfaction, and convince himself of the Truth of his Resurrection in the Manner, on which he insisted. *Thomas*, now fully satisfied in

that

Dec. 21. that Point, acknowledged him to be his Lord and his God; a Confession sufficient to confound those Hereticks, who denied God and Man to be one Person in *Jesus Christ.* St. *Gregory* the great in his twenty ninth Homily on the Gospels observes very justly that our Saint's Infidelity or Doubt was more useful to the Church than the ready Belief of the other Apostles, as it gave our Lord an Opportunity of assuring us of his Resurrection by such Proofs, as will admit of no Cavil, or Uncertainty.

Jo. 21. Some Days after the Apostles left *Jerusalem*, *Thomas* and some of his Collegues were employ'd in fishing in what the Gospel calls the Sea of *Tiberias*, or the Lake of *Genesareth*, where they pass'd the whole Night without any Success. The next Morning *Jesus* appear'd on the Shore; but they did not know him 'till he perform'd a Miracle in their Favour, and directed them to such a Draught of Fishes as open'd their Eyes. This, now, is all the Account the sacred Historian has left us of our Saint.

Parthia, and the neighbouring Countries are generally thought to have been the Scene of his Apostolical Labours after the Descent of the holy Spirit, according to the current Tradition of the Church at the Beginning of the III Century. Several of the Fathers are of Opinion that he travell'd into *Ethiopia*, and carried the Light of the Gospel into the *Indies*. St. *Chrysostom* tells us that our Apostle visited almost all the known World, and encounter'd all the Dangers and Difficulties which attended his Ministry with an Ardour and Intrepidity which made sufficient Amends for his former Incredulity and Weakness. It is usually thought that St. *Thomas* survived St. *Peter* and St. *Paul*; but Authors are divided about the Manner of his Death. It is highly probable that he glorified God by Martyrdom; and the most common Opinion places it at *Calamina*, a Town in *India*, not known to modern Geographers.

The Festival of St. *Thomas*, as seperate from the rest of the Apostles, was observed in the East with great Solemnity in the IV Century; and the *Grecians* honour his Memory in a particular Manner on the sixth of *October*. The *Roman* Martyrologe mentions the Removal of his Body to *Edessa* in *Mesopotamia* on the third of *July*; but observes the twenty first of *December*, as the Day of his Death.

The XXII Day. Dec. 22

St. ISCHYRION, MARTYR.

*D*ECIUS's Perfecution raged violently in *Alexandria*, and carried off great Numbers of Chriftians in that City during the Year 251, from which Place it foon made it's Way to other Parts of *Egypt*, as we learn from St. *Dionyfius*'s Account of the Matter, fent to *Fabius*, Bifhop of *Antioch*, a confiderable Fragment of which valuable Piece is ftill extant in *Eufebius*. The holy Patriarch of *Alexandria* is there very large in Commendation of feveral glorious Martyrs, who were torn in Pieces by the frantick Zeal of the Pagans in feveral Towns and Villages; and has recorded the Courage and Sufferings of *Ifchyrion*, as an Example of the Cruelty of the Enemies of the Faith, and the invincible Conftancy of its Votaries in that fevere Perfecution.

Ifchyrion, according to that Prelate, was engaged in an honourable Service under a Magiftrate, or chief Officer in fome Town of *Egypt*, whofe Name is not mention'd in the Account. He had no fooner enter'd the Family, but his Mafter required him to qualify himfelf for his Poft by facrificing to Idols; upon his firft Refufal he was feverely reproved, and loaded with injurious Terms; which were doubled on his perfifting in his Refolution. Provok'd at the Patience, with which the Saint bore all he could fay, the Officer forced a fharp Stick into his Bowels, and thus became the Executioner of his Servant. The Church commemorates his Victory on the twenty fecond of *December*, and places his Martyrdom at *Alexandria*

✤✤

St. CHEREMON Bifhop and MARTYR.

THE fame holy Bifhop, from whom we take our Account of St *Ifchyrion*, is the only Perfon, that has fpoken of *Cheremon*, whom the Church honours this Day as a Martyr. When the Perfecution firft broke out in *Egypt*, feveral of the Faithful, diffident of their own Strength, retired to avoid being expofed to fo hazardous a Trial, and in this they did but follow the Example of fome of their moft virtuous Paftors. The Hardfhips which they encounter'd in the Defarts, and on Mountains; and the violent or lingering Deaths which carried them off, when thus abondon'd to Hunger, Diftempers, the Rage of wild Beafts, and the Cruelty of Highwaymen,

Dec. 23 men, have secured them a Glory equal with that of such as fell by the Hands of the Persecutors. St. *Dionysius* tells us their Number was very considerable, and mentions *Cheremon* Bishop of *Nilopolis*, as one of the most illustrious Martyrs in that Way. That Prelate, loaded with Age and Infirmities, fled with his Wife to the Mountains of *Arabia*, infested by the *Saracens*, and other Barbarians. St. *Dionysius* adds that they were never seen after that Time, nor their Bodies found, though strict Search was made for them. The *Roman* Martyrologe honours our Saint together with the rest of that illustrious Number, who were lost in this Manner, and places their Festival on the twenty second of *December*.

The XXIII. Day.

St. THEODULUS, and his nine Companions, *Martyrs in* CRETE.

UPON the Publication of the Edict for persecuting the Christians under *Decius*, no Man was more active in seeing it executed than the Governour of the Isle of *Crete*, now call'd *Candia*, which soon became one large Field of Blood. Among the great Number of Martyrs, who fell a Sacrifice to his Aversion for the Name of *Christ*, none were more conspicuous than *Theodulus*, *Saturninus*, *Euporus*, *Gelasius*, *Eunicianus*, *Zeticus*, *Cleomenes*, *Agathopus*, *Basidides*, and *Euaristus*; who, being brought before the Governor from different Parts of *Crete*, united their Forces against the common Enemy in a Way that has made their Memory venerable to Posterity.

The three first were Inhabitants of *Gortyna*, where they had probably been grounded in the Faith by St. *Cyril*, Bishop of that City whose Life may be seen on the ninth of *July*; the rest were brought from four or five different Towns in the Island. The twenty third of *December* was the Day appointed for the Trial. Assoon as they appear'd in Court, they were order'd to sacrifice to *Jupiter*, in Obedience to the Will and express Command of his Imperial Majesty; upon their refusing to defile their Hearts or Hands with that detestable Act, the Judge assured them they should be put to the most severe Tortures, while the rest of their Country-men gave a loose to all the Pleasures and Diversions of that Day, which was in a particular Manner consecrated to the God, whose Worship they declined. Resolved to let no Confideration deter them from their Duty to the only true God, they anfwer'd they fhould look on all they could fuffer for that excellent Being as the moft fubftantial Pleafure they could enjoy in this World. The deluded Governour attempted to engage their veneration for *Jupiter*, his Mother *Rhea*, and his Wife *Juno* by enlarging in Commendation of thofe pretended Deities; but as the Story of thofe boafted Divinities, when told to the beft Advantage by their blind Votaries is extreamly abfurd and extravagant, this Account gave our Saints an opportunity of making feveral Remarks on their Genealogy, and Actions that could not be agreeable to the Governour, who therefore ftopp'd their Mouths with ordering them to be rack'd, and tortur'd for their impious Contempt of the Gods of the firft Rank. The Saints remaining the fame unalterable Afferters of the Vanity of Idols, and the Dignity of the one true God, 'though their Bodies were bruifed and torn in a moft barbarous Manner, the Governour pafs'd Sentence of Death on them, and they were beheaded the fame Day near *Gortyna*, then the Metropolis of the Ifland, and ordinary Refidence of the Governour. Their laft Breath was employ'd in an ardent Prayer that the Almighty would preferve the Faith of *Chrift* in that Country. The Fathers of the Council of *Crete* in 558, were perfwaded of the fuccefs of their Application to Heaven on that Subject, when writing to the Emperor *Leo*, they obferved that their Ifland had 'till then been guarded againft the Infection of Herefy at the Interceffion of the ten Martyrs. Both the *Greeks* and *Latins* honour their Memory on the Day of their Death.

St. SERVULUS.

IN the Time of St. *Gregory* the great, as he tells us in his Dialogues, *Servulus*, who had been afflicted with the Palfy from his Infancy, and had the additional Affliction of extreme Poverty, lay in the Porch of St. *Clement's* Church at *Rome*, and depended on the Contributions of thofe who pafs'd by for his Subfiftance. God, who is the beft Judge of what is proper for his Creatures, had placed him in this humble Station with a View of fanctifying him by Patience under his Sufferings, and the Practice of Submiffion to the divine Will, and more than made him amends for the Abfence of what the World calls Riches by giving him a plentiful Supply of Grace, which made him fubftantially rich. His Condition moved the Compaffion of all who faw him, and engaged them to relieve him 'till it was in his Power to support his Mother and Brother, who assisted him, and gave Alms to other miserable Objects, which he did with an edifying Cheerfulness.

Servulus had not the Advantage of Education; but, full of Veneration for the sacred Word of God, he bought the holy Scriptures, and begg'd the Religious who visited him, and receiv'd Part of their Subsistance from his Hands, to read those sacred Books to him, that he might get them by Heart. His continual Pains were so far from dejecting him, or distracting his Devotions, that they proved a constant Motive for raising his Mind to God, and his whole Time was spent in singing Psalms and Hymns in Honour of the supreme Being, whose Wisdom and Goodness he acknowledged with Love and Gratitude.

After several Years spent thus, he found his Distemper, which 'till then had render'd all his Limbs useless, seize his Vitals, from which he easily concluded that his End was near. Full of this Persuasion, he desired the Poor who lived on what he could spare, and the Pilgrims who depended on his Hospitality, to repeat some Psalms, 'till his Soul returned to his his Creator. He join'd his Voice with theirs, and expired in this holy Exercise, which, as he declared, was attended by the Choir of Angels, whose Melody he heard. We owe this Account to St. *Gregory* the Great, who adds this Observation; " such was the Life and Death of a Man whom " God sanctified in Poverty and continual Misery; who kept the Law of " God, and filled all the Duties of a Christian, according to his State, 'though " deprived of the Use of his Limbs, whose whole Behaviour loudly condemns " those, who when bless'd with good Health and a plentiful Fortune, nei- " ther do good Works nor suffer the least Cross with tolerable Patience." The Body of our Saint was buried in St *Clement*'s Church, and honour'd with many Miracles, according to the *Roman* Martyrologe, in which his Name occurs on the twenty third of *December*.

The XXIV Day.

St DELPHINUS Bishop of BOURDEAUX.

ST. *Delphinus*, whom the *Galican* Church deservedly esteems as one of the chief Ornaments of that Country, was raised to the Episcopal See of *Bourdeaux* before the Year 360, and probably soon after the Council of

Rimini

Rimini held in 359; for we find him employ'd in clearing *Aquitain* of the Remains of *Arianism*, which got footing there by the Bishops of that Council being surprized by the Hereticks, as has been related in the Life of S. *Phebadius* Bishop of *Agen* in the same Province, on the twenty fifth of *April*. *Delphinus* acted in Concert with that holy Bishop in this great Work; St. *Ambrose*, Bishop of *Milan*, writing to them, commends their Union form'd by christian Charity which animated all their Actions, and observes that the whole Church reap'd the Advantage of their holy Friendship.

Our Saint assisted in the Council of *Saragossa*, held against the *Pricillianists* in 380. Those Hereticks not appearing, 'though invited, were condemn'd by that venerable Assembly; after which *Gratian*, Emperor in the *West*, published an Order for driving all Hereticks out of his Dominions. Those who had been lately censur'd in the Council of *Saragossa*, divided and travel'd into different Countries, to avoid falling under the Lash of the Law, to which they would have been exposed if they had remain'd in a Body under the Pretence of Worship. *Instantius*, and *Salvian* two Bishops of *Priscilian*'s Party, and that Heresiarch, who receiv'd the Episcopal Character from their sacrilegious Hands, went for *Rome*, with a Resolution of making their Innocence appear before *Damasus*, then in St. *Peter*'s Chair. They took *Aquitain* in their Way, where they imposed on the ignorant well meaning People so successfully, that they were receiv'd like true Servants of God, and assisted in propagating their Errors. *Delphinus* perceiving their Art of insinuating themselves with the People, watched their Motions, and prevented the Infection from spreading in his Flock, by hindering them from making any Stay at *Bourdeaux*.

When we mention the Services, which our Saint did the Catholick Church, we must not forget, that under God, we owe the great *Paulinus*, Bishop of *Nola*, to his Care. That holy Prelate receiv'd his first Instructions in Religion, and the Sacrament of Regeneration from the Hands of *Delphinus*. *Paulinus* retain'd a grateful Sense of the Favour his whole Life, and has left us eight Epistles directed to his great Benefactor, full of large Commendations of his Virtue and Expressions of a filial Respect for our Saint.

Delphinus lived to a good old Age; some place his Death in the Close of 403, others at the Beginning of the following Year. His Name appears on the twenty fourth of *December* in the *Roman* Martyrologe.

Dec. 24   St. THRASILLA, and St. EMILIANA, Virgins.

GORDIAN, a *Roman* Senator, Father to St. *Gregory* the Great, had three Sisters who consecrated their Virginity to God, and devoted themselves to his Service in a particular Manner. *Thrasilla*, whom the Church honours this Day among her Saints was the eldest; and *Emiliana*, whose Name occurs on the fifth of *January* in the *Roman* Martyrologe, the youngest; as their holy Brother has given the Characters of his two worthy Aunts together, we thought it would not be amiss to follow his Example. *Thrasilla* and *Emiliana*, renouncing the Vanities of the World about the same Time, and receiving the sacred Veil on the same Day, started together in the glorious Course to Perfection, and were as much united by the Fervour of their Hearts as by Blood. They lived in their Father's House at *Rome* as retired as if in a Monastery; far removed from the Conversation of Mankind; and, exciting one another to Virtue by Discourse and Example, soon made a considerable Progress in a spiritual Life. They were so disengag'd from the World, mortified all their Senses so severely, and maintain'd so strict an Union with God, that they seem'd to have forgot their Bodies, and arose above all Considerations of human Nature. *Gordiana*, their Sister set out with the same Vigour, but flagg'd by the Way, and by Degrees admitted the World into her Heart to the Prejudice of the Almighty, to whom it had been offer'd. *Thrasilla* could not see this unhappy Change without Concern, and frequently bewail'd *Gordiana*'s Negligence and Relaxation to *Emiliana*; who joyn'd her in endeavouring their Sister's Reformation. As their Remonstrances on that Occasion were temper'd with all the Sweetness that natural Affection, and Charity could inspire, *Gordiana* seem'd much affected at them, and, full of Confusion, promised to be more faithful in the Discharge of the Duties of a State, which was her own free Choice; but these Impressions were soon worn out; *Gordiana* grew impatient of Silence, and Retirement, and shew'd but too plainly that she had no Relish for the Conversation of Persons whose Discourse turn'd on God, and spiritual Subjects.

   St *Gregory* tells us that *Thrasilla* was favour'd with a comfortable Vision toward the Close of her Days, in which St. *Felix* Pope appeared to her and invited her to a glorious Habitation. The same Author adds that she sicken'd the next Day; and, when in her Agony, call'd out to the Company, desiring them to make Room for *Jesus Christ*, whom she saw coming toward her, and then breath'd out her pious Soul into the Hands of God.

Thrasilla

Thrasilla died on the twenty fourth of *December*, and was follow'd by *Emiliana* on the eighth of *January* following; but we have no Account of the Year.

Dec. 25

The XXV Day.

The NATIVITY of JESUS CHRIST, commonly called CHRISTMAS Day.

AUGUSTUS CÆSAR having been several Years Master of the Roman Commonwealth, and given the whole Empire Peace a third Time, issued out an Order for taking an exact and particular Account of all his Subjects, that he might know their Number, and levying a Poll Tax on each of them according to their respective Circumstances. Twenty four Persons of known Probity and Experience were named for this Work; *Quirinus* whom the *Grecians* call *Cyrinus* was sent into *Syria*, with all necessary Powers for carrying it on; and, as *Palestine* was under the same Governour, *Judea* was of Course comprehended in that Commission. Upon the Publication of this imperial Edict, every one went to the Place, from which their Family first came; for which Reason *Joseph* left *Nazareth*, a small Town in *Galilee*, the Place of his Residence, and travel'd to *Bethlehem* in *Judea*, to give in his Name there with the blessed Virgin, who, as the Evangelist observes, was then pregnant. *Bethlehem* was at that Time a small Village about six Miles south of *Jerusalem*, situated on a craggy Mountain, and consisting only of a few poor Houses and Stables for the Use of the Inhabitants. While the holy Couple were there, the Time of our Lord's Appearance in the Flesh was accomplished, and his pure Mother was deliver'd of the Saviour of the World in a Stable; for, as the sacred Historian observes, there was no Room for them in the Inn; so great was the Concourse on that Occasion.

Luke 2.

The Birth of *Jesus Christ*, from which all who own his Name reckon their Time, happen'd according to the antient Tradition of the Church of *Rome*, which had better Opportunities than others of consulting the publick Registers of the Empire, on the twenty fifth of *December*; and that this was the current Tradition of the West in St. *Augustin*'s Time, appears from more than one Passage in that Father; who calls it an ancient and immemorial Custom.

The

Dec. 25. The Blessed Virgin deliver'd of the divine Infant without Pain, because he was conceived without Concupifence, swathed his tender Limbs, and laid him in a Manger. Some Shepherds, who were keeping their Flocks in the neighbouring Fields, were the first who received the comfortable Message of the Birth of the long expected *Messiah*. An Angel, appearing to them and spreading a Blaze of celestial Light about them, struck them with Surprize and Amazement. The heavenly Messenger bid them give over their Fears, assuring them that Night had produced a Subject of great Joy for them and the whole World; and then directed them to the Saviour of the World, by giving them those Marks of Humility, which were the distinguishing Characteristicks of him who took Flesh to make Satisfaction for our Pride, and teach us Humility both by Word and Example. *You shall find him* said the Angel, *swathed and lying in a Manger.*" He had scarce ended his Description of our Lord's Situation at *Bethlehem*, when he was joyned by a numerous Choir of glorious Spirits, who proclaim'd the Benefit which resulted to Mankind by the Birth of *Jesus Christ*, and the Glory due to God for the inestimable Favour, in the Words used by the Church at this Day before her solemn Sacrifice. *Glory be to God on High, and on Earth Peace to Men of good Will.* Assoon as the Angels left the Field, the Shepherds found their Hearts warm'd with a Desire of seeing the Blessed *Jesus*, whom they found according to the Angel's Direction, and communicated the happy News to all they met.

The Birth of a God, who thereby becomes Man for our Use, is an Object so truly great, so superlatively holy, so full of Wonders, and so instructive, that every Circumstance of that Mystery preaches most powerfully engages our Adoration, and challenges the most profound Gratitude. If we can comprehend what Man was after the Fall, we may conceive what we owe the Almighty for the Mercy of this Day, on which we commemorate the Salvation of Sinners, the Redemption of the most miserable of Slaves, the Collection of stray'd Sheep under the true Pastor, Strength given to the Weak, Light to the Blind, a Master and Model to the Ignorant; in short Salvation and Life bestow'd on the Dead.

In this Day's Mystery, as recorded by the Evangelist, we have in the Person of *Jesus Christ* an admirable Example of all the Virtues, which should compose the Character of a Christian. His Obedience to the Laws of a Pagan Emperor, his Humility in the Choice of the Place of his Nativity, his Love of Poverty, his Affection for Sufferings, his Contempt of the World and its Grandeurs, which appear'd in the several Circumstances of

his

his Birth, are so many admirable Lessons of Self-denial, Mortification, and holy Simplicity, which we receive this Day from our Infant Saviour.

Dec. 25

St. ANASTASIA, *Martyr.*

*A*NASTASIA according to the Account of her Martyrdom, descended of an illustrious Family at *Rome*, was educated in the Christian Religion by *Flavia* her Mother, a Woman of great Virtue and strict Piety. That excellent Lady dying, while our Saint was very young, *Anastasia* was put into the Hands of *Chrysogonus* a holy Priest, who finished what her Mother had began, and confirmed the Foundation which she laid. *Pretextatus* our Saint's Father, who was a Stranger to the Name of *Christ*, obliged her to marry *Publius*, who had nothing but his Birth to recommend him; for he was a Pagan, and guilty of the most criminal Extravagancies. That unhappy Debauchee wasted most of her Fortune by riotous Living; and, in Order to secure to himself that Part of it which she destin'd for the Relief of the Poor, put her under a Guard, and confined her as an impious Magician, and Enemy of Religion; the usual Epithets bestow'd by the Idolaters on the Practices of our holy Profession. He deprived her of all the Satisfactions of Life, and gave strict Orders that she should receive no Visits, especially from such as he apprehended would strengthen her in her Resolution of suffering all he could inflict rather than renounce her Faith or do any Thing unworthy of her great Master.

Chrysogonus, our Saint's Tutor and Director, was then in Prison for Religion, so that beside the Mortification of being separated from that excellent Guide, she had that of hearing he groan'd under several Hardships. She found Means to convey a Letter to him, in which she gave him an Account of her Situation, and begg'd the Assistance of his Prayers for her Deliverance either by Death or her Husband's Conversion. *Chrysogonus* addressed Heaven in her Favour, and then sent her an Answer, in which she was exhorted to Patience, and consoled with the Assurance of a Calm that would soon succeed the Storm. *Anastasia*'s hard Usage being considerably increas'd since the Receit of her holy Director's Letter, she wrote to him a second Time, let him know she could expect no other Relief than what Death would bring, and recommended herself once more to his Prayers in a very pressing Manner. *Chrysogonus*, inform'd of the Particulars of her Sufferings from the Woman who brought her Letter, employ'd the same

Dec. 25 Person to exhort her to Perseverance, and tell her from him that she was in the Way to the Glory which attends Martyrdom.

Publius, our Saint's Husband, travelling into the East, died soon after, which gave her her Liberty and the free Disposal of the remaining Part of her Fortune, which she cheerfully employ'd in relieving the Indigent, assisting the Sick, and comforting or releasing the Prisoners We are told that when *Chrysogonus* went to *Aquileia* by *Dioclesian*'s Order to take his Trial there, *Anastasia* follow'd him to that City. After his Death she spent her whole Time in visiting the Confessors under Confinement; which charitable Actions provok'd the Emperor so, that he put her into the Hands of *Florus* Governor of *Illyricum*, who attempted her Constancy by a barbarous Variety of Torments, and finding her invincible, order'd her to be burnt alive; which Sentence was immediatly executed.

The Author of our Saint's Acts tells us her Body was buried near *Zara* in *Dalmatia* by the Care of a Christian Lady. It was afterwards removed to *Sirmium*, the Capital City of *Pannonia*, and from thence to *Constantinople* by the Direction of the Emperor *Leo*, about the Year 460, where it remain'd the Object of universal Veneration, 'till that City was taken in the Year 1453. The *Grecians* celebrate the Memory of S. *Anastasia* on the twenty second of *December*, and place her in the first Class of Martyrs. The *Latin* Church commemorates her Victory on the twenty fifth of *December*, which is supposed to be the Day of her Death, and her Name is repeated every Day by all who use the *Roman* Missal.

The XXVI Day.

St. STEPHEN, the *Proto-Martyr*.

AFTER the Descent of the holy Spirit, the Church of *Jesus Christ* encreased daily, and the Members of that new form'd Body made a common Practice, on their embracing the Faith, of throwing their Fortunes at the Feet of the Apostles, who were empowered to make a common Stock of them for the Relief of such as wanted, and disburse what was barely necessary for the Maintainance of their former Owners. The Church of *Jerusalem* growing very numerous, the Apostles found themselves sufficiently employ'd in preaching, and were therefore obliged to commit the Administration of temporal Affairs to others. The *Greeks*, i. e. the Christians of

Act. 6.

other

other Countries, who spoke *Greek*, grumbled at the *Hebrews* or Natives of Dec. 26. *Palestine* about the unequal Distribution of the common Stock, which they urged was not employ'd as it ought to be for the Relief of their Widows. This Complaint, being urged with some Warmth, might have been attended with dangerous Consequences, had not the Apostles provided a speedy Remedy for the Abuse. In Order to proceed regularly in an Affair which so nearly concern'd the whole Church, they assembled the Faithful; observed to them that it was not proper for Them to relinquish the most important Duties of their Ministry for the Care of Tables; and recommended to them the Choice of seven Men of an unblemished Character, full of the holy Ghost and Wisdom, who might for the future be employ'd in that Way.

This Proposal was perfectly agreeable to the whole Assembly, who immediately pitched on *Stephen, a Man, full of Faith and the holy Spirit*, and six others, whom they presented to the Apostles. Those Governors of the Church begg'd the Blessing of Heaven on what they were doing, and then ordain'd them to the Office of Deacons by Imposition of Hands. Our Saint stands first in the List, which was what prevail'd with St. *Ireneus*, and others among the Ancients to stile him *Arch-deacon*, or Chief of the Deacons. We have no Account of the Place, or Time of his Birth; nor can we tell when or on what Occasion he engaged in the School of *Jesus Christ*. *Baronius* is of Opinion that he was a Student under *Gamaliel*, at the same Time with St. *Paul*; according to *Epiphanius* he was one of the LXXII Disciples; others date his Conversion on the Feast of Pentecost, and attribute it to St. *Peter*'s first Sermon. The Fathers give him the Character of great Erudition, and speak of his Discourse to the Jews at his Trial as a finished Piece of Eloquence.

The Apostolical Ordination conferr'd a fresh Supply of Grace on our holy Deacon, and the additional Gift of Miracles, which were so numerous and extraordinary, that the Enemies of the Gospel bent their whole Force and directed all their Malice against him; and the Zeal with which he preached made him the Object of the Aversion of the Jews. The Conspiracy was form'd against him by the *Libertines* (i. e. such as had been carried Captives to *Rome* by *Pompey*, and had since obtain'd their Freedom) those of *Cyrene* in *Libya*, *Alexandria*, *Cilicia* and *Asia*, who had each a distinct Synagogue at *Jerusalem*. At first they undertook to dispute with St. *Stephen*; but, finding themselves unequal to the Task, while their Adversary was powerfully assisted by the holy Ghost, they suborned a sufficient Number of false Witnesses, who deposed that the holy Deacon had spoken disrespectfully and

Dec. 26. even blasphemously of the Law and the Temple: *for*, continued they, *We heard him declare that this* JESUS *of* NAZARETH *will destroy this Place, and change the Traditions which* Moses *has left us.* This Charge being brought against him in the *Sanhedrim*, or great Council of the *Jewish* Church, *Caiphas*, the high Priest gave him Leave to make his Defence by asking him whether the Allegation already mention'd was true; and it pleas'd God to manifest his Innocence, and engage the Audience to a favourable Attention by diffusing a Beauty and Lustre in the Saint's Face, which appear'd more than human. *Stephen* began his Answer to that Question in a Manner which spoke his Deference for the Company, whom he called *Brethren* and *Fathers*.

Acts, 8.

He then expresses a profound Regard for the antient Patriarchs, is particular in Commendation of *Abraham*'s Faith and ready Obedience; gives a brief Account of *Joseph*'s Sufferings from the Hands of his Brethren, his Promotion in *Pharaoh*'s Court, and the Establishment of his whole Family in *Egypt* by his Interest: he takes Occasion from the History of *Moses* to mention the *Jews* perverse Dispositions, in rejecting that Prophet at his first appearing in that Character; and quotes his memorable Prophesy of our Saviour. The Saint proceeded in the next Place to give some Instances of the *Jews* Proneness to Idolatry; after which he endeavours to invalidate the Accusation urged against him by owning that the Tabernacle was made by God's Order and Direction, that the Words of the Law were the living Oracles of the Lord, &c. But then he takes Care to raise their Views to more sublime and spiritual Objects by observing to them, according to the Prophets, that God does not reside in Buildings raised by the Hands of Men. Perceiving by the extraordinary Light with which he was favour'd at that Time that his Discourse made little or no Impression on the Hearts of his Hearers, he address'd them in the following Words; " *Men with stiff Necks, and uncircumcised Hearts* " *and Ears, who always resist the holy Spirit, and in this imitate your Fathers.* " *Who among the Prophets have not your Fathers persecuted? They have like-* " *wise put those to Death, who foretold the coming of the Just Person, whom you* " *have betray'd and murther'd; You who receiv'd the Faith by the Ministry of* " *Angels,* " *but have not observed it.*

Deut. 18. 17.

This stinging Reproach touched them to the quick, and kindled them into a Rage, which was not to be extinguished but with the holy Deacon's Blood; but he, full of the holy Ghost raised his Eyes to Heaven, was favour'd with a Sight of the Glory which was to reward his Courage, and beheld his divine Saviour at the Right Hand of his Father, in a Posture which

spoke

spoke his Readiness to assist the Champion, and crown him as soon as he Dec. 27
should gain the Victory. Transported with the Vision, he cried out,
"*I see the Heavens open'd and the Son of Man standing at the right Hand of*
"*God.*" The *Jews*, hearing this Declaration, stopp'd their Ears, clamour'd
loudly against the Saint, fell on him with unbridled Fury, dragg'd him out of
Town, and stoned him, under Pretence of punishing him as a Blasphemer.
The Witnesses, who according to the Levitical Law were to begin the Exe- Deut.17.
cution in all capital Cases, threw their Cloaths at the Feet of *Saul*, who, ac- 7.
cording to his own Way of reasoning on that Occasion, partook of the Act. 22.
Crime of those who stoned the holy Martyr. While the enraged *Jews* were 20.
discharging a Shower of Stones on St. *Stephen*, he, full of the Spirit of his divine Master, begg'd the Sin of which they were guilty in shedding innocent
Blood might not be imputed to them, and recommended his Soul to *Jesus*,
for whom he suffer'd that violent Death. The Church this Day in a particular Manner recommends the Pardon of Injuries in her Collect, and leaves
her Children without Excuse, while she proposes the Example of a mere Man
to enforce this truly Christian Virtue.

The sacred Historian telling us that St. *Stephen fell asleep in the Lord*, has
left us a comfortable Idea of the peaceable and happy State of such as lay
down their Lives for the Faith, or finish their Course in a Manner acceptable
to the Almighty. St. *Luke* tells us that the venerable Body was buried Act. 8. 2.
by the Care of some devout Persons, who paid the Tribute of their Tears
to his Relicks. According to the Account given us by *Lucian*, from
whom we have received the History of that Discovery in the V Century,
they were deposited about twenty Miles from *Jerusalem*, by the Direction of
Gamaliel, and at his Expence. Our Readers are referr'd to the third of
August for a full Account of the Discovery of our Saint's Body, and the Miracles perform'd wherever they were carried. His Festival has been generally
observed on the Day after *Christmas-Day*, 'though the Church was not always
unanimous in fixing that great Festival.

✚✚✚

The XXVII Day.

St. JOHN, Apostle and EVANGELIST.

ST. *JHON*, whom the Gospel distinguishes by the Character of the
Beloved Disciple, and the *Grecians* by the Name of *the Divine*, was Son
of

of *Zebedee* and *Salome*, and younger Brother to St. *James* the Greater. *Zebedee* got his Living by the mean and Laborious Employment of Fishing, and his Sons had been engaged in the same humble Profession for some Time, when they were call'd by our Blessed Saviour. The Evangelical History assures us that on the first Invitation our Saint and his Brother quitted their Father, and their Nets, that is, all they had or hoped for in this World, and follow'd *Christ*. They were present together at the Cure of St. *Peter*'s Mother-in-Law, and the Resurrection of *Jairus*'s Daughter. They were afterwards receiv'd among the Apostles, and by our Lord called *Sons of Thunder*.

It is the general Opinion that St. *John* was the youngest of the Twelve, when he first engaged in the Service of his divine Master; but almost all that the Evangelists have recorded of our Saint being inseperable from their Account of his Brother, our Readers are referr'd to the twenty fifth of *July* for what concerns them both.

Our Apostle was sent in Company with St. *Peter* to *Jerusalem* the Night before our Saviour died to prepare all Necessaries for his last Supper; upon which Occasion St. *John* lay on his Lord's Bosom, according to his usual Privilege. *Jesus Christ* having eat the Paschal Lamb, with the Ceremonies prescribed by the Law, washed his Disciples Feet, and among other Predictions, assured them that one of their Number should betray him into the Hands of his Enemies. The Apostles, struck with Surprize, look'd one at another, and were onxious to know who among them could be so base and impious. Upon this Occasion St. *Peter* made a Sign to our Saint to ask our Lord whom he pointed at in the Declaration. St. *John* understood him, and made the desired Enquiry; to which *Jesus* answer'd he was the Man, who should receive a Sop from his Hands; so that according to the Signal, it appear'd to be *Judas Iscariot*.

Supper being over, the Eucharist instituted, and several important Instructions deliver'd to his Disciples, *Jesus*, attended by the Twelve, went to the Garden of *Gethsemani*, where our Saint, with his Brother and St. *Peter* were allow'd to see his Agony. The Gospel tells us that all the Disciples fled when they saw their Master in the Hands of his Enemies; but St. *Chrysostom* is inclined to except St. *John* on this Occasion, being of Opinion that He was the Disciple, who follow'd *Jesus Christ* to the high Priest's House, and afterwards introduced St. *Peter*; but this may be true, 'though we suppose he fled with the Rest at first. It is certain, however, that our Apostle was the only one who attended his dying Saviour in his last Moments; and his Courage and Affection which appear'd in that Action met with a glorious Reward.

Reward. *Jesus*, now ready to expire, substituted his beloved Disciple in his Dec. 27 Place, and bequeath'd his holy Mother to him; seeing the Blessed Virgin and the Apostle at the Foot of his Cross, he said to the former, " *Woman,* Jo. 19. " *behold your Son.*" to the latter " *behold your Mother,*" From that Moment Jo. 20. 6. St. *John* look'd on the Blessed Virgin as his own particular Charge, took her home, and provided her with all Necessaries as long as she lived.

He did not leave Mount *Calvary*, 'till the whole Tragedy of the Day v. 34. was over; and it is from him that we learn the sacred Body of our Redeemer, being pierced with a Spear by one of the Soldiers, yielded a Mixture of Water and Blood. As the Actions and Sufferings of St. *John* after our Lord's Crucifixion were the same with those of the Prince of the Apostles 'till they both left that Country, our Readers are referr'd to St. *Peter*'s Life for those Particulars. St. *John* was present at the famous Council of *Jerusa-* Gal. 2. 9. *lem*, where St. *Paul* tells us he appear'd as one of the Pillars of the Church; and was one of the last that left *Judea*. It is said that *Parthia*, was the Scene of his Apostolical Labours; and his first Epistle has been quoted by St. *Augustin*, and others under the Title of an Epistle to the *Parthians*; which is probably to be understood of the Jews dispersed through the Provinces of the *Parthian* Empire. Some are of Opinion that he had visited the Coasts of the *Lesser Asia* before he carried the Light of the Gospel into that Country. It is generally believed that he settled at *Ephesus* about the Year sixty six; and made that City the Place of his common Residence, according to St. *Ireneus*, who had good Opportunities of informing himself of that Particular. The Church of *Ephesus* was than govern'd by S. *Timothy*, whom the *Asiatick* Prelates in the Council of *Chalcedon* mention as it's first Bishop. But St. *John*, according to the Extent of his Apostolical Authority, had a general Inspection of that and the other Churches in *Asia*; for which Reason St. *Jerom* speaks of our Appostle as the Founder, and Governor of all the *Asiatick* Churches. His Preaching was attended by Miracles, most of which are unknown at present. St. *Epiphanius* tells us that the whole Tenor of his Conduct was such as became the exalted Character which he bore; and that his Way of Living was not unlike that of St. *James* Bishop of *Jerusalem*, who was remarkable for Austerity and Mortification.

Sweetness of Temper was the distinguishing Character of our great Apostle, which, however was never allow'd to break in upon, and prejudice the Vigour which was necessary for maintaining the Sanctity and Purity of the Gospel against all Sorts of Corruptions; as appears from his deposing a Priest, who wrote a sort of Romance containing the pretended Acts of St.

Paul

Dec. 27 Paul and St. *Thecla*, imagining those holy Persons honour'd by the Imposture. The *Cerinthians*, and *Ebionites*, who appear'd in his Time, and asserted Christ was mere Man, that found Employment for our Saint's Pen, and Tongue. His Aversion to those blasphemous Hereticks appear'd as much in his Actions as Words, and St. *Ireneus* gives us a remarkable Instance of his Horror for *Cerinthus*, which he says he learnt from St. *Polycarp*, S. *John*'s Disciple. Being one Day in a Bath, and understanding that Arch-heretick was in the same Place, he left it immediately, and declared he was apprehensive that the Building would fall on his Head, if he staid with that Enemy of God and Truth. This Action of our Saint, which is dated at *Ephesus*, agrees exactly with the Advice he gives the Faithful, to avoid all Communication with Hereticks even in the Duties civil Life; a Caution always used by the Church, in Regard of such as wilfully, deliberately, and maliciously reform'd the Faith; using greater Tenderness, for such as had unfortunately imbibed Errors in their Infancy.

2 Ep. 10.

St. *John* had labour'd in *Asia* many Years with a Success answerable to his Zeal for the Faith, when *Domitian* raised a Persecution against the Christian Church. We have already told our Readers what Share the Apostle had in the Severities inflicted by that Prince's Direction, as may be seen on the fourth of *May*. The Miracle of his Preservation did not work the desired Effect on the Emperor, who immediately order'd him into Banishment; and the Isle of *Patmos* in the *Archipelago* was the Place of his Exile, where he wrote the Book of Revelations. Several of the Antients, finding this Book full of insuperable Difficulties, and consequently, as they thought, useless if not dangerous, made some Difficulty of receiving it into the Canon of the Scripture; but all Objections against it were over-ruled when the World was convinced it was pen'd by our Apostle.

Domitian being kill'd toward the Close of the Year 96 the Senate repeal'd all his Acts, and *Nerva*, who succeeded that Prince, recall'd all the Exiles; which favourable Order gave S. *John* an Opportunity of returning to *Ephesus* after about a Year and half's Banishment. His great Age did not hinder him from making several Apostolical Visits to the Neighbouring Churches, where he made such Regulations as he found Necessary for establishing or preserving the Flock of *Jesus Christ*; and it was in the last Years of his Life that he recover'd a profligate Person, whose Conversion seem'd impossible. Our Saint undertook to instruct him in the Principles of Religion, when young, and finding him endow'd with a good Capacity and several promising

mising Qualifications, recommended him to the Bishop of the Place, telling him he left the young Man in his Hands in the Presence of God and the Church, as a Trust which he expected should be kept with the utmost Care, and Vigilance. The Bishop undertook the Charge, and gave him the most solemn Assurances of performing all he could desire or wish in Favour of the Person in Question. The young Man was grounded in the Faith, instructed in the Duties of Religion, and then baptized; after which the good Bishop, thinking his Pupil out of Danger, allow'd him the Liberty which was attended by most pernicious Consequences. Falling into bad Company he soon forgot the Precepts of the Gospel; and, passing from one Degree of Wickedness to another till he had stifled all Remorse, put himself at the Head of his debauched Associates, and took to the high Way. He had spent some Time in this unhappy State before St. *John's* Affairs allow'd him to make a second Visit to the Town where he had left him. He then asked the Bishop what was become of what he had committed to his Care; as soon as that Prelate understood the Saint spoke of the young Man, full of Grief and Confusion he fixt his Eyes on the Ground, and told him, with a Sigh, the young Man was dead. The Apostle, desiring to know the Manner of his Death, was told it was of a spiritual Nature, that the young Man was dead to God, and plunged into all Manner of Crimes and Debauchery. St. *John*, surprized and afflicted at the News, express'd his Concern by a deep Sigh and other Marks of a thorough Grief, reproached the Bishop with Negligence, and immediately mounted on Horseback in Quest of the lost Sheep, making his Way to the Mountain where he was inform'd the Captain and his Gang kept their Rendevous, he was stopp'd by one of their Number; but, instead of begging his Life, or offering any Composition for saving it, he declared he only desired to be conducted to the Commander of that desperate Company, and fall by his Hands, if his Death was inevitable.

The Captain expected his Arrival, completely arm'd; but as soon as he saw the Apostle he was seiz'd with a Mixture of Shame and Fear, threw down his Arms, and made off with the utmost Precipitation. The Saint, forgetting his Age, pursued him full Speed, and call'd to him in the following Words; " *Child*, said he, *why do you thus fly from your Father, a helpless,*
" *and unarm'd old Man? Have Compassion of me; fear not; there is still*
" *Room for Repentance and Hopes of Salvation: I will answer for you to* JESUS
" CHRIST; *I am ready to lay down my Life for you, as* JESUS CHRIST *laid down*
" *his for all Men; stay, and be assured that I am sent on this Errand by the*
" *same divine Saviour.*" Deeply affected at this Expostulation and Assurance,

Dec. 27 the Criminal stood still, fixt his Eyes on the Ground, and bath'd in Tears embraced this tender Father, but hid his right Hand, which had been guilty of the Excesses of his illegal Profession. The holy Apostle, seeing his Confusion, gave him fresh Assurances of Pardon, promised to engage the divine Mercy in his Favour, knelt down, pray'd for him, kiss'd his guilty Hand, now cleansed by his Penitential Tears; and receiv'd him once more into the Church, which he had deserted. To secure his Conquest, the great Apostle applied to Heaven for the Gift of Perseverance, and comforted him with such Passages of Scripture as were design'd for the Use of returning Prodigals.

The Faithful, considering St. *John* was the only surviving Apostle, and apprehending that his Death, which could not be far off, would prove an Advantage to the Hereticks, begg'd he would furnish them with Weapons against those early Reformers of the Faith; the united Petitions of the *Asiatick* Bishops, and Persons deputed from several illustrious Churches engaged him to compose his Gospel. St. *Jerom* tells us that Work was preceeded by a rigorous Fast, and publick Prayers. As the other Evangelists had been clear and large enough on what regarded the Humanity of *Jesus Christ*, St. *John* chose to insist particularly on the Proof of his Divinity in Opposition to the Errors of *Cerinthus*, *Ebion*, and the *Nicholaïtes*; and it appears from the Performance itself that he had another View in composing it, viz. to supply what had been omitted by the other Evangelists, especially the History of the first Year of our Saviour's publick Ministry, which had been touched but slightly by those inspired Writers. His three Epistles were written about the same Time; the first of which is full of Exhortations to Charity, and breaths the truly Christian Spirit of it's Author; the second is address'd to a Lady distinguished by her Virtue and Station, and her Children, whom he congratulates on their steady Adherance to the Truth, in Spight of all the Arts of Seducers, then abroad in the World: the third is directed to *Caïus*, whom he there commends for his Perseverance in the Faith, and his tender Regard for the Brethren of other Countries.

St. *John*, loaded with Years and the Infirmities inseperable from old Age, was now reduced to a very low Condition, and carried to Church by his spiritual Children. As he was not capable of making long Discourses in the Assemblies of the Faithful at *Ephesus*, their whole Entertainment, consisted in frequent Repetitions of that divine Command, " *Children, love one* " *another.*" His Disciples, weary with hearing the same Thing so often, asked him why he would not say somewhat new to them; to which he replied, " *This is our Lord's Command; perform but this, and you do enough.*"

An

An Answer truly worthy of the favourite Disciple of *Jesus Christ*, who had Dec. 28 learnt this essential Duty on his Master's Breast. The ninety ninth Year after our Saviour's Nativity is supposed to be that of our Saint's Death.

His Body was interr'd near *Ephesus*; where it reposed in the Year 431, when a general Council was held in that City. The 26th of *September* is kept in his Memory by the modern *Greeks*, which in their Menologe they call his *Translation*, or Death; but the *Roman* Martyrologe places his Festival on the twenty seventh of *December*.

The XXVIII Day.

The HOLY INNOCENTS.

HEROD, who had reign'd in *Judea* thirty six Years, and knew no Superior in that Country, was extremely surprised at the Arrival of the *Magi* from the East, and their Enquiry after the new born King of the *Jews*. That Prince, understanding the Person in Question was the expected *Messiah*, and that according to the Prophesies of the old Testament he must be born in *Bethlehem*, dismiss'd the Strangers with a strict Injunction to take *Jerusalem* in their Way home, and inform him of their Discoveries, that He, as he pretended, might go and adore the wonderful Infant; but his real Design was to establish his Authority and Title by the Death of his supposed Rival. His sanguinary Views were providentially defeated; and the *Magi* receiv'd an Order from Heaven to take another Road to their own Country. About the same Time an Angel appear'd to *Joseph*, and directed him to conduct the divine Child and his holy Mother into *Egypt*, to avoid the Rage of the incensed King, which was immediately done. Mat. 2

It was not long before *Herod* found the *Magi* had deceived him; whereupon he sent Orders for murthering all the Male Children of two Years old and under that Age in *Bethlehem*, and the adjacent Country; and St. *Matthew* observes that the Prophesy of *Jeremy* was then fulfill'd which says; *A Voice, and great Mourning and Lamentation were heard in Rama, Rachel weeping for her Children; and would not be comforted, because they are not.* To understand this Prediction, we are to remember that *Rachel*, the Mother of *Benjamin*, was buried between *Bethlehem* and *Rama*, and that in this Place, by an easy and common Figure, the Mothers of *Benjamin*'s Posterity are represented by *Rachel*. This Prophesy was fulfill'd in some Manner when *Nabuchodonosor* Jer. 31. 15. Gen. 35. 19.

carried

Dec. 27 carried off the two Tribes of *Benjamin* and *Juda*, but receiv'd its last Completion in the Massacre of the *Innocents*, whom the Church in all Ages reverenced as real Martyrs of *Jesus Christ*, who had the peculiar Advantage of dying instead of their Saviour.

It is not our Business to enquire into the precise Time of this Tragedy, a Point on which the Learned are much divided; it is enough to observe in this Place that it happen'd soon after our Saviour was carried into *Egypt*, according to the Evangelical History, and consequently after the Adoration of the *Magi*, and the Purification of the *Blessed Virgin*. As we therefore suppose, with the whole Church, that the Son of God was born, according to the Flesh, on the twenty fifth of *December*, and presented in the Temple on the second of *February*, the Massacre of the *Innocents* must be placed in that Month or at the Beginning of the next, because *Herod* died before the following *Passover*. The Western Church celebrates their Memory on the twenty eighth of *December*; those of *Greece* and *Asia* on the twenty ninth; the *Syrians* and other Eastern Nations on the twenty seventh of the same Month.

St. THEODORE, ABBOT.

THEODORE, whom the *Grecians* call the *Sanctified*, to distinguish him from other holy Men of the same Name, descended from one of the most considerable Families in the upper *Thebaïs*, was born about the Year 314, of Christian Parents, who educated him in Piety and Literature. It was at that Time usual in his Country to celebrate the Feast of the *Epiphany* with great Pomp and Solemnity, but such as had more the Air of Diversions and worldly Rejoicings, than Acts of Devotion; for Feasting and Visiting made up much the greatest Part of the Ceremonies on that Occasion, not unlike the preposterous and indecent Manner in which but too many Christians at this Day keep the most solemn Festivals appointed by the Church for the grateful Commemoration of the Benefits we have receiv'd from God, or the Mysteries of our holy Religion. The Reflections, which our Saint made on this Subject may serve therefore as a seasonable Admonition to such as continue the same Abuse among us to this Day. *Theodore*, considering seriously the Nature of Religious Joy, and the Design of what we justly call Holydays, 'though then but twelve Years old, said thus to himself, " Alas, " poor Theodore, *what good will it do you to be great and happy in this*
" *World,*

"World, if you are neither in the next? 'Tis in vain to think of securing those "Advantages both here and hereafter; if you expect the one, you must re- "nounce the other. The Way to eternal Happiness does not lie in the Pleasures "and Delights of this World; which must therefore be quitted, if you hope "for the Joys of Heaven." These Reflections made so strong an Impression on his Mind, that he left the Company, and retired to a remote Part of the House, indulged his Tears, and begg'd the Almighty would enlighten him, and direct him to the right Path. He was thus employ'd when his Mother found him alone, thoughtful and a Stranger to the Mirth that reign'd in the Family at that Time; she desired to know the Cause of what she saw, and press'd him to put on a more cheerful Countenance, and go with her to Dinner. *Theodore*'s Thoughts were turn'd a different Way, and all she could say would not prevail with him to discover them, or share in the Joys of the Day; from that Time, he pursued his Studies with great Application, lead a retired and mortified Life, never appearing but when his Duty to his Parents required it, and abstaining from every thing that could flatter or gratify the Senses.

The Saint had spent two Years thus in his Father's House, when he came to a Resolution of retiring to the Desart where he design'd to follow a set of Rules, by which he might form himself to a spiritual Life. As his unexperienced Age must then want some Hints in that Way, he entered among some holy Solitaries in the Neighbourhood, who met every Evening, and held Conferences on the written Word of God. He had been engaged in that edifying Conversation some Time, when the Character of St. *Pachomius*, who had lately built a Monastery in the Desart of *Tabenna*, inspired him with a Desire of making his Way to that excellent Man, and petition him to be admitted into his religious Community. Providence soon gave our Saint a favourable Opportunity of pursuing his devout Inclinations; for one of the Monks of *Tabenna*, making a Visit to the Hermitage, where *Theodore* then resided, and understanding his Inclination, conducted him to *Pachomius*, who receiv'd him without Difficulty, upon hearing his Character, as deliver'd by the Solitaries, who had been Eye Witnesses of his Fervour and Attention to the sacred Oracles, and Love of Mortification.

Theodore had not been long in the Monastery, before he appear'd to Advantage in that numerous Family of Saints, and was look'd on as a Model of Perfection, which God had directed thither for the Use of the whole Community. His Mother, who had probably lost her Husband since our Saint left her, was desirous of seeing her Son, whose Virtue made him doubly

Dec. 28 doubly dear to her; and prevail'd with several worthy Prelates to give her Letters which might facilitate the desired Interview, and press *Pachomius* to dismiss him. Thus provided she went to a Convent of Women not far from that of *Pachomius*, and govern'd by that Saint's Sister, where she met with a kind Reception, and was allow'd to wait the holy Abbot's Answer to her Request, as urged by the Bishops already mention'd. *Pachomius*, having perused his Packet, called for *Theodore*, told him his Mother desired to see him, and added that he was of Opinion that so reasonable a Request was not to be denied a Parent. *Theodore*, apprehending the Consequences of what at first Sight seem'd no more than his Duty, replied that he was always ready to act according to the Direction of his holy Superiour, but desired to be assured that *Jesus Christ* would at the last Day approve of his visiting his Mother, after having left her and the whole World for the Practice of Evangelical Councils; and that his Complaisance in this Point would not scandalize the religious Family, of which he had the Happiness to be a Member. *Pachomius* replied that what he had said on that Subject was rather a Proposal than a Command, so that he was at Liberty to act as he should judge most agreeable to that Perfection which his present State required, and recommended. *Theodore* thanked the Abbot for this favourable Answer, and immediatly resolved not to hazard his Peace by seeing his Mother. That Lady was at first much disturbed at the Disapointment; but the holy Community, who entertain'd her, endeavouring to console her under that Mortification, work'd so powerfully on her that she resolved to spend the Remainder of her Days among them.

Pachomius had made a sufficient Tryal of our Saint's Genius and Capacity, and the more learned he found him, the more Pains he thought himself obliged to take to render him humble and obedient; and had the Satisfaction of finding his Knowledge still inferior to his Virtue. The Community being one Day assembled to receive Instruction on Points of Spirituality, the Abbot order'd *Theodore* to deliver his Opinion on the Subject in Hand, who acquitted himself of that Commission in a Manner that surprized the whole Company. *Theodore* was then but twenty Years old, and as it was not usual for the young Monks to speak in the Conferences, some of the more advanced were so offended at his appearing on that Occasion, that they left the Place abruptly, before he had finished his Discourse. *Theodore* was allowed to proceed; and his holy Superior was so well satisfied with the Performance, that he gave the old Monks a severe Reprimand, and prescribed a suitable Penance for their Pride and Envy; Vices which insinuate themselves insensibly

insensibly into the most religious Characters. *Pachomius*, making a Jour-
ney to an Episcopal City in *Thebais*, where he had founded a Monastery,
was attended by our Saint and another of his Disciples, whom he commis-
sion'd to engage with a famous Philosopher of that Place, who had desi-
red to discourse with the Abbot or some of the most ingenious of his Monks.
The captious Philosopher open'd the Conference with asking them who was
he that died, and was never born? who was he that was born and never
died? and who it was that died without leaving a Carcase on the Earth,
subject to Corruption? *Theodore*, without the least Hesitaton, replied that the
Persons enquired after were *Adam*, *Enoch*, and *Lot*'s Wife; shew'd the same
quickness of Apprehension in the Solution of all the Difficulties proposed;
and concluded with a pressing Exhortation to the Philosopher to renounce all
vain and Airy Speculations, and make his Salvation his only Care.

Theodore had not pass'd his twenty fifth Year, when *Pachomius* employ'd
him in visiting several of his Monasteries, and about six Years after, retired
to another House and put that of *Tabenna* under his Direction. That holy
Abbot, desirous of making the Saint's Presence more serviceable to the
Community, obliged him to take the Order of Priesthood; and we may
judge of that great Man's Opinion of our Saint's Humility and other sa-
cerdotal Virtues, when we consider this Step was an Exception from his
common Practise, as has been observed on the fourteenth of *May*. *Theodore*,
succeeded to the Care and Inspection of all the Houses founded by his ex-
cellent Master about three Years after his Death, trod faithfully in his Steps
brought Monastick Discipline to great Perfection, and breathed out his pious
Soul into the Hands of his Creator on the twenty seventh of *April* 368,
being the fifty fourth Year of his Age. The *Grecians* honour his Memory
on the sixteenth of *May*; and his Name appears on the twenty eighth
of *December* in the Martyrologe; but the Reason of neither is known
at present.

The XXIX Day.

St. THOMAS *Arch-Bishop* of CANTERBURY, *Martyr*.

THOMAS, the Son of *Gilbert Becket*, was born at *London* on the twenty
first of *December* 1117; and the excellent Qualities, with which he was
endow'd, were carefully cultivated by a good Education. The Death of his
Father

Dec. 28 Father, which happen'd in 1138, left our Saint expofed to all the Temptations of the World, at an Age when the moſt dangerous Miſtakes are uſually committed. He was then in the Warmth of Youth, and every Way qualified to make a Figure in the World, and indulge himſelf in all its Pleaſures; but the divine Grace preſerved him from Corruption. *Thomas* had been his own Maſter about a Year, when he confider'd the Dangers that furrounded him while unemploy'd, and refolved to guard againſt them by reaffuming his Studies, which had been difcontinu'd for fome Time. In this View he went to *Paris*, where he learnt the Canon Law, and improv'd himſelf in other Branches of Literature which were neceſſary or uſeful for a Man, who at that Time had no Thoughts but thoſe of living in a fecular Station. As his Parents had fuſtain'd confiderable Loſſes, our Saint's Fortune was but fmall, which obliged him at his Return to accept of a handfome Poſt under a Merchant of *London*. His next Situation was in the Family of a Gentleman, of a plentiful Eſtate in the Country, where Variety of Diverfions were his only Employment, and his Virtue feem'd to be in great Danger from an idle and unprofitable Life; but it pleaſed God to open his Eyes by a Miracle. Being one Day in Purfuit of Game his Hawk made a Stoop at a Duck and dived after it into a River; *Thomas*, apprehenfive of lofing his Hawk, jumpt into the Water, without confidering the Confequence of that precipitate Action; the Stream which was very rapid, hurried him to a Mill; but the Wheel ſttopt immediatly, and allowed Time for taking him out.

This vifible Protection, and furprizing Efcape put him on ferious Thoughts, and proved a Motive for his applying to fomewhat more folid and worthy of a Chriſtian. Thus recover'd, he turn'd his Mind to Bufineſs, in which he gave fubſtantial Proofs of folid Judgment, uncommon Penetration, and inviolable Integrity. He fpent about two Years in the Service of a Man of Quailty, to whom he was to be related; and was then employ'd in fome publick Affairs of the City of *London*; but faw fo much Fraud and Injuſtice practiſed by thoſe with whom he was concern'd, that he refolved to confecrate himſelf to God in the Service of the Church. In this View he applied to *Theobald*, then Archbiſhop of *Canterbury*, who received him into his Family. That Prelate foon found what a Treaſure he poſſeſs'd in our Saint, and employ'd him in Affairs of the greateſt Confequence. He had not been a Year in the Archbiſhop's Service when he found Means to relieve the Church of this Iſland, which groaned under the Oppreſſions of *Henry* Biſhop of *Winchester*, Brother to *Stephen* then on the

Engliſh

English Throne, and Legate to the Pope, who abused his Authority to the manifest Prejudice of the Episcopal Dignity. As *Thomas* had suggested the Measures proper to be taken in that difficult Affair, *Theobald* engaged him to undertake an Embassy to *Rome*; where he succeeded so well, that his Holiness *Celestine* II, divested the Bishop of *Winchester* of the Legatine Power and conferr'd it on the Archbishop of *Canterbury*. This signal Service was soon after rewarded by the Archdeaconry of *Canterbury*, vacant by the Promotion of *Roger*, the last Incumbent, to the See of *York*, and the Provostship of *Beverly*.

Upon the Death of King *Stephen*, which happen'd in the Year 1154, *Henry* II succeeded to the Throne. That Prince had some good Qualities but a much larger Catalogue of Vices; he was politick and courageous; but his Passions were violent, his Desires perverse and irregular, and his Will his only Law. *Theobald*, well acquainted with the King's haughty and impetuous Temper, and seeing him surrounded by evil Counsellors, who had put his Predecessor on several Enterprizes prejudicial to the Rights of the Church, thought *Thomas* a proper Person to stem the Tide, and therefore took all Opportunities of recommending him to the King, who conceived so exalted an Opinion of him that he made him Chancellor of *England*, about the Year 1157.

Thomas raised, to this Dignity, fill'd all the Duties of his high Station in a Manner suitable to the Importance of the Trust, and the original Design of that Office. His House was open for all; there Innocence found a sure Protection; the Poor were furnished with Necessaries, and the Weak assisted against the oppressive Power of the Great. The King, finding the Archbishop had not imposed on him in the Character of our Saint, entrusted him with the Education of Prince *Henry* his Son, who would have been a great and good Prince, had he follow'd the Instructions of his excellent Governour. The Grandeur, in which he appear'd, the Favour of his Sovereign and the dazzling Lustre of a Court made no Alteration in his Humility, and Modesty; 'though the latter Virtue had been put to several Trials by the King's Direction: His Complaisance for his Prince, and the Nobility made him give cheerfully into all innocent Diversions; but at the same Time he practised a great Variety of secret Austerities on himself.

Beside the voluntary Mortifications, which the Chancellor used as so many Preservatives against the infected Air of the Court, it pleased God to raise him some that appear'd more shocking because inflicted by other Hands. Those whose ambitious Schemes were disconcerted by his Authority, and

Dec. 29 Vigilance, made it their Business to ruin his Credit with the King; to which End they gave a malicious Turn to his most innocent Actions, and insinuated that his Loyalty was not such as might justly be expected from a Man, who ow'd so much to the Royal Bounty. These Calumnies would not pass on his Majesty, who was but the more confirm'd in his Opinion of our Saint by the calm and Christian Manner in which he bore them. In the Year 1158 *Henry* gave him a fresh Proof in his Confidence in his Wisdom and Fidelity, by sending him to *France* to negotiate a Match between his Son *Henry*, and *Margaret*, Daughter to *Lewis the Young*. *Thomas* succeeded in this Embassy to his Master's Wish; the Marriage was concluded, with a Proviso only of deferring it's Solemnization 'till the Parties come to a proper Age. The Princess was deliver'd to the Chancellor, who brought her over, and put her into the Hands of *Robert of Newbury* for Education.

The See of *Canterbury* becoming vacant in the Year 1161 by the Death of *Theobald*, all Eyes were fix'd on the Chancellor to succeed in that important Post, and the common Opinion of the Nation placed him at the Head of the *English* Church. The King, who was then at *Falaise* in *Normandy*, design'd him for the Metropolitan See, and order'd our Saint, who attended the Court to prepare for his Return to *England*, where his Presence would be necessary. When *Thomas* went to take his Leave of his Majesty he was told that his Business in *England* was to take Possession of the Archbishoprick of *Canterbury*. The Chancellor, surprized at the Proposal, told the King, with a Smile, he had made a very odd Choice, and could not believe he really meant to confer that Dignity on him; but, finding him serious and resolved on the Affair, observ'd to him that the Promotion in Question would be the most effectual Means for satisfying the most malicious of his Enemies. " For, said the Saint, *your Majesty will in all Probability insist on such Things* " *as a Guardian of the Liberties of the Church cannot grant, and which my Con-* " *science will oblige me to refuse.*

The King was startled at this Freedom in one, who had 'till that Moment appear'd the most obsequious and complaisant, but persisted in his Resolution, and depended on making what Use he pleas'd of him, when raised to the Archiepiscopal See. *Henry* then commission'd some of the Nobility to attend the Chancellor into *England*, and promote his Election. *Thomas*, reflecting on the Dangers and Difficulties of the Post which was press'd on him with so much Warmth, and considering the King's unhappy Temper, and the restless Malice of those about him, made a long and vigorous Resistance; but the Cardinal of *Pisa*, Legate from the holy See, in *England* over-ruled.

over-ruled all his Scruples, and perfuaded him that God call'd him to that Dec. 29 Poſt, as a Man of invincible Courage, who would generouſly oppoſe every Attempt on the Rights and Liberties of the Church. The Clergy and Nobility met on this Subject in *Weſtminſter* Abbey, where his Election was oppoſed by the Biſhop of *London* and ſome others, who were apprehenſive that the King's Officers would plunder the Church with more Eaſe and leſs Interruption under a Prelate taken from the Court, and unuſed to oppoſe his Sovereign's Will; to which they added that it would be highly abſurd, and contrary to both divine and Eccleſiaſtical Laws to place a Man of his Way of Living at the Head of the *Engliſh* Church before he had given any Proofs of an Eccleſiaſtical Spirit. Theſe Objections, though very conſiderable in themſelves, were allow'd no Weight with ſuch as knew the Integrity and Courage of our Saint; for, after a long Debate, *Thomas* was declared duely elected on Whitſon-Eve 1162. He was then conducted to *Canterbury*, where he was ordain'd Prieſt, and the next Day conſecrated by the Biſhop of *Wincheſter*, aſſiſted by fourteen Prelates; when he was on the Road he expreſs'd a true Senſe of the Weight and Difficulty of what he undertook by deſiring one of the Clergy of his Church, a Man of ſingular Merit, to tell him what the World ſaid of him, being apprehenſive, as he ſaid, that ſome Freedoms would be taken with his Character, which he ſhould never know without the Aſſiſtance of a faithful Friend; and enjoyn'd him to apprize him of every falſe Step in his Conduct for his greater Security.

His Conſecration made a viſible Change in his Conduct; for, 'though he was always upright and full of excellent Sentiments of Religion, he now conſider'd himſelf as a living Sacrifice, and reſolved to devote all his Time and Thoughts to the Intereſts of the Church. As ſoon as he had receiv'd the *Pallium* from Pope *Alexander* III, he engaged in the Monaſtick State, which was eſtabliſhed in the Chapter of *Canterbury*, and 'though he appear'd in a Dreſs ſuitable to his Epiſcopal Dignity, he wore St. *Benedict*'s Habit, and a Hair Shirt under the Marks of that exalted Character. His uſual Practice was to riſe at two in the Morning, repeat *Matins*, and then waſh the Feet of thirteen poor Perſons, begging the Aſſiſtance of their Prayers for the Diſcharge of his Duty. This Act of Humility was done in the Night to expiate the Faults which he might have committed by Vanity while employ'd in the Affairs of the World. Thoſe miſerable Objects were diſmiſs'd with a handſome Alms; and, after a ſhort Repoſe, the holy Prelate aroſe and converſed with God in his written Word. At Break of Day twelve indigent Perſons were relieved at his Door, and at nine in the Morning a third

Dec. 29. third Company, amounting to an hundred, were assisted in a Manner suitable to their Necessities. The Sacrifice of the Mass was his next Employment, which he offer'd with a Mixture of Fear and Devotion, that warm'd his devout Heart and drew Tears from his Eyes. That Act of Religion was succeeded by a charitable Visit to the Hospitals, where he furnished the Patients with proper Remedies for the Distempers both of their Souls and Bodies; and continued in the Practice of such Works as became his Character 'till three in the Afternoon, the Time of his Dinner. His Meal was handsome, but frugal, and always attended by the Reading of some pious Book. After Dinner he held a Conference with learned and pious Persons on the holy Scripture, or the Affairs of his Diocese.

Having made his own Family an excellent Model for his whole Diocese, he enter'd on the Reformation of his Flock. Being sensible that the People were apt to take Example by the Clergy, he was particularly careful in the Choice of such as were design'd for the Care of Souls; and knowing that the Sanctification of the Flock usually depends on the Sanctity of the Pastors, he was very difficult and exact in his Examination of Persons, who offer'd themselves for holy Orders. As his Alms were bestowed out of the Revenues of his Bishoprick, he took Care to act the Part of a faithful Steward in perserving what Temporalities he found annex'd to the See of *Canterbury*, and recovering such as had been alienated by the Weakness or Negligence of his Predecessors. The Usurpers of the Episcopal Lands carried their Complaint to the King, who at that Time rejected them, and obliged them to acquiesce in the Archbishop's Conduct.

The Saint had not been above a Year in Possession of the Metropolitan See, before he was obliged to go to the Council of *Tours*, conven'd by Pope *Alexander* III, to remedy the Schism made by the Antipope, who took the Title of *Victor* III. His Reception on the Road to that City was little inferior to that of a crown'd Head for Magnificence and Respect. When he was near *Tours*, he was met by the People, the Magistrates, and a great Number of Prelates and Abbots. The Council was composed of seventeen Cardinals, a hundred and twenty four Bishops, four hundred and fourteen Abbots, and a great Number of inferior Ecclesiasticks, with his Holiness at their Head; but none of that venerable Company appear'd to greater Advantage than the Archbishop of *Canterbury*, from whom the rest were glad to learn how to guard against the Ambition and Avarice of the Laity, who made themselves Masters of the Church Lands, and infringed the Liberties of the Clergy; for the *Anathema* pronouced by the Fathers of that Council.

cil against such Usurpers, fell on those Ecclesiasticks who consented or gave Occasion to such Incroachments.

Dec. 29

At his Return, St. *Thomas* was receiv'd by the King with all imaginable Marks of Respect, and his Majesty seem'd particularly proud of having placed a Man of so much Merit in the two most conspicuous Stations in his Kingdom. The Bishopricks of *Worcester*, and *Hereford* had then been vacant for some Time, and the Revenues converted to the Use of the Crown; our holy Prelate took this Abuse so seriously to Heart that he allow'd the King no Ease 'till he gave his Consent for filling those Sees. The Conduct of the Saint in this Particular, his Resigning the Dignity of Chancellor, and putting the Decree of the Council of *Tours* in Execution alarm'd the King, and made the first Alteration in his Affections for our Prelate. But the Dispute about the Jurisdiction of the Civil Power over Ecclesiasticks was the fruitful Source of all the Evils which befell our Saint in the Sequel of his Life. St. *Thomas*, according to the Privileges the Clergy in those Days, asserted that though guilty of the most enormous Crimes they were to be judged ultimately by their Diocesan, and punish'd as the Canons of the Church direct, and that the secular Tribunal ought not to try them 'till being degraded, and thus reduced to the State of Laymen, they should incur the Penalty of the Laws by a fresh Transgression. The Archbishop shew'd himself resolved to act up to his Principles on the first Occasion that offer'd. A Priest, accused of Murther, was carried before the Bishop of *Salisbury*, pursuant to the Privilege already mention'd, and that Prelate was so warmly attack'd by the King's Officers to give the Ecclesiastick up to the Course of secular Justice that in all Appearance he would have complied, had not our Saint interfered, and exerted his Metropolitan Authority in Favour of what was then then the Right of the Clergy. Conformably to the Archbishop's Advice and Direction, the Priest in Question, proving guilty, was degraded, for ever render'd incapable of his Functions, and committed to a Monastery for the Remainder of his Life. In this and other Proceedings of the same Nature our Saint pleaded not only the standing Privileges of the Christian Church, as granted and secured by Princes of the greatest Wisdom and Piety, but also a Regulation made by the late King in the fifth Year of his Reign in an Assembly of the Clergy and Nobility, which constituted the Bishops of this Island sole Judges, wherever the Persons or Goods of Ecclesiasticks were concern'd.

Henry look'd on this Exemption as an Incroachment on the Royal Prerogative, and issued out his Orders for convening the Bishops of his Kingdom in *Westminster* Abbey. Having premised some Complaints which regarded
the

Dec. 29 the Primate in particular, his Majesty declared his Design of calling them together was to gain their free Consent for trying the Clergy in secular Courts, which he conceived to be the Right of the Crown, and the only effectual Means for stopping the Progress of such Crimes as could not be sufficienlty punished by the Canons of the Church. The Saint, upon hearing this Proposal, consulted with the Bishops, and then answer'd in the Name of his Collegues and the whole Clergy of this Nation, that the *English* Church was in legal Possession of the disputed Privilege; and that the Bishops were strictly obliged to insist on it; and begg'd his Majesty would be pleas'd to remember the Assurance which he gave in Writing on his Coronation Day of maintaining and defending the Rights of the Church, as he found them. *Henry*, incensed at this Reply, and finding the whole Assembly of Bishops united to that Primate, asked them whether they would observe the Laws and Customs of *England*, as they stood and had been observed by the Prelates under his Predecessors. Our Saint and his Collegues, perceiving the Question was captious and form'd to betray them into somewhat unworthy of their Stations, and Character, replied they were ready to comply with such Customs, as far as they did not clash with their Duty to God and his Church; a usual Restriction in all Oaths taken at that Time by the Bishops of this Island. The King, not being able to bring them to his Terms, told them, with some Warmth, he perceived they were united against him, and left the Place abruptly.

The next Day, the King dispatch'd a Message to the Archbishop, requiring him to surrender several Rents, and Revenues, which he had receiv'd with the Seals, and retain'd 'till that Time, and left the Town, without giving the Bishops Notice of his Departure, as usual, which they look'd on as a Mark of his highest Displeasure. Apprehending the Consequences of their Sovereign's Anger, they conjured our Saint to accomodate the Matter with the King, and consult the Peace of the *English* Church, which could not but suffer from that Prince, if exasperated. *Thomas* opposed their Reasons on this Subject with the same Force which he had used when answering the King; but their Prayers and Tears prevail'd with him to follow the King to *Oxford*, and assure him that upon understanding his Majesty's real Intentions, he was willing to change the Terms which had given him so much Offence. *Henry*, soften'd by this Condescension, call'd a Parliament at *Clarendon*, in *January* 1164, in which he required the Bishops to swear to observe the Customs of *England*, which made the Subject of the Dispute at *Westminster* the preceeding Year. The Archbishop had given the Matter a second Thought, and from

what

what he knew of the King's Temper, apprehended he would make a bad Dec. 29. Use of the Conceſſion, and therefore choſe rather to incur the Cenſure of Levity among Men by changing his Mind, than preſerve the Character of Wiſdom and Conſtancy at the Expence of his Duty to God and the Church. The King complain'd loudly of his Conduct, declared himſelf inſulted, diſſolved the Aſſembly, and left the Biſhops in the laſt Confuſion. *Henry* had ſcarce left the Place, when the Saint was ſurrounded by his Collegues, who were very urgent with him to have ſome Regard for the precarious Poſture of Affairs, and conſult the Intereſt of the Church, by a neceſſary Compliance with a Prince's Demands, whoſe Rage would kindle a Flame not eaſily to be extinguiſhed. *Thomas*, overcome by theſe preſſing Remonſtrances, made by Perſons of great Piety and Wiſdom, promiſed them the deſired Satisfaction; and was the firſt who laid himſelf under a ſolemn Obligation to obſerve the Cuſtoms of the Kingdom, without expreſſing any Reſtriction; in which he was follow'd by the other Prelates.

The King commiſſion'd ſome of the Nobility, whom he thought beſt acquainted with the Cuſtoms in Diſpute, or moſt obſequious to his Inclinations, to draw them up, and reduce them to ſeveral Articles, that the Biſhops might ſign them. *Thomas*, ſuſpecting the Courtiers in Commiſſion might offer ſome Cuſtoms for Subſcription, which did not deſerve that Name, deſired Time for examining the Particulars, for his own Security. His Requeſt was too reaſonable to be refuſed by Men, who pretended to proceed in a regular and legal Manner. As ſoon as the Aſſembly broke up, our Saint's Domeſticks canvaſs'd the Matter over very warmly; ſome of them commending his Prudence in accomodating himſelf to the Times, while others inſiſted on it that he had betray'd the Intereſt of the Church. One of the latter, who carried the Croſs before the Biſhop, had the Courage to let his Maſter know his Mind in ſuch Terms as made him own his Weakneſs, expreſs a profound Sorrow for what he had done, and reſolve to expiate his Fault by penetential Auſterities, and a voluntary Separation from the Altar. Soon after, the Archbiſhop diſpatched a Courier to his Holineſs, then at *Sens*, acquainted him with the whole Affair, begg'd his Abſolution, and Direction how to proceed. The Pope, who was no Stranger to the Matter, ſent him the deſired Comfort with all convenient Expedition, preſs'd him to re-aſſume his Functions, and exhorted him to act as became a Paſtor of the Church.

The King, underſtanding the Archbiſhop of *Canterbury* repented of his Oath, and was inclin'd to retract what Conſent he had given, gave a Looſe

Dec. 29. to his Passions, and let drop some Words which made it appear the holy Prelate's Life was in Danger. The Saint, finding himself incapable of doing any Good in *England*, and wishing to reserve himself for better Times, came to a Resolution of going over to *France* privately; but was driven back by contrary Winds. He made a second Attempt, with the same Success; from which he concluded his Design was opposed by the divine Will, and return'd to *Canterbury*. After a short Stay in that City, the Saint waited on his Majesty, hoping he might be happy enough to gain a favourable Hearing; but met with nothing but Reproaches for endeavouring to leave the Kingdom, contrary to one of the Customs insisted on at *Clarendon*.

The Archbishop, perceiving the King deaf to an Accommodation on any Terms but those which the holy Prelate judged prejudicial to the *English* Church, left the Court to avoid another Surprize, and resolved to assert the Cause of the Church, 'though his Life should pay for his Courage. The Bishop of *Evreux*, who had the King's Ear at that Time, employ'd himself very vigrously in that Affair, but could not prevail with his Majesty to make the least Abatement in the Articles drawn up at *Clarendon*; and our holy Prelate was as resolute in declaring he would not purchase his Peace at the Expence of his Conscience. *Henry*, finding he gain'd no Ground of the Saint, sent an Embassy to the Pope, desiring the Character of Legate might be bestow'd on the Archbishop of *York*, and our Prelate and his Collegues be obliged to observe the Customs of the Kingdom. His Holiness replied that it was neither reasonable nor just to translate an Honour to another See, which belong'd to that of *Canterbury*, more than to the Person of the Archbishop. The King, not satisfy'd with this Answer, dispatched a second Embassy to the Pope, with the same Demand, and the Persons deputed were instructed to insist on the Confirmation of the holy See in Favour of the Customs in Dispute. The Embassadors added, that the *English* Church was in no small Danger from the violent and revengeful Temper of the Prince on the Throne. The Pope would not hear of allowing the pretended Customs of *England* the Sanction insisted on; but, to prevent the Consequences of the King's Rage, he consented to the Translation of the Legatine Character to the Archbishop of *York*, but under such Restrictions as render'd it almost useless; for the new Legate was allow'd no Jurisdiction over the Person of our Saint or his Suffragans.

The King, incensed at the Limitation of a Power which he had desired might be lodged in the Hands of one devoted to his Interest, for oppressing the Archbishop of *Canterbury*, sent back the Pope's Brief with Contempt;
and

and refolved for the Future to give a Loofe to his Paffions without confulting any but fuch as were too weak or complaifant to oppofe him. Henry, being fecure of moft of the Bifhops in *England*, order'd a Charge to be drawn up againft our Saint, and affembled the Nobility and Prelates at *Northampton*, where the Archbifhop of *Canterbury* was condemn'd and his Goods confifcated. The Saint declared againft this irregular Proceeding, and appeal'd to the Sovereign Juftice of God. This Sentence was pronounced on *Thurfday October* eighth 1164; the next Day the King made a Demand of five hundred Pounds, which he faid he had lent our Saint when he was Chancellor; the Archbifhop alledged that the Sum in Queftion was a free Gift, but, as he own'd the Receit of the Money, he was obliged to give Bail for the Payment of it. On *Saturday* the King required an Account of the Revenues of feveral Bifhopricks and Abbeys which had been in his Hands during their Vacancy, and amounted to 230,000 Marks. This Propofal furprized the whole Affembly; and the Bifhop of *Winchefter* obferved that as the Sum mention'd, if ever receiv'd, was Part of what he might be charged with when Chancellor, and, as he had been releafed from all former Obligations, when he was elected to the See of *Canterbury*, he could not conceive how this Demand could be urged with any Shadow of Juftice. The other Prelates made large Difcourfes on the Matter before them, which all ended in advifing him either to fubmit to the King, or refign his Bifhopick for Peace fake. The Saint, perfuaded that the Intereft of the Church, and the Glory of God were at Stake, that his Compliance with the King's Will would be no better than betraying his Truft, and that he could not relinquifh his Poft without expofing his Flock to the Fury of the Wolf, reproaching the Bifhops with deferting him fhamefully in a Caufe common to them all, forbid them under holy Obedience to affift in giving Sentence againft him, and appeal'd to the holy See. *Gilbert*, Bifhop of *London*, one of his warmeft Adverfaries, appeal'd to the fame Tribunal from his Primate's Prohibition; and the Bifhops of *Winchefter* and *Salisbury* were the only Prelates, who advifed our Saint to maintain the Interefts of the Church; but they had not the Courage to give their Opinion publickly.

Thomas, finding himfelf thus abandon'd to the Rage of his Prince, prepared for it's worft Confequences by faying a Votive Mafs in Honour of St. *Stephen*; after which he made his Way to Court in his Pontifical Veftments, and enter'd the King's Appartment with his Crofs in his Hand. *Henry* refented this Act as an Infult done to his Majefty, and an Infinuation that he was an Enemy and Perfecutor of the Church; all were ready to flatter

flatter the King's Passions, and join him in declaring our Saint an ungrateful perjured Traitor. The Bishops were order'd to divide from the Nobility and consider what Punishment was due to the Archbishop. After a long Debate, not daring to act in Concert with the secular Power in condemning that Primate, they came to a Resolution of citing him before the holy See, as guilty of Perjury, and giving the King all possible Security of doing their best toward deposing him; upon Condition that all Proceedings against him should be immediately stopt. This Assurance was bound by an Oath, after which they went to the Archbishop and let him know what they had done. After much ill Treatment, and abusive Language, the holy Prelate left the Palace; and engaged the Bishops of *Worcester*, *Hereford*, and *Rochester* to ask the King's Leave for quitting the Kingdom; to which his Majesty replied he would propose the Matter in Council the next Day.

In the mean Time two Noblemen, our Saint's Friends, apprized him of a Design against his Life; whereupon he disguised himself, went over to *Flanders*, and from thence travell'd into *France*. The King, alarm'd at this suddain Retreat, assembled the Bishops and Nobility, and desired their Advice in the Affair. It was resolved to send a Deputation to the Pope, then at *Sens*, and urge the Charge of Perjury against St. *Thomas*. The Archbishop of *York*, and the Bishops of *London*, *Worcester*, *Chichester*, and *Exeter* undertook this Embassy, in which they were join'd by sufficient Numbers of the Nobility, attended by an magnificient Retinue.

The Saint had sent to the King of *France*, and desired Permission to take Shelter in his Dominions; but his Messengers were prevented by those dispatched from *England*, who deliver'd a Letter to *Lewis*, in which the King of *England* desired he would not receive *Thomas*, late Archbishop of *Canterbury*, who was a Traitor and a Fugitive. *Lewis*, shock'd at the Terms of this Epistle, asked the King's Deputies by whom and how the Archbishop had been deposed; express'd no small Surprize at this Treatment of a Man, to whom the *English* Crown had great Obligations, and assured them the Archbishop of *Canterbury* might depend on a safe Retreat in his Dominions. The next Day our Saint's Deputies reach'd *Compiegne*, where the King then resided, gave his Majesty a full Account of the holy Prelate's Sufferings, and receiv'd a gracious Assurance of Protection.

St. *Thomas*, thus encouraged, made a Journey to *Soissons*, where the King of *France* arrived the next Day, made him the first Visit, embraced him with a filial Affection, and made him a Profer of what was necessary for supporting

porting the Dignity of his Character. In the mean Time his Holiness gave Dec. 29 Audience to the *English* Deputies; not thinking it prudent to incense King *Henry*, he answer'd with Caution, and let them know he could not proceed any farther in the Archbishop's Absence, who was expected at *Sens* in a few Days. The Deputies pretended their Time was expired, and therefore did not wait his Arrival, but left *France* without taking his Holiness's Blessing. St. *Thomas* reach'd *Sens* soon after, attended by the King's Officers, where he was receiv'd very coldly by the Cardinals, but had Audience of the Pope, who order'd him to appear the next Day in the Consistory, and give a full Account of the Proceedings, and the Cause of his leaving *England*. The Saint discharged himself of that Commission in a pathetick and moving Manner; and in the Conclusion of his Discourse produced the Articles of *Clarendon*, protesting he had rather suffer a thousand Deaths than see the *English* Church reduced to such a State of Slavery, as was intended by the King, and his Adherents. The next Day our holy Prelate was again admitted to Audience in the Presence of the Cardinals, when he own'd that he had indeed been the unhappy Cause of the Storm raised in the *English* Church by engaging in the Episcopate out of Complaisance to his Prince, rather than according the Rules of the Church; that nothing hinder'd him from resigning his Post, while in *England*, but the Apprehension of leaving a pernicious Example, and giving temporal Princes a Handle for displacing the Pastors of Christ's Flock, according to the Dictates of their Passions; but that he then begg'd Leave to put the Church of *Canterbury* into his Holiness's Hands, that he might provide it with one more capable of governing it. He then took off his Episcopal Ring, presented it to the Pope, and retired.

The Consistory were divided on the Case before them; some were of Opinion that this favourable Opportunity of re-establishing a Calm in the *English* Church was not to be neglected, and that they ought to proceed to the Choice of an Archbishop, who should be more agreeable to the King. But his Holiness, and some others, better acquainted with, or more zealous for the Good of the Church declared for endeavouring the Restoration of the injured Prelate. The Majority giving into the latter Opinion, the Pope order'd our Saint to be call'd in, commended his Integrity and Modesty, return'd his Ring, advised him to continue his Endeavours in Favour of the Church, and assured him of the Friendship and Protection of the holy See.

His Holiness then sent for the Abbot of *Pontigny* and put our illustrious Exile into his Hands, with a particular Recommendation. St. *Thomas*, pleas'd with the Prospect of enjoying the Pleasures of a religious Retreat, to which,

Dec. 29 which he was then a Stranger, accompanied the Abbot to *Pontigny*, where he took the Habit of that House, gave heartily into all the penitential Austerities of the Community, and made confiderable Additions to them to expiate his Want of Vocation, and Weaknefs in once condefcending to what his more mature Thoughts could not approve of.

The Saint had not been long in Poffeffion of his new Happinefs, when the King of *England*, enraged at the favourable Reception which he met with abroad, confifcated all his Goods, and thofe of his Relations and Friends, banifh'd all who had any Connexion with him, without Exception of Age or Sex; obliged fuch of them as were arrived to the Ufe of Reafon to take an Oath to go in Queft of the holy Archbifhop, that the Sight of fo many unhappy and diftrefs'd Perfons might add to his Afflictions; and ftrictly forbid all his Subjects to pray for the factious Prelate, as he ftiled him. After this fevere Order, great Numbers came daily to *Pontigny*, and complain'd loudly of their Misfortunes, which proved the moft fenfible Mortification that the Saint ever felt. Providence, however, took them into it's Protection, they were kindly receiv'd in feveral diftant Countries, and fome of them lived better abroad than they could have expected at home.

Henry could not bear to fee his Endeavours for Revenge fall thus to the Ground, and therefore drew up ten new Articles, more prejudicial to the Liberties of the Church than thofe of *Clarendon*, which he publifhed in his Dominions, and required an Oath for obferving them. Being apprehenfive that the Archbifhop would lay an Interdict on the Kingdom of *England*, he gave ftrict Orders for watching all the Ports, and hindring the Paffage of Letters from the holy Prelate or the Pope. The Saint, however, found Means of writing to his Majefty and the Bifhops of this Nation, endeavouring to bring them to a Senfe of their Duty; but his charitable Admonitions fell fhort of their defired Effect, and the few Prelates, who were convinced of his Innocence and the Juftice of his Caufe, had neither Intereft nor Courage enough to ftem the Tide which bore hard upon them.

The Pope, returning to *Italy* in 1165, before he could bring St. *Thomas*'s Affair to a Conclufion, fignalized himfelf in that Prelate's Favour by declaring him Legate from the holy See in all *England*, except the Diocefe of *York*; in this Quality the Saint excommunicated feveral of his Countrymen who had invaded the Ecclefiaftical Jurifdiction, feiz'd the Church Lands, or adhered to the Antipope, who fucceeded *Victor* IU, and took the Name of *Pafcal*. The King was threaten'd with the like Cenfure, if he did not fubmit to the Authority of the Church, and do Penance for what was paft.

'Though

Though that haughty Prince did all in his Power to work himself into a Dec. 29 through Contempt of such Menaces, he could not dissemble his Apprehensions, and therefore conven'd his most faithful Councellors at *Chinon* in *Touraine* to know what was to be done. *Henry* complain'd of the Archbishop's Conduct with Tears, and reproached those present with Want of Concern for their Royal Master's Repose, which would have directed them to ease him of the Man who gave him so much Disquiet. The Archbishop of *Rouën* undertook to shew him the Unreasonableness and Uselessness of that violent Transport; but nothing could calm him 'till the Bishop of *Lizieux* proposed an Appeal to *Rome*, as the only Expedient in that Counjuncture. Thus, according to the Remark of the famous *John* of *Salisbury*, the King condemn'd his Opinion by his Practice, and had Recourse to *Rome* in his Extremity, at a Time when he was doing his utmost toward destroying the Right of Appeals to the holy See. As soon as the Assembly broke up the Bishop of *Lizieux* and *Sees* went to *Pontigny* to notify the King's Appeal against the Primates Sentence; the Archbishop of *Rouën* accompanied them out of a charitable Desire of negotiating a Reconciliation. The Saint was then at *Soissons*, begging the Assistance of the Blessed Virgin and St. *Gregory* the great in this important Affair, so that the King's Deputies lost their Labour. *Thomas* was now fully resolved to pronounce Sentence of Excommunication against the King on *Whitsunday* 1166; but deferr'd it on hearing his Majesty was then dangerously ill.

The King was scarce recover'd, when he wrote to the general Chapter of the *Cistercians*, complain'd that the Monks of *Pontigny* had harbour'd a Rebel and his profess'd Enemy, and threaten'd to destroy all the Monasteries of that Order in *England*, if they entertain'd him any longer. The Saint being inform'd of the Affair, let the Monks know he shou'd be extremely sorry that an Order which had entertain'd him so kindly in his Distress shou'd suffer on his Account, and therefore resolved to make them easy on that Point. With this View he sent the King of *France* the melancholy News; and that Prince order'd the Messenger to assure our holy Prelate of the Continuance of his Protection, and desire he wou'd choose the Place of his Residence. He pitched on the City of *Sens*, where he was receiv'd by the Archbishop, the Clergy, and the People with all Marks of Joy and Respect; and retired into a Monastery, where he was supplied with all that was necessary for a Man of his Rank at the King's Expence; when ever *Lewis* went to *Sens*, he visited the holy Archbishop, and consulted him in what regarded the Salvation of his Soul, and the Government of his Kingdom.

In

Dec. 29 In the mean time *John* of *Oxford* made a Journey to *Rome*, where he found Means to surprize the Pope into Measures, which gave the King of *England* an Advantage over St. *Thomas*. That artful Hypocrite assured his Holiness upon Oath that he had done nothing at the Schismatical Council of *Wurtzbourg*, prejudicial to the Church, or contrary to the Dignity of the Apostolical See, and solemnly abjur'd the disputed Customs of *England*; whereupon the Pope absolved him from the Excommunication pronounced by our Saint, and at his Persuasion dispatched two Legates to the *English* Court to examine the Matter between the King of *England*, and the Archbishop of *Canterbury*, suspending the Saint's *Legatine* Power for a Time.

William Cardinal of *Pavia*, and Cardinal *Otho*, the Persons entrusted with this important Affair, left *Rome* on the first of *January* 1167, but did not reach *Normandy*, where the King of *England* then was, till the latter End of the Summer; at their Arrival they found him and the King of *France* at Variance about the City of *Toulouse*, and other Articles. The Pope, having Intelligence of the Matter, sent an Order to the Legates to employ all Means in their Power for reconciling the two Potentates, before they enter'd on the Archbishop's Business. The Peace between the two Crowns was a Work of Time; and some Months pass'd before the Time and Place of the Conference with St. *Thomas* could be fix'd, which was held at last near *Gisors*, where the two Kingdoms joined. The Archbishop went thither, attended by several who had follow'd him into Banishment, among whom was the famous *John of Salisbury*, afterwards Bishop of *Chartres*, a Man of great Learning, and consummate Prudence, which Talents he employ'd with good Success in Favour of his holy Friend, who might otherwise have been surprized by the *Cardinal* of *Pavia*'s captious Proposals. The Conference ending without bringing Matters to an Issue, the Legates carried an Accout of their Proceedings to King *Henry*, and declared they had no Commission to go any farther. That Prince, enraged at the Miscarriage of his Design, storm'd violently against the Archbishop, and accused the Pope of Indifference to the Interest of the Crown of *England*. The Legates gave him no farther Satisfaction than that of receiving an Appeal of the Bishops, and publishing the apostolical Letters forbidding the Saint to lay an Interdict on the Kingdom of *England*, till farther Advice from the holy See. They ventured to exceed the Bounds of their Power to obliged the King, and undertook to absolve most of those, who had been excommunicated by the Archbishop of *Canterbury*; whereupon they were recall'd.

The

The King of *France*, mortified at this Delay, resolved to employ all his Dec. 29 Interest with *Henry* for restoring the injured Prelate to his See. His Holiness, being apprized of his Majesty's Disposition, wrote to him, and conjur'd him to undertake the Matter. *Lewis*, thus press'd enter'd on the Affair with an Ardour that shew'd his Affection for the Archbishop, and Concern for the Peace of the Church. He had several Conferences with the King of *England*, who was at last prevail'd to allow St. *Thomas* an Interview. Pursuant to this Leave the holy Prelate, being introduced to the King before a numerous Assembly, threw himself at his Majesty's Feet, but was immediately order'd to arise from the Ground, and declare his Business. The Saint begun with imploring that Prince's Mercy in Favour of the *English* Church, and attributed its Troubles to his own Sins; he then declared that he referr'd the whole Matter to his Royal Wisdom, and Discretion, and would stand to his Judgment, as far as was consistent with the Honour of God. *Henry*, who expected an absolute, unconditional Submission, was so offended at the Restriction, that giving a Loose to his Passion, he loaded him with Reproaches of Arrogance, and Ingratitude; and, then, turning to the King of *France*, observed to him that the Condition, with which the Archbishop's pretended Submission was clogg'd, would prove the fruitful Source of endless Disputes, it being easy for that Prelate to pretend that which is not agreeable to his Humour, is contrary to God's Honour. Having observed that the whole Assembly was surprized at the Warmth with which he had deliver'd himself, and pleas'd with the Mildness of the Saint's Answers, he had Recourse to Artifice, and gave his Cause the Appearance of Justice by this specious Proposal. " Sir, said he, speaking
" still to the King of *France*, I have been preceeded in the *English* Throne
" by several Princes some less and some more powerful than myself; and
" the Pelate before us came to the See of *Canterbury* when it had been
" honour'd with several great and holy Archbishops; now all I insist on
" is that he would only grant me the Satisfaction which the most worthy
" of those Prelates did not scruple to give to the least of my Predecessors."
This artful Declaration had the intended Effect; for the whole Company gave it as their Opinion that his Majesty could not make any farther Profer, and that a happy Conclusion of this troublesome Affair depended entirely on our Saint.

Had *Thomas* accepted the Proposal, his Conduct would have been sufficiently justified by that of St. *Anselm*, and other Archbishops of *Canterbury*, who had most strenuously opposed the King's of *England* on the

same

Dec. 29 same Subject. But, he knew *Henry* better than the rest of that august Assembly, and therefore made no Reply, being justly apprehensive that the *King* would make no Difficulty of breaking his Word after he had refused to admit of the Clause in Dispute. *Lewis*, dazzled with the false Lustre of the artful Proposal, asked the Archbishop with some Emotion, what he meant, and whether he pretended to be better or wiser than the many excellent Prelates, who had sat in the See of *Canterbury*; and declared that the desired Reconciliation depended entirely on him. " Yes, replied the Saint, " my Predecessors were certainly superiour to me both in Vertue and Know-" ledge; each of them retrenched some Abuse, but there is Employment " enough of that sort left for their Successors. Our Ancestors suffered Mar-" tyrdom rather than not preach the Name of *Jesus Christ*, and shall I be-" tray his Honour to ingratiate myself with a Man?" These Words set him and the Nobility of the two Kingdoms on Fire, who unanimously pronounced him Obstinate, and an Enemy to Peace; one of the most considerable among them protested that the Archbishop had render'd himself unworthy of their Majesties Favours and had forfeited the Protection of the *French* King. The two Princes seem'd equally incensed against him, and left the Assembly without taking Leave of our Saint; and *Henry* insulted him by telling him he had now the Satisfaction of a complete Revenge on the Enemy of his Crown and Dignity in the united Declarations of the Members of that honourable Company. *Lewis* grew very cool to the holy Prelate and discontinued his usual Allowance for some Time; but that Loss was in some Measure supplied by the charitable Contributions of several *French* Bishops.

Some Days after the King of *France*, giving the Matter a second Thought, could not but believe he had been to blame in pressing the Saint to a Compliance with *Henry*'s Terms, and sent for him. At his Entrance into *Lewis*'s Apartment the Archbishop found him sitting in a melancholy Posture, and expected nothing better than an Order for leaving his Dominions; but was agreeably surprized to see that Monarch, after some Moments pass'd in a profound Silence, threw himself at his Feet, and with Tears acknowledge him the only Person who saw clearly into *Henry*'s Intentions, beg to be absolved from the Crime which he had committed in joining with his Enemies at the late Conference, and assure him of a Continuance of his Favour and Protection. The Saint return'd this Acknowledgement with his Blessing, and Expressions of Gratitude; was conducted back to *Sens* in a magnificent Manner, and entertain'd there at the King's Expence, as before. This Action was highly disagreeable to all St. *Thomas*'s Enemies, but none re-

sented

sented it so highly as the King of England, who deputed the Archbishop of Sens, and the Archdeacon of Canterbury with a Message to his Majesty expressing his Dislike to it in very strong Terms. *Lewis* replied, that if *Henry* thought he had a Right to insist on the Customs of his Kingdom, his Majesty could not think it strange that he kept up the Practice of his Royal Predecessors in protecting the Afflicted, and especially such as suffer'd for Justice.

Dec. 29

Henry, thus disappointed in *France*, employ'd all Manner of Artifices, and Solicitations in *Germany* and *Italy* to procure the Archbishop of *Canterbury*'s Disgrace and Condemnation. He sent a new Deputation to *Rome*, to intimidate him, surprize him, and tire him into his Measures: and made considerable Offers to several Cities in *Italy*, if they would employ their respective Interests with his Holiness against the suffering Prelate. *Alexander*, still in St. *Peter*'s Chair, sent two Legates to the King of *England*, *Gratian*, and *Vivian*, and gave them such Instructions as might secure them from making any false Step in the Execution of their Commission. After several tedious Conferences, and warm Debates, the King promised to restore the Saint, and all who had suffer'd on his Account. But, the Legates not consenting to some Terms in the Agreement insisted on by the King, the whole Affair fell once more to the Ground; and, after some farther Endeavours to bring Matters to a happy Conclusion, *Gratian* and *Vivian* return'd to *Rome*.

The King, finding his Attempt for deposing the Archbishop of *Canterbury* miscarry, began now to endeavour to deprive him of all the Rights of his Metropolitan Dignity. The placing the Crown on the Heads of the *English* Monarchs had long been the Privilege of the Archbishop of *Canterbury*: The Prince then on the Throne, designing to give the Royal Title to *Henry* his eldest Son in his Life Time, pitch'd on the Archbishop of *York* for performing the Ceremony of his Coronation. The Pope, being apprized of the King's Design, wrote to that Prelate, strictly charging him not to usurp an Office that belong'd to our Saint, who also wrote to him on the same Subject. The King, incensed at this Interposition, which his officious Flatterers improved into an Affront to his Person and Dignity, published an Order obliging all his Subjects to abjure their Obedience to the Pope and the Archbishop of *Canterbury*. Several were complaisant or weak enough to take this Oath; and the Saint, sensibly afflicted at the Schism, wrote a Letter to his Diocese, and the whole *English* Church, full of Zeal, and Authority.

Ggg In

Dec. 29. In Spite of the Pope and the Archbishop, Prince *Henry* was crown'd at *Westminster* by the Archbishop of *York*, assisted by the Bishops of *London*, *Rochester*, and *Salisbury*. The News of this Usurpation of his Rights, and some Proceedings at *Rome* to the Prejudice of his primatial Authority, rouzed all our Saint's Fire and drew several bitter Complaints from his Pen, in a Letter to Cardinal *Albert*. *Thomas* wrote to his Holiness soon after, and conjured him in the strongest Terms not to defer the last and only Remedy any longer. The King of *France* was very pressing with him on the same Subject, and assured the Pope that his long Forbearance only harden'd King *Henry*'s Heart. The Archbishop of *Sens* made the same Complaint, and put his Holiness in Mind of the terrible Account he must one Day give for the Blood of his Brethren, who were in danger of being lost.

Alexander, thus attack'd on all Sides, wrote to the Archbishop of *York*, declared him suspended from all Ecclesiastical Functions; and laid an Interdict on the Prelates who had assisted at the young King's Coronation. At the same Time his Holiness directed the Bishops of *Rouën* and *Nevers* to make the last Proposal of Peace to the King of *England*, and interdict his whole Dominions, on his Noncompliance with the Terms offer'd. He wrote likewise to King *Henry*, commanding him in the Name of God and by Virtue of the Apostolical Authority, to be speedily reconciled to the Archbishop of *Canterbury*, if he would avoid incurring the Sentence of Excommunication from the holy See. This Thunder awaked the King of *England*, who now declared his Resolution of negotiating a Peace with the Pope's Legates, as soon as possible. These Prelates had received all necessary Instructions from our Saint how to proceed with that artful and penetrating Prince; and the Archbishop of *Sens*, who was join'd in that Commission, prevail'd with St. *Thomas* to go with them; in short the Peace was concluded on the Archbishop's own Terms, and he was assured of all the Respect, Favour, and Protection that he or his Church could desire. He then took his Leave of the King of *France*, and his Friends at *Sens* and *Pontigny*. *Lewis* was at that time at *Paris*, and our Saint on his Arrival in that City lodged in the Abbey St. *Victor*. The Regular Canons of that House desired their holy Guest to preach in their Church on the Octave of St. *Augustin*, and when he left them, found Means of securing his Hair Shirt, which they keep to this Day as a very valuable Relick.

Coming to *Witsan*, or as some write it *Guissan* in *Picardy*, the Saint dispatched the Pope's Letters into *England* to prepare his Way there; which Letters interdicted the Archbishop of *York*, and all who had assisted at Prince *Henry*'s

St. Thomas, Archbishop.

Henry's Coronation, and excommunicated or suspended several other Prelates Dec. 29 of this Kingdom, for different Reasons. As he was one Day walking on the Sea shore, *Milo* Dean of *Boulogne* brought him an Account of a Conspiracy form'd against him by his Enemies in *England*, who were resolv'd to kill or take him Prisoner at his Landing in any of the Ports of this Island. *Thomas* thank'd that Ecclesiastick for the Information and his kind Concern for his Person; but declared his Resolution of going where he was persuaded God call'd him. There was indeed but too much Truth in the News; for the Archbishop of *York*, the Bishops of *London* and *Salisbury*, join'd by some desperate Persons, had surprized the young King into a Permission to wait his Arrival and execute their Revenge on the holy Prelate. *Thomas* embark'd on the twenty ninth of *November* 1170, being the seventh Year of his Banishment, and landed safe at *Sandwich*. The Dean of *Salisbury*, commission'd by the King to reinstate our Saint in his See, perceiving the Conspirators, apprized of his Arrival, were making toward the Archbishop, stept up to them, declared his Royal Master's Orders, and prevailed with them to lay down their Arms. They reproached the Saint, however, with returning in a hostile Manner, and thundering out Excommunications and Interdicts against the Bishops. *Thomas* replied he had done nothing in that Affair, without the express Consent of his Majesty; the discontented Party grew cooler upon hearing the King named, and in a suppliant Manner desired those Prelates might be absolved; but the Archbishop defered the Consideration of that Affair till his Arrival at *Canterbury*, which City he reach'd next Day, and was received there with all Demonstrations of universal Joy.

The Saint had enjoy'd but one Night's Repose, when three Heads of the Conspirators, accompanied by the same Number of Ecclesiasticks, deputed by the Archbishop of *York*, and the Bishops of *London*, and *Salisbury*, went to the Archiepiscopal Palace, and in the King's Name demanded the Absolution of those Prelates. He was ready to grant their Request on certain Conditions, to which they would not submit, but prejudiced the young King against the Saint, and then made a Journey to *Normandy*; where they laid their Complaints before the Father of that Prince. The three Bishops reach'd that Country a few Days before *Christmas*, threw themselves at his Majesty's Feet, implored his Protection against the pretended Violences of our Saint, whom they represented as a turbulent Prelate, and an implacable Enemy of his royal Dignity. They gave so specious a Turn to their Calumnies that *Henry* really Thought the Saint disposed to lord it over the Clergy, and even spirit up the People to Rebellion. In this Persuasion, giving a

Dec. 29 Loose to his Passion, he pronounced a heavy Curse on all whom he had promoted, honour'd with his Friendship, and fed at his Table, who yet had neither Courage nor Affection enough for their Prince and Benefactor to do him Justice on one single Priest, who gave him more Disturbance than all the rest of his Subjects together. This Reproach afforded the Saint's Enemies a favourable Handle for executing their black Designs; four of them, resolved to ingratiate themselves with their Sovereign by removing the Disturber of his Peace, enter'd into a Conspiracy, which they executed in the following Manner. They landed in *Kent* on the Day holy to the Memory of *the Innocents*; and went to the Archbishop's Palace the next Morning, where they found him surrounded by Ecclesiasticks and Monks and told him they came from the King. The Saint order'd all the Company out of the Room that these pretended Deputies might communicate his Majesty's Orders with more Freedom and Secrecy. Upon hearing their Proposals, he found them so extravagant, that he had Reason to suspect they never came from the King. He then call'd in his Clergy, and desiring they might be Witnesses to what pass'd at that Interview; justified his whole Conduct to the Confusion of his Enemies; and assured them he was firmly resolved to act up to the Character of a true Pastor of the Church, whatever became of his own Life.

The Assassins left the Palace in a Manner that shew'd them resolved on some desperate Attempt; and soon after appear'd completely arm'd for the Undertaking. *Thomas* remain'd perfectly calm in his Chamber, and it was with some Difficulty that he was prevail'd with to take Shelter in the Church, where his Friends hoped he might be secure. The Saint had not been there long when the Ruffians and their Attendants forced their Way in, and put the Chapter into the utmost Consternation. Those Villains in a loud and menacing Tone asked where was *Thomas Becket*, that infamous Traitor. This Demand meeting with no Answer, they asked where the Archbishop was. Upon which the holy Prelate left his Seat, and declared he was the Person they sought, but denied the Title of Traitor. One of the Desperadoes commanded him to quit the Church, having some faint Remains of Respect for the holy Place. The Saint replied that he would not make his Escape, but was ready to die for Justice and the Liberties of the Church, and conjured them in the most solemn and awful Manner not to hurt his Monks, his Clergy, or his People. After some Endeavours to drag him out of the Church, the Assassins murther'd him before the Altar, and then made their Way to his House which they plunder'd with the Licentious-
ness.

ness of victorious Soldiers. Thus fell the holy Martyr on the twenty ninth of December, 1170.

The News of this execrable Fact spread an universal Confusion through *Canterbury*; the People flock'd to the Church in great Numbers; the Poor, the Widows, and the Orphans bewail'd the Loss of their common Father and best Friend; they express'd their Veneration for him by kissing his Hands and Feet, rubb'd their Eyes with the Blood shed for the Cause of God, and dipp'd their Cloaths in it as a valuable Relick. The venerable Body was buried privately to prevent the Attempts of the Saint's Enemies to carry it off, and throw it into some common Sewer. The many glorious Miracles perform'd at his Tomb were receiv'd as so many authentick Attestations from Heaven of this great Prelate's Sanctity and Justice of his Cause; which prevail'd with Pope *Alexander* III to canonize him with great Solemnity in the Year 1173, stile him a Martyr, and order the Observation of his Festival on the Day of his Death. *Stephen Langton*, Archbishop of *Canterbury*, order'd the sacred Relicks to be removed on the seventh of *July* 1223, a Translation which was commemorated annually on that Day by our devout Ancestors till the Change of Religion in this Country. 'Till that unhappy Time, the twenty ninth of *December* was observed with the same Exactness in *England* as the four preceeding Days; and the Catholicks among us continue that pious Custom to this Day.

The XXX Day.

St. SABINUS, *Bishop of* ASSISIUM, *Martyr, and his Companions.*

SABINUS was in Possession of the See of *Assisium* when the *Romans*, animated by the Edicts of *Dioclesian*, and *Maximian*, clamour'd for what they call'd Justice on the Christians, and declared for the Extirpation of that odious Sect in the Place of their publick Diversions. The Senate willing to satisfy the People and oblige the Emperor, published an Order on the twenty second of *April* 303, for putting all such as should be discover'd into the Hands of the Governor of the respective Towns, or the Judges of each particular Place, who were thereby authorised and required to oblige them to renounce their Religion, and sacrifice to the Gods. We are told that pursuant to this Order *Maximian* sent a Rescript to the Governor of *Tuscany*, directing

Dec. 30 directing the Confiscation of Goods, and inflicting corporal Punishments on those who should refuse or neglect to execute it.

By Virtue of this Authority *Sabinus*, and his two Deacons *Marcellus*, and *Exuperantius*, with several other Ecclesiasticks, were seiz'd at *Assisium* in *May*, and thrown into Prison by an Order from *Venustianus* Governor of *Tuscany* and *Umbria*; where they lay 'till that Magistrate came to Town; and then *Sabinus*, being carried before him, was press'd to offer Incense to *Jupiter*. The holy Bishop gave him a suitable Answer to the absurd Proposal, and being farther importuned to that detestable Act, express'd his Abhorrence of it by thrusting the Idol from him. *Venustianus*, incensed at his Boldness, which he resented as the highest Impiety, order'd his Hands to be cut off; after which *Marcellus* and *Exuperantius* were put on the Rack, and beaten unmercifully for a considerable Time. Finding them proof against all the Severities which he could inflict, the Governor gave Orders for tearing their Bodies with Iron Hooks, 'till they died under the barbarous Operation. They were thrown into a River, but soon after taken up and buried by a Priest on the last of *May*.

Sabinus was doom'd to a slower Martyrdom, for he was confined several Months, without any Relief but what he receiv'd from *Serena* a Christian Widow, whose Grandson recover'd his Sight by the Ministry of the holy Prelate. The Miracle just mention'd reached the Ears of *Venustianus*, who was much startled at the Account; and, having been long troubled with sore Eyes, sent for *Sabinus*, and let him know his Sentiments were then very different from what he had formerly entertain'd. He then threw himself at the Bishop's Feet, and begg'd his Assistance in the Care of both his Soul and Body. The Fervour of his Prayers, and Sincerity of his Intentions were rewarded with all he had asked; after some Instructions he receiv'd Baptism, and from that Moment found his Eyes perfectly well. His Wife and Children made the same Step; and the Conversion was follow'd by that of fourteen or fifteen Persons, who saw what God had done in Favour of *Venustianus*.

Maximian, being inform'd of what had happen'd, sent *Lucius* one of his chief Officers, to *Assisium*, with Orders to behead the Governor and his whole Family. After the Execution of this Sentence, *Lucius* went to *Spoleto*, where he brought *Sabinus* to his Trial; and, finding him inflexible, gave Directions for his being whipt to Death. *Serena*, who follow'd the Martyr to *Spoleto*, took Care of his Body, and buried it about a Mile from that Town on the seventh of *December*. 'Though the Martyrs of this Day suffer'd at different Times, as appears from their Acts, the Church honours their Memory together;

together; and the *Roman* Martyrologe places their Names on the thirtieth of *December*.

***

The XXXI Day.

St. SILVESTER, POPE.

SILVESTER, a Native of *Rome*, was Son to *Rufinus*, and *Justa*. His Mother, being left a Widow while our Saint was young, took a particular Care of his Education in Virtue and good Literature by putting him into the Hands of *Caritius*, or *Carinus*, a Priest of an unexceptionable Character and great Abilities. Being form'd under that excellent Master, he enter'd among the Clergy of *Rome*, and was ordain'd Priest by Pope *Marcellinus*, before the Peace of the Church was disturbed by *Dioclesian* and his Associate in the Empire. His Behaviour in that Station was such as recommended him to the publick Esteem; and upon the Death of *Melchiades*, which happen'd at the Beginning of the Year 314 he was thought worthy to succeed that holy Pope.

The only considerable Disturbance in the Church at that Time was caused by the *Donatists* in *Africa*, whose Schism had then subsisted above seven Years. The Emperor *Constantine* hoped he should remedy this Evil by naming some Bishops of *Italy* and *Gaul* to examine and decide the Affair in a Council at *Rome*, as has been related in the Life of St. *Melchiades* on the tenth of this Month. But, finding those Schismaticks refractory, and full of Complaints of the pretended Precipitation of that Council, and the small Number of it's Bishops, he was resolved to leave them no Shadow of Reason, or any thing that should look like an Excuse for their Disobedience. In this View a Council was call'd at *Arles* in the Year 314, where our Saint was represented by four Legates, two Priests, and as many Deacons. This venerable Assembly, consisting of thirty three western Bishops, was held on the first of *August* and confirm'd the Decisions of the Synod of *Rome*. Before the Council broke up, they made twenty two Canons, all which related to Church Discipline, and were directed to our Saint, desiring him to publish them through the whole Christian World.

Some Time after the Church of *Egypt* was disturb'd by the Rise of *Arianism*, which soon spread it's self through the whole East. *Constantine*, not having been able to stiffle this Flame when it first broke out, and apprehending

Dec. 31. ding it would make Havock in all the Provinces of the Empire, had Recourse to the last Remedy for extinguishing it, that is called an œcumenical Council, to which all the Prelates, who own'd his Authority, were invited, and those who were not Subjects of the *Roman* Empire had free Leave to assist at their Assembly, which was open'd at *Nice* on the nineteenth of *June* 325, and closed on the twenty fifth of the following *August*. As this Council represented the whole Church, *Silvester*, who was it's first Bishop, would have presided there, had his great Age allow'd him to make so long a Journey, for which Reason he deputed two Priests to act in his Name, and consent to the Decisions of the Bishops.

After almost twenty two Years spent in a punctual Discharge of all the Duties of his exalted Station, St. *Silvester* received the Reward of his Labours on the last Day of the Year 335, and was buried in *Priscilla*'s Ground about two Miles from *Rome*. Toward the Middle of the IX Century Pope *Sergius* II removed his Body to a Church, which afterwards bore the Saint's Name. His Veneration was publickly established, at least at *Rome*, in the VI Century, as is evident from a Homily pronounced by St. *Gregory* the Great on the Day devoted to his Memory, which is his ninth on the Gospels. Pope *Gregory* IX, who was promoted to the holy See in the Year 1227 made it a general Festival for the whole Church; which is observed by the *Latins* on the Day of his Death; but by the *Grecians* on the second of *January*.

The END.

An INDEX

Of the most remarkable Things in the Fourth Volume.

A
Apolinarius's Heresy, what, 342

B
Bishops of Rome, three first after the Apostles, the Order and Manner of their Succession disputed, 249

C
Canonization, what formerly, 334
Carmelites, their Regulation under St. Teresa, 75
Catholicks, who accounted such, 343
Cerinthians, their Errors, 386
Christians represented as Magicians, 280
    Weak not to despair, 73
Clergy and Religious, Valentinian's Law concerning them, 640
Communion under one Kind, used in the third Century, 224
Confessors, who accounted such, 368
    When first publickly venerated, 178
Crosses worn by Christians in the fourth Age, 346, 347

D
Danegelt, what, 64
Dead, Prayers for them always the Church's Practice, 137
Death, Sentence thereof wisely regulated by St. Ambrose and Theodosius, 326

E
Easter, it's Observation fixt by the Council of Nice, 244
Ebionites, their Errors, 386
Ecclesiasticks, their Exemption from Jurisdiction of the Civil Power, causeth much Trouble in England, 399
Edward, King, why stiled Confessor, 64
Evil, the King's, why so called, 65
Eucharist reserved for the Sick in the third Century, 224

E
Eutyches endeavours to impose upon the Western Bishops, 282
    His Heresy, what, ibid

F
Faults of a few not chargeable on a whole Body, 250
Feasts of the second Rank, what in England, 345
Festivals, Christian, abused, 390

G
Gospel of St. John particularly insists on Christ's Divinity, 388

H
Heart's Sincerity excuseth Errors of Judgment, 342
Holy Innocents, how Christian Martyrs, 390
Hymns introduced into the Church Service by St. Ambrose, 321

I
Images, their Veneration, that Doctrine explained, 263
Jovinian's Heresy, 323

K
Knowledge of one's self, the first Step to a new Life, 213

L
Law, Civil, necessary in all Professions, 212
Luciferians, their Error and Schism, 341 & 354

M
Marriage, second, not unlawful, 311
Martyrs, who so accounted, 226, 240, 371
Monothelites, their Heresy, 185

N
Nuns, their Inclosure not so strict before the Council of Trent, 70

Ordeal

INDEX

O
	Page
Ordeal, Trial, what,	65
Origen's Method of teaching,	213

P
Pantheon, Temple, why preserved,	134
Paris, a general Resort for Students,	282
Popes, the first, why stiled Martyrs,	117
Pope, the Center of Christian Unity,	342
Princes, wicked, want not vile Instruments,	108
Unhappiness in being obliged to see with the Eyes of others,	65
Purgatory, Necessity of such a Place,	136
The Council of Trent thereon,	137

Q
Questions, intricate, not to be proposed to weak or perverse Minds,	298

R
Relicks of Saints, Veneration paid to them proved from the Heathens Care to destroy them,	53
Revelations of St. John, St. Dionysius's Opinion thereof,	225
Romances, pernicious Amusements,	68

S
Sabellian Hereticks, their Tenets,	225
Saints, All, their Festival, why observed,	133
Veneration, whereon founded,	ibid
Not derogatory to God's Power,	ibid
Their Errors of short Duration and they after shine with greater Lustre,	192
In some Actions to be admired, not imitated,	337
Salvation, whereon it depends,	298
Schismaticks cannot be Martyrs or Confessors,	257
Supremacy of the Bishop of Rome own'd in the third Century	227

T
Thais, the remarkable Means of her Conversion,	30
Thomas, St. his Doubting how useful to the Church,	370

V
Visitants, secular, dangerous in Nunneries,	71
Virgin, Blessed, her Presentation, that Festival why observ'd	241

FINIS.